THE CAMBRIDGE HANDBOOK OF MARKETING AND THE LAW

This handbook examines a wide range of current legal and policy issues at the intersection of marketing and the law. Focusing on legal outcomes that depend on measurements and interpretations of consumer and firm behavior, the chapters explore how consumers form preferences, perceptions, and beliefs, and how marketers influence them. Specific questions include the following: How should trademark litigation be valued and patent damages assessed? What are the challenges in doing so? What divides certain marketing claims between fact and fiction? Can a litigant establish secondary meaning without a survey? How can one extract evidence on consumer behavior with the explosion of social media? This unique volume at the intersection of marketing and the law brings together an international roster of scholars to answer these questions and more.

JACOB E. GERSEN is Sidley Austin Professor of Law at Harvard Law School, Affiliate Professor in the Department of Government, and Director of the Food Law Lab, which supports academic research on the legal treatment of food in society. He is also the coeditor of *Food Law & Policy*.

JOEL H. STECKEL is Professor of Marketing at New York University Stern School of Business. Steckel was the founding president of the INFORMS Society for Marketing Science and has published numerous articles in publications including *Journal of Marketing Research*, *Marketing Science*, *The Trademark Reporter*, *University of Pennsylvania Journal of Business Law*, *University of Chicago Law Review*, and *Emory Law Journal*.

The Cambridge Handbook of Marketing and the Law

Edited by

JACOB E. GERSEN

Harvard Law School

JOEL H. STECKEL

New York University

CAMBRIDGE
UNIVERSITY PRESS

Shaftesbury Road, Cambridge CB2 8EA, United Kingdom

One Liberty Plaza, 20th Floor, New York, NY 10006, USA

477 Williamstown Road, Port Melbourne, VIC 3207, Australia

314–321, 3rd Floor, Plot 3, Splendor Forum, Jasola District Centre, New Delhi – 110025, India

103 Penang Road, #05-06/07, Visioncrest Commercial, Singapore 238467

Cambridge University Press is part of Cambridge University Press & Assessment, a department of the University of Cambridge.

We share the University's mission to contribute to society through the pursuit of education, learning and research at the highest international levels of excellence.

www.cambridge.org
Information on this title: www.cambridge.org/9781108470018
DOI: 10.1017/9781108699716

© Cambridge University Press & Assessment 2023

This publication is in copyright. Subject to statutory exception and to the provisions of relevant collective licensing agreements, no reproduction of any part may take place without the written permission of Cambridge University Press & Assessment.

First published 2023

A catalogue record for this publication is available from the British Library

Library of Congress Cataloging-in-Publication Data
NAMES: Gersen, Jacob E., editor. | Steckel, Joel H., editor.
TITLE: The Cambridge handbook of marketing and the law / edited by Jacob E. Gersen, Harvard Law School, Massachusetts; Joel H. Steckel, New York University.
DESCRIPTION: Cambridge, United Kingdom ; New York, NY : Cambridge University Press, 2023. | Series: Cambridge law handbooks | Includes bibliographical references and index.
IDENTIFIERS: LCCN 2022062000 (print) | LCCN 2022062001 (ebook) | ISBN 9781108470018 (hardback) | ISBN 9781108699716 (epub)
SUBJECTS: LCSH: Law–Economic aspects–United States. | Marketing–Law and legislation–United States. | Law–United States–Statistical methods.
CLASSIFICATION: LCC KF385 .C36 2023 (print) | LCC KF385 (ebook) | DDC 343.7307–DC23/eng/20230524
LC record available at https://lccn.loc.gov/2022062000
LC ebook record available at https://lccn.loc.gov/2022062001

ISBN 978-1-108-47001-8 Hardback

Cambridge University Press & Assessment has no responsibility for the persistence or accuracy of URLs for external or third-party internet websites referred to in this publication and does not guarantee that any content on such websites is, or will remain, accurate or appropriate.

*To Ben, Phil, Jaemin, Natalie, Mina, and Nina,
our most challenging cases, and to Felice and Jeannie,
our favorite lawyers.*

Contents

List of Figures	*page* xi
List of Tables	xiii
List of Contributors	xv
Introduction Jacob E. Gersen and Joel H. Steckel	1

PART I UNDERSTANDING CONSUMER BEHAVIOR

1 The Purchase Funnel and Litigation   9
   Laura O'Laughlin and Catherine Tucker

2 Implications of the Consumer Journey to Traditional Consumer
   Surveys for Litigation   36
   Chad Hummel, Ben Mundel, and Jerry Wind

3 "They Ruined Popcorn": On the Costs and Benefits of
   Mandatory Labels   63
   Cass R. Sunstein

4 Valuation of Personal Data: Assessing Potential Harm from
   Unauthorized Access and Misuse of Personal Information in
   Consumer Class Actions   78
   Vildan Altuglu, Lorin M. Hitt, Samid Hussain, and Matteo Li Bergolis

PART II UNDERSTANDING MARKETING PHENOMENA

5 The Persistence of False Reference Prices: Theory and
   Empirical Evidence   105
   Yiting Deng, Richard Staelin, and Joel E. Urbany

6	Brand Value, Marketing Spending, and Brand Royalty Rates Dominique M. Hanssens, Lorenzo Michelozzi, and Natalie Mizik	149
7	On Puffery Rebecca Tushnet	172
8	Search Engine Advertising, Trademark Bidding, and Consumer Intent Anindya Ghose and Avigail Kifer	185

PART III METHODOLOGICAL ADVANCES

9	Choice Experiments: Reducing Complexity and Measuring Behavior Rather than Perception Joel H. Steckel, Rebecca Kirk Fair, Kristina Shampanier, and Anne Cai	207
10	Use of Conjoint Analysis in Litigation: Challenges, Best Practices, and Common Mistakes Rene Befurt, Niall MacMenamin, and Aylar Pour Mohammad	221
11	Piece Problems: Component Valuation in Marketing and in Patent and Tort Law Saul Levmore	236
12	Marketing Analysis in Class Certification Randolph E. Bucklin and Peter Simon	250
13	Damages Estimation in Consumer Deception Class Actions: Legal and Methodological Issues August T. Horvath	270
14	Taking a Second Look at Secondary Meaning: A Marketing Perspective on Circuit Court Factors Peter N. Golder, Michael J. Schreck, and Aaron C. Yeater	293
15	Social Media Evidence in Commercial Litigation Tom Wesson, Erich Schaeffer, Brenda Arnott-Wesson, Mark Pelofsky, David Heller, and Bree Glaviano	312

PART IV HOW THE LAW PROTECTS

16	Law as Persuasion Bert I. Huang	347

17	The Coca-Cola Bottle: A Fragile Vessel for Building a Brand Jacob E. Gersen and C. Scott Hemphill	361
18	Poor Consumer(s) Law: The Case of High-Cost Credit and Payday Loans Shmuel I. Becher, Yuval Feldman, and Orly Lobel	384
19	Eating Law Stephen Ansolabehere and Jacob E. Gersen	415

Figures

2.1	Why the stimulus–response model is inaccurate and incomplete	page 46
2.2	McKinsey's customer decision journey (CDJ)	49
2.3	Futures Company's purchase fish	51
2.4	Safeguards in DIRECTV purchase process	53
2.5	Consumer decision journey for buying a corporate credit card	54
2.6	Customers go through a journey	60
2.7	Knowledge of contract terms	61
2.8	Modified disclosures did not change behavior	62
5.1	Effects of competition on promotional activities	114
5.2	Effects of the extent of sophisticated consumers by the end of the game on promotional activities	115
5.3	Effects of the extent of sophisticated consumers at the beginning of the game on promotional activities	115
5.4	Effects of competition on total industry profit	116
5.5	Effects of the extent of sophisticated consumers by the end of the game on total industry profit	117
5.6	Distinguishing fake from true discounts	124
7.1	Three images from DIRECTV's comparative advertising	182
9.1	Example stimulus for three groups in *Hobbs* v. *Brother*	213
9.2	Example dependent measure outcomes from *Hobbs* v. *Brother*	213
9.3	Example four-group experimental setup to disentangle the effects of two separate claims	215
10.1	Example of a standard CBC task	224
10.2	General supply and demand curves	234
15.1	Social media mentions of Lance Armstrong in connection with doping allegations	314

15.2	Peak monthly social media mentions of Lance Armstrong, Alex Rodriguez, and Maria Sharapova in connection with doping allegations	315
15.3	Percentage of all online conversations connecting Armstrong to doping allegations compared to other benchmark topics	316
15.4	Number of social media posts mentioning "pink slime"	326
15.5	Consumer engagement with posts about pink slime on the ABC News Facebook page	327
15.6	Consumer engagement with posts about pink slime on the ABC World News Facebook page	327
15.7	Social media posts spreading ABC's allegedly damaging and misleading claims about BPI and LFTB	328
15.8	Number of social media posts mentioning "pink slime"	329
17.1	Coca-Cola patents and the 1916 production bottle	368
17.2	Patent #1 and the Whistle patent	370
17.3	Prior art patents cited in *Coca-Cola Co.* v. *Whistle Co.*	371
19.1	Comparison of cooking oil ingredient lists	435
19.2	Comparison of POM Wonderful and Coca-Cola juice bottles	443

Tables

5.1	Consumer utility	page 111
5.2	Examples of three possible promotions	138
6.1	Comparison of the top-30 most valuable brands in 2020 according to Interbrand, Millward Brown, Forbes, and Brand Finance	168
6.2	Percentage change in brand valuations between 2019 and 2020 according to Interbrand, Millward Brown, Forbes, and Brand Finance	170
8.1	Chapter overview	189
12.1	Issues, methods, example cases, and outcomes	269
14.1	Factors considered by circuit courts in secondary meaning tests	295
14.2	Barriers, actions, and marketplace outcomes: exemplars and related circuit court factors	297
14.3	Conceptual favorability of establishing secondary meaning	310
16.1	Saving two by sacrificing one	353
18.1	Behavioral phenomena, their impact and mitigating/de-biasing tools	412
19.1	What do people care about when deciding about food?	425
19.2	Effects of GMOs on price, taste, cooking, healthiness, and purchase	430
19.3	Probit estimates relating beliefs about products to purchase preferences	431
19.4	Effects of bovine growth hormone (BGH) label on price, taste, nutrition, healthiness, and purchase preferences	433
19.5	Cooking oil experiment effect summaries	435
19.6	Consumer beliefs about product attributes after information disclosure	437
19.7	Summary of product, price, health, and taste bundles	438
19.8	Effect of sugar content and sugar percentages	440

19.9	Yogurt, sugars, and price	442
19.10	Consumer views about POM and Minute Maid juices	444
19.11	Relationship between beliefs about juice attributes and purchasing preference	445

Contributors

Vildan Altuglu, Vice President at Cornerstone Research

Stephen Ansolabehere, Frank G. Thompson Professor of Government at Harvard University

Brenda Arnott-Wesson, Managing Partner/Founder at Voluble Insights

Shmuel Becher, Associate Professor at Victoria University of Wellington, Wellington School of Business and Government

Rene Befurt, Principal at Analysis Group

Randolph Bucklin, Peter W. Mullin Chair in Management, Professor of Marketing at the University of California, Los Angeles, Anderson School of Management

Anne Cai, Manager at Analysis Group

Yiting Deng, Assistant Professor of Marketing at University College London, UCL School of Management

Yuval Feldman, Mori Lazarof Professor of Legal Research at Bar-Ilan University School of Law

Jacob Gersen, Sidley Austin Professor of Law at Harvard Law School

Anindya Ghose, Heinz Riehl Chair, Professor of Business at New York University, Stern School of Business

Bree Glavano, Voluble Insights

Peter Golder, Professor of Marketing at Dartmouth College, Tuck School of Business

Dominique Hanssens, Distinguished Research Professor of Marketing, Emeritus, at University of California, Los Angeles, Anderson School of Management

David Heller, Voluble Insights

Scott Hemphill, Moses H. Grossman Professor of Law at New York University School of Law

Lorin Hitt, Zhang Jindong Professor of Operations, Information and Decisions at University of Pennsylvania, Wharton School

August Horvath, Partner at Foley Hoag LLP

Bert Huang, Michael I. Sovern Professor of Law at Columbia Law School

Chad Hummel, Partner at Sidley Austin LLP

Samid Hussain, Senior Vice President at Cornerstone Research

Avigail Kifer, Cornerstone Research Principal

Rebecca Kirk Fair, Managing Principal at Analysis Group

Saul Levmore, William B. Graham Distinguished Service Professor of Law at University of Chicago Law School

Matteo Li Bergolis, Principal at Cornerstone Research

Orly Lobel, Warren Distinguished Professor of Law at University of San Diego School of Law

Niall MacMenamin, Executive Vice President at Compass Lexecon

Lorenzo Michelozzi, Principal at Cornerstone Research

Natalie Mizik, Professor of Marketing, J. Gary Shansby Endowed Chair in Marketing Strategy at University of Washington, Foster School of Business

Ben Mundel, Partner at Sidley Austin LLP

Laura O'Laughlin, Vice President at Analysis Group

Mark Pelofsky, Principal at Voluble Insights

Aylar Pour Mohammad, Associate at Analysis Group

Erich Schaeffer, Chief Operating Officer at Voluble Insights

Michael Schreck, Vice President at Analysis Group

Kristina Shampanier, Executive Vice President at Compass Lexecon

Peter Simon, Vice President at Analysis Group

Richard Staelin, Gregory Mario and Jeremy Mario Professor, Emeritus, at Duke University, Fuqua School of Business

Joel H. Steckel, Professor of Marketing at New York University, Stern School of Business

Cass Sunstein, Robert Walmsley University Professor at Harvard University

Catherine Tucker, Sloan Distinguished Professor of Management Science at Massachusetts Institute of Technology, Sloan School of Management

Rebecca Tushnet, Frank Stanton Professor of the First Amendment at Harvard Law School

Joel E. Urbany, Professor of Marketing at University of Notre Dame, Mendoza College of Business

Tom Wesson, Associate Professor of Strategic Management at York University, Schulich School of Business

Jerry Wind, Lauder Professor Emeritus of Marketing at University of Pennsylvania, Wharton School

Aaron Yeater, Managing Principal at Analysis Group

Introduction

Jacob E. Gersen and Joel H. Steckel

This volume emerged from the notion that marketers and lawyers often talk about the same things. They may use different names, but essentially the things they talk about are the same. For example, while marketers talk about brands, lawyers talk about trademarks. However, relatively late in the process of editing this volume, we, as editors, had a somewhat unsettling realization. Throughout the planning and editing process for this book, we had been laboring under, not unrelated, but certainly not identical, views about the domain of marketing and the reach of law. We had no real common understanding of what marketing is, what marketing theory entails, and how the law shapes and governs marketing activities. Such a state of affairs is part of the inevitable risk of bringing together a group of scholars from two distinct disciplines. Fortunately, the realization helped us recognize that both marketing and law are sometimes vessels into which users can pour whatever content they wish. At the start, therefore, we thought it wise to dispense with some misconceptions and offer at least some working definitions of the terms and ideas we encounter in this volume.

For those outside of the field, marketing sometimes tends to reduce to advertising, promotional materials that describe and hock an already produced good or product. Similarly, for nonlawyers, law sometimes is about courts and judges, rather than the more expansive set of legal rules from statutes, regulations, and local government bodies. For those working on the inside of marketing and law, each field tends to encompass a far more wide-ranging, nearly imperialist vision.

In his landmark book *The Practice of Management*, Peter Drucker, the legendary management guru, wrote: "If we want to know what a business is, we have to start with its purpose. And its purpose must lie outside the business itself. In fact, it must lie in society since a business enterprise is an organ of society. There is one valid definition of business purpose: to create a customer."[1] To do that, a company has to

---

[1] Drucker, Peter F. (1954), *The Practice of Management*, Harper Collins.

produce and deliver goods and services that provide value to a large enough group of consumers at prices that are reasonably attractive to them. Indeed, without revenue and the resulting profit from those customers, the rest of business strategy is pointless.

Marketing is the business function that focuses on how to extract revenue from the customer. It creates value for them by providing benefits that customers want. Marketing recognizes that people do not buy products; they buy benefits. When one of us goes to a hardware store, we do not buy an electric drill; we buy holes in our walls. If we go to a haberdashery store, we do not buy a necktie; we buy enhanced appearance. Therein lies the value the drill and necktie provide.

The pre-1980s view of marketing focused on selling the product, manipulating and distorting the message when necessary largely though advertising and promotion. The focus was on making a sale. This older, and now somewhat dated, view of marketing is more in line with the lay and maybe lawyer's view of marketing.

The more modern view focuses on creating customer satisfaction and building relationships between firms and customers. In the modern view, marketing has an external focus. It is based on research to assemble information about customers, competition, and the marketing environment in order to match the demands of customers with the company's capabilities. In such a view, the product is a variable; it cannot be fixed. If a firm is going to create and deliver superior value, the product must be variable and vary according to customer needs. The firm needs to decide what that superior value is and then what goods and services will deliver that value.

In sum, marketing consists of three stages of value delivery to its customers. First, the firm chooses what value to deliver to its customers. This involves selecting target customers and assessing their needs. Second, it must provide the value. This involves the design and pricing of the product or service as well as determining how the product or service will be distributed. Finally, the value gets communicated to potential customers. Only then does the pre-1980s view of marketing, the component of marketing that emphasizes communication tools (e.g. advertising, promotion, distribution, salesforce) come into play. To the outsider, and perhaps the lawyer, it is this pre-1980s' view that the idea of marketing tends to connote.

Law's domain also tends to be somewhat broader than the lay understanding. Just as the term marketing tends to connote advertising and sales, the term law tends to connote courts and judges. But modern law is constant and ubiquitous, consisting of the body of federal statutes, administrative regulations, federal common law, state common law, state statutes, local ordinances, and so on.

What then is a book concerned with marketing theory and law about? Is it about law and business? Law and the structure of the firm? Allowable and unallowable legal practices? Given the expansive nature of both modern marketing and law, we risk writing a book about everything and therefore about nothing. As part of an initial effort and imposing some modest structure and intellectual discipline, we have chosen to focus on a constellation of problems and recurrent puzzles that have arisen in litigation over the marketing of products, mainly in the United States. These problems often relate to consumer confusion, valuation, and gaps between expectations of either products or legal protections. The volume is organized into four parts.

Part I focuses on understanding consumer behavior. In their chapter "The Purchase Funnel and Litigation," O'Laughlin and Tucker explain the purchase funnel – sometimes known as the "consumer decision journey" or the "consumer buying path" – is a valuable analytical framework for informing the finder-of-fact in litigation matters. Unlike most economic analyses, the purchase funnel recognizes that the consumer must pass through a series of distinct hurdles progressing from awareness to consideration, conversion, and post-purchase. Laying out these steps can pinpoint the impact of an alleged offense in a large variety of litigation contexts.

In their chapter "Implications of the Consumer Journey to Traditional Consumer Surveys for Litigation," Hummel, Mundel, and Wind take this one step further and generalize the purchase funnel (i.e. the consumer journey) to account for active empowered consumers. They present implications of this modern view of consumer behavior for the consumer surveys that often form the core evidence in false advertising cases.

Cass Sunstein's "They Ruined Popcorn: On the Costs and Benefits of Mandatory Labels" canvasses the challenges of using cost–benefit analysis to evaluate mandatory labeling policies. Because tastes often evolve and there is an actual welfare loss involved when consumers learn things they would rather not know, the welfarist case for more information is not nearly as straightforward as sometimes suggested.

In their chapter "Valuation of Personal Data: Assessing Potential Harm from Unauthorized Access and Misuse of Private Information in Consumer Class Actions," Altuglu, Hitt, Hussain, and Bergolis discuss misuse of consumer information. In particular it delves into the evaluation of alleged harm created as a result of misuse or unauthorized disclosure of private information. The chapter focuses on consumer class actions, the usual mechanism by which consumers seek compensation for alleged loss of privacy.

Part II focuses more expressly on understanding marketing phenomena. Deng, Staelin, and Urbany contribute a chapter entitled "The Persistence of False Reference Prices: Theory and Empirical Evidence." Both popular press accounts and a growing wave of deceptive pricing cases indicate that the practice of firms stating a misleading reference price (i.e. the price from which the product is being discounted) appears to be as common as ever today. The chapter explains this persistence and outlines conditions under which the persistence benefits firms.

In "Brand Value, Marketing Spending, and Royalty Rates," Hanssens, Michelozzi, and Mizik note that marketing expenditures both enhance brand value and drive sales. They discuss some modern marketing science methods that help distinguish between brand and marketing contributions to firm revenue and profits.

They discuss these principles and techniques in the context of various legal disputes on brand royalty rates.

Rebecca Tushnet's "On Puffery" explores how courts address puffery, nonfactual claims that are generally said not to be used by consumers, but that nevertheless make up a broad swath of advertising and therefore presumably matter to someone. Using a series of recent cases, Tushnet reveals the weakness of existing judicial doctrine and draws into focus precisely how important puffery is for advertising, and how important it should be to the legal regulation of those practices.

Ghose and Kifer's chapter studies trademark bidding, the practice of rival firms bidding for a search ad placement when a consumer performs an online search for a competitor's brand. The chapter, entitled "Search Engine Advertising, Trademark Bidding, and Consumer Intent," examines whether, and under what conditions, the presence or absence of trademark bidding results in harm to consumers by contributing to confusion or inhibiting consumer price search.

Part III turns to methodological advances. In "Choice Experiments: Reducing Complexity and Measuring Behavior rather than Perception," Steckel, Kirk Fair, Shampanier, and Cai show how simple A/B or test control experiments can be useful in assessing materiality in false advertising and trademark protection cases.

Befurt, MacMenamin, and Mohammad's chapter, "Use of Conjoint Analysis in Litigation: Challenges, Best Practices, and Common Mistakes," outlines the application of conjoint analysis in litigation. Conjoint analysis may be the most significant tool developed by academic marketing researchers. Also known as tradeoff analysis, conjoint analysis addresses questions of how important the attributes of a product (including price) are in determining consumer choice and market share. As such, conjoint analysis is useful in examining consumer fraud, false advertising, and patent infringement cases.

Saul Levmore's chapter, "Piece Problems: Component Valuation in Marketing and in Patent and Tort Law," brings together the component valuation problem in patent law, the comparative negligence analysis in tort law, and conjoint analysis in marketing to explore how the strategies employed by courts in these latter cases might be informed by the conjoint analysis mindset.

In their chapter "Marketing Analysis in Class Certification," Bucklin and Simon note that much of the class certification process involves assessments regarding the similarity – or lack thereof – in class members' situations. This has made marketing and its analytic toolkit for examining markets at the disaggregate level well suited to provide insight into key issues in class certification. The chapter describes the analytic data-based tool set and presents examples of its use.

Horvath's chapter, "Damages Estimation in Consumer Deception Class Actions: Legal and Methodological Issues," explains the importance of class damages models in recent false-advertising cases. He describes the analyses that have been proffered and the issues raised with them. He concludes by analyzing the strategies that have been successful.

In the spirit of this volume, Golder, Schreck, and Yeater develop a marketing perspective on the legal concept of secondary meaning. In their chapter, "Taking a Second Look at Secondary Meaning: A Marketing Perspective on Circuit Court Factors," they integrate factors traditionally considered by courts into a framework of barriers to achieving secondary meaning, actions to overcome these barriers, and marketplace outcomes reflecting the success of these actions. Golder and his coauthors base their work on the presumption that these barriers govern the probability that a firm will be able to establish secondary meaning.

In "Social Media Evidence in Commercial Litigation," Wesson et al. demonstrate that analyzing what people post on social media sites can yield powerful evidence for use in commercial litigation. They view social media as a natural way of listening into people's conversations about products, services, brands, trademarks, and patents. The authors suggest that social media analyses could substitute for the more established consumer surveys

Part IV focuses on how the law protects marketing. Bert Huang's chapter, "Law as Persuasion," revisits the classic trolley problem in moral philosophy as a way of inquiring into law's persuasive properties or, if you will, marketing of moral ideas and intuitions. The chapter asks not so much how law does or ought to regulate marketing, but rather how law might be conceived of as marketing practice itself.

In their chapter "The Coca-Cola Bottle: A Fragile Vessel for Building a Brand," Gersen and Hemphill use one of the most famous examples of trade dress protection – the Coca-Cola bottle – to explore the relationship between patent protection, branding, and trademark. Coca-Cola was perhaps the most successful innovator to leverage design patent protection into trade dress protection in its effort to build and protect brand.

In "Poor Consumers(s) Law: The Case of High-Cost Credit and Payday Loans," Becher, Feldman, and Lobel explore how consumer law does and should respond to instances of allegedly counterproductive decision-making in the context of high-cost credit and loans. By linking behavioral economics and the psychology of poverty and scarcity, the authors offer several policy recommendations.

Finally, Ansolabehere and Gersen's "Eating Law" presents the results from a series of choice experiments involving consumer confusion and preference about food and beverage product attributes. They suggest that while marketing claims near to health can create a halo effect for other product attributes, consumers generally make reasonable inferences about underlying product attributes from available information.

Obviously, these chapters, written as they were by leading marketing scholars, legal scholars, and practitioners, have both a heterogeneous object of inquiry and a heterogeneous method. Indeed, our goal as editors was to assemble a constellation of related scholarship from a broad range of perspectives in the hope of illustrating and furthering the emerging research as the interaction of law and marketing.

PART I

Understanding Consumer Behavior

1

The Purchase Funnel and Litigation

Laura O'Laughlin and Catherine Tucker[*]

This chapter explains why the purchase funnel – sometimes known as the "consumer decision journey" or the "consumer buying path" – is a valuable analytical framework for marketing experts engaged to provide an external expert opinion to inform the finder of fact in litigation matters. The value inherent in the purchase funnel framework is that, unlike most economic analyses or analyses grounded in the strategy literature, the purchase funnel does not treat consumers as making a single discrete decision. Instead, it recognizes that for each decision that any one consumer makes, the consumer must pass through a series of distinct hurdles progressing from awareness to consideration, conversion, and post-purchase. Laying out these steps can be helpful in a large variety of litigation contexts. Specifically, this framework can assist the finder of fact in understanding the following:

- Why a simple regression analysis in a damages case that tries to map a single variable to a purchase decision may not adequately capture a more complex purchasing process.
- When a patented product feature under dispute might be important in the purchasing process, and what other factors might also influence a customer purchase decision.
- When a particular instance of a disputed use of a trademark or trade dress might be relevant for a customer's decision-making, or for a customer's state of knowledge at the time they are exposed to a trademark or trade dress.
- How different types of advertising or disclosures might have different types of influence at various points in the purchase process.

[*] The authors wish to profusely thank Joe Bourdage and Grace Brittan, both of Analysis Group, for their invaluable research assistance.

In general, the purchase funnel as a framework has wide applicability and features that make it practically helpful in litigation. First, as we discuss in Section 1.1, this framework is one of the oldest in marketing, with the advantages of having myriad academic articles written on it as well as being broadly used in industry. Second, the purchase funnel is intuitive – anyone who has bought something can recognize the different stages in the consumer journey in their own behavior. The purchase funnel framework helps people on the bench, in the jury box, or otherwise past the bar translate their own insights about their everyday behavior as a consumer to new contexts in an organized and rigorous way. Third, it is a way of adding structure in contexts where it is otherwise hard to find a formal structure – such as consumer purchasing behavior or consumers' navigation of the digital world.

This chapter starts by describing more thoroughly the framework and its historical grounding in the academic literature. It then discusses the use of the framework to disentangle cause and effect in four particular litigation contexts: consumer protection, antitrust, and intellectual property (including both patent and trademark litigation).

1.1 WHAT IS THE PURCHASE FUNNEL?

Perhaps one of the oldest theories in marketing is the purchase funnel, which lays out the series of hurdles that a potential customer must overcome if they are to purchase a new product or service. In 1898, advertising executive E. St. Elmo Lewis made one of the earliest attempts at describing this process. Lewis laid out four steps through which a customer engages an advertisement, which he called AIDA: A – Attention, I – Interest of the Customer, D – Desire, and A – Action. Through AIDA, an advertiser would introduce a product to the consumer, convince the consumer of their need for the product, and, ideally, sell them the product at the end of the exchange. In the 1920s, firms adopted the more common "funnel" framework still recognized today.[1] The image of the funnel reflects the idea that, although firms might engage consumers at various phases of their shopping behavior, consumers inevitably drop off at each phase. The funnel shared with AIDA the underlying goal of tracing the consumer experience from introduction to sale.

Since this early work, many consumer behavior specialists have tried to understand the nuances and drivers of the precise stages within the purchase funnel and the interaction between these stages. This emphasis on the understanding of consumer behavior led some researchers to relabel the purchase funnel the "consumer buying path" or the "consumer journey" in order to reflect the consumer-centric nature of the behavior it described. Newer research suggests that the purchase process tends to be far more iterative and less straightforward than earlier models

---

[1] Edward K. Strong, Jr., "Theories of Selling," 9 J. Applied Psych. 76 (1925).

assumed.² These academic insights from the 1990s were formalized in a report from McKinsey & Company, which emphasized the idea of an iterative purchase decision journey rather than a funnel. The McKinsey report studied 20,000 consumers across five industries: automobiles, skin care, insurance, consumer electronics, and mobile telecoms. Through an analysis of online purchase data, the McKinsey report proposed that consumers may start their search with some brands in mind and that their choices may expand as they shop and learn more about a product category.³ The report highlighted the interplay of awareness and consideration in the purchase process, as consumers may learn about new products even as they move closer to making a purchase. This ongoing research confirms why the purchase funnel continues to be a helpful framework precisely because of the ease with which it can be updated as technology and advertising methods change.⁴

Broadly, the modern consumer buying path maps consumer purchase behavior into four phases that determine whether or not a consumer purchases or repurchases a product: awareness, consideration, conversion, and post-purchase.

Phase 1: Awareness. In the awareness phase, consumers become aware of either the brand or the product. Firms may introduce the brand or product through digital or traditional advertising, or consumers gain awareness through digital or traditional word of mouth. The awareness phase may be relevant for both new and existing brands. If customers are already aware of a brand, advertising can create something called the "mere exposure" effect, whereby repeated exposure can help prompt brand affinity and draw attention to new products from a particular brand.⁵ Sometimes the barrier at this phase is a simple lack of "problem recognition" – that the consumer does not realize they have a problem or recognize the problem the firm is trying to solve.⁶

Phase 2: Consideration. In the consideration phase, a consumer's role is generally less passive. At this stage, consumers gather more information about the products or services in their "consideration set." As their preferences become more refined, consumers may introduce or eliminate products based on price, perceived

---

² Demetrios Vakratsas & Tim Ambler, "How Advertising Works: What Do We Really Know," 63:1 *J. Mktg.* 38 (1999).
³ David Court, Dave Elzinga, Susan Mulder & Ole Jørgen Vetvik, "The Consumer Decision Journey," 3:3 *McKinsey Q.* 96–107 (2009).
⁴ For example, Mark Ritson argued that "[t]he sales funnel precedes the invention of television, direct mail, telemarketing, cinema ads, the internet and smartphones. Each and every one of these technologies has changed the tactical options available to advertisers, but the essential challenge of advertising strategy and the enduring value of a properly derived sales funnel remain undimmed." Mark Ritson, "If You Think the Sales Funnel Is Dead, You've Mistaken Tactics for Strategy," *Mktg. Wk.* (Apr. 6, 2016), www.marketingweek.com/mark-ritson-if-you-think-the-sales-funnel-is-dead-youve-mistaken-tactics-for-strategy/.
⁵ Robert B. Zajonc, "Attitudinal Effects of Mere Exposure," 202 *J. Personality & Soc. Psych.* 1 (1968).
⁶ Gordon C. Bruner & Richard J. Pomazal, "Problem Recognition: The Crucial First Stage of the Consumer Decision Process," 5 *J. Cons. Mktg.* 53 (1988).

quality, connection to the product, affinity for the brand's mission, or other factors. Consumers in the consideration phase look for differences among competing products, and may turn to customer reviews, review websites, and other digital information sources.

Phase 3: Conversion. The next phase is conversion. At this point, a consumer likely has decided which product to buy, if any, and price becomes an even more important factor. Often, consumers who appear to have selected a product do not actually follow through on the purchase for various reasons, such as social influences, lack of availability, high price, financial status, or time pressure.[7]

Phase 4: Post-purchase. The final phase, post-purchase, can be a critical part of the consumer buying path. This phase determines how the purchaser talks about the product or service to other consumers and whether the consumer becomes a repeat customer (reentering the funnel). A consumer reentering the purchase funnel after trying the product once may have a different experience, passing through stages more quickly or even skipping stages. For example, a consumer who had a positive experience with the brand may simplify their buying experience in the future, not giving serious consideration to other alternatives. In the case of smaller, more frequently purchased items such as household cleaners or bath tissue, the consumer may develop a purchase routine defaulting to one brand, without considering others. Alternatively, consumers who did not like the brand, or are open to variety, may reenter the purchase funnel with the intention of considering other alternatives.

1.2 USING THE PURCHASE FUNNEL TO DISENTANGLE CAUSE AND EFFECT IN LITIGATION

Many litigation cases grapple with questions of how a particular business action influences market outcomes. The rest of this chapter provides examples of how the purchase funnel can be used in a variety of litigation cases. To prove a link between actions and outcomes, litigators have typically relied on economists to "prove" the link through techniques such as regression analysis. However, an expert opinion exclusively based on regression analysis may incorrectly infer a causal link between the at-issue conduct and the endpoint. For many cases, a closer examination of the consumer decision-making process reflected in the purchase funnel can complement – or contradict – econometric assumptions of causality.

Understanding the purchase funnel and the decisions that consumers make at each step can clarify the data-generating process and help the expert design and calibrate an analytical model. In consumer protection matters, plaintiffs may argue that an allegedly incorrect representation or deceptive practice changes consumer purchasing decisions and causes consumers to pay more – or purchase more – than

---

[7] Monika Kukar-Kinney & Angeline G. Close, "The Determinants of Consumers' Online Shopping Cart Abandonment," 38 *J. Acad. Mktg. Sci.* 240 (2010) at 44–48.

they would with "correct" information. In antitrust cases, the focus is similarly on harm to consumers who have purchased a product or service arising from the exercise of market power. In intellectual property matters, parties could allege that a new product using patent-infringing technology caused an older product from a competing company to lose consumer purchases. In trademark infringement cases, parties will debate whether the alleged trademark infringement caused consumer confusion. A framework that follows the consumer buying path may both improve a regression analysis and help the expert lay out the "narrative" behind statistical relationships.

In this section we apply the purchase funnel approach to litigation matters involving consumer protection, antitrust, and intellectual property, including both patent and trademark matters. We show that the purchase funnel can identify the mechanisms behind consumer decisions at each step in the buying process, helping the expert to design and calibrate statistical models linking actions and outcomes. Using a mix of well-known and less well-known cases in each of these areas, we illustrate the usefulness of the purchase funnel approach to matters where legal theories of consumer behavior are at the center of judicial decision-making.

1.2.1 The Funnel and Consumer Protection

Class actions involving consumer protection, false advertising, and other allegations of misleading firm behavior often hinge on issues related to consumer perception and decision-making. Identifying where and how perception changes, and how the change in perception impacts decisions, may depend on where consumers are within the purchase funnel. A recent California class action concerning the popular beverage kombucha, which alleged violations of California's Unfair Competition Law (UCL), California's False Advertising Law (FAL), California's Consumer Legal Remedies Act (CLRA), and breach of express warranty, highlights precisely these issues.[8] The plaintiff took issue with a dry tea-bag product, "Yogi Green Tea Kombucha," which is manufactured and sold by defendant East West Tea Company LLC. The plaintiff argued that East West Tea Co. advertised and sold its product as containing "Organic Kombucha," despite the product containing no kombucha as understood by the plaintiff.[9] The plaintiff argued further that East West Tea Co. cannot market the tea-bag product as kombucha because the product does not contain "live organisms," which the plaintiff argued is a "common understanding" of the meaning of kombucha.[10]

---

[8] *Cohen v. E. W. Tea Co.*, No. 17-2339, 2018 U.S. Dist. LEXIS 130151 (S.D. Cal. Aug. 2, 2018).
[9] Ibid. at 2.
[10] Ibid. at 4.

In consumer "class action" lawsuits, one or more plaintiffs file a lawsuit on behalf of all individuals who have common claims against one or more defendants.[11] For a class action lawsuit to proceed, the class must first be "certified." Two of the factors that must be met for class certification are that there are questions of law or fact common to the class (commonality) and that the claims of the named plaintiff or plaintiffs are typical to the class (typicality).[12] The plaintiff or plaintiffs must also demonstrate the existence of a common methodology for assessing damages.

In this case, East West Tea Co. filed a motion to dismiss the case on the ground that their product's labeling does not mislead the "reasonable consumer," a crucial test that the court uses to govern claims under the UCL, FAL, and CLRA. Under the test, the plaintiff must demonstrate that the "reasonable consumer" is "likely to be deceived" by the at-issue label.[13] Likelihood of deception is proved affirmatively if the court concludes that "it is probable that a significant portion of the general consuming public or of targeted consumers, acting reasonably under the circumstances, could be misled."[14]

Considering the at-issue tea product in *Cohen v. East West Tea Company LLC* through the purchase funnel processes of awareness, consideration, conversion, and post-purchase can inform an analysis of the effect of the label "Organic Kombucha" on consumer behavior. This analysis can provide an assessment of whether consumers in the proposed class suffered a common and typical impact – creating a case for class certification – and whether or not the label likely deceived the "reasonable consumer." In the remainder of this section, we describe consumers' interactions with the at-issue product at each stage of the funnel. We describe how expert analyses targeted at various stages of the purchase funnel can speak to critical issues within the stages of a class action case, including class certification, damages, and defendants' motions to dismiss.

Awareness. Most kombucha products on the market are bottled, refrigerated beverages typically made by fermenting brewed tea with sugar and a sourdough starter-like "symbiotic culture of bacteria and yeast" known as SCOBY. The resulting beverage often contains probiotic bacterial cultures.[15] Although kombucha has "been brewed in homes for centuries," the commercial product is a relative newcomer to the North American beverage market.[16] To date, in the United States,

---

[11] Fed. R. Civ. P. 23(b).
[12] Fed. R. Civ. P. 23(a).
[13] *Freeman v. Time*, 68 F.3d 285, 288–90 (9th Cir. 1995).
[14] *Lavie v. Procter & Gamble Co.*, 105 Cal. App. 4th 496, 508 (Cal. Ct. App. 2003).
[15] Elaine Watson, "Do Consumers Expect Kombucha to Contain Live Organisms? Court Gives Green Light to Lawsuit," *Food Navigator USA* (Aug. 2018), www.foodnavigator-usa.com/Article/2018/08/21/Do-consumers-expect-kombucha-to-contain-live-organisms-Court-gives-green-light-to-lawsuit#.
[16] The first US commercial brand, GT Kombucha, was founded in 1995. Kombucha Brewers International, *History of Kombucha Brewing* (2019), https://kombuchabrewers.org/about-us/history-of-kombucha-brewing/.

there is no industry consensus or currently existing FDA regulation defining kombucha, and manufacturers of kombucha products use different methods and add-ins to create their products.[17]

In the complaint, the plaintiff's counsel asserts that all putative class members "would not have purchased the Kombucha Products absent Defendant's misrepresentation regarding the composition of the Kombucha Products."[18] In other words, the complaint makes it clear that the Kombucha plaintiffs believe that class members were aware of the health benefits of ready-to-drink kombucha and purchased Yogi Green Tea Kombucha in ready-to-brew tea bags for that reason. The Kombucha Complaint further asserts that "the Plaintiff's claims are typical of the claims of the Class Members because … all Class Members have been deceived (or were likely to be deceived) by Defendant's false and misleading advertising claims about the composition of Defendant's products."[19]

Despite the Kombucha plaintiffs' claims of common harm and typicality in consumer deception, there may be large variations in consumer awareness of the product category, as well as variations in what consumers understand the product label to mean. For example, some purchasers of "Yogi Green Tea Kombucha" may not be aware of the brewed, ready-to-drink kombucha product category at all. The "kombucha" label on "Yogi Green Tea Kombucha" may stand out to a particular type of consumer who is variety-seeking, and therefore open to the various alternatives displayed on the dry-tea shelf at the supermarket. To this consumer, the not-at-issue elements of product packaging, including the word "NEW" printed in a sticker-like way on the tea box, could increase the likelihood that they notice the label and become aware of the product with or without attending to the term "kombucha." Prior consumer awareness of the brewed, ready-to-drink kombucha product category may also play a role in the impact of the at-issue representations. Some consumers, like the named plaintiff, may be aware of an association between kombucha and "live organisms," and perhaps they have knowledge of the typical kombucha brewing process. Perhaps a subset of these consumers have even brewed their own kombucha in the past. Other informed consumers may have a more vague level of awareness: they know that kombucha contains certain healthful vitamins, antioxidants, or other beneficial ingredients, and assume that "Yogi Green Tea Kombucha," though not the refrigerated drink they are familiar with, also contains some of these nutrients. Because consumers enter the purchase funnel with different levels of awareness, an analysis of class-certification-related issues may hinge on establishing the extent of consumers' awareness surrounding the specific "Yogi

---

[17] For example, some products are pasteurized, and some use coffee as a base product, instead of tea. Watson, "Do Consumers Expect Kombucha."
[18] Class Action Complaint at 3, *Cohen v. E. W. Tea Co.*, No. 17-2339 (S.D. Cal. Nov. 17, 2017).
[19] Ibid. at 13.

Green Tea Kombucha" product and the brewed, ready-to-drink kombucha product category.

An expert retained at the class certification stage of this case may research consumer awareness of the kombucha product category as a starting point of their opinion. Because kombucha is a relatively new and growing product category in the United States, the expert could analyze consumers' information-seeking behavior to establish an appropriate context. For example, an analysis of historical Internet searches for "kombucha," including its proximity to keywords such as "probiotic," "bacteria," "cultures," and other terms related to the plaintiff's alleged "live organisms" understanding could show the prevalence of this association among other terms, for example "health," "benefits," or even "alcohol content." This contextualizing analysis could extend to mentions of "kombucha" in online articles, blogs, online forums, or on social media, and inform a review of the network of associations that exist around the kombucha product category. Such an analysis could also detect developments and changes in these associations over time.

Under the awareness step of the purchase funnel framework, the expert could also conduct a survey to assess current consumer familiarity with the kombucha product category. Following established survey design best practices, the expert could gauge respondent awareness of several established and developing food and beverage product categories, including red-herring product categories.[20] For respondents who indicate awareness of kombucha, the survey could pose open-ended questions, asking respondents to describe the beverage and any associations they have with it (hot or cold, sweet or sour, etc.). An analysis of the survey results would build evidence for the network of associations that exist around kombucha.

Another survey aimed at exploring consumer awareness of the product category could examine the at-issue product specifically. After screening past or prospective purchasers among the relevant population, the survey would display an image of "Yogi Green Tea Kombucha" and sort the subjects into groups based on whether or not they have previously seen or purchased the product. Those who have purchased the product would resemble members of the proposed class, while the non-purchasers would resemble the general public. The survey could then allow consumers to examine all sides of the at-issue product's packaging and respond to questions expressing their understanding of the package's claims or associations.

These potential studies targeted at the awareness stage would allow the testifying expert to demonstrate whether or not there is a coherence in consumer awareness of the kombucha product category or differences between consumer groups with varying awareness levels. To the extent that there is coherence, expert analysis could

---

[20] Examples of developing categories could be other foods and beverages that have grown in popularity in the past decade, including hummus, sriracha sauce, sparkling water, and cold brew coffee. A red herring product category could be something plausible, like "sassafras oil," which exists but is unavailable in the United States for regulatory reasons.

also provide insight into the expectations and associations with kombucha among consumers with various levels of awareness of the product category. Analyses honed at the awareness stage of the purchase funnel may ultimately demonstrate the difficulties in certifying a class of consumers who are all assumed to have the same associations with the word "kombucha."

Consideration. At the consideration stage of the purchase funnel, the consumer seeks information about products in the product category and considers various alternatives. As with the awareness stage, an analysis of consumer behavior at the consideration stage can also show that questions of commonality and typicality in a proposed class require rigorous treatment.

A key insight at the consideration stage is that the amount of research and length of the consideration period varies across products. Purchase decisions are often classified by the level of involvement consumers have during the purchase process, on a spectrum that ranges from low to high involvement. For a high-involvement purchase, like a new car, consumers typically seek out greater amounts of information and spend more time considering options, up to many years in advance.[21] For low-involvement purchases, consumers conduct little research, if any, before purchase. Consumers typically have low involvement with most low-cost, frequently purchased products which would likely include ready-to-drink kombucha beverages and tea bags.[22] For certain consumers, this lack of research or low involvement might increase consumer susceptibility to product claims. The low cost and low risk associated with purchasing Yogi Green Tea Kombucha gives consumers little incentive to research competing claims. At best, the consumer repurchases the product; at worst, the partially used box joins other half-used boxes of tea bags in consumer cupboards.

In *Cohen v. East West Tea Company LLC*, the channel through which a consumer first becomes aware of the product may affect the length and involvement of the consideration period and considerable differences in the types of channels used may be problematic for a conclusion of commonality. Consumers who encountered Yogi Green Tea Kombucha for the first time on a supermarket shelf may purchase the item without even noticing the kombucha-related label – some other feature, such as the "green tea," the "USDA Organic" label, or the Yogi brand may instead drive their consideration. Other consumers, whose first exposure to Yogi Green Tea Kombucha came through a print or digital advertisement, may conduct more research in advance of purchase and be less susceptible to any allegedly false claims. Commonality in the class would require that all members of the class considered and ultimately purchased the tea for a narrow band of reasons related

---

[21] Keith Clarke & Russell W. Belk, "The Effects of Product Involvement and Task Definition on Anticipated Consumer Effort," 6 *Advances in Consumer Rsch.* 313–14 (1979).

[22] Philip Kotler & Kevin L. Keller, chapter 6 in *Marketing Management* 202 (15th ed.), Pearson Prentice-Hall (2016).

to the term "kombucha" in the product name. Such analyses would likely undermine the Kombucha plaintiff's claims of commonality.

A consumer's consideration set consists of the potential brands and products that the consumer considers purchasing for the same purpose. For example, some consumers may evaluate Yogi Green Tea Kombucha in the same product category as ready-to-drink kombucha: both are purportedly healthy beverages. Perhaps these consumers have differing amounts of knowledge about the typical kombucha brewing process. Conversely, some consumers who regularly purchase brewed, ready-to-drink kombucha or who understand the kombucha brewing process might not include traditional kombucha and Yogi Green Tea Kombucha in the same consideration set. These consumers may not consider purchasing Yogi Green Tea Kombucha or tea-bag products at all, or they may consider the tea bags against other non-kombucha tea products, coffees, herbal teas, or a range of other grocery and pharmaceutical products.

The assumed drivers behind consumer consideration of the at-issue product may have consequences for class certification and the success of a motion to dismiss. In this case, the plaintiff alleged that she purchased the tea product as a result of the package's "Organic Kombucha" representation and the package's claim that the tea "combine[s] Green Tea with Kombucha to supply antioxidants to support your overall health." The plaintiff argued that she would not have purchased Yogi Green Tea Kombucha "but for Defendant's misrepresentation that the tea did in fact contain Organic Kombucha." In response, East West Tea Co. argued that the product's packaging clarifies any ambiguity about the definition of kombucha and that the product does not fail the reasonable consumer test. Because the product's packaging contains instructions to boil the tea bag in hot water, the company argued, the reasonable consumer would conclude that there could be no live kombucha-specific organisms "present in the tea bag when the tea is boiled."[23]

The court sided with the plaintiff, denying the defendant's motion to dismiss in August 2018. The court could not conclude that consumers were unlikely to be deceived and noted that case law is "mixed ... on whether ambiguity regarding the definition of a word merits a motion to dismiss." How a reasonable consumer defines kombucha is "a question of fact," the court determined. With no "approved nor agreed upon definition of kombucha," the plaintiff had made a plausible case that consumers had been deceived. Had the defendants undertaken an analysis of consumers' consideration of Yogi Green Tea Kombucha, the court might have been able to rely on empirical evidence to disentangle the general ambiguities noted in the court's opinion.[24]

---

[23] *Cohen v. E. W. Tea Co.*, No. 17-2339, 2018 U.S. Dist. LEXIS 130151 at *9 (S.D. Cal. Aug. 2, 2018).

[24] Ibid. at *8–9.

Conversion. At the conversion stage, the value that consumers place on the kombucha label becomes an important question. In other words, does the at-issue label make all consumers more or less likely to purchase the tea product? At what price? Or at what price for certain consumers, if any? For example, consumers who are aware of the brewed, ready-to-drink kombucha product category and associate kombucha with health benefits may be more inclined to purchase Yogi Green Tea Kombucha. Other consumers, whose consideration sets include both Yogi Green Tea Kombucha and other tea-bag products and supplements, may be more inclined to purchase the product for claims unrelated to the "Organic Kombucha" labeling. At the same time, the claims may not affect the decisions of consumers who understand Yogi Green Tea Kombucha to be distinct from traditional kombucha. The list of potential effects of the at-issue claim on different types of consumers goes on, and includes the type of consumer who would be a member of the proposed class: those "who would not have purchased the Kombucha Products absent" the alleged misrepresentation of its composition.

An expert at this stage might conduct a survey experiment to isolate the effect of the at-issue label and packaging on the purchase of Yogi Green Tea Kombucha. After screening for qualified past and prospective purchasers, the expert would randomly assign respondents to two experimental groups. One group, the control group, would view the original Yogi Green Tea Kombucha packaging, and the other group, the test group, would view the same package but with an alteration that tests the allegations of the case. For example, the package that the test group sees could have a disclaimer stating the differences between the product and brewed, ready-to-drink kombucha, or an alteration to the product's name, perhaps simply "Yogi Green Tea with Antioxidants," such that the "kombucha" association is removed. Both groups of respondents would then be asked about their likelihood of purchasing the tea product. In a properly designed experiment among the relevant population, any significant difference between groups would demonstrate the impact of the at-issue claim on consumers' purchase intent. Conversely, such a study could show that the at-issue claim is not at all material to consumers' decisions, which may aid an argument about what drives the purchase decisions of the "reasonable consumer."

This type of analysis would also be informative should the case proceed to the damages phase. If the class were to be certified, the court would determine appropriate damages to be owed to those who purchased the tea as a result of the alleged misrepresentations. An informed analysis at the conversion stage would demonstrate the extent to which the at-issue packaging and representations are actual purchase drivers for the tea product. An expert demonstrating how various consumers entered the purchase funnel, formed a consideration set that includes the product, and ultimately came to purchase the product could provide empirical evidence against the singular narrative that the plaintiff advanced on behalf of the class.

Post-purchase. The post-purchase stage determines whether or not consumers would buy the product again. At this stage, the at-issue "organic kombucha" label could again have multiple effects on post-purchase consumer evaluation of the product. For example, previous consumers of traditional kombucha who expected Yogi Green Tea Kombucha to be the same may be disappointed and be less likely to purchase the product again. Other consumers, who do not associate the product with the kombucha product category or are unaware of traditional kombucha, may consider repurchasing the product for reasons other than the at-issue representations.

During the damages phase of such a case, the extent of the injury could depend in part on consumer evaluation of their experience(s) with the at-issue product. In a world in which the product's packaging is found to contain misrepresentations of the type alleged by the Kombucha plaintiff, consumers who would not have bought the product at all but for the misrepresentations suffer an injury different to those who paid a price premium for a green-tea product with the allegedly false "kombucha" labeling. Consumers who would not have bought the product at all could be compensated for the full price of the product, whereas consumers who paid a price premium might only be compensated for the incremental amount they paid for the product. In a class action lawsuit, there needs to be a common method for assessing damages within the class. In this case, consumers suffering different types of harm should not be considered in the same class for a damages analysis, as a common method cannot reflect these different types of harm.

1.2.2 *The Funnel and Antitrust Litigation*

In 1998, the US Department of Justice famously accused Microsoft of illegally bundling its Internet Explorer browser with the Windows operating system in order to limit the potential market for Netscape Navigator and other rival Web browsers. The behavior was alleged to have resulted in stifled innovation and higher prices.[25] In 2001, a US appeals court upheld that Microsoft had abused its near-monopoly in the operating system market to promote its software products. After the decision, AOL-Time Warner, the then-parent company of Netscape, sued Microsoft for three times the amount of damages that the company had incurred over the seven-year period of Microsoft's illegal bundling behavior. Counsel for AOL-Time Warner claimed that "there [was] no question that Microsoft's conduct violated the law and harmed competition and consumers."[26]

In antitrust cases, plaintiffs (which can include enforcers and/or competing firms) claim that consumers are harmed from the defendant's exercise of market power.

---

[25] Complaint at 11, *United States v. Microsoft Corp.*, No. 98-1232 (D.D.C. May 18, 1998).
[26] David Teather, "Netscape Sues Microsoft for Unfair Practice," *The Guardian* (Jan. 2002), www.theguardian.com/media/2002/jan/23/citynews.business.

One type of potential antitrust violation is bundling, as in *United States* v. *Microsoft* and *Netscape* v. *Microsoft*. Bundling is when the seller of a product requires consumers to purchase another product as well. Bundling can have both costs and benefits for consumers. Bundling can lower supplier production costs, or reduce consumer transaction and information costs.[27] Bundling behavior can also harm competition and consumers by reducing competition, which is said to ultimately harm consumers through price increases or a decrease in choice. In the Microsoft cases, the questions of harm focused on whether the bundling of Internet Explorer with Windows would lead Microsoft to hold monopoly power in the browser industry as a result of its near-monopoly in the operating system market, resulting in stifled innovation in the development of Web browsers.

The purchase funnel provides a framework for evaluating the potential effects of the alleged anticompetitive behavior during the purchase process and assessing the extent of consumer harm. In particular, an evaluation of the Web browser dispute through the lens of the purchase funnel can provide reasonable insight into whether, but for Microsoft's bundling behavior, consumers would instead have purchased and used Netscape Navigator.

Awareness. Web browsers were a novel product in the mid-1990s. Netscape launched Netscape Navigator, the first commercial Web browser, in late 1994.[28] Microsoft debuted Internet Explorer eight months later, initially as an add-on package for Windows 95.[29] Both companies were early participants in the rapidly growing market for home access to the World Wide Web. In 1997, the year in which Microsoft integrated Internet Explorer 4.0 with Windows, 18 percent of US households had a home Internet connection, a figure that would spike to over 40 percent by the year 2000.[30]

During this period, many consumers were unaware of Web browsers. In 1995, only 3 percent of consumers with a home Internet connection had used the World Wide Web.[31] Microsoft's bundling may have actually benefited consumers

---

[27] Christian Ahlborn, David S. Evans & A. Jorge Padilla, "The Antitrust Economics of Tying: A Farewell to Per Se Illegality," 49 *Antitrust Bull.* 287 (2004).

[28] David Shedden, "Today in Media History: The First Commercial Web Browser, Netscape Navigator, Is Released in 1994," *Poynter* (Oct. 2014), www.poynter.org/reporting-editing/2014/today-in-media-history-the-first-commercial-web-browser-netscape-navigator-is-released-in-1994/.

[29] Jimmy Daly & Cherilyn Winkler, "A Visual History of Internet Explorer," *StateTech Mag.* (Aug. 2013), https://statetechmagazine.com/article/2013/08/visual-history-internet-explorer.

[30] "Percentage of Households with Internet Use in the United States," *Statista* (Sept. 2018), www.statista.com/statistics/189349/us-households-home-internet-connection-subscription//.

[31] Sixty-five percent of these consumers used email at least once every few weeks, which required an Internet connection but not necessarily access to the World Wide Web. "Americans Going Online ... Explosive Growth, Uncertain Destinations," *Pew Rsch. Ctr.* (Oct. 16, 1995), www.pewresearch.org/politics/1995/10/16/americans-going-online-explosive-growth-uncertain-destinations/; "World Wide Web Timeline," *Pew Rsch. Ctr.* (Mar. 11, 2014), www.pewinternet.org/2014/03/11/world-wide-web-timeline/.

(and Netscape as well) by raising awareness of browsers in general. Court documents from the Microsoft antitrust case highlight the limited awareness that consumers had of the Web browser category. In his Findings of Fact, US District Judge Thomas Penfield noted that "[t]he inclusion of Internet Explorer with Windows at no separate charge increased general familiarity with the Internet and reduced the cost to the public of gaining access to it."[32]

While Netscape's market share dropped from more than 70 percent in 1995 to less than 20 percent after the bundling began, vastly more consumers were using Web browsers to connect to the Internet.[33] An analysis that considers the purchase funnel would necessarily incorporate the large difference in awareness of the Internet and changes in this awareness over time, growth in home Internet connections, and increasing adoption of home PCs. But for Microsoft's bundling of Internet Explorer with its operating system, awareness of browsers might not have been so high. An analysis of the awareness phase of the purchase funnel might leverage internal marketing documents produced by the parties such as consumer brand-awareness research and other metrics tracking brand strength vis-à-vis competitors in key consumer segments. Such documents would likely indicate low overall awareness of Internet browsers (and Netscape in particular) among consumers considering their first purchase of a Windows PC.[34] An expert would be able to leverage such evidence to weaken counterfactual growth projections for Netscape market share. Evidence of limited or growing awareness of Internet browsers would dispute the proposition that, but for Microsoft's bundling, the same consumer would have bought the Netscape Navigator browser.

Consideration. For consumers who were newly aware of the browser product category, the bundling could potentially preclude any consideration of other browsers. Having a browser pre-installed for free on a personal computer makes the search for other browser options unnecessary, unless consumers are aware of alternatives and actively seek them out. For many everyday Windows users, the operating system's capability to run its pre-installed software was likely among the most salient qualities in choosing to purchase or upgrade. A *New York Times* review of Windows 98, for example, noted that "the most noticeable change [compared to Windows 95] is that Windows 98 blurs the distinction between information that resides on a local hard disk and information that exists on the Internet," which consumers accessed through Internet Explorer.[35]

---

[32] *United States v. Microsoft Corp.*, 84 F. Supp. 2d 9, 110 ¶408 (D.D.C. Nov. 5, 1999).
[33] Complaint at 7 ¶11, *Netscape Commc'ns Corp. v. Microsoft Corp.*, No. 02-97 (D.D.C. Jan. 22, 2002).
[34] Klint Finley, "The Sorry Legacy of Internet Explorer," *Wired* (Jan. 2016), www.wired.com/2016/01/the-sorry-legacy-of-microsoft-internet-explorer/.
[35] Peter H. Lewis, "Windows 98, The Tuneup," *NY Times* (Apr. 30, 1998), www.nytimes.com/1998/04/30/technology/windows-98-the-tuneup.html.

For another type of consumer, who was either aware of other Web browsers or already using Netscape Navigator, other browsers may have entered their consideration set. Some consumers clearly preferred Netscape Navigator, either out of tech-savvy preference for the browser's features compared to Internet Explorer or existing familiarity. After Internet Explorer was released for free and Navigator began losing market share, the company seemed to recognize that its profits would come from consumers who valued advanced tech or familiarity, and accordingly invested in continued development of their Web software and methods to direct traffic to their popular home page. After charging $50 or more for Navigator in the years after its free initial launch, Netscape again made the browser free for noncommercial users in January 1998.[36] The *New York Times* noted in November 2000 that "[i]n no other industry do the two market leaders invest so much money and effort in their products and then distribute them free."[37]

As discussed below, even loyal Netscape users may have still switched to Internet Explorer at the conversion stage of the funnel. An analysis of the consideration phase could incorporate an evaluation of different product attributes that consumers weighed (if at all) when selecting a browser. Such analysis could be informed by natural language processing of consumer reviews and expert reviews in the popular press, revealing perhaps that certain technical stumbles with buggy products such as Netscape Navigator 2 alienated influential customer groups, making these groups more open to considering alternatives.

Conversion. Well-regarded contemporaneous sources found Netscape Navigator to be the technically superior browser, pointing to Netscape's pioneering introduction of innovative browser features such as JavaScript that later became bedrock components of Web browsing.[38] Pointing to Netscape Navigator's drastic market share drop from more than 70 percent in 1995 to less than 20 percent after the bundling of Internet Explorer with Windows, antitrust enforcers alleged that the bundling limited competition beyond what should reasonably be expected, artificially restricting the choices available to consumers. Even if the browser itself was nominally free, as Netscape was starting in 1998, other "costs" of switching browsers included convenience and time costs from researching the product, downloading it, and installing it on a personal computer. The comparable monetary, convenience, and time costs of using Internet Explorer on a Windows PC was zero. To late 1990s Web users, "some logging on for the first time, the differences [between Netscape Navigator and Internet Explorer] were negligible. The deciding factor was that

---

[36] "Netscape: A History," BBC News (Feb. 10, 2000), http://news.bbc.co.uk/2/hi/in_depth/business/2000/microsoft/635689.stm.
[37] David Pogue, "State of the Art; Netscape 6 Browser: Mixed Bag," NY *Times* (Nov. 30, 2000), www.nytimes.com/2000/11/30/technology/state-of-the-art-netscape-6-browser-mixed-bag.html/.
[38] David Flanagan, *JavaScript: The Definitive Guide* (5th ed., 2006).

Microsoft owned Windows 95."[39] For users of Windows who were aware of and would consider using Netscape Navigator, the "cost" of switching browsers could have been enough to preclude consumers from using Netscape, despite its other benefits. Alternatively, the aforementioned technology missteps by Netscape may have been enough to encourage formerly devoted Netscape customers to try alternative browsers.

Today, the explosion of free browsers creates another barrier – complexity. Although there were not as many choices during the "browser wars" of the late 1990s as there are today, consumers still had options. Faced with an abundance of nominally free choices that may nonetheless require trial and error to find the "best" choice, it is easy to understand why consumers experience choice overload and simply stick with the default option pre-installed on their computer.

Proper consideration of consumer behavior can help analyze the extent to which consumer decisions and purchases would have been different had the alleged actions not been taken. Any regression analysis tracking the conversion phase endpoint of profits, sales, or adoption against key dates, without regard to influencer perception, consumer behavior, and emerging competitive incentives in a rapidly growing market, would be necessarily incomplete. The use of a funnel helps identify when regression analysis captures appropriately a "but-for" world or instead misses out on key parts of consumer behavior.

Post-purchase. In the post-purchase phase of the browser purchase funnel, consumers evaluate whether to continue using Internet Explorer or to try an alternative browser. Network effects and the installed base effect would encourage consumers to continue using Internet Explorer and also attract new customers to Internet Explorer.

Economists use "network effects" to describe contexts in which a good or service offers increasing benefits the more users it has. In the case of multi-sided platforms, there are direct and indirect network effects. Direct network effects affect users on the same side of the platform – for example, a fax machine becomes more useful as other people also use fax machines. Indirect network effects flow across to users on another side of the platform. For example, Uber would not be a very useful app for a rider if there were no drivers using the platform. Similarly, drivers would not want to use the Uber app if no riders were using it.[40] In the case of browsers, one side of the platform is users, and the other side is developers who develop content for websites or programs that run on websites.[41] Developers want to write code for websites on browsers that many consumers use. Users want to use the browser that is compatible

---

[39] Matt Blitz, "Later, Navigator: How Netscape Won and Then Lost the World Wide Web," *Popular Mechs.* (Apr. 2019), www.popularmechanics.com/culture/web/a27033147/netscape-navigator-history/.
[40] Catherine Tucker, "Network Effects and Market Power: What Have We Learned in the Last Decade," *Antitrust* (Spring 2018).
[41] Timothy F. Bresnahan, Network Effects and Microsoft, Stanford U. Manuscript (2001).

with most websites. This leads to a positive feedback loop where both consumers and developers wanted to use the browser with the most users – Microsoft Internet Explorer.

Once the majority of consumers were using Internet Explorer, the "installed base effect" would incentivize consumers to continue using it. The installed base effect occurs when there are benefits of compatibility with other consumers.[42] For example, standardization of the keyboard or other machinery makes learned skills more transferable. Using Microsoft Word software makes it easier to transfer files to others. Website programmers began to optimize page displays for the Internet Explorer browser as this would ensure a uniform browsing experience for the largest potential group of consumers. In this case, the installed base effect means that, even if a new browser was superior, consumers would be reluctant to adopt a new browser unless all other users did so as well. Such effects cannot be incorporated easily into an endpoints-based regression analysis.

At the time of the settlement in *Netscape v. Microsoft* in 2003, Internet Explorer had a 95 percent market share of the browser market.[43] Netscape Navigator languished for several more years before AOL-Time Warner, which had purchased Netscape in 1999, pulled support for the browser in March 2008.[44] Advances in technology and changes in consumer preferences have since allowed other companies to enter the Web browser market and flourish. As of 2019, Microsoft browsers (Internet Explorer and its 2015 sequel, Microsoft Edge) still arrive pre-installed on Windows PCs, but Microsoft browsers are no longer the market leader. As in the period of the Netscape–Microsoft browser wars, other browser companies continue to give away browsers for "free," with new dimensions of competition including browser personalization, synchronization with other applications, privacy, and speed. The most popular worldwide browser today, Google Chrome, competes against the Microsoft browsers, Apple Safari, Mozilla Firefox (itself an open-source offshoot of Netscape), and others in a market that is no longer winner-take-all.[45] In 2019, the most popular browsers in the United States were Google Chrome (48 percent market share) and Apple Safari (32 percent), followed by Internet Explorer (4.8 percent), Microsoft Edge (4.5 percent), and Mozilla Firefox (4.4 percent). In the end, Microsoft's bundling of Internet Explorer with its operating system did not lead to a monopoly in the browser market, as consumers became aware of and converted to other browsers.

---

[42] Joseph Farrell & Garth Saloner, "Installed Base and Compatibility: Innovation, Product Preannouncements, and Predation," 76 *Am. Econ. Rev.* 940 (1986).
[43] "Microsoft's Internet Explorer Losing Browser Share," *BBC News* (May 4, 2010), www.bbc.com/news/10095730.
[44] Jonathan Fildes, "Final Goodbye for Early Web Icon," *BBC News* (Feb. 29, 2008), http://news.bbc.co.uk/2/hi/technology/7270583.stm.
[45] "Browser Market Share United States of America," *GlobalStats* (Sept. 2019), https://gs.statcounter.com/browser-market-share/all/united-states-of-america.

1.2.3 The Funnel and Patent Infringement

In 2011, Apple, Inc. sued rival smartphone maker Samsung for alleged infringement of the company's trademarks, trade dress, and design and utility patents on the original iPhone, beginning a pivotal lawsuit in the "smartphone patent wars."[46] These patents covered several recognizable smartphone features, including the app-grid layout of the iPhone home screen, the tap-to-zoom feature, the rounded corners of the phone, and the home button.[47] Apple alleged that Samsung copied the features in order to gain an edge in the early market for touchscreen smartphones.

In patent infringement cases, the patent holder must establish the validity of the patents and rely on technical experts to attest that the patents were infringed. Assessing damages hinges on questions of whether the patents actually created value for Samsung or caused harm to Apple. A common approach to estimating damages in intellectual property (IP) cases is hypothetical negotiation: If, prior to the alleged infringement, the conflicting parties had negotiated a reasonable royalty for the IP, what rate would they have agreed on? The determination of a royalty rate depends on product value, and therefore consumer behavior. A firm would only agree to pay a royalty insofar as the intellectual property increased sales or the amount that consumers were willing to pay. The purchase funnel is again a useful framework for assessing the impact, if any, of the at-issue product features. Such an analysis may consider how and where along the consumer buying path the alleged patent infringement would have impacted consumer behavior.

Apple can reasonably claim that the company invented the touchscreen smartphone category, as the iPhone was among the first touchscreen phones of its kind when it debuted in January 2007. At the time, media interest in the product category exploded: the *New York Times* noted that there were over 11,000 print articles published about the iPhone between its January unveiling and its June launch.[48] Two weeks before the launch, a marketing research survey found that 64 percent of American mobile phone users were aware of the new touchscreen phone.[49] By 2009, the iPhone was the most popular mobile phone in the United States. Of the top ten most popular mobile phones that year, no other phone was in the

---

[46] Complaint, *Apple Inc. v. Samsung Elecs. Co.*, No. 11-1846 (N.D. Cal. Apr. 15, 2011); Jack Nicas, "Apple and Samsung End Smartphone Patent Wars," NY *Times* (June 27, 2018), www.nytimes.com/2018/06/27/technology/apple-samsung-smartphone-patent.html; Jacob Kastrenakes, "Apple and Samsung Settle Seven-Year-Long Patent Fight Over Copying the iPhone," *The Verge* (June 27, 2018), www.theverge.com/2018/6/27/17510908/apple-samsung-settle-patent-battle-over-copying-iphone.

[47] Nilay Patel, Matt Macari & Bryan Bishop, "Apple vs. Samsung: Inside a Jury's Nightmare," *The Verge* (Aug. 23, 2012), www.theverge.com/2012/8/23/3260463/apple-samsung-jury-verdict-form-nightmare.

[48] David Pogue, "The iPhone Matches Most of Its Hype," NY *Times* (June 27, 2007), www.nytimes.com/2007/06/27/technology/circuits/27pogue.html?module=inline.

[49] "Survey: High Awareness, Strong Demand for Apple iPhone," *Mktg. Charts* (June 2007), www.marketingcharts.com/industries/technology-694.

touchscreen-only smartphone category.[50] In 2010, Samsung released the first of its Android OS products, the Galaxy line of smartphones and tablets. Within forty-five days of launch, Samsung sold 1 million Galaxy S units in the United States, at a base price equal to a comparable iPhone 4. In comparison, Apple sold 3 million iPhone units within three weeks of launch.[51] *Time* Magazine awarded the Galaxy S smartphone second place in its list of the Top 10 Gadgets of 2010, proclaiming that "[i]n phones, 2010 was the year of the Android."[52] In a series of lawsuits, Apple alleged that the home screen, shape, and other features of Samsung Android OS devices bore design cues similar to the iPhone. Specifically, in the first lawsuit, Apple alleged that Samsung "chose to infringe Apple's patents, trade dress, and trademark rights through the design, packaging and promotion of its Galaxy mobile phones and the Galaxy Tab computer tablet, and similar products," which caused sustained damage and irreparable harm to Apple.[53] In the second lawsuit, Apple alleged that new products introduced by Samsung infringed on "many of the same design patents, utility patents, trademarks, and trade dress rights" at issue in the first case, but also infringed "additional utility patents."[54] In this case, the purchase funnel framework can evaluate whether Apple suffered sustained damage and irreparable harm attributable to the alleged patent, trademark, and trade dress infringement.

Awareness. The at-issue patents could have created value for Samsung by increasing consumer awareness of early Samsung touchscreen smartphones. Awareness can come from a variety of sources, such as advertisements, observing a product on the street or at a store, social media, or seeing a friend or colleague's phone.

To evaluate whether the at-issue features could influence the awareness stage of the buying process, one should determine whether the features were even presented in the various ways consumers became aware. Because many of the at-issue features are part of the phone's outward design (e.g. home button, rounded corners), consumers interact with the at-issue features when becoming aware of Samsung smartphones. In fact, many of the at-issue features – including the rounded-corner

---

[50] "Most Popular Mobile Phones in Use in the U.S. from January through October 2009," *Statista* (2020), www.statista.com/statistics/266378/market-share-of-mobile-phones-in-the-us-in-2009/.

[51] A 16 GB Samsung Galaxy S and a 16 GB iPhone 4 were both priced at roughly $200 with a two-year contract, before other incentives. Seth Weintraub, "Samsung: 1 Million Galaxy S Smartphones in 45 Days in the US," *Fortune* (Aug. 29, 2010), https://fortune.com/2010/08/29/samsung-1-million-galaxy-s-smartphones-in-45-days-in-the-us/; Other iPhone 4 Press Conference Notes: "Over 3 Million Sold, White Models Coming, International Releases July 30th," *MacRumors* (July 16, 2016), www.macrumors.com/2010/07/16/other-iphone-4-press-conference-notes-over-3-million-sold-white-models-coming-international-releases-july-30th/

[52] Doug Aamoth, "Top 10 Gadgets," *Time* (2010), http://content.time.com/time/specials/packages/article/0,28804,2035319_2033840_2033837,00.html.

[53] Complaint, *Apple Inc.* v. *Samsung Elecs. Co.*, No. 11-1846 (N.D. Cal. Apr. 15, 2011).

[54] Complaint at 2, *Apple Inc.* v. *Samsung Elecs. Co.*, No. 12-630 (N.D. Cal. Feb. 8, 2012).

design and the touchscreen functionality – were on prominent display in Samsung's marketing. A review of company sales scripts for in-store visits could reveal whether store employees were instructed to highlight the allegedly infringing features or not. A thorough expert analysis of produced advertising data and marketing information can determine where consumers could be exposed to the allegedly infringing designs, as well as evaluate the extent to which consumers were exposed to them. Similarly, internal market research documents may have information on how consumers learned about a product, and whether it was through a channel that tended to emphasize the at-issue features.

Consideration. In the consideration stage, consumers seek out further information about the Samsung and Apple smartphones and other alternatives. An expert could evaluate whether and to what extent the allegedly infringing features are highlighted in consumers' search processes. For example, one can evaluate whether the allegedly infringing features were mentioned on social media, used as keywords in Google searches, or discussed on websites comparing smartphone alternatives.

A social media analysis can highlight whether the allegedly infringing features are regularly discussed by actual and potential consumers on social media platforms. Another helpful source might be Google analytics data, which can analyze how consumers navigate to Samsung or Apple websites, and the relationship between the consumer Internet information search and Google search terms. If, for example, many consumers searched for one of the allegedly infringing features such as "tap-to-zoom," and then clicked on a link toward Samsung's website (or toward a mobile phone carrier website's Samsung product page), this may be evidence that consumer consideration of Samsung was impacted by the feature. With Google analytics data, an expert can analyze these trends in aggregate to see whether and to what extent consumers search for these features (versus others), and the rate at which consumers searching for these allegedly infringing features end up at Samsung's website, rather than Apple's.

Conversion. If the at-issue features were valuable to consumers, Samsung's alleged infringements may have increased the likelihood that consumers would ultimately purchase a Samsung smartphone over the iPhone, or increased the price that consumers were willing to pay for the phone.

To determine whether the allegedly infringing features impacted conversions, a marketing expert could design a survey to actually test whether these features matter to consumers in their decision process. The study would survey consumers who are already considering purchasing an iPhone, and are therefore at or near the conversion stage of the funnel. One group would be shown the Samsung phone with the allegedly infringing features and the second group would be shown a version of the Samsung phone without the allegedly infringing features. Both groups would then be asked whether they would purchase the Samsung phone presented to them or the iPhone. A difference in purchase intent or lack thereof would provide evidence as to the materiality of the allegedly infringing features.

For consumers who would have purchased the Samsung smartphone without the allegedly infringing features, the question becomes whether the consumers paid more for the smartphone than they would have otherwise. In many patent infringement cases, and in *Apple* v. *Samsung*, a marketing expert may conduct a conjoint survey to determine the value of the at-issue features, which can be expressed as a relative preference, a willingness to pay, or as a price premium depending on the approach used. A reliable conjoint survey needs to realistically reflect the actual purchase process and contain features that seem to matter to consumers when making an actual choice, in addition to the at-issue features. In fact, immediately prior to the launch of Samsung's Galaxy line, a survey of smartphone users found that 85 percent of surveyed participants listed the user interface and 71 percent listed the style/design of the smartphone as the most or second most important features when choosing a new smartphone.[55] Judge Koh recognized the importance of certain features such as battery life, operating system, GPS, processors, and media player functionality as primary drivers of choice, arguing in her March 2014 *Order Denying Apple's Renewed Motion for Permanent Injunction* that "numerous features that were not tested ... [and] are highly important to consumers."[56] The purchase funnel framework can provide insight into whether a conjoint survey does reflect the actual consumer evaluation (consideration) then purchase (conversion) process.

Post-purchase. In the post-purchase phase, consumers evaluate their satisfaction with the product, and consider whether they will repurchase it in the future. In the case of smartphones, high switching costs and network effects can encourage consumers who purchase a Samsung phone once to continue purchasing it for subsequent future phone upgrades. Such "lock-in" would compound the effect of the allegedly infringing features by increasing future purchases, even if Apple was granted a permanent injunction.

First, consider switching costs for smartphones. Switching smartphone brands requires purchasing new accessory products, such as phone cases, chargers, and docks that may not be compatible with the previous device particularly if the brand is different.[57] Consumers must also transfer data, apps, and media content, which can be more difficult when switching between Apple and Samsung operating systems. In recent years, Samsung has made this process easier, but during the litigation period, consumers needed to transfer contacts, music, and calendar events using separate methods. There is also a cost of learning a new operating

---

[55] Sangita Subramanian, "Dynamically Adapting Design and Usability in Consumer Technology Products to Technology and Market Life-cycles: A Case Study of Smartphones," PhD Diss. Mass. Inst. of Tech. (2009).
[56] *Apple Inc.* v. *Samsung Elecs. Co.*, No. 11-1846, U.S. Dist. LEXIS 29721, *82 (N.D. Cal. Mar. 6, 2014).
[57] Cadie Thompson, "Ditching Apple for Android? What You Need to Know," CNBC (Oct. 9, 2013), www.cnbc.com/2013/10/09/ditching-apple-for-android-what-you-need-to-know.html.

system. All of these costs can discourage users from switching platforms to Apple, exasperating the effect of the alleged infringement.

Further, network effects could compound the impact of the allegedly infringing features. As described above, when there are network effects, consumers benefit when more users join the platform. iPhone users experience direct network effects through iMessage (i.e. iPhone users benefit from iMessage where more users also have an iPhone). There are also indirect network effects from the interaction between users and app developers. Users benefit when there are more apps available to them. Similarly, app developers benefit when there are more users on the platform to use their app. Prior to the proliferation of Samsung smartphones, Apple would have had an edge over Samsung because of its robust App Store and the benefits of iMessage. If more consumers purchased Samsung smartphones due to the allegedly infringing features, the Samsung platform would benefit from increased network effects. For example, more consumers using Samsung smartphones would incentivize developers to create more apps on the Android platform, increasing the value of Samsung smartphones to consumers. If Samsung did actually gain users from the allegedly infringing features, it could have a lasting benefit for Samsung and Android OS smartphones due to network effects.

By the second quarter of 2018, Android OS devices had captured 88 percent of all new smartphone sales worldwide, with Samsung holding a 21 percent share to Apple's 12 percent.[58] As discussed, the allegedly infringing features could impact consumers at any point in the purchase funnel, or be overwhelmed by more salient non-infringing features that were introduced at the same time. Simply examining Apple sales before and after the introduction of the Samsung smartphone would miss the nuances of how, whether, and to what extent the at-issue features impact the smartphone consumer path to purchase (and repurchase) along the funnel.

1.2.4 The Funnel and Trademark Infringement

In trademark infringement cases, "the crucial issue ... is whether there is any likelihood that an appreciable number of ordinarily prudent purchasers are likely to be misled, or indeed simply confused, as to the source of the goods in question."[59] These issues of consumer confusion arose in a series of two cases involving the Alzheimer's Association and the Alzheimer's Foundation of America (AFA).[60]

---

[58] "Global Mobile OS Market Share in Sales to End Users from 1st Quarter 2009 to 2nd Quarter 2018," *Statista* (2020), www.statista.com/statistics/266136/global-market-share-held-by-smart phone-operating-systems/; "Global Smartphone Market Share: By Quarter," *Counterpoint Rsch.* (Aug. 2019), www.counterpointresearch.com/global-smartphone-share.

[59] *Plus Prods. v. Plus Discount Foods*, 722 F. 2d 999, 1003 (2d Cir. 1983).

[60] First Amended Complaint, *Alzheimer's Disease and Related Disorders Ass'n d/b/a Alzheimer's Ass'n v. Alzheimer's Found. of Am., Inc. d/b/a Alzheimer's Found.*, No. 10-5013 (S.D.N.Y. July 30, 2010); Amended Complaint, *Alzheimer's Found. of Am. v. Alzheimer's Disease and Related Disorders Ass'n*, No. 10-3314 (S.D.N.Y. July 14, 2010).

The Alzheimer's Association, the senior mark, was founded in 1980 and is the world's largest funder of Alzheimer's research. The AFA, the junior mark, was founded in 2002 with the primary purpose of providing optimal care and services to individuals living with Alzheimer's disease, their families, and their caregivers. The AFA held registration to the trademarks "Alzheimer's Foundation of America" and also the shorter phrase "Alzheimer's Foundation" used in conjunction with its logo.

Beginning in 2007, the two nonprofit organizations were involved in various trademark infringement litigations. The original basis for the litigation surrounded consumer confusion in non-digital donations via check. In later litigation, the lawsuit centered on digital advertising and keywords. The Alzheimer's Association alleged that the AFA's purchase of "Alzheimer's association" as a keyword in search engine advertising constituted trademark infringement. For example, a Google search of "Alzheimer's association" showed the AFA's ad as the top result, with the main header as "Alzheimer's Foundation – alzfdn.org" with the tagline "An Association of Care and Support. Reach Out to Us for Help." Ultimately, the judge dismissed the claims, ruling that the Alzheimer's Association failed to prove that the AFA's keyword purchases and search engine result taglines were likely to cause consumer confusion.[61] Like many prior cases, the judge found that the use of a competitor's name in keyword advertising does not constitute trademark infringement.[62]

In many trademark and trade dress cases, the parties engage experts to conduct the likelihood of consumer confusion through surveys, such as the traditional *Squirt* and *Eveready* format surveys. However, these surveys should not be adopted without first considering the relevant population of consumers – particularly where the consumers are in the purchasing process. Although the plaintiffs in the second Alzheimer's case put forward surveys to demonstrate likelihood of confusion, the judge gave the plaintiffs' surveys little weight due to significant flaws. The purchase funnel can provide an alternative framework to evaluate the potential for and extent of consumer confusion.

Awareness. At the awareness stage, consumers may become aware of brands, products, and causes on social media or become exposed through other advertising channels. Confusion in trademark cases can be evaluated at this stage through social media mentions. For example, in this case, consumers who are confused might mention AFA on social media, but the content of their post might indicate that they were confusing AFA with Alzheimer's Association. For example,

---

[61] *Alzheimer's Disease & Related Disorders Ass'n v. Alzheimer's Found. of Am., Inc.*, 307 F. Supp. 3d 260, 285-97 (S.D.N.Y. Apr. 20, 2018).

[62] *1-800 Contacts, Inc. v. Lens.com, Inc.*, 755 F. Supp. 1151 D. Utah (Dec. 14, 2020), rev'd on other grounds, 722 F.3d 1229 (10th Cir. July 16, 2013); *Gen. Steel Domestic Sales, LLC v. Chumley*, No. 10-1398, 2013 U.S. Dist. LEXIS 64932 (D. Colo. May 7, 2013); *Hearts on Fire Co. v. Blue Nile, Inc.*, 603 F. Supp. 2d 274 (D. Mass. Mar. 27, 2009).

Alzheimer's Association has an online community forum called "ALZConnected," an online tool that helps those facing Alzheimer's develop an action plan called "Alzheimer's Navigator," and a safety service called "MedicAlert +" that provides assistance when someone with the disease has a medical emergency. These product names are specific to Alzheimer's Association, so mentions of these services while tagging AFA or including other AFA identifiers might provide evidence of confusion.

Consideration. The potential for and level of consumer confusion will depend greatly on how informed (and involved) consumers are in the consideration process. Consumers conduct two types of searches on search engines: navigational and non-navigational. Navigational searches are those where the consumer searches a specific keyword as a shortcut to find a specific webpage such as the trademark owner's website. Clear examples of navigational search terms in this case would be "Alzheimer's Association" or "Alzheimer's Foundation of America," where each organization's full name is specifically included as keywords. Non-navigational searches in this case are those where the consumer is using the keyword for another reason, such as finding information about a product or service or looking for competitors or other alternatives. Consumers could also use a non-navigational search term when they are very early in the purchase funnel, and not yet considering the trademark owner's product or service at all.[63] Examples of non-navigational searches would be "Alzheimer's" or "Alzheimer's donation." While in theory, consumers conducting a navigational search could be at risk of being confused by the allegedly infringing ad, recent research indicates that companies engaging in competitor keyword advertising are unlikely to be successful in attracting consumers engaging in navigational searches.[64]

Even then, due to the largely descriptive organization name "Alzheimer's Association," a search using these keywords could potentially be classified as navigational or non-navigational. The judge in the case agreed, noting that "because of the weakness of the mark, it is not easy to disaggregate the consumers searching for the Association as a specific organization from those searching generically for an Alzheimer's charity when they type 'Alzheimer's Association' or some similar derivation into a web browser."[65]

Because there is ambiguity in this case as to whether the trademark "Alzheimer's Association" is a navigational or non-navigational search term, an expert could conduct an analysis to measure the effect of the at-issue advertisements or search engine results pages. The effect of the ad (or keyword campaigns) on these

---

[63] Stefan Bechtold & Catherine Tucker, "Trademarks, Triggers, and Online Search," 11 *J. Empir. Leg. Stud.* 718 (Dec. 2014).
[64] Ibid.
[65] *Alzheimer's Disease & Related Disorders Ass'n v. Alzheimer's Found. of Am., Inc.*, 307 F. Supp. 3d 260, 290-91 (S.D.N.Y. Apr. 20, 2018).

consumers can be measured using Google analytics data from A/B tests. For example, one could compare the rate at which consumers click on the plaintiff's website when the allegedly infringing ad is present versus when it is not. If there is no difference in the rate of clicking on the plaintiff's website, then one can conclude that the ad had no effect on consumer confusion at this stage.

It is of course entirely possible that consumers who encounter the at-issue ad while in the consideration phase might include those who search for "Alzheimer's association" while looking for an Alzheimer's organization in general, without prior knowledge of either the plaintiff (Alzheimer's Association) or defendant (AFA). For these consumers, either organization might be an option for them. They may look at the websites for both organizations to determine which one better fits their needs. Empirically, an evaluation of website bounce rates and time spent on the website can provide indication of deep consideration or confusion. Consumers spending a short amount of time on the defendant AFA's website before returning to the search engine results page would provide evidence that certain consumers quickly realized their mistake (if they were searching specifically for the Alzheimer's Association) and were not confused.

Conversion. To determine whether an appreciable number of consumers would be confused at the conversion phase in our example Alzheimer's case, an expert should examine the level and salience of information presented to consumers on the donation webpage, where a potential donor converts to an actual donor. On the current AFA website, the AFA logo and "Alzheimer's Foundation of America" organizational name are clearly presented in multiple places on the AFA donation page. The judge agreed with this assessment, reasoning that "[o]n the donation page, there are many references to 'AFA' or 'Alzheimer's Foundation of America,' and no references to the Association or use of any the Association Marks. At no point while on the AFA website during the donation process would a consumer see any of the Association Marks."[66]

Ultimately, only a small portion of consumers may have been confused by the at-issue AFA keyword advertising, given that they must (1) mistakenly click on the AFA ads thinking that they are related to the Alzheimer's Association and (2) make donations on a webpage that displays AFA's full name and logo in multiple places. Therefore, the question becomes whether the expert is able to identify this subset of consumers – those who accidentally click the defendant's ad and make a purchase – from other consumers who were not confused by the keyword advertising after continuing to browse the search engine results page or the defendant AFA's website. As illustrated by the court opinion, expert survey evidence failed to show exactly how many consumers were truly confused. In this instance, party-sponsored studies might

---

[66] *Alzheimer's Disease & Related Disorders Ass'n v. Alzheimer's Found. of Am., Inc.*, 307 F. Supp. 3d 260, 273 (S.D.N.Y. Apr. 20, 2018).

have been supplemented with website clickstream data, showing how long and how far consumers progress within the parties' websites after clicking on particular ads.

Post-purchase. In the post-purchase phase, consumers may write reviews about the organization that they donated to. Consumers that are confused may write things specific to the other organization in their reviews. One could do a text analysis of online reviews for Alzheimer's Association and AFA to determine whether consumers are reviewing their interactions with one organization but attributing it incorrectly to the other organization. Similar to the social media analysis described in the awareness stage, one could search AFA reviews for details and programs specific to the Alzheimer's Association (such as ALZConnected, Alzheimer's Navigator, and MedicAlert+). Mentions of these services in AFA reviews would provide evidence of confusion in the post-purchase phase. Also, an analysis of past donors and repeat donation behavior could show that there are many consumers that contemporaneously donate to and continue to donate to both organizations.

As discussed, a simple statistical examination of the number of donations or website visits before and after the at-issue keyword ads draws a line between two dots and assumes causality, ignoring how consumers move along the purchase funnel. An analysis that fails to take into account the increasing amount of information that consumers gather along each step of the funnel is subject to many confounding factors and cannot account for the context in which consumers interacted with the alleged trademark infringement.

1.3 CONCLUSION

As discussed throughout this chapter, a deeper analysis of the consumer decision-making process allows the expert to disentangle hypothesis from causation in the context of litigation. Although parties to litigation often lean upon economists to draw causal links between actions and endpoints via regression analysis, such analyses often obscure complex mechanisms and interactions that motivate consumers along the purchase funnel of awareness, consideration, conversion, and repurchase. A standard analysis focused only on endpoints or a particular phase in the purchase funnel may incorrectly infer a causal link between the at-issue conduct (an allegedly deceptive product label) and the endpoint (such as increased sales of an at-issue product) without considering underlying complexities in behaviors across consumers that may belie this causality assumption. By explicitly considering consumer and firm behavior at each step of the purchase funnel, a marketing expert applying this framework can avoid pitfalls that are assumed away by an endpoint-focused approach.

Given the increased demand for empirical and theoretical proof of impact in litigation cases, frameworks such as the purchase funnel can provide a valuable complement or alternative to statistics for triers of fact to consider. Applying the marketing framework to questions of impact can help fill the gap between statistical models and human behavior, thereby ensuring that the statistical relationship is correctly specified and, where it cannot be completed, providing the "story" based on which conclusions can be drawn. Determining where the alleged bad acts occurred in the purchase funnel process can direct fact finders to critical questions of impact, whether in estimating damages or in examining commonality and typicality.

2

Implications of the Consumer Journey to Traditional Consumer Surveys for Litigation

Chad Hummel, Ben Mundel, and Jerry Wind

2.1 INTRODUCTION AND THE LEGAL CONTEXT

The traditional legal framework for assessing liability for false and misleading advertising is whether the advertising is likely to deceive consumers acting reasonably under the circumstances. Typically, the plaintiff also has to show materiality – that the allegedly deceptive advertising would be important in a consumer's decision to purchase the product or service.[1]

This basic legal standard applies in private false advertising litigation under federal law (for example, under the Lanham Act), under state false advertising laws, and in litigation under federal regulatory law (for example, section 5 of the FTC Act).[2] When false advertising is based on so-called implied claims or omissions or inadequate disclosures regarding terms and conditions for sales, the traditional "stimulus-response" approach for assessing liability needs to be closely examined and even revisited, particularly in connection with the advertising for high-involvement purchases.[3] This chapter offers support for a more sophisticated and relevant approach in such cases, one which closely examines the consumer journey to the purchase decision; recognizes that consumers are empowered and active rather than passive recipients of advertising, they are not homogeneous in how they view and process advertising; considers multiple potential touchpoints for information about the

---

[1] While this chapter focuses on individual consumers, the same principles apply to organizational buying.

[2] FTC (Federal Trade Commission). This chapter does not offer an alternative method of analyzing advertising claims that can be shown to be literally false or unsubstantiated to the extent required by law or regulation.

[3] Even though involvement depends on the consumers, product/service categories that exhibit one or more of the following characteristics are considered high involvement: High price, complex features, large differences between alternatives, high perceived risk, long-term commitments, high potential reflection on self-image. Verbeke, W., & Vackier, I. (2004). "Profile and effects of consumer involvement in fresh meat." *Meat Science*, 67(1), 159–68.

advertised product; and focuses on whether by the time of purchase the consumer knows the true facts.

The key to prosecuting deceptive advertising cases in which the subject advertising (or stimulus) does not contain literal falsity was (and still is) proving that a substantial proportion of consumers are likely deceived. Anecdotal testimony from actually deceived consumers could provide some evidence of likely deception. More commonly, however, likely deception is proved in litigation through the use of consumer perception experiments involving a test group exposed to the adverting in question and a control group exposed to the same or similar advertising but without the questionable elements. The objective of these experiments is to quantify the percentage of consumers likely to take away false messages after viewing a stimulus. Courts have held that if 20–25 percent or more consumers (net of a control) take away a false impression after viewing a stimulus in isolation, the "likely to deceive" element of the false advertising cause of action can be satisfied.[4] In recent civil actions by government regulators (including the FTC), the government has argued that the element of likely deception occurs if a substantial percentage of consumers "don't know" the true material facts about a product or service based on the review of a single stimulus.[5]

Both of these methods of proving likely deception ignore reality. Consider the following examples in which liability for false advertising based on implied claims or inadequate disclosure is unfair and makes no sense:

1. A consumer perception experiment which displays one stimulus to consumers and reveals that 20 percent of those surveyed and who viewed that ad in isolation under artificial survey conditions take away a false message from the ad; however, data shows that consumers who actually buy the product, and who viewed that ad in a real-world context, are not deceived about the tested issue. How is that single stimulus-response experiment determinative of false advertising liability? It ignores how actual consumers process advertising – are they skeptical of advertising in general; have they done independent research about the product or service; have they used the product before; was other information about the product or service available during the purchase process that served to accurately inform the consumer prior to purchase? These are but a few factors that should inform a complete "likely to deceive" analysis.
2. A single piece of advertising does not disclose all the material terms and conditions relevant to a consumer purchase decision. In a traditional

---

[4] In *Novartis Consumer Health, Inc. v. Johnson & Johnson Merck Consumer Pharmaceuticals Co.*, 290 F.3d 578 (3d Cir. 2002).
[5] See e.g. *FTC v. DIRECTV* (N.D. Cal. 2018) and *FTC v. FleetCor* (ND Ga. 2020).

"stimulus-response" experiment based on that single advertisement, consumers are likely to answer in high percentages that they "don't know" the relevant information. In recent cases, the FTC has asserted that this result is equivalent to likely deception. They conflate a lack of knowledge with deception. Again, this analysis misses the mark, and more egregiously so. In the purchase of high-involvement products, this analysis again ignores that consumers can and do perform independent product research, the advertiser likely makes necessary disclosures during other segments of the consumer journey to purchase, and consumers have multiple means of obtaining necessary information and are thus (for multiple reasons) likely to be fully informed at the time they make the decision.

In both examples given, the consumer is not likely deceived by the advertising in the real world during the purchase decision.

One can argue that this is really a debate about whether the advertising (which in isolation causes false impressions or fails to convey all necessary information) actually harms consumers, but this chapter provides a framework for analyzing whether such advertising is actually likely to deceive consumers acting reasonably under the circumstances. The framework is based on the growing acceptance by both academics and practitioners of the consumer journey as a dominant paradigm for understanding consumer behavior. With this consumer journey framework in mind, we propose a new experimental survey methodology. This methodology, unlike the traditional stimulus–response surveys, tries to take into account the entire consumer journey by analyzing real customers at the end of their purchase decision.

The chapter starts with a short review of what we know about the consumer journey and its challenge to the stimulus–response model of advertising. This is followed by a discussion of an ideal consumer journey-based research design to determine if consumers are deceived. The ideal research design is then illustrated with an actual case – the *FTC* v. *DIRECTV*, in which we employed the idealized design on behalf of DIRECTV. The chapter concludes with lessons learned and implications.

2.2 THE CONSUMER JOURNEY

Essential to the stimulus–response model of consumer behavior and its follow-up, hierarchy-of-effect models, is the assumption of a passive consumer whereby advertising is a one-way interaction and "marketers assume they can control what consumers think about brands through marketing communications, especially advertising." As William Weilbacher put it, "advertising is not a stimulus in the outmoded behavioral psychology stimulus–response model of human information processing. Advertising, if it is attended to at all, is nothing more than a net addition to everything the consumer has previously learned and retained about the brand."[6]

While the old stimulus–response assumption might have been plausible in the early to mid-twentieth century when consumers had relatively little knowledge and thus relatively little power compared to advertisers, the world has changed drastically since that time. Specifically, advances in science, technology, and media have shifted power to consumers such that today's empowered, skeptical, and informed consumers play a far more active role in the commercial sphere.

In this section, we will briefly discuss characteristics of modern consumers that support the fact that consumers do not follow a stimulus–response model but rather a complex, dynamic, and idiosyncratic journey.

2.2.1 *The Context*

2.2.1.1 Empowered Consumers

The proliferation of computers, smartphones, and increasingly wearable technology and connected devices means that for most consumers, the digital world is never more than a click or voice command away.[7] This machine–human interaction has not only changed how we communicate, learn, shop, etc., but *how* we communicate, learn, and shop. For example, a 2015 study by Microsoft found that the average attention span had dropped from twelve seconds to eight seconds since 2000, but our ability to multitask had drastically improved.[8] The study authors suggest that these changes result from "the brain's ability to adapt and change itself over time," meaning the brain has evolved to adapt to the digital age. New data from a 2019 study found that "accelerating popular content" has driven an increase in productivity and consumption of content which leads to more "rapid exhaustion" of attention resources.[9] As early as 2014, McKinsey found that "two-thirds of smartphone and tablet users say mobile has meaningfully changed the way they shop."[10] Additionally, a 2017 Nielsen study focusing on Facebook product marketing noted a "38% of brand recall, 23% of brand awareness, and 25% of purchase intent"

---

[6] Weilbacher, W. M. (2003). "How advertising affects consumers." *Journal of Advertising Research*, 43(2), 230–34.
[7] This chapter includes data from the early 2000s to show that the consumer journey principles are not a new phenomenon. While the underlying principles have been known for some time, courts and litigants have been slow to recognize their implications for false advertising cases.
[8] McSpadden, K. (2015, May 14). "You now have a shorter attention span than a goldfish." *Time*. https://time.com/3858309/attention-spans-goldfish/
[9] www.eurekalert.org/news-releases/490177
[10] Ericson, L., Herring, L., & Ungerman, K. (2014, Dec. 1). "Busting mobile-shopping myths." McKinsey & Company. www.mckinsey.com/industries/retail/our-insights/busting-mobile-shopping-myths

resulting from "video impressions that are under two seconds."[11] Our brains have evidently adapted to digitalized advertisement despite this shorter attention span.

This new "era of interactivity" driven by technological change has transformed the way brands and consumers interact. While marketing used to be "pushed" onto consumers by companies through traditional advertising, direct marketing, etc., "consumer-driven marketing" is increasingly important as today's empowered consumer has seized "control of the process," actively "pulling" information helpful to them.[12] Consumers feel almost "obligated to shop around … the proliferation of sophisticated sites and technologies has made it much easier for consumers to compare brands" based on a 2017 review.[13] Google asserts that when consumers "want or need something, we tune in via convenient, self-initiated bursts of digital activity."[14] Consumers no longer have to rely on what they are told through means of advertising but rather can pull information and opinions from a variety of sources. In fact, on an average day, Google serves 25 percent of North American Internet traffic, clearly dominating the search engine market with a market share of 92 percent in June 2021.

2.2.1.2 The "Always On" Consumer

The ability of consumers to be connected to the Internet and each other anywhere and anytime thanks to the widespread use of mobile and digital technologies has given rise to an "always on" consumer who "snacks" on digital content throughout the day – while waiting in line, during a commercial break, or even while their dinner date is in the bathroom. A McKinsey survey found that smartphone owners in the United Kingdom check their device an average of more than 150 times a day,[15] and a 2013 study conducted by IAB UK, in partnership with RealView, showed that we now use devices to fill downtime, with 52 percent agreeing with the statement "when I have downtime, I hardly ever just sit and think, I prefer to check my smartphone" and 37 percent admitting to checking their phones when out with friends.[16] In 2021, a similar study by RealView noted that "93% of the total internet population aged 15 and over use smartphones."[17] A 2015 survey by Google

---

[11] www.marketingdive.com/news/facebook-why-mobile-video-ads-must-work-fast/446217/
[12] Court, D., Elzinga, D., Mulder, S., & Vetvik, O. J. (2009). "The consumer decision journey." *McKinsey Quarterly*, 3, 96–107. www.mckinsey.com/business-functions/marketing-and-sales/our-insights/the-consumer-decision-journey
[13] www.mckinsey.com/about-us/new-at-mckinsey-blog/ten-years-on-the-consumer-decision-journey-where-are-we-today
[14] Adams, L., Burkholder, E., & Hamilton, K. (2015). "Micro-moments: Your guide to winning the shift to Mobile." *Google*. https://think.storage.googleapis.com/images/micromoments-guide-to-winning-shift-to-mobile-download.pdf
[15] Ericson et al., "Busting mobile-shopping myths."
[16] "IAB UK – Realview: How people really use connected devices." IAB UK. (2014). www.slideshare.net/IAB_Europe/iab-uk-realview
[17] www.iabuk.com/research/ipsos-iris-93-online-population-use-smartphones

found that 68 percent of respondents check their phone within fifteen minutes of waking up in the morning,[18] and a study by Mitek and Zogby Analytics found that 87 percent of respondents always have their smartphone at their side, day and night.[19] A 2020 study show that 87.8 percent of people "feel uneasy about leaving their phone at home," so much so that 55.4 percent of people even said they look at their phone while driving.[20]

Furthermore, studies show that people will often shop during these occasions. For example, a report by AOL found that 46 percent of shoppers say, "I look at stuff to buy online almost every day [even if I'm not actually making purchases]."[21] With this in consideration, stemming from a 2019 analysis by Episerver, 62 percent of online shoppers purchase something at least once per month, 26 percent of online shoppers purchase something once a week, and 3 percent claim they shop every day.[22]

This "always on" phenomenon is also driven by the proliferation of social media outlets. Social media has essentially created a space, with great speed and reach, where consumers are encouraged to stay "active" throughout the day and to actively engage with brand content, as well as each other.

2.2.1.3 The Spontaneous Consumer

The always-on consumer is a spontaneous consumer. Searching and looking at products/services all the time makes a consumer more aware of what's out there, which helps shape their own preferences. This awareness, in combination with guaranteed quick access to online shopping outlets (e-commerce) and easy-to-use app interfaces and e-transactions, give consumers the confidence to be more spontaneous in their purchasing. AOL found that 43 percent of tablet/smartphone owners agree to the statement "I find myself buying stuff that I didn't plan to" versus only 29 percent of non-owners.[23] Keep in mind that 2021 data suggests it takes 0.05 seconds for consumers to form an opinion about a website.[24] A study by Ehrenberg-Bass found that in-store the average consumer spends only thirteen seconds purchasing a brand and online consumers spent on average only nineteen seconds to purchase, with a majority spending less than ten seconds.[25]

---

[18] Adams et al., "Micro-moments."
[19] Mitek & Zogby Analytics (2014). *Millennials, selfies and the changing face of mobile commerce.* Mitek Systems, Inc.
[20] www.reviews.org/mobile/cell-phone-addiction/
[21] Aol Advertising (2014). "Draper, buying at speed: How technology empowers the always-on shopper."
[22] www.oberlo.com/blog/online-shopping-statistics
[23] Aol Advertising, "Draper, buying at speed."
[24] www.sweor.com/firstimpressions
[25] Anesbury, Z., Nenycz-Thiel, M., Dawes, J., & Kennedy, R. (2015). "How do shoppers behave online? An observational study of online grocery shopping." *Journal of Consumer Behaviour*, 15 (3), 261–70.

2.2.1.4 Multi-Screen Consumers

The number and variety of technologies available to consumers – from computers to smartphones to tablets to glasses and other AI – is growing, and consequently so is the trend towards concurrent use of multi-screens.

For example, a Google study found 91 percent of consumers "turn to their phones for ideas in the middle of a task."[26] An AOL study found that 81 percent of smartphone owners watch TV while using their smartphone, and 66 percent use smartphones and computers simultaneously.[27] A 2016 Google survey found that "66% of smartphone users turn to their smartphones to learn more about something they saw in a TV commercial."[28] This trend has continued: a January 2019 study shows that 54.2 million individuals simultaneously used their TV and the Internet in 2018.[29]

A recent 2019 study found that 46.8 percent of mobile in-store users use in-app discounts, 43.3 percent search for product information, and 33.6 percent of consumers compare prices with competitors.[30]

2.2.1.5 Multi-Touchpoint Consumers

The simplistic notion that people respond reflexively to stimuli such as ads fails to account for the fact that consumers' brains are not blank slates when they view an advertisement. Advertising is only one of the many stimuli/sources of information that can potentially influence an individual's purchasing decision. Assuming a consumer processes an advertisement at all, the context of all their past experiences influences the process. The actual impact of any given advertisement is mediated by the consumer's memories.

The findings from Keller Fay Group's TalkTrack study of touchpoints referenced in word-of-mouth conversations demonstrate the range of touchpoints that may influence a customer. Many of these touchpoints are not controlled by the brand (e.g. something in the store, another website, online customer reviews). Furthermore, the influence of all these touchpoints is mediated by the conversations the consumer is having around them and their own experience.

---

[26] "Micro-moments: How consumers rely on mobile to meet their needs." (2016, June). Think with Google. www.thinkwithgoogle.com/marketing-strategies/app-and-mobile/micro-moments-consumer-mobile-needs/
[27] "The new multi-screen world: Understanding cross-platform consumer behavior." (2012). Google. https://services.google.com/fh/files/misc/multi-screen_infographic.pdf
[28] "4 new moments every marketer should know." (2015, June). Think with Google. www.thinkwithgoogle.com/marketing-strategies/app-and-mobile/4-new-moments-every-marketer-should-know/
[29] www.statista.com/topics/2531/second-screen-usage/
[30] www.pymnts.com/news/mobile-payments/2019/in-store-smartphones/

It is important to note that the importance of the various touchpoints varies by product categories, context, and obviously the consumer.

2.2.1.6 Omnichannel Consumers

As a result of flipping from screen to screen or device to device, shoppers are increasingly moving between channels during the shopping process. This practice of using channels "interchangeably and seamlessly" during the search and buying process has been described as omnichannel shopping.[31]

In general, while a fraction of consumers who research a product on any given device (smartphone, tablet, laptop, or in-store) will purchase on that same device, a significant portion will switch to a different device to make the final purchase.

2.2.1.7 High Expectation Consumers/Personalization

Consumers are becoming accustomed to immediate accessibility, ease in navigation, and personalized experiences/products and services.

Personalization of the purchasing experience is one of the more prominent trends among consumers. A 2017 survey, conducted by Evergage, indicated that 63 percent of all respondents rated personalization of website content, app interface, email, and mobile messages as very or extremely important to their organization, and 88 percent of business owners believe that prospective customers already expect a personalized experience. According to a 2019 report, "80% of users who qualify themselves as frequent shoppers will only shop with brands that personalize the experience."[32]

Technology makes it easier than ever to personalize, and there are two approaches to personalization:

(1) Using data on the customer purchase behavior and analytics to recommend personalized products and services. For example, Netflix makes customized recommendations for what movies you would like to watch next.
(2) Designing a platform that allows the customer to personalize their offerings, such as a 100-flavor vending machine or Converse shoes that offers customization).

---

[31] Verhoef, P. C., Kannan, P. K., & Inman, J. J. (2015). "From multi-channel retailing to omni-channel retailing: Introduction to the special issue on multi-channel retailing." *Journal of Retailing*, 91(2), 174–81.
[32] "Privacy & Personalization: Consumers share how to win them over without crossing the line." https://smarterhq.com/blog/personalization-statistics-roundup

2.2.1.8 The Skeptical Consumer

In the process of becoming empowered, the consumer has also become increasingly skeptical of marketers.

A 2014 Forrester study found that "only 22% of consumers trust emails from companies or brands, just 13% trust ads on websites, and no more than 32% trust ads in any channel."[33] This low level of trust in advertising has continued as consumer trust in all institutions, including businesses, continues to erode, as evident from the annual Edelman Trust Barometer.[34]

2.2.1.9 The Nonrational, Emotional, and Intuitive Consumer

With its foundations in the idea of "salesmanship," advertising came to focus on the communication of a rational message as the means of persuading a consumer to act. The hierarchy-of-effect models were thus formed with the assumption that brand purchases are primarily "a direct result of a conscious, rational consumer choice process."[35] However, studies show that humans are far from rational actors. Instead, people do not consciously process most inputs and often base decisions on intuition and affect.

In direct contrast to the assumption of purchasing decisions as conscious choices, evidence shows that consumers do not make overt, conscious decisions before they buy a particular brand.[36] Rather, they rely on nonrational intuition.

2.2.1.10 Pre-Shopping: Zero Moment of Truth (ZMOT)

In 2005, Procter & Gamble coined the term "the first moment of truth" (FMOT) to describe the moment "when a consumer stands in front of the shelf and chooses a product from among many competitive offerings."[37] Extending this idea, Google published a series of writings on what it termed the "Zero Moment of Truth" (ZMOT), that is, all of the thoughts, search, and decisions that occur before the consumer arrives at this critical "First Moment of Truth."[38] This is further supported

---

[33] "Marketers: Consumers don't trust your campaigns" (2014, Apr. 14). *Forrester*. www.forrester.com/press-newsroom/marketers-consumers-dont-trust-your-campaigns/
[34] www.edelman.com/trust/2021-trust-barometer
[35] Weilbacher, W. M. (2003). "How advertising affects consumers." *Journal of Advertising Research*, 43(2), 230–34.
[36] Barnard, N., & Ehrenberg, A. (1997). "Advertising: Strongly persuasive or nudging?" *Journal of Advertising Research*, 37(1), 21–31; Ehrenberg, A., Barnard, N., Kennedy, R., & Bloom, H. (2002). "Brand advertising as creative publicity." *Journal of Advertising Research*, 42(4), 7–18.
[37] Procter & Gamble Annual Report, 2006. www.annualreports.com/HostedData/AnnualReportArchive/p/NYSE_PG_2006.pdf
[38] Lecinski, J. (2011). "Winning the zero moment of truth: ZMOT." *Google*.

by a 2020 research study showing that "53% of shoppers always do research before they buy."[39]

2.2.1.11 Satisfaction

While the purchase is after the "climax of the journey" for the brand and retailer, it is only the beginning of the story for the consumer. As one author phrased it, for the consumer, "there is the tension between the excitement of purchase and fear of having made the right decision." Whether the person's final conclusion is of excitement or regret is entirely dependent on the post-purchase experience. P&G used the term the "second moment of truth" to describe the moment "when the consumer uses the product and evaluates how well the product meets his or her expectations."[40]

Consequently, marketing executives consistently rank satisfaction as one of their most important priorities.[41] While satisfaction in and of itself is not that important, executives care about it as it is believed to translate into advocacy (Net Promoter Score), customer loyalty,[42] engagement behaviors,[43] and increased Custom Lifetime Value (CLV).[44]

Given what we know about the historical heterogeneity of consumer behavior and the changes in them, as briefly outlined above, the contemporary view of advertising and consumer behavior can be illustrated in Figure 2.1.

The simple fact that a firm advertises does not guarantee that the message is received, read, correctly perceived, believed, deemed relevant, considered important, and compels a person to consider the advertised product or service, let alone purchase it. Nor is advertising likely to have a direct impact on consumers.

While our discussion focuses here on consumers, these points are also relevant to organizational buying behavior. For organizational buyers, each of these facts is present. In addition, they also have to focus on the organizational factors, including having a more complex buying center, buying situation, and buying processes.[45]

---

[39] www.pardot.com/blog/the-zero-moment-of-truth-what-is-it-why-should-you-care/
[40] Procter & Gamble Annual Report, 2006.
[41] Larivière, B., Keiningham, T. L., Aksoy, L., Yalçin, A., Morgeson, F. V., & Mithas, S. (2016). "Modeling heterogeneity in the satisfaction, loyalty intention, and shareholder value linkage: A cross-industry analysis at the customer and firm levels." *Journal of Marketing Research*, 53(1), 91–109.
[42] Aksoy, L. (2013). "How do you measure what you can't define? The current state of loyalty measurement and management." *Journal of Service Management*, 24(4), 356–81.
[43] Brodie, R. J., Hollebeek, L. D., Jurić, B., & Ilić, A. (2011). "Customer engagement: Conceptual domain, fundamental propositions, and implications for research." *Journal of Service Research*, 14(3), 252–71.
[44] Larivière et al., "Modeling heterogeneity."
[45] Webster, F. E., & Wind, Y. (1972). *Organizational Buying Behavior* (Foundations of Marketing). Prentice-Hall.

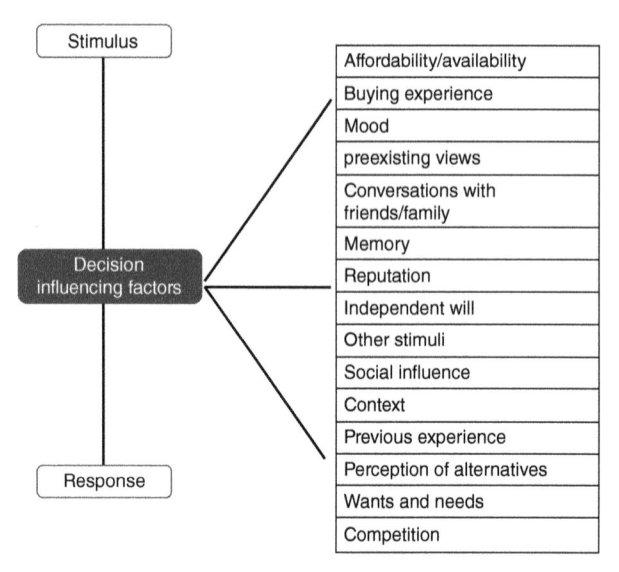

```
          ┌───────────┐
          │ Stimulus  │
          └─────┬─────┘
                │              ┌──────────────────────────────┐
                │              │ Affordability/availability   │
                │              ├──────────────────────────────┤
                │              │ Buying experience            │
                │              ├──────────────────────────────┤
                │              │ Mood                         │
                │              ├──────────────────────────────┤
                │              │ preexisting views            │
                │              ├──────────────────────────────┤
                │              │ Conversations with           │
                │              │ friends/family               │
                │              ├──────────────────────────────┤
        ┌───────┴────────┐    │ Memory                       │
        │ Decision       │────┤ Reputation                   │
        │ influencing    │    ├──────────────────────────────┤
        │ factors        │    │ Independent will             │
        └───────┬────────┘    ├──────────────────────────────┤
                │              │ Other stimuli                │
                │              ├──────────────────────────────┤
                │              │ Social influence             │
                │              ├──────────────────────────────┤
                │              │ Context                      │
                │              ├──────────────────────────────┤
                │              │ Previous experience          │
          ┌─────┴─────┐       ├──────────────────────────────┤
          │ Response  │       │ Perception of alternatives   │
          └───────────┘       ├──────────────────────────────┤
                              │ Wants and needs              │
                              ├──────────────────────────────┤
                              │ Competition                  │
                              └──────────────────────────────┘
```

FIGURE 2.1. Why the stimulus–response model is inaccurate and incomplete

The consumer journey described for businesses can be even more complex than for individual consumers.

2.2.2 *The Consumer Journey*

2.2.2.1 The Concept

Reframing the question to focus on the consumer has led to the emergence of a relatively new framework known as the customer journey. In most examples of consumer journey maps, the journey is depicted horizontally, in contrast to the traditional stimulus–response models that portray consumer behavior as a vertical funnel-type linear model (like the Awareness–Interest–Desire–Action model triggered by advertising or other stimuli targeted at a passive consumer). For the consumer journey map, researchers start with the consumer and work backwards to trace all their interactions with the brand – before, during, and after purchase. Siddharth Galkwad, practice head of digital experience at Dell digital business services, defines a journey map as "an illustrated representation of a customer's expectations, experiences, and reflections as it unfolds over time across multiple stages and touchpoints while using a product or consuming a service."[46] In today's day and age, according to a 2020 analysis by Salesforce, a consumer journey can

---

[46] "Customer journey mapping – the heart of digital transformation." Knowledge@Wharton (2015, Nov. 4). https://knowledge.wharton.upenn.edu/article/customer-journey-mapping-is-at-the-heart-of-digital-transformation/

include "interactions over social media email, livechat or other channels" that help tell "the story of your customers' experiences."[47]

Mapping the customer journey provides marketers, researchers, and courts with the lens to look at the total experience of customers in a holistic manner. Specifically, once one has mapped the customer journey for each business/customer segment, one can begin identifying the "pain points" or "frictions" in the journey, i.e. any barriers, challenges, or roadblocks between the consumer and the purchase, including confusing website navigation, a hard-to-understand store layout, poor in-store/online help, a complicated checkout process/long checkout line, out-of-stock items, difficulty identifying a previously purchased item for repurchase, difficulty sharing a positive/negative experience with others, etc. Once identified, marketers can focus on alleviating these pain points and removing the frictions.

Additionally, in the spirit of positive psychology – a school of psychology grounded "in the belief that people want to lead meaningful and fulfilling lives, to cultivate what is best within them, and to enhance their experiences of love, work, and play"[48] – brands should also think about how they can add "happiness points" to the journey. These "pain points" and "happiness points" demonstrate the models' emphasis on emotions and feelings, transforming consumer journey mapping into a unique management tool, or, in other words, "an empathy mapping exercise."[49]

It should be noted that "customer journey maps should be updated frequently and often can involve an ongoing investment" and "different customer segments will have different journeys, so journeys should be understood at a segment level."[50] Also, according to the 2020 Salesforce review, "customer expectations are changing for all businesses as customers demand an omnichannel approach to marketing and sales."[51] Over time, new customer journey maps better reflect the change in the technological and social environment.

This framework has become a cornerstone of modern marketing, as exemplified by the increasing number of companies focused on helping companies understand and map the customer journey.

2.2.2.2 The Advantages to the Consumer Journey Framework

The consumer decision journey (CDJ) has many advantages over the outdated purchase funnel. First and foremost, this framework produces a holistic picture of

---

[47] www.salesforce.com/uk/blog/2016/03/customer-journey-mapping-explained.html
[48] https://ppc.sas.upenn.edu/
[49] Rosenbaum, M. S., Otalora, M. L., & Ramírez, G. C. (2017). "How to create a realistic customer journey map." *Business Horizons*, 60(1), 143–50.
[50] "Customer journey mapping – the heart of digital transformation." Knowledge@Wharton (2015, Nov. 4).
[51] www.salesforce.com/uk/blog/2016/03/customer-journey-mapping-explained.html

the consumer experience, rather than narrowly focusing on advertising messaging, which makes up only a small fraction of the touchpoints a consumer has with a brand. By following the customer (as opposed to prescribing reactions), the CDJ accounts for the heterogeneity of purchase journeys resulting from the consumer's interactions, the product/service being offered, and the context. This framework allows researchers to understand the "truth" as to what consumers understand and know, as opposed to the artificial stimulus response model that focuses on the reaction to a single ad in isolation.

Consumer journey mapping also allows managers to see all of the potential organizational touchpoints at each stage of the journey, enabling them to develop strategic initiatives and engagements for each touchpoint (sometimes referred to as expanding the vertical axis).[52] This translates in the legal space to allow courts to assess whether consumers are deceived when all engagements and touchpoints are considered.

The approach is also advantageous in that its framework and theories are not built on the assumption of rationality and active cognition from the consumers. It is, instead, an "evidence-driven method that drives action."[53]

The exercise of customer journey mapping necessitates that a company maps how purchase journeys vary between consumers (men vs. women; stressed consumers vs. relaxed consumers), between products/services (a durable vs. a service, a high-priced item vs. a low-priced item), between contexts (on a weekend vs. a weekday, on a sunny day vs. a rainy day), and the interaction between all three (e.g. how a twenty-year old woman who is an expert in cosmetics purchases lipstick on a weekday). By using tools such as journey mapping to analyze these differences and the influences on them, companies can find ways to transform bad experiential touchpoints into good ones for potential consumers with different demographics and product preferences. So, too, researchers in false advertising cases can consider how different journeys impact consumer perception and behavior.

Furthermore, the fact that the CDJ incorporates the connection between pre-purchase, purchase, post-purchase, and the next purchase, as well as the introduction of the loyalty loop, addresses one of the major failings of the purchase funnel, which is its inability to distinguish between different buying situations (new task, modified rebuy, and straight rebuy).

2.2.2.3 Popular Illustrative Frameworks

Marketers have proposed several general frameworks for mapping the journey. Most frameworks began as linear, horizontal journeys with three main stages: pre-

---

[52] Rosenbaum et al., "How to create a realistic customer journey map."
[53] Fichter, D., & Wisniewski, J. (2015). "Customer journey mapping." *Online Searcher*, 39(4), 74.

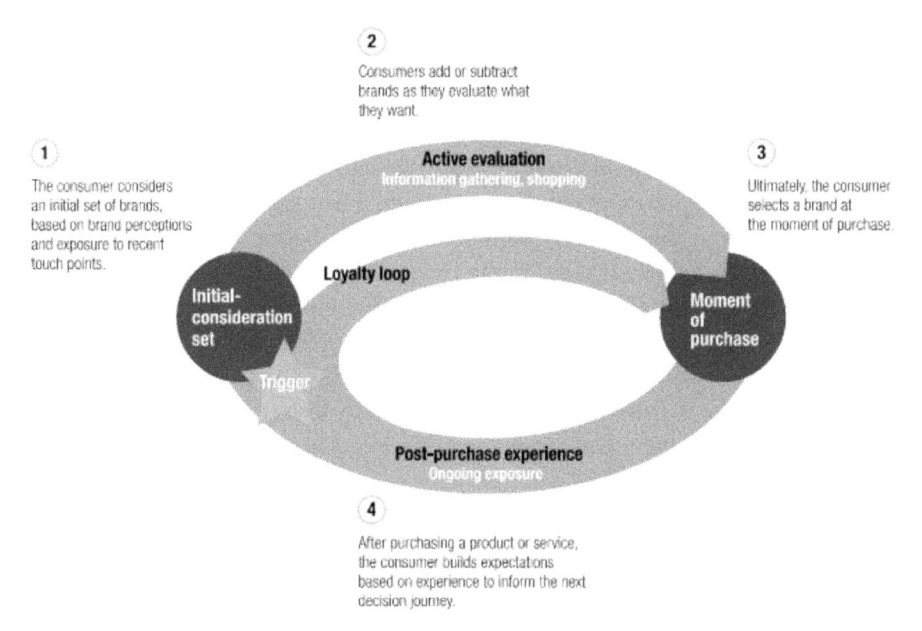

FIGURE 2.2. McKinsey's customer decision journey (CDJ)
Court et al., "The consumer decision journey."

purchase, purchase, and post-purchase.[54] Over time, these models have evolved to better capture the digital, as well as the physical and emotional aspects of the consumer journey.

One of the most popular frameworks is McKinsey's Consumer Decision Journey (see Figure 2.2). Introduced in 2009 but still used in 2021, the McKinsey "Consumer Decision Journey" models "how people move from initially considering a product or service to purchasing it and then bonding with the brand."[55] It has since become "the new standard in thinking about the path consumers take from awareness through purchase and importantly, even after purchase."[56] They picture the consumer journey as a circular journey with a primary loop as well as a loyalty loop. The primary has five main components: a trigger, initial consideration set, active evaluation (information gathering, shopping), a moment of purchase, and post-purchase experience (ongoing exposure). The loyalty loop eliminates the extended consideration and evaluation phase, such that consumers are delivered from the trigger directly to the moment of purchase and from post-purchase back to

---

[54] Rosenbaum et al., "How to create a realistic customer journey map."
[55] www.smartinsights.com/marketing-planning/marketing-models/mckinseys-consumer-decision-journey/
[56] Wheeler, S. R. (2015). *Architecting Experience: A Marketing Science and Digital Analytics Handbook.* World Scientific.

trigger, "locking them within [the loyalty loop]."[57] The strength of this model is in its simplicity. McKinsey has distilled a complex journey into four primary stages.

The circular nature of today's consumer journey directly contradicts the "funnel metaphor" previously used. Instead, the number of brands under consideration during the active evaluation phase may now actually expand rather than narrow as consumers seek information and shop a category. The graphic illustrates the notion that the end of one purchase process is potentially the beginning of the next, which will then be affected by learnings in the first purchase and its aftermath.[58]

A 2014 article in the *Harvard Business Review* presented research from interviews with marketers from a wide variety of fields. "According to these marketers, *the primary problem with the funnel is that the buying process is no longer linear.* Prospects don't just enter at the top of the funnel; instead, they come in at any stage. Furthermore, they often jump stages, stay in a stage indefinitely, or move back and forth between them."[59]

There are other consumer journey frameworks to consider. Futures Company offers a complementary approach advocating the "purchase fish" model (see Figure 2.3) as a representation of the "fluid, yet interconnected, flow of inputs and decisions in today's retail environment."[60] Unlike other models that funnel from the top, this model illustrates how "empowered" consumers can choose for themselves different paths that all ultimately lead to the head. The "fish" is bigger in the front than at the back, as more happens upfront. Shoppers enter at a variety of points and then "swim around" between the different points, moving sometimes quickly and sometimes more slowly, to eventually make decisions that can loop around and affect inputs after the purchase itself.[61] Recent conversations in 2020 about the "purchase fish model" emphasize its importance. Individuals recognize the value of touchpoints given the complexity of living in the age of "e-commerce, live-streaming, and social commerce."[62]

The meanderings throughout the fish demonstrate the complexity of consumer behavior by considering the detailed steps in the marketing and sales process that are relevant in the modern environment. The purchase fish model emphasizes consumer engagement and the existence of this network of touchpoints that spans from

---

[57] Edelman, D. C., & Singer, M. (2015, Nov.). "Competing on customer journeys." *Harvard Business Review,* 93(11), 88–100. https://hbr.org/2015/11/competing-on-customer-journeys

[58] Court et al., "The consumer decision journey."

[59] https://hbr.org/2014/05/marketing-can-no-longer-rely-on-the-funnel (emphasis added). See also Kotler, P., & Keller, K. (2014). *Marketing Management* (15th ed.). Pearson, chapter 6, "Analyzing consumer markets," 195. ("Consumers don't always pass through all five stages – they may skip or reverse some.")

[60] Burdett, L., Smith, J. W., Curry, A., Gildenberg, B., & Mader, S. (2013). *The future shopper: How changing shopper attitudes and technology are re-shaping retail.* Kantar Consulting. www.warc.com/Content/4275a808-4f4b-44e1-98aa-b4c4b73efce8

[61] Burdett et al., "The future shopper."

[62] www.warc.com/newsandopinion/opinion/warc-from-home-path-to-purchase--what-is-it-and-how-is-it-changing/en-gb/3556

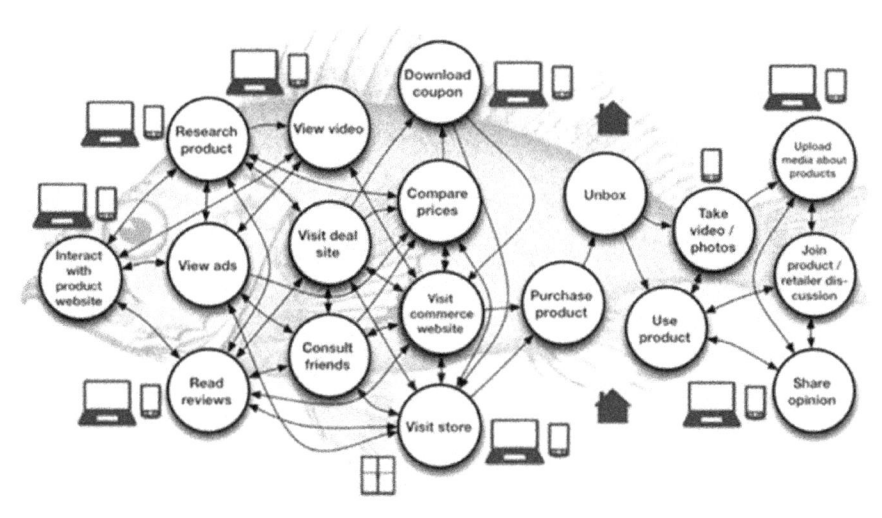

FIGURE 2.3. Futures Company's purchase fish
Burdett et al., "The future shopper."

research to the online community. This model is an example of taking a multichannel approach to addressing consumer needs.

The purchase fish model nicely identifies even more potential stops on the journey than the McKinsey model. The fish may be more complex than is necessary for the purposes of explaining the CDJ to judges and juries. But it provides a list of possible steps on the journey that can be tailored to particular industries, products, and cases.

2.2.2.4 Micro-Moments as Part of the Journey

The customer-centric customer journey framework is certainly a great improvement from the marketer-centric purchase funnel, though still limited by the fact that it looks at human behavior in the context of that person as a consumer. The term "customer journey" itself implies that an individual's behavior has a "destination" (e.g. making a purchase). Realizing that in reality, a single destination does not direct people's behavior, in 2015 Google introduced the concept of "micro-moments."

Micro-moments are defined as "intent-rich moments when decisions are made and preferences shaped."[63] Google sees them as "critical touchpoints within today's consumer journey [such that] when added together, they ultimately determine how that journey ends." Specifically, they find there are four major categories of micro-moments during which people are open to the influence of brands:

---

[63] Ramaswamy, S. (2015, Apr.). "How micro-moments are changing the rules." *Think with Google*. www.thinkwithgoogle.com/marketing-strategies/app-and-mobile/how-micromoments-are-changing-rules/

- I-want-to-know,
- I-want-to-go,
- I-want-to-buy, and
- I-want-to-do moments.

The key to this concept is that it respects the fact that people exist in this world outside of their role as consumers; thus, it does not make sense to construct a narrative for human behavior that centers only on consumption. Most people do not go about their day consciously thinking about their role in the commercial sphere. Needs, biases, beliefs ultimately drive people's behavior and aspirations that are far more influential than any marketing campaign could be. The concept of micro-moments frees marketers from trying to "overpower" these deeply entrenched behavior drivers and encourages them to focus on the moments that consumers actively welcome the influence of marketers.

Immediate gratification brought about by the advancement of technology and the central theme of this model is crucial in ensuring that consumers are satisfied, no matter where they are in the buying, pre-purchase, and post-purchase process. According to Google, brands need to capture and deliver in those split seconds of need – when consumers are actively researching or looking to purchase to fulfill a need

2.2.2.5 Examples of the Consumer Journey in Litigation

Figures 2.4 and 2.5 show pathways for customer journeys in two cases we have worked on. Figure 2.4 depicts the pathway a potential purchaser of DIRECTV satellite television would embark on to make a purchase decision. As shown, there are many safeguards and decision points a firm can design to force potential customers to learn more about the product after the advertisements.

Figure 2.5 shows a purchase journey for consumers making a purchase decision for a credit card. The potential customer obtains information from a wide variety of sources separate from the credit card company and, in addition, obtains information from the credit card company, both from the ad and from other sources.

The consumer journey has significant implications for advertising and advertising research as well as regulators. The next section will focus on the research implications.

2.3 IDEAL ADVERTISING RESEARCH DESIGN THAT CAPTURES THE CONSUMER JOURNEY

Once it is recognized that the journey represents customer behavior better than the outdated stimulus–response and funnel models, it has substantial implications for how best to test whether advertising is likely to deceive reasonable consumers and also whether potentially false advertising has caused any damage. This section

Implications of the Consumer Journey

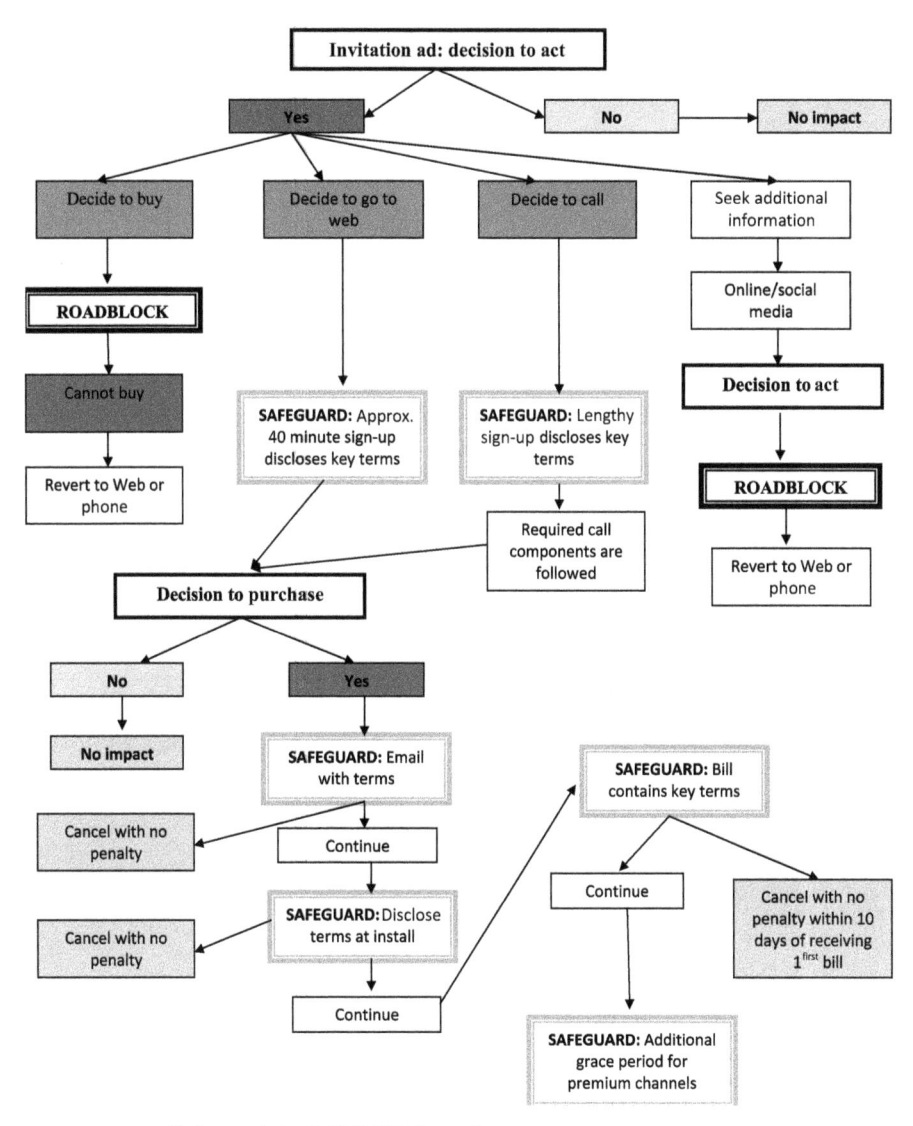

FIGURE 2.4. Safeguards in DIRECTV purchase process

outlines ideal advertising research, recognizing the key implications of the CDJ, to determine whether advertising or marketing is likely to deceive reasonable consumers. One of the primary goals of this experimental methodology is to increase external validity based upon the literature on customer behavior. Not all of these features can be used in every experiment, but researchers should consider them, and, when possible, design them as part of their studies to enhance external validity.

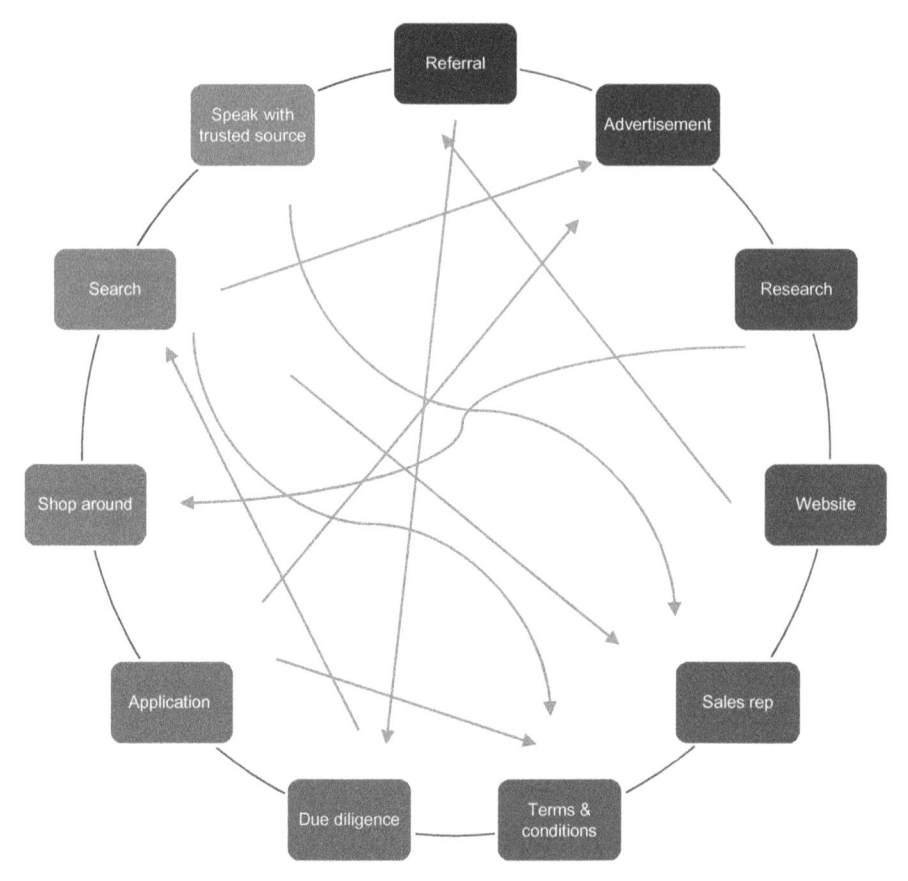

FIGURE 2.5. Consumer decision journey for buying a corporate credit card

2.3.1 Test Actual Customers

Researchers should endeavor to use actual customers in their studies, as opposed to panels of survey takers.

When conducting research, we are accustomed to using panels of survey takers, students, and others survey participants. The goal when doing so is to ensure the survey participants match the demographics of the actual population of customers as closely as possible along key dimensions of age, income, gender, etc. Using panels of survey participants is well-accepted, however, only because it is cheaper and easier than surveying the actual customers of interest. The panel methodology has obvious drawbacks. Most notably, the panel of participants has not gone through the entire customer journey as real customers do. Therefore, they may not perceive the advertising in the same way as actual customers do, and they may not behave in the same way as actual customers do.

When possible, researchers should use the company's actual customers in the research. By testing actual customers, you can capture their entire journey. This means the test can consider the actual customer's preexisting views and the outcome of their research, analysis, and the entire journey. A panel respondent, by contrast, only views a stimulus and responds. Moreover, by testing actual customers, researchers can avoid an error resulting from the differences between panel respondents and actual customers.

2.3.2 Use Business-as-Usual (Test) and Modified (Control) Stimuli

To determine whether advertising is deceptive, one should use a test vs. control experiment. Considering the CDJ, the best way is to use a business-as-usual (BAU) stimulus – either an actual ad that the company uses or an actual sign-up process. By doing this, you can test the real stimuli at issue.

For the control, the researcher should modify the BAU stimulus. There are several potential ways to do this, depending upon the specific allegations in the case. If an ad is allegedly deceptive, one could remove the alleged deception from the actual ad used. If the allegation is one of failure to disclose then one could improve the disclosures in the modified stimuli.

In either scenario, the control is crucial. It is important to ensure that the control is as close as possible to the BAU stimulus but fixes the alleged problem (removes the alleged deception or improves the alleged inadequate disclosures, as examples). Depending on the allegations in the case, it may be useful or necessary to use more than one control to allow for testing individual claims and combinations of claims.

Once the BAU and control stimuli are set, actual prospective customers should be randomly assigned to either the BAU or control stimulus for the survey.

2.3.3 Use All Sign-Up Methods and in as Natural a Context as Possible

Companies increasingly allow customers to purchase their products and services through different methods: phone, online, and in person (to name a few). The idealized research design includes actual company customers from each sign-up method and creates BAU and modified stimuli for each. Ideally, the survey experience would be as close to the real-world customer experience as possible, with the modified control only revised to address the alleged problems.

If possible, the ideal design could modify the actual final buying process by creating an additional path to purchase for the control. In these cases, when a customer is at the point of purchase, they are randomly assigned to either the test or control stimulus.

2.3.4 Survey Soon after the Purchase Decision

Now that you have a group of actual customers to include in your experiment – those that signed up with the BAU stimulus and the control stimulus – it is best to survey them shortly after they make their purchase decision. Memories fade, and researchers will get the best information soon after the consumer makes their purchase decision.

2.3.5 Recognize "Don't Know" as a Valid Option

For some types of surveys, some researchers recommend not giving respondents the option of "don't know" or "don't recall the answer." However, it is crucial to provide this option in deception surveys. First, respondents may forget information, and researchers do not want to encourage them to guess. Second, some customers do not care or do not have an opinion on certain things. Researchers also have to recognize that respondents who say they "don't know" were not necessarily deceived or lied to. For example, if you surveyed customers who just left the grocery store and asked them how much they were charged for a gallon of milk, some percentage of respondents would likely say they "don't know." That does not mean they were deceived; it may mean they simply did not care what the price was or that they forgot.

2.3.6 Test Behavior, Not Just Perception

Because the idealized research design tests actual customers (and not just hypothetical customers), researchers can study actual customer behavior and not just survey questions. While survey answers provided very useful information, observing actual customer behavior can provide additional useful insights into research questions.

For example, if advertising is allegedly deceptive, researchers could see if conversion rates are higher for the BAU stimulus or the modified stimulus that take out the allegedly deceptive ad. If conversation rates are not statistically different, that would suggest that the allegedly deceptive statements are not material to a purchase decision. Analyzing actual customer behavior can be even more insightful than asking purchase intent questions.

Similarly, if the allegation in a case is that customers were not informed of all the fees and conditions before signing up, a researcher could analyze conversion rates with improved disclosures. If there were no statistically significant differences between the business-as-usual disclosures and the improved disclosures, that would suggest that the allegedly inadequate disclosures were not material.

2.3.7 Learn about Journey/Sources of Info

In the survey questionnaire, we recommend asking respondents about their journey to purchase. In our experience, researchers can get rich information from customers about how they came to make the purchase decision (what their decision set was, what research they did, whether referred by friends and family, etc.). Many of these facts can help analyze whether customers are likely to be deceived. Ideally, this question will include both open-ended questions and closed-ended questions.

2.3.8 Calculate Net Deception

Once data is collected, it is crucial to analyze it correctly. We have seen too many litigation parties attempt to analyze the data without considering the control or the critical measure of "net deception." The entire purpose of doing modified disclosures is to have a control to benchmark the test against. A complementary and equally important measure is testing whether the difference between the test and control groups is statistically significant. Use that control in the interpretation of the data.

For example, if the study showed that 20 percent of respondents in the BAU were incorrect about the terms of a product but that 20 percent were similarly wrong in the modified/control group, that would suggest there is 0 net deception. Studies have shown that it is impossible to get 100 percent informed rates, even with crystal-clear disclosures. Therefore, a control must be used when determining if the disclosure is inadequate. The same principles apply to deceptive advertising.

These research design elements help researchers take into account the CDJ and thereby increase external validity. By using these tools, researchers can better determine whether today's customers are likely to be deceived and provide more reliable information to parties and courts.

This research design also has important implications for damages, as well as liability. In false advertising cases, damages are often calculated in the form of "restitution." Some consumers may be deceived by false advertising but will learn the information prior to purchase (through the consumer journey). Because these consumers have full information at the time of purchase they are not harmed. This research design can identify these consumers, and therefore provides additional information for damages.

The next section discusses a real-world case where we used this idealized research design.

2.4 THE DIRECTV CASE

2.4.1 Background on the Case

In 2015, the FTC sued DIRECTV, alleging that its online, TV, and print advertisements failed to disclose certain conditions of its satellite TV services adequately, including that:

(i) DIRECTV required a twenty-four-month commitment to obtain a discounted offer;
(ii) the introductory discount price lasts twelve months;

(iii) the price in the second year of the commitment is higher than the introductory discounted price;
(iv) canceling before the end of the commitment period triggers an early cancelation fee; and
(v) a three-month free premium channel programming (such as HBO and Showtime) package automatically rolls over to the regular price if the customer does not call to cancel after the third month of service (collectively, the "Conditions of Purchase").

DIRECTV defended the case, arguing that while it did not (and could not) disclose all of these conditions of purchase in a thirty-second TV commercial or a single-page print ad, it disclosed all of the conditions of purchase repeatedly during the customer's journey to sign up with DIRECTV (both before and even after the purchase decision). DIRECTV argued that for particularly high-involvement purchases, and where no customer could purchase the service directly from an advertisement, the rest of the consumer journey should be considered. This argument was based on the CDJ.

The FTC's case, however, was based on the outdated stimulus–response theory. The FTC rejected DIRECTV's consumer journey argument, i.e. that disclosures and information provided outside of the single advertisement should be considered. Indeed, under the FTC's view, if DIRECTV had advertised its satellite TV service and concluded at the end of a TV spot "prices start at $29.99 per month, call for details," it would be deceptive because the ad did not include all of the pricing information. That argument ignores the reality of advertising and marketing today.

At trial, the FTC had very limited evidence. The FTC ignored the customer journey and relied most heavily on a "facial review" of DIRECTV's advertising – meaning it asked the court to look at the ads and conclude without any extrinsic evidence that the messages were deceptive. The FTC did have a traditional stimulus/response copy test of one version of DIRECTV's website. It tested that website with a panel of potential DIRECTV customers (not actual customers). Still, it did not take into account information customers learned outside of the website and did not replicate the normal conditions of a DIRECTV customer making a purchase decision.

We designed a survey to address whether DIRECTV customers were aware of the conditions of purchase and whether DIRECTV's advertisements were deceptive. The survey methodology followed the idealized survey design discussed in the prior section.

2.4.2 Study Objectives

The objective of the study was to assess whether actual DIRECTV customers were deceived regarding the conditions of purchase at the end of their journey (immediately after purchase). The specific objectives of the study were as follows:

- To survey and gather data about new DIRECTV subscribers' knowledge, immediately after subscription and prior to activation of services, of the following conditions of purchase of DIRECTV's services.
- To assess differences, if any, in new subscriber knowledge based on the DIRECTV sales method (phone, web, or both) through which they subscribed.
- To assess impacts, if any, of subscription processes with modified disclosures on new subscriber knowledge of the conditions of purchase and to measure the net deception, if any, in customers who were incorrect in their knowledge about the conditions of purchase.
- To assess differences, if any, in new subscriber knowledge of certain conditions of purchase based on whether they self-identified as being price-sensitive or non-price-sensitive subscribers.
- To evaluate certain aspects of the subscription process of DIRECTV new subscribers, including considerations and sources of information used in the purchase decision

2.4.3 Study Methodology

Key to the design is the incorporation of the test and control ads in the natural flow of subscribing to the DIRECTV service. This required modifying the regular flow of subscribing and a randomization process which randomly assigned prospects to either the test or control stream. This allowed the prospect to view the stimulus in its natural context toward the end of the consumer journey at a time they approached DIRECTV on their own. Once the prospect completed the purchase process and subscribed, we had invaluable info on the conversion rate to the test and control ads. In addition, we could now select a random sample of customers and send them a traditional web survey invitation asking them to participate in a follow-up survey. Again, a time when consumers expect a follow-up contact from the company they just bought a service from by web or phone.

Each of the actual 2,872 DIRECTV customers in the experiment either went through the regular sign-up process on the web or by phone – known as the business-as-usual process (the "test") – or through a modified process that had alternative methods of disclosing the conditions of purchase at issue in this case (the "control"). The web control sign-up process included modified disclosures of the conditions of purchase that complied with what the FTC previously stated would have been proper disclosures. The phone script control was revised to include more prominent disclosures.

The web survey included a combination of closed-ended and open-ended questions. The key deception questions asked respondents to identify what they knew about the conditions of purchase that the FTC alleged were inadequately disclosed (promotional pricing, contract term, early cancelation fee, etc.).

2.4.4 Study Results

The substantial majority of surveyed consumers engaged in the extensive consumer journey and knew the conditions of purchase at issue, and very few gave incorrect answers about the conditions. In general, there were no material differences in knowledge of conditions between those who subscribed by phone or on the web. The methods of subscribing (web, phone, or a combination) were equally effective in communicating the conditions to consumers.

Generally, there was no statistically significant difference between consumer knowledge of conditions between the test and control and no statistically significant difference between consumers who were not informed about the terms between the test and control. In other words, based on the experiment, the disclosures in the business-as-usual (test) and modified control were equally effective in communicating the conditions to consumers. Figure 2.6 shows the extensive consumer journey that DIRECTV customers go through.

Figure 2.6 shows survey results confirming that DIRECTV customers engage in a complex journey prior to purchase. It shows that recommendations by friends and family and Internet searches, not advertising, were the top source of information for

Q19: What one source of information, did you consult first before deciding to subscribe to DIRECTV satellite TV service? (Please select a single response)

	Total		Web		Phone		Web then Phone	
	Test -a-	Control -b-	Test -c-	Control -d-	Test -e-	Control -f-	Test -g-	Control -h-
# Respondents	1171	1116	272	245	857	817	42	54
Friends or Family	46%	44%	39%	32%	47%	46%	36%	39%
Online/Internet Research	22%	25%	38%	45%	19%	21%	41%	44%
Advertisements	7%	7%	3%	2%	8%	8%	5%	2%
Consumer Reports	1%	1%	1%	2%	1%	1%	7%	-
Previous Subscriber	1%	2% a	<1%	1%	1%	2% e	2%	-
I don't remember	4%	4%	4%	2%	4%	4%	-	2%
I didn't research / None of these	16%	15%	13%	13%	18%	15%	5%	13%

FIGURE 2.6. Customers go through a Journey

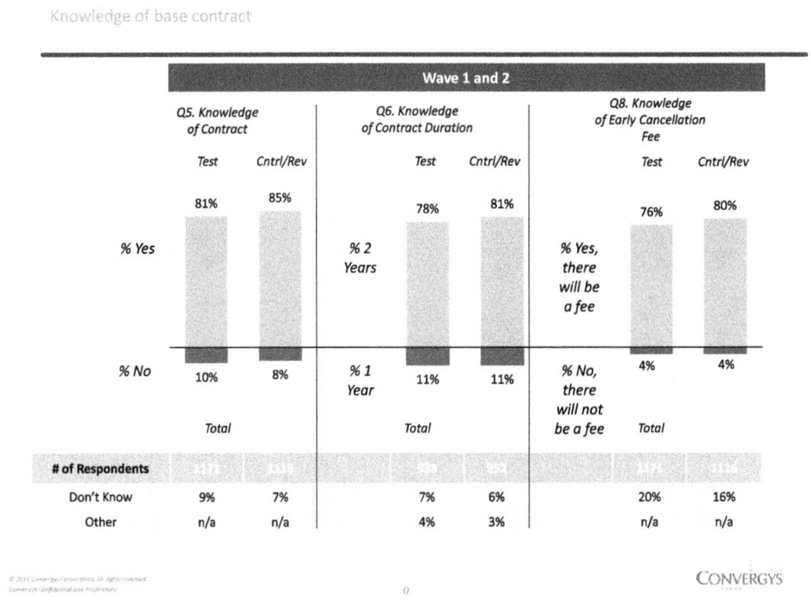

FIGURE 2.7. Knowledge of contract terms

prospective customers. The survey also showed that most customers relied on multiple sources of information prior to signing up.

In addition, Figure 2.7 shows that the respondents did understand the key contract terms and that there are no statistically significant differences between the test and control groups.

Since there is no statistically significant difference between the test and control groups, we concluded that there was no net deception. No disclosures will ever result in 100 percent or perfect consumer understanding and recollection of the terms of a complex transaction for many reasons. If the disclosures were deceptive – or lacking in clarity – there would have been a large difference across the board between the DIRECTV disclosures and the modified disclosures.

Finally, as seen in Figure 2.8, we looked at actual customer behavior and compared conversation rates (views/purchase) between the customers that viewed the business as usual disclosures (test) vs. those that viewed the modified website (control) flows. Because the rates were nearly identical, we concluded that the enhanced disclosures did not affect purchase decisions.

2.4.5 Resolution of the Case

The DIRECTV case went to trial in 2017. After the government presented its case, based upon the stimulus–response theory, DIRECTV moved for judgment on partial findings (without presenting a defense case or this study). After the briefing,

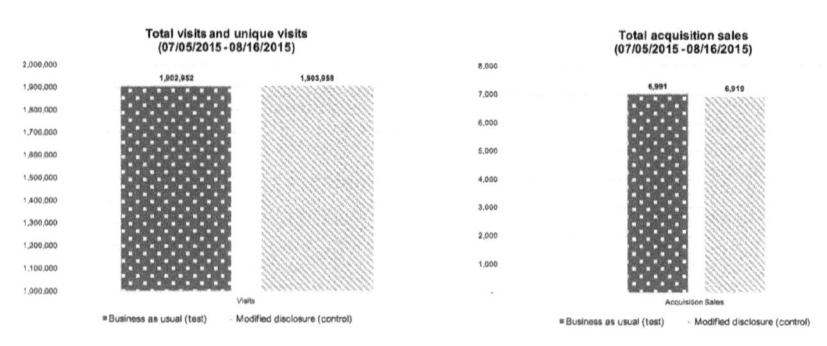

FIGURE 2.8. Modified disclosures did not change behavior

the court granted DIRECTV's motion on the deceptive advertising claim. (Though the court denied DIRECTV's motion as to a single claim under the Restore Online Shoppers Confidence Act). Based upon the judge's decision, the FTC dropped the case and did not go forward with the remaining claim. Thus, this survey, while defended in deposition, was never presented to the court. But we hope that the description of it here will be helpful to researchers as they think about how best to analyze allegations of deceptive advertising.

2.5 CONCLUSION

This chapter has shown that the outdated stimulus–response model does not accurately reflect consumer behavior for either individuals or organizations. Marketers and businesses have moved on from this obsolete model and understand that consumers engage in a much more expansive and nuanced consumer journey to purchase. On this consumer journey, potential customers obtain information from a wide variety of sources, view advertising skeptically, and continue to learn more even post-purchase.

Unfortunately, some government regulators of advertising and marketing are not up-to-date. Contrary to the well-accepted practices in the field, the government has brought false advertising cases that rely exclusively on the outdated stimulus–response model. There is hope, however. Courts have already begun rejecting false advertising cases that rely on this outdated marketing and customer behavior view.[64] We hope both courts and regulators move past the stimulus–response model and adopt a standard based on the consumer journey. For cases in which there is no false statement and consumer perceptions and understanding are necessary, the consumer journey presents a valid mode of analysis.

---

[64] See *FTC v. DIRECTV*.

3

"They Ruined Popcorn"

On the Costs and Benefits of Mandatory Labels

Cass R. Sunstein[*]

When should government mandate labels? When would mandatory labels have desirable consequences for social welfare? How can those consequences be measured? When would labels do more good than harm?

These questions arise in many contexts, involving (for example) calorie labels, mortgage disclosures, energy efficiency labels, fuel economy labels, credit card disclosures, labels for genetically modified food, nutrition facts panels, country of origin labels, graphic warnings for cigarettes, and much more. Some of these labels are designed to enable consumers to protect themselves from risks, involving money or health. Some of them attempt to protect third parties or respond to moral concerns – as, for example, when labels offer information that has bearing on animal welfare. Some of them respond to some kind of consumer (or interest-group) demand for government action, whether or not risks are involved.

In all of these cases, assessment of welfare effects can be challenging. Sometimes government agencies know far too little to make any kind of projection of likely effects, and they simply confess that fact. Sometimes they can engage in "breakeven analysis," explaining that if the benefits reach a certain level, the costs of labels will be justified. Sometimes agencies are able to quantify the benefits and costs of mandatory labels, or at least significant subsets of them, either by using endpoints (economic savings or health benefits) or by measuring private willingness to pay for labels. Sometimes they can point to human dignity, equity, or distributional concerns.

As we shall see, the costs of labels may be higher than is readily apparent, because they may produce subtle decreases in consumer welfare – as, for example, when

---

[*] This chapter draws on Cass R. Sunstein, "On Mandatory Labeling, with Special Reference to Genetically Modified Foods," 165 U. Pa. L. Rev. 1043 (2017); Cass R. Sunstein, "Ruining Popcorn," 58 J. Risk & Uncertainty 121 (2019); and Oren Bar-Gill et al., "Drawing False Inferences from Mandated Disclosures," 3 Behav. Pub. Pol'y 209 (2019).

calorie labels lead people to buy goods that are lower-calorie but less tasty, or when energy efficiency labels lead people to purchase appliances that cost less to operate but are less attractive. The point was captured in a reaction of one government official to mandatory calorie labels: "They ruined popcorn!"

As we shall see, private willingness to pay is the best approach in theory, because it should capture everything that consumers stand to gain from labels. But obtaining a useful measure raises serious empirical, normative, and conceptual challenges. A central reason is that to be worth using, willingness to pay should be informed, and often consumers lack the information that would enable them to decide how much to pay for (more) information. Another reason is that in some of the relevant contexts, preferences may be labile and endogenous. Once informed about health risks associated with certain foods, for example, people might (begin to) develop different tastes. On optimistic assumptions, for example, salt and sugar labels can lead to transformations in tastes. Ex ante willingness-to-pay figures will be insufficiently informative on that count, which creates serious problems for welfare analysis.

3.1 PRODUCT LABELING IN GENERAL

3.1.1 *Market Failure?*

When should government require products to be labeled? Suppose that we care about social welfare, suitably specified, and answer that labels should be required when they would do more good than harm. It is easy to imagine labels that are unnecessary, that are costly to impose, that are widely ignored by consumers, that mislead consumers, or that promote the interests of powerful private groups, not of the public as a whole. It is also easy to imagine labels that help consumers to save money, to avoid serious risks, to protect third parties, or to register their deepest moral commitments. Under the standard economic approach, the initial question is whether there is a market failure. In many cases, we expect the market to produce the necessary information on its own (Beales et al. 1981). In other words, sellers are expected to disclose relevant information voluntarily. Mandatory disclosure is needed only when voluntary disclosure fails.

When offering accounts of market failure under the requirements of prevailing executive orders, agencies usually ask about what consumers are likely to demand. A standard market failure, often invoked by agencies themselves, involves *incomplete information*. Sometimes consumers lack the information that would enable them to make (sufficiently informed) choices, and government provides that information in order to make the market work efficiently.

It is true, of course, that consumers sometimes insist on product-related information, and hence the market will provide it; there is no need for a mandate. But consumers might not have the information that would put them in the position to demand disclosure of (further) information, and it might not be rational for them to attempt to acquire that information. Consider the health risks posed by trans fats, which raise highly technical questions. Rational ignorance on the part of consumers might lead them not to acquire information from which they would ultimately benefit. Without that information, they might lack the knowledge that would lead them to even ask for labels. For that reason, a government response might be appropriate.

A further problem stems from the fact that information has the characteristics of a public good, which means that the market will not generate enough of it. Acting on their own, each consumer might not seek information from which all or most consumers would benefit. Mandatory labels overcome a collective action problem.

Yet another problem arises when the point of disclosure is to protect third parties. Often consumers want to know whether products are harming people, but even if they do not, disclosure might be required in order to reduce that harm. Suppose, for example, that disclosure of information is designed to reduce the risks of second-hand smoke, to prevent harms to animals (such as elephants or dolphins), to protect vulnerable groups (as with disclosure of "conflict minerals"), or to protect American jobs (as with "country of origin" or "made in America" labels). If third parties are at risk, we have a standard argument for government intervention. To the extent that GM food is thought to pose risks to the environment, a market failure seems to be involved. It is true, of course, that the preferred response to such risks is some kind of corrective tax, not disclosure. But if a tax is unavailable, for political or other reasons, then disclosure might seem to be a reasonable second-best.

There are behavioral issues as well. If risks are not sufficiently salient, then consumers might not demand relevant information about them, even if those risks are not exactly trivial. In principle, disclosure could therefore increase consumer welfare (Gabaix and Laibson 2006). Or suppose that health risks are long-term; if so, then "present bias" might lead consumers not to demand information about them (O'Donoughue and Rabin 2015). It is true that in the face of present bias, disclosure might not do much good; present-biased consumers might not care about what they learn. But perhaps information could be provided in a way that would reduce present bias. For example, labels might be graphic or specifically focus people on what might happen in the long term.

3.1.2 Producer Behavior

Notwithstanding these points, a standard argument predicts voluntary disclosure even if consumers do not demand it. Assume that for whatever reason (rational or not), consumers would choose non-GM foods if they were given the information that would enable them to do so. Specifically, assume that consumers are willing to pay $10 for GM salmon and $20 for non-GM salmon. Further, assume that GM salmon costs $5 to produce, whereas non-GM salmon costs $7 to produce. Finally, assume that, initially, half the salmon on the market is GM and half is not. Without any labeling, the consumer would not know what kind of salmon they are buying and would, therefore, be willing to pay $15 (= 0.5*$10 + 0.5*$20). This state of (consumer) ignorance benefits the producers of GM salmon and harms the producers of non-GM salmon.

But this state of ignorance is not an equilibrium. The non-GM sellers will voluntarily add a "No GMOs" label so that they can charge $20, rather than $15 per salmon (as long as the cost of adding such a label is less than $5 per salmon). The GM salmon will not be labeled, but GM labeling would not be necessary – rational consumers would infer that non-labeled salmon is GM. As Bar-Gill and Board (2012, 237) explain, "An implication of this result is that mandatory disclosure of product-attribute information is often unnecessary."

In the example just given, the relevant quality dimension is binary (GMO or non-GMO). A similar argument predicts voluntary disclosure when the relevant quality dimension is continuous. Assume that different microwave ovens in the market emit radiation in the range of 0–10 mW/cm^2, with levels of radiation distributed uniformly (such that, for example, the number of microwave ovens emitting no radiation is equal to the number of ovens emitting 1 mW/cm^2 of radiation, and equal to the number of ovens emitting 2 mW/cm^2 of radiation, and so on). Without any labeling, consumers would not be able to distinguish low-radiation ovens from high-radiation ovens and would attribute the average radiation level, 5 mW/cm^2, to any oven they consider purchasing. Producers of low-radiation ovens, with radiation levels below 5 mW/cm^2, would be harmed by this state of consumer ignorance. These producers would voluntarily disclose their ovens' radiation levels.

Now consumers would know the radiation levels of all ovens with levels below 5 mW/cm^2. And when considering a non-labeled oven, the consumer would assume an average radiation level of 7.5 mW/cm^2. But then producers with radiation levels of 5–7.5 mW/cm^2 will voluntarily disclose. Only producers with radiation levels of 7.5–10 mW/cm^2 will remain silent, and so consumers would attribute an average radiation level of 8.75 mW/cm^2 to a non-labeled oven. Now producers with levels of 7.5–8.75 mW/cm^2 will voluntarily disclose. And so on, until complete unraveling is achieved and all information is voluntarily disclosed.

As a real-world example analogous to the question of GM food, consider the example of gluten-free foods. Some people (including those with celiac disease) are allergic to food that contains gluten. At least to date, we do not observe statutory disclosure requirements ("Warning: this product contains gluten"). Instead we see voluntary labels, saying (for example) that products are "gluten free." The FDA has issued guidance for such labels (US FDA 2016). On admittedly optimistic assumptions, voluntary labels provide sufficient information.

3.1.3 Markets That Do Not Unravel

This happy unraveling story, however, does not always play out. Failure of voluntary disclosure occurs for several reasons – some neoclassical and some behavioral. Starting with the standard, neoclassical reasons, note that the unraveling result assumes that voluntary disclosure is truthful. But imperfect enforcement might lead to false disclosures, which government must correct – and once government is in the business of correction, it may be essentially mandating a label.

In addition, voluntary disclosure might fail when there is no standardized format or metric for disclosing information. Without standardization, consumers might not be able to make the required distinctions, in which case voluntary disclosure will be insufficient. And if the point of disclosure is to protect third parties, the unraveling story might not work because consumers might not care enough about third-party effects to respond to the various informational signals. True, consumer indifference would also mean that mandatory labels would be ineffective. But it is plausible to think that consumers care *somewhat* – enough to make mandatory labels work but not enough to promote unraveling.

Behavioral economics suggests an additional and perhaps stronger reason for skepticism about voluntary disclosure. The unraveling result assumes that consumers attend to and draw rational inferences from silence – from the absence of a label. But attention is limited (Kahneman 1973), and such inferences can be quite difficult to draw, especially when consumers are receiving numerous signals at the same time (as is true for food) and when there are multiple quality levels or continuous quality dimensions. Suppose, for example, that some products come with labels saying "low fat" or "low sugar." Would consumers necessarily infer that products lacking such labels are high in fat or sugar? Or would many consumers not think much or at all about the question of fat or sugar?

A standard neoclassical argument is that in a generalization of the "lemons equilibrium" (Mullainathan and Shafir 2013) competition might occur over easily observed characteristics, such as price, and less or not at all over less observable characteristics, such as ingredients (Akerlof 1970). The behavioral suggestion (or exclamation point) is that in view of the scarcity of attention, this limited kind of competition is highly likely. And even if consumers pay attention to the relevant ingredient (salt, sugar, fat), they might be unable to draw a fully rational inference from the absence of disclosure.

For example, those who are purchasing cereal or milk might attend to a variety of product attributes, and unless high fat or high sugar content is brought to their attention, many of them might not consider those ingredients at all. If many consumers would not pay attention or draw a negative inference (or a sufficiently negative inference) from the absence of a label, voluntary disclosure might fail. Such failure justifies the consideration of mandatory disclosure, at least in principle.

The Affordable Care Act, for example, mandates calorie labels, and there is a plausible argument on their behalf based on the considerations just sketched.

3.1.4 "Does Not Contain" Labels vs. "Contains" Labels

There are many differences between a system in which products without some characteristic say "Does Not Contain X" and one in which products with some characteristic say "Contains X." As we have seen, "Contains X" offers far more salient information to consumers with bounded attention. In addition, "Contains X" might offer a distinctive signal, suggesting that private and public institutions think that something is wrong with X.

"Does Not Contain X" might also promote a desirable form of sorting. Suppose that 10 percent of the population is troubled by X, whereas 90 percent is not; suppose that both groups are informed and rational. If so, there is no need for "Contains X." Those who want to avoid X can easily do so, and those who have no interest in avoiding X need not be troubled by the issue.

On a certain view of the facts, "Does Not Contain X" is the right approach both to gluten-free and to GM food. People who are allergic to gluten should know what to look for. The principal problem is that if they are inattentive, they might become sick simply by virtue of the fact that the issue has not been brought to their attention. (Compare labels saying "Contains peanuts" or "Contains shellfish," which may be especially important if consumers are inattentive or if it is not self-evident that the relevant food contains either.) With "Does Not Contain" labels, consumers can easily avoid GM food if that is what they want to do. But this approach is not a solution if GM food has harmful systemic effects or threatens to cause environmental harm (or if relevant interest groups want to stigmatize GM food).

3.2 COSTS AND BENEFITS

Even if there is a market failure, the question remains: do the benefits of labels justify the costs? If it would be expensive to comply with a labeling requirement – say, $800 million annually – the question whether the benefits are sufficient would be put in stark relief. We could easily imagine disclosure requirements that do little good, perhaps because consumers pay no attention to them. If so, such requirements would be unjustified on cost–benefit grounds. We could also imagine disclosure requirements from which consumers and third parties would benefit greatly.

As we shall see, agencies have not always responded well to the difficulty of quantifying the costs and benefits of disclosure requirements. In fact, they have adopted four distinctive approaches, imposing increasingly severe information-gathering demands on agencies. It is not always easy to explain why they choose one or another in particular cases.

The first approach – and it may be the most candid – is to confess a lack of knowledge by acknowledging that, in light of existing information, some costs and (especially) benefits simply cannot be quantified (Beales et al. 1981; *Investment Co. Institute* v. *Commodity Futures Trading Comm'n* 2013). The problem with this approach is that it suggests that the decision to proceed is essentially a stab in the dark. When the stakes are high, that seems unacceptable, certainly for policymakers.

The second approach involves "breakeven analysis," by which agencies describe what the benefits would have to be in order to justify the costs – and suggest that the benefits are indeed likely to be of the requisite magnitude. In principle, this approach is better than a simple confession of ignorance, and it is often the best path forward. But it involves a high degree of guesswork, and it may be a mere conclusion, a kind of *ipse dixit*, masquerading as an analytic device. Without a great deal of discipline, it too may not be so different from a confession of ignorance.

The third approach is to attempt to specify outcomes in terms of (say) economic savings or health endpoints. The advantage of this approach is that it actually points to concrete benefits, and it attempts to measure and to monetize them. But it too runs into difficulties. The first is that agencies may lack anything like the information that would enable them to venture such a specification. The second and more interesting is that, for reasons I will explore, even an accurate specification will not give a complete picture of the actual benefits, and, in crucial respects, it will almost certainly overstate them. In brief, the problem is that people might experience significant losses as well as gains as a result of the label (for example, if they switch to a product that is inferior along certain dimensions), and an account of endpoints will ignore those losses.

The fourth approach is to identify consumers' willingness to pay. As a matter of abstract principle, that approach is (mostly) the right one, because it should capture the full universe of losses and gains from the label. At the same time, it runs into serious and perhaps insuperable normative, conceptual, and empirical challenges. As we shall see, the most obvious problem is that it is difficult to elicit people's *informed and unbiased* willingness to pay for labels. The most interesting problem involves the potentially labile character of some preferences.

3.3 COSTS

On the cost side, some of the questions are relatively straightforward. Regulators may well be able to learn the total cost of (for example) producing fuel economy labels and placing them on new vehicles. The principal difficulty arises *when the information itself imposes costs on consumers*. It is a mistake to ignore those costs, even if they prove difficult to quantify, and even if consumers enjoy a net benefit (Levy et al. 2016). Those costs come in several different forms. Some of them will usually be low – but not always.

3.3.1 A Small Cognitive Tax

First, a cost is involved in reading and processing the information. For each consumer, that cost is likely to be quite low, but across a large number of purchasers, it might turn out to be significant. Information disclosure is, in a sense, akin to a paperwork burden. To be sure, consumers are not compelled to read and process what is disclosed. But even for those who seek to ignore it, its very presence may operate as a kind of cognitive tax. Because people have limited bandwidth, that tax may not be safely ignored. (If there is a Hell, it may well be filled with warnings.)

3.3.2 Ruining Popcorn, 1: A Hedonic Tax on Those Who Do Not Change Their Behavior

Second, and more importantly, the cost may be hedonic, not cognitive. Suppose that smokers are given information about the adverse health effects of smoking or that visitors to chain restaurants are given information about the caloric contents of food. Many members of both groups will suffer a hedonic loss. Consider, for example, smokers who cannot quit and customers who decide to choose high-calorie foods notwithstanding the labels. In hedonic terms, such people will lose, rather than gain, if they are miserable or at least sadder at the time of purchase.

It is important to note that the hedonic costs might be incurred in the present, while the health benefits are likely to occur in the future. If people do not care sufficiently about their future selves (recall the phenomenon of "present bias"), they might give insufficient weight to those benefits. The point is not that people are free from present bias. It is only that hedonic costs, whenever they occur, must be counted in the overall analysis.

To be sure, there is a normative question whether regulators should count, as costs, the adverse hedonic effect of truthful information. Is it a cost, or a benefit, if people learn, truthfully, that they have diabetes or cancer? On net, that might well be a benefit, at least if they can do something about the problem. But there is a cost as well, and a large one, even if the net effect is positive. If we are operating within a welfarist framework, the hedonic loss must be treated as a cost. It might turn out to be low, but regulators should not ignore it (as they typically do).

Compare: Many people do not want to get blood tests, even if doctors advise them to do so, because they do not want to bear the hedonic cost of less-than-good results. The failure to get the tests might be a product of a behavioral bias (for example, present bias), but it might also be a product, in part, of a rational aversion to negative information.

3.3.3 Ruining Popcorn, 2: A Hedonic Tax on Those Who Do Change Their Behavior

Even if people might be able to quit smoking or end up choosing lower-calorie items, and will hence enjoy a high net benefit, they will incur a cost by seeing something that inflicts pain. In principle, that cost should also count, even if it is greatly outweighed by benefits. The point, then, is not that the hedonic cost is necessarily a trump card; if people make different choices once they are informed, the presumption should be that they are better off. But *by how much?*

To answer that question, the hedonic cost must be taken into account. For many people, a calorie label imposes a serious cost, simply because it informs them that the delicious cheeseburger they are about to eat is also going to make their belly bulge.

3.3.4 *A Consumer Welfare Loss*

There is a fourth loss, in the form of forgone consumer surplus. Suppose that people decide that on balance, they should have a salad rather than a cheeseburger, on the ground that the latter has many more calories. If they choose the salad because of the label, they are probably better off on balance – and, in a sense, they are sadder but wiser (and healthier). They are sadder to the extent that they enjoy their meal less. Assessment of the magnitude of the loss poses serious conceptual and empirical challenges, but there is no question that it exists, and that it might turn out to be a significant fraction of the benefits. In principle, a decision to forgo the hamburger might make people only modestly better off, if the hedonic loss is almost as high as the health gain.

Suppose, for example, that consumers are choosing between two essentially equivalent cars; that on average the more fuel-efficient one would cost $2,000 less annually to operate because of its fuel efficiency; that the less fuel-efficient one would cost $500 more upfront; and that because of the fuel-economy label, they select the fuel-efficient car. For each such consumer, we might be tempted to say that the label has produced $1,500 in gains. But in actual practice, the effects of a fuel-economy label will be much more complicated to assess. Some consumers will end up purchasing cars that are more fuel-efficient but inferior along some dimension, so that they will gain $1,500 minus X, where X refers to the desirable features of the unchosen car that they otherwise prefer. It is hard for public officials to know whether X is, on average, $100, or $1,000, or $1,450.

3.3.5 *The Problem of Endogenous Preferences*

All this assumes that preferences are consistent and exogenous. In some contexts, however, that assumption is not correct. This point complicates the foregoing analysis and creates a risk that analysis of costs will ignore shifts in tastes that are induced by labels themselves.

Suppose that at Time 1, people enjoy hamburgers a lot and enjoy salads only a little. Now suppose that having seen the labels, people switch at Time 2 because they want to make healthier choices. At Time 2, they suffer costs as a result of the switch; they miss hamburgers (delicious!) and they do not much like salad (boring!). But at Time 3, people might come to dislike hamburgers (disgusting!) and to love salad (fresh!). In principle, preference change must be taken into account by the considered cost–benefit analysis, though doing so presents serious challenges: it might be difficult to know the magnitude of the change and even the sign (perhaps those who switch to salad will crave hamburgers and grow to despise salad).

3.4 BENEFITS

On the benefits side, the assessment is even more challenging (Allcott and Kessler 2015). If the government mandates a fuel-economy label, agencies should project the economic and environmental benefits from the mandate. But to do that, they have to *know the effect of labels on behavior*. In principle, a randomized controlled trial would be valuable and perhaps necessary for that purpose. If one group sees a particular label and a similar group sees a different label (or no label), regulators should be able to specify the effect of the label on purchasing decisions. Armed with that information, they could estimate economic and environmental consequences (at least if they could generalize from the trial).

Unfortunately, it is sometimes difficult or impossible to run randomized controlled trials. In these circumstances, making any kind of projection of how consumers will react to a label is exceedingly difficult. An additional problem is that for the reasons given thus far, the projection would not give an adequate estimate of the (net) benefits. We have seen that if people are buying cars that are more fuel-efficient but otherwise highly undesirable, there will be a welfare loss. For that reason, regulators might explore the issue from another direction (Thomson and Monje 2015). Rather than asking about the economic savings from the fuel-efficient car, they might ask an entirely different question: *how much would consumers be willing to pay for a fuel-economy label?*

Under ideal conditions and under plausible assumptions, and bracketing the endogeneity issue, the right question for regulators to ask involves willingness to pay; they should not focus on the economic benefits that consumers might receive if (for example) they purchase more fuel-efficient cars. The reason is that on optimistic assumptions, the willingness-to-pay question ought to capture everything that matters to consumers. (Of course it is true that the question will not fully capture third-party effects, nor will it capture welfare effects if preferences are endogenous.)

As an empirical matter, however, it is not easy to obtain a reliable answer to that question, or anything close to it. To be sure, we might simply ask people. Online experiments might tell us something important. Field experiments would be even better. We might be able to learn a great deal from such experiments; this is an area in which considerable progress should be expected in the future.

A pervasive challenge is that for people's answers to be relevant, it would be important to provide pertinent information – for example, about the potential benefits (purely economic and otherwise) of labels. Providing that information is no simple endeavor, not least because offering some numbers about those potential benefits would be important, and any numbers might "anchor" consumers and hence bias their answers. Suppose that the problem of anchoring could be overcome and that informed consumers would be willing to pay (say) $10, on average, for fuel-economy labels. If so, we might have some sense of the benefits, at least if behavioral biases are not distorting people's answers.

Unfortunately, however, such biases might well produce distortions; consider present bias and optimistic bias, which may lead to unduly low willingness to pay. In any case, survey evidence is imperfectly reliable, in part because of the familiar problems with contingent valuation studies, in part because of the immense difficulty of informing consumers in a sufficiently neutral way.

For health-related disclosures, the problem is even harder. One goal of calorie labels, for example, is to reduce obesity, which causes an assortment of health problems, including premature mortality. Regulators have established ways to turn health endpoints into monetary equivalents. For example, a statistical death is now valued at about $9 million (Loureiro et al. 2006; Sunstein 2014). But how many premature deaths would be prevented by calorie labels? And what would be the effect of such labels on adverse health outcomes short of death?

To answer such questions, regulators have to undertake two tasks. First, they must begin by making some prediction about the effect of calorie labels on what people choose to eat. Second, they have to follow that prediction by specifying the health consequences of lower levels of caloric intake. At least it can be said that if they can accomplish those tasks, they will have some sense of the benefits of the labels, once (and this is a third task) they turn the various consequences into monetary equivalents. After undertaking all three tasks, regulators will have specified endpoints – but for the reasons given, a specification of endpoints will overstate benefits because it will not include various cognitive and hedonic losses.

Alternatively, we could (again) ask how much people would be willing to pay for calorie labels (Gruber and Mullainathan 2002). As before, asking that question is, in principle, preferable to an effort to assess health states, because the answer will capture all variables that matter to consumers (US FDA 2011; Bronsteen et al. 2015). Also, as before, there are formidable challenges in using surveys to elicit reliable numbers free from biases of various kinds. And if preferences are endogenous and labile, willingness-to-pay numbers might greatly understate the welfare gain from labels. Recall that people might develop tastes for the products to which they shift. (I am also bracketing the questions raised by addictive goods, such as cigarettes, for which labels might be beneficial on welfare grounds precisely because they help break the hold of the addiction. Note that cigarette taxes appear to make smokers happier (Gruber and Mullainathan 2002).

In light of these challenges, regulators have two imperfect options. First, they can work on the two relevant tracks to try to produce answers: exploring endpoints and enlisting surveys. On prominent occasions, they have tried the former (OSHA 2016). Second, they can acknowledge the difficulties, confess that they cannot surmount them, and use "breakeven analysis," by which they ask what the benefits would have to be in order to justify the costs, and then do what they can to generate a reasonable lower bound. Suppose, for example, that an energy-efficiency label for refrigerators would cost $10 million annually and that 8 million refrigerators are sold in the United States every year. Even if the average consumer saves only $0.50 annually as a result of the label, the cost will be made up in just three years. Breakeven analysis can be crude, but in some cases, it will suggest that the argument for labels is either very strong or very weak.

3.5 THIRD PARTIES – AND MORALITY

Some actual or imaginable labels are meant to protect third parties, not consumers as such. Suppose that some or many consumers are concerned about the use of certain minerals to finance mass atrocities, and they favor labeling, or some kind of disclosure requirement, so that consumers can decline to purchase products that contain such minerals. Or suppose that consumers care about where goods were made, perhaps because they want to purchase products from their own nation or perhaps because they do not want to purchase products from nations that do not respect human rights. They might seek "country of origin" labels for that reason. Or suppose that some or many consumers care about the welfare of animals in general or certain animals in particular; because they do, they seek labels to reflect how animals were (mis)treated.

In some of these cases, the third-party effects are not obscure, and the real challenge is how to quantify them. As before, it is necessary to begin by making some projections about consumer behavior. To what extent would consumers change their purchasing habits in response? Even if that question can be answered, it would be necessary to tie any such changes to reduced harm or increased benefit for third parties. And even if that problem can be resolved, it would be necessary to quantify and monetize the resulting effects. It is no wonder that in the context of conflict minerals, the agency concluded that quantification was not possible (*Nat'l Ass'n of Mfrs. v. SEC* 2015). Perhaps it should have engaged in some form of breakeven analysis, explaining that the requirement was likely to survive cost–benefit analysis even if its effect were modest. But perhaps it lacked the information that would have allowed it to make that analysis plausible.

Some disclosure requirements, including mandatory labels, are not simple to defend within a standard cost–benefit framework, not for the reasons I have been sketching, but because considerations of equity, distributional effects, or human dignity are involved. When values of this kind are involved, it is perfectly legitimate for agencies to consider them. It might well be sufficient for agencies simply to point to such considerations and not to fold them into a cost–benefit analysis. Agencies are authorized to give independent consideration to equity and human dignity. If the statutory goal is to achieve distributional goals by transferring resources from some people to others, then cost–benefit balancing is not the rule of decision, and it is not all that matters. A rule might have costs in excess of benefits, in the sense that the losers lose more than the winners gain, but perhaps the winners are poor or otherwise deprived, and perhaps have a special claim to attention under the relevant law or as a matter of principle.

I have suggested that if quantification of the benefits of labels is required, the question might be: how much would (informed) consumers be willing to pay for such labels? Within a certain framework, that question is the right one. But even if we put the difficulties to one side, it is not at all clear that the framework is the right one. If the issue involves human dignity, equity, or distributional considerations – or any kind of harm to third parties – why should the proper analysis depend on how much people are willing to pay for it? It seems senseless to say that labels motivated by distributive goals should be imposed to the extent that people are willing to pay for them.

To say this is not to say that consequentialist considerations do not matter at all. Insofar as harms to third parties are involved, cost–benefit analysis can be used, acknowledging the empirical problems sketched earlier. Insofar as the issue involves equity or dignity, break-even analysis might be useful. To the extent that distributive goals are involved, a key question is whether such goals would, in fact, be promoted by labels or disclosure. That question would seem relevant to the "conflict minerals" problem. Some kind of means–ends analysis, explaining how the means are connected to the ends, would seem indispensable to an evaluation of labels that are designed to promote distributive goals (or for that matter equity or human dignity). Agencies should be expected to undertake that analysis – or to explain why they cannot.

3.6 TAKING STOCK

In numerous contexts, the US Congress has required or authorized federal agencies to impose disclosure requirements. In all those contexts, executive agencies are required, by executive order, to catalogue the benefits and costs of disclosure requirements, and to demonstrate that the benefits justify the costs. Such agencies face persistent challenges in projecting benefits, and they use four different approaches: a refusal to do so on the ground that quantification is not feasible; break-even analysis; projection of end states, such as economic savings or health outcomes; and estimates of willingness to pay for the relevant information.

Each of these approaches raises serious questions and runs into strong objections. In principle, the right question generally involves willingness to pay. But in practice, people often lack enough information to give a sensible answer to the question how much they would be willing to pay for (more) information. (How much would you be willing to pay for information about the presence of chemical XYZ in your favorite food, when you know little or nothing about chemical XYZ or its effects?)

We have also seen that when preferences are labile or endogenous, even a sensible answer may fail to capture the welfare consequences, because people may develop new tastes and values. In these circumstances, a break-even analysis is the very least that should be required, and it is sometimes the most that agencies can do. If it is accompanied by some account of potential outcomes, acknowledging uncertainties, a break-even analysis will often show that mandatory disclosure is justified on welfare grounds – and often that it is not.

REFERENCES

Akerlof, George A. (1970) "The Market for 'Lemons': Quality Uncertainty and the Market Mechanism," 84 Q.J. ECON. 488.

Allcott, Hunt & Judd B. Kessler (2015) "The Welfare Effects of Nudges: A Case Study of Energy Use Social Comparisons," 2 (Nat'l Bureau of Econ. Research, Working Paper No. 21,671), www.nber.org/papers/w21671.

Bar-Gill, Oren & Oliver Board (2012) "Product-Use Information and the Limits of Voluntary Disclosure," 14 AM. L. & ECON. REV. 235, 237.

Beales, Howard et al. (1981) "The Efficient Regulation of Consumer Information," 24 J.L. & ECON. 491, 502.

John Bronsteen et al. (2015) *Happiness and the Law* (University of Chicago Press).

Gabaix, Xavier & David Laibson (2006) "Shrouded Attributes, Consumer Myopia, and Information Suppression in Competitive Markets," 121 Q.J. ECON. 505, 511.

Gruber, Johnathan & Sendhil Mullainathan (2002) "Do Cigarette Taxes Make Smokers Happier?," www.nber.org/papers/w8872.

Investment Co. Institute v. Commodity Futures Trading Comm'n, 720 F.3d 370, 372–75 (D.C. Cir. 2013).

Kahneman, Daniel (1973) *Attention and Effort* (Prentice-Hall), 13–17.

Levy, Helen et al. (2016) "Tobacco Regulation and Cost–Benefit Analysis: How Should We Value Foregone Consumer Surplus?" (Nat'l Bureau of Econ. Research, Working Paper No. 22,471), www.nber.org/papers/w22471.pdf.

Loureiro, Maria L. et al. (2006) "Do Consumers Value Nutritional Labels?" 33 EUR. REV. AGRIC. ECON. 249, 263.

Mullainathan, Sendhil & Eldar Shafir (2013) *Scarcity: Why Having Too Little Means So Much* (Times Books).

Nat'l Ass'n of Mfrs. v. SEC, 800 F.3d 518 (D.C. Cir. 2015), 547.

Occupational Safety and Health Administration (OSHA) (2016) Improve Tracking of Workplace Injuries and Illnesses, 81 Fed. Reg. 29,624, 29,628 (proposed May 12) (to be codified at 29 C.F.R. pts. 1904, 1902).

O'Donoghue, Ted & Matthew Rabin (2015) "Present Bias: Lessons Learned and to Be Learned," 105 AM. ECON. REV. 273, 274–75.

Sunstein, Cass R. (2014) *Valuing Life: Humanizing the Regulatory State* (University of Chicago Press).

Thomson, Kathryn & Carolos Monje (2015) Memorandum from Kathryn Thomson, Gen. Counsel & Carlos Monje, Assistant Sec'y for Policy, U.S. Dep't of Transp., to Secretarial

Officers & Modal Adm'rs, U.S. Dep't of Transp. 2 (June 17), www.transportation.gov/sites/dot.gov/files/docs/VSL2015_0.pdf

U.S. Food & Drug Administration (FDA) (2011) Food Labeling; Nutrition Labeling of Standard Menu Items in Restaurants and Similar Retail Food Establishments, 76 Fed. Reg. 19192 (proposed Apr. 6).

U.S. Food & Drug Administration (FDA) (2016) Gluten and Food Labeling, www.fda.gov/Food/GuidanceRegulation/GuidanceDocumentsRegulatoryInformation/Allergens/ucm367654.htm

4

Valuation of Personal Data

Assessing Potential Harm from Unauthorized Access and Misuse of Personal Information in Consumer Class Actions

Vildan Altuglu, Lorin M. Hitt, Samid Hussain, and Matteo Li Bergolis

4.1 INTRODUCTION

Data is the lifeblood of the digital economy. Much of the data in use today is generated by the everyday activities of consumers as they communicate, shop, travel, work, or engage in routine interactions with other consumers, businesses, and government entities through digital systems, platforms, and media. This has led to an enormous accumulation of data about individual consumers that can directly or indirectly provide information about their characteristics, preferences, activities, or behaviors.

Given this massive accumulation of information, the opportunities for disputes over the use or misuse of consumer information has concurrently increased. In this chapter we address a key component of such disputes – evaluating the alleged harm created as a result of misuse or unauthorized disclosure of personal information, with a special focus on assessing such alleged harm in the context of consumer class actions.

Class actions are a common mechanism by which consumers seek compensation for injury from alleged loss of privacy or other remedies to prevent similar loss in the future. The analysis of the value of privacy is relevant both for the purposes of class certification and for determination of damages. To certify a class, it is necessary to demonstrate that alleged harm can be determined through a common method or proof.[1]

---

[1] If one cannot determine whether a particular putative class member was harmed without undertaking an individual inquiry, then a class is generally not certified. "The District Court held, and it is uncontested here, that to meet the predominance requirement respondents had to show (1) that the existence of individual injury resulting from the alleged antitrust violation (referred to as 'antitrust impact') was 'capable of proof at trial through evidence that [was] common to the class rather than individual to its members'; and (2) that the damages resulting from that injury were measurable 'on a class-wide basis' through use of a 'common methodology.'" *Comcast Corp. et al. v. Behrend et al.*, 133 S. Ct. 1426, 1433 (2013), pp. 2–3. See also Campbell, M. D., B. Stamps Todd, S. Hussain, V. Altuglu, and M. Li Bergolis (2021)

Should the class be certified, a reliable method must be employed for the determination of damages that are not pre-specified by statute.[2]

As will be developed in detail in our discussion, a crucial aspect of assessing the value consumers may place on privacy, and thus the potential harm resulting from perceived privacy violations (e.g. the change in this value) depends critically on the nature of the information, whether the information was indeed private (e.g. information was not previously disclosed), and consumers' preferences for privacy. To the extent that these factors vary across settings or across consumers, such variation needs to be addressed by any method attempting to determine the value of privacy. The variation across consumers, in addition, may affect whether it is appropriate or possible to use a common method to determine the value of privacy.

Different methods from marketing and economics, including analysis of market data, demand modeling, hedonic price analysis, or preference elicitation techniques such as conjoint analysis or contingent valuation studies have been proposed, and in some cases implemented, to assess the value of privacy in the consumer class action context. The reliability of these methods is, in part, determined by their ability to address potential variation across consumers in the nature of their private information and preferences over this information. In addition, the reliability of these methods, all of which were developed for other purposes, depends on their ability to address some unique aspects of the privacy valuation context. Perhaps the most important of these features is the so-called "privacy paradox," which is the observation that there is typically substantial divergence between consumers' stated preferences for privacy (i.e. expressed preferences) and their behaviors regarding disclosure of private information or willingness to engage in efforts to protect their privacy (i.e. revealed preferences).[3]

In the subsequent discussion we will first focus on sources of heterogeneity in the nature of personal information and consumer preferences over data privacy that provide the context in which valuation methods will need to be employed. We will then focus on a discussion of various methods that have been proposed in recent consumer class actions involving personal data, which we divide into two broad

---

"Damages," chapter 3 in *The American Bar Association Trial & Insurance Practice Section Class Action Book*, 3rd ed. (ABA Publishing).

[2] "[A] model purporting to serve as evidence of damages ... must measure only those damages attributable to that theory. If the model does not even attempt to do that, it cannot possibly establish that damages are susceptible of measurement across the entire class for purposes of Rule 23(b)(3)." *Comcast Corp. et al. v. Behrend et al.*, 133 S. Ct. 1426, 1433 (2013), p. 7. See also Campbell et al., "Damages."

[3] Spiekermann, S., J. Grossklags, and B. Berendt (2001), "E-Privacy in 2nd Generation E-Commerce: Privacy Preferences versus Actual Behavior," *Third ACM Conference on Electronic Commerce*, Tampa, pp. 38–47; Norberg, P. A., D. R. Horne, and D. A. Horne (2007), "The Privacy Paradox: Personal Information Disclosure Intentions versus Behaviors," *Journal of Consumer Affairs*, 41(1), pp. 100–26; Adjerid, I., E. Peer, and A. Acquisti (2018), "Beyond the Privacy Paradox: Objective versus Relative Risk in Privacy Decision Making," *MIS Quarterly*, 42(2), pp. 465–88.

categories: (1) *invasion-of-privacy* settings, where personal information was allegedly misused by the receiving party, and (2) *data-breach* settings, where personal information was improperly accessed by unrelated third parties. Examples of the former include cases related to the alleged misuse of data by technology and social media firms that collect or manage this information upon sign-up or through the use of the service.[4] Examples of the latter include the often well-publicized cases involving misappropriation of customer and payment card information in a variety of industries, such as retail, healthcare, hospitality, and telecommunications.[5] While invasion-of-privacy and data-breach cases share many similarities, one crucial difference involves the benefits consumers may accrue from the use of their data. Specifically, invasion-of-privacy claims typically occur in the context of an economic relationship where the use of information may have both costs and benefits to the consumer. There are no such compensating benefits to consumers in data-breach matters, because typically the breached data can be accessed by malicious actors.

4.2 BACKGROUND: PERSONAL INFORMATION AND PREFERENCES FOR DATA PRIVACY

Personal information is often associated with the concept of "personally identifiable information" or PII. PII typically involves identifying information about the consumer, such as name, address, email, or social security number, but can also include information that is directly connected to a consumer, such as payment card information, geolocation, purchase history, messaging content, or a contacts list. To the extent that a wide variety of information can be combined in a way that connects back to an individual consumer, the scope of what is considered PII is likely to evolve and expand over time.

---

[4] See e.g. *In Re: Facebook Privacy Litigation*, Case No. 10-cv-02389-JW; *In Re: Facebook, Inc. Consumer Privacy User Profile Litigation*, Case No. 18-md-02843-VC; *Fraley et al. v. Facebook, Inc.*, Case No. 11-cv-01726; *Brown et al. v. Google*, Case No. 20-cv-03664-SVK; *Rodriguez et al. v. Google*, Case No. 20-cv-04688-RS.

[5] See e.g. "Chipotle Says Hackers Hit Most Restaurants in Data Breach," *Reuters*, May 26, 2017, www.reuters.com/article/us-chipotle-cyber/chipotle-says-hackers-hit-most-restaurants-in-data-breach-idUSKBN18M2BY; "Wendy's Update on Payment Card Security Incident," *Wendy's Press Release*, July 7, 2016, https://s1.q4cdn.com/202642389/files/doc_news/archive/6bc91c58-7baa-4bc5-bf80-fef45d14d014.pdf; "Notice of Unauthorized Access to or Acquisition of Chili's Grill & Bar Guest Data," *Chili's Press Release*, Sept. 20, 2018, www.newsandpress.net/notice-of-unauthorized-access-to-or-acquisition-of-chilis-grill-bar-guest-data/; *In re Barnes & Noble Pin Pad Litigation*, Case No. 12-cv-08617, US District Court for the Northern District of Illinois; *In re Zappos.com, Inc. Customer Data Security Breach Litigation*, MDL No. 2357, US District Court for the District of Nevada; *Vetter, et al. v. Marriott International, Inc.*, Case No. 19-cv-00094, US District Court for the District of Maryland, Southern Division; *In re: Anthem, Inc. Data Breach Litigation*, Case No. 15-MD-02617-LHK, US District Court for the District of Maryland, Southern Division; *Vash v. T-Mobile US Inc.*, Case No. 21-cv-03384, US District Court for the Northern District of Georgia.

Not all PII is private in all circumstances, however. For example, privacy advocates and scholars have recognized that information is not private if it has already been disclosed.[6] In today's digital world, different individuals may disclose varying degrees of their personal information (such as their names, birthdates, friends, photos), through their activities in various social media apps or other online channels.[7] For example, the Pew Research Center, which conducts periodic surveys on consumers' use of online services, has reported that, in 2021, 69 percent of adults used Facebook, and that 72 percent of online adults used multiple social networking sites.[8] Thus, the extent to which PII is private may affect the privacy value of this information.

The way PII is generated, captured, and transferred is quite diverse. In some cases, it is the result of a deliberate action by a consumer to share information with a broader group (perhaps even the general public) such as creating a public social media profile, making a post or comment on a social media platform, or providing a product review or recommendation. In other cases, the information is generated as a necessary by-product in the pursuit of another activity – for instance, an online purchase that involves the transfer of payment card information as well as other information such as name, home address, and telephone number. Information is also generated in the background by normal online and offline interactions in ways less obvious to the consumer – for instance, advertisers gather clickstream data as consumers move from site to site on the Internet (in some cases which can be tied directly to a consumer), software applications on a consumer's computer or mobile device may exchange information (such as identity, location, contacts) to provide services, and consumers may regularly interact with various technologies that capture digital traces in traditionally offline activities such as public video cameras or through interactions with an increasingly wide range of networked smart devices (including, for instance, appliances and vehicles).

There is also considerable diversity in the way information is used. A number of the examples given involve situations where the usage of data is likely well understood by the consumer. For example, consumers generally understand that their social media posts will appear at a minimum to a group of social media "friends," or that the payment and shipping information they provide will be used to fulfill an order. But more recent technical innovations may involve applications of information that are less obvious to consumers. For example, consumers' browsing behavior and past purchase history might be used by third parties to tailor online experiences, such as search results, or making product recommendations and setting

---

[6] Solove, D. J. (2008), *Understanding Privacy*, Harvard University Press, pp. 69–70.
[7] This type of personal information sharing may also be conducted through offline activity.
[8] "Social Media Fact Sheet," *Pew Research Center*, Apr. 7, 2021, www.pewresearch.org/internet/fact-sheet/social-media/. Social network use may be even higher within certain demographics. See e.g. "Social Media Use in 2021," *Pew Research Center*, Apr. 7, 2021, www.pewresearch.org/internet/2021/04/07/social-media-use-in-2021/.

prices. The use of the data may also be completely unobserved, such as a merchant reselling information to other commercial entities for use in advertising, customer research, or product development, or used internally within a company for marketing or product design purposes.

On the one hand, the vast quantities and variety of information that are now available about consumers create many opportunities for information use that can create value for both consumers and companies. Many of these opportunities are well-understood and anticipated by the individual providing the information. Social media and online commerce, for one, could not exist without the free flow of at least some types of information (one of the key distinguishing characteristics of social media is the public profile[9]), and the fact that vast numbers of consumers participate in these services suggests the presence of considerable value to these participants. In addition, the ability of businesses to offer services for free depends on the ability to obtain an alternative revenue stream (typically from a third party), and many of these business approaches involve the use of consumer information. For instance, Google uses information about consumers' past and current search queries to target ads.[10] Here, consumers provide information that is used for a secondary purpose (targeted advertising) but receive a benefit in return (high-quality or relevant search results).

On the other hand, the diversity of end-uses, especially emerging end-uses that arise because of improvements in technology or by the ability to combine data in new ways, may create situations where the use of private information may be unexpected and some consumers could perceive or actually experience it as detrimental, while others may not. For example, some consumers may be surprised when they receive a "retargeting" email suggesting that they purchase a product left abandoned in an online shopping cart (not realizing that this information was being tracked and associated with them). Some consumers could also be potentially adversely affected if their browsing history or past purchase history was used to determine that they would be willing to pay more for a product, and thus were offered or paid a higher price for a product as a result.[11]

These concerns could become more significant when information – intentionally or inadvertently – is transferred or obtained by third parties which makes it more difficult for consumers to anticipate how the information is used, or to connect the provision of information to an economic benefit (e.g. when purchase history is used to identify and recommend products that consumers may be interested in). In some

---

[9] Boyd, D. M., and N. B. Ellison (2008), "Social Network Sites: Definition, History, and Scholarship," *Journal of Computer-Mediated Communication*, 13, pp. 210–30.

[10] Google's list of "[r]easons you might see an ad" includes, for example, "Your current search query" and "Previous search activity." See "Google Ads Help – Why you're seeing an ad," https://support.google.com/ads/answer/1634057?hl=en.

[11] Odlyzko, A. (2004), "Privacy, Economics, and Price Discrimination on the Internet," *Economics of Information Security*, 12, pp. 187–211; Acquisti, A., and H. R. Varian (2005), "Conditioning Prices on Purchase History," *Marketing Science*, 24(3), pp. 367–81.

cases, such as a data breach incident, information can be misused by third parties in a way that can generate a potential direct financial loss to some consumers through the third party's fraudulent use of the information (e.g. payment card or debit account information), or a potential indirect loss to the consumer through any time and expenses spent by the consumer to monitor for potential identity theft incidences.

A final source of diversity in the nature of information exchange is the differences across the consumers themselves. Consumers vary widely in their propensity to share information as well as the types of transactions they perform and their own individual characteristics, which can influence the value of any particular piece of information.[12] Consumers also vary in their level of awareness of the potential opportunities for use and reuse of information and their preferences over this use and reuse. Furthermore, these preferences and behaviors are not constant. Consumers may share different information in different contexts, and change their information-sharing behaviors over time. For example, some consumers may show an elevated concern for data privacy immediately following an adverse public event such as a publicized data breach. Recent research has also indicated that consumer behavior can be substantially affected by small changes in how information is presented, further underscoring the fact that preferences for privacy can be context-specific.[13]

4.3 CHALLENGES ASSOCIATED WITH ASSESSING AND QUANTIFYING ALLEGED HARM IN INVASION-OF-PRIVACY CASES

There have been a number of recent cases in which consumers allege that businesses have obtained and used private information without consent. For instance, plaintiffs in *Facebook, Inc. Consumer Privacy User Profile Litigation* alleged that Facebook allowed thousands of third-party apps to access user content (such as personally identifying information about statuses, relationships, photos, and videos), and that it sold access to this information to numerous business partners (such as Netflix, Lyft, and Airbnb).[14] According to the plaintiffs, Facebook did not disclose these practices and did not ask for users' consent.

---

[12] See e.g. Palen, L., and P. Dourish (2003), "Unpacking 'Privacy' for a Networked World," *Proceedings of the SIGCHI Conference on Human Factors in Computing Systems*, pp. 129–36; John, L. K., A. Acquisti, and G. Loewenstein (2011), "Strangers on a Plane: Context-Dependent Willingness to Divulge Sensitive Information," *Journal of Consumer Research*, 37 (5), pp. 858–73; Acquisti, A., L. K. John, and G. Loewenstein (2012), "The Impact of Relative Standards on the Propensity to Disclose," *Journal of Marketing Research*, 49(2), pp. 160–74.

[13] John, Acquisti, and Loewenstein, "Strangers on a Plane"; Brandimarte, L., A. Acquisti, and G. Loewenstein (2012), "Misplaced Confidences: Privacy and the Control Paradox," *Social Psychological and Personality Science*, 4(3), pp. 340–47.

[14] Plaintiffs' claims stem from the so-called Cambridge Analytica Scandal. According to the plaintiffs, a third-party app developer gleaned data from 87 million Facebook users and sold

In another example, plaintiffs in *In re: Vizio, Inc., Consumer Privacy Litigation* alleged that Vizio secretly installed software in millions of its Smart TVs to collect highly specific data about consumers' viewing histories and preferences.[15] Vizio allegedly shared the data with third-party advertisers and media content providers, so that they could deliver targeted advertisements and other content in real time.

As a factual matter, whether certain conduct can be considered invasion of privacy depends critically on whether the information was indeed private, and whether the consumer provided consent. Both of these considerations are subject to substantial uncertainty. Moreover, whether there is both a factual basis for an invasion-of-privacy claim as well as the potential injury from any invasion of privacy depends on the conditions that would have prevailed "but for" the invasion of privacy. For instance, a consumer may be unlikely to sustain a claim of injury for the disclosure of their home address or birth date if such information is posted in public forums such as an online directory or a social media site. Indeed, in an environment where substantial amounts of information are routinely made available in online forums, the scope of information that can be legitimately considered private may have narrowed considerably.

With a few exceptions (e.g. health information, certain types of financial information), privacy under the current US law is governed by contractual agreements between a user of a service and the service receiving the information. These agreements are typically disclosed in the form of "privacy policies" and may simply be available for review or may be directly presented to the user in written or online form (often through some type of "clickwrap" agreement policy).[16] The uncertainty in consent arises because the agreements may be structured in general terms such that there is uncertainty as to whether a particular practice is covered or would be expected to be covered by the terms of a privacy agreement. There is also academic research suggesting that consumers may not read or seriously consider privacy policies and other types of information presented in clickwrap contracts.[17]

---

it to Cambridge Analytica, a political intelligence firm, which allegedly used the data for inferring political orientations of the users and sending targeted ads prior to the 2016 presidential elections. See Plaintiffs' Second Amended Consolidated Complaint, *In Re: Facebook, Inc. Consumer Privacy User Profile Litigation*, Case No. 18-md-02843-VC, Aug. 4, 2020, pp. 1–5. Facebook has been the subject of a number of other privacy-related lawsuits. See e.g. *In Re: Facebook Privacy Litigation*, Case No. 10-cv-02389-JW; *Fraley et al. v. Facebook, Inc.*, Case No. 11-cv-01726; *In Re: Facebook Biometric Information Privacy Litigation*, Case No. 15-cv-03747.

[15] See Second Consolidated Complaint, *In re: Vizio, Inc., Consumer Privacy Litigation*, Case No. 8:16-ml-02693-JLS, United Stated District Court for the Central District of California Santa Ana Division, Mar. 23, 2017, pp. 1–5.

[16] See e.g. "Data Policy," *Facebook*, www.facebook.com/about/privacy/update; "Twitter Privacy Policy," *Twitter*, https://twitter.com/en/privacy.

[17] Jensen, C., C. Potts, and C. Jensen (2005), "Privacy Practices of Internet Users: Self-Reports versus Observed Behavior," *International Journal of Human-Computer Studies*, 63, pp. 203–27.

There are generally two theories of harm that have been pursued in recent privacy cases. The first theory of harm predicates that an intrinsic value of privacy is lost upon the disclosure of private information. This value is typically viewed as independent of the actual type and amount of private information accessed and of the use (if any) that the intruder makes of this information.[18] For example, in *Brown v. Google LLC and Alphabet Inc.*, plaintiffs claimed damages partly because Google's tracking of web browsing activity without users' consent "intruded upon the Plaintiffs' solitude or seclusion" in a manner that was "highly offensive to a reasonable person."[19]

The second theory of harm considers private data akin to assets or intellectual property that has an economic value, either because such data can be traded in certain markets (either legal or illegal), or because the entities that gleaned such data use it for financial gain. Different types of information may have different economic value, and unauthorized appropriation of private information by third parties may cause economic loss to the rightful owners.[20]

Regardless of the alleged harm, analyzing potential economic harm from asserted privacy violations should account for the cost–benefit trade-off when individuals' information is accessed, disclosed, or discovered. There are many situations in which a person receives a benefit from revealing otherwise private information. For instance, researchers have examined the implications of retailers' access to shoppers' past purchase history in setting product prices and determining product recommendations.[21] Although these practices may impose a cost on some consumers (i.e. enabling price discrimination), they also provide benefits such as customized products or helping consumers pick products that better suit their needs. Other contexts involve similar trade-offs.[22] Some researchers have accordingly suggested that privacy concerns arise not as an abstract loss of value, but because consumers do not feel they are receiving a proper cost–benefit trade-off for providing their private information.[23] This view suggests that any assessment of damages from

---

[18] See e.g. Complaint and Demand for Jury Trial, *Brown et al. v. Google LLC and Alphabet Inc.*, Case No. 5:20-cv-3664-SVK, United States District Court Northern District of California, June 2, 2020, ¶¶ 145–54.

[19] See e.g. ibid.

[20] See e.g. Plaintiffs' Second Amended Consolidated Complaint, *In Re: Facebook, Inc. Consumer Privacy User Profile Litigation*, Case No. 18-md-02843-VC, Aug. 4, 2020, pp. 248–52.

[21] See e.g. Odlyzko, "Privacy, Economics, and Price Discrimination"; Acquisti and Varian, "Conditioning Prices on Purchase History."

[22] For example, in the context of e-commerce and online advertising, consumers may perceive advertisers' access to information about their online behavior (such as search entries) as a cost. However, targeted advertising might benefit consumers in identifying products they are interested in, and in avoiding unwanted marketing communications or spam. See Lenard, T. M., and P. H. Rubin (2010), "In Defense of Data: Information and the Costs of Privacy," *Policy & Internet*, 2(1), pp. 149–83.

[23] See e.g. Samuelson, P. (1999), "Privacy as Intellectual Property," *Stanford Law Review*, 52, pp. 1125–73, at p. 1134 and footnote 48.

loss of privacy requires an assessment of both the costs and benefits of accessing allegedly private information to the consumer, which is inherently an individualized inquiry.

Several empirical approaches have been proposed in order to assess and quantify the damages allegedly caused by unauthorized access and misuse of private information. We will discuss each of these in detail.

4.3.1 Damages Based on Alleged Loss of the "Intrinsic" Value of Privacy

A theory of damages for loss of the "intrinsic" value of privacy postulates that individuals ascribe a certain economic value to the integrity of private information, and that such value is automatically lost when third parties access private information without prior consent.[24]

The intrinsic-value-of-privacy theory has its origins in theories related to the societal value of privacy and some of the early privacy-related disputes surrounding the public release of unauthorized recordings or photographs.[25] This approach is attractive from the perspective of a plaintiff in a consumer class action setting because it sidesteps the need to characterize the nature of the information disclosure (only requiring that the disclosure be "unconscionable"), and because the positioning of privacy interest as a general interest to society allows for abstracting it away from the preferences of individual consumers.[26]

However, the use of common, intrinsic value of privacy as a basis for damages appears generally inappropriate when applied to mass-market business-to-consumer interactions for at least two reasons. First, where this theory has been applied, the injury is considered to apply to the society as a whole, and is not particular to a customer or transaction. Indeed, taken literally, this theory would imply that consumers who did not use the service at issue or those who have not engaged in the type of transaction at issue would have incurred the alleged harm from invasion of privacy in the same manner as the consumers who used the service or transaction at issue and whose privacy was allegedly invaded.

Second, on a more practical level, the concept that there exists a common, uniform injury associated with invasion of privacy is at odds with how privacy and invasion of privacy have been typically discussed and analyzed in economics. As noted earlier, a consistent finding of much of the academic, practitioner, and policy literature on privacy is that the perception of privacy varies considerably across

---

[24] See e.g. Complaint and Demand for Jury Trial, *Brown et al. v. Google LLC and Alphabet Inc.*, Case No. 5:20-cv-3664-SVK, United States District Court Northern District of California, June 2, 2020.

[25] "Several theorists view privacy's value as originating from the very condition of privacy itself. Privacy, in other words, is understood as having an intrinsic value." See Solove, D. J. (2008), *Understanding Privacy*, Harvard University Press, p. 84.

[26] "When something has intrinsic value, we value it for itself." See ibid., p. 84.

individuals and across contexts.[27] Different individuals may have different expectations regarding whether their information is public or private, different levels of concern for the privacy of their information, and even the same individual may display different privacy preferences for the same information in different contexts.[28] As a result, there is no reason to believe that there is a unique, "intrinsic" value that is lost with lack of prior consent, and that any injury associated with lack of prior consent would be uniform across individuals. Consumers' privacy preferences are likely to depend on individual-specific factors such as the type and amount of information potentially exposed to third parties and individuals' subjective expectations about the ways in which any third parties will likely use this data.

For example, in the context of private contacts data stored on mobile devices, some contacts will be private, personal connections that people have entered into their mobile devices individually, while others will be information relating to other types of relationships (e.g. retailers, information services) that may have been placed into their mobile contacts database by automated tools.[29] These "contacts" therefore represent a variety of interactions that users may have had online or offline, some of which users may consider to be more or less private than others.[30] Hence, different individuals may attach different values to prior consent (and for different types of information), and for some individuals, prior consent may not be important at all.

Given that this theory implies a common loss across all consumers, it may be appealing to proponents of theories of loss of the "intrinsic" value of privacy to

---

[27] See e.g. Smith, H. J., S. J. Milberg, and S. J. Burke (1996), "Information Privacy: Measuring Individuals' Concerns about Organizational Practices," *MIS Quarterly*, 20(2), pp. 167–96; Acquisti, A., L. Brandimarte, and G. Loewenstein (2015), "Privacy and Human Behavior in the Age of Information," *Science*, 347(6221), pp. 509–14; Martin, K., and K. Shilton (2016), "Why Experience Matters to Privacy: How Context-Based Experience Moderates Consumer Privacy Expectations for Mobile Applications," *Journal of the Association for Information Science and Technology*, 67(8), pp. 1871–82; Nissenbaum, H. (2004), "Privacy as Contextual Integrity," *Washington Law Review*, 79, pp. 101–39; Acquisti, A., L. K. John, and G. Loewenstein (2013), "What Is Privacy Worth?" *Journal of Legal Studies*, 42(2), pp. 249–74.

[28] See e.g. Palen and Dourish, "Unpacking 'Privacy' for a Networked World," pp. 129–36; John, Acquisti, and Loewenstein, "Strangers on a Plane"; Acquisti, John, and Loewenstein, "The Impact of Relative Standards on the Propensity to Disclose," pp. 160–74.

[29] For instance, Gmail users who "sync" their iPhone with their Gmail account will automatically import contacts data from anyone who has sent the user an email. See "Contacts Help – See Google Contacts on your mobile device or computer," https://support.google.com/mail/answer/118271?hl=en. According to a study involving smartphones using the Android operating system, 84 percent of the 200 participants in the study connected their Google/Gmail accounts to contacts on their phones, 70 percent connected their Facebook accounts, while 17 percent connected their Yahoo! accounts. Only 11 percent of the participants in the study did not sync their phones with any of these services. See Bentley, F., and Y. Chen (2015), "The Composition and Use of Modern Mobile Phonebooks," *Proceedings of the 33rd Annual ACM Conference on Human Factors in Computing Systems*, pp. 2749–58, at p. 2752.

[30] According to Bentley and Chen ("The Composition and Use of Modern Mobile Phonebooks"), participants in a study of users' contact information could not recognize over 29 percent of their twenty-five randomly selected contacts. See ibid., p. 2752.

employ expressed preference methods such as surveys to determine an average loss across a representative consumer population such as contingent valuation or conjoint analysis.

There are several inherent problems with applying survey-based methodologies in the privacy context. First, methods such as contingent valuation (where consumers are essentially asked to place a specific value on a privacy-related feature) can produce inflated values, and have encountered significant criticism in the scientific community.[31] Conjoint studies are less subject to the criticisms leveled specifically for contingent valuation, but have related problems that privacy may not be a product "feature" that is typically considered by consumers and thus can generate a similarly inflated value by "focalism bias."[32]

Second, all expressed preference methods, where consumers state preferences directly or imply preferences based on their survey responses (such as in a choice-based conjoint survey setting), can yield unreliable results due to the "privacy paradox." According to this well-established phenomenon, consumers will often express a significant interest in privacy when asked in the abstract but will behave as if their value is much lower in real market settings.[33]

Finally, surveys attempting to measure the value of privacy can at best measure the value of privacy for the survey respondents only, which is then aggregated to create some type of average value of privacy that is extrapolated to the class as a

---

[31] See e.g. Hausman, J. (2012), "Contingent Valuation: From Dubious to Hopeless," *Journal of Economic Perspectives*, 26(4), pp. 43–56. In particular, contingent valuation is subject to three main problems: hypothetical bias; discrepancy between willingness to pay (WTP) and willingness to accept (WTA); and embedding effect. See Hausman, "Contingent Valuation," p. 43. Hypothetical bias arises when respondents answer hypothetical questions with which they have little or no real market experience. Respondents' stated behaviors and preferences therefore tend to differ from observed real market choices, and survey results regarding WTP tend to be inflated. See Hausman, "Contingent Valuation," pp. 44–46. The discrepancy between WTP and WTA – i.e. the difference between the value that a given respondent would be willing to pay to avoid a negative outcome versus the value they would be willing to receive to accept a negative outcome – that is typically observed in contingent valuation studies reflects the fact that contingent valuation studies often elicit inaccurate and inconsistent valuations from respondents. See Hausman, "Contingent Valuation," pp. 46–47. Finally, the embedding effect is the tendency of contingent valuation studies to obtain preferences that change conditional on whether a good is considered alone or as a part of a group of goods. The presence of this bias further reflects the inability of contingent valuation studies to reliably infer respondents' valuations. See Hausman, "Contingent Valuation," pp. 47–49.

[32] Kahneman, D., and D. Schkade (1998), "Does Living in California Make People Happy? A Focusing Illusion in Judgments of Life Satisfaction," *Psychological Science*, 9(5), pp. 340–46; Kahneman, D., A. B. Krueger, D. Schkade, N. Schwarz, and A. A. Stone (2006), "Would You Be Happier if You Were Richer? A Focusing Illusion," *Science*, 312(5782), pp. 1908–10.

[33] Spiekermann, Grossklags, and Berendt, "E-Privacy in 2nd Generation E-Commerce"; Norberg, Horne, and Horne, "The Privacy Paradox"; Adjerid, Peer, and Acquisti, "Beyond the Privacy Paradox"; Acquisti, Brandimarte, and Loewenstein, "Privacy and Human Behavior in the Age of Information," p. 510; Kokolakis, S. (2017), "Privacy Attitudes and Privacy Behaviour: A Review of Current Research on the Privacy Paradox Phenomenon," *Computers & Security*, 64, pp. 122–34.

whole. But even if one assumes that this average value is measured correctly, it still relies on the assumption that all consumers have the same value, which is inconsistent with all of the sources of potential heterogeneity identified by academic researchers. In addition, such an assumption can be contradicted by the survey itself due to the variation in the values used to create the average. Sometimes the variation in valuation is so large that it can render the average meaningless.

Overall, the inability of expressed-preference methods to reliably measure the value of privacy is reflected in the large variation observed across academic studies that have attempted to use these types of methods to estimate the value of privacy. For example, Hann et al. estimated willingness to pay for protecting website users from secondary use of their personal information to be between $39.83 and $49.78, on average, while a later study by the same authors estimated this value to be between $7.98 and $11.68, on average.[34]

4.3.2 Damages Based on the Alleged Value of Private Information

Theories of damages concerning the loss of value of private information are based on the claim that private information is personal property, which may have a certain economic value, and consumers are harmed when this information is accessed without consent and/or compensation. For example, plaintiffs in *Facebook, Inc. Consumer Privacy User Profile Litigation* claimed that "users' content and information is property," and that "users were harmed when Facebook took their property."[35] Furthermore, they alleged that "there is economic value to users' data"[36] that was allegedly accessed without consent.

Several empirical approaches have been proposed for measuring the economic value of such data, which will be discussed in detail.

4.3.2.1 Measuring the Market Value of Personal Data

The first proposed damages method aims at measuring the value of personal data by looking at "transaction" prices. However, it is difficult, if not impossible, to pinpoint a unique market value for private data. Unlike an asset such as a home or a car – for which there is an established marketplace in which one can obtain a price from observed transactions – there is no marketplace for personal data. While some data

---

[34] Hann, I., K. Hui, T. S. Lee, and I. P. L. Png (2002), "Online Information Privacy: Measuring the Cost–Benefit Trade-Off," *Twenty-Third International Conference on Information Systems*, pp. 1–10; Hann, I., K. Hui, T. S. Lee, and I. P. L. Png (2007), "Overcoming Online Information Privacy Concerns: An Information-Processing Theory Approach," *Journal of Management Information Systems*, 24(2), pp. 13–42.

[35] Plaintiffs' Second Amended Consolidated Complaint, *In Re: Facebook, Inc. Consumer Privacy User Profile Litigation*, Case No. 18-md-02843-VC, Aug. 4, 2020, pp. 248–50.

[36] Ibid., p. 249.

brokers such as SavvyConnect compensate individuals in exchange for collecting their personal information such as the individual's browsing history on a mobile device,[37] the prices observed in these settings are likely to be context-dependent and difficult to generalize to other settings. For example, the personal data exchanged in this setting may involve complete browsing history collected over extended periods of time or over multiple devices – thus, the compensations observed in these exchanges cannot reliably approximate the value of browsing history data relating to a specific timeframe, specific sites, or a specific device.[38] Furthermore, the compensations offered by data brokers may cover not just personal data but also tasks undertaken by the individual, such as participation in market research surveys on some regular basis.[39] Finally, some of these data brokers may maintain curated panels that focus on particular types of individuals, and thus compensation provided to this specific group of individuals may not be representative of a general population of, say, credit card users.[40]

While there may be well-established commercial markets for some consumer information, the prices and terms of trade in these markets are divorced from the terms that would apply to consumers. For instance, "list vendors" aggregate and sell private data (such as data on individuals who might have certain health conditions) to third-party users.[41] However, the prices paid are from the list vendor to a commercial user, and do not involve the consumers whose information is being transacted. In addition, the transacted data is typically sold in bulk, including the information of thousands of individuals, and may be further combined with other types of personal data or processed in various ways to facilitate specific applications, such as importing the data into contact management software for sales prospecting.[42] For some of these applications, such as conducting a mass mailing or training

---

[37] In its terms and conditions, SavvyConnect states that "[b]y agreeing to participate in a market research project, you are agreeing to download a software application ('SavvyConnect' or the 'Software') onto your laptop, desktop portable computer, or mobile device to allow information regarding your internet activity to be monitored, collected, stored, aggregated and distributed by Luth Research to its market research clients and any of their third party service providers as part of a market research project." See "Terms and Conditions," Survey Savvy, www.surveysavvy.com/savvyconnect_terms.

[38] For example, SavvyConnect describes itself as a software that "uses safe, cutting-edge technology to collect data as you surf the web" and encourages its users to "[d]ownload SavvyConnect on your smartphone, tablet and/or PC." SavvyConnect, www.surveysavvy.com/savvyconnect.

[39] "[i]f you pass the in-depth screening portion of the survey and complete the body of the survey, [SurveySavvy] will credit your account the amount mentioned in the invitation." Survey Savvy, "How It Works," www.surveysavvy.com/how_it_works.

[40] For example, SavvyConnect has a minimum activity threshold that requires users to have at least seven days of browsing history each month. See "SavvyConnect VIP Participation Requirements," *Survey Savvy*, www.surveysavvy.com/savvyconnect/vip-requirements.

[41] See e.g. "Ready-Made Lists," *Exact Data*, www.exactdata.com/ready-made-lists.html.

[42] See e.g. "Exact Data makes it easy to create targeted consumer and business email lists to help you acquire and retain your ideal customers," *Exact Data*, "Email Marketing Solutions," www.exactdata.com/email-marketing.html.

predictive models to identify potential customers or purchase patterns, the information may only have value because it involves a large number of consumers rather than a specific consumer. As such, these list prices cannot be meaningfully deconstructed to estimate a price for the data of a given individual.

In recent matters, plaintiffs have argued that transactions on the "Dark Web," where malicious actors are able to exchange and monetize compromised personal data, can provide an indicator of the market value of personal data.[43] For example, plaintiffs in *Facebook, Inc. Consumer Privacy User Profile Litigation* alleged that login information to Facebook accounts can be sold for approximately $5.20 each on the Dark Web.[44] There are several issues related to using Dark Web transactions data to assess the value of personal data. First and foremost, the Dark Web does not constitute a legal market or a marketplace that individual consumers would use to monetize their data. According to basic economic principles, market prices reflect arm's length transactions between willing buyers and sellers.[45] However, the Dark Web is not a "market" in which individual consumers would willingly sell access to their private information and receive a payment for it. Dark Web participants engage in such transactions to obtain private information to commit fraud – for example, the price of date-of-birth information on the Dark Web reflects the value of this type of data in relation to illicit activities such as identity theft, which may be very different from the value expressed in legitimate transactions, such as when advertisers legitimately buy data in order to perform targeted advertising. In addition, Dark Web prices are not even transaction prices, but rather list prices at which the data is offered to potential buyers.[46] Furthermore, the data exchanged in these so-called markets is unlikely to be comparable to the data that was infringed.[47]

---

[43] Declaration of Ian Ratner, CA, CBV, CPA/ABV, ASA, CFE, *In Re: Yahoo! Inc. Customer Data Security Breach Litigation*, Case No. 16-md-02752-LHK (N.D. Cal. July 14, 2018), ¶¶ 11–21, 24–28; Plaintiffs' Second Amended Consolidated Complaint, *In Re: Facebook, Inc. Consumer Privacy User Profile Litigation*, Case No. 18-md-02843-VC, Aug. 4, 2020.

[44] Plaintiffs' Second Amended Consolidated Complaint, *In Re: Facebook, Inc. Consumer Privacy User Profile Litigation*, Case No. 18-md-02843-VC, Aug. 4, 2020, p. 249.

[45] The "Fair Market Value" is the "[p]rice at which property will change hands between a willing buyer and seller when all relevant factors are considered and the seller is not compelled to sell nor the buyer compelled to buy." See Oldham, G. E. (1993), *Dictionary of Business and Finance Terms*, Barnes & Noble, p. 82, https://archive.org/details/dictionaryofbusiooooooldh/page/82/mode/2up?q=%22fair+market+value%22.

[46] Such list prices can also vary considerably depending on the type of information packaged and its comprehensiveness. For example, the observed list prices for sets of personally identifiable information (PII) – such as an individual's social security number, date of birth, and full name – ranges from $1 to $75 on the Dark Web. See Rowley, O. (2017), "Analysis: Pricing of Goods and Services on the Deep and Dark Web," *Flashpoint*.

[47] In *Yahoo! Inc. Customer Data Security Breach Litigation*, plaintiffs considered using the Dark Web prices for email login information and social media login information to determine the value of the breached personal data of Yahoo! account holders. According to the plaintiff, the Dark Web price of login details for a Yahoo or Gmail account was around $1. See Declaration of Ian Ratner, CA, CBV, CPA/ABV, ASA, CFE, *In Re: Yahoo! Inc. Customer Data Security*

4.3.2.2 Measuring the Price Premium for Data Privacy Protection

An alternative damages methodology tries to assess the economic value of privacy by measuring the price premium for privacy protection that is allegedly embodied in the purchase price of the privacy-infringing product or service. For example, in *Vizio, Inc. Consumer Privacy Litigation*, purchasers of Vizio smart TVs alleged that these devices unknowingly collected detailed data about users' viewing histories and shared these with third parties. According to the plaintiffs, had they known the truth about Vizio's data collection and dissemination practices, they would not have purchased Vizio smart TVs, or would have paid a lower price for them.[48] In these types of cases, plaintiffs have proposed using conjoint analysis (an expressed preference method) to measure the alleged price premium attributable to privacy protection.

Conjoint analysis typically involves a survey where consumers are presented with a series of products with different attribute levels (e.g. product characteristics such as, say, the screen size, resolution, and speed of a laptop computer, as well as price), and are asked to make selections among them. The premise of this method is that, by observing how consumers choose in this setting, statistical methods can be used to make inferences about the average willingness to pay for different attributes included in the analysis, such as protection of personal data from third-party access.[49] Conjoint methods are widely used and demonstrated to be useful for research in product design and development.[50] However, there are substantial limitations of the conjoint method when applied to the privacy context, especially

---

Breach Litigation, Case No. 16-md-02752-LHK (N.D. Cal. July 14, 2018), ¶¶ 21, 24–28, and Table 2.

[48] Second Consolidated Complaint, *In re: Vizio, Inc., Consumer Privacy Litigation*, Case No. 8:16-ml-02693-JLS, United Stated District Court for the Central District of California Santa Ana Division, Mar. 23, 2017, ¶¶ 160, 190, 204, 226, 249, 253.; See also Second Amended Consolidated Class Action Complaint, *In re: Brinker Data Incident Litigation*, Case No 18-cv-00686-TJC-MCR, United States District Court for the Middle District of Florida Jacksonville Division, ¶ 9; Third Amended Class Action Complaint, *Antman et al. v. Uber Technologies, Inc.*, Case No. 3:15-01175-LB, United States District Court for the Northern Division of California San Francisco Division, ¶ 64; Plaintiff's Third Amended Consolidated Class Action Complaint, *In re: Zappos.com, Inc. Customer Data Security Breach Litigation*, Case No. 3:12-cv-00325-RCJ-VPC, United States District Court for the District of Nevada, ¶ 7; Plaintiff's Amended Consolidated Class Action Complaint, *In re: Sonic Corp. Customer Data Breach Litigation*, Case No. 1:17-md-02807-JSG, United States District Court for the Northern District of Ohio Eastern Division at Cleveland, ¶¶ 64, 66–69.

[49] See e.g. Green, P. E., and V. Rao (1971), "Conjoint Measurement for Quantifying Judgmental Data," *Journal of Marketing Research*, 8(3), pp. 355–63; Green, P. E., and V. Srinivasan (1990), "Conjoint Analysis in Marketing: New Developments with Implications for Research and Practice," *Journal of Marketing*, (54)4, pp. 3–19.

[50] See e.g. Cattin, P. and D. Wittink (1982), "Commercial Use of Conjoint Analysis: A Survey," *Journal of Marketing*, 46(3), pp. 44–53; Green and Srinivasan, "Conjoint Analysis in Marketing."

attempts to use conjoint methods to determine an alleged "price premium" attributable to privacy protection.

First, academic studies show that the conjoint method cannot reliably estimate privacy valuations.[51] As discussed earlier, one of the main problems related to expressed preference methods such as conjoint surveys involves response biases due to the so-called privacy paradox. These response biases generate inflated values of privacy relative to the value suggested by individuals' actual behavior in real-world settings.[52] Furthermore, academic literature shows that consumers' stated privacy valuations are strongly influenced by environmental cues, such as question framing.[53] As a result, there is no reason to believe a conjoint survey would reliably capture how privacy concerns could have affected choices in a real-world setting. For example, a literal interpretation of a conjoint design could be that a consumer would be willing to pay different amounts for a fast-food item depending on the degree of privacy protection offered for their credit card information. It is unlikely that this type of decision would occur to a consumer in a normal fast-food transaction, but it could induce a behavioral change when such a trade-off is presented in a survey setting.

Second, in cases where the product at issue is free (e.g., mobile applications such as Facebook which consumers can use without payment), conjoint analysis cannot be used to estimate a monetary value for privacy. In a typical conjoint survey, a key variable that is manipulated is the price associated with a product based on the bundle of attributes it contains.[54] When the actual price is zero, any product options that have nonzero prices in the conjoint survey would immediately be nonrepresentative of the actual market. Furthermore, research has shown that consumers often behave differently when a product is free (i.e. price is zero) versus when it has a nonzero price.[55] For instance, one study showed that a price reduction from $15 to $1 caused substantially less of a demand increase than a price reduction from $14 to

---

[51] See e.g. Acquisti, Brandimarte, and Loewenstein, "Privacy and Human Behavior in the Age of Information," p. 510: "explicit investigations of privacy valuation spotlight privacy as an issue that respondents should take account of and, as a result, increase the weight they place on privacy in their responses." See also Acquisti, John, and Loewenstein, "What Is Privacy Worth?"

[52] Spiekermann, Grosslags, and Berendt, "E-Privacy in 2nd Generation E-Commerce," pp. 38–47; Norberg, Horne, and Horne, "The Privacy Paradox"; Adjerid, Peer, and Acquisti, "Beyond the Privacy Paradox"; Acquisti, Brandimarte, and Loewenstein, "Privacy and Human Behavior in the Age of Information," p. 510.

[53] Acquisti, Brandimarte, and Loewenstein, "Privacy and Human Behavior in the Age of Information," p. 511.

[54] Conjoint analysis involves statistical techniques developed to evaluate consumers' product choices and determine the trade-offs they make among the attributes of a product or service. Green and Srinivasan, "Conjoint Analysis in Marketing."

[55] Shampanier, K., N. Mazar, and D. Ariely (2007), "Zero as a Special Price: The True Value of Free Products," *Marketing Science*, 26(6), pp. 742–57; "Free! Why $0.00 is the Future of Business," WIRED, Feb. 25, 2008, www.wired.com/2008/02/ff-free.

$0, even though the change in prices is the same.[56] As a result, reliable economic inferences about consumers' willingness to pay for the attributes of a free product, in particular attributes on the privacy of data, cannot be made using conjoint analysis.

Third, a conjoint analysis, by itself, is not capable of determining the effect on the market price of a product due to changes in the product's attributes. It is well established in the literature that willingness-to-pay measures derived from conjoint analysis are not market prices, since they only look at consumer preferences for product attributes and do not account for any supply factors, such as competitors' actions, costs of production, and manufacturers' willingness to sell.[57] For instance, a certain service may be altered (or not offered at all) if consumers do not agree to certain types of data collection or use, companies could switch from free to paid for certain types of information services (e.g. not offering an ad-supported free app and instead requiring payment), and other product attributes may be changed (e.g. additional features or offering guarantees for remediation of privacy-related problems).[58] Competitors may respond by altering their privacy policies, prices, or other product attributes. Indeed, in the privacy context it may be especially likely that supply responses are focused on non-price changes, which would make it unusually challenging to provide a rigorous but credible model of supply behavior. In other words, assessing the price of a product in a but-for world with disclosure about lack of privacy protection requires analyzing both demand and supply in the but-for world, as but-for price is jointly determined by demand and supply. Conjoint analysis can only assess one part of the price-setting equation (i.e. it can measure demand), hence it cannot measure the price premium allegedly paid for data privacy protection.

4.3.2.3 Measuring Unjust Enrichment Due to Privacy Violation

This damages approach attempts to compensate for unauthorized use of private information through restitution of the profits or revenues that the infringing third party allegedly unjustly obtained from this information. For example, plaintiffs in *Facebook, Inc. Consumer Privacy User Profile Litigation* claimed unjust enrichment

---

[56] Ibid.
[57] "Conjoint Analysis ... is designed to measure and simulate demand in situations where products can be assumed to be comprised of bundles of features. ... WTP measures only a shift in the demand curve and not what the change in equilibrium price will be as the feature is added or enhanced." See Allenby, G., J. Brazell, J. Howell, and P. Rossi (2013), "Using Conjoint Analysis to Determine the Market Value of Product Features," *Proceedings of the Sawtooth Software Conference*, Oct. 2013, pp. 341–55, at p. 342.
[58] For example, it has become commonplace for companies to offer free credit monitoring as a service following a data breach. Indeed, such services are already available for free in many cases. See e.g. "Monitor Your Credit. For Free. For Everyone," CreditWise, https://creditwise.capitalone.com/home.

damages due to alleged commercial benefits Facebook received from its alleged unauthorized gathering and sharing of plaintiffs' data.[59]

Reliable estimates of privacy value based on an unjust enrichment theory requires the ability to distinguish and isolate the portion of a firm's revenues or profits that is directly attributable to the alleged misuse of private data. This is typically difficult to do, as numerous concomitant factors may influence a firm's revenues and profits. For example, plaintiffs in *Facebook, Inc. Consumer Privacy User Profile Litigation* claimed a restitution of "the money [Facebook] has collected from advertisers and others that corresponds to the user data that is the subject of this lawsuit."[60] However, advertisement revenues are influenced by a multitude of factors, such as the size and prospective growth of the user base of a social network, its level of user engagement, and the availability of competing online and offline advertising alternatives which would be capable of hosting the same advertisements. Identifying the portion of the advertisement revenues that is solely due to the alleged misuse of users' data would therefore be highly difficult and perhaps impossible to do. Further, the fact that a business may benefit from the use of private information does not preclude benefits to consumers. The use of private information to expand the size of a commercial social network, for instance, can benefit consumers as well.[61] Any method used to calculate privacy value based on unjust enrichment claims may therefore need to offset the benefits individuals accrued from the disputed use of their data.

4.3.2.4 Challenges Associated with Assessing and Quantifying Potential Harm in Data Breach Cases

In the past decade, data breaches have become increasingly common, with consumers receiving multiple data breach notifications within a given timeframe.[62] Industry research indicates that in the United States alone, over 11,000 breach incidents have been reported between January 2005 and May 2020, involving over 1.6 billion compromised records.[63] A 2016 study showed that roughly

---

[59] Plaintiffs' Second Amended Consolidated Complaint, *In Re: Facebook, Inc. Consumer Privacy User Profile Litigation*, Case No. 18-md-02843-VC, Aug. 4, 2020, pp. 348–49.

[60] Ibid., ¶ 988.

[61] Findings in academic research have shown that users' contributions to social media services are greater when there is a larger audience to consume the content. Zhang, X. (M.), and F. Zhu (2011), "Group Size and Incentives to Contribute: A Natural Experiment at Chinese Wikipedia," *American Economic Review*, 101(4), pp. 1601–15.

[62] See Ablon, L. et al. (2016), "Consumer Attitudes toward Data Breach Notifications and Loss of Personal Information," *RAND Corporation*, at pp. x–xi, 1; See also "Cyber Incident & Breach Trends Report," *The Internet Society*, Jan. 25, 2018, at p. 4. Companies are not always required to notify the public of a breach, and some state laws even provide exemptions in the case of small breaches. See Ablon et al., "Consumer Attitudes toward Data Breach Notifications," p. 6.

[63] "Data Breaches," *Identity Theft Resource Center*, www.idtheftcenter.org/data-breaches/?utm_source=ITRC&utm_medium=Home.

36 million US adults received more than one notification of data breach in the year 2014–15 alone.[64]

Malicious parties can target multiple companies in the same industry. Food and accommodation establishments, for example, have been among the most commonly breached institutions, with the following quick-service restaurant establishments experiencing data breaches within the last five years: Wendy's (2016), Arby's (2017), Chipotle (2017), Panera Bread (2018), Chili's (2018), Landry's (2019), and McDonald's (2021).[65] In addition, certain PII such as payment card information are commonly breached. According to a 2016 study, among the individuals who had received data breach notifications, 49 percent indicated that their credit card information was compromised in the most recent breach instance.[66] The ubiquity of data breach incidents alone makes it difficult to establish that a specific set of consumers were economically harmed due to a specific data breach incident. Thus, establishing causality – a necessary condition for damages – in data breach matters is challenging.

The main alleged injury from breached PII is the experience or threat of identity theft. However, historical evidence and academic literature suggest that only a small number of consumers will experience any type of identity theft. And determining who experienced or will likely experience identity theft in the future, and the extent of their injury, is difficult. In the following, we describe the different types of economic injury claims, and challenges in quantifying each claim.

4.3.3 Time Spent/Loss of Productivity to Address the Breach

One type of damages claimed in data breach matters is based on the direct and opportunity costs of time and effort consumers spend dealing with the actual and potential consequences of the data breach. These can include time and effort spent to identify fraudulent charges, to cancel existing payment cards and make requests for new ones to be issued, to close accounts that were fraudulently opened in their

---

[64] See Ablon et al., "Consumer Attitudes toward Data Breach Notifications," pp. xi, 6. These figures do not include breaches or compromised records that have gone unreported, "[s]ince most incidents are not reported to executives, law enforcement, regulators or the public."

[65] "2012 Data Breach Investigations Report," *Verizon*, at p. 10; "2016 Data Breach Stats," *Identity Theft Resource Center*, Jan. 2017; "Hackers Stole Credit Card Information From Thousands of Arby's Customers," *Fortune.com*, Feb. 9, 2017; "Most Chipotle Restaurants Hacked with Credit Card Stealing Malware," *CNN*, May 28, 2017; "Panera Bread's Website Exposed Customer Data, Security Expert Says," *NBCNews.com*, Apr. 3, 2018; "Chili's Restaurants Were Hit by a Data Breach That Exposed Customers' Credit-Card Information," *Business Insider*, May 14, 2018; "Credit Card Breach Affects 60 National Restaurant Chains – Here's What You Need to Know," *NBC TODAY*, Jan. 8, 2020; "McDonald's Hit by Data Breach," *CNN*, June 11, 2021.

[66] Ablon et al., "Consumer Attitudes toward Data Breach Notifications," p. 19.

name, to freeze credit, and to purchase credit monitoring and identity theft protection services (or sign up for free services offered by the breached institution), among others.[67]

Quantifying such damages on a class-wide basis involves several challenges. First, academic and industry studies suggest significant variation in whether consumers undertake any efforts after a data breach, and the types of effort they undertake. For example, according to a 2016 survey by the RAND Corporation, while 24 percent of participants closed or switched their bank account upon notification of a breach, 22 percent took no action at all.[68] Similarly, a 2014 study by the Ponemon Institute found that the most frequent response to a data breach notification from an organization was to ignore it and take no action.[69] Second, significant variation is bound to exist in the extent of effort (e.g. number of hours or days spent) undertaken by the consumers, rendering damages calculations difficult to execute reliably. For those consumers who were reviewing their credit card statements regularly even before the data breach, another complication involves isolating the additional time these individuals spent above and beyond their normal practices.[70] Further, reliably quantifying lost productivity on a class-wide basis is difficult as it is bound to require individualized inquiry regarding labor market opportunities of many individuals that are not similarly situated. Use of averages in such settings is not likely to be reliable.

---

[67] See e.g. Second Amended Consolidated Class Action Complaint, *In re Barnes & Noble Pin Pad Litigation*, Case No. 1:12-cv-08617, United States District Court for the Northern District of Illinois, ¶¶ 95, 111, 125; Second Amended Consolidated Class Action Complaint, *In re: Brinker Data Incident Litigation*, Case No. 18-cv-00686-TJC-MCR, United States District Court for the Middle District of Florida Jacksonville Division, ¶¶ 9, 51–56; Consolidated Class Action Complaint, *In re: The Home Depot, Inc. Customer Data Breach Litigation*, Case No. 14-02583-TWT, United States District Court for the Northern District of Georgia Atlanta Division, ¶¶ 187, 214, 221; Third Amended Class Action Complaint, *Antman et al. v. Uber Technologies, Inc.*, Case No. 3:15-01175-LB, United States District Court for the Northern Division of California San Francisco Division ¶¶ 63–64, 78, 126; Plaintiffs' Third Amended Consolidated Class Action Complaint, *In re: Zappos.com, Inc. Customer Data Security Breach Litigation*, Case No. 3:12-cv-00325-RCJ-VPC, United States District Court for the District of Nevada, ¶ 7; Consolidated Class Action Complaint, *Echavarria et al. v. Facebook, Inc.*, Case No. 18-cv-05982-WHA, United States District Court for the Northern District of California, ¶¶ 14–15, 201, 211; Plaintiffs' Amended Consolidated Class Action Complaint, *In re: Sonic Corp. Customer Data Breach Litigation*, Case No. 1:17-md-02807-JSG, United States District Court for the Northern District of Ohio Eastern Division at Cleveland, ¶¶ 64–81, 215.
[68] Ablon et al., "Consumer Attitudes toward Data Breach Notifications," p. 30.
[69] "The Aftermath of a Data Breach: Consumer Sentiment," *Ponemon Institute* 2014, at p. 5.
[70] According to the US DOJ Bureau of Justice Statistics, 84.4 percent of non-victim consumers (defined as those who did not experience identity theft in the prior twelve months) engaged in actions to reduce the risk of identity theft, and that 75.2 percent of them checked their bank or credit statements. "Victims of Identity Theft, 2014," US Department of Justice, Bureau of Justice Statistics, Revised Nov. 2017, at p. 12.

4.3.4 Monetary Costs of Identity Theft Monitoring and Prevention

Another type of damages claim is based on what consumers already paid or would likely pay for credit and identity theft monitoring and prevention services.[71] These may include a range of services such as "credit freezes" with credit reporting agencies, identity theft insurance, and credit monitoring services.[72] The main challenge with respect to quantifying these types of damages relates to determining which class members incurred or would be likely to incur such costs, as not everyone will sign up for credit monitoring services. As a remedial offering, breached institutions may offer breach victims free credit monitoring services for a specific amount of time (these services are typically offered to cover one or two years post-breach). Any class members who have taken advantage of these types of offerings, and who have not paid for additional credit monitoring services due to the breach, would not need to be compensated for such costs. The rate at which breached

---

[71] See e.g. Second Amended Consolidated Class Action Complaint, *In re Barnes & Noble Pin Pad Litigation*, Case No. 1:12-cv-08617, United States District Court for the Northern District of Illinois, ¶¶ 95, 111, 125; Second Amended Consolidated Class Action Complaint, *In re: Brinker Data Incident Litigation*, Case No. 18-cv-00686-TJC-MCR, United States District Court Middle District of Florida Jacksonville Division, ¶ 9; Consolidated Class Action Complaint, *In re: The Home Depot, Inc. Customer Data Breach Litigation*, Case No. 14-02583-TWT, United States District Court for the Northern District of Georgia Atlanta Division, ¶¶ 187, 214, 221; Third Amended Class Action Complaint, *Antman et al. v. Uber Technologies, Inc.*, Case No. 3:15-01175-LB, United States District Court for the Northern Division of California San Francisco Division, ¶¶ 63, 78, 126; Plaintiffs' Third Amended Consolidated Class Action Complaint, *In re: Zappos.com, Inc. Customer Data Security Breach Litigation*, Case No. 3:12-cv-00325-RCJ-VPC, United States District Court for the District of Nevada, ¶ 7; Consolidated Class Action Complaint, *Echavarria et al. v. Facebook, Inc.*, Case No. 18-cv-05982-WHA, United States District Court for the Northern District of California, ¶¶ 14, 201, 211; Plaintiffs' Amended Consolidated Class Action Complaint, *In re: Sonic Corp. Customer Data Breach Litigation*, Case No. 1:17-md-02807-JSG, United States District Court for the Northern District of Ohio Eastern Division at Cleveland, ¶¶ 64, 79–81, 215.

[72] See e.g. Second Amended Consolidated Class Action Complaint, *In re Barnes & Noble Pin Pad Litigation*, Case No. 1:12-cv-08617, United States District Court for the Northern District of Illinois, ¶ 125; Second Amended Consolidated Class Action Complaint, *In re: Brinker Data Incident Litigation*, Case No. 18-cv-00686-TJC-MCR, United States District Court for the Middle District of Florida Jacksonville Division, ¶ 9; Consolidated Class Action Complaint, *In re: The Home Depot, Inc. Customer Data Breach Litigation*, Case No. 14-02583-TWT, United States District Court for the Northern District of Georgia Atlanta Division, ¶¶ 187, 214, 221; Third Amended Class Action Complaint, *Antman et al. v. Uber Technologies, Inc.*, Case No. 3:15-01175-LB, United States District Court for the Northern Division of California San Francisco Division, ¶ 126; Consolidated Class Action Complaint, *Echavarria et al. v. Facebook, Inc.*, Case No. 18-cv-05982-WHA, United States District Court for the Northern District of California, ¶¶ 14, 201, 211; Plaintiffs' Amended Consolidated Class Action Complaint, *In re: Sonic Corp. Customer Data Breach Litigation*, Case No. 1:17-md-02807-JSG, United States District Court for the Northern District of Ohio Eastern Division at Cleveland, ¶¶ 64, 79–81; *In re: Marriott International Inc. Consumer Data Security Breach Litigation*, Case No. 8:19-md-02879-PWG United States District Court for the Southern Division of the District of Maryland, ¶ 270.

individuals sign up for these types of free credit monitoring services may be informative about the rate at which they might sign up for similar services for a fee. Thus, to the extent that a small percentage of class members enroll in free credit monitoring services (something that has commonly been observed in data breaches to date),[73] it may be difficult to argue that many or most class members would enroll in services which actually cost money. Second, it is possible to have a debate on what service needs to be provided. Services vary from free to quite expensive, based on the package of services, with the more expensive services bundling insurance, remediation services, and other things. Establishing a connection between a particular (paid) credit monitoring service and an event could be particularly challenging given the range of offerings at different prices.

4.3.5 Diminished Value of Breached PII

Damages claims can also be based on diminution in the value of breached individuals' personal and financial information.[74] These types of damages are premised on the idea that the breached information is a form of intangible property that has a specific monetary value. As discussed earlier, the challenge with quantifying this type of damage is the lack of a "market price" for the breached information.[75] There is no market in which an individual can obtain a price for most of their personal data. Most individuals will not monetize their PII at all whether through the Dark Web (a purported marketplace for data per the plaintiffs in a number of class actions) or by joining consumer panels such as SavvyConnect.

---

[73] For example, according to a *New York Times* article, only about 3.3 million individuals (out of 147 million individuals eligible for settlement) signed up for the free credit monitoring services offered by Equifax. See "Equifax Breach Affected 147 Million, but Most Sit Out Settlement," *New York Times*, Jan. 22, 2020, www.nytimes.com/2020/01/22/business/equifax-breach-settlement.html.

[74] See e.g. Second Amended Consolidated Class Action Complaint, *In re Barnes & Noble Pin Pad Litigation*, Case No. 1:12-cv-08617, United States District Court for the Northern District of Illinois, ¶¶ 95, 111; Second Amended Consolidated Class Action Complaint, *In re: Brinker Data Incident Litigation*, Case No. 18-cv-00686-TJC-MCR, United States District Court for the Middle District of Florida Jacksonville Division, ¶ 9; Third Amended Class Action Complaint, *Antman et al. v. Uber Technologies, Inc.*, Case No. 3:15-01175-LB, United States District Court for the Northern Division of California San Francisco Division, ¶¶ 63, 126; Plaintiffs' Third Amended Consolidated Class Action Complaint, *In re: Zappos.com, Inc. Customer Data Security Breach Litigation*, Case No. 3:12-cv-00325-RCJ-VPC, United States District Court for the District of Nevada, ¶ 7; Consolidated Class Action Complaint, *Echavarria et al. v. Facebook, Inc.*, Case No. 18-cv-05982-WHA, United States District Court for the Northern District of California, ¶¶ 14, 201, 211; Plaintiffs' Amended Consolidated Class Action Complaint, *In re: Sonic Corp. Customer Data Breach Litigation*, Case No. 1:17-md-02807-JSG, United States District Court for the Northern District of Ohio Eastern Division at Cleveland, ¶¶ 64, 81, 215.

[75] See discussion in Section 4.3.2.

4.3.6 Risk of Future Economic Injury

Another common damages claim in data breach cases involves alleged damages relating to the risk of future injury. The underlying premise of this damage is that the negative consequences of a data breach may not be imminent, and breached individuals should be compensated for the "long term" impact of the data breach. In other words, the typical argument is as follows: the breached PII (payment card information, social security number, mailing address, etc.) may not be misused immediately after the unauthorized access of the data, but this information will be available in the Dark Web for a long time to come and can be subject to misuse at any point in the future.[76] The challenges one faces in estimating these damages are multidimensional.

First, to properly calculate this type of damage, one needs to be able to isolate the *incremental* risk associated with the data breach for each individual in the future. As of now, it is not possible to identify changes in risk associated with a specific breach versus other data breaches. Given the ubiquity of data breaches, determining the causal relationship between a particular data breach and a particular adverse event (fraudulent charges) is nearly impossible.

Second, different types of PII are susceptible to different types of potential harm and, depending on the PII at issue, one needs to account for this variation in quantifying damages. For example, if PII at issue is limited to information available on a payment card, an identity theft outcome is probably unlikely. In this scenario, potential harm can also be limited or not exist at all, considering that most payment card issuers have policies and cancel fraudulent charges when informed by cardholders.[77] Payment cards are also easily cancelable and replaceable, after which

---

[76] See e.g. Second Amended Consolidated Class Action Complaint, *In re Barnes & Noble Pin Pad Litigation*, Case No. 1:12-cv-08617, United States District Court for the Northern District of Illinois, ¶¶ 95, 111; Second Amended Consolidated Class Action Complaint, *In re: Brinker Data Incident Litigation*, Case No. 18-cv-00686-TJC-MCR, United States District Court for the Middle District of Florida Jacksonville Division, ¶¶ 9, 55; Third Amended Class Action Complaint, *Antman et al. v. Uber Technologies, Inc.*, Case No. 3:15-01175-LB, United States District Court for the Northern Division of California San Francisco Division, ¶¶ 63, 78, 126; Plaintiffs' Third Amended Consolidated Class Action Complaint, *In re: Zappos.com, Inc. Customer Data Security Breach Litigation*, Case No. 3:12-cv-00325-RCJ-VPC, United States District Court for the District of Nevada, ¶ 7; Consolidated Class Action Complaint, *Echavarria et al. v. Facebook, Inc.*, Case No. 18-cv-05982-WHA, United States District Court for the Northern District of California, ¶¶ 14, 201, 211; Plaintiffs' Amended Consolidated Class Action Complaint, *In re: Sonic Corp. Customer Data Breach Litigation*, Case No. 1:17-md-02807-JSG, United States District Court for the Northern District of Ohio Eastern Division at Cleveland, ¶¶ 64, 80–81, 215.

[77] "$0 Liability on Unauthorized Charges," *Citigroup*, www.cardbenefits.citi.com/Products/0-Liability-on-Unauthorized-Charges; "Online Security Guarantee," *Wells Fargo*, www.wellsfargo.com/privacy-security/guarantee/.

there is little to no further risk of fraud.[78] Indeed, stolen payment card data displays rapidly deteriorating prices on the cyber black market over time. According to a 2018 study presented to the US House Financial Services Committee, "[i]mmediately after a large breach ... freshly acquired credit cards command a higher price – as there is greater possibility for the credit cards to still be active. Over time, prices fall because the market becomes flooded ... leveling off as the data becomes stale or if there has been significant time since the last breach."[79] While a freshly acquired US credit card may initially be valued at $15 on the black market, the value can drop to as low as $0.75 as the data becomes more stale.[80]

Moreover, it is difficult to predict who will be impacted. For example, in 2016 only 31.7 percent of individuals who were affected by a data breach reported being a victim of subsequent identity fraud, which is indicative of the varying levels of risk faced after a breach.[81] The probability that an individual will be subject to future identity theft can also vary across individuals based on a variety of factors such as prior incidence of identity theft, number of companies that have an individual's PII, and the type of PII that was compromised.

Perhaps somewhat paradoxically, the long-term impact of identity theft was found to be positive in some instances as those impacted become more vigilant: "the immediate effects of fraud on consumers are typically negative, small, and transitory. After those immediate effects fade, identity theft victims experience persistent, positive changes in credit characteristics, including improved risk scores (indicating lower default risk)."[82]

4.3.7 Unjust Enrichment

This type of damage is based on the premise that breached consumers should be entitled to the money consumers paid to the company during the period of the data

---

[78] "What to Do When You Receive a Data Breach Notice," *Privacy Rights Clearinghouse*, Revised Feb. 7, 2019, www.privacyrights.org/consumer-guides/what-do-when-you-receive-data-breach-notice. The identity theft outcomes for social security information, on the other hand, may be different and can involve opening new financial accounts and filing fraudulent tax returns, among others. See "5 Kinds of ID Theft Using a Social Security Number," LifeLock, www.lifelock.com/education/5-kinds-of-id-theft-using-social-security-number/.
[79] Ablon, L. (2018), "Data Thieves: The Motivations of Cyber Threat Actors and Their Use and Monetization of Stolen Data," Testimony Presented before the House Financial Services Committee, Subcommittee on Terrorism and Illicit Finance, Mar. 15, p. 11.
[80] Ablon, "Data Thieves," Table 4 at p. 12.
[81] Tatham, M., "Identity Theft Statistics," *Experian*, Mar. 15, 2018, www.experian.com/blogs/ask-experian/identity-theft-statistics/.
[82] Blascak, N., et al. (2016), "Identity Theft as a Teachable Moment," Federal Reserve Bank of Philadelphia, Payment Cards Center. The study concludes that "[t]he patterns we find in the data are consistent with the conjecture that some consumers were less attentive to their credit records before experiencing a severe identity theft event ... Thus, at least for some consumers, identity theft or fraud may serve as a teachable moment, increasing their attention to credit information." See p. 3.

breach.[83] In other words, according to this theory, prior to or at the point of transacting with consumers, if the company revealed it could not properly safeguard consumers' PII or what the expected risk of breach is, consumers would not have transacted with the company. This requires that firms can reasonably estimate the probability of a data breach and consumers can rationally evaluate different levels of risks across different alternative companies. Moreover, as with a number of other theories that involve a commercial relationship, the appropriate economic injury will not typically be the entire price paid, but the difference between the price paid and the utility of the product or service delivered.

4.4 CONCLUSION

In sum, private information or PII may be valuable depending on the type of information, the context in which it is used, whether the data is indeed private, and in relation to the specific party that makes use of the data and the party that can monetize it. Different consumers may have different valuations of this information due to their preferences for privacy, past behaviors, and contextual factors that may vary over time. These factors need to be properly accounted for in trying to assess and quantify the potential harm from the perspective of consumers in a consumer class action setting.

---

[83] See e.g. Second Amended Consolidated Class Action Complaint, *In re: Brinker Data Incident Litigation*, Case No. 18-cv-00686-TJC-MCR, United States District Court Middle District of Florida Jacksonville Division, ¶ 9; Plaintiffs' Amended Consolidated Class Action Complaint, *In re: Sonic Corp. Customer Data Breach Litigation*, Case No. 1:17-md-02807-JSG, United States District Court for the Northern District of Ohio Eastern Division at Cleveland, ¶¶ 64, 66–69.

PART II

Understanding Marketing Phenomena

5

The Persistence of False Reference Prices

Theory and Empirical Evidence

Yiting Deng, Richard Staelin, and Joel E. Urbany

5.5.1 INTRODUCTION

A general premise of consumer protection is that greater consumer information and more competition in a market should increase the tendency of firms to behave fairly and honestly.[1] In the case of deceptive promotional pricing, greater consumer information comes from having more consumers in the market being attentive to and knowledgeable of reference promotional pricing (i.e. showing a regular price along with the sales price).

5.1.1 *False Promotion: The FTC's Position*

Based in large part upon these two premises, i.e. more competition and knowledgeable consumers, the Federal Trade Commission (FTC) put a stop to its regulation of "fictitious pricing" over forty years ago. This hands-off policy was explained by future FTC Commissioner Robert Pitofsky in his landmark 1977 *Harvard Law Review* article.[2] The use of fictitious reference prices – referred to here as *false promotion*[3] – is the common seller practice of including exaggerated (false)

---

[1] See Howard Beales, Richard Craswell, and Steven C. Salop. "The efficient regulation of consumer information," 45(1) JOURNAL OF LAW AND ECONOMICS 491 (1981); Michael B. Mazis, Richard Staelin, Howard Beales, and Steven Salop. "A framework for evaluating consumer information regulation," 45(1) JOURNAL OF MARKETING 11 (1981).
[2] Robert Pitofsky, "Beyond Nader: Consumer protection and the regulation of advertising," 90 HARVARD LAW REVIEW. 661 (1977).
[3] In the legal, marketing, and economics literatures, different terms are used for the practice involving the use of reference prices that are exaggerated or have rarely/never actually been charged. These include "fake discounts" (Donald Ngwe, *Fake Discounts Drive Real Revenues in Retail* (Harvard Business School, 2018)), "fictitious pricing" (David Adam Friedman, "'Dishonest search disruption': Taking deceptive-pricing tactics seriously," UC DAVIS LAW REVIEW ONLINE 121 (2018), and "false bargains" ("FTC Guides Against Deceptive Pricing," www.lawpublish.com/ftc-decprice.html). Throughout the chapter, we will use the

comparison prices when offering a product or service at a reduced sale price. The goal of such communication is primarily to showcase a significant was/is comparison to inflate the expected savings that the customer would receive by purchasing the promoted item. Pitofsky's analysis held that – unlike judging product quality – it was straightforward for consumers to judge competitive prices in a market, and that "where consumers are fully capable, through common sense or simple observation, of protecting their interests against advertising exaggerations or distortions, there would be no reason for the law to intervene."[4]

While Pitofsky offered other reasons for pulling back on the regulation of this practice,[5] central to his thought process was the assumption that consumers will police the competitive market by identifying when price claims are exaggerated and ignoring those claims in their decision-making. Pitofsky, Shaheen, and Mudge later reiterated this assumption with additional confidence, buoyed by the emergence of a powerful price search tool (the Internet).[6] In their writings, they encouraged states to follow the FTC's lead and to stop prosecuting firms for false promotion.

5.1.2 A Recent Surge in Litigation

In light of these assumptions and encouragement from the FTC, one might expect that false promotion activity would have declined and that regulatory attention would have dwindled to an occasional complaint. In fact, it's gone the other way. Casual observation and regular reporting in the popular press and Internet content suggest that the practice is as prevalent as ever, if not more.[7] Dozens of deceptive

---

term "false promotion" to connect our analysis to the analytic model developed by Deng et al. (Yiting Deng, Richard Staelin, Wei Wang, and William Boulding, "Consumer sophistication, word-of-mouth and 'false' promotions," 152(10) *JOURNAL OF ECONOMIC BEHAVIOR & ORGANIZATION* 98 (2018), which is detailed in Section 5.2.

[4] Pitofsky, "Beyond Nader," p. 671.

[5] Pitofsky was writing at a time of evolving principles of advertising regulation at the FTC, following a period during which the commission had gotten into "nit-picking, literalistic disputes over the meaning of words in ads," and was regulated with the apparent aim of protecting established sellers against "competition from cheaper substitutes" (Pitofsky, "Beyond Nader," p. 674). He instead called for a set of rules that improved the information environment for consumers – i.e. that emphasized "required disclosure of accurate and important product information" that consumers could use for effective decision-making. Regarding fictitious pricing, one significant concern was that restricting the practice of comparison price exaggeration would create a tool with which established, service-based retailers could confront through litigation the competition emerging from the new category of discount chains. Pitofsky argued that this would reduce the social good of lower prices for consumers.

[6] Robert Pitofsky, Randal Shaheen and Amy Mudge, "Pricing laws are no bargain for consumers," 18 *ANTITRUST* 62 (2004).

[7] Writing in a blog called CPG Matters in 2019, attorneys Stephanie Sheridan and Meegan Brooks note that "Over the last few years ... more than 150 lawsuits have blanketed the retail community, alleging that more than 80 retailers have deceived consumers through their price advertising practices." False promotion has been discussed widely in both the popular press and in the blogs of law firms that seek to offer services in defense of this practice. Examples include

pricing suits have been filed over the past ten years, including those against such high-profile firms as Overstock.com, Nordstrom, JC Penney, Amazon.com, Columbia Sportswear, Kate Spade, and, most recently, Old Navy.

The outcomes of these cases have varied widely, ranging from outright dismissal to multimillion dollar settlements or penalties paid by defendant firms. Friedman attributes this variance to "piecemeal state actions" and varying legal philosophies across different jurisdictions.[8] A particularly challenging issue is the difficulty of estimating a consumer's financial loss from a transaction in which inflated comparison prices are alleged to have influenced their judgment and purchase behavior.

5.1.3 What's Missing in the Arguments: A Model of the Firm

In deceptive pricing cases, a central part of the plaintiff's complaint is that consumers were deceived or tricked into buying a product from a firm because it communicated a high, exaggerated comparative price (e.g. "Regular Price") with a lower sale price. This comparison made the promoted product look to be of higher quality and better value than it would have in the absence of the exaggeration. Establishing the potential intent to deceive is based in large part on documenting the firm's prices and sales over time. The intent to deceive is argued by plaintiffs to be reflected in defendant firms' limited or no sales of the promoted item at inflated advertised comparative prices.

In deceptive pricing cases, the plaintiffs' presentation often centrally consider arguments around consumer psychology – i.e. how consumers interpret and respond to false promotions.[9] These arguments normally rely on the relatively

---

Sarah Shemkus, "Don't fall for deceptive pricing practices," BOSTON GLOBE (Dec. 16, 2016); Andrew Lustigman and Morgan Spina, "Deceptive pricing: Unlawful trickery or skillful selling?," LAW.COM/NEW YORK LAW JOURNAL (Aug. 24, 2018); Suzanne Kapner, "The dirty secret of Black Friday 'discounts,'" WALL STREET JOURNAL (Nov. 25, 2013); Ben Popken, "JCPenney, Sears, Macy's and Kohl's sued for 'fake' sale pricing" (2016), www.nbcnews.com/business/consumer/jcpenney-sears-macy-s-kohl-ssued-fake-sale-pricing-n694101; Manatt.com, "Deceptive pricing suits continue to proliferate," Manatt, Phelps & Phillips, LLP (2019), www.manatt.com/insights/newsletters/advertising-law/deceptive-pricing-suits-continue-to-proliferate

[8] David Adam Friedman, "Reconsidering fictitious pricing," 100 (Feb.) MINNESOTA LAW REVIEW (2016).

[9] Examples include: *Colorado v. May Dept Stores Co.*, 849 P.2d 802 (Colo. Ct. App. 1992), *Commissioner of Competition v. Sears Canada Inc.* Tribunal File No. CT-2002-004; *Hinojos v. Kohl's Corp.*, 718 F.3d 1098, 1102 (9th Cir. 2013); *People v. Overstock.com, Inc.*, No. RG10546833, 2014 WL 657516, at *12–13 (Cal. Super. Ct. Feb. 5, 2014). While Section 5.3 of this chapter provides an overview of empirical research in consumer behavior relevant for deceptive pricing cases, we would refer the reader in search of deeper insight into legal applications of this research to other sources, including: Dhruv Grewal and Larry D. Compeau. "Comparative price advertising: Informative or deceptive?" 11(1) JOURNAL OF PUBLIC POLICY & MARKETING 52 (1992); Dhruv Grewal and Larry Compeau. "Interpretations of semantic phrases in comparative price advertisements: Some preliminary evidence on a public policy issue." ACR NORTH AMERICAN ADVANCES (1993); Larry D.

extensive literatures in psychology, marketing, and economics that address the impact of comparison/reference prices (both fictitious and non-fictitious) on consumer judgment and behavior.

In contrast, defendant firms tend to lead with the economics of the consumer's decision-making. Advertised reference prices are said to have limited or no impact on consumer judgment and the firm's sales, due in large part to the primacy (to consumers) of promoted sale prices rather than reference prices. Consumers are assumed to actively search for competitive options with a primary goal of finding the lowest selling prices and with a skeptical, disbelieving eye for comparison prices. In addition, the defendant firm will generally seek to demonstrate that its offered sale prices are the equal or better of its market competitors, ensuring no consumer harm.

In sum, defendant firms tend to argue that false promotions have little impact on consumers. Such effects are either made irrelevant by sale price competition or rendered ineffective by the consumer's extensive search focusing on finding low sale prices, with limited or no attention to inflated comparison prices. These arguments raise an important question which has yet to be addressed in the literature: why do firms consistently engage in a pricing practice that, when pressed in a courtroom, they argue bears little fruit?

In this chapter, we seek to explore the following questions:

1. Are financial incentives sufficient to encourage false promotion?
2. Does greater competition drive out false promotion?
3. Does greater consumer sophistication drive out false promotion?
4. Does false promotion impact industry, firm, and consumer welfare?

The next section of this chapter examines questions 1–3 through the structure of an analytic model. It is followed by Section 5.3, which reviews existing theory and empirical evidence around the abovementioned four questions, using the analytic model's mechanisms for both consumer response and firm pricing behavior as a foundation for such discussions. Section 5.4 presents conclusions.

Compeau, Dhruv Grewal, and Rajesh Chandrashekaran. "Comparative price advertising: Believe it or not," 36(2) JOURNAL OF CONSUMER AFFAIRS 284 (2002); Friedman, "Reconsidering Fictitious pricing"; David Adam Friedman, "'Dishonest search disruption': Taking deceptive-pricing tactics seriously," 121 UC DAVIS LAW REVIEW ONLINE (2018). Patrick J. Kaufmann et al., "Deception in retailer high-low pricing: A 'rule of reason' approach," 70 JOURNAL OF RETAILING (1994); Ngwe, *Fake Discounts Drive Real Revenues in Retail*; Joel E. Urbany, Mitchell Olsen, Vamsi Kanuri, and Frank Germann, *Evaluating Harmless Deception* (Mendoza College of Business, University of Notre Dame, Working Paper, 2020); R. Van Loo, "Broadening consumer law: Competition, protection, and distribution," 95(1) NOTRE DAME LAW REVIEW (2019).

5.2 MODEL

5.2.1 *Overview*

The goal of this section is to provide deeper insights into the implications of the FTC's decision not to actively regulate "fictitious pricing." We do this by discussing in some detail a model put forth by Deng et al. that directly addresses the questions listed above.[10] Specifically, their model parsimoniously captures two situations. In both situations competing firms sell similar products to the same set of consumers. However, in one the firms have the option of offering (1) real promotions (i.e. lowering the retail price below the normal price), (2) false promotions (i.e. falsely stating the regular normal price being higher than it is and then discounting that factitious normal price), or (3) not offering any promotion. In the second, the firms are limited, either by choice or regulation, to only the first or third options, i.e. false promotions are not an option. The customers are of two types. The first are sophisticated (i.e. they can detect false promotions). Not only do these consumers lower their evaluation of products sold under a false promotion, but they also subsequently inform some of the naïve consumers (those who, before being informed, believe all promotions are real promotions). After being informed, these formerly naïve consumers become sophisticated on future purchase occasions.

We choose an analytic model based on a small set of assumptions versus, say, an empirical model, since the analytic model approach clearly lays bare the underlying assumptions and the mechanism of action that is driving the results. It also provides a framework for assessing the veracity of the FTC's current position that competition and sophisticated consumers will lead the market to self-correct, thereby eliminating the need to regulate the practice of false promotions. With this noted, we recognize that many of the reading audience may lack familiarity with mathematical models and this approach for analyzing complex interactions between firms and consumers. Therefore, in this discussion, we not only focus on potential policy implications but also provide guidance on the underlying assumptions and the implications of these assumptions.

5.2.2 *Model Setup*

The Deng et al. model is highly appropriate for this discussion, since it captures the key elements of the FTC's premise, namely competition, the presence of sophisticated consumers, and the ability of these consumers to pass this knowledge on to naïve consumers through word of mouth (WOM). As with most analytic models, their model places heavy emphasis on parsimony, thereby allowing the reader to see

---

[10] Deng, Staelin, Wang, and Boulding, "Consumer sophistication, word-of-mouth and 'false' promotions."

"all the moving parts" without the distraction of complexity. In the case of Deng et al. this approach results in three broad components of the model: the general environment, the consumers' demand function (i.e. how consumers evaluate each offering and decide to buy), and the rules of the game (i.e. how the firms decide on prices, and promotional strategies). These three components are necessary to allow the model builders to determine the equilibrium outcomes of this game.

General Setting. The model captures competition by allowing the market to be composed of two firms (instead of the more complex setting of many firms), with one parameter (d) to capture the distance between the two firms: when d is larger, the degree to which these two firms compete is lower. In this way, the model is able to look at the effects of competition on the final outcomes of interest. It also contains two types of consumers. A fraction λ of them are sophisticated and able to identify if a promotion is false. The rest $1-\lambda$ of the consumers are naïve, and they do not question whether a promotion is false. If the sophisticated segment of the market sees that the industry is practicing false promotions, it passes this knowledge on to a subset of naïve consumers who then become sophisticated in the next period. This ability to pass knowledge on requires the model builders to have at least two periods, one for the sophisticated consumers to learn about industry practices, and the second to pass this knowledge on to some of the naïve consumers. The efficiency of WOM is captured by a parameter ϵ, which measures how many naïve consumers become sophisticated in the second period. Thus, in the second period, the fraction of sophisticated consumers would remain λ if neither firm offers a false promotion in the first period, and increase to $\lambda + \epsilon$ if at least one firm offers a false promotion in the first period.

In each period, each firm decides whether to offer a price promotion on its product. If a firm decides not to offer a promotion (denoted as N), it then sells the product at its list price p. If a firm decides to offer a real promotion (denoted as T), it must first choose the optimal discount rate α, which reduces the price from p to $p-p\alpha$. Thus, larger values of α imply a deeper discount. If the firm decides to offer a false promotion (denoted as F), it first artificially inflates the list price to $p/(1-\alpha)$, and then claims the discounted price to be p. For example, if the regular list price is $100, and the discount rate is 20 percent, then under a real promotion, the final price would be $80. Under a false promotion, the firm would inflate the list price to $125 and offer the product at $100 which is 20 percent off the inflated list price.

Consumer Demand. The consumers' evaluation of both firms' offerings is based on four distinct attributes, the inherent value of the product (v), the mismatch costs associated with the individual consumer's taste for this product and/or the actual costs incurred going to the retail location (x), the selling price (after any promotion of the product), and the increase (decrease) in value if the product is believed to be on promotion (on false promotion). This last attribute implies that, if the consumer believes the product is under a real promotion, then their evaluation of the offering goes up, i.e. the consumer gets additional utility thinking that they bought the

TABLE 5.1. *Consumer utility*

		\multicolumn{3}{c}{Consumer belief}		
		N	T	F
Firm strategy	N	$v-p-x$	–	–
	T	–	$(1+\alpha)v-(1-\alpha)p-x$	–
	F	–	$(1+\alpha)v-p-x$	$(1-\alpha)v-p-x$

product on "deal." Such behavior is in line with empirical evidence and will be discussed at greater length in Section 5.3.1. This added utility increases with the discount rate, reflecting that consumers love deeper discounts. However, if the consumer believes the product is under a false promotion, then they get disutility by believing that the price is unfair,[11] that they are being "tricked" by the firm, and the firm is engaged in "poor" marketing practices. Similar to the utility associated with feeling good about getting a good deal, the consumer's disutility associated with feeling tricked also increases with the discount rate. Note, however, that even if the consumer knows that the promotion is false, this consumer may still buy from the retailer offering this false promotion. This could occur if the product closely matched the consumer's tastes or the consumer found it more convenient to go to that retail store.

One explicit result of Deng et al.'s assumed consumer demand function is that sophisticated consumers value a real promotion the highest, a false promotion the lowest, and a no promotion in between, all else being equal. In contrast, the naive consumers value a real promotion the highest, followed by a false promotion, and value a no promotion the least. This ordering is because false promotions are still evaluated higher than the normal selling price (although both have the same price) due to the additional utility associated with getting a "good deal," but their evaluations are lower than those of the real promotions, since the effective price is higher and consumers always prefer lower prices to higher prices.

These basic assumptions are captured in terms of consumer utility (evaluation) which is found in Table 5.1. For example, if the consumer buys a product under the condition of no promotion, the consumer would get the intrinsic value of v, and incur two decreases in utility, the first by paying the price p and the second associated with the product not perfectly matching the consumer's taste as captured by the parameter x. Similarly, if this consumer believes the promotion is a real promotion and the promotion is indeed real, this consumer gets an intrinsic value of $(1+\alpha)v$ from purchasing the product, where αv is due to believing the product is on sale, and suffers both from a disutility cost of $(1-\alpha)p$ for having to pay for the discounted product, and from a mismatch cost of x.

---

[11] See Lan Xia, Kent B. Monroe, and Jennifer L. Cox, "The price is unfair! A conceptual framework of price fairness perceptions," 68(4) JOURNAL OF MARKETING 1 (2004).

Deng et al. restrict the range of v (the intrinsic value of the product), p (the stated regular price), and d (the degree to which the two firms are competing or conversely are differentiated) to ensure that the market is fully covered when the final price is p. This assumption of the market being fully covered implies that at least some consumers find both products provide them with positive utility and is a standard assumption made in many game-theoretic models. It has two major implications. First, it means that the two firms are always competing, i.e. the actions of one firm will affect the actions of the other firm, since at least some consumers are considering both offerings. Second, industry demand does not expand when prices are dropped, although demand can shift between the firms depending on their particular price and promotional strategy. However, as discussed more fully subsequently, total demand in their model can shrink if both firms adopt false promotions.

Rules of the Game. In each period, each firm sets prices (in this case, it is the size of the discount because the normal retail price is assumed to be fixed at p, which represents the manufacturer suggested retail price), conditional on the other firm's price. The firms have foresight in that they can anticipate what will happen in subsequent periods. The firm's goal is to maximize long-term profits, in this case two-period profits. In contrast, consumers are not strategic, but instead only think about maximizing their one-period consumption value. In each period, a consumer can purchase at most one product. They decide which firm to purchase from, and they can also decide not to make a purchase if their utility from purchasing is negative. Firms settle on solutions where there is no advantage to move – this is referred to as an equilibrium solution.

5.2.3 Model Analysis

In the situation where there is no regulation, each firm can take one of the three promotion strategies T, F, and N, in each period. Consequently, there are nine promotion strategy profiles: {N, N}, {N, T},{N, F}, {T, N}, {T, T}, {T, F}, {F, N}, {F, T}, and {F, F}. In each strategy profile, the first letter denotes the strategy of firm 1 and the second letter denotes the strategy of firm 2 for that period. Similarly, if there is regulation, there are only four promotion strategy profiles each period.

The analytic model's goal is to compare and contrast the firms' decisions under both situations and, importantly, under the situation without regulation, to characterize the occurrence of false promotions under different market environments as characterized by parameters d, v, p, λ, and ϵ. Deng and her coauthors do this by systematically varying these parameters and then solving the two-period game to obtain the equilibrium strategy of each firm in both periods.

Their first step is to derive the optimal discount for each firm under each of the nine promotion strategy profiles. When there is no promotion (N), the discount is zero and the price is the original list price p. Under a real promotion (T), the optimal discount is the discount that would lead to the highest profit given the other firm's strategy. Under a false promotion (F), the optimal discount mimics that of T. For instance, when firm 1 chooses F and firm 2 chooses T, firm 1 claims a discount rate that is the same as its own discount rate when both firms choose T, and inflates its regular price accordingly. Firm 2 in turn obtains its optimal price conditional on firm 1's pricing strategy. Based on the optimal prices under all promotion strategy profiles, they derive the equilibrium of this two-period game using the concept of subgame perfect Nash equilibrium (SPNE). In words, SPNE means that at every stage of the two-period game, the obtained solution is in Nash equilibrium, i.e. neither firm finds it in its best interest to switch promotional strategies or discount rates. These equilibrium solutions are a function of the market environment and the consumer parameters, i.e. d, v, p, λ, and ϵ.

This general setup allowed them to explore multiple questions related to the occurrence of false promotions and changes in industry profit as a function of the size of the sophisticated segment, the effectiveness of WOM, and the degree of competition between firms. It also allows us to use their results to more thoroughly explore the validity of the FTC's implicit assumption that competition and sophisticated consumers in the market will reduce the prevalence of false promotions.

Results. Deng et al. start their analysis by first exploring what the industry would look like if the FTC were to disallow the practice of false promotions. They then compare strategies and profits to an industry that allows false promotions as an option, i.e. they use the regulated industry as the benchmark.

They find that if false promotions are not allowed, then when competition is high (small d), the unique equilibrium is that both firms offer real promotions in both periods and obtain lower profits than if they never promote. Such a solution is often referred to as a "prisoner's dilemma," where players' strategic behavior leads to suboptimal decisions for all players. When competition is low (large d), the equilibrium outcome is that, in each period, one firm offers a real promotion while the other does not promote. So the occurrence of promotional activities reduces from 100 percent to 50 percent. Thus, competition in a regulated market that does not allow false promotions leads to lower prices (and profits) and the existence of deeper (and real) discounts.

When false promotions are allowed, at least from the FTC's point of view, the equilibria are more complicated. Deng and her coauthors provide closed-form solutions for some market conditions, while for others they conducted numerical simulations and solved the equilibrium outcomes under more than 6 million different market environments characterized by parameters d, v, p, λ, and ϵ. They used these results to determine the effects of different environmental parameters on promotional outcomes and industry profits.

We summarize many of their findings next. We first look at their findings concerning how the occurrence of false promotions in an unregulated market changes with the level of competition. Figure 5.1 shows in each period, averaged over all of the solutions generated, the percentage of times a real promotion (T), a

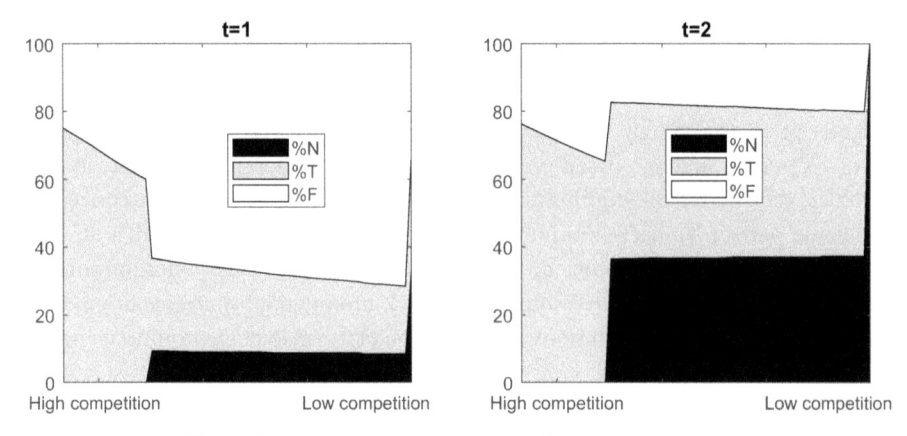

FIGURE 5.1. Effects of competition on promotional activities

false promotion (F), and no promotion (N) occur under different competition levels, i.e. for different levels of d. (In other words, for each level of d all the other parameters were allowed to vary across their total allowable range.) Note that when the competition is the most intense,[12] and false promotions are unregulated, we see the modal strategy is to give real promotions. However, even though competition is most intense, firms still offer false promotions under some market conditions. Simply put, competition can reduce the use of false promotions, but it alone is not powerful enough to stop the practice of offering false promotions. In fact, even when there is no differentiation between firms, over 20 percent of the solutions showed firms giving false promotions in both the first and second periods.

As might be expected, in the first period decreases in the competitive level lead to increases in the firm offering false promotions and decreases in the use of real promotions. However, at some point, as competition becomes less fierce, firms stop offering promotions (true or false) all the time. The selection of no promotions occurs more in the second period. Somewhat counterintuitively, false promotions occur less in the second period even though there is no further penalty for offering a false promotion. Deng et al. conjecture this firm behavior to be driven by the larger sophisticated population in the second period coming from the large occurrence of first-period false promotions.

Next, we consider the remaining self-regulating mechanism, i.e. the existence of sophisticated consumers. We note that the Deng et al. analysis combines the two mechanisms, i.e. the initial size of the sophisticated segment and the effectiveness of WOM, by looking at how the occurrence of false promotions changes with the extent of sophisticated consumers by the end of the game, $\lambda + \epsilon$. Figure 5.2 shows, in each period, the percentage of times when there is a real promotion (T), a false

---

[12] In Figure 5.1, competition increases moving from right to left since d is inversely scaled such that *smaller* values reflect *more* competition.

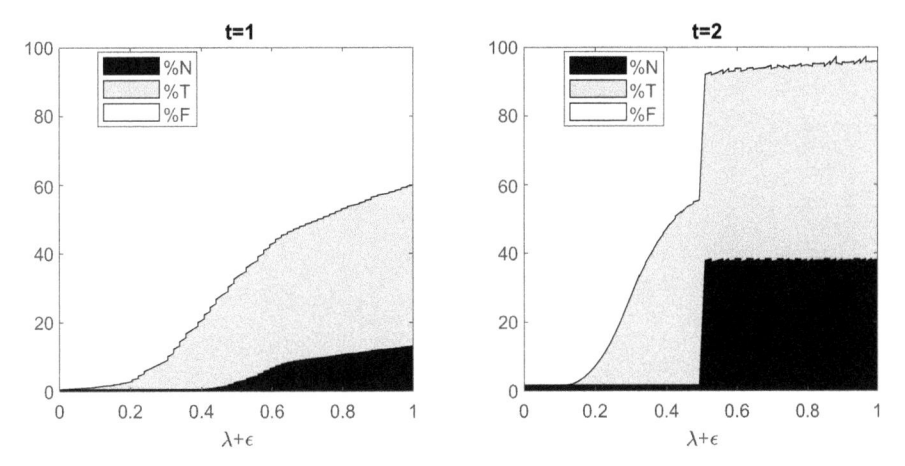

FIGURE 5.2. Effects of the extent of sophisticated consumers by the end of the game on promotional activities

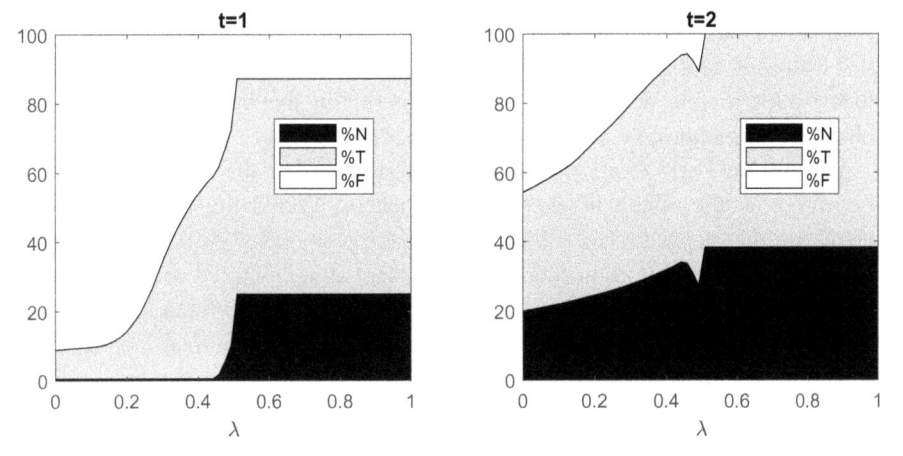

FIGURE 5.3. Effects of the extent of sophisticated consumers at the beginning of the game on promotional activities

promotion (F), and no promotion (N) under different values of $\lambda + \epsilon$ (again allowing all the other parameters to vary across their permissible ranges). As expected, in both periods, the occurrence of false promotions decreases with $\lambda + \epsilon$. However, interestingly, false promotions are not eliminated even under high values of $\lambda + \epsilon$. Such an occurrence is because the undesirable prisoner's dilemma can be circumvented by offering a false promotion.

We then unlink the effects of WOM and the initial size of the sophisticated market segment and look at the prevalence of the three promotional strategies as a function of λ only. The results are shown in Figure 5.3. Two interesting observations come from this figure. First, even when 100 percent of the population is sophisticated initially, firms still find it in their best interest to offer false promotions in the

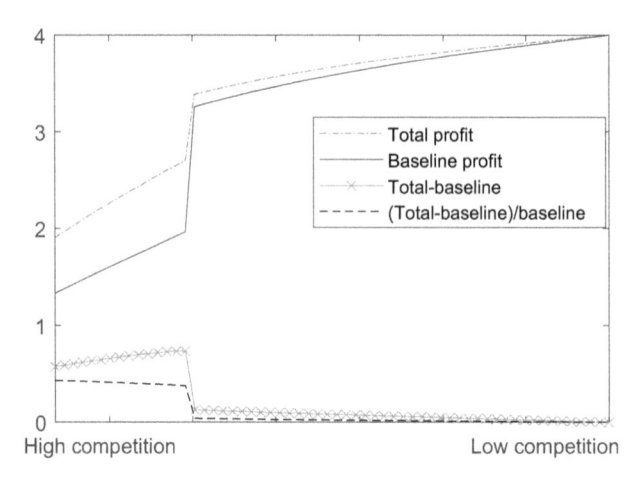

FIGURE 5.4. Effects of competition on total industry profit

first period, albeit at a lower rate than if the proportion of sophisticated consumers is less than 50 percent. However, in the second period this is no longer true. It appears that by having a longer time horizon (in this case a second period), firms are willing to take a hit, thereby decreasing the proportion of time that both firms are driven to offer real promotions, i.e. arrive at the prisoner's solution.

We use the Deng et al. findings to investigate whether the industry as a whole benefits from the option to offer false promotions. Would the industry welcome regulation that stopped retailers from offering false promotions? As before, we look at the effect of the level of competition and the extent of sophisticated consumers by the end of the game. Figure 5.4 shows, for different values of competition level, the total industry profit with the option of false promotions, the baseline total industry profit when false promotions are not allowed, the difference between the two, and the difference normalized by baseline profit. As might be expected, as the market becomes less competitive, industry profit increases either with or without the option of false promotions, and the difference between the two decreases, implying a smaller net increase in total profit by allowing for false promotions. Thus, in a highly competitive market, the option to offer false promotions leads to a larger increase (which is about 40 percent on average in their model) in industry profit. Only at low levels of competition do we see the percentage increase over baseline decrease to lower levels. These results imply that regulation will be fought harder in highly competitive industries.

Recall that these authors assumed that the market is fully covered unless both firms offer false promotions. Thus, real promotions do not change the total industry demand but only affect the firms' market shares. When both firms offer false promotions, some sophisticated consumers with high mismatch costs (i.e. find that neither product meets their needs well) will forgo the purchase, leading to a decrease in total industry demand. Therefore, the higher industry profit when false promotions are allowed is driven by higher sales margins instead of higher demand.

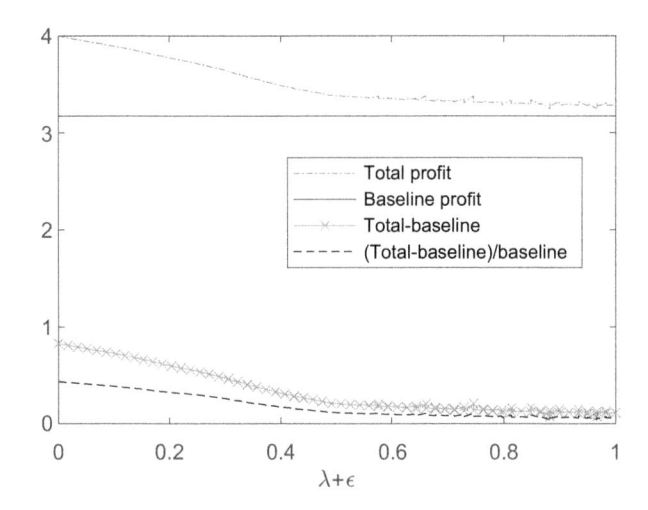

FIGURE 5.5. Effects of the extent of sophisticated consumers by the end of the game on total industry profit

Similarly, Figure 5.5 shows the results repeated for different values of $\lambda + \epsilon$. As expected, as the market includes more sophisticated consumers, the benefit of introducing false promotions to the market becomes less significant.

5.2.4 Discussion

The main objective of this section was to look at the implications of competition and the degree of sophistication among consumers to self-regulate the market, thereby providing supporting evidence of the FTC's decision to basically ignore false promotions. The overarching conclusion is that, although both increases in competition and the size of the sophisticated market segment decrease the prevalence of false promotions (thereby supporting the FTC's priors), the Deng et al. results show that in many environments, firms find it in their best interest to offer false promotions even when competition is fierce and/or the size of the sophisticated segment is large. Only when at least 50 percent of the consumers were sophisticated initially did we observe no false promotions and even then this only occurred at the end of the game. Moreover, left to their own devices, the industry is better off if firms have the option to offer false promotions. The underlying mechanism for this finding is that, if one firm offers a real promotion, the competing firm at times finds its best response to this promotional strategy is not to also offer a real promotion, but instead to offer a false promotion. The net effect is to dampen competition, since prices are no longer being driven to the lowest levels for both firms.

In making all these observations, the reader should take into consideration that the Deng et al. model represents a stylized world, much simpler than the actual retail environment. Yet hopefully their model provides the reader with a deeper understanding of the effects of the different market conditions on the prevalence of false promotions and the validity of basic premises of what will occur under different market conditions. Thus, it is probably reasonable to assume that competition will reduce the prevalence of false promotions, all else being equal, but it is probably not reasonable to assume that competition will eliminate such a practice. Likewise, having most of the consumer segment being aware of false promotions, being able to tell others about this, and showing a distaste for such a practice is not enough to stop the practice of firms offering false promotions as long as the firm has a long-term time horizon. Finally, the reason for all this occurring is because, with the option for offering false promotions, firms no longer have to respond to their competitor's real promotion by also offering a real promotion. Instead, they can offer a false promotion (rather than no promotion or a real promotion), knowing that they will "tick off" some consumers, but they still can attract naïve consumers and a fraction of the sophisticated consumers who find their product offering more in tune with their personal tastes.

5.3 REVIEW OF EVIDENCE ON THE FINANCIAL INCENTIVES FOR FALSE PROMOTION

Up until now, our discussion of false promotions has been in the stylized world of the Deng et al. analytic model, which is characterized by a set of assumptions, equations, and rules of how the players (firms and consumers) interact. Although this approach provides depth and clarity of insight about the market actors and outcomes, it can lack some degree of realism due to the need to make specific assumptions about market structure and player characteristics in order to isolate particular phenomena to study.

In this section we look for confirming (and disconfirming) evidence on how the "real world" marketplace outcomes match up to what we learn from the Deng et al. analysis. We do this by comparing the analytic results with existing empirical and conceptual evidence that addresses the four questions raised in our introduction section, i.e.:

1. Are financial incentives sufficient to encourage firms to engage in false promotion?
2. Does greater competition drive out false promotion?
3. Does greater consumer sophistication drive out false promotion?
4. Does false promotion impact industry, firm, and consumer welfare?

5.3.1 Question 1. Are Financial Incentives Sufficient to Encourage Firms to Engage in False Promotion?

The Deng et al. analysis leads to the conclusion that profit-maximizing firms in a competitive market will use false promotion under a surprisingly wide array of conditions, even when a significant proportion of the consumer market is sophisticated and/or even when competition is intense. These conclusions are based on the explicit assumption that consumers react favorably to a "sale" and that they gauge the sale based, at least in part, on the difference between the sale price and the stated normal price. Two recent studies respectively by Jindal and Ngwe provide empirical evidence that directly addresses this specific assumption and show that not only do consumers react positively to higher stated before-sales prices (holding fixed the sale price), but also that increasing this stated normal price figure has major profit implications for firms.[13] However, before discussing these two studies, it is useful to first briefly review the research on consumer response to promotions in general, in order to give the reader a sense of the empirical modeling tradition that has emerged in marketing using transactional data.

5.3.1.1 Examining Reference Price Effects with Transactional Data

Marketing researchers have long used consumer panels to capture, over time, objective records of purchases. Initially these panels were made up of households that had agreed to share that information, along with surrounding context (e.g. price and advertising levels in place at the time of each transaction). Since the 1960s, marketing scientists used such data to build models of consumer response to marketing stimuli.

In the early 1980s, marketing scientists started using scanner panel data to analyze consumer choice. A pioneering paper by Winer uses scanner panel data of 1,318 households in a single city to examine consumer choice in the coffee category.[14] These data captured daily histories of coffee purchases for over a year. Winer built an empirical model of brand choice which included not only the effects of price (P), but also the effects of a reference price against which the consumer could determine if the current price was a "good deal." Specifically, he added to the choice model an estimate of each household's own unique *internal reference price* (IRP, representing brand price expectations held in memory). Household IRPs were estimated for each brand in each period using recent past prices to which the household would have likely been exposed. The remarkable result in Winer's analysis was that for two of the three coffee brands studied, purchase probability was affected significantly by *both* the brand's price (a negative effect of P) *and* the difference between the price P and the consumer's internal reference price for that brand (a positive effect of IRP – P).[15]

---

[13] Pranav Jindal, "Perceived versus negotiated discounts: The role of advertised reference prices in price negotiations," 59(3) JOURNAL OF MARKETING RESEARCH 578 (2022). https://doi.org/10.1177/00222437211034443; Ngwe, *Fake Discounts Drive Real Revenues in Retail*.

[14] Russell S. Winer, "A reference price model of brand choice for frequently purchased products," 13(2) JOURNAL OF CONSUMER RESEARCH 250 (1986).

[15] Note that if the IRP is lower than the offered price, this term would decrease sales. We discuss this more in footnote 20.

The negative effect of P is expected, i.e. consumers are less likely to choose a brand at competitively higher prices. However, the positive effect of [IRP − P] was new to the literature, suggesting that the higher the IRP, relative to the price, the more likely consumers were to buy the product (holding the selling price fixed). In other words, consumers are implicitly influenced in their choices by the comparison of an observed price to their own intuitive sense of what the brand "ought to cost" and this positive effect on choice probability was separate from the standard allocative effect of the selling price.

The many papers published following Winer's original work examined variations of internal reference price effects.[16] Of particular interest is the research by Mayhew and Winer, who added *external* reference prices – that is, prices that sellers promoted in advertising and in-store as their *regular* prices.[17] Using a panel dataset of 185 households focusing on purchases in the yogurt category over two years, Mayhew and Winer found that adding a predictor capturing the difference between sale price P and external reference price (ERP)[18] significantly improved the prediction of brand choice after accounting for the effects of both selling price P and the [IRP − P] predictor.[19] In fact, Mayhew and Winer concluded initially that "external reference prices have much greater effects on brand-choice decisions than internal reference prices do," although they later tempered that point to suggest that it was an important future research question.[20]

---

[16] A ten-year retrospective on the literature that subsequently blossomed as a result of Winer's original paper can be found in Kalyanaram and Winer's work (Gurumurthy Kalyanaram and Russell S. Winer, "Empirical generalizations from reference price research," 14(3) MARKETING SCIENCE G161 (1995). Note that a key insight from this work was the need for brands to pay attention to how the patterns of their pricing and promotions would shape consumer price expectations and thus future sales and firm revenue. Greenleaf's work (Eric A. Greenleaf, "The impact of reference price effects on the profitability of price promotions," 14 (1) MARKETING SCIENCE 82 (1995)) subsequently presented a model showing that a brand would need to account for this effect of past prices on internal reference prices in order to maximize profits.

[17] Glenn E. Mayhew and Russell S. Winer, "An empirical analysis of internal and external reference prices using scanner data," 19(1) JOURNAL OF CONSUMER RESEARCH 62 (1992).

[18] In the marketing literature, external reference prices are often referred to as advertised reference prices (ARPs). It is probably more common to see the acronym ARP in court filings for deceptive pricing cases. However, we'll use the ERP acronym to distinguish external from internal reference prices.

[19] Mayhew and Winer additionally distinguished between sale prices that represented a *loss* relative to the internal reference price and sale prices that represented a *gain*. Consistent with Kahneman and Tversky's Prospect Theory (Daniel Kahneman and Amos Tversky, "Prospect theory: An analysis of decision under risk," 47(2) ECONOMETRICA 263 (1979)), they found that sale prices that were higher than expected prices (losses) were much more influential than sale prices that were lower than expectations (gains).

[20] It is not surprising that ERP has a larger impact than IRP, since the former is observable at the time of purchase and the latter is more fallible and requires the consumer to recall pricing history from memory. This difference is also probably magnified by the length of the purchase cycle, with longer cycles reducing the salience of pricing history.

This early work, based upon actual transactions in the marketplace, supported the conceptual thinking that had been emerging in other fields of study, that consumers instinctively use both internal *and* external reference prices in their decision-making in addition to just the current price.[21] The two studies described next build upon this tradition to analyze transactions data and provide specific insight into the financial incentives associated with both true and false promotions.

5.3.1.2 Financial Incentives for Using False Promotion: Recent Evidence

The studies discussed above focused attention on consumer response to promotions and in particular to the response to IRP and ERP. (In the parlance of the Deng et al. utility model, the inclusion of a term for the effect of deal.) We next look at two recent empirical studies based on transactions data that not only estimate the effects of ERP holding the sales price fixed, but also relate these effects to firm's financial outcomes associated with both true and false promotions. Both studies focus on durable product categories, which are generally more expensive than nondurables and purchased less frequently.[22]

5.3.1.2.1 *Jindal: Anchoring in Price Negotiations* Jindal used transactional data obtained from a very large durable goods retailer to examine how the firm's posted reference price (ERP) and advertised price (P) affected consumer behavior and the resulting implications for the retailer.[23] The environment studied was one where consumers can negotiate with the salesperson to get a final purchase price that is even lower than the advertised sales price. Jindal first looked at how ERP and P affected the resulting discount realized by the consumer. His data covered almost 29,000 consumers who made 43,534 orders in the two-year period between 2015 and 2017 for over 150,000 unique Stock Keeping Units (SKUs) that were classified into fifty narrowly defined subcategories and further organized into six broader categories. Besides the offered P and ERP, the dataset includes wholesale cost of the product to the retailer, realized price paid by the customer, P^*, brand, product, consumer background, and other factors. The observations in the dataset only represent actual purchases that consumers made from the retailer and thus do

---

[21] Kahneman and Tversky, "Prospect theory"; Richard Thaler, "Mental accounting and consumer choice," 4(3) MARKETING SCIENCE 199 (1985).
[22] Generally speaking, durable product categories are more relevant for the study of false promotions because virtually all litigation has involved durables. In addition, consumers' price expectations (IRPs) for durables may generally be held with more uncertainty given less frequent purchase. As such, ERPs suggested by sellers may have a greater impact on consumer judgment for durables. Many of the early studies in the reference price modeling literature were focused on frequently purchased products (such as coffee and yogurt), using data that had become increasingly accessible through scanner panel companies.
[23] Jindal, "Perceived versus negotiated discounts."

not allow Jindal to estimate the effects of P and ERP on the decision to buy or negotiate.

Due to confidentiality restrictions, Jindal presented all his findings in terms of rescaled pricing units (although he analyzed the data on the true prices). To give the reader a feel for the data, he presented the average of the disguised prices (while maintaining the relative price and cost figures). These averages along with other relevant data are as follows:

(A)	External reference price (ERP): "Regular" price	$453
(B)	Offered price P: Sale price promoted vs. ERP	$351
(C)	Apparent savings % [(A) − (B) / (A)]	23%
(D)	Realized price P^*: Final price paid after negotiating	$340
(E)	Realized discount after negotiation [(B) − (D) / (B)]	3%
(F)	Percentage of consumers who negotiate	81%
(G)	Percentage of sales sold at ERP	0%

This example points out a number of important features of the data. First, all of the sales were below the stated ERP figure, i.e. no sales occurred at the listed ERP. Second, even after seeing the product offered at a lower sales price, 81 percent of consumers were able to get an even lower price, albeit only 3 percent lower on average. All this is of particular relevance since the author states that the store's ERP was in line with competing retailers' sales prices, i.e. the focal firm's ERP was similar to the sales prices charged by other competing firms. However, these competing retailers often had a higher ERP. (In terms of the Deng et al. model, the focal retailer was offering a true promotion and the competitors were offering a false promotion.)

Jindal investigated the impact of the ERP on the size of the final discount (which effectively translates to the paid price) after controlling the announced sales price and a wide range of methodologically relevant factors. He finds that *an increase of the "Regular" price (ERP) by $1 produces a reduction of negotiated discount level* by 6.6 cents, i.e. the final price paid is higher by 6.6 cents. In short, the higher the ERP stated alongside the selling price, the higher is the retailer's profit margin on the sale, conditional on the consumer buying. Jindal then supplemented his transactional data with a lab experiment in order to provide deeper insights into the underlying mechanism driving his results. He found that increases in the ERP both decrease the probability that a consumer will negotiate for a lower price than the sales price, and decrease the amount of additional discount received by this negotiating consumer. In other words, the increase in the ERP has a double whammy. He goes on to say that "Despite the increase in negotiated price, an increase in IPD increases purchase likelihood in bargaining scenarios. The result is a positive, significant effect of IPD on the seller's revenue."[24]

---

[24] Jindal, "Perceived versus negotiated discounts," p. 594, where IPD represents the initial perceived discount determined by the seller's choice of ERP in our notation.

There are two observations about Jindal's results relevant to our question 1 about the financial incentives for false promotion. First, as confirmed by communications with the author, the actual announced discounts always exceeded 50 percent, yet on average 81 percent of the consumers negotiated to lower the paid price even more. Importantly, the estimated effect of increasing the firm's posted "Regular prices" (ERPs) is to significantly reduce consumers' desire to negotiate and increase the retailer's margins and profitability. Second, Jindal's conclusions (as quoted in the previous paragraph) *illustrate precisely* the profit incentive that might start some retailers down the path to inflating ERPs. This is exactly the decision calculus – and the temptation – that firms in the Deng et al. model face. In this way, Jindal's results provide a supporting affirmative answer to our question 1, illustrating that there is a profit incentive for a retailer to inflate its ERPs. In the case of the focal retailer studied by Jindal, that retailer apparently felt constrained by competition, in that, although the retailer never sold any items at its ERP, it did use ERPs based on its competitors' actual selling prices. In contrast, in the next subsection we will discuss Ngwe's analysis of a firm that had no qualms about substantially inflating its ERPs (presented as list prices), and profited from it.

5.3.1.2.2 Ngwe: Fake Discounts Drive Real Revenue Ngwe provides additional insights on how ERPs affect demand using a unique proprietary transactional database of over 16 million unique consumers of a major fashion goods manufacturer.[25] This vertically integrated manufacturer sells its products through two different channels: in-city retail stores and outlet stores normally located in malls at least thirty miles from the downtown area. Ngwe confined his analysis to items sold in the outlet stores. These items can be partitioned into two groups. The first were items that were initially sold in the in-city stores and later moved to the outlet stores to be put on sale at a price substantially below the initial in-city selling price. In this case, the ERP used was the initial selling price in the in-city store. The second group of products were items that came directly from the factory and never were previously available. Similar to the in-city items, each item coming directly from the factory had a stated ERP (list price) and a stated sale price P which was (substantially) lower than the stated ERP. However, unlike those items initially sold in the in-city stores, those coming directly from the factory were never sold at the stated ERP. This quasi-experiment allowed Nwge to partition the observed (total) discount, i.e. [ERP − P*] for each unique product into two components, the first associated with a fake "list" price, and the second associated with the real "list" price. Figure 5.6 provides an example of his approach. In this example, the current sales price ($125) is lower than the true list price ($175, which was the maximum price at which the item had been offered and sold). This difference between ERP and the price paid, P*, is because the retailer systematically lowered the sales price over time on all items in

---

[25] Ngwe, *Fake Discounts Drive Real Revenues in Retail*.

```
Fake list price          $ 279
[posted ERP]                           ⎤
                                       ⎥  FAKE
                                       ⎦  discount
                              ⎤
                              ⎥  FULL
                              ⎥  discount
True list price          $ 175⎥                ⎤
[actual max price at which    ⎥                ⎥
the item has been sold]       ⎥                ⎥  REAL
                              ⎦                ⎦  discount

Sale price               $ 125
```

FIGURE 5.6. Distinguishing fake from true discounts

the outlet store. Other than this difference in the veracity of the ERPs, Nwge showed there were no significant observable differences (e.g. quality, average initial sales price, etc.) between these two sets of products.

Ngwe developed a standard discrete choice model to estimate the effects of the firm's discounts (both real and "fake" discounts) after controlling for the stated selling price, the product age, and several other product characteristics, on the probability that a consumer will purchase an item.

He found both real and fake discount terms were significant predictors of demand above the effects of the sales price, with *fake discounts having a substantially larger effect than real discounts*. Ngwe interpreted this as follows:

> Comparing coefficients, we see that a $1 increase in a product's list price [read this as ERP] has the same effect on purchase probabilities as a $0.77 decrease in selling price, all else held constant. Considering that a firm can increase a firm's list price [on items coming directly from the factory] at virtually no cost, this has potentially huge consequences for producer and consumer welfare.[26]

Nwge supplemented this analysis by estimating consumers' prior knowledge of prices on the magnitude of the effects of both types of promotions on the likelihood of purchase. He proxied this prior knowledge in two ways. In the first, he used how long the mall outlet had been open, presuming that the longer it is open, the more likely that consumers are better informed about the store's pricing policies and thus the existence of fake ERPs. In the second, he used the distance between the outlet store and the in-city store, assuming that the closer the two stores, the greater the average consumer's awareness of the differences in product range between the two channels. In both instances, the results provide suggestive evidence that the more experience consumers have with products, the less likely they will be responsive to fake discounts.

Summary. Perhaps the most central unanswered question to date in the debate about false promotion is whether there are financial incentives for a firm to use it. As

---

[26] Ngwe, *Fake Discounts Drive Real Revenues in Retail*, p. 14.

discussed, the Deng et al. analytic model identifies many conditions in which firms engage in false promotion because it increases their profits. The two recent empirical studies reviewed in this section do not contradict that conclusion. Examining real consumer transactions, these studies together find that regular or list price ERPs representing both true and false discounts significantly influence consumer demand and the opportunity for profit gains by the firm.

While the Jindal and Ngwe studies provide pioneering insight into the main effects of true and false promotions on demand and profit opportunities, we need to look to other literature for answers to the other questions raised in the Deng et al. analysis. Do increases in competitive intensity and consumer sophistication affect firm incentives to reduce or eliminate false promotions? These questions are addressed in Sections 5.3.2 and 5.3.3.

5.3.2 *Question 2: Does Greater Competition Drive Out False Promotion?*

"[R]obust competition is the best single means for protecting consumer interests."[27]

Timothy Muris
Chairman, Federal Trade Commission, 2000–2004

The recent empirical studies just reviewed clearly indicate financial incentives associated with the use of false promotions. Yet are such incentives driven out as markets get more competitive? FTC Chairman Muris' quote reflects a standard assumption in economics that competition reduces firm power and increases consumer welfare. Generally, in the economics literature, more competition refers to growth in the *number* and *substitutability* of *competitors* in a market.[28] However, another way of thinking about competition is from the consumer side. For example, Lee et al. measure competitive intensity by the percentage of consumers who consider (at a given price) multiple offerings.[29] A somewhat similar approach found in the marketing literature is to measure competitiveness with cross-elasticities between brands (i.e. changes in sales of Brand A in response to a price change by Brand B).[30] These latter two definitions are in concert with marketing concepts of

---

[27] Timothy Muris, "The interface of competition and consumer protection," Paper presented at Fordham Corporate Law Institute's 29th Annual Conference on International Antitrust Law and Policy, New York (2002).

[28] See Sumit Agarwal, Changcheng Song, and Vincent Yao, "Banking competition and shrouded attributes: Evidence from the US mortgage market," (Oct. 20, 2022). https://ssrn.com/abstract=2900287 or http://dx.doi.org/10.2139/ssrn.2900287.

[29] Eunkyu Lee, Richard Staelin, Weon Sang Yoo, and Rex Du, "A 'meta-analysis' of multibrand, multioutlet channel systems," 59(9) MANAGEMENT SCIENCE 1950 (2013).

[30] See Greg M. Allenby and Peter E. Rossi, "Quality perceptions and asymmetric switching between brands," 10(3) MARKETING SCIENCE 186 (1991); Johannes Auer and Dominik Papies, "Cross-price elasticities and their determinants: A meta-analysis and new empirical generalizations," 48 JOURNAL OF THE ACADEMY OF MARKETING SCIENCE 584 (2020). A relevant, but less frequently used measure of competitive intensity is how competitive

differentiation, i.e. firms shield themselves from intense competition by offering unique attributes that appeal to different segments of the market. Taken together, these two different views of measuring competitive intensity imply that competition increases not only with more firms, but also with a greater proportion of consumers considering multiple offerings and thus being sensitive to the actions of the firms. Both forces drive firms, in their quest to win consumers, to also look for greater efficiency[31] and as such drive out the less efficient firms, which, in the case of false promotions, might be tempted to substitute dishonest representations for honest representations of their offerings in order to compete.

In this section, we briefly explore this perspective, labeling it Competition Proposition 1. We then contrast it with a competing school of thought (Competition Proposition 2) which offers the polar opposite proposition: greater competition may actually *motivate* competitors to hide or distort information about their offerings rather than step up to compete on price and quality. Finally, we go back to the Deng et al. model and show how it provides a third take on why firms might still offer false promotions under greater competition.

5.3.2.1 Competition Proposition 1: Competition Deters False Promotion

Armstrong describes a market behaving efficiently as one in which "only those firms which give consumers what they want can prosper."[32] Such a definition provides an articulation of the position presented by FTC Chairman Muris and follows in the steps of Chairman Pitofsky summarized early in the chapter.[33] It also is in concert with the marketing concept that firms should provide their customers with offerings that best meet their needs (i.e. maximize their utility). However, Armstrong qualifies this description by highlighting that this competitive self-discipline is strong only "when all product attributes and prices are easily observed and evaluated at the time of sale, when search costs are not significant, when consumers sample offers from

---

brands react to *each other*. Competitive reaction elasticities capture, for example, changes in the price of Brand A in response to a price change by Brand B, separate from cross-elasticity in demand between the two brands, see Peter S. H. Leeflang and Dick R. Wittink, "Competitive reaction versus consumer response: Do managers overreact?," 3(2) INTERNATIONAL JOURNAL OF RESEARCH IN MARKETING 103 (1996).

[31] See Chad Syverson, "Market structure and productivity: A concrete example," 112(6) JOURNAL OF POLITICAL ECONOMY 1181 (2004).

[32] Mark Armstrong, "Interactions between competition and consumer policy," 4(1) COMPETITION POLICY INTERNATIONAL 97 (2008) at p. 100.

[33] See Timothy J. Muris, *Creating a Culture of Competition: The Essential Role of Competition Advocacy* (US FTC, 2002); Timothy J. Muris and Paloma Zepeda, "The benefits, and potential costs, of FTC-style regulation in protecting consumers," 8 COMPETITION LAW INTERNATIONAL 11 (2012).

multiple suppliers, and when most consumers are capable of making reasonably good decisions concerning the product in question."[34]

Economists often refer to the conditions stated by Armstrong as "full information." Such conditions may seem obvious enough to be assumed implicitly. However, there is some evidence that the number of firms and the level of consumer sophistication in a market are not independent forces. Instead, they are inextricably linked. The effect of competition as measured by the number of firms and described by Muris and Armstrong depends in part on the alertness and knowledge of the consumer market in being able to fully understand and act rationally on the actions of the firms. Put somewhat differently, the key mechanism required for greater firm competition to monitor the marketplace is the ability of consumers to "detect and punish" firms that provide "non-desired" offerings (or in our case non-desired promotions).

Kahneman, Knetsch, and Thaler report the results of experiments showing that buyers believe it is fair for a firm to raise its price to defend its profit, if that profit is threatened by increases in the cost of inputs, but it is unfair to raise price in an effort to exploit excess demand or limited supply.[35] Feinberg, Krishna, and Zhang suggest consumers care about not only price offered to themselves but also price available to other consumers, and that their choices can be affected by perceived price unfairness.[36] Simply put, there appears to be other factors than just the actual price that consumers consider when determining if the price is "non-desired" and thus they should punish the firm.

In sum, a key requirement for Competition Proposition 1 to operate is a healthy consumer information environment, thereby endowing consumers the power to reward the best suppliers and punish those less effective and potentially less honest. This proposition finds its roots in the classical models of economic competition and assumes actors on both sides of the market are knowledgeable and informed about their options and market conditions.

5.3.2.2 Competition Proposition 2: Competition Motivates False Promotion

An alternative to Proposition 1 is that increased competition leads firms to take actions that foster false pricing and communications behavior. Before discussing the

---

[34] Armstrong, "Interactions between competition and consumer policy," p. 100.
[35] Daniel Kahneman, Jack L. Knetsch, and Richard Thaler, "Fairness as a constraint on profit seeking: Entitlements in the market," 76(4) AMERICAN ECONOMIC REVIEW 728 (1986). Daniel Kahneman, Jack L. Knetsch, and Richard H. Thaler, "Fairness and the assumptions of economics," 59(4) JOURNAL OF BUSINESS S285 (1986).
[36] Fred M. Feinberg, Aradhna Krishna, and Z. John Zhang, "Do we care what others get? A behaviorist approach to targeted promotions," 39(3) JOURNAL OF MARKETING RESEARCH 277 (2002).

mechanism for why this might occur, we first look at the evolution of false promotions and propose the likely path dependence of these practices in the retail marketplace.

5.3.2.2.1 Casual Empiricism: More Intense Retail Competition and Fictitious Sales Harkrader details the evolution of the retail trade post-World War II and the competitive conditions that created a takeoff point for false promotion practices.[37] Department stores had for decades relied on selling merchandise in multiple quality tiers with standard markup pricing (which matched manufacturers' suggested prices), while competing with other stores directly on service. In the 1950s, however, the entry of discount retailers disrupted this market by competing on price instead of service. They did this by lowering their costs with such actions as locating in low-cost suburban locations, reducing staff by implementing customer self-service, and eliminating most other services provided by department stores. Discounters then advertised their low prices "flamboyantly." As competition got more intense, this "triggered a chain reaction of extravagant pricing claims by both kinds of merchants, often abetted by inflated manufacturers' retail price lists and tickets."[38] In 1958, the FTC issued its "Guides Against Fictitious Pricing."

This scenario renewed itself in the 1970s and 1980s as "a rash of store openings intensified competition and forced retailers to look for new ways to stand out."[39] This increased competition was accompanied by a new dynamics of promotional pricing that lead regularly to the promotion of fictitious "regular" prices. Kapner described this pricing as follows: "A supplier sells the sweater to a retailer for roughly $14.50. The suggested retail price is $50, which gives the retailer a roughly 70% markup. A few sweaters sell at that price, but more sell at the first markdown of $44.99, and the bulk sell at the final discount price of $21.99."[40]

This cultural "sale mentality" has grown stronger rather than weaker. For example, when Ron Johnson took over as CEO of JC Penney in 2011, he found consumers receiving "an average discount of 60%, up from 38% a decade earlier. The twist was that consumers weren't saving more. In fact, the average price paid by customers stayed about the same over that period. What changed was the reference initial price (i.e. ERP), which increased by 33%."[41] According to this *New York Times* article, these practices were not limited to bricks-and-mortar outlets. In 2014,

---

[37] Carleton A. Harkrader, "Fictitious pricing and the FTC: A new look at an old dodge," 37 *ST. JOHN'S LAW REVIEW*. 1 (1962). See also Friedman, "Dishonest search disruption."
[38] Harkrader, "Fictitious pricing and the FTC," 5.
[39] Kapner, "The dirty secret of Black Friday 'discounts.'"
[40] Ibid.
[41] Farhad Manjoo, "Online deals for holiday shopping: Buyer beware," *THE NEW YORK TIMES* (Dec. 10, 2014).

two organizations researched 54,000 online deals around Black Friday, comparing advertised selling prices to other available prices on the Internet. They reported only 300 (less than 1 percent) to be good deals – i.e. deals representing legitimate savings.

The recent escalation of competition appears to have drawn retailers into a game of false promotions and reinforces Harkrader's comment decades ago: "whether businessmen might have preferred to operate otherwise or not, price competition forced them to advertise comparatively as their competitors did."[42] A number of firms that decided not to play in this game have paid a heavy price. For example, Sears' highly publicized switch away from heavy price promotion to an everyday low pricing (EDLP) strategy in the late 1980s led to a 63 percent drop in net income[43]. Despite a creative and energetic effort to alter JC Penney's heavy discounting promotional strategy, Mr. Johnson was unable to overcome his customers' need to feel like they were saving money. The company's stock price dropped over 50 percent in the last twelve months of Mr. Johnson's eighteen-month tenure as CEO.

In sum, historical patterns of retail competition suggest that, rather than reducing the incidence of false promotion, more intense competition is a *cause of it* or at least is associated with it. A firm may have little choice but to join the false promotion game and, once in, finds it highly unprofitable to leave. (That is not to imply that the firms have lower profits, only that false promotion is the equilibrium solution and thus no player wants to depart from this promotional strategy.)

In the next section, we discuss a recently proposed theory that might explain why competition may in fact increase, rather than decrease, false promotion. This theory implies that firms have an incentive to create complexity in order to gain market power especially in situations where they would otherwise not be able to exert such power. We then contrast this theory with the Deng et al. analytic model, which assumes that false promotions provide a mechanism that enables firms to maintain higher margins than they would if they never used false promotions, independent on the level of information complexity in the environment.

5.3.2.2.2 Firms Exploiting Boundedly Rational Consumers as Competitive Intensity Increases Since the Nobel Prize-winning work of George Stigler,[44] economists and researchers in marketing have sought to explain why prices differ across competitors for similar items. Over the last fifteen years, a literature has blossomed with an interesting explanation: prices differ because of noise or complexity (at times unnecessarily) produced by firms. Gabaix and Laibson were among the first to examine analytically how market noisiness could in fact be managed by

---

[42] Harkrader, "Fictitious pricing and the FTC," 5.
[43] Gwen Ortmeyer, John A. Quelch, and Walter Salmon, "Restoring credibility to retail pricing," 33(1) MIT SLOAN MANAGEMENT REVIEW 55 (1991).
[44] George J. Stigler, "The economics of information," 69(3) JOURNAL OF POLITICAL ECONOMY 13 (1961).

firms strategically in order to shield themselves from competition.[45] Their underlying assumption was that noise created by firms – e.g. complexity in product features or price and financing – reduces consumers' ability to know the true value or cost of a good with certainty.[46] Gabaix and Laibson model consumers' utility to be a function of both true value and noise, suggesting that noise about products initially creates positive utility for consumers (for example, in the form of more sophisticated products) but has an overall inverted-U-shaped relationship with value, peaking and then declining as noise grows. (In marketing lingo, when the firm differentiates its offering by adding new attributes, it provides real value at first. However, at some point the addition of attributes adds less value than the added confusion.)

Gabaix and Laibson's model has firm i decide on the price p_i and the level of product complexity σ_i. This level of complexity not only determines the intrinsic value of the product, but also affects "the standard deviation of the noise that will be perceived by the consumer."[47] Firm i chooses p_i and σ_i to maximize profits in an environment where consumers vary in their sophistication.

One of the results coming from their model is that increasing competition "tends to exacerbate the incentives for excess complexity" and "contradicts the standard economic intuition that competition increases consumer welfare."[48] One possible interpretation is that, if a firm does not have the best quality, it is incentivized to create noise or confusion to make assessment of its product difficult. Another viewpoint (coming from marketing strategy) has the firm, in the face of increased competition, creating variety in its product lines with the intent of meeting the needs of specific niche consumer markets. These extra features may result in (unintended) consumer confusion. What is important, however, is that, irrespective of the underlying mechanism that leads firms to add more complexity, Gabaix and Laibson's finding implies that increases in the number of competitors result in the information environment becoming more complex.

When firms add "noise," they seek to influence a customer's path to purchase, but without necessarily enabling all the consumers to obtain full disclosure of all the important facts. Examples include communication of false reference prices at which the item has never or only rarely been sold, shrouding additional fee or contract information until after purchase,[49] or attracting customers with a very low advertised

---

[45] See Xavier Gabaix and David Laibson, "Competition and consumer confusion," *HARVARD AND MIT MIMEO* (2004); Xavier Gabaix and David Laibson, "Shrouded attributes, consumer myopia, and information suppression in competitive markets," 121(2) *QUARTERLY JOURNAL OF ECONOMICS* 505 (2006).
[46] Note that their use of the term "noise" does not necessarily represent nonrelevant information. Instead they use this term to denote "complex" information that may not be easily understood by all consumers, i.e. it adds "noise" during the evaluation/decision-making process.
[47] Gabaix and Laibson, "Competition and consumer confusion," 8.
[48] Ibid., 20, 21.
[49] Gabaix and Laibson, "Shrouded attributes, consumer myopia."

price, only to lead them to purchase higher-priced options by making it difficult to find the low-priced item (i.e. by bait and switch[50]). All these firm actions are designed to exploit consumer naiveté, lack of information, or myopia by increasing complexity and thereby hiding information. What is most important here is that the theoretical model of Gabaix and Laibson implies that these behaviors should increase with competitive intensity.

A number of recent papers build upon the concepts of Gabaix and Laibson to look specifically at adding complexity associated with the pricing decision. Carlin models firms that choose both (1) price (e.g. interest rate) and their complexity (e.g. technical language in price disclosures) and shows that as competition increases, firms find it in their best interest to add complexity.[51] Chioveanu and Zhou develop an analytic model in which firms set prices and choose price frames.[52] Gamp and Krahmer allow firms to choose both price and quality levels, where quality can either be superior or inferior (deceptive).[53] In each model, firms have some opportunity to create confusion for consumers, and find it profitable to do so under many circumstances.

Carlin's paper is interesting in that it provides deeper intuition than just an inverted-U-shaped utility curve on why firms might want to add obfuscation in more competitive environments. He notes that a given firm faces a double-whammy when competition increases. First, just by sheer numbers, the probability that a firm will win business from the sophisticated consumer segment shrinks. Second, with more competitive options to evaluate, the consumer's search and choice task becomes more challenging (i.e. the cost of search rises) – and thus there will be *fewer consumers* who will take the time to evaluate all of them. As such, the firm's chance of winning a sophisticated consumer's business declines even more. Consequently, it turns to attracting naïve consumers by adding more "extraneous" information. Making more noise (creating more uncertainty) in fact increases the size of the naïve consumer segment beyond just the effects associated with the addition of more consumer offerings.

---

[50] Glenn Ellison and Sara Fisher Ellison, "Search, obfuscation, and price elasticities on the Internet," 77(2) ECONOMETRICA 427 (2009).

[51] Bruce I. Carlin, "Strategic price complexity in retail financial markets," 91(3) JOURNAL OF FINANCIAL ECONOMICS 278 (2009).

[52] Ioana Chioveanu and Jidong Zhou, "Price competition with consumer confusion," 59(11) MANAGEMENT SCIENCE 2450 (2013). Chioveanu and Zhou define price frames as different methods of presenting price that make competitive comparison difficult, e.g. inconsistent use of unit prices or complex tariff schemes, or varying price presentation over time. They provide an example of changing price presentation frames over time for the Body Shop (cosmetics retailers), which "offered a '$10 off for any $20 purchase on November 27, 2012; it changed to a deal of 'up to 50% off' on October 2, 2012; and it offered a deal of 'buy 2 get 2 free' on October 7, 2012" (p. 2450).

[53] Tobias Gamp and Daniel Krähmer, "Deception and competition in search markets." No. crctr224_014_2018. University of Bonn and University of Mannheim, Germany (2018).

Regardless of the underlying mechanism, as summarized by Spiegler, it appears that:

> [fostering] competition in a market with rational consumers (increasing the number of competitors, introducing an attractive outside option) may have adverse welfare effects when consumers are limited in their ability to evaluate complex objects. The reason is that firms respond to increased competition by obfuscating, rather than by acting more competitively.[54]

Finally, there is empirical support for these ideas. An example is a study by Agarwal, Song, and Yao, which examined the effects of deregulation of financial services on banks' contract design for adjustable rate mortgages (ARMs).[55] They find that deregulation dramatically increased competition, by producing a 38 percent increase in the number of competitive banks and a 13 percent increase in loan activity in states in which the law was implemented (vs. those in which it was not implemented). However, at the same time as this increased competition, the deregulated banks were "shrouding" *less favorable* back-end terms (shorter fixed terms in months and higher reset margins hidden in contracts) while promoting *more favorable* front-end terms (lower initial interest rates).

Greater Competition and the Probability of Getting Caught. It should be noted that Competition Proposition 2 (i.e. competition *motivates* false promotion and other deceptive firm behaviors), is modeled explicitly around conditions in which consumer search and understanding are more limited. As such, the "detect and punish" mechanism that is so critical to Competition Proposition 1 (i.e. that competition *deters* false promotion) is absent or substantially weakened. A central concept that would support Competition Proposition 2, then, is simply that a firm generally has a lower *probability of getting caught* in deception, either by the consumer or by some other mechanism such as a regulator. Some recent work in marketing analyzes the impact of this concept in explaining the likelihood that a firm will follow the rules of the game. Branco and Villas-Boas build an analytic model in which firms must compete following a set of rules determined by laws, regulations, and social practices or pressures, which directly affect profitability by impacting the marginal cost of production, as well as the expected liability if the rules are broken. Regarding increasing competition, their chief conclusion is: "The intuition is that with more competition, firms have less to lose if they are caught breaking the market rules and therefore are more likely to be less careful about respecting those rules."[56]

This discussion does not require consumer monitoring of the rules, but instead is entirely dependent on the firm's costs and the probability of getting caught.

---

[54] Ran Spiegler, "Competition over agents with boundedly rational expectations," 1(2) THEORETICAL ECONOMICS 207 (2006) at p. 209.

[55] Agarwal, Song, and Yao, "Banking competition and shrouded attributes."

[56] Fernando Branco and J. Miguel Villas-Boas, "Competitive vices," 52(6) JOURNAL OF MARKETING RESEARCH Russell S. Winer, a reference price model of brand choice for frequently purchased 801, 804 (2015).

However, if breaking the rules also implies that the firm provides "noisy" information to the consumer, thereby decreasing the consumer's ability to detect the firm breaking rules, then both explanations imply the same thing, i.e. increased competition leads to more false promotions.

Linking this to the earlier discussion, greater competition and a condition of bounded rationality for consumers (i.e. more limited search and knowledge), are likely to have a powerful joint effect in reducing the probability that a firm will get caught in deception. These conditions would provide important explanations for the persistence of false promotions.

5.3.2.3 Deng et al. Analysis: Greater Competition Is a Weak, Conditional Deterrent

Deng et al. do not explicitly model changes in the information environment, but instead vary the amount of "noise" by varying the percentage of the population that are naïve/sophisticated and the effectiveness of WOM, neither of which is assumed to be a function of the level of competition. Thus, their model setup is not directly comparable with the model of Gabaix and Laibson and those that built on their model structure. Still, it is interesting to compare findings across the different models. The Deng et al. analytic model, although showing a general decrease in the prevalence of false promotions with increases in competitive intensity, also finds that even at the highest level of competition (i.e. there is no spatial or product differentiation between the two offerings), false promotion still occurs over 20 percent of the time. At first, this result may seem counterintuitive and against all of the prior results of pure competition. However, the Deng et al. results are averaged over all possible consumer knowledge settings. In some of these settings, there were a small number of (or no) sophisticated consumers or a small (or no) effect of WOM. In these instances, extreme competitive intensity (even pure competition) is not able to completely protect consumer interests.

The absence of many sophisticated consumers and/or little WOM is akin to having substantial information noise. Put slightly differently, if increased competition decreases the number of sophisticated consumers and/or the efficiency of WOM, the Deng et al. model also shows that the firms will be more likely to offer false promotions. However, their model does not rely on adding noise to the system, only the existence of two types of consumers. Therefore, their explanation is less about adding noise and more about reducing the tendency of firms to only compete using real promotions. In this way, they show that false promotion is another way of softening competition.

5.3.2.4 Summary

The current section suggests two propositions that make diametrically opposed predictions about the relationship between level of competition and incidence of false promotion. While there are likely to be many different conditions moderating this relationship, we focus centrally on each proposition's respective assumptions about the strength of the consumer policing mechanism. Proposition 1 works if there is a sizable segment of sophisticated consumers in the marketplace who actively detect deceptive behavior and punish it with their patronage choices. Proposition 2 is based on the assumption that consumers are boundedly rational, searching more limitedly and thus less omniscient about market conditions, an environment which has been shown analytically and empirically to lead firms to provide noisy information as competition increases. The Deng et al. analysis provides some support for both propositions. It does not assume (or show) that firms will produce noisier information at higher levels of competition, and shows that the frequency of false promotions decreases with increases in competition. However, it also shows that as long as there exists a significant segment of naïve consumers, firms will offer false promotions even at the highest levels of competitive intensity, i.e. competition will not eliminate the occurrence of false promotions. Next in Section 5.3.3, we will present relevant empirical findings about the extent of consumers' information search and their response to false promotions in durables markets.

5.3.3 Question 3: Does Greater Consumer Sophistication Drive Out False Promotion?

5.3.3.1 Consumer Segments

The tradition of representing different segments of consumers in analytic pricing models began with Salop and Stiglitz.[57] In the spirit of parsimony, they assumed there existed only two types of consumers, one with high search costs, the other with lower search costs. This convention of assuming two different consumer segments was quickly adopted by others who similarly sought to explain how consumer information shaped firms' pricing behavior.[58] Deng et al. do not model consumer search behavior per se, since both naïve and sophisticated consumers are assumed to be aware of prices at both competitive stores each period. However, they recognize that there are two different segments of consumers with respect to how they process this information. We next discuss the external validity of these two assumed segments and the implications of this segmentation in terms of the FTC's assertion that a large number of consumers can self-regulate any misleading price advertising behavior that might exist in the marketplace.

---

[57] Steven Salop and Joseph Stiglitz, "Bargains and ripoffs: A model of monopolistically competitive price dispersion," 44(3) REVIEW OF ECONOMIC STUDIES 493 (1977).

[58] See Hal R. Varian, "A model of sales," 70(4) AMERICAN ECONOMIC REVIEW 651 (1980); Louis L. Wilde and Alan Schwartz, "Equilibrium comparison shopping," 46(3) REVIEW OF ECONOMIC STUDIES 543 (1979).

As discussed earlier, Deng et al.'s two segments are labeled as "naïve" and "sophisticated" consumers. Both segments get positive utility from all promotions they believe are true, but only sophisticated consumers are able to detect false promotions from which they get negative utility. What's more, they spread the word about false promotions when they see them. In this way, they are tougher than assumed by the FTC.

The Deng et al. analytic model indicates that the sophisticated segment must be at least 50 percent of all consumers for sellers to shift completely away from false promotions and, even then, this only occurs at the end of their game. Deng and her coauthors do not discuss the likelihood of at least 50 percent of the market being composed of sophisticated consumers, but numerous papers in marketing and psychology provide estimates of the size of this consumer segment. We discuss this evidence in more detail next.

5.3.3.2 What Proportion of Consumers Actively Search for Price (a Qualification of Sophisticates)?

As noted, naïve and sophisticated consumers in the Deng et al. model do not vary in their current-period search behavior per se, but Sophisticates must be confident enough in their price knowledge to know when they see a false promotion. A reasonable extension is that Sophisticates are the more experienced segment who have conducted more search over time and are attentive to all prices in their search. This premise was the foundation for the approach used by Nwge when he explored the heterogeneity of responses to false promotion and found that, in situations where there was more opportunity for consumers to gather competitive pricing information, the response to false promotions was less.

Research in marketing suggests that consumer segments that conduct extensive searches are a minority of the consumer population. Documenting this lack of extensive search behavior goes back at least to the early 1970s.[59] This long empirical literature on search is summarized by Moorthy, Ratchford, and Talukdar in the following way: "A puzzling but consistent empirical finding is that consumers exhibit very limited pre-purchase information-search activity, even for high-ticket durable goods."[60] This heterogeneity in consumer search has been observed in a variety of contexts. For example, Furse, Punj, and Stewart discovered a "high

---

[59] See Joseph W. Newman and Richard Staelin, "Multivariate analysis of differences in buyer decision time," 8(2) JOURNAL OF MARKETING RESEARCH 192 (1971); Joseph W. Newman and Richard Staelin, "Prepurchase information seeking for new cars and major household appliances," 9(3) JOURNAL OF MARKETING RESEARCH 249 (1972).

[60] Sridhar Moorthy, Brian T. Ratchford, and Debabrata Talukdar, "Consumer information search revisited: Theory and empirical analysis," 23(4) JOURNAL OF CONSUMER RESEARCH 263 (1997). See also Beales, Craswell, and Salop, "The efficient regulation of consumer information."

search" (price-driven) segment and a "self-reliant" segment in a large-scale study of consumer automobile purchasers.[61] Each of these consumer groups spent more time on searches than the other groups and considered a larger number of makes and models. Together, however, the high-search and self-reliant segments accounted for only 17 percent of the consumer population. In retail grocery markets, a similarly small proportion of consumers (22–24 percent) regularly shop two or more stores.[62] Shopping two or more stores on a given day to "cherry pick" price specials – once thought by retail executives to be the price-search strategy of the *majority* of consumers – actually describes only 7 to 13 percent of consumer households.[63] These findings are not limited to shopping in bricks-and-mortar environments. Studies of price dispersions and consumer online search reach surprisingly similar conclusions.[64] For example, Johnson et al.'s study of online search in the book, music, and travel categories led them to conclude: "Our results suggest that people visit few stores online despite the fact that consumers are 'just a mouse click away' from other stores."[65] A longitudinal study on consumer search in the automobile market by Dehdashti, Ratchford, and Namin examined the consumer segments identified in Furse, Punj, and Stewart study discussed above and find that the Internet had become a more central search tool for some segments.[66] However, the two "heavy search" segments identified in this new research accounted for only 24 percent of the consumer population.[67]

---

[61] David H. Furse, Girish N. Punj, and David W. Stewart, "A typology of individual search strategies among purchasers of new automobiles," 10(4) JOURNAL OF CONSUMER RESEARCH 417 (1984).

[62] See Joel E. Urbany, Peter R. Dickson, and Alan G. Sawyer, "Insights into cross-and within-store price search: retailer estimates vs. consumer self-reports," 76(2) JOURNAL OF RETAILING 243 (2000); Joel E. Urbany, Peter R. Dickson, and Rosemary Key, "Actual and perceived consumer vigilance in the retail grocery industry," 2(1) MARKETING LETTERS 15 (1991).

[63] Edward Fox and Stephen J. Hoch, "Cherry-picking," 69 JOURNAL OF MARKETING 46–62 (2005).

[64] Michael R. Baye, John Morgan, and Patrick Scholten, "Information, search, and price dispersion," 1 HANDBOOK ON ECONOMICS AND INFORMATION SYSTEMS 323 (2006); Xing Pan, Brian T. Ratchford, and Venkatesh Shankar, "Price dispersion on the Internet: A review and directions for future research," 18(4) JOURNAL OF INTERACTIVE MARKETING 116 (2004).

[65] Eric J. Johnson, Wendy W. Moe, Peter S. Fader, Steven Bellman, and Gerald L. Lohse, "On the depth and dynamics of online search behavior," 50(3) MANAGEMENT SCIENCE 299 (2004). See also Jun B. Kim, Paulo Albuquerque, and Bart J. Bronnenberg, "Online demand under limited consumer search," 29(6) MARKETING SCIENCE 1001 (2010); Bart J. Bronnenberg, Jun B. Kim, and Carl F. Mela, "Zooming in on choice: How do consumers search for cameras online?," 35(5) MARKETING SCIENCE 693 (2016).

[66] Yashar Dehdashti, Brian T. Ratchford, and Aidin Namin, "Who searches where? A new car buyer study," 6(2) JOURNAL OF MARKETING ANALYTICS 42 (2018); Furse, Punj, and Stewart, "A typology."

[67] Dehdashti, Ratchford, and Namin did identify a separate "self-reliant" segment similar to Furse, Punj, and Stewart, but did not categorize it as a heavy search segment. In recent years, this segment showed more moderate search, focused primarily on books and car ratings.

A number of researchers have built models to explain *why* rational consumers might not continue to look for the lowest price, but instead exhibit the type of limited search behavior discussed above. The common thread across these studies is the idea that consumers search *sequentially*.[68] In sequential search, a consumer rank-orders unsearched options based upon uncertain estimates of their likely value for money. Once the top candidate is searched, it serves as a "bird in the hand," and the benefit of searching further is evaluated by considering the chance that one of the remaining options has greater value. Search stops when the expected value of the best unsearched option (after subtracting search cost) is less than the value of the option in hand. Higher search costs will lessen the expected value of unsearched alternatives and reduce search, as will factors that enhance the value of the best option in hand.

This sequential model provides an intuitively appealing account of search behavior and appears to be an accurate description in many durables markets.[69] It also conforms to the observation over many years that consumer search is surprisingly limited and, accordingly, the segment of actively searching consumers in a market is relatively small. "Small" would mean proportions of actively searching consumers in the range of 15–25 percent in most markets. This is far below the 40–50 percent that Deng et al. find necessary to discipline the market for false promotions.

In sum, if we use this 15–25 percent benchmark as a rough surrogate for the representation of Sophisticates in the market, we conclude that they do not appear in large enough numbers to drive the market to a fully honest equilibrium devoid of false promotion. Even with this noted, there is another reality that appears to further shrink the market policing power of the Sophisticates. Specifically, other (nonrational) behaviors have been identified which suggest that at least some of the Sophisticates will *not* punish a firm's false promotion. They will instead be taken in by it. We summarize some of these behaviors.

5.3.3.2.1 A Puzzling, yet Robust Finding about Consumer Response to False Promotions Let's say you are in the market for a television set and seven stores carry them locally. One day you see that one of the stores is advertising a TV brand with features that interests you. The TV is on sale for $319 at this store. With this as the backdrop, envision an experimental study in which different groups of participants are presented with different offers, varying only in the presence and level of a "Regular Price" in the offer. Consider the three offers in Table 5.2.

---

[68] Martin L. Weitzman, "Optimal search for the best alternative," 47(3) ECONOMETRICA 641 (1979).
[69] See Jun B. Kim and Carl F. Mela, "Zooming in on choice"; William L. Wilkie and Peter R. Dickson, *Shopping for Appliances: Consumers' Strategies and Patterns of Information Search* (Marketing Science Institute, 1985); Moorthy, Ratchford, and Talukdar, "Consumer information search revisited."

TABLE 5.2. *Examples of three possible promotions*

	(A)	(B) (Control)	(C) (True promotion)	(D) (False promotion)
		Sale! Now $319	Sale! Reg. $419 Now $319	Sale! Reg. $799 Now $319
Believable savings (index)		100	105	73
Estimated average market price		$343	$361	$467
Perceived offer value (index)		100	115	131
% buying at advertiser, no search		19%	24%	35%
Gross profit* (index)		100	126	233

*Assumes $319 price and 40% unit gross margin.

The particular study by Urbany, Bearden, and Weilbaker involved a computer-based shopping simulation in which participants could, at a cost, "travel" to competing stores for price information.[70] Columns B, C, and D in Table 5.2 show three different advertisements given to different groups in the study. The column B ad offers no reference price as a control, while C and D present ads with plausible (true) and exaggerated (false) reference prices, respectively. Column A presents a subset of the variables measured during this simulated shopping experience, the first three taken prior to the search task and the last two outcome measures.

The results tell a clear, if somewhat paradoxical story. Participants who saw the false promotion "Reg. $799, Now $319" (Column D) found it significantly less believable than did those who saw the other ads. Yet of the three ads, *the false promotion* had the *greatest influence* on participant beliefs and produced the highest sales conversion and by far the highest gross profit for the advertising retailer.

This result is surprising in that it goes against the standard economic assumption that consumers are rational. A rational consumer should only consider the price needed to buy the product. All other information about what might have been the past price is not relevant. Yet we saw in Section 5.3.1 that reference prices do affect consumer behavior. What is surprising in the described experiment is that this effect

[70] Joel E. Urbany, William O. Bearden, and Dan C. Weilbaker, "The effect of plausible and exaggerated reference prices on consumer perceptions and price search," 15(1) *JOURNAL OF CONSUMER RESEARCH* 95 (1988).

occurs even when consumers do not find the reference price believable. Importantly, this effect has been replicated many times in the literature,[71] and emerges as a central conclusion in Compeau and Grewal's meta-analysis of thirty-eight different reference price studies.[72] These authors conclude that their meta-analysis "leaves little doubt that comparative price advertisements work ... Overall, the potential for deception seems rife because external reference prices have a strong influence on consumers, even when they are exaggerated."[73]

Anchoring and (at least Some) Susceptible Sophisticates. The most widely acknowledged behavioral explanation for this inflated reference price effect is *anchoring*, a subtle "power of suggestion" appearing in the form of information that happens to be processed early in a judgment task. The effect of that early information, even if it is considered irrelevant or is discounted, tends to linger as one goes through the task, affecting judgments that occur later.[74] Essentially, once seen, a high, inflated "Regular" price in a false promotion is difficult to "unsee." Biswas et al. describe it this way:

---

[71] See Scot Burton, Donald R. Lichtenstein, and Paul M. Herr, "An examination of the effects of information consistency and distinctiveness in a reference-price advertisement context," 23(24) JOURNAL OF APPLIED SOCIAL PSYCHOLOGY 2074 (1993); Balaji C. Krishnan, Sujay Dutta, and Subhash Jha, "Effectiveness of exaggerated advertised reference prices: The role of decision time pressure," 89(1) JOURNAL OF RETAILING 105 (2013).

[72] Compeau and Grewal, "Comparative price advertising," p. 263.

[73] Ibid. There are naturally boundary conditions to this effect. For example, in the same study, Urbany, Bearden, and Weilbaker found that the exaggerated reference price ad was less influential in determining search at a very low sale price ($279). This was because this sale price was recognized as a very good price by a large proportion of participants, leading about 40 percent of them to go straight to the advertising store to buy, independent of the advertisement they saw. Similarly, Suter and Burton (Tracy A. Suter and Scot Burton, "Believability and consumer perceptions of implausible reference prices in retail advertisements," 13(1) PSYCHOLOGY & MARKETING 37 (1996)) found that those who were most skeptical of a false promotion in some cases reported deal evaluations that were less influenced or not influenced by an inflated reference price than those who believed it more (although price expectations were affected similarly for both groups).

[74] See Amos Tversky and Daniel Kahneman, "Judgment under uncertainty: Heuristics and biases," 185(4157) SCIENCE 1124 (1974); Burton, Lichtenstein, and Herr, "An examination of the effects of information"; Gretchen B. Chapman and Eric J. Johnson, "Anchoring, activation, and the construction of values," 79(2) ORGANIZATIONAL BEHAVIOR AND HUMAN DECISION PROCESSES 115 (1999). The earliest mention of anchoring was Lichtenstein and Slovic's (Sarah Lichtenstein and Paul Slovic, "Reversals of preference between bids and choices in gambling decisions," 89(1) JOURNAL OF EXPERIMENTAL PSYCHOLOGY 46 (1971) at p. 54) observation that preference reversals for gambles tended to occur when a subject "starts with the amount to win and adjusts it downwards to take into account the other attributes of the bet." Tversky and Kahneman (in "Judgment under uncertainty") examined anchoring directly, exposing experimental subjects to random information before asking them to make judgments. They famously report the often-cited finding that the random number obtained from the spin of a wheel had a significant impact on participants' later estimates of the number of African countries in the UN.

[A]n initial starting point (relevant or irrelevant) is used as the anchor for a judgment or estimation of values of unknown objects. This anchor is then adjusted to reflect implications of other information provided by external sources such as the semantic or focal cues. However, the adjustments are generally insufficient and lead to estimates that are biased in the direction of the initial anchor.[75]

The anchoring effect has been widely studied and validated in both experimental and real-market contexts (see, for example, Beggs and Graddy's study of art auctions in the *American Economic Review*, which reports "finding strong support for anchoring," as distinct from rational learning[76]). In the context of false promotion, an important implication is that some sophisticated consumers who recognize an inflated reference price as false can still be influenced by it in a way that favors the false promoter.

The anchoring and (incomplete) adjustment phenomenon is not the only possible biasing factor in the consumer's search process. If we continue following the customer's journey from perception to actual behavior, there is another potential effect of the abnormally high valuation that an exaggerated reference price can produce. We provide more detail next.

5.3.3.3 Search Disruption

Consistent with the logic of limited search (Section 5.3.3.2), there has been discussion, both in the marketing literature and in legal circles, that promotional tactics such as false promotions potentially have the effect of disrupting search – that is, to *encourage consumers to stop or limit their search* and to purchase from the firm that is presenting the offering deceptively. Lindsey-Mullikin and Petty review twelve different "bargain assurance" tactics which have the potential to reduce search deceptively.[77] Similarly, Friedman discusses a variety of tactics (including fictitious price discounts) as having the capacity for "dishonest search disruption."[78] The results found in Table 5.2 provide a clear illustration of such a disruption. Compeau and Grewal's meta-analysis cited earlier provides additional empirical support for the search disruption account.[79] They find both the presence of external/advertised reference prices (vs. their absence) and increases in reference prices – to the point of implausibility – significantly *reduced* consumers' intentions to

---

[75] Abhijit Biswas, Chris Pullig, Balaji C. Krishnan, and Scot Burton, "Consumer evaluation of reference price advertisements: Effects of other brands' prices and semantic cues," 18(1) JOURNAL OF PUBLIC POLICY & MARKETING 52 (1999) at p. 62.
[76] Alan Beggs and Kathryn Graddy, "Anchoring effects: Evidence from art auctions," 99(3) AMERICAN ECONOMIC REVIEW 1027 (2009).
[77] Joan Lindsey-Mullikin and Ross D. Petty, "Marketing tactics discouraging price search: Deception and competition," 64(1) JOURNAL OF BUSINESS RESEARCH 67 (2011).
[78] Friedman, "Dishonest search disruption."
[79] See Compeau and Grewal, "Comparative price advertising."

search.[80] Somewhat analogous are the previously reported findings of Jindal, that show higher ERP leads to fewer consumers negotiating discounts.

A real marketplace example of how the presence of ERPs can disrupt the search process is included in the findings of *California v. Overstock.com*. This legal case concerned claims that Overstock's use of inflated external "compare at" prices violated both California's False Advertising Law and its Unfair Competition Law. The state argued that Overstock's ERPs on its website were higher than the actual comparative market prices at which similar items were sold elsewhere. With the hopes of demonstrating that these comparative prices had no impact on consumer decision-making, Overstock.com undertook tests where it removed the "compare at" prices and observed the percentage change in customers who stopped searching, i.e. they bought the product on the website. They found that displaying ERPs in pricing statements (versus not showing them) increased the probability that customers complete the buying process by between 0.3 and 13 percent. Put slightly differently, these increased sales conversions reflect consumers' decisions to stop searching elsewhere. Although later studies that used better controls showed smaller effects than early tests, Judge Wynne Carvill argued in his decision that – because that most products in the tests were commodities – the Overstock tests likely underestimated the overall effect of including the ERPs for other categories in which effects would likely be larger. He concluded that even a 1 percent gain in sales conversion attributable to inflated ERPs (called ARPs at trial) was sizable, noting that "those in the best position to know at Overstock firmly believed that ARPs affected consumer behavior in a material, positive way ... a 1% increase in conversion rate is viewed as a 'home run' by a retailer like Overstock (Trial at 916) and the raison d'etre for using ARPs."[81] By our calculation, with rough estimates of daily website visitors and $1.5 billion in annual revenue around the time of the case, a 1 percent increase in the rate at which website visitors stopped their search and made a purchase at Overstock.com translates to an incremental $15 million in sales revenue annually.[82]

---

[80] Also see Dhruv Grewal, Kent B. Monroe, and Ramayya Krishnan, "The effects of price-comparison advertising on buyers' perceptions of acquisition value, transaction value, and behavioral intentions," 62(2) JOURNAL OF MARKETING 46 (1998); Albert J. Della Bitta, Kent B. Monroe, and John M. McGinnis, "Consumer perceptions of comparative price advertisements," 18(4) JOURNAL OF MARKETING RESEARCH 416 (1981).

[81] PEOPLE OF THE STATE OF CALIFORNIA, Plaintiff, vs. OVERSTOCK.COM, INC., Defendant. No. RGlo–546833 TENTATIVE RULING AND PROPOSED STATEMENT OF DECISION, Jan. 3, 2014.

[82] This assumes annual sales of $1.5 billion, 1 million website visitors per day, a conversion rate of 3.71 percent which grows by 1 percent to 3.747 percent when comparison prices are added to the prices presented on the website (the conversion rates come from Test 4, which the Overstock.com expert felt was most reliable). The increased conversion provides 371 additional purchasers per day, worth an average of $110.77 for incremental revenue attributable to inflated comparison prices of $41,096 daily and $15 million annually. The revenue and visitor numbers come from the company's website (www.overstock.com/16-sweet-facts-about-overstock).

5.3.3.4 Summary: Consumer Vigilance around Price Does Not Appear to Be Sufficient to Police the Market for False Promotions

The analytic model presented in Section 5.2 of this chapter provides the guidance that – in light of firms' economic motivations – false promotion can only be driven out of a market with *a sizable army* of sophisticated consumers. Empirical research in marketing, however, suggests that in most consumer markets, the size of the more knowledgeable (sophisticated) segment of price searchers is not likely to be large enough to win that battle (or even close). To make matters worse, it has been well-established empirically that – as a likely result of anchoring – at least a portion of those skeptical consumers may be taken in by the very promotional claims that they recognize to be false.

The implications of these findings are significant. The Deng et al. model incorporates the two important forces – specifically legal, intense competition and vigilant, sophisticated consumers who pass on information to less informed consumers – needed to lead firms to reduce or even eliminate false promotions. However, one of the model's key insights is around the *absolute levels* of these forces required to largely minimize deceptive promotions. These levels are quite large, and are not likely to occur in the actual marketplace.[83] Importantly, the empirical evidence reviewed in Sections 5.3.2 and 5.3.3 shows the interaction of these two forces resulting in the likelihood that the magnitude of consumer force is limited in very competitive environments. In addition, recent empirical analyses of *firm transactional data* show (a) there is a clear opportunity for firms to increase their profits by exaggerating ERPs if they chose to (study by Jindal), and (b) there exists actual, significant incremental revenue and profit returns directly attributable to false promotion (study by Ngwe).

As such, the evidence reviewed here fits the observation that false promotions have persisted and there is little evidence that they will shrink over time. From a regulatory perspective, then, the question becomes – does it matter? Section 5.3.4 provides brief consideration of the complex issue of how false promotion may affect industry, firm, and consumer welfare.

5.3.4 Observations about Welfare

The issue of consumer information and firm behavior – with false promotion being an important subset – has received substantial attention in the economics, law, and marketing literatures in the past thirty years. That attention, along with both the

---

[83] Note that this is not intended to be a statement about the realism of the Deng et al. model (or lack thereof). It is instead a statement about the low likelihood that competition and consumer sophistication serve as strong policing mechanisms for controlling or eliminating deception in the actual marketplace.

Deng et al. analysis and the empirical evidence presented in this chapter, all give strong indication that false promotions are a persistent economic phenomenon in the marketplace.

Given this, the question still remains, "Does this practice affect welfare in the market?" Even if FTC leadership conceded that false promotions do in fact influence consumer judgment and choice, their stance over the last forty years would suggest it doesn't matter. If markets are price-competitive (in part, the FTC might add, *because of* aggressive promotional advertising!), then consumers following even falsely exaggerated price promotion ads will find their way to low prices, thus avoiding harm. The following discussion provides a brief set of observations about consumer, firm/industry, and total or societal welfare.

5.3.4.1 Consumer Welfare

The concept of consumer welfare is well established in both the economics and legal literatures, albeit with slightly different emphases. In legal proceedings, welfare is thought of in the form of injury or harm. In an incisive review of frameworks for damages analysis in consumer class actions involving deception, August Horvath (Chapter 13 in this volume) elaborates on two central damages models; restitution and benefit-of-the-bargain. Restitution essentially involves the wrongdoing seller returning an amount to the consumer to compensate for the inflated price the consumer paid as a result of the advertising that falsely boosted the product's value. As Horvath describes, restitution captures "the amount that the consumer paid minus the amount that the consumer would have had to pay to purchase the product in the but-for world where the false claim was not made." The second damages model – benefit-of-the-bargain (also known as expectations damages[84]) – uses a similar "but-for" logic, but based instead upon the consumer's perception of the value that was promised by the seller (and their willingness to pay for it) rather than actual market prices. This latter model takes the perspective of seeking to "place the parties where they would have been if the transaction had been completed successfully with all promises kept."[85] As such, it determines damages by comparing the value that consumers saw in the product as advertised (falsely) with the value they would have received if the seller had presented the product truthfully.

Each model, then, is faced with the challenge of estimating prices in a counterfactual "but-for" world; the models differ in that restitution damages depends upon estimates of actual market prices while benefit-of-the-bargain damages instead generally focus on consumer perceived value and willingness to pay.

---

[84] Mark A. Allen et al., "Reference Guide on Estimation of Economic Damages," in *NATIONAL RESEARCH COUNCIL REFERENCE MANUAL ON SCIENTIFIC EVIDENCE* 3rd ed. (National Academies Press, 2011). https://doi.org/10.17226/13163.
[85] Horvath, Chapter 13 in this volume.

This framing of welfare is similar in spirit to that found in economics. In this latter case the standard definition of consumer welfare is consumer surplus – i.e. the difference between the price paid and the price the consumer is willing to pay with full information about the product and the competitive offerings. This definition makes clear there are three "prices" associated with measuring consumer welfare (and thus any injury) in false promotion situations. Importantly, two of these prices can be hard to determine, i.e. the perceived value of the offering and the prices associated with competitive offerings. We look at these two components next.

The first measurement issue concerns determining if there are any differences between consumers' valuation of a falsely promoted product at the time they actually purchased it and the valuation they *would have had* with accurate reference price information. The challenge with estimating whether consumers are led to misperceive value based upon false promotions centers on how to estimate the counterfactual "valuation the consumer would have had with truthful information." Perhaps the most promising approach – conjoint analysis – has been used increasingly to identify the true value of attributes and to evaluate damages in patent and advertising deception litigation. Moreover, leading experts have provided significant insights into valid applications of this technique.[86] With this noted, the actual application of conjoint analysis remains inconsistent and controversial.[87] Horvath (Chapter 13 in this volume) provides an interesting account of how the use of conjoint analysis has evolved in class action cases of consumer deception.

The ambiguity associated with linking the price paid by the plaintiff-consumer and the actual competitive price information against which to compare it is twofold. One difficulty is *timing*, i.e. getting accurate price information from competitive firms to align with the specific time of the transaction in question. A second and larger concern is *comparability*, i.e. finding the *same item* with the *same feature set* as that purchased at other stores to determine potential loss. Comparability is especially challenging in durable product categories in light of the common manufacturer strategy of creating different branded variants for competitive retailers in a given market.[88]

Setting these issues aside, and even with guidance from the two central damages frameworks discussed by Horvath (restitution and benefit-of-the-bargain), there appear to be varying methods and standards for assessing financial harm.

---

[86] See Greg M. Allenby et al., "Valuation of patented product features," 57 JOURNAL OF LAW AND ECONOMICS 630–31 (2014); Greg Allenby et al., "Calculating reasonable royalty damages using conjoint analysis," 45 (Spring) AIPLA QUARTERLY JOURNAL 234–35 (2017).

[87] See, for example, Suneal Bedi and David Reibstein, *Damaged damages: Errors in patent and false advertising litigation* (Kelley School of Business Research Paper, 2019).

[88] Cf. Mark Bergen et al., "Branded variants: A retail perspective," 33 JOURNAL OF MARKETING RESEARCH 9–10 (1996); Steven M. Shugan, "Pricing When Different Outlets Offer Different Assortments of Brands," in ISSUES IN PRICING: THEORY AND RESEARCH (Timothy Devinney ed. Lexington Books, 1988).

Friedman's work cited earlier reports that many cases have been ruled in favor of defendant firms because plaintiffs have been unable to demonstrate pecuniary harm.[89] He also provides an insightful discussion of the very different standards of judicial judgments between California and Illinois, where Illinois gives stricter attention to a standard of financial injury, and puts little weight on false valuation compared to California. Hamilton and Werner summarize four different methods commonly used for estimating class-wide financial damages in false promotion cases,[90] but also note that "providing defensible estimates ... has remained a significant stumbling block."[91] They illustrate this assertion by pointing out variation in judicial opinion even *within jurisdiction*. The California Central District Court granted class certification against JC Penney in 2015 based upon plaintiffs' damage estimates applying the full refund, profit disgorgement, and actual discount methods (the case was later settled for $50 million), while the same court ruled *against* these methods in a case against Kohl's less than a year later.[92]

5.3.4.2 Firm/Industry Welfare

Analytic models probably offer the most effective way to investigate, in general, the impact of false promotion practice, as well as its regulation, on firm and industry surplus and, thus, consumer welfare. As noted earlier, Deng et al. find that industry profits generally increase when firms use false promotions, although this effect is larger when competition is greater and consumer sophistication is weaker. Another analytic model, constructed by Armstrong and Chen, investigates the effects of regulation in a market where firms can post false promotions.[93] These researchers set up a model where a monopolist sets first and second period prices, product quality, and a reference price in the second period. They do this in an environment with or without regulation, and where the consumers are either all sophisticated or all naïve. In this way, they rule out the effects of competition and only focus on the

---

[89] Friedman, "Reconsidering fictitious pricing."
[90] These methods include: (1) *Full refund*, in which the plaintiff asks for an amount equal to the price they paid for the falsely advertised product; (2) *Profit disgorgement*, which involves seeking a payment equal to the defendant firm's profit on selling the item; (3) *Actual discount*, which applies the falsely advertised discount level to an estimate of the true reference price to determine the price that "should have been paid," then returns the portion actually paid over that amount; and (4) A *"Price–value differential"* approach, which most resembles consumer surplus (i.e. estimates the actual value of the item purchased, and again returns the portion paid over that amount).
[91] Stephen Hamilton and Dan Werner, "Keys to estimating damages in deceptive pricing cases," Weblog, Law360.com (2017).
[92] See ibid., footnote 3.
[93] Mark Armstrong and Yongmin Chen, "Discount pricing," 58(4) ECONOMIC INQUIRY 1614 (2019).

effects of informed consumers.[94] They also only allow for the existence of false promotions in the second period.

These authors, like Deng et al., find a number of conditions under which firms improve profitability by posting a false promotion (i.e. stating a higher first-period price than they actually charged in that period when they post second-period prices). Conclusions about industry profitability, however, depend upon the specific regulatory scenarios assumed for each model setting and the types of inferences that consumers make from seeing the first-period price. Not surprisingly, the authors find that the monopolist firm – and thus industry – was most profitable in a "laissez-faire" regulatory regime with naïve consumers who trust firms' price claims. However, the consumer welfare implications on the impact of regulation depend on the type of inferences consumers make from seeing the reference price. If consumers infer the quality level from the reference price used, a move to regulation improves efficiency and leads to higher quality (and higher first-period prices) compared to what the firm would do with no regulation. In addition, if second-period consumers are naïve, these consumers gain benefit compared to no regulation. In contrast, if consumers infer that since the item is on sale, the initial price was set too high for the quality, then a move to regulation only results in the firm charging a higher price (than if there was no regulation), but the firm does not increase the quality level, thereby reducing consumer welfare.

These are interesting findings since they directly address the impact of regulation in an industry (albeit an industry composed of one firm) that discounts its offerings over time. What may be most noteworthy is that the results depend significantly on how consumers view the reference price. Is it a sign of quality, or is it a sign of a poor choice of the initial (first-period) price? To the best of our knowledge, little is known about the inferences, if any, that consumers make about firm behavior when making their evaluation and purchase decisions. Do they really play the "sophisticated" game of inferring what the firm was doing last period in setting prices and qualities, or do they just look at the ERP and the sales price and determine if the sale is a "good deal"?

5.4 CONCLUSIONS

We began this chapter by noting that the FTC's decision to stop regulating false promotions was not informed by a formal analysis or empirical research. Although logically defended from the perspective of a rational model with competition and well-informed consumers as disciplining forces, their analysis is not particularly helpful for evaluating the mechanisms which might predict escalation of both discounting frequency and exaggeration of the reference prices.

---

[94] Another way of viewing their model is that all the firms are in total collusion, and thus this single firm represents the combined market.

We see three distinct research phases/approaches which together explain why false promotion persists. The first focuses on consumer behavior and identifies factors such as the explanatory power of transaction utility,[95] the robust effect of falsely inflated reference prices on even skeptical consumers,[96] and the potential disrupting effect of false promotion on already-limited consumer search.[97] Second, there are recent analytic models which demonstrate both the clear economic incentives that firms have for engaging in false promotion[98] and the potential accelerating impact that more intense competition may have on firms' efforts to obfuscate or deceive.[99] Third, we discussed two recent papers, respectively by Jindal and Ngwe, with large-scale data and empirical models that directly examine the effect of reference prices and false reference prices on consumer decisions and firm financial outcomes, each finding statistically and financially significant effects.

We agree with the assessment of Rhodes and Wilson that "Despite its prevalence and policy importance, false advertising remains understudied."[100] At the same time, we would note that there is a rich foundation of perspective and insight that has blossomed in economics, law, marketing, and psychology on the subject. Further, many of the papers cited in our chapter show a good deal of cross-fertilization. A paper that simultaneously cited work published in the *American Economic Review*, *Harvard Law Review*, *FTC Guides*, and the *Journal of Consumer Research* would have been a rarity even twenty years ago. Today, however, one can find many such examples of scholars studying false advertising/promotion who are drawing upon multiple disciplinary and methodological points of view.

In sum, there is little doubt that false promotion is a persistent economic phenomenon. There are at least two important questions that remain. First, does

---

[95] See e.g. Thaler, "Mental accounting and consumer choice"; Winer, "A reference price model."

[96] E.g. Grewal and Compeau, "Comparative price advertising"; Grewal and Compeau, "Interpretations of semantic phrases in comparative price advertisements"; Krishnan et al., "Effectiveness of exaggerated advertised reference prices."

[97] E.g. Beales, Craswel, and Salop, "The efficient regulation of consumer information"; Friedman, "Reconsidering fictitious pricing"; Friedman, "Dishonest search disruption"; Kaufman et al., "Deception in retailer high–low pricing"; Moorthy, Ratchford, and Talukdar, "Consumer information search revisited"; Urbany, Olsen, Kanuri, and Germann, Evaluating Harmless Deception; Urbany, Dickson, and Sawyer, "Insights into cross-and within-store price search"; Urbany, Dickson, and Key, "Actual and perceived consumer vigilance in the retail grocery industry"; Urbany, Bearden, and Weilbaker, "The effect of plausible and exaggerated reference prices."

[98] E.g. previously cited studies by Deng, Staelin, Wang, and Boulding, "Consumer sophistication, word-of-mouth and 'false' promotions"; Armstrong and Chen, "Discount pricing."

[99] E.g. previously cited study by Gabaix and Laibson, "Competition and consumer confusion"; Gabaix and Laibson, "Shrouded attributes, consumer myopia"; and the study by Ellison and Ellison, "Search, obfuscation, and price elasticities on the Internet."

[100] Rhodes, A. and Wilson, C. M. "False advertising," 49 RAND JOURNAL OF ECONOMICS, 348, 365 (2018). https://doi.org/10.1111/1756-2171.12228.

this practice affect welfare in a way that creates disproportionate gains and losses in the marketplace? Director Pitofsky was clearly quite passionate about his hypothesis of "no harm, no foul." Today, we have the joint benefit of behavioral, analytic, and econometric research traditions on which to draw to give that hypothesis a thorough test. Second, if society feels that the answer to the first question is "Yes, welfare is affected adversely and thus, needs to be addressed," then what are the possible solutions? One is via regulation. The Deng et al. model clearly demonstrates that firms would be worse off in terms of profits and consumers would see lower prices via true sales promotions if firms no longer had the option of competing using false promotions. A second approach would be education to strengthen consumer opposition to this practice. Again, the Deng et al. model shows that a larger proportion of knowledgeable consumers in the market reduces the prevalence of false promotions, but does not eliminate them. It would take a stronger consumer reaction, perhaps by increasing the disutility associated with potentially buying a product that was falsely promoted or consumers forming alliances and starting class actions against firms that use false promotions. Finally, competing firms may use the Lanham Act[101] to bring private lawsuits against another competitor for false advertising. Although this Act has normally been used for trademarks, the Supreme Court's decision in the 2014 *Pom Wonderful, LLC v. The Coca-Cola Company* case[102] legitimized a firm's application of the Lanham Act in bringing claims of false advertising against a competitor, increasing the likelihood of such cases in the future. Lawsuits brought forward by firms against their competitors may provide greater deterrence since larger firms bring more resources to such battles than do consumer class action lawsuits, the latter often financed via contingency fees.[103] Only time will tell which, if any, approach might be most effective.

---

[101] Lanham (Trademark) Act (Pub.L. 79–489, 60 Stat. 427, enacted July 5, 1946, codified at 15 U.S.C. § 1051 et seq. (15 U.S.C. ch. 22)
[102] *Pom Wonderful, LLC v. The Coca-Cola Company*, Oyez, www.oyez.org/cases/2013/12-761.
[103] Cases financed through contingency fees are essentially funded by the law firms who take them on. Bedi and Marra describe this practice as follows: "Contingency fee agreements allow illiquid or risk constrained litigants to permit lawyers to bear some or all of the financial costs and risks of litigation, in exchange for the attorney receiving a share of the rewards if the matter succeeds." See Suneal Bedi and William Marra, "The shadows of litigation finance," 74 VANDERBILT LAW REVIEW 563 (2021).

6

Brand Value, Marketing Spending, and Brand Royalty Rates

Dominique M. Hanssens, Lorenzo Michelozzi, and Natalie Mizik[*]

According to the American Marketing Association, a brand is defined as "a name, term, design, symbol, or any other feature that identifies one seller's goods or service as distinct from those of other sellers."[1] But to the brand owners, customers, employees, and investors, a brand is much more than just a name. A strong brand is a prized asset for many corporations. It can energize and engage the employees, create alignment around common values, and promote emotional and intellectual engagement at work. Strong brands can create positive associations in the consumer's mind and reduce purchasing risk and search costs in buying situations. Not surprisingly, strong brands often outsell the competition, realize higher repeat purchase rates, are able to charge premium prices, and can command customer loyalty over a long time.

Owners of strong brands often continue to invest heavily in costly marketing initiatives, even after they have achieved a prominent position in the market. For example, in 2019 Nike and Procter & Gamble each spent about 10 percent of their global annual revenue on advertising, while Coca-Cola spent about 11 percent.[2]

---

[*] The views expressed herein by Lorenzo Michelozzi are those of the author; they do not necessarily reflect those of Cornerstone Research. The authors thank Steven R. Dixon of Steptoe & Johnson LLP for his help in identifying recent transfer pricing disputes related to brand valuation.

[1] "Definition of Brand," American Marketing Association, www.ama.org/the-definition-of-marketing-what-is-marketing.

[2] Nike, Inc., *Annual Report Pursuant to Section 13 Or 15(D) of the Securities Exchange Act of 1934 for the Fiscal Year Ended May 31, 2019* (July 23, 2019), www.sec.gov/Archives/edgar/data/320187/000032018719000051/nke-531201910k.htm, at pp. 33, 37; The Procter & Gamble Company, *Annual Report Pursuant to Section 13 Or 15(D) of the Securities Exchange Act of 1934 for the Fiscal Year Ended June 30, 2019* (Aug. 6, 2019), www.sec.gov/Archives/edgar/data/80424/000008042419000050/fy181910-kreport.htm, at pp. 10, 40; The Coca-Cola Company, *Annual Report Pursuant to Section 13 or 15(D) of the Securities Exchange Act of 1934 for the Fiscal Year Ended December 31, 2019* (Feb. 24, 2020), https://investors.coca-colacompany.com/filings-reports/annual-filings-10-k, at pp. 50, 68.

A part of these marketing expenditures may serve as an investment contributing to building and supporting the brand asset, thereby increasing a firm's revenues in future years. However, these expenditures are typically fully expensed in the accounting reports in the year in which they occur. As such, by treating an investment as an expense, current accounting practices generate a disconnect in the timing of revenue and expense recognition. This disconnect creates a challenge for understanding and properly estimating the portion of the company revenue that is attributable to the brand asset effects and the portion attributable to the ongoing marketing initiatives.

The challenges of distinguishing between the effects of brand versus marketing spending on firm performance have prompted a rich and varied research agenda in marketing science. They have also created several scenarios in litigation in which the relative importance of each is the key question. As an example, when a brand has global reach and the international divisions of the brand owner are independently managed, these divisions may pay royalties to the brand owner. These fees, in turn, can have a major effect on the taxable earnings of the brand owner in its home country and may come under the scrutiny of tax authorities.

In this chapter we first discuss the various ways in which brands serve as assets for the firm and the metrics where brand effects can be observed empirically. Then we discuss some modern marketing science methods that may help distinguish between brand and marketing contributions to firm revenue and profits. Finally, we discuss these principles and techniques in the context of various legal disputes on brand royalty rates.

6.1 BRANDS ARE VALUABLE ASSETS AND THEIR ROLE AND BENEFITS DIFFER FOR DIFFERENT STAKEHOLDERS AND ACROSS INDUSTRIES

Brands are valuable intangible assets.[3] Firms can choose to market their products under one common brand name ("branded house" or "umbrella" branding strategy) or manage a diverse portfolio of product brands ("house of brands" strategy) in the marketplace. Corporate brands and product brands play different roles in the market, but both can be crucial in creating value for organizations and their stakeholders.

Academic research on branding has provided important insights on key issues, such as, naming effects (Dinner et al. 2019; Lowrey and Shrum 2007; Melnyk et al. 2012; Peterson and Ross 1972; Sood and Keller 2012), brand extensions and co-branding strategies (Bottomley and Holden 2001; Cao and Sorescu 2013; Lane and Jacobson 1995), measurement of brand equity (e.g. Ailawadi, Lehmann, and Neslin 2003; Fischer 2007; Goldfarb, Lu, and Moorthy 2009; Srinivasan, Park,

---

[3] Some sections of the chapter draw heavily from Mizik (2014) and Dinner et al. (2019).

and Chang 2005), financial performance impact of brand perceptions (Mizik 2014; Mizik and Jacobson 2008), and brand valuation (Barth et al. 1998; Mizik and Jacobson 2009).

Branding can be used to communicate the positioning and strategic intent of the firm and can affect the ongoing loyalty of customers, employees, business partners, investors, regulators, and other stakeholders. The loyalty and support of these key constituencies is critical to the financial success of a firm. Branding can inform relevant stakeholders about managerial mindset and future firm behavior. It is often a reflection of the internal vision and strategy and can be viewed as a signal of management commitment. It can reduce uncertainty and help firm stakeholders make better inferences and form better expectations about their relationship with the company.

For customers, corporate branding can serve the following functions and provide the following benefits (the list is not exhaustive):

- serve as a source identification for the product/service;
- signal quality;
- reduce perceived risk of purchasing the product/service;
- reduce search costs;
- create emotional attachment or relationship;
- be a tool for self-expression, serve as a symbolic device and substitute for religious practice.

All these effects can manifest in some or all of the following product market measures related to the existing firm's products and services: price premium, quantity premium, higher repurchase frequency, longer attachment (loyalty), greater likelihood of a more positive response to product extensions and new product introductions as compared with these measures for an unbranded product. High brand equity with consumers can also lead to lower marketing support requirements for existing operations. Stronger brands might require lower advertising and branding outlays as a percentage of revenues they generate. Further, great brands can be leveraged to benefit the firm's future products through increased likelihood of trial and adoption decreasing marketing costs of new product introductions.

For *employees*, corporate brands can:

- communicate the company's identity, vision, and ideas;
- promote corporate alignment around common values and goals;
- help establish the norms of corporate citizenship;
- energize and engage the employees;
- promote emotional and intellectual engagement at work.

Corporate brand effects on employees have been documented in mergers and in research on executive compensation. Mergers tend to negatively affect employee morale: acquisitions increase the turnover of senior management teams and stifle employment, wages, and productivity. Bommaraju et al. (2018) examined the impact of mergers and acquisitions on sales force performance and found that a merger with a poorer-image firm dilutes salespeople's organizational identification and impairs their individual performance. Tavassoli, Sorescu, and Chandy (2014) demonstrated the significance of employee-based brand equity in an executive pay context: firms with better brands can pay their top executives less. Overall, the effects of strong brand equity on employees may be observed in higher motivation and productivity, lower production costs, and lower labor costs.

For investors, business partners, regulators, competitors, and other stakeholders, brands can serve as a signal of:

- strategic focus and the direction of corporate strategy;
- competitive posturing;
- earnings quality.

The benefits of brand equity with investors, creditors, and business partners may be observed in lower cost of capital, more favorable credit terms, larger credit lines, and more favorable response to earnings announcements. Brand equity with the regulators and government can be reflected in a higher likelihood of securing government contracts, more favorable contract terms, and a lower likelihood of investigations and prosecution. High brand equity with local communities where the company is located or is considering opening facilities can be observed in more favorable leasing terms, an easier process for acquiring land, building permits, and obtaining concessions such as additional government investment in local infrastructure to support the firm's operations.

6.2 THE FINANCIAL VALUATION OF BRAND ASSETS IS MULTIFACETED

As a result of the factors noted in the previous section, branding may contribute directly to the company success because it is a value-generating market-based asset impacting customer behavior (e.g. it may have demand-shifting effect) and employee behavior (costs-shifting effect). It can also affect the behavior of other stakeholders (e.g. regulators, business partners) and increase the likelihood of new contracts or more favorable contractual arrangements. This mechanism is referred to as the "brand-as-asset" perspective. Effective branding can help enhance and/or preserve brand equity for customers and employees, expand appeal of firm products to new segments, generate new incremental value to customers and employees through improved image and better marketing of firm products. As a result of this expected new value creation (increased sales and/or decreased costs), successful branding efforts can affect the stock market valuation (i.e. the equilibrium expectation of future performance) of the firm.

Signaling is another mechanism that can potentially explain branding effects on firm valuation. Under the signaling perspective, brands do not impact the behavior of customers, employees, regulators, and other constituents directly. Instead, under the signaling view, branding strategy only serves as a signal to the investment community of how well the firm is doing financially. Branding strategy can signal the strategic direction and vision, managerial intent, and commitment to stated business goals. This signal can affect the evaluations of the business risk of the firm and the discount factor investors use for valuing its expected future cash flows. The signaling and brand-as-asset effects are not mutually exclusive. Both mechanisms might be present and operate simultaneously.

Because these mechanisms through which brands benefit different stakeholders and thus impact a firm's bottom line are complex, measuring the total financial impact of a brand remains a challenge. Similarly, existing conceptualizations and measurement proposed in the literature so far tend to capture only a few of the many facets through which brands contribute to firm value.

6.2.1 Challenges in Brand Asset Measurement

While brands are widely acknowledged as valuable intangible assets with long-term benefits and are viewed as central to the success of many firms (Aaker 2011; Keller 2012; Keller and Lehmann 2006), the full scope and the dynamics of brands' financial impact are not well understood (Mizik 2014).

Several authors have noted the prevalence as well as the negative implications of focusing on readily available short-term brand performance metrics in evaluating brand performance (Dekimpe and Hanssens 1999; Jedidi, Mela, and Gupta 1999; Lodish and Mela 2007). In particular, they argue that the proliferation of immediate response data (e.g. scanner and Internet data) and the paucity of long-term performance metrics are weakening the powerhouse brands, sometimes beyond recovery, and driving myopic allocations of marketing budgets toward activities that yield an immediate and incontrovertible boost to sales at the expense of the long-term investments into brand building. They conclude that "it's time for changes in how companies measure brand performance" (Lodish and Mela 2007, p. 106).

Indeed, the need to quantify brands' contribution to the financial bottom line is one of the great challenges facing marketing managers. In the absence of a readily observable performance impact, managers are likely to forgo marketing initiatives geared toward enhancing long-term marketing assets with superior returns and replace them with initiatives of potentially lower value but with more immediate and quantifiable financial outcomes (Lodish and Mela 2007; Paul 1994; Pauwels et al. 2004).

Several challenges hinder marketers' ability to evaluate marketing's contribution to the bottom line. First, most of the marketing assets are intangible and, as such, are inherently difficult to measure. As a result, construct definitions and marketing metrics have little consistency – even those collected within a single industry (Kimbrough and McAlister 2009). Second, standardized marketing metrics data collection over time is still scant (Pauwels et al. 2005), resulting in rather limited time-series data of marketing metrics. Poor data availability limits the use of traditional time-series approaches for assessing the full dynamic impact of marketing assets.

These challenges are particularly evident in branding research. Marketing researchers agree that brands have long-term effects. Most of the brand valuation models, however, rely on current product-market performance measures (e.g. Ailawadi, Lehmann, and Neslin 2003; Keller and Lehmann 2006). As Srinivasan, Park, and Chang (2005) and Goldfarb, Lu, and Moorthy (2009) point out, these approaches (e.g. conjoint measurement) do not address the brands' long-term future performance effects and, as such, do not capture the brands' total financial impact.

6.2.2 Conceptualizations and Measurement of Brand Equity in the Marketing Literature

Many conceptualizations of brand equity exist in the literature, but most are consistent with Farquhar's (1989) definition: brand equity is the value a brand adds to the firm's offering. Keller and Lehmann (2006) review the brand equity literature and argue that, although brands may live in consumers' (and other stakeholders') minds, their impact and value are reflected on three levels: customer mindset, product-market outcomes, and, ultimately, the stock market value of a firm.

6.2.2.1 Customer Mindset Metrics

Brands can provide value to consumers. They help reduce consumer search costs and perceived risk, guarantee quality, and create/enhance consumption experiences (e.g. Aaker 2011; Erdem 1998; Keller 2012; Schmitt 1999). Brands can be represented in consumers' minds through a particular knowledge structure that may encompass familiarity, perceptions, attitudes, and relationships.

The elements of this knowledge structure can be assessed to measure customer mindset-based brand equity, e.g. with surveys. The content and the structure of brand knowledge and attitudes affect consumer behavior toward the brand, consumer response to marketing effort, and the probability of brand choice over time (i.e. loyalty). Scholars have proposed several theoretical models of consumer knowledge, attitude, and relationship structure (Aaker 2011; Keller 2012). Most of these models focus on the consumer's familiarity with and understanding of the brand, attitudes, perceptions of quality, relevance, and the strength of the relationship or loyalty to the brand.

Customer mindset brand measures are useful because they are diagnostic; that is, they reflect the sources of brand strength and managers can use them to guide branding initiatives and brand-development programs. However, these measures are also commonly criticized because (1) they do not provide a single, simple measure of brand performance, as they are typically assessed through multiple-item surveys, and (2) although they are related to brand performance, they do not reflect a brand's financial value. As such, they are not very useful in gauging financial returns to brand investment (i.e. marketing productivity) and determining appropriate spending levels.

6.2.2.2 Product-Market Outcomes

Product-market outcome measures of brand equity are often represented with a dollar value. Several product-market measures have been proposed and used to assess brand equity. Most popular measures are based on the price premium or market-share premium a brand commands over a generic or its competitors (Park and Srinivasan 1994; Sethuraman 1996). Ailawadi, Lehmann, and Neslin (2003), however, argue that revenue premium is superior to both price and share premiums because it captures the trade-off between the price and demand and summarizes the overall performance premium. Yet others (e.g. Goldfarb, Lu, and Moorthy 2009) argue that profits – rather than the price, share, or revenue premium – provide a better metric of brand value because profit measures incorporate the costs of creating, maintaining, and managing the brand.

Srinivasan, Park, and Chang (2005) also advocate a profitability-based measure of brand equity. They define brand equity as the annual incremental dollar contribution (i.e. incremental revenue minus incremental variable costs), which is obtained by a brand relative to a base product. The authors, however, also note a limitation of this measure. Specifically, they note that because this measure (similar to the other product-market-based measures) reflects only the contemporaneous (one-year) financial impact and not future performance impact, it does not reflect the *total* financial contribution of a brand. As such, they conclude that additional analyses are needed to determine the total value of the brand equity.

To ascertain the total value of a brand, many brand equity models advocated by consulting firms rely on earnings-decomposition and brand-growth multipliers. That is, product-market brand outcomes such as brand-induced profits or sales are first computed and then weighted by a "multiplier" to arrive at the final valuation. Knowles (2003), for example, suggests multipliers that range from 0.9 to 2.5 of annual sales. In general, the earnings-decomposition approaches have been criticized (e.g. Fernandez 2001) because they rely heavily on subjective judgment rather than data analysis to decide (1) what portion of profits is due to brand and (2) what brand multiplier is appropriate. The comparison of the recent brand valuation data from the leading industry providers presented in the Appendix highlights these issues and the inconsistencies in the estimates.

6.2.2.3 Financial-Market Valuation

When a brand is viewed as an asset, its value can be defined as the total sum of all cash flows (current and future) attributable to this brand. The full brand value is revealed at the time of a brand acquisition, or it can be assessed by aggregating the brand's overall franchise and licensing income (Mahajan, Rao, and Srivastava 1994). Brand acquisitions, however, are relatively rare events, and many brands are not franchised or licensed in the open market.

Simon and Sullivan (1993) proposed using the "residual" market value as a measure of brand equity after all other tangible sources of firm value have been accounted for. This approach, however, is limited because the residual market value also reflects many other intangible assets unrelated to branding or marketing (e.g. management quality, growth prospects, patents, proprietary scientific knowledge, innovation, and technology strategy).

Some studies have linked consumer mindset brand metrics (e.g. Aaker and Jacobson 1994, 2001; Mizik and Jacobson 2008) and product-market-based brand metrics (Barth et al. 1998) directly to stock returns to assess their future financial impact.[4] They report that some brand-related constructs have long-term financial implications beyond their immediate impact on same-year profits. Mizik and Jacobson (2009) have shown that customer-based brand metrics increase the explanatory power of enterprise valuation (forecasting) models. Johansson, Dimofte, and Mazvancheryl (2012) examined the relative predictive power of a customer mindset (EquiTrend) measure versus a financial product-market-based brand equity (Interbrand) measure during the 2007–2009 financial crisis and concluded that a consumer-based metric is a superior predictor of firm performance. Mizik (2014) quantified the total performance impact of brands over time and reported that, on average, the immediate (same-year) effect is only 3 percent of the total impact, with 97 percent of the returns occurring in subsequent years. There exists, however, a significant variation in these breakdowns across different industries. Although some recent studies have come closer to quantifying the total impact brands have on a firm's bottom line, more research and richer data for brand metrics are needed to fully measure the multifaceted benefits that brands, as assets, can provide to their owners.

6.3 RECOGNIZING THE DISTINCT IMPACT OF BRAND AND MARKETING SPENDING ON BUSINESS PERFORMANCE IN LICENSING AGREEMENTS

As discussed earlier, strong brands can offer numerous benefits to their owners and these benefits can materialize in different domains of firm operations and can be

---

[4] One needs to control for same-year profits for brand metrics to reflect future impacts only.

reflected in various performance metrics. One important point, however, is that brands, as any other asset, require *investments*, first in brand development, and subsequently in brand maintenance.

The structure of trademark licensing agreements reflects these considerations. With licensing contracts, the licensee is granted the right to use the trademark and thus take advantage of the goodwill established by the licensed mark. In consideration of this grant, the licensee pays royalties to the trademark owner (Calboli 2007). Importantly, licensing contracts also impose obligations regarding ongoing marketing investments, which can fall entirely on the licensee or be distributed between the licensee and the owner. It is also common for the owner to retain some form of control over these activities with the aim of preserving and increasing the value of the licensed mark.[5] Franchising contracts as well as intracompany transfer pricing agreements for trademarks or other marketing intangibles share similar features (Lagarden 2014; PricewaterhouseCoopers 2013; Palmatier, Stern, and El-Ansary 2016).[6]

It is a challenge to distinguish between the financial returns that accrue and are directly attributable to a brand asset itself versus the financial returns that accrue to the ongoing marketing effort undertaken as a part of normal business operations. Consider a hypothetical example in which a "strong" brand A and a "weak" brand B achieve the same revenue in a given market, but brand B must spend more on marketing to attract and retain customers than brand A. In this case – assuming that a licensee takes on responsibility for marketing support and holding all else equal – brand A should command a higher brand royalty payment than brand B because it provides greater value to a prospective licensee.

While the logic of this hypothetical example is straightforward, determining an appropriate royalty rate is in fact a complex undertaking. In principle, one would have to understand the business performance components determining the profitability of firms, particularly those components related to firm brand *and* nonbrand ongoing marketing spending. Thus, one would need to consider and find a way to determine a few key quantities:[7] (1) the portion of the overall contemporaneous firm

---

[5] See, for example, Oliver Herzfeld, *How to Establish a World-Class Corporate Brand Licensing Program: Part 2*, Forbes (May 22, 2017), www.forbes.com/sites/oliverherzfeld/2017/05/22/how-to-establish-a-world-class-corporate-brand-licensing-program-part-two/.

[6] Franchising contracts often include a sign-up fee in addition to the payments of royalties, and may require regular contributions toward advertising expenses (Blair and Lafontaine 2011). Intracompany transfers of marketing intangibles can also be structured as intracompany sales or cost-sharing agreements (Lagarden 2014). Marketing intangibles include but are not limited to trademarks, trade names, corporate reputation, the existence of a developed sales force, and the ability to service and train customers (PricewaterhouseCoopers 2013).

[7] In the situations where the researcher seeks to understand the entire value contribution of brands, one should also carefully examine (1) any potential benefits and synergies that accrue through reductions in other, non-marketing cost components and (2) the expected duration and the pattern of the returns accruing due to the brand asset. For example, strong brands are likely to have a more loyal customer and employee base extending the benefits into future

revenue that is attributable to firm marketing assets vs. the portion of the revenue that is attributable to other tangible and intangible assets owned by the firm (e.g. patents, distribution rights, customer lock-in due to technology standards, etc.); (2) the breakdown of the marketing-related revenue into the brand-induced portion and the portion generated through other nonbrand assets and ongoing marketing spending; (3) the portion of marketing spending that goes toward brand-building/maintenance (i.e. the brand reinvestment component of marketing spending) and its effectiveness in building the brand versus the portion of marketing spending that goes toward other marketing activities (e.g. market research). This is not a trivial task and it may not be possible to fully accomplish it in practical applications.[8]

Nonetheless, to gain some insight into these issues one can examine the extent to which the brand asset and the ongoing marketing spending impact contemporaneous company sales and how the brand asset is affected by marketing spending. Both brand strength and marketing spending tend to fluctuate over time and across brands, as managers strive to make marketing budget allocation decisions between brand-building/support and other marketing activities to maximize the impact of their marketing investments. To the extent that data on brand sales, marketing spending, and brand strength are available, one may be able to assess their relative importance using econometric techniques.

There is a vast scientific literature on the estimation and interpretation of *sales response* or *marketing-mix* models. While functional forms vary, such models allow for simultaneous modeling of the effects of brand asset and marketing mix elements (e.g. pricing, promotions, advertising, sponsorship campaigns, etc.), environmental variables (such as the state of the economy and seasonal indicators), and competition (e.g. competitive marketing spending and competitive prices), in order to assess their relative importance. Because both marketing spending and brand assets can have delayed or carryover effects on sales, such models can also be specified to explicitly accommodate the dynamics of these effects over time.

---

periods and they might help secure a more qualified and motivated labor force, thus lowering labor and manufacturing costs of the enterprise.

[8] In practice, royalty rates do not solely reflect the strength of the mark being licensed but also additional considerations, which complicates the analysis further. For example, intracompany transfer agreements may comprise the transfer of multiple intangible assets (Lagarden 2014). Franchise contracts often grant franchisee access to training services or input purchase programs that reduce costs in addition to gaining the right to use the franchised mark (Blair and Lafontaine 2011). Finally, the licensing terms between unrelated parties will also reflect the need to balance the licensee and the owner's diverging objectives and incentives (see, for example, Palmatier, Stern, and El-Ansary 2016 at pp. 246–49 for a discussion in the context of franchising agreements). These divergences are likely to be less severe in the context of an intracompany transfer, in which the trademark owner has a direct line of control to the subsidiary that will use and monetize the mark. Nevertheless, common transfer pricing practice is to try to align the terms of intracompany agreements to what they would have been had the transaction taken place at arm's length between unrelated parties (PricewaterhouseCoopers 2013).

Market response models can be estimated using econometric techniques based on data across time periods or across both time periods and cross-sectional units. Two key parameters of interest are the marketing spending's and the brand asset's marginal effects on contemporaneous sales. When high-quality brand and marketing spending data are available (i.e. measurement error in the independent variables is not a concern), examining the relative importance of the parameter estimates for brand and marketing spending measures may inform on the legally relevant question: "What is the importance of brand asset vs. marketing spending?"

To obtain accurate estimates of these effects, the market-specific conditions that moderate them need to be taken into account. Brand perceptions and brand strength and their effects can vary significantly across international markets and adaptation to local market conditions is an important part of international marketing strategy (Steenkamp and Geyskens 2014). The same brand can have vastly different effects in one regional market vs. another (for example, the power of the Chevrolet brand is likely higher in the US market than in the European market). Similarly, if a brand ceases all marketing support for a sustained period of time, or is unavailable to consumers for a sufficiently long time, its impact on consumer perceptions and behavior is likely to deteriorate. Likewise, frequent price promotions, which tend to significantly lift short-term sales, may erode the brand's image as consumers realize they can wait for the next price promotion and avoid purchasing the brand at full price.

A few important additional factors need to be taken into consideration. First, *increasing sales may not be the only strategic business objective of the firm*. Another objective may be to increase prices and profitability. Second, when there is an *intermediary* in the supply chain between brand and consumer (for example, a retailer or dealer), part of the firm's marketing may be aimed at motivating the intermediary to order a larger inventory of the advertised product. Thus the marketing spend drives distribution, which, in turn, drives consumer sales. In such situations, additional econometric equations can be specified to make price levels or distribution a function of marketing spending and other drivers. The specifics of such multi-equation models are described in Hanssens, Parsons and Schultz (2001). Further, brand effects can also be reflected in the differential *persistence of sales* across brands. All else being equal, a strong brand would likely have a higher sales persistence than a weak brand. This effect can also be modeled directly in the sales response function by specifying the effects of lagged sales on current sales.

Sales response models, however, even when properly specified, do not provide a complete measure of brand impact. As described earlier, strong brands offer value to *several* of the firm's stakeholders (consumer, employees, investors, etc.), possibly over long time horizons, whereas the sales response models primarily capture the *consumer demand* effects of branding and marketing effort. In the context of royalty rate setting, though, the evaluation of branding and marketing effects on sales provides useful insights for practical applications, as we discuss in the next section.

6.4 APPLICATION TO LEGAL DISPUTES ON BRAND ROYALTY RATES

The concepts described have found application in recent transfer pricing disputes between the Internal Revenue Service (IRS) and US-based multinationals. These companies operate in multiple foreign markets through local subsidiaries reporting back to a central location (headquarters) in the United States.

These foreign subsidiaries typically undertake substantial marketing activities in the markets they serve to support the company's brands. Examples include the Kraft Heinz Company, the Ford Motor Company, and Procter & Gamble:

- The Kraft Heinz Company markets its brands across the globe. Its foreign subsidiaries oversee local operations and undertake marketing campaigns in the markets they serve.[9]
- Ford Motor Company is a multinational automaker with operations all over the world. Local managers of Ford run marketing campaigns and offer products tailored to local conditions.[10]
- Procter & Gamble markets personal care and household products across the globe. Over the years, it has tailored its product offerings and distribution channels to accommodate the market conditions in the countries it serves.[11]

---

[9] For example, Kraft Heinz Australia operates like a local company and undertakes campaigns tailored to the Australian market. Heinz UK and Ireland has created over a 100 new products in recent years. See Vanessa Mitchell, *Kraft Heinz CMO: Get to the Human Truth behind Brands*, CMO from IDG (Nov. 22, 2018), www.cmo.com.au/article/649889/kraft-heinz-cmo-get-human-truth-behind-brands/; *About Heinz – Heinz UK and Ireland*, Heinz, http://web.archive.org/web/20190217215808/https://www.heinz.co.uk/Our-Company/About-Heinz/Heinz-UK-and-Ireland.

[10] For instance, in Germany and Britain (Ford's first and third markets in Europe by volume) the company has been creating and shooting advertising campaign tailored to consumer sensibilities in these two countries rather than continuing to adapt advertisements created for the European market as a whole. The management team of Ford China launched a China Turnaround Plan to improve their understanding of local customers, introduce new products tailored to local consumers, and strengthen relationships with dealers. See Leonie Roderick, *Ford Shifts to Local Advertising as It Looks to Become More "British-Centric,"* Marketing Week (July 27, 2017), www.marketingweek.com/2017/07/24/ford-british-centric/; Robert Ferris, *Why China Is Getting Tougher for Ford, GM and Other Automakers*, CNBC.com (Dec. 24, 2018), www.cnbc.com/2018/12/24/why-china-is-getting-tougher-for-ford-gm-and-other-automakers.html.

[11] For example, in the 1990s Procter & Gamble managed to make its brand Joy the top selling detergent in Japan thanks to an innovative compact packaging that made the product more profitable for retailers than competitors' brands. The brand's compact packaging saved shelf space, enabling retailers to stock more of it and reduce restocking costs (Winer and Dhar 2011). Recently, Procter & Gamble innovated on its marketing in China to adapt to local changes and appeal to a younger generation of consumers. The company has introduced new tooth-whitening products using cold light technology, rolled out digital shelves that present personalized multimedia content to prospective shoppers, and partnered with local e-commerce platforms Alibaba, JD, and Tencent. Yuan Shenggao, *P&G Plans New Strategy to Attract Younger Consumers*, China Daily (June 21, 2018), http://global.chinadaily.com.cn/a/201806/21/WS5b2b02b5a3103349141dd747.html.

In their day-to-day operations, the foreign subsidiaries not only carry out and fund marketing activities in the local markets, but also use intangible assets, such as patents, trade secrets, or trademarks owned by headquarters. To the extent that these assets contribute to the revenues and profits generated by the foreign subsidiaries, headquarters are entitled to receive some compensation for their use.

The specific contractual and organizational arrangements vary across multinationals and include intracompany sales, licensees, or cost-sharing agreements for the development of the intangibles that may require an initial buy-in payment (Lagarden 2014; PricewaterhouseCoopers 2013). Regardless of the particular arrangement chosen, headquarters take a cut of the subsidiaries' revenues and/or profits (expected revenues and/or profits in the case of an intracompany sale or a buy-in payment for a cost-sharing agreement). Although these intracompany payments are known as transfer prices in the argot of accounting and taxation, in essence they resemble (ongoing or expected) royalty fees that subsidiaries pay to headquarters.

The Internal Revenue Service has challenged these transfer pricing arrangements on numerous occasions, demanding that US-based multinationals extract higher compensation from their foreign subsidiaries for the trademarks and other intangibles. If the IRS and the challenged multinational cannot come to an agreement on how to adjust these payments, litigation ensues. Recent cases include:

- *Veritas Software Corporation v. Commissioner of Internal Revenue.* In 2006, Veritas, a software company, sued the IRS's determination that the buy-in payment from its Ireland-based subsidiary for certain assets, including marketing intangibles, was too low.[12]
- *Medtronic, Inc. and Consolidated Subsidiaries v. Commissioner of Internal Revenue.* Medtronic filed a Tax Court petition in 2011 to challenge the IRS's determination that the royalty paid by its Puerto Rico subsidiary for several intangibles – including a trademark – was too low.[13]
- *Amazon.com Inc. & Subsidiaries v. Commissioner of Internal Revenue.* In a case much like Veritas, Amazon sued the IRS in 2012, disputing the IRS's determination that the buy-in payment received from its

---

[12] *Veritas Software Corp. & Subs. v. Commissioner*, 133 T.C. 297 (T.C. 2009). See also Amy Bennett, *Symantec Disputes $1 Billion IRS Back Taxes, Penalties Bill*, IT World (June 29, 2006); Robert Willens, *Veritas Scores a Major Transfer-Pricing Victory*, CFO.com (Dec. 21, 2009), www.cfo.com/accounting-tax/2009/12/veritas-scores-a-major-transfer-pricing-victory/; Barton W.S. Bassett, William F. Colgin, Jr. & Neal A. Gordon, *Veritas v. Commissioner: Tax Court Decision Exposes Flaws in Common IRS Cost-Sharing Buy-In Theories*, Lexology (Dec. 16, 2009), www.lexology.com/library/detail.aspx?g=19aaf6d5-ad86-4723-bbc1-86fd84a86673.

[13] *Medtronic, Inc. v. Commissioner of Internal Revenue*, 2016 T.C. Memo 112 (T.C. 2016). See also Michael Macagnone, *Medtronic Fights IRS Over Sealed Docs In $561M Tax Row*, Law 360 (May 22, 2015), www.law360.com/articles/659414/medtronic-fights-irs-over-sealed-docs-in-561m-tax-row.

Luxembourg subsidiary for its intangible assets, including trademarks, tradenames, and domain names, was too low.[14]
- *The Coca-Cola Company v. Commissioner of Internal Revenue.* In 2015, Coca-Cola filed an action in the Tax Court disputing the IRS's determination that Coca-Cola was inadequately compensated by the royalties from seven of its foreign affiliates for the use of Coca-Cola's intellectual property, including its trademarks and formulas.[15]
- *Facebook, Inc. and Subsidiaries v. Internal Revenue Service.* In 2016, Facebook filed an action to dispute the IRS's determination that the company did not receive an adequate buy-in payment for intangible property, including marketing intangibles, that it contributed to a cost-sharing arrangement.[16]

Compensation for the trademarks and other marketing intangibles that headquarters receive from their foreign subsidiaries is a key point of contention in these disputes. The parties seek the courts to determine an appropriate *quantum* based on the analysis of accounting and transfer pricing experts they have retained. These experts and the courts therefore need to form an understanding of the relative contribution to sales and profits in the local markets of the brand licensed by the headquarters and the marketing carried out by the foreign subsidiaries. This would not be possible without the insights of marketing science.

Marketing researchers are involved in these disputes to provide these insights and educate the transfer pricing experts and the courts. Common questions that marketing experts are asked to weigh in on include:

- Can the impacts of branding and marketing on business performance be measured? Are there limitations to this measurement?
- Do branding and marketing motivate intermediaries in the supply chain? If so, how?
- How persistent are the impacts of branding and marketing on business performance? What are their useful lives?
- How is brand equity created in the various local markets and what is the contribution of local marketing activities in creating and maintaining brand equity?

---

[14] *Amazon. com, Inc. & Subs. v. Commissioner*, 148 T.C. 108 (T.C. 2017). See also *US: Important US Tax Controversies in 2017*, International Tax Review (Aug. 16, 2017), www.internationaltaxreview.com/Article/3746116/US-Important-US-tax-controversies-in-2017.html?ArticleId=3746116; Angel Gonzalez, *Amazon Wins $1.5 Billion Tax Battle with IRS*, Seattle Times (Mar. 23, 2017), www.seattletimes.com/business/amazon/amazon-wins-15-billion-tax-battle-with-irs/.

[15] *Coca-Cola Company & Subsidiaries v. Commissioner of Internal Revenue*, 155 T.C. 10 (T.C. 2020). See also *Coca-Cola Fights Back $9.4 Billion Transfer Pricing Adjustment*, Bloomberg Tax (Dec. 15, 2015), www.bna.com/cocacola-fights-94-n57982065115/.

[16] *Facebook, Inc. & Subsidiaries v. Commissioner of Internal Revenue*, Petition, Docket No. 21959–16 (Oct. 11, 2016). See also Julie Martin, *Facebook Battling IRS in Tax Court over Royalty Income from Related Irish Company*, MNE Tax (Oct. 13, 2016), https://mnetax.com/facebook-battling-irs-royalty-income-following-intangibles-transfer-irish-sub-17616.

Measuring branding and marketing impact. As explained in the previous section, market response models may help to evaluate the relative impact of brands and marketing activities on sales outcomes. Marketing researchers can contribute their expertise in these disputes by estimating such models or by analyzing and assessing models that the multinational firm may have commissioned during the ordinary course of business. Providing a careful interpretation of these analyses is particularly important in this context. As explained in the prior sections, market response models only provide a partial view of the impact of both branding and marketing on a firm's bottom line. Branding contributes to a firm's bottom line in more ways than just sustaining or growing sales. At the same time, ongoing marketing is essential to maintain the health of a brand.

Branding and marketing impact on intermediaries. Most multinational firms rely on intermediaries to sell their products to consumers. Motivating these intermediaries to carry the firm's product is therefore necessary (although not sufficient) to generate revenues and profits. Branding and marketing work together to foster the support of these intermediaries. For example, retailers are more inclined to offer shelf space to a brand that consumers know and value. However, they also respond to how strongly the firm is supporting the brand with ongoing marketing activities, which they anticipate to impact consumer demand. Thus, in the context of transfer pricing disputes, marketing researchers can contribute their expertise by describing and analyzing how these interdependencies play out and evolve in a dynamic marketplace.

Persistence of branding and marketing impact. In a competitive and dynamic marketplace the impact of branding and marketing is anything but permanent. Nevertheless, it can be persistent. Evaluating the persistence of branding and marketing on sales or other market outcomes (their useful life) is one of the central issues in these types of dispute. If branding or marketing did not have persistent effects, then the goodwill that they generate would have to be constantly reconstituted in the marketplace. If that were the case, the foreign subsidiaries would have to recreate brand equity afresh every year, and headquarters could not demand a royalty rate for the use of the trademarks. Marketing researchers can provide their expertise to put the persistence of branding and marketing impact in perspective. For example, recent research demonstrated that consumer attitudes toward brands persist over time (Mizik 2014), but at the same time, ongoing marketing affects these perceptions (Hanssens et al. 2014). Similarly, research has shown that successful ongoing marketing can have long-lasting impacts on sales (Ataman, Mela, and van Heerde 2008; Ataman, van Heerde and Mela 2010; Bronnenberg, Mahajan, and Vanhonacker 2000; Dekimpe and Hanssens 1995; Lodish et al. 1995).

Creating and maintaining brand equity in the local markets. The subsidiaries of US-based multinationals often conduct and fund ongoing marketing activities to introduce, build, and maintain the firm's brands in their local markets. One important consideration in these disputes is the extent to which both the branding and the marketing are tailored to local market conditions. The more tailored they are, the more "adapted" the brand may be considered, and the lower the royalty that headquarters may extract. Marketing researchers can bring their expertise to bear on these considerations. They can evaluate how the same brands are perceived in different markets and the degree to which ongoing marketing is tailored to local demographic, economic, and cultural conditions.

6.5 CONCLUSIONS

Brands can be important assets owned by the firm that impact the firm's financial performance in the long run, on multiple dimensions. They are often at the heart of legal disputes, notably on the determination of royalty rates (or other payment arrangements) that reflect a brand's contribution to the profitability of a business. Insights that have been generated in marketing research can shed light on some of these issues. Marketing principles and metrics can be used to answer specific questions that are relevant to the courts adjudicating these cases.

BIBLIOGRAPHY

Aaker, David A. (2011) *Brand Relevance: Making Competitors Irrelevant*, John Wiley & Sons.
Aaker, David A., & Robert Jacobson (1994) "The Financial Information Content of Perceived Quality," 31 *Journal of Marketing Research* 191.
  (2001) "The Value Relevance of Brand Attitude in High-Technology Markets," 38 *Journal of Marketing Research* 485.
Ailawadi, Kusum L., Donald R. Lehmann, & Scott A. Neslin (2003) "Revenue Premium as an Outcome Measure of Brand Equity," 67 *Journal of Marketing* 1.
Ataman, M. Berk, Carl F. Mela, & Harald J. Van Heerde (2008) "Building Brands," 27 *Marketing Science* 1036.
Ataman, M. Berk, Harald J. Van Heerde, & Carl F. Mela (2010) "The Long-Term Effect of Marketing Strategy on Brand Sales," 47 *Journal of Marketing Research* 866.
Bahadir, S. Cem, Sundar G. Bharadwaj, & Rajendra K. Srivastava (2008) "Financial Value of Brands in Mergers and Acquisitions: Is Value in the Eye of the Beholder?," 72 *Journal of Marketing* 49.
Barth, Mary A., et al. (1998) "Brand Values and Capital Market Valuation," 3 (1/2) *Review of Accounting Studies* 41.
Blair, Roger D., & Francine Lafontaine (2011) *The Economics of Franchising*, Cambridge University Press.
Bommaraju, Raghu, et al. (2018) "The Impact of Mergers and Acquisitions on the Sales Force," 55 *Journal of Marketing Research* 254.
Bronnenberg, Bart J., Vijay Mahajan, & Wilfried R. Vanhonacker (2000) "The Emergence of Market Structure in New Repeat-Purchase Categories: The Interplay of Market Share and Retailer Distribution," 37 *Journal of Marketing Research* 16.
Bottomley, Paul A., & Stephen J. S. Holden (2001) "Do We Really Know How Consumers Evaluate Brand Extensions? Empirical Generalizations Based on Secondary Analysis of Eight Studies," 38 *Journal of Marketing Research* 494.
Calboli, Irene (2007) "The Sunset of Quality Control in Modern Trademark Licensing," 57 *American University Law Review* 341.

Cao, Zixia, & Alina Sorescu (2013) "Wedded Bliss or Tainted Love? Stock Market Reactions to The Introduction of Cobranded Products," 32 *Marketing Science* 939.
Dekimpe, Marnik G., & Dominique M. Hanssens (1995) "The Persistence of Marketing Effects on Sales," 14 *Marketing Science* 1.
Dekimpe, Marnik G., & Dominique M. Hanssens (1999) "Sustained Spending and Persistent Response: A New Look at Long-Term Marketing Profitability," 36 *Journal of Marketing Research* 397.
Dinner, Isaac M., et al. (2019) *Branding a Merger: Implications for Merger Valuation and Future Performance*, Working Paper, https://ssrn.com/abstract=1756368.
Erdem, Tulin (1998) "An Empirical Analysis of Umbrella Branding," 35 *Journal of Marketing Research* 339.
Farquhar, Peter H. (1989) "Managing Brand Equity," 1 *Marketing Research* 24.
Fernandez, Pablo (2001) *Valuation of Brands and Intellectual Capital*, Working Paper, https://papers.ssrn.com/sol3/papers.cfm?abstract_id=270688.
Fischer, Marc (2007) *Valuing Brand Assets: A Cost-Effective and Easy-to-Implement Measurement Approach*, Report 07-107 MSI Working Paper Series.
Goldfarb, Avi, Qiang Lu, & Sridhar Moorthy (2009) "Measuring Brand Value in An Equilibrium Framework," 28 *Marketing Science* 69.
Hanssens, Dominique M., et al. (2014) "Consumer Attitude Metrics for Guiding Marketing Mix Decisions," 33 *Marketing Science* 534.
Hanssens, Dominique M., Leonard J. Parsons, & Randall L. Schultz (2001) *Market Response Models: Econometric and Time Series Analysis* (2nd ed.), Kluwer Academic Publishers.
Jedidi, Kamel, Carl F. Mela, & Sunil Gupta (1999) "Managing Advertising and Promotion for Long-Run Profitability," 18 *Marketing Science* 1.
Johansson, Johny K., Claudiu Dimofte ,& Sanal Mazvancheryl (2012) "The Performance of Global Brands in the 2008 Financial Crisis: A Test of Two Brand Value Measures," 29 *International Journal of Research in Marketing* 235.
Keller, Kevin Lane (2012) *Strategic Brand Management: Building, Measuring, and Managing Brand Equity* (4th ed.), Pearson.
Keller, Kevin Lane, & Donald R. Lehmann (2006) "Brands and Branding: Research Findings and Future Priorities," 25 *Marketing Science* 740.
Kimbrough, Michael D., & Leigh McAlister (2009) "Linking Marketing Actions to Value Creation and Firm Value: Insights from Accounting Research," 46 *Journal of Marketing Research* 313.
Knowles, Jonathan (2003) "Value-Based Brand Measurement and Management," 5 *Interactive Marketing* 40.
Lagarden, Martin (2014) "Intangibles in a Transfer Pricing Context: Where Does the Road Lead?," 21 *International Transfer Pricing Journal* 331.
Lane, Vicki, & Robert Jacobson (1995) "Stock Market Reactions to Brand Extension Announcements: The Effects of Brand Attitude and Familiarity," 59 *Journal of Marketing* 63.
Lodish, Leonard M., & Carl F. Mela (2007) "If Brands Are Built over Years, Why Are They Managed over Quarters?," 85 *Harvard Business Review* 104.
Lodish, Leonard M., et al. (1995) "A Summary of Fifty-Five In-Market Experimental Estimates of the Long-Term Effect of TV Advertising," 14 *Marketing Science* G133.
Lowrey, Tina M., & L. J. Shrum (2007) "Phonetic Symbolism and Brand Name Preference," 34 *Journal of Consumer Research* 406.

Mahajan, Vijay, Vithala R. Rao, & Rajendra K. Srivastava (1994) "An Approach to Assess the Importance of Brand Equity in Acquisition Decisions," 11 *Journal of Product Innovation Management* 221.

Melnyk, Valentyna, Kristina Klein, & Franziska Voelckner (2012) "The Double-Edged Sword of Foreign Brand Names for Companies from Emerging Countries," 76 *Journal of Marketing* 21.

Mizik, Natalie (2014) "Assessing the Total Financial Performance Impact of Brand Equity with Limited Time-Series Data," 51 *Journal of Marketing Research* 691.

Mizik, Natalie, & Robert L. Jacobson (2008) "The Financial Value Impact of Perceptual Brand Attributes," 45 *Journal of Marketing Research* 15.

(2009) "Valuing Branded Businesses," 73 *Journal of Marketing* 137.

Palmatier, Robert W., Louis W. Stern, & Adel L. El-Ansary (2016) *Marketing Channel Strategy: An Omni-Channel Approach* (8th ed.), Routledge.

Park, Chan Su, & Vern Srinivasan (1994) "A Survey-Based Method for Measuring and Understanding Brand Equity and Its Extendibility," 31 *Journal of Marketing Research* 271.

Paul, Jonathan M. (1994) *Managerial Myopia and the Observability of Future Cash Flows*, Working Paper, https://papers.ssrn.com/sol3/papers.cfm?abstract_id=2788.

Pauwels, Koen, et al. (2004) "New Products, Sales Promotions, and Firm Value: The Case of The Automobile Industry," 68 *Journal of Marketing* 142.

Pauwels, Koen, et al. (2005) "Modeling Marketing Dynamics by Time Series Econometrics," 15 *Marketing Letters* 167.

Peterson, Robert A., & Ivan Ross (1972) "How to Name New Brands," 12 *Journal of Advertising Research* 29.

PricewaterhouseCoopers (2013) *International Transfer Pricing: 2013/2014*, www.pwc.com/gx/en/international-transfer-pricing/assets/itp-2013-final.pdf.

Schmitt, Bernd H. (1999) *Experiential Marketing: How to Get Consumers to Sense, Feel, Think, Act, Relate to Your Company and Brands*, Simon & Schuster.

Sethuraman, Raj (1996) "A Model of How Discounting High-Priced Brands Affects the Sales of Low-Priced Brands," 33 *Journal of Marketing Research* 399.

Simon, Carol J., & Mary W. Sullivan (1993) "The Measurement and Determinants of Brand Equity: A Financial Approach," 12 *Marketing Science* 28.

Skinner, Douglas J. (2008) "Accounting for Intangibles – A Critical Review of Policy Recommendations," 38 *Accounting and Business Research* 191.

Sood, Sanjay, & Kevin Lane Keller (2012) "The Effects of Brand Name Structure on Brand Extension Evaluations and Parent Brand Dilution," 49 *Journal of Marketing Research* 373.

Srinivasan, Shuba, & Dominique M. Hanssens (2009) "Marketing and Firm Value: Metrics, Methods, Findings and Future Directions," 46 *Journal of Marketing Research* 293.

Srinivasan, Vern, Chan Su Park, & Dae Ryun Chang (2005) "An Approach to the Measurement, Analysis, and Prediction of Brand Equity and Its Sources," 51 *Management Science* 1433.

Steenkamp, Jan-Benedict E. M. and Inge Geyskens (2014) "Manufacturer and Retailer Strategies to Impact Store Brand Share: Global Integration, Local Adaptation, and Worldwide Learning," 33(1) *Marketing Science*, 6.

Tavassoli, Nader T., Alina Sorescu, & Rajesh Chandy (2014) "Employee-Based Brand Equity: Why Firms with Strong Brands Pay Their Executives Less," 51 *Journals of Marketing Research* 676.

Winer, Russell S., & Ravi Dhar (2011) *Marketing Management* (4th ed.), Pearson.

APPENDIX

Industry Valuation of the Brands: Top-100 Lists

The current state of knowledge regarding marketing assets' contribution to the bottom line is rather limited (Srinivasan and Hanssens 2009) and does not allow for measurement of probable future benefits with sufficient precision and certainty, which under Generally Accepted Accounting Principles (GAAP) is a requirement for balance sheet recognition. Intangibles such as brands are unique economic resources, but, tellingly, internally generated brands are not on the balance sheets of their owners. Many marketing intangibles are not separable from the enterprise, property rights for intangibles are often not well defined, there are no liquid secondary markets for intangibles, and it is difficult to write contracts for intangibles (Skinner 2008). As such, it is understandable why at the present there is no agreement on how to value them.

Bahadir, Bharadwaj, and Srivastava (2008) have examined the accounting treatment of brand assets in mergers and acquisitions transactions. When a firm is acquired, there is an opportunity for its brands to be added to the balance sheet of the acquirer. Bahadir, Bharadwaj, and Srivastava (2008), however, document significant heterogeneity and subjectivity in the accounting treatment of brands, further underlining the lack of a consistent valuation approach. They conclude that brand value "is in the eye of the beholder."

Consider, for example, Table 6.1, which presents top-30 listings of the brand value estimates from the "100 most valuable brands" published in 2020 by leading brand valuation providers Interbrand, BrandZ/Millward Brown, Forbes, and Brand Finance.[17]

As shown in Table 6.1, little agreement exists with respect to the valuation of the same brand despite the fact that these valuations are computed using similar

---

[17] Table 6.1 was compiled by Type 2 Consulting. See Jonathan Knowles, *Brand Valuation: Comparison of the 2020 Brand Value League Tables*, Type 2 Consulting (Oct. 20, 2020), www.slideshare.net/jpoknowles/2020-brand-valuation-review.

TABLE 6.1. *Comparison of the top-30 most valuable brands in 2020 according to Interbrand, Millward Brown, Forbes, and Brand Finance*

Rank	Interbrand		Millward Brown		Forbes		Brand Finance	
	Brand	Brand value ($ millions)	Brand	Brand value ($ millions)	Brand	Brand value ($ millions)	Brand	Brand value ($ millions)
1	Apple	322,999	Amazon	415,855	Apple	241,200	Amazon	220,791
2	Amazon	200,667	Apple	352,206	Google	207,500	Google	159,722
3	Microsoft	166,001	Microsoft	326,544	Microsoft	162,900	Apple	140,524
4	Google	165,444	Google	323,601	Amazon	135,400	Microsoft	117,072
5	Samsung	62,289	VISA	186,809	Facebook	70,300	Samsung	94,494
6	Coca-Cola	56,894	Alibaba	152,525	Coca-Cola	64,400	ICBC	80,791
7	Toyota	51,595	Tencent	150,978	Disney	61,300	Facebook	79,804
8	Mercedes-Benz	49,268	Facebook	147,190	Samsung	50,400	Walmart	77,520
9	McDonald's	42,816	McDonald's	129,321	Louis Vuitton	47,200	Ping An	69,041
10	Disney	40,773	MasterCard	108,129	McDonald's	46,100	Huawei	65,084
11	BMW	39,756	AT&T	105,833	Toyota	41,500	Mercedes-Benz	65,041
12	Intel	36,891	Verizon	94,662	Intel	39,500	Verizon	63,692
13	Facebook	35,178	Coca-Cola	84,022	Nike	39,100	China Construction Bank	62,602
14	IBM	34,885	IBM	83,667	AT&T	37,300	AT&T	59,103
15	Nike	34,388	Marlboro	58,247	Cisco	36,000	Toyota	58,076
16	Cisco	34,119	SAP	57,585	Oracle	35,700	State Grid	56,965
17	Louis Vuitton	31,720	The Home Depot	57,585	Verizon	32,300	Disney	56,123
18	SAP	28,011	Moutai	53,755	VISA	31,800	Agricultural Bank of China	54,658

19	Instagram	26,060	**Louis Vuitton**	51,777	Walmart	29,500	WeChat	54,146
20	Honda	21,694	UPS	50,748	GE	29,500	Bank of China	50,630
21	Chanel	21,203	Nike	49,962	Budweiser	28,900	The Home Depot	50,508
22	J P Morgan	20,220	Disney	48,802	SAP	28,600	China Mobile	49,023
23	American Express	19,458	PayPal	48,453	Mercedes-Benz	28,500	Shell	47,529
24	UPS	19,161	Starbucks	47,753	IBM	28,200	Saudi Aramco	46,768
25	IKEA	18,870	Xfinity	46,973	Marlboro	26,800	VW	44,897
26	Pepsi	18,603	Netflix	45,889	Netflix	26,700	YouTube	44,476
27	Adobe	18,206	**Walmart**	45,783	**BMW**	25,900	Tencent	44,091
28	Hermes	17,961	Spectrum	42,917	American Express	25,100	Starbucks	41,043
29	GE	17,961	Instagram	41,501	Honda	24,500	Wells Fargo	40,881
30	YouTube	17,328	Accenture	41,437	L'Oreal	22,800	**BMW**	40,483
Value of six common brands:		931,062		1,614,198		878,600		774,036
Value of top-30 brands:		1,670,419		3,450,509		1,704,900		2,135,578
Value of top-100 brands:		3,947,544		2,542,000		4,988,811		2,321,938

Source: Jonathan Knowles, *Brand Valuation: Comparison of the 2020 Brand Value League Tables*, Type 2 Consulting (Oct. 20, 2020), www.slideshare.net/jpoknowles/2020-brand-valuation-review

Note: Only six brands (Amazon, Apple, Disney, Facebook, Google, Microsoft) are common across all four lists in the top-30 listings. Thirteen brands (shown in bold) are common to three of the lists.

approaches that should, in principle, yield approximately the same estimate of brand value. Specifically:

- Two different brands occupy the first spot across the four league tables – Amazon and Apple – and the valuation of the top brand across the four lists varies between $221 billion and $416 billion.
- Only six brands are common to all four lists (Amazon, Apple, Disney, Facebook, Google, Microsoft) in the top-30 listings.

TABLE 6.2. *Percentage change in brand valuations between 2019 and 2020 according to Interbrand, Millward Brown, Forbes, and Brand Finance*

Brand	Change 2020/19 BF 20 v. 19	Change 2020/19 Forbes	Change 2020/19 MB	Change 2020/19 IB	Consensus?
Amazon	18%	40%	32%	60%	Yes
BMW	0%	−13%	−12%	−4%	Yes
Facebook	−4%	−21%	−7%	−12%	Yes
MasterCard	8%	24%	18%	17%	Yes
Netflix	8%	72%	34%	41%	Yes
Nike	7%	6%	5%	6%	Yes
Accenture	−4%	15%	6%	2%	No
American Express	6%	−3%	−16%	−10%	No
Apple	−9%	17%	14%	38%	No
Cisco	7%	4%	−9%	−4%	No
Citi	−9%	4%	−17%	−6%	No
Coca-Cola	5%	9%	4%	−10%	No
Disney	23%	17%	−14%	−8%	No
FedEx	−5%	−4%	−23%	5%	No
Google	12%	24%	5%	−1%	No
HSBC	−4%	13%	−19%	−14%	No
Huawei	5%	6%	9%	−9%	No
IBM	2%	−10%	−3%	−14%	No
IKEA	−9%	3%	−5%	3%	No
Intel	−6%	2%	17%	−8%	No
J P Morgan	15%	10%	−11%	6%	No
McDonald's	19%	5%	−1%	−6%	No
Mercedes-Benz	8%	−14%	−9%	−3%	No
Microsoft	−2%	30%	30%	53%	No
Samsung	4%	−5%	7%	2%	No
Siemens	−7%	−8%	−9%	2%	No
Starbucks	5%	5%	4%	−5%	No
Toyota	11%	−7%	−3%	−8%	No
UPS	1%	6%	−8%	6%	No
VISA	−3%	18%	5%	15%	No

- The total value of the six common brands ranges from $774 billion (Brand Finance) to $1.61 trillion (Millward Brown).
- The aggregate value of the top-30 brands on each list varies between $1.67 trillion (Interbrand) and $3.45 trillion (Millward Brown).

Furthermore, as shown in Table 6.2,[18] there is a lack of consensus on whether each of the thirty brands included on all four top-100 lists in 2019 and 2020 has increased or decreased in value from 2019 to 2020:

- There is consensus on the direction of the change in value for only six of the thirty common brands (four brands increasing in value, and two declining in value).
- For the other twenty-four brands, there is disagreement about whether the brand had increased or decreased in value.

---

[18] Ibid., p. 9

7

On Puffery

Rebecca Tushnet

Puffery is a concept that purports to be about things consumers ignore and don't rely on. It is in fact a concept about things courts ignore and won't rule on. At the moment, marketing and other empirical work has essentially nothing to say about puffery in the courts; puffery consists of precisely the elements of advertising for which courts neither require nor allow empirical evidence of consumer reaction.[1] That doesn't make the doctrine wrong, but it does mean that explanations for the doctrine should not be founded on unsupported, mostly unsupportable judicial assertions about how consumers think and what advertising claims they disregard. Instead, this chapter will argue, puffery should be about what kinds of advertising claims are too difficult to evaluate for their truth in judicial settings. That's an epistemological determination that judges are actually well qualified to make, unlike the idea that consumers don't rely on puffery.

7.1 PUFFERY AS DOCTRINE

In modern advertising law in general, only factual misstatements are actionable.[2] Opinions can be actionable if they have the character of facts, e.g., if opinions are offered by experts or if they suggest the existence of undisclosed facts.[3] There are

---

[1] This is often decided as a matter of law. See e.g. *Perkiss & Liehe v. Northern Cal. Collection Serv., Inc.*, 911 F.2d 242 (9th Cir. 1990) (puffery determinations are for court as matter of law), *In re Century 21–RE/MAX Real Estate Advert.* Claims Litig., 882 F. Supp. 915 (C.D. Cal. 1994) (refusing to consider plaintiff's evidence that public could be misled by claim because statement was puffery as matter of law).

[2] See e.g. *Coastal Abstract Serv. Inc. v. First Am. Title Ins. Co.*, 173 F.3d 725 (9th Cir. 1999).

[3] See e.g. FTC Policy Statement on Deception, § III (Oct. 14, 1983) ("Claims phrased as opinions are actionable ... if they are not honestly held, if they misrepresent the qualifications of the holder or the basis of his opinion or if the recipient reasonably interprets them as implied statements of fact ... [R]epresentations of expert opinions will generally be regarded as representations of fact.").

even a few cases finding falsity where no reasonable person could have held the expressed opinion, the more tangible facts being what the speaker knew them to be.[4] But puffery is an overlay onto the fact/opinion divide: it allows courts to reject liability for what might look like factual, verifiable claims (such as "the cheapest prices in the universe," or even "the cheapest prices in West Virginia"[5]) because they are too exaggerated or vague to be believed by reasonable consumers. The Fifth Circuit wrote, for example, that "non-actionable 'puffery' comes in at least two possible forms: (1) an exaggerated, blustering, and boasting statement upon which no reasonable buyer would be justified in relying; or (2) a general claim of superiority over comparable products that is so vague that it can be understood as nothing more than a mere expression of opinion."[6] The Federal Trade Commission (FTC) has reasoned similarly.[7]

One additional piece has to be understood before the scope of the problem is understandable: advertising law, like trademark law, is probabilistic. If 25 percent of consumers (net of control) are confused or deceived, almost any court would grant relief.[8] Deception, that is, doesn't need to be universal to be actionable by a competitor, or by the FTC.[9] Deception doesn't even need to be the most likely outcome for a given target consumer as long as a substantial number of consumers are likely to be deceived.

But these rules apply only when the advertising is not puffery. Courts maintain, without evidence, that consumers don't rely on puffery, and they rely on their own

---

[4] See e.g. *In re Countrywide Financial Corp. Secs. Litig.*, 588 F. Supp. 2d 1132, 1144 (C.D. Cal. 2008) ("[T]he [complaint] adequately alleges that [the defendant's] practices so departed from its public statements that even 'high quality' became materially false or misleading; and that to apply the puffery rule to such allegations would deny that 'high quality' has any meaning.").

[5] *Imagine Medispa, LLC v. Transformations, Inc.*, 999 F. Supp. 2d 873 (S.D. W. Va. 2014) ("West Virginia's Lowest Price Weight Loss and Skin Care Clinic" and "Lowest Prices in WV!" didn't refer to any specific services or products, and drew no direct comparisons but instead were "broad, vague exaggerations or boasts on which no reasonable consumer would rely"); *General Steel Domestic Sales, LLC v. Chumley*, 129 F. Supp. 3d 1158 (D. Colo. 2015) (boast "Awarded Best in the Industry" was puffery, "as no reasonable consumer would rely on such an assertion without first inquiring further into the nature and credibility of the entity granting the award"); *Hackett v. Feeney*, 2011 WL 4007531 (D. Nev. 2011) (a boast that a particular theatrical performance was "Voted #1 Best Show in Vegas," when no such "vote" ever occurred, was puffery).

[6] *Pizza Hut, Inc. v. Papa John's Int'l, Inc.*, 227 F.3d 489 (5th Cir. 2000).

[7] *C&H Sugar Co.*, 119 F.T.C. 39, 44 (1995) ("The term 'puffery' as used by the Commission here generally includes representations that ordinary consumers do not take literally, expressions of opinion not made as a representation of fact, subjective claims (taste, feel, appearance, smell) and hyperbole that are not capable of objective measurement.").

[8] See e.g. *McNeil-PPC, Inc. v. Pfizer Inc.*, 351 F. Supp. 2d 226 (S.D.N.Y. 2005) (noting that courts consider 20 percent to be a significant number of consumers for purposes of Lanham Act liability).

[9] Consumer class actions work differently, though some states – including California, the source of much class action litigation – rebuttably presume that each member of a class is deceived if an ad is deceptive.

judgment to determine what advertising is puffery and what is at least plausibly factual.[10] This treatment is fundamentally normative, and it has distributional consequences – it is about how consumers should behave, not about what advertisers should say. As Learned Hand wrote, "There are some kinds of talk which no sensible man takes seriously, and if he does he suffers from his own credulity."[11] The influential treatise *Prosser & Keeton on the Law of Torts* says that an advertiser has a privilege "to lie his head off, so long as he says nothing specific."[12] Some courts even think that advertising is mostly puffery.[13]

Ivan Preston argues that current puffery doctrine is a mistaken evolution from nineteenth-century cases involving individual buyers and sellers that held that buyers couldn't sue for fraud based on statements that they could easily have verified or disproved themselves.[14] When buyers were unable to verify the claims, however, the law provided them redress. But as the puffery doctrine developed, he argued, it turned into a rule that consumers treated certain claims as meaningless and therefore rejected them at the outset. He argues that this new rule was not only unconnected to its historical foundation in fraud law, but also was inappropriate for modern mass advertising where the complexity of factual claims combined with their sheer volume mean that consumers can't actually investigate most of the factual claims they receive.[15]

7.2 THE PROBLEM: PUFFERY WORKS

The articulated justification for the puffery rule is, unfortunately, divorced from facts about consumer behavior. The conventional justification of the doctrine cannot admit that puffery *actually works*, in the sense of getting consumers to buy things, because it is supposed that consumers do not rely on puffery – its lack of credibility is supposedly why there's no need for legal intervention.

---

[10] Ivan L. Preston, "Puffery and Other 'Loophole' Claims: How the Law's 'Don't Ask, Don't Tell' Policy Condones Fraudulent Falsity in Advertising," 18 *J.L. & Com.* 49 (1998).
[11] *Vulcan Metals Co.* v. *Simmons Mfg. Co.*, 248 F. 853 (2d Cir. 1918).
[12] W. Page Keeton et al., *Prosser & Keeton on the Law of Torts* § 109, at 756–57, West Group (5th ed. 1984).
[13] See e.g. *Guidance Endodontics, LLC* v. *Dentsply Int'l, Inc.*, 708 F. Supp. 2d 1209 (D.N.M. 2010) ("[T]he larger the audience the more likely it is that the statement is puffery"; in marketing materials, "a seller is expected to cast his wares in the best possible light to tempt consumers to buy his product rather than any other").
[14] Preston, "Puffery and Other 'Loophole' Claims," 74–78.
[15] Ibid., 78–86. Preston argues that, in the modern economy, consumers are likely to see advertisers as experts with special access to the facts, including facts about competing products. Moreover, if the advertiser is communicating in a mass medium, consumers are likely to believe that its claims are valid across a large group of consumers. As a result, he argues, consumers will give greater deference to their statements – treating them as inherently less subjective and more verifiable – than they would to the statements of a single individual. Ibid., 91–92.

But broad, general claims are popular with advertisers because they often do work.[16] For example, C&H Sugar was ordered in 1977 not to call its brand "superior" to or otherwise different from other granulated sugars without substantiation.[17] In 1995, it successfully argued that it shouldn't be barred from using ads such as "I love C&H the best" or "C&H tastes best," because its competition was free to make similar unsubstantiated claims. The FTC granted the modification, because competing ad campaigns were able to "take advantage of C&H's inability to counter claims that ... constitute puffery." The underlying problem was that "[t]he homogeneous nature of the product means that there are few truthful, nondeceptive comparisons that can be made among competing products. In order to promote their brands, sugar refiners must rely on ... subjective endorsement claims ... or objective product source and origin claims which are precisely the kinds of claims prohibited by the existing order."[18] But, of course, if C&H needed puffery to compete, then puffery was affecting consumer behavior.

And sugar is unlikely to be unique among puffed products. Advertisers both want to affect consumers and seem likely to have greater-than-average insight into what might affect consumers in the sale of their particular thing. In other words, if we ask why a message appears in ads, the obvious answer seems to be: to get to the sale. One thing we might do when advertising claims are challenged in court, then, would be to presume that claims in ads matter to consumers.[19] The key questions we should have would be about whether a significant group of consumers receives a factual message specific enough to be falsified. We could also still recognize that there are parts of ads that aren't claims as such – for example, elements of ads that function to attract attention, thence to deliver a factual claim. But even if we screen out attention-getting, the concept of unbelievability adds nothing useful to the question

---

[16] See ibid.
[17] See *C&H Sugar Co.*, 119 F.T.C. 39 (1995) (rehearing), rev'g 89 F.T.C. 15 (1977).
[18] Ibid. at 46–47. See also *Clarification of Three Provisions of a 1972 Order Concerning Safety Claims for Its Tires*, 112 F.T.C. 609, 610 (1989) (advisory opinion) (allowing "generalized safety claims" without substantiation, such as "quality you can trust"). The FTC, however, then suggested that "I love C&H the best" or "C&H tastes best" are capable of being substantiated. But then it went on to say that claims not relating to "health, safety, nutritional quality, or purity ... will not be deemed to contain an implied comparison under this order." Thus, taste claims would be allowed. Ivan Preston argues that this conclusion is both paradoxical – the better taste claim is concededly capable of being substantiated – and wrong. Preston, "Puffery and Other 'Loophole' Claims."
[19] In *Schick Manufacturing, Inc. v. Gillette Company*, 372 F. Supp. 2d 273 (D. Conn. 2005) the court noted that "[b]ecause of the expense of television advertising, companies have a very short period of time in which to create a 'reason to believe' and are generally forced to pitch only the key qualities and characteristics of the product advertised." The court thus concluded:

> It is clear that whether the M3 Power raises hairs is material. Gillette's employees testified that television advertising time is too valuable to include things that are "unimportant." Furthermore, in this case, hair extension is the "reason to believe" that the M3 Power is a worthwhile product. The magnitude and frequency of that effect are also, therefore, material.

of falsifiability. While it's possible that a sufficient exaggeration *means* that no falsifiable factual message has been conveyed, we really don't know that at the wholesale level, without looking at the specific exaggeration and the market.[20]

There is one defense of puffery that might be able to sidestep the question of its effectiveness: if we decide that puffery can't be regulated, then every market participant has roughly equal access to the technique, contingent on how good their ad agencies are. And large numbers of them are apparently in need of it: The president of the American Advertising Federation said that without puffery, advertisers "would, in effect, be denied the ability to compete on anything other than factual grounds. Thousands of products do not compete on factual grounds because they are essentially the same."[21]

That level playing field might be thought to justify a certain amount of judicial restraint, though it ignores dynamic and distributional effects. Among other things, it seems that contradictory factual information may not be enough for a competitor to beat back the positive effects of puffing.[22] And "everybody can do it" as a justification raises the problem of the market for lemons: if consumers are expected to disregard self-interested claims, it becomes very hard for truthful advertisers to convince consumers of their unusual probity, resulting in welfare losses.[23] Even if you accept the equal-playing-field defense of puffery, though, I think it fits well into my description of puffery as a litigation management doctrine rather than one that has much to do with consumer perceptions.

7.3 EXAMPLES OF THE CONTRADICTION OF WORKING PUFFERY IN CURRENT DOCTRINE

Two examples from the FTC, and a few from the courts, demonstrate that the current conception of puffery as meaning something about actual consumer perception is not working very well.

---

[20] See *Hansen Beverage Co. v. Vital Pharm., Inc.*, 2010 WL 1734960 (S.D. Cal. 2010) (the claim that an energy beverage "will leave you 'amped' to the max in minutes, ready to tear apart the weights and wear out the treadmill like a tiger released from its cage!" was puffery); *Blue Cross v. Corcoran*, 558 N.Y.S.2d 404 (App. Div. 1990) ("Remember, if you don't have Blue Cross, you're not covered" so obviously false that it was neither intended nor likely to be taken literally by people of average education and intelligence); *Gillette Co. v. Norelco Consumer Prods. Co.*, 946 F. Supp. 115 (D. Mass. 1996) (ad for a dry shaver portrayed wet shavers as snakes biting, bees stinging, and flamethrowers burning: it was not deceptive to exaggerate their underlying meaning "beyond the point of believability, in order to ensure that that underlying message is conveyed").

[21] Preston, "Puffery and Other 'Loophole' Claims."

[22] See Michel Tuan Pham & A. V. Muthukrishnan, "Search and Alignment in Judgment Revision: Implications for Brand Positioning," 39 *J. Marketing Res.* 18 (2002) (discussing puffery as "abstract positioning" about superiority such as "The best pen money can buy" versus specific performance claims). In some circumstances, it may even take anti-puffing to beat puffing. See ibid., 27–28 ("There is nothing special about this pen" worked better than negative statements about specific attributes to change subjects' views).

[23] See George A. Akerlof, "The Market for 'Lemons': Quality Uncertainty and the Market Mechanism," 84 *Q.J. Econ.* 488 (1970).

The first comes from the FTC Endorsement Guides. If puffery is about subjectivity and variation among consumers' understanding, and if reasonable consumers don't rely on puffery, then the FTC's approach to endorsements is wrong. The FTC takes the position that an endorser has to disclose connections to an advertiser when they wouldn't be obvious from context (for example, when the endorser is appearing in a traditional thirty-second TV ad, no separate disclosure is necessary) and when knowledge of the connection would be relevant to the consumer in weighing the endorsement. So far, so good.

But the FTC – quite rightly, I think – requires disclosure even when the endorser is otherwise just offering their opinion: these clothes are so cool! This hair color looks fabulous on me! Failure to disclose the connection is deceptive where the audience is likely to believe that the speech is uncompensated opinion.[24] But, critically, in that situation, "the deception can only be material if vague, fact-free claims made by a sufficiently credible source affect purchase decisions."[25] If the underlying claim is pure immaterial puffery of the kind on which consumers are irrefutably presumed not to rely – and the underlying claim in a social media endorsement *is* indeed often exactly that kind of claim – how can it possibly be important to consumers to know that the endorser is being compensated?

The answer is that consumers, in general, want opinions to be in some sense authentic, and they care about whether a speaker is getting paid; their influence will be less if that payment is disclosed. As I have written elsewhere, the evidence indicates that consumers use a message's source to judge its trustworthiness, and they are likely to rely on the opinions of people they judge sufficiently relatable (or desirable). The effect is multiplied when the endorsements are multiplied, simulating the wisdom of crowds. "Even better from the marketer's perspective, people don't understand why they find the repeated, multiple-source claim plausible. They attribute it to the inherent truth value of the claim rather than to the repetition, making them particularly vulnerable to manipulation of this type."[26]

In an endorsement situation, the fact of a financial connection is itself verifiable, so its absence can be misleading, even if all that gets said in an endorsement are claims that consumers weren't supposed to be relying on as a matter of law. The endorsement guidelines thus inherently, if covertly, recognize that puffery does work. Puffery's effectiveness is why it is important to regulate undisclosed endorsements even if they don't make other factual claims. A disclosure requirement gives us a factual hook of sufficient specificity that the courts and the FTC can handle:

---

[24] For example, the FTC took the position that "tagging a brand in an Instagram picture is an endorsement of the brand and requires an appropriate disclosure." See *CSGO Lotto Owners Settle FTC's First-Ever Complaint Against Individual Social Media Influencers*, Federal Trade Commission, Sept. 7, 2017.
[25] Rebecca Tushnet, "Attention Must Be Paid: Commercial Speech, User-Generated Ads, and the Challenge of Regulation," 58 *Buffalo L. Rev.* 721, 776 (2010).
[26] Ibid., 748–49 (footnotes omitted).

determining whether there was in fact a relationship and whether it was adequately disclosed.

The second example comes from the FTC Green Guides, which specifically address the heterogeneity of meaning. In puffery discussions, courts often say that vagueness matters: some words or statements are too vague to have one specific meaning. But there are different possible meanings of vagueness: a statement might be too vague even for an individual to get a specific message in response to the statement, but the statement might also have a lot of varying interpretations among heterogeneous consumers, at least some of whom have specific definitions in mind. A court considering whether "America's Favorite Pasta" was puffery endorsed the latter view for that phrase, saying that "favorite" might mean most-purchased, but it might also mean that people liked it best but couldn't often afford it.[27] But then the court said that "America's Favorite Pasta" was therefore nonactionable puffery. Yet if the thought is that different consumers will fill out words like "favorite" with different meanings, then we might, if we put the empirical work in, actually figure out what those meanings are and whether they're shared across a substantial number of relevant cases, and thus whether a substantial number of relevant consumers are deceived. At the very least, if that endeavor is not worth undertaking, we should explain why not.

The possibility of multiple falsifiable meanings with greater practical significance is not merely theoretical, as the Green Guides demonstrate. The FTC's general rule for advertisers is that they have to substantiate factual claims that are conveyed to a substantial number of relevant consumers. Relying on its own research into the meaning of general environmental benefit claims ("green" and "eco-friendly"), the FTC found that substantial numbers of consumers understood a variety of things from those claims. Sixty-one percent of consumers thought that a product labeled "green" without further qualification would be made from made from recycled materials; 59 percent thought that it would be recyclable; 54 percent thought it would be made with renewable materials; 53 percent thought it would be biodegradable; 48 percent thought it would be made with renewable energy; 45 percent thought it would be nontoxic; 40 percent thought it would be compostable; and 27 percent thought it would have no negative environmental impact.[28] These numbers dropped – though they were still high enough that they might count as deceptive to a substantial number of consumers – when the "green" claims were qualified with a specific attribute.[29] As a result, the FTC's guidance to advertisers

---

[27] *Am. Italian Pasta Co. v. New World Pasta Co.*, 371 F.3d 387, 393–94 (8th Cir. 2004).

[28] FTC, *Green Guides Statement of Basis and Purpose* (2012).

[29] For example, when the phrase was qualified to be specific to recycling, "green – made with recycled materials," 26 percent of surveyed consumers took away other implied claims; the result was similar for "green – made with renewable energy." Without "green," but with "made with recycled materials," 18 percent of consumers took away other implied claims. Ibid. This suggests that even a qualified "green" claim might be deceptive unless the advertiser can substantiate the other implied claims.

indicates that they shouldn't make unqualified general environmental claims, not despite their vagueness but because of it.[30]

A variation of this phenomenon of multiple but factual meanings is when the defendant says something that's usually so vague that it's puffery – like "high quality" – and there are simply no plausible circumstances in which that's true for any definition of the term. For example, the FTC prevailed against a defendant who advertised the opportunity to buy high-quality cars at below-market prices, where the evidence established that the cars were actually in poor condition and, in the unusual case where the cars were in good condition, they sold for market price.[31] In at least some circumstances, then, it's feasible to figure out the various meanings of a multiple-meaning term and their distribution. Sometimes, we could in fact evaluate whether a substantial number of consumers are likely to be deceived by a false meaning or meanings of a multi-meaning claim. In these kinds of situations, the general benefits of giving advertisers leeway to make claims are outweighed by the costs of consumer deception, especially given advertisers' ability to make truthful claims instead (e.g. "made with recycled materials" instead of "environmentally friendly").

In the examples above, the FTC has asserted its authority over what might be called deceptive puffery because of its institutional commitments to protecting consumers as they are, not as we would have them be. Unfortunately, courts have used the concept of puffery to let advertisers off the hook for deceptiveness that helps no one and that could easily have been replaced by truthful alternatives. For

---

[30] Green Guides, § 260.4 General Environmental Benefit Claims:

> (b) Unqualified general environmental benefit claims are difficult to interpret and likely convey a wide range of meanings. In many cases, such claims likely convey that the product, package, or service has specific and far-reaching environmental benefits and may convey that the item or service has no negative environmental impact. Because it is highly unlikely that marketers can substantiate all reasonable interpretations of these claims, marketers should not make unqualified general environmental benefit claims ...
> Example 1: The brand name "Eco-friendly" likely conveys that the product has far-reaching environmental benefits and may convey that the product has no negative environmental impact. Because it is highly unlikely that the marketer can substantiate these claims, the use of such a brand name is deceptive.

> The FTC indicated, however, that properly qualified "eco-friendly because it's made with recycled material" type of claims would be acceptable if they didn't also convey other false messages.

[31] See *Vallery* v. *Bermuda Star Line, Inc.*, 532 N.Y.S.2d 965 (City Civ. Ct. 1988) (advertising for a cruise ship touting "a very special kind of luxury" with "impeccable taste, in the design and furnishings of the beautifully appointed lounges, dining room and cabins," combined with pictures and other representations that the cabins would be "beautiful" and "luxurious," supported a consumer fraud claim where the plaintiffs' cabin was actually dirty and furnished with broken, damaged, and outworn furniture). But see *Intertape Polymer Corp.* v. *Inspired Techs., Inc.*, 725 F. Supp. 2d 1319 (M.D. Fla. 2010) (finding vague superiority claims to be puffery despite internal testing evidence suggesting that the advertiser knew that its product performed worse than that of the challenger).

example, *Johnson v. Mitsubishi Digital Electronics America, Inc.*[32] involved an advertiser's claims that its television was "1080p" (the best available technology). The TVs, however, could not display a 1080p signal. Instead, at best they could display an upconverted 1080i (interlaced) signal from a 1080p device. The upconversion process results in undesirable artifacts like feathering that make the viewing experience worse.

The *Johnson* court nonetheless concluded that, although Mitsubishi designated its television set as a 1080p television set, the phrase 1080p "does not convey a specific claim that is recognizable to the targeted customer." Instead, 1080p only had meaning for engineering professionals, and the court pointed to the plaintiff's own testimony that what he wanted was a top-of-the-line set ("top of the line" being classic puffery). Because he didn't understand what 1080p meant, the claim was puffery to him.

Yet it is evident that 1080p had a specific meaning; it wasn't a vaguer "top of the line" or "really good." Further, consumers didn't need to know the technical requirements for 1080p televisions in order to be moved to act by that designation any more than they need to know how their statins work or why the drugs are called statins. If a consumer receives a message that they think is factual, credible and material, even if they can't be particularly specific about the details, then they can be harmed if that message is false. And it was really easy to prove that 1080p was false. But focusing on the precision of consumer understanding leads to errors like that of the *Johnson* court.

7.4 THE PROPER BOUNDARIES OF PUFFERY

Puffery may indeed be effective in influencing purchases without being either provable or falsifiable in conventional judicial terms. Thus, a determination that a claim is pure puffery should arguably trump evidence that it actually influences consumers – but only if the reason for finding puffery is the difficulty of proof of truth, rather than that the challenged claim has multiple possible meanings or is unbelievable in the abstract.

One implication of my argument is that exaggeration should be rejected as a separate defense or category of puffery. The question should always be what factual message consumers are likely to receive, if any. If the claim is "we'll save you a million dollars on car insurance," we can ask whether a substantial number of consumers receives a message that they can expect to save a significant amount compared to other insurers, and whether that message is false. The lawyers' fighting would of course shift to whether the inquiry into falsity was a manageable judicial task – how much is enough to be significant savings? It might be that consumers don't have a specific enough idea of significance to falsify the claim, unless there

---

[32] 578 F. Supp. 2d 1229 (C.D. Cal. 2008).

were no savings at all. Still, courts forced to consider heterogeneous groups of consumers at the outset might be moved to look more rigorously for falsifiable meanings in an ad, where appropriate.

The proper boundary of falsifiability, then, should have to do with the difficulty of getting reliable results from consumers, or of figuring out what the possible factual meanings are. This reformulation wouldn't eliminate the category of puffery. For example, Ivan Preston, in his article about puffery, points to consumer research asking respondents whether ad claims were "completely true," "partly true," or "not true at all." Twenty-two percent said that "State Farm is all you need to know about life insurance" was completely true, and 36 percent said it was partly true. Even higher percentages found Pan Am's claim to be "the world's most experienced airline" completely or partly true; Texaco's "you can trust your car to the man who wears the star" obtained similar levels of agreement.[33] Preston claims that, if consumers were responding to puffery in the way the law presumes, they would have answered "not true at all." But the researchers didn't give consumers the option of responding "neither true nor false," and even if they had, we still wouldn't know what they thought those phrases *meant*, or how to falsify them. Those slogans therefore strike me as examples that would still be nonactionable puffery even if we abandoned the fiction that consumers don't rely on puffery.

Better treatment of puffery would also help us understand when images can convey false messages. The Second Circuit has reasoned that, "[u]nlike words, images cannot be vague or broad."[34] It went on to hold that, while one standard definition of puffery – general claims of superiority that are so vague as to be meaningless – fits images badly, the other – "an exaggerated, blustering, and boasting statement upon which no reasonable buyer would be justified in relying" – could be applied. But that analysis is backwards. Not all images have completely transparent meanings; especially in ads, images need to be interpreted.[35] Images absolutely could convey a vague or broad meaning, depending on what the ad was doing.

But the abandonment of verifiability and focus on reasonable reliance leads courts to judge consumers instead of ads – and to find consumers wanting. In the Second Circuit case, DIRECTV ran Internet ads showing unwatchable TV images

---

[33] Preston, "Puffery and Other 'Loophole' Claims," 80–81. In another study cited by Preston, a researcher used different versions of a car ad, one using facts such as "27 miles per gallon" and the other using puffery such as "truly excellent gas mileage." Consumers rated the importance and credibility of these claims essentially the same, though courts would usually call the latter claim puffery. See Morris B. Holbrook, "Beyond Attitude Structure: Toward the Informational Determinants of Attitude," 15 *J. Marketing Res.* 545 (1978).

[34] *Time Warner Cable, Inc. v. DIRECTV, Inc.*, 497 F.3d 144 (2nd Cir. 2007).

[35] See e.g. *Rhone-Poulenc Rorer Pharms., Inc. v. Marion Merrell Dow, Inc.*, 93 F.3d 511 (8th Cir. 1996) (determining that an image of two gas pumps with different prices, as used to draw an analogy with drugs, represented that the two drugs had identical performance characteristics).

182   Rebecca Tushnet

FIGURE 7.1. Three images from DIRECTV's comparative advertising

contrasted to sharp and clear images, labeled "Other TV" and "DIRECTV," and inviting consumers to "Find out why DIRECTV's picture beats Cable" (Figure 7.1).

The district court had agreed with Time Warner that DIRECTV's own rationale for running the ads – that consumers were highly confused about HD technology and needed to be educated that both digital equipment and digital signals were required to experience HD quality – was reason to think that consumers might rely on the ads. The court of appeals found that the district court clearly erred. The court found it difficult to imagine that any consumer, no matter how unsophisticated, could be fooled into thinking cable's picture quality would be that bad.[36] That's a problem of the court's imagination; a consumer might know that ordinarily their cable wouldn't be anything near that bad. But why would a consumer transitioning to the new HDTV technology have been confident about what cable would look like when they attached an analog cable feed to their new HDTV?

---

[36] The "other TV" images in the Internet ads were extremely bad – "unwatchably blurry, distorted, and pixelated, and ... nothing like the images a customer would ordinarily see using Time Warner Cable's cable service," according to Time Warner's senior network engineer. Indeed, the pixelation was "not the type of disruption ... that could naturally happen to an analog or non-HD digital cable picture." 497 F.3d at 160. The court accepted DIRECTV's argument that even a person who didn't know anything about cable would know that Time Warner couldn't supply an unwatchable signal and still survive in the market. The comparison of DIRECTV picture quality to basic cable picture quality was so "obviously hyperbolic" that no reasonable buyer would be justified in relying on it. Ibid. at 161. See also *Wysong Corp. v. APN, Inc.* 889 F.3d 267 (6th Cir. 2018) (holding that "it is not plausible that reasonable consumers believe most of the (cheap) dog food they encounter in the pet-food aisle is in fact made of the same sumptuous (and more costly) ingredients they find a few aisles over in the people-food sections," even though some pet foods, such as the plaintiff's, did contain premium cuts of meat).

It is quite common for advertisers to imply factual claims, especially with images; too readily deeming those implications to be puffery allows deception to go unchecked. Edward F. McQuarrie and Barbara J. Phillips point out that "[i]t is rare to find a magazine ad that makes a straightforward claim like 'Tide gets clothes clean.' Instead, detergent ads claim to make your clothes 'as fresh and clean as sunshine,' or show a picture of a measuring cup filled with blue sky." They argue that using images as metaphors makes consumers more likely to pay attention to an ad, encouraging them to use their imaginations to interpret the image, which is more fun than just getting explicit information.[37] In most cases, that's no problem: as long as Tide gets clothes clean, an image that implies this is fine.[38] The difficult question, which puffery doctrine tends to obscure rather than clarify, is *what message* does the image convey?

A related way to think about the problems posed by multiple meaning involves cost–benefit analysis. For example, with the Green Guides, it appears that even an explicit claim such as "made with recycled materials" may imply other (likely false) messages about environmental benefit to a nontrivial number of consumers. As long as we think that "made with recycled materials" is an important piece of information for a much larger group of consumers, it still makes sense to allow the claim to be made. We could require additional disclosures disclaiming any additional environmental benefit, but those disclosures would likely generate potential confusions of their own.[39] The best result in terms of maximizing consumer understanding and

---

[37] One benefit for advertisers is that this process is more convincing: "Consumers are less likely to argue against associations they came up with themselves, and more likely to remember and act on them." But depending on how consumers use their imaginations, they might draw truthful or misleading conclusions. McQuarrie and Phillips found in their empirical research that when comparing ads using straightforward claims, verbal metaphors, or visual metaphors, all three ads communicated the same basic message. Nonetheless, the metaphors left consumers with more positive thoughts toward the product – they even reported receiving factual claims not explicitly present in the ad – and visual metaphors did better than verbal metaphors. Moreover, the visual metaphors worked immediately, whereas verbal metaphors required further prompting. Edward F. McQuarrie & Barbara J. Phillips, "Indirect Persuasion in Advertising: How Consumers Process Metaphors Presented in Pictures and Words," 34 J. Adver. 7 (2005).

[38] McQuarrie and Phillips conclude that

> [L]egal protections may need to evolve beyond a focus on whether a claim made in words is true or false. ... [I]t is not reasonable to infer from a picture of a bottle made of berries that the cleaning product contained therein is made of all-natural ingredients. Nonetheless, based on the evidence of this study, it is an empirical fact that such inferences do spontaneously occur when consumers are exposed to pictorial metaphors. Whether the legal system can evolve to address the possibility of misleading pictorial claims remains to be seen.

Ibid., at 19.

[39] See e.g. Oren Bar-Gill et al., Drawing False Inferences from Mandated Disclosures, *Behavioral Pub. Pol'y*, Feb. 15, 2018, www.cambridge.org/core/journals/behavioural-public-policy/article/drawing-false-inferences-from-mandated-disclosures/B39AD28CC0167B80609C433294F29C63/core-reader#.

minimizing consumer misunderstanding – which are unfortunately not opposites, given consumer heterogeneity – might therefore to be to accept "made with recycled materials" as the least deceptive, most informative version of alternative possible claims. As Richard Craswell has argued with respect to control ads in empirical tests of deceptiveness, identifying the least deceptive version of a claim that has both truthful and potentially deceptive elements allows us to take into account the interests of different groups of consumers and of the information regulation system as a whole.[40]

But this type of balancing of costs and benefits doesn't require the existing legal category of puffery, nor does current puffery doctrine obviously help explain what benefits the nondeceived consumers might be getting. By current definition, if the claim is puffery then consumers are supposedly not getting specific truthful information at all, though maybe they're getting enjoyment from a cool ad.

A clearer understanding of puffery could help us when we ask, "is there anything lost to the nondeceived group if we get rid of or reformulate the part of the message that's causing the deception?" Indeed, Preston argues that, since puffs generally imply facts, and since advertisers could benefit even more from adding explicit truthful statements if they could do so, a puff without an accompanying fact claim is likely to be fraudulent. That is, an advertiser that has safety tests (or some other tests) showing its tires to be the best should logically advertise that it has conducted such tests rather than simply claim to be the best. If it makes only the weaker puff, then it is trying to fool people into thinking that some kind of superiority exists.[41]

Even if one doesn't agree with Preston's condemnation of puffery, it is still a doctrine that is presently – and by design – detached from actual consumer reaction to advertising claims. Courts require tools to manage the conceptual boundaries of falsity in advertising. My argument is not that they should be deprived of those tools, but that conforming the concept of puffery to ideas of judicial capacity, rather than assertions about consumer behavior, would better reflect the role that puffery plays in managing litigation. That approach would be much more honest about courts' knowledge of human reactions to specific advertising. It would also help courts avoid mistakes when consumer understanding of a seemingly indeterminate term may actually be discoverable and its potential deceptiveness testable.

---

[40] Richard Craswell, "'Compared to What?' The Use of Control Ads in Deceptive Advertising Litigation," 65 *Antitrust L.J.* 757 (1997).
[41] Preston, "Puffery and Other 'Loophole' Claims," 98.

8

Search Engine Advertising, Trademark Bidding, and Consumer Intent

Anindya Ghose and Avigail Kifer[*]

8.1 INTRODUCTION

Online advertising has quickly become one of the most important avenues through which brands reach consumers. It is lauded as one of the most effective ways for a business to grow, acquire new customers, and spread information.[1] By some estimates, Internet advertising is a nearly $300 billion business.[2]

Understanding online consumer search behavior is paramount for any firm operating in a competitive market, as well as for any advertising platform or intermediary. The payoffs from a successful online advertising strategy can incentivize a variety of firm behaviors, whose implications for competition and consumer welfare can be analyzed through a marketing lens. In particular, the mechanics of search engine advertising encourages the practice of "trademark bidding," in which rival firms attempt to display ads whenever consumers search for a competitor's trademark. The effects of trademark bidding, however, largely depend on consumer intent – what a consumer intended to do when they typed in a search query.

The focus of the first part of this chapter will be on understanding and analyzing consumer intent, and how online ads might affect this analysis. In particular, we ask:

---

[*] The views expressed herein are solely those of the authors, who are responsible for the content, and do not necessarily represent the views of Cornerstone Research.

[1] Clifford Chi, "Online Advertising: Everything You Need to Know in 2019," *Hubspot*, Aug. 2, 2018, https://blog.hubspot.com/marketing/online-advertising; Dave Chaffey, "Global Social Media Research Summary 2019," *Smart Insights*, Feb. 12, 2019, www.smartinsights.com/social-media-marketing/social-media-strategy/new-global-social-media-research/; Zack Kaplan, "The Upside of Facebook's Unprecedented Power," *Vox*, May 17, 2016, www.vox.com/2016/5/17/11683858/facebook-zack-randall-media-digital-distribution; Cydney Hatch, "Understanding Internet Advertising: The Basics," *Disruptive Advertising*, Feb. 22, 2018, www.disruptiveadvertising.com/marketing/internet-advertising/.

[2] "Digital Advertising in 2022: Market Trends & Predictions," *Insider Intelligence*, Apr. 20, 2022, https://www.insiderintelligence.com/insights/digital-advertising-market-trends-predictions/.

- How does the presence of ads on search engine results pages affect consumer behavior?
- How do we determine what consumers intend to do when they submit a particular search query?

In the second part of the chapter, we evaluate whether the presence or absence of trademark bidding results in harm to consumers, and in what way, by asking:

- Does trademark bidding contribute to consumer confusion?
- Does trademark bidding encourage or inhibit consumer price search?
- Does trademark bidding affect the presence of the "most relevant" ads in search engine results?
- Does trademark bidding affect consumer search costs, and, if so, how?

8.1.1 Search Engine Advertising

Search engine advertising is a common form of online advertising, in which retailers pay search engines to run ads whenever a consumer searches for certain phrases. This type of advertising is, not surprisingly, highly competitive: its audience consists of consumers with a digital footprint and expressed interest in a particular topic. In July 2009, over 100 billion searches were conducted worldwide.[3] In 2019, industry estimates implied that Google alone responded to 5.8 billion global searches per day (70,000 searches per second, or 2 trillion searches per year).[4] Current estimates also indicate that more than 60 percent of all searches are completed on a mobile device or a tablet, adding yet another dimension to marketing strategy.[5] Competition is further increased by the limitations that search engines place on the number of ads to appear on any one results page.

Multiple firms will compete and bid for the same few ad slots on a search engine page, which vary in value based on their position on the page. Ads displace organic search results, or the non-paid-for links that appear in direct response to a consumer's search query. Thus, though ads generate revenues, search engines must limit the number of ad spots, though the way in which search engines have optimized this tradeoff for space has evolved over time.[6]

---

[3] Manish Agarwal and David K. Round, "The Emergence of Global Search Engines: Trends in History and Competition," *Competition Policy International*, 7, no. 1, Spring 2011 pp. 115–34.

[4] Meg Prater, "25 Google Search Statistics to Bookmark ASAP," *Hubspot*, May 7, 2019, https://blog.hubspot.com/marketing/google-search-statistics.

[5] Mobile Share of Organic Search Engine Visits in the United States from 3rd Quarter 2013 to 4th Quarter 2021," *Statista*, Mar. 2, 2022, https://www.statista.com/statistics/297137/mobile-share-of-us-organic-search-engine-visits/.

[6] See Ginny Marvin, "Google Continuing to Test 4 Text Ads in Search Results," *Search Engine Land*, Dec. 8, 2015, https://searchengineland.com/google-continuing-to-test-4-text-ads-in-search-results-237905; Ananya Bhattacharya, "Google Has Been Quietly Placing More Ads in Search Results," *Quartz*, Feb. 2, 2017, https://qz.com/900349/google-goog-has-been-quietly-placing-more-ads-in-search-results/.

In addition to limiting the number of ad spots, search engines must be selective about the ads they run. As a multi-sided platform, search engines must be responsive to both consumers and advertisers. Search engines rely on consumers' eyeballs (in exchange, consumers receive indexed search results that are responsive to their queries), and they rely on advertisers for revenues (in exchange, advertisers receive an audience). For this reason, merely running the ads of the highest bidders may not be in the best interests of the search engine: if an irrelevant ad displaces a relevant, organic search result, frustrated consumers could switch to another search engine or another source of information. Ad spots on that search engine's pages would be less valuable and less attractive to advertisers, and the search engine's revenues could fall. Simply, the primary challenge for the search engines is to sort through ads in a way that caters to consumers while maintaining attractiveness to advertisers.

Search engines and consumers play a repeated game, which means that search engines need to sort ads based on relevance, usefulness, and quality, to ensure that consumers return. However, it also means that search engines can gather the data from successive interactions with the same consumers to improve results and further ensure their return.[7]

Advertisers, for their part, need to devise ways to successfully compete with other advertisers and organic search results to grab consumer attention. These strategies differ from those used in traditional advertising due to the mechanics underlying search engine algorithms. Broadly, for each ad submitted to a search engine's advertising service, an advertiser must bid on keywords, which may be single words or phrases, and specify whether the keywords should appear in or match exactly to a consumer's search query. Then, every time a consumer initiates a search query, the search engine identifies the set of ads that match keywords from the consumer's search, and runs an auction to rank the ads. The winners of the auction then appear on a search engine results page.[8]

The advertiser has two strategic components to consider: the bid amount and the ad itself. All else being equal, a higher bid leads to a higher probability of success. However, the ad itself can also contribute to a successful outcome. Google, Bing, and other search engines assign each ad a value, which Google calls a "quality score." This

[7] Aidan Crook, "Adapting Search to You," *Bing Blogs*, Sept. 14, 2011, http://blogs.bing.com/search/2011/09/14/adapting-search-to-you; Thom Craver, "Bing Adds Adaptive Search, Customized by Your Search History," *Search Engine Watch*, Sept. 15, 2011, www.searchenginewatch.com/2011/09/15/bing-adds-adaptive-search-customized-by-your-search-history/; "Ad Rank," *Google*, https://support.google.com/adwords/answer/1752122; Chris Roat, "Improving Ad Rank to Show More Relevant Ad Extensions and Formats," *Google*, Oct. 22, 2013, https://adwords.googleblog.com/2013/10/improving-ad-rank.html; Frederick Vallaeys, "Quality Score Explained by a Former Googler," *Search Engine Land*, July 12, 2013, http://searchengineland.com/quality-score-explained-by-a-former-googler-166007.

[8] "The Ad Auction," *Google*, https://support.google.com/adwords/answer/1704431; "About Ad Position and Ad Rank," *Google*, https://support.google.com/adwords/answer/1722122; "Learn how Microsoft Advertising Works," *Microsoft*, https://help.ads.microsoft.com/#apex/ads/en/53102/0.

score is a function of the ad's characteristics and its expected usefulness to the consumer. Included in these calculations are predictions (based on data collected from previous and similar consumer searches) of the number of clicks the ad would receive when matched to keywords in a query, the ad's relevance (i.e. the closeness of the relationship between the keyword and the ad), and the landing page experience (i.e. the relevance of an advertiser's landing page to consumers that clicked on the ad).[9]

The advertiser has little control over certain inputs to the quality score, but can certainly affect inputs such as relevance and the landing page experience. In fact, large brands may have marketing teams that focus on "search engine strategy" and try to optimize the content and presentation of an ad to maximize its chances of winning the ad auction.

Smaller or lesser-known brands, on the other hand, may not be able to "win" on relevance. For such brands, advertising strategy may include piggy-backing off of well-recognized brands and attempting to intercept consumers on their way to the well-recognized brands' pages. This can involve bidding on another trademark in ad auctions, a practice known as trademark bidding, whose legality has been hotly contested. These actions could be seen as tricking, confusing, assisting, or informing consumers, depending on which brand is describing the auction outcome.

8.1.2 Trademark Bidding

The practice of trademark bidding has frustrated many online advertisers in the past. Concerns include trademark infringement, the loss of sales to consumers who are intercepted and steered away from visiting the trademark owner's site, the possibility that trademark bidding engenders consumer confusion, and the speculation that it increases search costs. Those in favor of trademark bidding postulate that the ads that appear as a result provide informational value, exposing consumers to new brands or to the prices of other brands' products. Analyses of the effects of trademark bidding thus must also consider consumer intent: what did the consumer intend to do with a search query containing a trademark, and was that consumer harmed by seeing the ads of competitors?

These analyses of consumer intent are informed by the content of search queries, the resulting consumer click behavior, and, perhaps less obviously, the device(s) on which the relevant searches were performed. The introduction of Internet-connected mobile devices has added several new dimensions to the search environment (and resulting analyses of consumer intent): consumer location, context, weather, time of day, trajectory, crowdedness, and so on.[10] A consumer searching for information about a clothing store while standing outside of one may have a

---

[9] "About Quality Score," *Google*, https://support.google.com/adwords/answer/7050591; "About Ad Relevance," *Google*, https://support.google.com/adwords/answer/1659752; "Landing Page Experience: Definition," *Google*, https://support.google.com/adwords/answer/1659694.

[10] Anindya Ghose, *TAP: Unlocking the Mobile Economy*, MIT Press, 2017.

different purpose than when they search for this information from home. Propensity to react to online ads (e.g. by clicking on the ad or purchasing the product) while "on the go" may be different from propensity to do so while sitting in front of a desktop computer.

In addition, because mobile search occurs on smaller screens, search costs for consumers may increase relative to those incurred when using personal computers.[11] On smaller screens, fewer ads show "above the fold" (on the first screen), likely decreasing a consumer's propensity to click on the ads they would need to scroll down to see, indicating higher search costs. However, mobile devices may have also reduced search costs by allowing search to happen anytime and anywhere. If not accounted for, the changes in consumer behavior caused by the changes in search costs might lead to inaccurate or biased conclusions about consumer intent.

Finally, analyses of consumer intent are also informed by the trademark itself: how well-known is it? How is it used in the lexicon? What does it represent? For this reason, it is useful to think of trademark bidding as occurring in two forms. In the first form, a firm bids on the brand name of a product (e.g. a shoe retailer bids on "Nike," or a kitchen appliance store bids on "Cuisinart"). In the second form, a firm bids on a trademark that is associated with a category of goods (e.g. a clothing store bids on "Bloomingdale's").

TABLE 8.1. *Chapter overview*

Issues to be addressed	• Does trademark bidding contribute to consumer confusion?
	• Would restrictions on trademark bidding encourage or inhibit consumer price search?
	• Would restrictions on trademark bidding affect the presence of the "most relevant" ads in search engine results?
	• Does trademark bidding affect consumer search costs, and if so, how?
Methods	• Analysis of ad performance data
	• Analyses of query data
	• Consumer choice models
	• Consumer search models
Relevant cases	See e.g.
	• *Travelpass Group, LLC, et al., v. Caesars Entertainment Corporation, et al.*, Case No. 5:18-cv-153 *In re 1-800 Contacts, Inc.*, FTC Docket No. 9372
	• *Sazerac Brands, LLC et al. v. Jack Daniel's Properties, Inc.*, Case No. 3:15-cv-00849
	• *Multi Time Mach., Inc. v. Amazon.com, Inc.*, 804 F.3d 930 (9th Cir. 2015)
	• *Digby Adler Grp. LLC v. Image Rent a Car, Inc.*, 79 F. Supp. 3d 1095, 1102 (N.D. Cal. 2015)
	• *Rosetta Stone Ltd. v. Google, Inc.*, 676 F.3d 144 (4th Cir. 2012)

---

[11] Ibid.

8.2 UNDERSTANDING CONSUMER INTENT

Before diving into a discussion of whether trademark bidding hurts or harms consumers, we need to understand how to interpret consumer behavior when faced with ads on a search engine results page.

To facilitate discussion, we introduce four "industry standard" terms:

- Impression: the appearance of an ad in a search engine results page.[12]
- Click-through rate (CTR): the percentage of an ad's impressions that result in a click.[13]
- Conversion: an action where a consumer, after clicking on an ad, performs an advertiser-defined action, such as an online purchase or a call to the business.[14]
- Conversion rate: the percentage of an ad's clicks that result in a conversion.[15]

8.2.1 How Does the Presence of Ads on Search Engine Results Pages Affect Consumer Behavior?

A typical search engine results page appears with paid ads and organic links. There are usually a number of paid ads at the top of the page (and sometimes also on the bottom and sides), whose presence and ordering is determined in part by factors that advertisers can control. Organic links make up the rest of the page. Their presence and ordering, on the other hand, cannot be affected by advertisers or domain owners.

As a result, the content of the top-ranked results for paid ads and organic links can be very different: there may be no relationship between the ads displayed and the top organic links. In fact, consumers may find some or all of the ads to be much less relevant to their searches than the organic links in the same page view. Under some circumstances, for example, an organic link that appears further down on a page could be more relevant than the first (paid) link on the page. However, because the attractiveness of a search engine to consumers depends on its ability to display relevant results, search engines have a strong incentive to run ads that are as relevant as possible. For this reason, search engines will cap the number of ads they display (and they will not, for that matter, always fill up all the reserved ad slots). Also for this reason, it is logical to assume that sometimes search engines might behave as though

---

[12] "Impressions: Definition," *Google*, https://support.google.com/google-ads/answer/6320?hl=en.
[13] "Clickthrough Rate (CTR): Definition," *Google*, https://support.google.com/adwords/answer/2615875.
[14] "Conversion: Definition," *Google*, https://support.google.com/adwords/answer/6365.
[15] A "conversion" is defined by the advertising retailer. Because different retailers define conversions in different ways, comparisons of ad performance across retailers are less reliable than comparisons of ad performance within retailers. "Conversion Rate: Definition," *Google*, https://support.google.com/adwords/answer/2684489.

some ads for rival firms or products (i.e. ads resulting from trademark bidding) are relevant to a consumer's search for another firm or product.

In addition to influencing the attractiveness of search engines, the presence of ads on a page can also influence consumer click behavior. One study found that the presence of a paid link for a major nationwide retailer led to higher total (organic and paid) CTRs and conversion rates for that retailer. Further, higher CTRs on paid links were associated with higher CTRs on organic links (and vice versa).[16]

Research has also demonstrated that increasing the number of ads on a search engine results page can shift clicks from a retailer's organic link (which is pushed down the page as more ads occupy the top spots) to its paid link (one of the ads on the top of the page). A large-scale field experiment on the Bing search engine studied the relationship between CTRs on organic and paid links, and the number of ads displayed in response to trademark searches. The researchers varied the number of ads displayed (keeping the ad of the "focal brand" in the top position) and found that the presence of additional ads could shift clicks from the focal brand's organic link to its paid link. The further down on the page the organic link, the less likely the consumer would scroll down to find it when the paid link was available.[17]

This result seems intuitive, but it confirms two important ideas: (1) the number of ads that are triggered in response to a search query containing a trademark term affects consumer clicks, and (2) online search is costly for the consumer. If it were equally effortless to click on a paid link at the top of a page and on an organic link further down, then the experiment would have been unlikely to uncover statistically significant results.

Similarly, a separate field experiment demonstrated that additional ads at the top of the results page, but below the focal brand's ad, generally *increased* the CTR on the focal brand's ad.[18] The researchers found that, because CTRs on organic links decreased as the number of ads increased, some of the clicks on the top ad were likely at the expense of the organic link. Still others documented the substitution between paid and organic links using data from field experiments conducted by eBay: "almost all (99.5 percent) of the forgone click traffic from [eBay's] turning off brand keyword paid search [on Yahoo! and Bing] ... was immediately captured by natural search traffic from the [search engine] platform."[19]

---

[16] Sha Yang and Anindya Ghose, "Analyzing the Relationship between Organic and Sponsored Search Advertising: Positive, Negative, or Zero Interdependence?" *Marketing Science*, 29, no. 4, 2010 pp. 602–23.

[17] Andrey Simonov et al., "Competition and Crowd-Out for Brand Keywords in Sponsored Search," *Marketing Science*, 37, no. 2, 2018 pp. 200–15.

[18] David Reiley et al., "Northern Exposure: A Field Experiment Measuring Externalities between Search Advertisements," *Proceedings of the 11th ACM Conference on Electronic Commerce*, 2010, pp. 297–304.

[19] Thomas Blake et al., "Consumer Heterogeneity and Paid Search Effectiveness: A Large-Scale Field Experiment," *Econometrica*, 83, no. 1, 2015, pp. 155–74.

This effect has been observed in industry studies as well. Google researchers compared two scenarios: (1) consumers searching for a brand name and not seeing an ad for that brand (but seeing that brand's organic link in the top-ranked organic slot); and (2) consumers searching for a brand name, seeing an ad for that brand, and *also* seeing the brand's organic link in the top slot. They found that the presence of the ad doubled the number of clicks the brand received.[20]

In sum, the academic literature and evidence from the industry indicate that increasing the number of ads displayed in trademark searches (that is, increasing the physical distance between a brand's ad and its top organic link) can shift consumer clicks from organic links to paid ads. Trademark bidding can increase the number of such ads, increasing the shift in clicks, and consequently increasing the advertising expense for the trademark owner (as ads are priced per click). To the extent that this increase in advertising expense trickles through to consumer prices, or that the increase in ads leads to higher search costs or greater consumer confusion, trademark bidding may harm consumers. On the other hand, to the extent that an increase in ads increases the amount of information available to and prominently displayed for consumers, and facilitates price search, trademark bidding may be net beneficial.

8.2.2 How Do We Know What Consumers Intended to Do When They Submitted a Particular Search Query?

A consumer who visits a search engine and types a query containing the phrase "water heaters" may be interested in learning about types of water heaters, in identifying where to buy them, or possibly even in remembering the word for "teapot." Because of the variety in the goals and purposes that may underlie seemingly identical queries, advertisers and advertising platforms alike devote resources to correctly guessing consumer intent. By successfully interpreting queries and presenting a set of links that are relevant to the consumer, a search engine can attract repeat visits from the consumer. By identifying the words or phrases that are most likely to indicate that a consumer is interested in their product, and then strategically bidding for their ads to appear in search engine results when those words or phrases are typed, an online advertiser can successfully market its wares. Misinterpreting consumer intent can be costly. Accurately and consistently identifying a consumer's goals can be lucrative.

Consumer intent can be revealed through the text of the query itself, through clicks on links and subsequent actions, such as purchases or additional clicks on a website, or through a consumer's search history. However, consumers are heterogeneous, and there is no one rule of thumb that reliably classifies a certain action of

---

[20] David Chan et al., "Impact of Ranking of Organic Search Results on the Incrementality of Search Ads," *Google*, Mar. 19, 2012, https://ai.google/research/pubs/pub37731.

any one consumer into one category or another. Furthermore, what may be the most telling clue to consumer intent – the consumer's search history – is largely unavailable to researchers studying consumer behavior.[21] Regardless, on average, consumer behavior can be categorized and interpreted through careful analysis.

With that caveat, the academic literature typically classifies search queries into three overarching categories:[22]

- Informational: these queries aim to locate content on a particular topic – consumers are hoping to answer a specific question.
- Navigational: the intent of navigational queries is to reach a particular website. It may be more convenient to navigate through the search bar than to type in the URL, or the consumer may not know the URL.
- Transactional: consumers searching with the desire to interact with a website – to perhaps make a purchase, or contact a business, for example – engage in transactional searching.

Identifying navigational searches is of primary concern in understanding the effects of trademark bidding.

Navigational queries. Generally, academic literature and industry research suggest that informational queries contain generic language, navigational queries contain brand names and trademarks, and transactional queries likely contain exact product or brand names (e.g. Google Pixel 3) or action verbs (e.g. "buy" or "order"). For example, Google's Search Quality Rating Guidelines, aimed at helping Google Search Quality Raters evaluate search results as part of Google's quality control process, indicate that queries such as "amazon" or "target website" – navigational queries, as defined above – are specific, clear, and unambiguous enough that a results page prioritizing a link to Amazon.com or Target.com "fully meets" the consumer's intent.[23]

In this way, Google's guidelines reflect an understanding that consumers searching for a brand name or trademark intend to navigate to that retailer's website or to obtain information about that retailer. To facilitate these searches, in many of the search results pages, Google also displays a "Knowledge Graph" containing

---

[21] The reason behind this unavailability is largely practical due to the sheer volume of data that would need to be stored such that a researcher could identify a consumer's search history leading up to any given search.
[22] See Andrei Broder, "A Taxonomy of Web Search," *ACM SIGIR Forum*, 36, no. 2, 2002, pp. 3–10; Daniel Rose and Danny Levinson, "Understanding User Goals in Web Search," *Proceedings of the 13th International Conference on World Wide Web*, 2004, pp. 13–19; Bernard Jansen et al., "Determining the Information, Navigational, and Transactional Intent of Web Queries," *Information Processing and Management*, 44, no. 3, 2008, pp. 1251–66.
[23] General Guidelines, "Google Search Quality Rating Program," *Google*, Sept. 5, 2019, https://static.googleusercontent.com/media/www.google.com/en//insidesearch/howsearchworks/assets/searchqualityevaluatorguidelines.pdf.

information about the people, places, and things searched for, when relevant.[24] The Knowledge Graph appears for searches containing brand names or trademarks. In addition, Google currently allows official representatives of a business to suggest changes to the Knowledge Graph card, further reflecting the understanding that consumers searching for a particular retailer are conducting navigational searches.[25]

Academic papers have also recognized that consumers who search for a particular retailer are likely to do so with a navigational intent. One paper, for example, studied the paid search advertising of a nationwide retailer. The authors estimated the relationship between CTRs, conversion rates, characteristics of the search query (such as whether the query contained retailer-specific information), and attributes of the ad displayed (such as the ad's position on the search results page among other ads, the length and specificity of the keyword that triggered the ad, and the ad's landing page quality). They determined that ads appearing in response to queries containing retailer-specific information were associated with higher CTRs and higher conversion rates – a difference of 14.7 percent and 50.6 percent, respectively.[26] In other words, queries with brand names were highly likely to be navigational.

However, note that there is a distinct difference between queries containing brand names of a product and queries containing trademarks of a retailer. A consumer may submit a search query with a brand name such as "Samsung Galaxy S7 Edge" with an informational intent to learn about the product; a navigational intent to find the Samsung webpage referencing the product; or a transactional intent to purchase the phone from the retailer's website, through a wireless carrier along with a plan, or from a diversified retailer such as Best Buy. Search queries that involve a retailer's trademark, on the other hand, are typically made with a navigational intent. That is, a consumer searching for a retailer's brand name, such as "Best Buy," generally does so with the intent to navigate to Best Buy's website.

Navigational vs. informational searches. In the online advertising space, retailers might bid to display ads in response to searches containing their own trademarks, in an effort not to lose navigational searchers who intended to reach their websites ("defensive advertising") or to strengthen the relationship with the customer and emphasize the retailer's advantages over the competition ("offensive advertising"). The goals behind trademark bidding conducted by non-trademark owners may similarly be to advertise competitive strength, but also to attempt to redirect navigational searchers away from their original target.

---

[24] Danny Sullivan, "Google Launches Knowledge Graph to Provide Answers, Not Just Links," *Search Engine Land*, May 16, 2012, https://searchengineland.com/google-launches-knowledge-graph-121585.

[25] "Update Your Google Knowledge Panel," *Google*, https://support.google.com/websearch/answer/6325583?p=kg_edit&rd=1.

[26] Anindya Ghose and Sha Yang, "An Empirical Analysis of Search Engine Advertising: Sponsored Search in Electronic Markets," *Management Science*, 55, no. 10, 2009, pp. 1605–22.

A 2010 policy change in Europe, leading to Google's relaxing its policy on who could bid on which trademarks in ad auctions, provided an ideal setting for economists to study the effect of the appearance of ads by competing retailers in search engine results pages on consumer browsing behavior. In a recent paper, researchers divided search queries into groups depending on whether or not they contained a brand name alone or with other words. Their hypothesis was that navigational queries were more likely to contain the brand name alone, and were more likely to use the search results as a shortcut to the brand name owner's site. They revealed that because of the policy change, which allowed the appearance of ads by advertisers other than the brand name owner (i.e. trademark bidding), consumers using navigational queries (i.e. queries that contained only the brand name) were less likely to reach the brand name owner's website, and consumers using nonnavigational queries (i.e. queries that contained the brand name and other words) were more likely to do so.

Interestingly, this effect was more pronounced for less well-known brand names.[27] The authors also caveat that though the policy change allowing trademark bidding made it more difficult for consumers to navigate to a brand name owner's website, it did not necessarily lead to lost profits for the brand name owner: the consumer may well have been able to navigate to another website that sold the same product.

Note that the difference between a brand name (like Samsung Galaxy) and a retailer trademark (like Best Buy) proves to be important in this study: the policy change did not necessarily lead to lost profits for the brand name owner because the owner can sell a brand through multiple retailers. A retailer trademark owner, on the other hand, has no such recourse. In other words, while a Samsung may not have lost a sale due to the policy change in Europe, a Best Buy likely did.

8.3 THINKING ABOUT CONSUMER HARM: A CASE STUDY

Consider a scenario where an online advertiser bids on its rival's trademarks, and is sued for trademark bidding. In this case, we may see extensive analyses of consumer confusion. Consider, simultaneously, a scenario where the advertiser and the rival agree not to engage in trademark bidding, or where some other restrictions on trademark bidding are imposed. In this case, we may see additional analyses relating to competition among advertisers. Allegations may include:

- Preventing competitors from providing "truthful and nonconfusing information";
- Preventing search engines from displaying the most relevant ads; and
- Increasing consumer search costs relating to the search for sneakers.

---

[27] Stefan Bechtold and Catherine Tucker, "Trademarks, Triggers, and Online Search," *Journal of Empirical Legal Studies*, 11, no. 4, 2014, pp. 718–50.

Marketing science techniques can be used to address each of these allegations. In the following sections, we parse these allegations into four discrete analyses. The first addresses consumer confusion; the second investigates the effects of the agreements on price search; the third analyzes whether the ads that were prevented from appearing were relevant in the first place; and the last explores whether consumer search costs were impacted. Each analysis, in effect, studies whether consumers were harmed.

For each section, we also discuss the type of data best suited to answer the questions at hand. Typically, the data available will govern (more frequently, limit) the types of analyses that may in fact be performed. For expository purposes, imagine that the focal firm, Sneakers R Us, is an online retailer of sneakers.

8.3.1 Does Trademark Bidding Contribute to Consumer Confusion?

One of the big questions in such a case concerns consumer confusion. Sneakers R Us, like many trademark owners, believes that consumers are likely to be confused if they type "Sneakers R Us" into the search engine bar and see an ad for any other sneaker retailer appear.[28] Such consumers, under this argument, seek information about Sneakers R Us or intend to visit the Sneakers R Us website, and would assume that the paid ad links in the search results page would direct them to that website.

Why might these consumers' assumptions be incorrect? A competitor, such as the also fictional "SneakerShop," is motivated to bid for search terms that are related to sneakers, so that its advertisements show up when consumers search for that product. This retailer is also motivated to bid for search terms related to its competitors' trademarks, such as "Sneakers R Us," so that its advertisements show up when consumers search for competitors.

The job of the marketing academic is to determine the consumer intent behind a query (what did the consumer intend to do when they typed "Sneakers R Us" into the search engine?) and to identify whether the resulting behavior indicated that a consumer was confused.

The counterargument to the consumer confusion claim could be that simply bidding on trademarked terms, without attempting to masquerade as another trademark, is not going to cause confusion. Consumers that click on the "SneakerShop" link are not naive, the counterargument would state, and in reality benefit from the information provided by the unexpected advertisement: that there are alternatives to the wares of Sneakers R Us.

Short of intercepting and interviewing the consumer as they conduct the search, how might an economist demonstrate intent and confusion? As in any analysis, the specific context and industry of the advertisers must be taken into account in order

---

[28] Note that it is unlikely that a search engine's algorithm would allow a competitor's ad to appear instead of – or even in a more prominent spot than – a "Sneakers R Us" ad.

to correctly interpret consumer behavior. Several metrics commonly collected by search engines and online advertisers, such as the CTR, can steer the investigation in the right direction.

CTR-based analysis of consumer confusion. The academic literature suggests that consumers who search for Sneakers R Us with a navigational intent are more likely to click on a Sneakers R Us ad than on another advertiser's ad.[29] They are also more likely to engage with the Sneakers R Us website after clicking on the ad. On the other hand, consumers who perform informational or nonnavigational searches are not necessarily more likely to click on a Sneakers R Us ad over another advertiser's ad, or make a purchase after clicking on the ad.

The first step in analyzing consumer intent and reaching conclusions about consumer confusion, thus, is to calculate and compare the rates of engagement with the ads that appeared in response to a query that contained Sneakers R Us keywords. Search engines collect such statistics. Datasets like Google Ads and Bing Ads contain information on each ad's keywords, impressions, clicks, cost, rank, conversions, quality score, and the match type of each keyword, aggregated across some unit of time.[30]

Consider the following two scenarios arising from a search that triggers Sneakers R Us keywords: (1) the CTR on Sneakers R Us ads is significantly higher than the CTR on competitors' ads, controlling for ad rank; and (2) the CTR on Sneakers R Us ads is similar to the CTR on "SneakerShop" ads, controlling for ad rank.

According to the academic literature, Scenario (1) would strongly indicate that consumers searched for Sneakers R Us and intended to reach the site. It would also suggest that consumers were not, on average, confused by other ads that appeared on the search engine results page.

We would also expect that the conversion rate of a Sneakers R Us ad would be high relative to the conversion rate of a non-Sneakers R Us ad that appears in response to a query containing Sneakers R Us keywords. Furthermore, the academic literature predicts that the cost per click and cost per conversion on a Sneakers R Us ad triggered by a Sneakers R Us trademark search would be lower than the cost per click and per conversion on rivals' ads.[31] Data that indicate otherwise could suggest that consumers were, in fact, confused between the ads.

---

[29] Ghose and Yang, "An Empirical Analysis of Search Engine Advertising."
[30] "Match type" is an option an advertiser can select in its bid on a keyword that relays to the search engine the degree of specificity with which it should match a keyword to a query. A "broad match," for example, allows the search engine to match the keyword to queries that contain misspellings, synonyms, and variations of the keyword. A "phrase match" instructs the search engine to match the keyword to queries that contain the exact keyword or phrase and close variations with additional words before or after. An "exact match" requires that the query matches the keyword exactly or is a close variation of the exact term with the same meaning. After the matching process, the search engine then can choose the ads to display from the set of matched ads. We do not discuss match type in this chapter. See "About Keyword Matching Options," *Google*, https://support.google.com/google-ads/answer/7478529?hl=en.
[31] See Ghose and Yang, "An Empirical Analysis of Search Engine Advertising."

In Scenario (2), consumers are searching for "Sneakers R Us" but are clicking on Sneakers R Us and SneakerShop ads with equal frequency. Such an outcome could indicate several things. For example, consumers may have been conducting navigational searches, but were confused by the SneakerShop ad and clicked on it thinking that it would lead to the Sneakers R Us site. Alternatively, consumers may have been conducting navigational searches and intended to reach the Sneakers R Us site, but received information about the existence of SneakerShop and chose to explore the SneakerShop site instead.

Confusion, in this scenario, would likely be marked by a high bounce-back rate, defined as a high percentage of consumers that leave the SneakerShop website without clicking anywhere else, and a low "dwell time," defined as the time spent on the SneakerShop landing page.[32]

8.3.2 Would Restrictions On Trademark Bidding Encourage or Inhibit Consumer Price Search?

Restrictions on trademark bidding could only inhibit price search if at least some consumers used Sneakers R Us keywords in queries intended to allow them to compare prices ("comparative searches") *and* if some of the ads blocked from appearing in response to Sneakers R Us keywords contained price information. The best data to evaluate these questions would be query data from Google, Bing, or other popular search engines. Query data could contain summaries of the queries, keywords associated with the queries (as determined by the search engine), and the set of advertisers, ad campaigns, and ad groups (as submitted by the advertiser to the search engines) that appeared in response to the queries, aggregated across some unit of time. In addition, it could contain measures relating to ad performance, such as impression counts, clicks, and conversions. Comscore also provides interesting data with similar fields (the Comscore Web Behavior Panel), and is commonly used by academics.[33]

Focusing first on consumer search: statistics on query data are particularly useful to address questions on comparative searches. The proportion of searches containing comparative language, such as "cheaper," "better," "vs," "expensive," or "competitor," would be particularly revealing. If the proportion were high, consumers likely

---

[32] The bounce-back rate measures the number of times per click that a user returns to the search engine results page instead of remaining on the landing page. The dwell time measures the length of time that a user stays on the landing page. See "Bounce Rate," *Google*, https://support.google.com/analytics/answer/1009409?hl=en; Duane Forrester, "What Is Dwell Time & Why It Matters for SEO," *Search Engine Journal*, Feb. 21, 2019.

[33] Comscore collects detailed online browsing and transaction data from internet users, whose activity is channeled through Comscore proxy servers. It reports the search queries a user ran, all the ads displayed (as well as the text of those ads), and any clicks on the paid and organic links that appeared. Because Comscore also collects information on organic links, it provides another dimension to internet search analyses.

were conducting price searches, and could potentially be harmed by a reduction in ads from Sneakers R Us' competitors.

The added complication in this case is that the question of whether Sneakers R Us is cheaper than SneakerShop is not a straightforward one. Because sneakers are highly differentiated products, a consumer needs to compare prices of specific brands, rather than the overall price levels of two retailers that sell a variety of brands.

Focusing next on the informational content of the blocked ads, price information in the blocked ads presumably would have allowed consumers to price shop. However, to argue that price search was inhibited, one would need to demonstrate that consumers commonly relied on these types of searches for price information, as opposed to searches for generic phrases like "cheap sneakers" or brand names of sneakers such as "Nike Air Zoom Structure." Google Trends provides a tool allowing users to compare frequencies of search terms over time and could be used to analyze the question of whether, and how frequently, consumers were using terms like "cheap sneakers" or using brand names in searches.

On the other hand, the blocked ads may not have contained price information. In that case, a consumer would have had to click on the blocked ads and navigate the respective landing pages to collect price information. In that case, the analysis would revert to one discussed in Section 8.2, concerning consumer intent.

8.3.3 Would Restrictions On Trademark Bidding Affect the Presence of the "Most Relevant" Ads in Search Engine Results?

The next question asks whether restrictions on trademark bidding could distort search engine results such that search engines are no longer able to present the most relevant sets of ads to consumers. Since advertisers are unable to affect organic search results, this question is specifically about the set of ads that appear at the top of the page.

Answering this question requires the construction of a counterfactual – the ad layouts (the set and ordering of ads on a page) that would have appeared in response to search queries *but for* the restrictions on trademark bidding – and a prediction of how consumers would have behaved in terms of clicks and conversions. Such a prediction is developed by first restrictions preferences using data from searches affected by the restrictions, and then applying the preference estimates to the "but-for" ad layouts to determine a consumer's likelihood to click on and further interact with one ad over another.

Creating the "but-for" set of ad layouts. The creation of a "but-for" world is difficult largely for two reasons: first, we do not have access to the algorithms used by search engines to choose, rank, and display ads; and second, we would observe neither the characteristics of the ads nor the identities of the advertisers that would have bid to display their ads, in the absence of the restrictions at issue. Each of these issues provides difficulties on its own. Even if we had information on the universe of advertisers that would choose to advertise on Sneakers R Us keywords in the absence of the restrictions at issue, we would not know (without access to the search engine algorithms) when and where the ads would appear or even how many there would be. Conversely, even if we could replicate the algorithms, we would not know which advertisers would bid on competitor trademarks.

Still, under some circumstances, it may be possible to construct the "but-for" world of ad layouts. The next step would be to estimate consumer preferences in the real world, and apply these preferences to searches in the "but-for" world.

Estimating consumer preferences. To estimate consumer preferences, economists typically model consumer choices using "logistic regression models." In cases where consumers can choose among more than two options, the model expands into a "multinomial logistic regression."

These models position a consumer's "click" as a choice that depends on a variety of factors, such as what was searched for, what ads appeared (and in what order), the identity of the advertisers, and certain consumer characteristics, among other things. The estimation would reveal how important each of these factors is in the consumer's click decision. An economist can then predict how a consumer will behave when faced with other, counterfactual, ad layouts.

For example, the estimation could reveal that the number of words in a consumer's query strongly and directly predicts likelihood of clicking on the ad belonging to the trademark searched for. It could also reveal, for instance, that younger users are more likely to click on the first ad in an ad layout, regardless of the keywords in their queries.

These preferences can then be applied to the "but-for" sets of ad layouts to predict the number of clicks and conversions on the ads that were prevented from appearing, relative to the actual ads that appeared for Sneakers R Us. Significant changes in CTRs can be interpreted as suggestive that the "most relevant" ads were, in fact, prevented from appearing. The results of this model should not be proposed as conclusive evidence, however, as they do not incorporate analyses of consumer confusion or changes in search costs.

8.3.4 *Does Trademark Bidding Affect Consumer Search Costs, and If So How?*

Advertisements do not have the best reputation in American culture – they can be seen as annoying, distracting, or useless. However, ads may provide price information, allowing consumers to compare prices without spending additional time perusing websites, or alerting consumers to the presence of new or previously unknown brands. While consumers may benefit from the information the additional ads provide, the benefit is neither guaranteed nor boundless. In addition, the problem of choice overload – where a decision is made more difficult by the presence of additional choices – also applies to consumers researching products on the Internet.

One of the issues underlying complaints concerning online advertisements is the presence of "search costs." Advertisements can clutter a page, potentially shift relevant content out of sight, and be generally distracting. This can make it more difficult for a consumer to conduct a search. In the context of online search, consumer search costs could include the costs of scrolling, of looking at an additional ad, of clicking on an additional link, or of processing additional information. While search costs on the Internet seem to be markedly lower than in other contexts (consumers do not, for example, need to drive to another store to observe prices of competing products), they are not zero.[34]

Search costs in most contexts are difficult to quantify as they are rarely explicitly measurable. Furthermore, the estimate of their magnitude depends on whether the consumer appears to search sequentially (i.e. scrolls through and rejects each successive option because they predict the next option is likely to be better, until deciding that the marginal cost of an extra search exceeds the expected marginal benefit) or nonsequentially (i.e. a priori decides to evaluate a certain number of options before making a choice).[35] The academic literature, including recent studies in economics and marketing, generally assumes that consumers search sequentially on search engines.[36]

Search costs may also be affected by whether the consumer is searching on a desktop or a smartphone, as discussed in the introduction. Although smartphones and other Internet-connected mobile devices provide consumers with more "instant" access to information, the difference in screen size of a mobile device compared to a PC means that users must scroll down to find links on a mobile device's search engine results page that would otherwise appear in a single view on a computer.[37] This in turn increases the importance of ad rank, as well as the consequences of trademark bidding.[38]

---

[34] See Dale Mortensen, "Job Search, the Duration of Unemployment, and the Phillips Curve," *American Economic Review*, 60, no. 5, 1970, pp. 847–62; Song Yao and Carl Mela, "Sponsored Search Auctions: Research Opportunities in Marketing," *Foundations and Trends in Marketing*, 3, no. 2, 2009, pp. 75–126.

[35] Weitzman, in single-agent scenarios, and Reinganum, in multi-agent scenarios, have laid theoretical foundations for sequential search models. Martin Weitzman, "Optimal Search for the Best Alternative," *Econometrica*, 47, no. 3, 1979, pp. 641–54; Jennifer Reinganum, "Strategic Search Theory," *International Economic Review* 23, no. 1, 1982, pp. 1–17.

[36] See Jun Kim et al., "Online Demand under Limited Consumer Search," *Marketing Science*, 29, no. 6, 2010, pp. 1001–23; Sergei Koulayev, "Search for Differentiated Products: Identification and Estimation," *RAND Journal of Economics*, 45, no. 3, 2014, pp. 553–75; Yuxin Chen and Song Yao, "Sequential Search with Refinement: Model and Application with Click-Stream Data," *Management Science*, 63, no. 12, 2016, pp. 4345–65.

[37] Anindya Ghose et al., "How Is the Mobile Internet Different? Search Costs and Local Activities," *Information Systems Research*, 24, no. 3, 2012, pp. 613–31.

[38] Ibid.

Despite the complexities in analyzing search costs, understanding the directionality and significance of changes to the search environment is crucial for understanding whether consumers are harmed or not.

Given the appropriate data, economists typically estimate search costs by tailoring one of several canonical search costs models to the specific setting at hand. These models typically involve specifying a consumer's utility function, search method (sequential or nonsequential), distribution of search costs, and choice set.

For sequential search models, the economist must also outline the consumer's decision tree: at each decision tree node, the consumer evaluates the choice in front of them, considers the expected utility from following all the possible paths ahead, and decides whether or not to stop searching. Once the model is specified, the model parameters are then calibrated against consumers' actual search behavior. The dollar value of a consumer's expected reward from continuing to search would be equal to the cost of searching through exactly one more option.

For nonsequential search models, the economist writes out the consumer's total cost of searching through n choices. The consumer's optimal number of choices is the number n at which the expected value of choosing among n options minus the expected value of choosing among $n+1$ options equals the consumer's cost of looking at that $(n+1)$th option.

If the addition of ads from retailers competing with Sneakers R Us increases consumer search costs, then one could conclude that such ads harm consumers. Industries with high search costs can be less competitive, as the costs make it more difficult for a consumer to learn about prices and find the best deal.

8.4 WHAT THE FUTURE MAY HOLD

Moving beyond the world of search engine advertising, a host of similar issues are relevant in the broader context of display advertising on the Internet.

Traditionally, display ads and search ads were considered by advertisers and media planners to serve different purposes. That is, display ads were meant to be used (and viewed as more effective) in an earlier stage in the path to purchase journey to create brand awareness, and search ads were meant to be used (and viewed as more effective) in a later stage in the path to purchase journey to create conversions. Today, advances in tracking technologies have allowed brands to identify both potential consumers and those who have expressed initial interest. In other words, advertisers can now effectively use display ads and search ads across the consumer purchase journey: to increase brand awareness, to increase a consumer's propensity to visit a brand's website, and to increase a consumer's propensity to make a purchase.[39] In fact, from an advertiser's

---

[39] Vilma Todri et al., "Trade-Offs in Online Advertising: Advertising Effectiveness and Annoyance Dynamics across the Purchase Funnel," *Information Systems Research*, 31, no. 1, 2020, pp. 102–25.

perspective, display ads are often interchangeable with search ads, and are often treated as such in ad budget allocation decisions.[40]

As a result, trademark bidding can have meaningful effects for both search ads and display ads. In addition, consumer confusion can arise in this ecosystem if consumers believe that the publishing of an ad by a platform is tantamount to endorsement of the brand or the content by the platform. A parallel issue arose during the 2016 US presidential election, where some social media sites were criticized for inadvertently running fake news stories that consumers did not realize were fake, due to the reputability of the sponsoring platform.

Another source of confusion can arise if the creative or design element of a display or search ad by a given brand closely resembles a competing brand. Conversely, a digital ad from a well-known brand positioned next to one containing extreme content (such as violence, terrorism, pornography, or drug trafficking) might undermine the reputation and quality perception of that brand. While this kind of confusion from digital advertising may not arise for a savvy user, the general lack of awareness about how digital ads are bought and sold can lead to such confusion in the minds of other consumers. Issues of "brand safety" will come into play, requiring attention from both brands and publishers.

As data-collection technologies improve and online advertising platforms gain access to more information about viewers, it may become possible to both better understand consumer intent and more accurately and effectively deliver ads to a target audience. Importantly, advertising algorithms enhanced by big data can also allow smaller, less well-known brands to reach consumers. Both scenarios could be welfare enhancing, if accomplished thoughtfully and with consumer privacy preferences in mind.

---

[40] A. Ghose and V. Todri, "Towards Digital Attribution: Measuring the Impact of Display Advertising on Online Consumer Behavior," *MIS Quarterly*, 40, no. 4, 2015, pp. 889–910.

PART III

Methodological Advances

9

Choice Experiments

Reducing Complexity and Measuring Behavior Rather than Perception

Joel H. Steckel, Rebecca Kirk Fair, Kristina Shampanier, and Anne Cai

9.1 INTRODUCTION

Surveys in trademark, trade dress, and false advertising cases often focus on liability. For example, in trademark cases, the focus of survey evidence has often been on whether consumers confuse the two marks. Similarly, survey evidence in false advertising cases has focused on whether the at-issue advertising claim misleads or deceives consumers. Surveys that address these issues of alleged confusion or deception measure consumer "perception," and the results are often the centerpiece of a plaintiff's liability arguments. While such questions may be central to cases that seek an injunction or aim to prevent the issuance of a new trademark, they are less relevant in questions of impact or injury.

In contrast, for patent infringement cases, the question generally raised in survey research has been one of "materiality" – that is, whether and to what extent consumers would *purchase* the product due to the consumer benefit derived from the patented feature. To assess or measure harm in such matters, the key question is often whether the product features covered by the patent are at the nexus of demand for the product. Thus, not surprisingly, surveys in patent cases more often go beyond consumer perception, and instead focus on the questions of purchase drivers and consumer choices.

Given the increasing emphasis in false advertising and trademark protection cases on impact and measures of damage, the "materiality" question can be as relevant, if not more relevant, than a question of perception.[1] In damages cases, such as those

---

[1] See, for example, Order, *J-B Weld Company, LLC v. The Gorilla Glue Company*, US District Court for the Northern District of Georgia (Atlanta Division), Civil Action No.: 1:17-cv-03946-LMM, Oct. 17, 2018, discussed in more detail below. See also Findings of Fact and Conclusions of Law, *State of Washington v. Comcast Cable Communications Management, LLC, et al.*, Superior Court of Washington in and for the County of King, No. 16-2-18224-1 SEA, June 6, 2019; *Singleton v. Fifth Generation, Inc.*, US Dist. LEXIS 170415 (N.D.N.Y. 2017).

brought by a class of consumers or a competitor, the question of consumers' perception may be supportive of liability, but the critical issue is whether and how consumers respond to the alleged confusion, deception, or infringement. In particular, the outcome of cases may depend on whether the allegedly confusing or misleading elements would affect consumers' purchase decisions. Rather than merely assessing how consumers *perceive* the allegedly confusing mark or allegedly misleading label, the cases may hinge on whether consumers *bought* a product of a certain brand due to the at-issue mark or patent, or the allegedly misleading elements of its label.

For example, in *J-B Weld Company, LLC v. The Gorilla Glue Company*, J-B Weld Company alleged that Gorilla Glue misled consumers and misrepresented that the GorillaWeld product was an epoxy. The plaintiff alleged that Gorilla Glue's "false and misleading statements and deception have [had] and will have a material effect on purchasing decisions, such as by consumers and retail customer[s]."[2] In the court's order on summary judgment, the court highlighted that the plaintiff "must establish materiality" regardless of whether or not the allegedly misleading claim is found to be literally false, or literally true but misleading.[3] J-B Weld Company's failure to offer any evidence that Gorilla Glue's statements were material to actual consumer purchasing decisions led the court to grant summary judgment in favor of Gorilla Glue.[4]

In this chapter, we will discuss methodologies that can be used to explore how consumers behave rather than what they think, and how to address these questions in each of three legal settings: trademark/trade dress infringement, patent infringement, and false advertising/consumer protection. In the context of litigation in particular, a simple choice experiment can lead to a robust and stable conclusion in an efficient and cost- and time-saving manner.

Establishing materiality is often a requirement under federal and state laws. Under section 43(a) of the Lanham Act, plaintiffs must demonstrate that the alleged deception "has a material effect on purchasing decisions."[5] Similarly, under the Consumer Protection Act Standard, "only material misrepresentations and omissions are actionable."[6] An act or practice is deceptive if it "could be of material

---

[2] First Amended Complaint, *J-B Weld Company, LLC v. The Gorilla Glue Company*, US District Court for the Northern District of Georgia (Atlanta Division), Civil Action No.: 1:17-cv-03946-LMM, Feb. 12, 2018, at ¶¶ 56–59.
[3] Order, *J-B Weld Company, LLC v. The Gorilla Glue Company*, US District Court for the Northern District of Georgia (Atlanta Division), Civil Action No.: 1:17-cv-03946-LMM, Oct. 17, 2018, at p. 22.
[4] Ibid., at pp. 26–27.
[5] Ibid., at p. 20.
[6] Findings of Fact and Conclusions of Law, *State of Washington v. Comcast Cable Communications Management, LLC, et al.*, Superior Court of Washington in and for the County of King, No. 16-2-18224-1 SEA, June 6, 2019.

importance to a customer's decision to purchase the company's services."[7] The materiality standard also exists for state laws. For example, under section 350 of New York's General Business Law, a plaintiff is required to demonstrate that "the act, practice or advertisement was misleading in a material respect" and that "the plaintiff was injured as a result of the deceptive practice, act or advertisement."[8] Some state laws require plaintiffs to establish causation. For example, under Florida's Deceptive and Unfair Trade Practices Act (FDUTPA), a consumer claim must have three elements: a deceptive act or unfair practice, causation, and actual damages.[9]

9.2 METHODS OF ASSESSING MATERIALITY

When trying to assess materiality, parties may be inclined to conduct a survey to ask consumers directly about hypothetical situations, such as "Would you still buy X if it did not have Y?" or even a series of direct closed-ended questions regarding the importance of specific attributes, performance claims, or advertisements. Despite the simplistic appeal of such an approach, these questions cannot reliably assess the impact of an at-issue element on consumer behavior.

These types of direct appeals are subject to the introduction of bias by focusing respondents on the elements of interest. For example, if respondents are asked "Would you still buy your smartphone if it had lower battery life?" they focus on battery life and none of the other features of a smartphone that may influence their purchase. As a result, they may overstate the importance they give to battery life relative to how they prioritize it when actually deciding which smartphone to purchase.[10] Academic literature has demonstrated this "focusing illusion" – when considering a single factor, respondents are prone to exaggerate its importance. For example, a study published in *Science* found that respondents exaggerated the contribution of income to their happiness, while in reality respondents with above-average income were barely happier than others.[11] Additionally, direct

---

[7] *Indoor Billboard/Washington, Inc. v. Integra Telecom of Washington, Inc.*, 162 Wn. 2d 59, 78, 170 P.3d 10 (2007).

[8] See, for example, *Ackerman v. Coca-Cola Company and Energy Brands, Inc.*, 2013 WL 7044866 (E.D.N.Y. 2013); *Singleton v. Fifth Generation, Inc.*, 2017 US Dist. LEXIS 170415 (N.D.N.Y. 2017).

[9] See, for example, *Fitzpatrick v. Gen. Mills, Inc.*, 236 F.R.D. 687 (S.D. Fla. 2010), *vacated on other grounds*, 635 F.3d 1279 (11th Cir. 2011); *Coleman v. CubeSmart*, 328 F. Supp. 3d 1349 (S.D. Fla. 2018); *Lombardo v. Johnson & Johnson Consumer Cos.* 124 F. Supp. 3d 1283 (S.D. Fla. 2015).

[10] This phenomenon is known as "the focusing illusion." As an example, Kahneman et al. found that "[w]hen people consider the impact of any single factor on their well-being – not only income – they are prone to exaggerate its importance." Kahneman, D., A. B. Krueger, D. Schkade, N. Schwarz, and A. A. Stone, "Would You Be Happier if You Were Richer? A Focusing Illusion," *Science*, 2006, Vol. 312, pp. 1908–10.

[11] Ibid.

questions may provide respondents with hints as to the purpose of the survey and result in respondents providing answers they think the survey is looking for, rather than providing their actual preferences.[12]

In addition to introducing bias into responses, research has demonstrated that individuals are unable to accurately assess and express their preferences when directly asked, as they may not have a clear understanding of their internal decision-making process. In fact, since at least the 1970s, academics have acknowledged the shortcomings of asking consumers for their preferences directly, and noted consumers' inability to access their own true motivations.[13] As a result, these explicitly stated preferences may differ from those that consumers would reveal when making an actual decision. The methods outlined in the following attempt to estimate more closely such "revealed" preferences, albeit using hypothetical scenarios.

9.2.1 Conjoint Surveys as an Indirect Method of Assessing Materiality

Conjoint surveys are a widely used indirect method to assess materiality, particularly in patent litigation and false advertising. Conjoint surveys can overcome the biases and limitations of attempting direct elicitation of stated preferences. In simple terms, a conjoint survey generally asks each respondent to perform between eight and sixteen choice tasks, each of which presents the respondent with a set of products from the same product category (e.g. smartphones) with varying attribute levels to choose from (e.g. the smartphones could vary on price, brand, screen size, battery life, and memory). As discussed in Chapter 10, when a large number of respondents complete these tasks, the choice data can be used to assess consumers' preferences associated with each attribute or attribute level.[14]

Conjoint analysis is a sophisticated and complicated tool that was originally developed to gather consumer insights into the new product development process. When well-designed, conjoint analysis (or simply "conjoint") can be a powerful instrument that provides detailed information about consumer preferences. However, a well-designed [for consistency] conjoint requires consideration of a number of different factors, including incentive alignment, selection of six to eight

---

[12] This is known as the "demand effects" or "demand artifacts" phenomenon. See, for example, Sawyer, A. G., "Demand Artifacts in Laboratory Experiments in Consumer Research," *Journal of Consumer Research*, Mar. 1975, Vol. 1, No. 4, pp. 20–30, at p. 20. See also Simonson, I. and R. Kivetz, "Demand Effects in Likelihood of Confusion Surveys: The Importance of Marketplace Conditions," *Trademark and Deceptive Advertising Surveys: Law, Science and Design*, ed. Shari Seidman Diamond and Jerre B. Swann, American Bar Association, 2012, pp. 243–59.

[13] Nisbett, Richard E. and Timothy DeCamp Wilson, "Telling More Than We Can Know: Verbal Reports on Mental Processes," *Psychological Review*, May 1977, Vol. 84, No. 3, pp. 231–59.

[14] For a detailed explanation of conjoint survey design and analysis, see Orme, B. K., *Getting Started with Conjoint Analysis*, 3rd ed., Research Publishers, 2014.

key attributes to include, selection of the levels of each of those attributes, and descriptions of them. This design process typically requires extensive testing that is often time-intensive and expensive. Further, once the data is collected, appropriate data analysis (e.g. hierarchical Bayesian analysis paired with estimation of supply and market simulations) is another minefield into which errors can creep.

As a result of this complexity, conjoint surveys are often misapplied in litigation matters, and their results are often misinterpreted. In one recent case, for example, a proposed conjoint study was criticized for equating willingness to pay with market price, and for not capturing the relevant products in the marketplace.[15] In another case, a conjoint was critiqued for not being able to quantify a hypothetical sales reduction and for not accurately reflecting realities of the marketplace, though the court noted in this case that these critiques would at best go toward weight and not admissibility.[16] Further, due to the large quantity of detailed data yielded by conjoint surveys, isolated responses can be construed by the other side to undermine the relevance and robustness of the overall results. Given these limitations and the time-intensive and expensive process typically required to design a reliable conjoint, more straightforward approaches to assessing materiality can often be useful alternatives.

9.2.2 Simple Choice Experiments to Measure Causation

While conjoint surveys can provide much more detailed information about consumer preferences, sometimes choice experiments can be a more straightforward option. If the research question is one of causation, a simple choice experiment can be an effective and more direct method to isolate the effect of a particular feature on consumers' purchase decisions regarding a complex product with many salient features. An appropriate choice experiment must be constructed based on factors such as the type of product, how or through what channels the product is sold or advertised, and the target population. This type of research is often similar to the research done to inform a conjoint study, but in a much more concentrated and focused manner.

9.2.2.1 Setting Up a Choice Experiment

In a typical choice experiment, as in most surveys, potential respondents must first pass a screening procedure to ensure that they reflect the target population. For

---

[15] Opposition to Motion for Class Certification, *Stockinger, et al. v. Toyota Motor Sales, U.S.A., Inc.*, US District Court, Central District of California, Case No. 2:17-cv-00035-VAP, Oct. 21, 2019, Exhibit A, pp. 7–9.

[16] Order Granting in Part and Denying in Part Motions to Exclude Expert Opinions, *Apple Inc. v. Samsung Electronics Co., Ltd.*; *Samsung Electronics America, Inc.*; *and Samsung Telecommunications America LLC*, Northern District of California, San Jose Division, Case No. 12-cv-00630, Feb. 25, 2014, pp. 24, 30, 32–33, and 36.

example, if the product at issue is a smartphone, the relevant target population may be consumers who purchased a new smartphone in the past three months or are planning to do so in the next three months. Respondents are then randomly assigned to one of two groups (although there can be more groups if the causality of multiple attributes needs to be dissected). The random assignment allows the researcher to create two situations in which participants are effectively the same but are faced with a scenario that differs only by the item of interest. This approach is what allows the researcher to establish causality, and this is also why the study is called an "experiment."

In essence, this procedure resembles the testing of drugs, where one group is given the new drug while the other gets the old drug (or a placebo). Random assignment guarantees that the two groups are statistically the same, and that the accused feature or trademark or claim – whichever is varied between the groups – is what actually drives the difference in outcomes. And, as in medical studies, respondents are not aware which group they are in. Further, unlike in medical studies, respondents do not even know that there are multiple groups, which reduces the likelihood of the respondents being able to guess the purpose of the study.

After the randomized group assignment, a choice experiment presents respondents with the at-issue product along with, say, two competitor products. Respondents in the test group see the at-issue product with the at-issue attribute (e.g. trademark or allegedly misleading statement), while the respondents in the control group are shown the at-issue product with the at-issue attribute replaced with a "placebo" or "but-for" claim or attribute. That is, the adjusted phrase or logo or shape is one that plaintiffs do not find to be deceptive or confusing to consumers, or infringing on a patent or a trademark or trade dress. For example, if the at-issue claim is that a cream "removes wrinkles," a claim in the control group could be "reduces appearance of wrinkles" if plaintiffs consider that claim nondeceptive. Aside from the at-issue attribute, all else would be the same between the two experimental groups. Figure 9.1 presents excerpts from the test and control stimuli in the *Hobbs v. Brother* choice experiment.

In such an experiment, the "dependent measure" would be the choices respondents make – specifically, the share of respondents choosing the at-issue product. To assess whether the at-issue attribute has a material effect on consumers' purchase decisions, we would compare the share of respondents choosing the at-issue product in each of the two groups. For example, if there is no statistically significant difference in the share, the at-issue attribute, product feature, trademark, or product claim has no material impact on consumer choice (and, as a corollary, the price premium on the at-issue attribute is zero). Figure 9.2 presents the outcome in the *Hobbs v. Brother* choice experiment.

A further simplified approach to a choice experiment could – instead of presenting an array of products and asking respondents to choose – present only the focal

Product Details

The Brother DCP-7065DN Multifunction Laser Printer offers three-in-one functionality, versatile network connectivity, and professional-grade printing for home offices and small businesses.

Bring a high-performance, versatile printer to your small business or home network with the Brother DCP-7065DN Multifunction Laser Printer. This printer is fully network-ready and features an integrated Ethernet jack that lets you connect it to your network. It can print up to 24 pages per minute, ensuring that it can keep up with heavy print loads. And with its built-in scanner and copier, this printer is an ideal solution for all of your business' document-creating needs.

- Network-ready; Ethernet an Hi-Speed USB 2.0 connectivity
- Up to 2400 × 600 dpi print resolution
- Automatic duplex print/copy/scan
- Prints and copies up to 24 ppm
- 10,000-page monthly duty cycle
- Supports a variety of "scan-to" features including email, file, image, and OCR
- High-quality color scanning up to 19200 dpi
- Unscannable margins of only 3mm on each edge
- 3-in-1 functionality lets you copy, print, and scan
- Adjustable, 250-sheet capacity paper tray for letter- or legal-size paper
- 25-page automatic document feeder copies and scans multiple pages
- Approx. 8.5 seconds to print first page
- Convenient, walk-up copying, no PC required
- 32MB memory
- Backed by a 1-year limited warranty

Control Group:
No unscannable margin disclaimer.

Test Group 1:
" • Unscannable margins of only 1mm on each edge"

Test Group 2:
" • Unscannable margins of only 3mm on each edge"

FIGURE 9.1. Example stimulus for three groups in *Hobbs* v. *Brother*.
Kenneth Hobbs v. Brother International Corporation, et al., No. 2:15-CV-01866-PSG-VBK, Expert Report of Joel H. Steckel, PhD, June 28, 2016 (C.D. Cal. 2016).

	Control Group (No Disclaimer)	Test Groups (With Disclaimer for Brother)
Brother	33%	31%
HP	33%	31%
Canon	25%	29%
None of the above	9%	10%
Total	100%	100%

FIGURE 9.2. Example dependent measure outcomes from *Hobbs* v. *Brother*.
"*Suppose you were choosing a multi-function printer with scanning and copying capabilities. Which device would you purchase?*".
Kenneth Hobbs v. Brother International Corporation, et al., No. 2:15-CV-01866-PSG-VBK, Expert Report of Joel H. Steckel, PhD, June 28, 2016 (C.D. Cal. 2016).

product to respondents and ask for likelihood of purchase of that product. In an experiment in which the dependent measure is likelihood of purchase (e.g. on a 0–10 scale), we would compare the mean likelihood of purchase between the two groups and assess whether there is a statistically significant difference.[17] Note that the predictive power of a dependent measure assessing purchase likelihood can vary depending on the type of scale used, and the strength of the relationship between respondents' stated intentions and ultimate purchase behavior can vary with the types of products that are studied and the ways in which data is collected.[18] For example, Morwitz, Steckel, and Gupta found that intentions are more closely correlated with ultimate purchase behavior in purchases of existing products than of new ones; in purchases of durable products than of nondurable goods; in purchases with short rather than long time horizons; when respondents are asked to provide intentions to purchase specific brands or models instead of at the product category level; when purchases are measured in terms of trial rates as opposed to total market sales; and when purchase intentions are collected in a comparative mode instead of monadically.[19]

In addition to determining whether the appropriate dependent measure is share of choice or likelihood of purchase, designing a choice experiment can involve a number of other considerations, depending on the nature of the product or allegations. For example, the brands of the products shown could be anonymized, if the at-issue claims are too widely associated with the brands, or if specific attributes or claims are being tested apart from the brand effect. However, in a trademark case, if the goal is to isolate the impact of the brand on the likelihood of purchase, anonymization does not make sense, but the development or identification of an appropriately realistic control brand will be critically important.

Another consideration is how narrowly we want to define the feature of interest, and whether we want to dissect the impact of its components. For example, if the allegedly misleading claim states that a product is "All natural" with "No preservatives," a two-group experiment can be conducted in which the control version of the product mentions neither the term "natural" nor "preservatives." Alternatively, a four-group experiment can be conducted in which one group sees the as-is version, the second sees a version without the "All natural" claim but with

---

[17] Experiments using likelihood of purchase as the dependent measure have been accepted by courts. See, for example, *State of Washington v. Comcast Cable Communications Management, LLC, et al.*, No. 16-2-18224-1 SEA, Expert Report of Professor Ravi Dhar, June 4, 2018 (King County Superior Court).

[18] See, for example, Kalwani, Manohar U. and Alvin J. Silk, "On the Reliability and Predictive Validity of Purchase Intention Measures," *Marketing Science*, 1982, Vol. 1, No. 3, pp. 243–322; Juster, F. T., "Consumer Buying Intentions and Purchase Probability: An Experiment in Survey Design," *Journal of the American Statistical Association*, 1966, Vol. 61, pp. 658–96; Granbois, D. H. and J. O. Summers, "Primary and Secondary Validity of Consumer Purchase Probabilities," *Journal of Consumer Research*, Mar. 1975, Vol. 1, No. 4, pp. 31–38; Day, Dianne, et al., "Predicting Purchase Behaviour," *Marketing Bulletin*, 1991, Vol. 2, pp. 18–30.

[19] Morwitz, Vicki G., Joel H. Steckel, and Alok Gupta, "When Do Purchase Intentions Predict Sales?" *International Journal of Forecasting*, 2007, Vol. 23, No. 3, pp. 347–64.

	"No preservatives" claim	*Without* "No preservatives" claim
"All natural" claim	**Group 1: As-is** "All natural" claim "No preservatives" claim	**Group 2:** "All natural" claim *Without* "No preservatives" claim
Without "All natural" claim	**Group 3:** *Without* "All natural" claim "No preservatives" claim	**Group 4:** *Without* "All natural" claim *Without* "No preservatives" claim

FIGURE 9.3. Example four-group experimental setup to disentangle the effects of two separate claims

the "No preservatives" claim, the third sees the "All natural" claim but not the "No preservatives" claim, and the fourth group sees neither of the two claims. Such an approach would allow us to establish whether one of the claims impacts consumer demand, and if so, which one that is. The same approach also allows us to capture interaction effects. For example, "No preservatives" may only drive demand when it is accompanied by the "All natural" claim, but not on its own. Such choices may be dependent on the extent to which plaintiffs have alleged deception by each component of the claim, or in the context of the overall packaging. Figure 9.3 presents a potential design evaluating both the individual and joint impact of the "All natural" and "No preservatives" advertising claims.

The technique of using a simple choice experiment has been accepted in court and cited in decisions. For example, in *Kenneth Hobbs v. Brother International Corporation, et al.*, the at-issue claim involved a printer's alleged inability to scan the margin at the edge of a page. A simple choice experiment was designed to assess the impact, if any, of that at-issue claim on consumers' purchase decisions. Respondents (past and potential purchasers of a multifunction printer) were randomly assigned to one of three groups. One group was presented with the printer advertising materials similar to those in the marketplace. That is, no mention of the unscannable margin was included. A second group was presented with the same materials but the unscannable margin and its size were mentioned in the specifications. The third group saw materials similar to those presented to the second group, but with the size of the unscannable margin reduced. All three groups were presented with advertising materials for two competing printers.

Respondents were then asked to indicate which of the three printers they would purchase. By comparing the share of respondents in each of the three groups that chose the at-issue printer, the expert found that a printer's inability to scan the area at the edge of a page did not affect which printer consumers chose, as all other elements of the experiment were exactly the same except for the at-issue attribute.[20]

9.2.2.2 Simple Choice Experiment Outcomes

As mentioned earlier, the main outcome or dependent measure of a choice experiment is the share of respondents choosing the focal product in each experimental group (or alternatively, the mean likelihood of purchase in each group if no competitor products are shown). When a choice experiment is properly designed, one can compare the outcomes of the groups to determine whether and to what extent the adjusted attribute, feature, claim, trademark, or product introduction influences consumer decision-making.

If shares are not statistically significantly different between experimental groups, one can conclude that the at-issue attribute (e.g. an advertising claim, patented feature, trademark, or trade dress) is not material to consumer purchase decisions. If one finds a result with no statistical significance, the choice experiment has essentially killed two birds with one stone: The results imply lack of materiality and thus no liability, as well as zero damages. Even if the case is still at the class certification stage, such an outcome essentially says: "Don't worry about commonality, don't worry about perception. Even if all consumers are identical and the product creates misleading perceptions, *it will not affect market outcomes.*" As in the *Hobbs v. Brother* case, the choice experiment's finding that there was no materiality was likely the logic behind the court's decision not to certify the class. As such, this approach can be a particularly economical one for the defense side.

On the other hand, if the market share of the at-issue product is statistically significantly higher in the test group shown the at-issue attribute than in the control group without the at-issue attribute, these inputs can be used to calculate damages using certain assumptions. In the case of such an outcome, the question of whether the allegations are true may come back into play. That is, while it is necessary to demonstrate materiality, materiality alone, without confusing or misleading consumers, is not sufficient. As such, it may also be beneficial to conduct perception studies to focus more narrowly on liability to determine the extent to which an allegedly false statement or infringed trademark leads to consumer confusion (or deception). For example, if an *allegedly* misleading statement contributes to consumer purchase decisions, but the statement is determined *not* to be misleading, there is no liability. Similarly, if an allegedly infringing trademark drives sales, but no confusion is found among consumers about the sources or affiliations of the

---

[20] Expert Report of Joel H. Steckel, PhD, *Kenneth Hobbs v. Brother International Corporation, et al.*, No. 2:15-CV-01866-PSG-VBK, June 28, 2016 (C.D. Cal. 2016), at pp. 3, 5–6, 14.

product, then there is still no liability. In these situations, complementing a materiality study with a perception or awareness study would be a suitable two-pronged approach.

9.3 WHEN THE KEY ATTRIBUTE IS PRICE: ASSESSING DAMAGES

Choice experiments can be used in many cases to assess damages. Often, a critical question is to assess the value held by a consumer or the price premium they paid. Such a question implicitly includes a second key attribute: price. Specifically, how much extra did the consumer pay because of the presence of the key attribute, product feature, trademark, or claim?

The construction of a choice experiment involves a choice between the product or service as offered and a similar product or service without the key attribute. A critical question is often whether the offering without the key attribute requires a reduced price to secure comparable support from respondents. A respondent's choice between those two alternatives provides some information about how much the respondent values the product feature, trademark, or product claim. At this point, a conjoint analysis would vary the scope of product attributes systematically to estimate the implied willingness to pay for each attribute. However, information about consumer value in the context of overall market prices can be obtained by varying the price as a second factor in a choice experiment. The discount amount at which a consumer is indifferent to the variance in cost between paying the reduced price and retaining the key attribute at full price represents the value the consumer places on the attribute.

One approach is to vary the size of the discount leading to the reduced price among respondents. That way (in theory) the researcher determines the size of the discount at which the respondent flips to the alternative that does not have the key attribute. Unfortunately, though, these judgments are not necessarily independent.

The approach we recommend here is to randomly vary the discount leading to the reduced price across respondents. In such an experiment, each respondent makes a single choice. In the example below, the discount at which the probability of a randomly selected consumer choosing the reduced price as opposed to retaining the key attribute is 1/2, which reflects indifference to the value placed on the key attribute. To obtain this discount, one can compute a logistic regression of the following form:

$$Ln\,(p/1-p) = a + b(DISCOUNT),$$

where p represents the conditional probability of choice in the population given the discount and Ln is the natural log. We then take that logistic regression and solve for the "DISCOUNT" at which $p = 1/2$. That discount, easily shown to be $-a/b$, reflects the consumer value of the key attribute.

9.4 WHEN TO USE A SIMPLE CHOICE EXPERIMENT INSTEAD OF A CONJOINT

Although simple choice experiments as described earlier and conjoint surveys are similar tools that answer similar questions, a choice experiment is typically less complex to design and implement. Also, choice experiments are often superior to conjoint analysis in terms of internal and external validity.

First, since conjoint analysis requires the specification of a meaningful relatively complete set of product attributes or features that govern consumer choice, a simple choice experiment can be more effective at isolating the causal impact of the key allegations without artificially focusing respondents' attention on them. In other words, a well-designed choice experiment that minimizes demand effects is less likely to artificially inflate the value of the at-issue feature for respondents.

Second, and relatedly, a simple choice experiment reflects how consumers process information in the real world better than a conjoint analysis does. While each respondent is typically required to make eight to twelve choices in a conjoint survey, a simple choice experiment only requires each respondent to make one choice, and is therefore less likely to generate respondent fatigue. Because of this reduction in choices required, simple choice experiments do not have to reduce product descriptions to only six to eight attributes, as is recommended for conjoint surveys, and they can provide more detailed product descriptions that encompass more of the relevant information that consumers may encounter in the marketplace. Additionally, unlike a conjoint, which depends on the variation of a number of attributes, a choice experiment does not create nonexistent products beyond the but-for version of the focal product. As a result, the choice experiment requires less preliminary research and less need for focus groups to understand what features consumers consider important in order to appropriately capture the marketplace and determine what is relevant to consumers.

Third, a simple choice experiment measures causation in a more straightforward manner, actually holding all else equal. The experimental design provides the ability to isolate the attribute(s) at issue to measure the effect of the allegations, which cannot be accomplished without a control group.[21] In contrast with a conjoint survey, a simple choice experiment does not require researchers to make hundreds of design decisions related to attributes and attribute levels. As such, for a choice experiment, the design, programming, and analysis of the study are much simpler, and a choice experiment therefore typically results in substantially lower costs and faster timelines. Furthermore, while conjoint surveys generate more detailed information about consumer preferences, an advantage of the straightforward nature of a choice experiment is that it does not allow the other side to

---

[21] Diamond, Shari, "Reference Guide on Survey Research," *Reference Manual on Scientific Evidence*, 3rd ed., National Academies Press, 2011, pp. 398–400.

undermine the relevance and accuracy of the study by mischaracterizing individual responses.

Fourth, the simple nature of the choice experiment welcomes the possibility of an "incentive alignment" in the study design. A study has incentive alignment if participants have incentives to make choices in the study that would be consistent with the participants' actual preferences. While rarely done in a litigation setting, promising respondents that they may actually receive the product they chose in the study is likely to increase the external validity of the study. For example, in a study of incentive-aligned conjoint analysis, researchers found that when respondents could actually receive the meal they chose, the incentive-aligned choice conjoint had better predictive power than a hypothetical choice conjoint.[22] Incentive alignment has also been used in litigation on a few occasions. In *Apple* v. *Samsung*, Dr. John Hauser conducted a survey in which "respondents were informed that one in 20 respondents would be selected at random to win the option for cash and a smartphone or a tablet."[23] Additionally, in a matter before the Copyright Royalty Board, Dr. Daniel McFadden also used incentive alignment in his conjoint[24] – though Dr. McFadden's implementation of incentive alignment in this matter was critiqued by Dr. Hauser for being unrealistic and confusing to respondents and creating demand artifacts, among other issues.[25]

While well-designed incentive alignment can be beneficial for external validity, incentive alignment can easily become a logistical nightmare. For one thing, the researcher has to track down the respondents potentially months after the study. Furthermore, unless the researcher wants to provide this huge payout, the incentive is usually presented as a chance to get the product. In other words, it is a lottery and one may run into issues with local gambling laws. More critically, in a conjoint setting it is quite hard to give the respondents the product they chose in the study because most of the products in conjoint studies simply do not exist, due to the numerous permutations of brands, price levels, and product features. In contrast, in a choice experiment, all products exist, except, possibly, for the control group, the

---

[22] Ding, Min, Rajdeep Grewal, and John Liechty, "Incentive-Aligned Conjoint Analysis," *Journal of Marketing Research*, Feb. 2005, Vol. 42, No. 1, pp. 67–82 at p. 67. See also Ding, Min, "An Incentive-Aligned Mechanism for Conjoint Analysis," *Journal of Marketing Research*, May 2007, Vol. 44, No. 2, pp. 214–23; Ding, Min, John R. Hauser, et al., "Unstructured Direct Elicitation of Decision Rules," *Journal of Marketing Research*, Feb. 2011, Vol. 48, No. 1, pp. 116–27.
[23] Expert Report of John R. Hauser, *Apple Inc. v. Samsung Electronics Co., Ltd.; Samsung Electronics America, Inc.; and Samsung Telecommunications America LLC*, Northern District of California, San Jose Division, Case No. 12-cv-00630, Aug. 11, 2013, p. 27.
[24] Testimony of Daniel L. McFadden, *In the Matter of: Determination of Royalty Rates for Digital Performance in Sound Recordings and Ephemeral Recordings (Web IV)*, Docket No. 14-CRB-0001-WR, US Copyright Royalty Board, Oct. 6, 2014, pp. 14–15.
[25] Rebuttal Testimony of John R. Hauser, ScD, *In the Matter of: Determination of Royalty Rates for Digital Performance in Sound Recordings and Ephemeral Recordings (Web IV)*, Docket No. 14-CRB-0001-WR, US Copyright Royalty Board, Feb. 23, 2015, pp. 33–43.

product without the feature at issue. One possibility is to provide a respondent choosing such a product with the same product *with* the feature, without making the respondent worse off.

When designed and conducted properly, a simple choice experiment is an alternative to both perception studies and conjoint analysis. Its advantage over perception studies, on the defense side, is that it allows skipping over perception into materiality, which is the ultimate measure of the market outcome, though in some circumstances a perception study and a materiality study can complement each other. And relative to conjoint surveys, choice experiments can be much simpler and more straightforward, often yielding both more robustness and lower costs.

10

Use of Conjoint Analysis in Litigation

Challenges, Best Practices, and Common Mistakes

Rene Befurt, Niall MacMenamin, and Aylar Pour Mohammad

10.1 INTRODUCTION

Conjoint analysis is a commonly used methodology in marketing – it can provide crucial information for new product development,[1] product line extensions,[2] design of product packaging,[3] pricing,[4] and various other applications for which it is important to understand consumer preferences. Because conjoint analysis can help market researchers, managers, and ultimately anyone else answer the question of which attributes of a product impact consumer purchase decisions, and to what extent, the method has become more and more frequently applied in the realm of litigation cases.[5] For example, in the legal domain, conjoint surveys can contribute to understanding and determining purchase reasons, consumer valuations, and potentially associated damages in matters with claims regarding product liability, false advertising, lack of disclosures, data/privacy breaches, infringement of intellectual property, and antitrust issues. Even though conjoint analysis seems to be a useful instrument when tackling certain legal challenges involving consumer purchase decision-making, courts have frequently rejected conjoint analyses from allowable evidence due to concerns regarding the validity or applicability of its results. The reasons for factfinders' skepticism are manifold and range from lack of

---

[1] See, for example, Pullman, M. E., Moore, W. L., & Wardell, D. G. (2002). "A comparison of quality function deployment and conjoint analysis in new product design." *Journal of Product Innovation Management: An International Publication of the Product Development & Management Association*, 19(5), 354–64.

[2] See, for example, Lee, M., Lee, J., & Kamakura, W. A. (1996). "Consumer evaluations of line extensions: A conjoint approach." *Advances in Consumer Research*, 23.

[3] See, for example, Silayoi, P., & Speece, M. (2007). "The importance of packaging attributes: A conjoint analysis approach." *European Journal of Marketing*, 41(11/12), 1495–1517.

[4] See, for example, Dobson, G., & Kalish, S. (1993). "Heuristics for pricing and positioning a product-line using conjoint and cost data." *Management Science*, 39(2), 160–75.

[5] See, for example, Iyer, S. (2018). "Conjoint analysis in litigation." In *Handbook of Marketing Analytics*. Edward Elgar.

specific expertise to misapplications of the technique. While lack of expertise can be preempted through careful selection of a proficient expert, the process of conducting a reliable conjoint analysis presents hurdles and challenges to anyone: sometimes, conjoint analysis is simply an unsuitable methodology for the question at hand, and at other times intricate aspects of the survey design or sample selections are disregarded. In the same vein, experts have expressed on various occasions that the application of the conjoint methodology may run into conceptual problems such as ignoring supply-side factors when determining consumers' loss for a specific product characteristic that may have been promised but was not provided. This chapter outlines common applications of conjoint analysis in litigation, describes the basic concepts and approaches in properly applying conjoint analysis, and points to misapplications of conjoint analysis in litigation matters. It will also make evident how conjoint survey design, data analysis, and use of results in litigation matters depend on the complexities of each case.

10.2 PRIMER ON CONJOINT ANALYSIS

Marketing researchers have used conjoint analysis in business contexts since the early 1970s, and have improved the technique over time, expanding its application in the market research industry and ultimately leading to its use in litigation.[6] In simple terms, conjoint analysis can be described as a combination of survey and statistical techniques. It involves the collection of survey data and the analysis of those data to estimate consumer preferences for certain products and their specific attributes.[7] In particular, conjoint analysis can shed light on which attributes affect consumers' purchase decisions, and to what extent they do so.

The underlying theory of conjoint analysis stems from decision-making theories that postulate that while consumers buy a product as a whole, we may, unbeknownst to us, decompose the complete product into its attributes and trade off one attribute against another. The theory behind conjoint analysis further assumes that consumers derive an overall benefit or "utility" from the purchase of a product, and that this overall utility is the sum of the utilities we derive from the individual attributes that comprise the product. Hence, although we literally pick a product as a

---

[6] Green, P. E., & Srinivasan, V. (1978). "Conjoint analysis in consumer research: issues and outlook." *Journal of Consumer Research*, 5(2), 103–23; Green, P. E., & Srinivasan, V. (1990). "Conjoint analysis in marketing: New developments with implications for research and practice." *Journal of Marketing*, 54(4), 3–19; Wittink, D. R., & Cattin, P. (1989). "Commercial use of conjoint analysis: An update." *Journal of Marketing*, 53(3), 91–96; Wittink, D. R., & Cattin, P. (1981). "Alternative estimation methods for conjoint analysis: A Monte Carlo study." *Journal of Marketing Research*, 18(1), 101–106; Green, P. E., & Rao, V. R. (1971). "Conjoint measurement for quantifying judgmental data." *Journal of Marketing Research*, 8(3), 355–63; Green, P., & Wind, Y. (1975). "New techniques for measuring consumer evaluations of products and services." *Harvard Business Review*, 53, 107–17.

[7] Rao, V. R. (2014). *Applied Conjoint Analysis* (p. 389). Springer.

whole from a supermarket shelf, theory suggests that we actually make our choice such that the combined (or "conjoined") utility arising from all (relevant) attributes is maximized and exceeds that of the remaining products on the shelf.[8] Of note is that the attributes involved in this choice process can be tangible or intangible – it is important for a product choice that we understand the benefits resulting from the products. For example, in a conjoint survey the potential attributes of a smartphone may include battery life, display size, storage capacity, brand, and price; and each of these attributes may be observed and judged in real-life choice situations based on their "attribute levels." In turn, the attribute levels of a smartphone's storage capacity can be 64GB, 128GB, or 256GB, and the levels of a brand attribute may be Apple, Samsung, Sony, and Nokia. Conjoint surveys present combinations of such attributes and attribute levels to respondents in the form of hypothetical products (called profiles), and let respondents ultimately choose the one they prefer most.[9] To make sure that each respondent provides sufficient data, conjoint surveys repeatedly present choice tasks with different attribute level combinations and let the survey taker chooses several times.

The result from such a conjoint survey are so-called choice data that reflect numerous "purchase" decisions. By analyzing these data using well-established statistical methods, a researcher can estimate how much utility a consumer may gain by choosing one attribute level over another.[10] For example, for some consumers the jump from 128GB to 256GB storage capacity may be very useful to accommodate for frequently taking videos, whereas other consumers with no affinity to videography would gain very little utility from an expanded memory capacity.

Generally, conjoint surveys can be conducted using different approaches to present respondents with product attributes. Some of these approaches are adaptive and present combinations of selected attributes dynamically while the survey is being conducted, whereas others rely on the presentation of entire products based on a predefined, complete set of attributes.[11] The latter approach is the underpinning of the most widely applied conjoint survey method: Choice Based Conjoint analysis (CBC).[12] In a CBC survey, respondents are asked a series of choice tasks regarding which product they would choose, if any, based on descriptions of each product's individual attributes or features – and reflecting how we choose products in real life; that is, in their entirety.

Figure 10.1 provides an example of a standard CBC task. In this task, respondents have to choose one of the alternative golf balls provided to them, or choose not to

---

[8] Iyer, "Conjoint analysis in litigation."
[9] Ibid.
[10] Ibid.
[11] Orme, Bryan K. (2006). *Getting Started with Conjoint Analysis: Strategies for Product Design and Pricing Research*, Research Publishers, chapter 5.
[12] Ibid., chapter 5.

If you were considering buying golf balls for your next outing and these were the only alternatives, which would you choose?
(1 of 14)

Brand:	High-Flyer Pro, by Smith and Forester	High-Flyer Pro, by Smith and Forester	Long Shot, by Performance Plus	
Performance:	Drives 10 yards farther than the average ball	Drives 15 yards farther than the average ball	Drives 15 yards farther than the average ball	None: i wouldn't purchase any of these
Price:	$6.99 for package of 3 balls	$6.99 for package of 3 balls	$10.99 for package of 3 balls	
	Select	Select	Select	Select

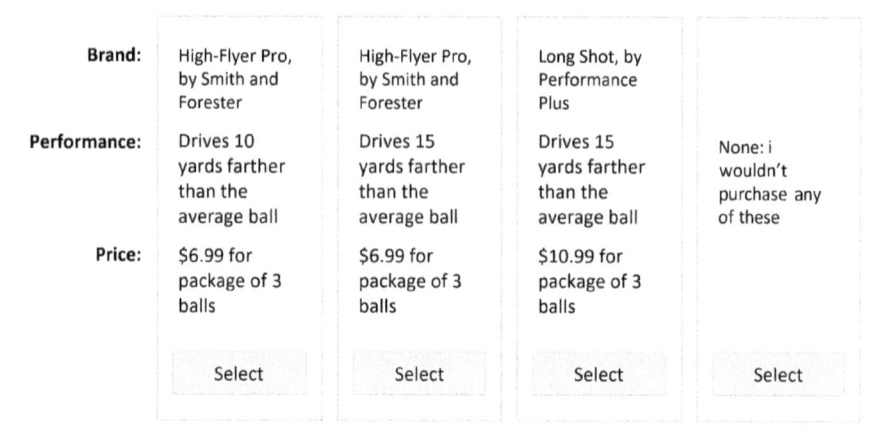

FIGURE 10.1. Example of a standard CBC task.
"CBC Tutorial and Example," *Sawtooth Software*, https://sawtoothsoftware.com/help/lighthouse-studio/manual/cbc-tutorial.html

purchase any of them. Respondents are asked to assume that all attributes of these alternative golf balls are exactly the same, except for the three attributes of brand, performance, and price. In this task, the brand attribute has two levels (*High-Flyer Pro, by Smith and Forester* and *Long Shot, by Performance Plus*), the performance attribute has two levels (*Drives 10 yards farther than the average ball* and *Drives 15 yards farther than the average ball*), and the price attribute also has two levels ($6.99 *for package of 3 balls* and $10.99 *for package of 3 balls*).

In a conjoint survey for litigation purposes, one (or more) of the attributes included in the choice tasks would involve the item at issue – the content of false advertisement, a benefit from a disputed patent, or (the main element of) a disputed disclosure. Respondents are expected to trade off these displayed product attributes with one another and thereby reveal their preference for each individual attribute and attribute level relative to other attributes and attribute levels. As price is usually included as one attribute in the survey, a researcher can conduct analyses that allow them to estimate the perceived monetary value of each level of product attributes for respondents. This can serve as a proxy for their willingness to pay (WTP) for a specific attribute level relative to another.[13]

We next provide discussion as to how the method can contribute to various applications in litigation.

---

[13] Ben-Akiva, M., McFadden, D., & Train, K. (2019). "Foundations of stated preference elicitation: Consumer behavior and choice-based conjoint analysis." *Foundations and Trends® in Econometrics*, 10(1–2), 1–144.

10.3 APPLICATIONS OF CONJOINT ANALYSIS IN LITIGATION

In the last few years, conjoint analyses have found their way into numerous litigations. Bryan Orme, CEO of Sawtooth Software and supplier of the most widely distributed and used conjoint analysis software, noted that "Sawtooth Software's conjoint tools and literature are wielded as battle axes to wage multi-billion dollar lawsuits in Silicon Valley," indicating the importance of the method not only for market research applications but also in courtrooms across the country.[14] At this point in time, conjoint analyses have been applied in product liability,[15] false advertising/mislabeling,[16] class certification,[17] data/privacy breach,[18] and intellectual property matters (e.g. patent infringement).[19]

10.3.1 *Product Liability, False Advertising/Mislabeling and Class Certification*

Product liability cases typically have the parties asking the question: what would consumers' valuation for a product be if they are assumed to have known at the time of purchase that the product they acquired came with a defect? In a number of these cases, survey experts have proffered conjoint analysis as a way to measure the effect of disclosing a defect on consumer valuations. In other words, these experts conduct conjoint analyses to help the factfinder with understanding consumer decision-making in a "but-for" world where consumers are assumed to have known about the allegedly undisclosed defects. As we would not expect that the defect associated with the product at issue were disclosed in the real world, conjoint analyses can "simulate" consumer decision-making in a but-for world by providing product choices that inform consumers about the potential occurrence of a defect.

---

[14] Orme, Bryan (2012) "The Apple vs. Samsung 'Patent Trial of the Century,' Conjoint Analysis, and Sawtooth Software," at www.sawtoothsoftware.com/download/apple_v_samsung_conjoint_analysis.pdf

[15] See, for example, *Claudia Morales et al. v. Kraft Foods* and *Thomas Davidson, et al. v. Apple, Inc.*

[16] See, for example, *Barbara Schwab et al. v. Philip Morris et al.*, *Claudia Morales et al. v. Kraft Foods*, *Singleton v. Fifth Generation, Inc.*, *Townsend v. Monster Bev. Corp.*, and *Erin Allen, et al. v. Conagra Foods, Inc.*

[17] See, for example, *Erin Allen, et al. v. Conagra Foods, Inc.*

[18] See, for example, In re: Premera Blue Cross Customer Data Security Breach Litigation, case number 3:15-md-2633, in the U.S. District Court for the District of Oregon.

[19] See, for example, *Apple Inc. v. Samsung Electronics Co., Ltd., Samsung Electronics America, Inc., and Samsung Telecommunications America, Llc*, *Fractus, S.A. v. Samsung et al.*, *Microsoft Corporation v. Motorola, Inc.*, *Odyssey Wireless, Inc. v. Apple Inc.*, *Samsung Electronics America, Inc., LG Electronics U.S.A., Inc., LG Electronics Mobilecomm U.S.A., Inc.*, *Oracle America, Inc. v. Google Inc.*, and *TV Interactive Data Corporation v. Sony Corporation et al.*

For example, in the *Davidson et al. v. Apple, Inc.* matter,[20] plaintiffs allege that the iPhone 6 and 6 Plus "suffer from a material manufacturing defect that causes the touchscreen to become unresponsive to users' touch input." Plaintiffs conducted a conjoint survey to analyze the value consumers attach to specific product attributes, and hence estimate the valuation of the product by consumers if they are assumed to have known about the touchscreen defect at the time of purchase.

Similar to product liability cases, matters involving false advertisements or mislabeling revolve around the question of what consumers' valuation for a product would be had the advertisement/label truthfully remarked upon the topic at issue. Conjoint analysis can provide insight into whether the promised consumer benefit had value (next to numerous other attributes a product might include), and what that value may have been to consumers at the time they made their purchase decision. Again, conjoint analyses may be suited to simulate a purchase decision similar to one that we may observe in reality, except the advertisement/label would not show the at-issue claim to respondents.

In recent years, class action matters involving false advertisement, product liability disputes, or data/privacy breach have proffered the results from conjoint analyses more frequently. Especially when transaction data for the products at issue are not available, too sparse, or would take too many resources to obtain, conjoint surveys have been considered by numerous plaintiffs to learn about the consumers' purchase decisions and valuations for certain product attributes. However, as we will point out later, numerous of these attempts lacked in craftsmanship or conceptual integrity and were rejected by various courts.

One example in which a conjoint analysis has been accepted by the court in a false advertisement matter is the *Hasemann v. Gerber Products Co.* matter.[21] Here, the court granted class certification based in part on the plaintiff's proposed use of conjoint analysis. Plaintiffs claimed that defendant's misrepresentations on the product label and in advertising regarding allergies falsely inflated the price of "Good Start Gentle" infant formula (GSG), such that those who purchased GSG paid more for that product than they would have had the product been marketed honestly. Plaintiff's damages methodology was based on conjoint analysis combined with hedonic regression, an econometric analysis based on transaction data. The defense pointed to errors in the conjoint survey design and argued it was impossible to isolate the challenged allergy message in the defendant's advertising because the challenged marketing representations were always promoted alongside other unchallenged product attributes. However, the court found that the plaintiff's

---

[20] Plaintiffs' Third Motion to Certify Class, *Thomas Davidson, et al. v. Apple, Inc.*, United States District Court for Northern District of California, No. 16-CV-04942-LHK, Mar. 2019.

[21] Memorandum & Order, *Jennifer Hasemann and Debbie Hoth v. Gerber Products Co.*, No. 15-CV-2995 (MKB) (RER), *Jeremy Greene and Cetaria Wilkerson v. Gerber Products Co.*, No. 16-CV-1153 (MKB) (RER), *Wendy Manemeit v. Gerber Products Co.*, No. 17-CV-93 (MKB) (RER), United States District Court for Eastern District of New York, Mar. 31, 2019.

proposed conjoint analysis in this specific matter sufficiently accounted for the individual product attributes at issue, and granted class certification.

10.3.2 Intellectual Property

In intellectual property matters such as patent disputes, the application of conjoint analysis relies on a similar approach as described for false advertisement and product liability matters: it seeks to provide insight as to whether the attribute at issue and its resulting consumer benefit(s) had value (next to numerous other attributes a product might include), and what that value may have been to consumers at the time they made their purchase decision.

One of the hurdles of surveying issues related to patents arises from the technical language through which a patented technology is frequently described in the patent application. Generally, a researcher should expect that technical patent descriptions are difficult for consumers to understand, and that they need to be translated into concrete, understandable benefits. In other words, a crucial issue for the use of conjoint analyses in patent litigations is the selection of the benefit arising from the patented technology, and the presentation of the benefit arising from a non-infringing alternative. For example, an online conjoint survey assessing consumers' valuation for a smartphone that unlocks via biometric recognition should offer respondents phones with face recognition and phones with fingerprint unlock. A properly conducted conjoint analysis in patent litigation requires a very specific understanding of consumer benefits arising from multiple available technologies – without such an understanding, survey respondents are likely not able to assess how much utility they assign to a certain attribute while taking the conjoint survey.

Once the conjoint survey is designed, fielded, and analyzed, results from it can be used in reasonable royalty and lost profits calculations, for example, as evidence speaking to but-for profits, royalty rates, apportionment, or whether the patented attribute has a substantial impact on consumer demand.[22]

For example, the court admitted the plaintiff's conjoint analysis for use in patent damages in *Odyssey Wireless v. Apple, Samsung and LG Electronics*.[23] The plaintiff conducted a conjoint survey to determine the value that customers would be willing to pay for the "upload speed" attribute of smartphones. Defendants argued that the survey focused on only certain attributes of a smartphone, focused only on high-end smartphones even though the at-issue products were not high-end smartphones, and contained other flaws relating to framing and clarity of the questions. The court found that the defendants' challenges to the conjoint analysis had to go to the weight

---

[22] See, for example, *TV Interactive Data Corporation v. Sony Corporation et al.*
[23] *Odyssey Wireless, Inc. v. Apple Inc., Samsung Electronics America, Inc., LG Electronics U.S.A., Inc., LG Electronics Mobilecomm U.S.A., Inc.*

of the survey, not its admissibility, and denied the motion to exclude the expert reports and testimony of the plaintiff's survey expert.

10.3.3 Antitrust/Mergers

Antitrust and merger matters often involve estimating market conditions in a hypothetical world involving changes in competitive dynamics pre- and post-merger. Conjoint analysis is used to estimate market shares, price changes, and diversion ratios due to mergers. Conjoint analysis can be used to model but-for sales under certain scenarios, such as if one of the merging parties were to increase prices for its products. Similarly, surveys of business-to-business customers in bidding markets can be conducted to more accurately determine the competitive choice set for recent contracts. Consequently, diversion ratios can be estimated from conjoint survey results.[24]

In conclusion, the acceptance of a conjoint survey by courts is far from a shoo-in. Since the science and industry practices are still evolving, the method itself comes with various technical and conceptual challenges of varying degrees. Not surprisingly, conjoint analysis has been accepted by courts in some cases and rejected in others. In the next section we discuss considerations when conducting conjoint analysis, including best practices for designing conjoint surveys, and examples in which courts have rejected conjoint analyses because best practices were not followed.

10.4 IMPORTANT CONSIDERATIONS WHEN CONDUCTING CONJOINT ANALYSIS

Conjoint analysis – with all of its complexities – can be informative to the factfinder if the survey and analysis overcome various technical and conceptual challenges. That is not to say that conjoint analysis itself is an unreliable method: when courts have accepted or rejected conjoint analyses, it was not that the conjoint method's theoretical underpinnings were the issue, but rather the implementation and application of the survey instrument and data resulting from it was found insufficient. For example, for certain product categories, conjoint analyses may estimate reliable values of consumer valuations but the implementation of these results by damages experts – or lawyers arguing a specific damages theory – may be the main problem in the court's opinion.

10.4.1 General Best Practices in Designing Conjoint Surveys

Conjoint analysis is a method that requires careful survey design and data analytics to provide reliable results. Furthermore, while conjoint analysis can be helpful for

---

[24] Kirk Fair, R., Befurt, R., & Cotton, E. (2018): "The Tyranny of Market Shares: Incorporating Survey-Based Evidence into Merger Analysis," *Corporate Disputes* (July–Sept.).

understanding consumer behavior, decision-making drivers, and consumers' valuations of products and product attributes, the method itself is not automatically the best methodology for all scenarios in which a researcher seeks to understand consumer purchase decisions. In fact, designing and implementing a conjoint survey and analyzing the data can be a time-consuming and expensive process that may not lend itself to each and every type of purchase decision. For some product categories or research questions, simpler alternative methodologies may be preferable. For instance, when evaluating whether a certain sentence in an insurance policy may have misled consumers about the benefits the policy offers them, a simple experimental analysis in which respondents are randomly assigned to either the treatment or the control groups can suffice when evaluating liability.

Similar to other survey methods, there are several best practices to consider when designing conjoint surveys. Not complying with these best practices may cause errors that, depending on the case, can lead to rejection of the conjoint survey in court. Here we discuss some of the best practices in the field along with common mistakes in designing conjoint surveys.

First, it is crucial to define a relevant target population for the survey and draw a representative sample of survey respondents from that target population. The target population may simply include a firm's defined target customers, or may be comprised of individuals whose perceptions, purchase situations, demographics, and various other potential aspects are relevant to the subject of the study.[25] The target population for a product mislabeling claim, for example, may consist of individuals who had purchased or intend to purchase the at-issue product in the past or next six months. It may be further narrowed to individuals aged eighteen and older, and then potentially to a person who is the primary decision-maker in the household regarding the at-issue product. The sample of survey respondents drawn from the target population should be representative of the target population, in terms of both demographic characteristics and other aspects relevant for a particular study. For example, in the case of a cosmetic product for which the majority of consumers are female, the sample may be comprised of the same proportion of female respondents as the target population. Selecting a representative sample generally allows the conclusion that the results of the study apply to the defined target population.

Failure to follow such best practices may result in exclusion of a conjoint survey. For example, in the *Fluidmaster, Inc. Water Connector Components* matter, the court granted the defendant's motion to exclude the plaintiff's proposed conjoint survey, citing concern that the combination of methodological issues – including sample selection – with the survey rendered it unreliable.[26] The claims in the case

---

[25] Diamond, Shari Seidman (2011). *Reference Manual on Scientific Evidence: Third Edition*, Chapter: "Reference guide on survey research," National Academies Press.
[26] *In re Fluidmaster, Inc., Water Connector Components Prods. Liab. Litig.*, United States District Court for the Northern District of Illinois, Eastern Division, No. 14-cv-5696, MDL No. 2575, Jan. 16, 2018.

involved alleged design defects in plumbing products designed and manufactured by the defendant that connect plumbing fixtures such as a toilet or kitchen sink faucet to the main water supply. The defendant argued that the conjoint survey did not measure damages for the plaintiff's theory of liability, and its methodology and assumptions were unreliable. The court granted the defendant's motion to exclude the plaintiff's survey expert partly because the survey selected a nonrepresentative sample of respondents.

Second, it is important to develop nonbiased survey questions and stimuli. The selection of product attributes should include the most salient drivers of consumers' choice processes in the real world.[27] That is, "the menus of products and their descriptions [should be] designed to realistically mimic a market experience."[28] In fact, a frequent critique leveled against conjoint surveys is the risk of bias arising from turning respondents' attention toward attributes that stand out from more typical, realistic, and salient decision-making drivers. Especially when the attribute of interest stands out due to its exotic character, lack of shopping context, specificity, or overly rich presentation,[29] respondents may be tipped off as to which feature is at the center of the research. For example, due to the nature of consumer surveys, it may not be possible to include all attributes and attribute levels of a product in the conjoint study. The survey designer then has to select a number of product attributes and attribute levels. Generally, including exotic or irrelevant attributes and excluding attributes that are key in consumer decision-making (such as brand in certain product categories) creates a "focusing bias" that can artificially inflate the estimated utility (or partworth) and ultimately the consumer valuations of the at-issue attribute.[30] The researcher should consider providing a theory for including and excluding certain product attributes (and attribute levels) in the survey. A potential approach is to refer to prior studies that identified the most important attributes of a particular product category for consumers or to rely on empirical research, such as results from focus groups with relevant consumers.[31] Of course, focus groups or interviews can be specifically conducted for each conjoint study prior to designing the attributes and attribute-level descriptions. Empirical research and careful pretests of the attribute descriptions in a conjoint survey can be helpful to avoid potential

---

[27] Rao, *Applied Conjoint Analysis* (p. 389).
[28] Ben-Akiva, McFadden, & Train, "Foundations of stated preference elicitation."
[29] For example, in *Oula Zakaria v. Gerber Prods. Co.*, the plaintiff's expert survey was shown to be biased because the at-issue product label was presented with a yellow sticker that gave the label "undue prominence" and implicitly encouraged respondents to pay extra attention to the label. See, Opinion, *Oula Zakaria v. Gerber Prods. Co.*, United States District Court for the Central District of California, No. LA CV15–00200 JAK (Ex), Aug. 9, 2017.
[30] See, for example, Schkade, D. A., & Kahneman, D. (1998). "Does living in California make people happy? A focusing illusion in judgments of life satisfaction." *Psychological Science*, 9(5), 340–46; Kahneman, D., Krueger, A. B., Schkade, D., Schwarz, N., & Stone, A. A. (2006). "Would you be happier if you were richer? A focusing illusion." *Science*, 312(5782), 1908–10.
[31] See, for example, Murphy, M., Cowan, C., Henchion, M., & O'Reilly, S. (2000). "Irish consumer preferences for honey: A conjoint approach." *British Food Journal*, 102(8), 585–98.

bias from presenting the at-issue attribute(s) or attribute levels in ways that are different from presenting other attributes or attribute levels. For instance, if one were to describe the at-issue attributes using pictures or videos and the remaining attributes using simple text, it can be expected that pictures and videos artificially increase respondents' interest in those attributes even though the interest in the real world would be minimal. In the same vein, using biased and leading language in describing attributes can direct respondents' attention or shape their attitudes toward that attribute in a one-sided, biasing way.[32]

For example, in the *Fluidmaster, Inc. Water Connector Components* matter,[33] one of the reasons why the court granted the defendant's motion to exclude the plaintiff's survey expert pertained to methodological issues regarding the selection of attributes that, especially in combination with unrepresentative sample of respondents, rendered the proposed survey unreliable. The conjoint survey in this case included five attributes with no explanation for their selection, and potentially focused respondents on the selected attributes without determining whether they played an actual role in consumers' real-world decision-making. The court restated the methodological issues described by the defendant as "artificially assign values among an arrangement of potentially unimportant attributes."

Third, the survey designer should follow accepted guidelines for implementing a feasible number of attributes and attribute levels in a conjoint survey. As mentioned, in the real world, products are made up of many attributes that consumers consider when making purchase decisions. Designing a conjoint survey to include too many attributes and levels may overload respondents, causing fatigue, disinterest, and reduced attention to choice tasks. Each of these challenges may lead to unreliable results. Ultimately, the researcher should seek a balance between too many and too few product attributes and levels – and rely on the academic and industry literature. In general, typical conjoint surveys that let respondents choose from a full set of products include around six or fewer attributes, and may describe these attributes through two to five levels.[34] Furthermore, the attribute levels should cover the range of possibilities for the product of interest.[35]

Fourth, it may be important for a conjoint analysis to be used in litigation to define the correct but-for world. In many litigation matters, one step in estimating damages is to define the but-for world in which the defendant's alleged conduct did not occur. In a conjoint survey, the but-for world is portrayed in the levels of the at-issue attribute: one level reflects the actual world, and another level reflects the but-for world. For example, if a plaintiff alleges that a claim on the label of the

---

[32] Diamond, *Reference Manual on Scientific Evidence*.
[33] *In re Fluidmaster, Inc., Water Connector Components Prods. Liab. Litig.*, United States District Court for the Northern District of Illinois, Eastern Division, No. 14-cv-5696, MDL No. 2575, Jan. 16, 2018.
[34] Orme, *Getting Started with Conjoint Analysis*, p. 43.
[35] Ibid., p. 44.

defendant's product is false, the but-for world may be reflected by a label with a claim that is modified so that it is not false.

Fifth, for many product categories a reliable conjoint survey should at least in part create a realistic decision-making setting. Researchers have added realism to their studies by, for example, using images or video,[36] or allowing for interaction with the stimuli to better understand characteristics such as start-up times on electronic devices. Another element that can induce additional realism is offering the option of not purchasing a product. In other words, such a "no choice" option allows respondents to postpone a purchase decision, or to determine that none of the available options are sufficiently attractive to pay the respective price for them. One way researchers provide this "no choice" option is by using the "dual-response" choice designs in which they first ask respondents to choose among product alternatives, and in a subsequent question ask respondents if they would or would not actually buy the product they had chosen.[37]

Sixth, the descriptions and questions in the conjoint survey should be clear and unambiguous. "When unclear questions are included in a survey, they may threaten the validity of the survey by systematically distorting responses if respondents are misled in a particular direction, or by inflating random error if respondents guess because they do not understand the question. If the crucial question is sufficiently ambiguous or unclear, it may be the basis for rejecting the survey."[38]

Conjoint researchers consider these best practices important to achieve reliable results. However, the list of additional guidelines and requirements for conjoint surveys is long and the design of instructions, attribute presentations, and choice tasks needs substantial expertise. As mentioned in case examples throughout this chapter, courts have been scrutinizing conjoint surveys carefully and have excluded surveys of doubtful quality on various occasions.

10.4.2 Considering Consumer Demand, Supply-Side Reactions, and Equilibrium Prices

One of the more recent topics regarding the application of conjoint analysis pertains to determining consumers' valuations for a certain product attribute or claim at issue. These valuations are typically expressed as a consumer's willingness to pay (WTP); that is, they represent the *maximum* amount that the consumer would be willing to spend.[39] This amount can vary substantially across consumers, and, for the

---

[36] Loosschilder, G. H., Rosbergen, E., Vriens, M., & Wittink, D. R. (1995). "Pictorial stimuli in conjoint analysis." *Market Research Society Journal*, 37(1), 1–15.
[37] Brazell, J. D., Diener, C. G., Karniouchina, E., Moore, W. L., Séverin, V., & Uldry, P. F. (2006). "The no-choice option and dual response choice designs." *Marketing Letters*, 17(4), 255–68.
[38] Diamond, *Reference Manual on Scientific Evidence*, p. 388.
[39] Varian, H. R., & Varian, H. R. (1992). *Microeconomic Analysis* (Vol. 2), Norton.

purchase of a product, generally has to be greater or equal to the price of a product for the consumer to make this purchase.

To transfer the concept of consumer valuations or WTP into the world of conjoint analysis, consider consumers who are in the market for a smartphone and who specifically wonder whether they should acquire a smartphone with a high-resolution screen. Leaving aside manufacturers' cost or pricing for a minute, conjoint analysis lets us determine how much higher consumers' valuations for a high-resolution smartphone screen are *compared* to a mid-resolution smartphone screen. However, assuming that a conjoint survey determines that respondents' average valuation of a high-resolution screen over a mid-resolution screen is $250 across all respondents, one cannot simply conclude that manufacturers would offer a smartphone with such a screen for $250 more than a smartphone with a mid-resolution screen. Instead, an economist may consider that suppliers in a competitive market environment would offer a phone with an upgraded high-resolution screen at marginal cost – which may be substantially different than the average demand-side willingness-to-pay observed by the conjoint analysis. Hence, conjoint surveys can help us estimate demand and demand-side WTP, but not the equilibrium price that one would find in the market.[40]

In contrast to average willingness-to-pay, equilibrium prices may be determined by the intersection of supply and demand (see Figure 10.2). In simple terms, the demand curve is estimated using conjoint analysis. The supply curve – the prices at which the producer would be willing to sell given quantities – are based on marginal costs to supply the product and competitive dynamics. The intersection of supply and demand determines the equilibrium price – in both the real world and in the but-for world. Comparison between the real-world price and quantity and the but-for price and quantity may then provide an estimate of the price premium and the change in market share associated with the at-issue attribute.

In some cases, courts have rejected conjoint analyses that did not include the added step of estimating prices using inputs for both supply and demand. For example, in *Oula Zakaria v. Gerber Prods. Co.*, a damages class seeking compensation for the alleged overpayment for infant formula based on a misleading label was decertified.[41] The opinion stated, in part "[t]he conjoint analysis is not sufficiently tethered to actual market conditions, including pricing and premiums."[42] Accounting for supply factors based on an assumption that in the but-for world, sales volumes would equal that in the actual world may not comport with reality. Lower

---

[40] Ben-Akiva, McFadden, & Train, "Foundations of stated preference elicitation"; Allenby, G., Brazell, J., Howell, J., & Rossi, P. (2013, Oct.). "Using conjoint analysis to determine the market value of product features." *Proceedings of the Sawtooth Software Conference* (p. 341).
[41] Opinion, *Oula Zakaria v. Gerber Prods. Co.*, United States District Court for the Central District of California, No. LA CV15–00200 JAK (Ex), Aug. 9, 2017.
[42] Ibid., p. 18.

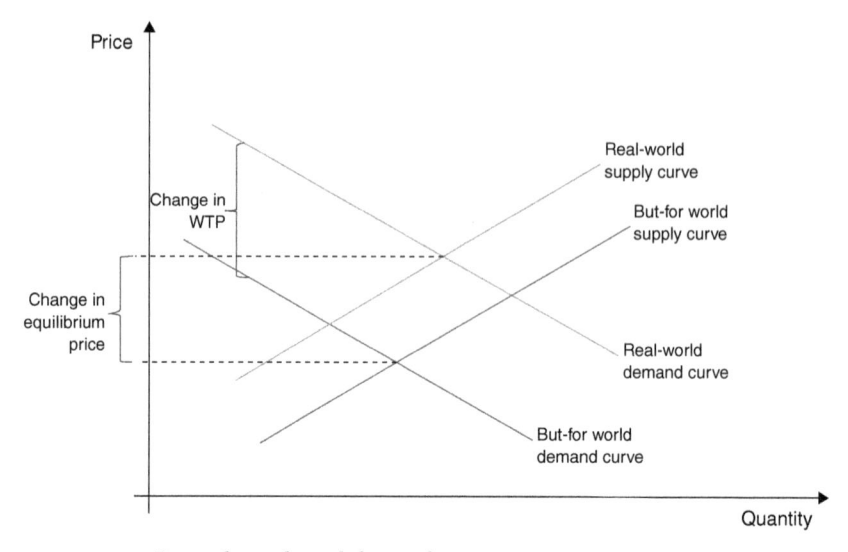

FIGURE 10.2. General supply and demand curves

demand in a but-for world would likely also reduce the quantity of sales (unless supply is perfectly inelastic).[43] Similarly, in *In re General Motors LLC Ignition Switch Litigation*, the court granted summary judgment for the defendants, finding that the plaintiff's conjoint analysis did not provide sufficient evidence supporting its "difference-in-value" theory of damages.[44] Plaintiffs claimed that they were suffered economic injury because their cars with safety defects were worth less than cars without safety defects. In making this claim, plaintiffs relied on a conjoint analysis to measure the difference between what plaintiffs actually paid and what they would have been willing to pay had they known about the defects. The plaintiff's conjoint analysis estimated willingness to pay – the change in demand between the actual and but-for worlds – but did not account for supply-side reactions, assuming instead that the supply of cars would remain unchanged in both worlds. The plaintiff's theory of damages, however, was based on the difference in market value, not the difference in willingness to pay. That is, the theory required that the plaintiff measured the equilibrium price, accounting for demand and supply, in the actual and but-for worlds. Hence, the court found that plaintiff's conjoint analysis did not meet its evidentiary burden for its "difference-in-value" damages claim, and granted

---

[43] Allenby, G. M., Brazell, J., Howell, J. R., & Rossi, P. E. (2014). "Valuation of patented product features." *Journal of Law and Economics*, 57(3), 629–63.
[44] Opinion and Order, *In re General Motors LLC Ignition Switch Litigation*, United States District Court for Southern District of New York, No. 14-MD-2543 (JMF) and 14-MC-2543 (JMF), Aug. 6, 2019.

summary judgment for the defendants regarding the damages claim.[45] Although the plaintiff's survey expert was not excluded, that issue was irrelevant given the court's ruling on summary judgment. Of note is that the inclusion of actual market prices and quantities in the conjoint survey may be sufficient for certain applications and courts. When market data for products in the but-for world are not available, however, estimation of the but-for marginal costs and competitive dynamics in the relevant market may be required to account for supply factors.

In summary, conjoint analysis can help market researchers, managers, and the factfinder in court to better understand consumer decision-making for various product categories and services. However, as the method becomes more and more frequently applied in litigation cases, it is crucial that conjoint survey design and data analyses abide by method-specific guidelines and standards. If these standards are ignored, the validity of conjoint surveys becomes questionable and may lead to outcomes that neither the academic research community nor courts are willing to accept.

---

[45] "[L]aw requires that benefit-of-the-bargain damages be calculated based on the difference in *market* value between the product as warranted and the product as sold and defines market value as the product of *both* a consumer's willingness to pay *and* a merchant's willingness to sell, when *neither* are under any compulsion to do so. Applying that law, the court is compelled to conclude that Boedeker's analysis does not, without more, suffice to prove that any of the Bellwether State plaintiffs suffered benefit-of-the-bargain damages based on a difference in value. Because there is no more – that is, plaintiffs point to no other evidence from which a factfinder could find damages based on a difference in value – there is an 'absence of evidence' on an 'essential element' of plaintiff's claims for such damages." Opinion and Order, *In re General Motors LLC Ignition Switch Litigation*, United States District Court for Southern District of New York, No. 14-MD-2543 (JMF) and 14-MC-2543 (JMF), Aug. 6, 2019, pp. 42–43.

11

Piece Problems

Component Valuation in Marketing and in Patent and Tort Law

Saul Levmore[*]

The problems referred to in the title of this chapter concern evaluating a given variable when it is one of several that have combined to bring about a result. In some cases, there is an easy market solution. Imagine that you contract to buy a house and then the beautiful kitchen stove, one of many things that attracted you to the property, is destroyed before you close the transaction or occupy the property. How much should the price now be reduced? Here there is an upper limit based on the cost of a comparable replacement appliance. A more precise valuation would also be easy if identical houses, lacking this one feature, had recently been sold. The stove is just a piece of the larger transaction and, with these convenient facts, there is not much of a "component valuation problem." Additionally, the stove is unlikely to have been of greater value because of its interaction with other items in the house; colors and sizes are fairly standardized. "Conjoint analysis" – a term that usually refers to survey evidence that tries to elicit the value of a component – is therefore unnecessary, or at least uncomplicated, because value does not depend on an interaction among variables in a way that is not directly observed. It is also interesting because it does not present a difficult game theory problem, or result that might be described in common parlance as something that depends on the relative bargaining skill of the parties.

In contrast, consider an important patent case, discussed shortly, concerning a company that adds three components, ABC, to a product in order to fetch a higher price and capture a larger market share. It turns out that the use of A knowingly infringed on the patent of another. What are the damages owed to this patent holder? It would be convenient if the two parties had recently bargained for the right to use A and nearly come to an agreement – though this would introduce relative bargaining power rather than some clean measure of value; it would also be nice if A were the only new feature in the product sold, instead of being combined

---

[*] I am indebted to Thomas Cotter and Jonathan Masur for discussions about Patent Law.

with B and C. In these cases, we would know the value of A to the breaching party or to the market. I aim to show that this component valuation problem in patent law is often like the "conjoint analysis" question in marketing research, a topic also discussed presently. I then show that it is also comparable to tort law's difficulty in carrying out the doctrine of comparative negligence, after a factfinder determines that multiple parties' negligence caused an injury. I like to think that drawing attention to the resemblance if not the equivalence of these matters is part of a connective tissue between the literature and practice of marketing and of law. Finally, I suggest that some solutions to the problem in one area might be useful, or hint at untried solutions, in another. As we will see, it is probably impossible to find a single, perfect solution that fits all cases in these areas (or even all that arise in any one of these fields), but it is interesting to think that areas of law might be informed by the marketing literature, and vice versa.

11.1 GETTING INCENTIVES RIGHT IN PATENT LAW

A good starting point is *Cornell University v. Hewlett Packard*.[1] It is a difficult case to understand or summarize, even for lawyers, unless they have expertise in patent law as well as judicial equivocation. The critical points for the present purpose can be refashioned as follows: Cornell had a patent on a method (though that is a loaded word in patent law) for speeding up computer processing. HP earned billions of dollars selling a product that it knew included Cornell's innovation, and arguably it encouraged its customers to infringe on Cornell's patent, and it did so without acquiring Cornell's consent. HP's product combined the Cornell innovation, which we will call A, with other advances in computer processing. Let us refer to HP's accompanying features, not wrongfully taken from Cornell, as B and C. Cornell objected and sought a recovery in the amount of HP's gain. Eventually, Cornell was found to have a valid patent on A.[2] HP enjoyed a huge advantage over competitors, and its large profits came from the combination, ABC – though the court seemed skeptical that HP's success had much to do with the presence of Cornell's piece. Patent law can be understood as attempting to recreate the value that the owner would have extracted from the infringer,[3] although once there is a finding (as there

---

[1] *Cornell Univ. v. Hewlett Packard*, 609 F. Supp. 2d 279 (2009). See Elizabeth Bailey, Gregory Leonard, & Mario Lopez, "Making Sense of 'Apportionment' in Patent Damages," 22 *Colum. Sci. & Tech. L. Rev.* 255, 259 (2011) ("In short, Judge Rader identified the portion of the revenue of the overall product (the server) that was closely related to the patented technology, namely the processor, and then used that revenue as the royalty base").

[2] Verdict & Settlement Summary, *Cornell Univ.*, No. 2008 WL 3166856 (N.D.N.Y. June 9, 2008).

[3] See 35 U.S.C. § 284, stating that damages awarded for infringement shall be "in no event less than reasonable royalty for the use made of the invention by the infringer, together with interest." I try to avoid the question of the relationship between "reasonable" royalty and the "game" that is played between the parties.

was) that HP knowingly used the patented A, we might expect courts to be generous in valuing the patent, though rarely so far as to extract all the gains that the infringer derived from infringing on the patent.[4] To the extent that courts occasionally come close to an "entire market value rule," likely drawn from lost profit claims – but perhaps with an eye on deterrence – we might imagine Cornell's recovering: (1) all the profit HP earned from these sales, arguably attributable (even if barely so) to the ABC improvement and advantage over its competitors. I will call this (1) a "maximum-market-value rule."[5] It is far more likely, and perhaps more law-abiding, for courts to aim at a smaller number, reflecting the benefit that A alone added to HP's profit.[6] After all, if Cornell and HP had bargained, it is the value-added of A to HP that they would have divided. Therefore, a court might give Cornell: (2) the total value-added by the inclusion of A, or (3) an amount reflecting a guess as to how the parties (or perhaps typical parties) would have divided the profit attributable to A through contract negotiation. Option (3) is a fraction of (2). I will call (2) the "value-added rule," and (3) the "estimated-bargained-for rule." Of course, if Cornell markets its patent to many users, the price might be lower, akin to the "reasonable royalty" measure of damages, familiar to patent lawyers.[7] If we go down this road, the list of possible results increases; it will include "infringement damages," because HP might be said to have deliberately infringed. But inasmuch as my goal is not to

---

[4] Compensation for patent infringement has traditionally not been punitive. See *Dowagiac Mfg. Co. v. Minn. Moline Plow Co.* 235 U.S. 641 (1915), quoting *Tilghman v. Proctor*, 125 U.S. 136, 145 (1888) ("It is inconsistent with the ordinary principles and practice of courts of chancery, either, on the one hand, to permit the wrongdoer to profit by his own wrong, or, on the other hand, to make no allowance for the cost and expense of conducting his business, or to undertake to punish him by obliging him to pay more than a fair compensation to person wronged"). However, a court may under the Patent Act increase up to three times any damages found by a jury or otherwise assessed. 35 U.S.C. § 284.

[5] Essentially, the market value rule allows compensation for the value of an item as sold where the value for a patented component part is inseparable from the value of the whole. *Cornell Univ.*, 609 F. Supp. 2d at 286, quoting *State Indus., Inc. v. Mor–Flo Indus., Inc.*, 883 F. 2d 1573, 1580 (Fed. Cir. 1989) ("When applied, this rule 'permits recovery of damages based on the value of the entire apparatus containing several features, where the patent related feature is the basis for customer demand'").

[6] In the *Cornell* case, while the court acknowledges that there is no market for the patented process itself, it awards damages based on "the smallest salable infringing unit" of HP's servers and workstations – their processors – to approximate the benefit HP acquired from Cornell's patent. *Cornell Univ.*, 609 F. Supp. 2d at 287–88.

[7] The Patent Act calls for damages adequate to compensate for infringement in no event less than a reasonable royalty. If the patent owner lost profits as the result of infringing activities, the profits lost may be a measure of damages. If there were no lost profits or they cannot be ascertained with reasonable accuracy, an amount adequate to compensate for the infringement not less than a reasonable royalty is the measure of damages. A reasonable royalty is sometimes said to be a floor for damages, meaning the damage award may be no lower. This means that if there is a basis for awarding damages under both the lost profits and royalty measures, the damage award may be based on the measure that yields the larger amount. This does not mean that in other situations damages may be greater than a reasonable royalty." "§9:26, Two basic measures of damages," 2 *Patent Law, Legal and Economic Principles* § 9:26 (2nd ed. 2015).

explore patent law, but to analogize from the way it grapples with component valuation problems, I will avoid subjecting readers to the details of damages in patent law, especially since they can be found in excellent analyses elsewhere.[8] Returning instead to option (2), the value-added rule, note that while it exploits the value of A, somehow separated from BC, and certainly separated from HP's larger product in which ABC was contained, it plainly discourages patent infringements. This is because if HP had bargained for the right to use A, as reflected in (3), the estimated-bargained-for rule, it would presumably have done better than giving away all the marginal profit. Such an intermediate recovery avoids giving Cornell undeserved credit for HP's unobjectionable use of BC.

It must be noted that finding the value-added by the inclusion of A is even harder than already suggested. Courts might want to reward the company that thought of *combining* the three elements, ABC. At times that innovator will be a patent holder like Cornell, but it is more interesting when a company like HP, which might never have used A on its own, used A exclusively in combination with BC. For our purpose, it will be sufficient to recognize that (2), looking for the value-added, may be closer to (1), the maximum value, than it first seems; if courts find it appropriate to reward the innovative step taken by the apparent infringer in combining the patented element with other elements, courts might (learnedly or intuitively) upgrade (2) to a level we can designate as (4), a "maximum-conjoined-bargain rule." This rule blends the conventional idea of marginal value (of A) with the value of combining it with other elements.

There are, to be sure, other possibilities. Courts might, instead of estimating the bargain, as in (3), impose a "default-split rule," which we can call option (5). The court might give Cornell one-half of the value-added, or even half of the total value of ABC in a perfectly competitive market. The rule is a default rule because eventually parties will bargain in its shadow and stay out of court. The division in half can be understood as freeing courts of the need to imagine a bargain between parties that might have different bargaining prowess. In the litigated case, the court eventually imagined a royalty based on (2), the value-added rule, but it might have done otherwise if the parties had not taken extreme positions, and had instead offered testimony aimed at estimating the bargain, as reflected in rule (3).[9]

---

[8] Greg Allenby, Jeff Brazell, John Howell, & Peter Rossi, "Valuation of Patented Product Features," 57 *J. L. & Econ.* 629 (2014).

[9] The decision is analyzed in www.wac6.com/wac6/2010/10/patent-damages-apportionment-and-the-cornell-case.html. For some excellent discussion of the component valuation problem, see Allenby et al., "Valuation of Patented Product Features," as well as J. Gregory Sidak & Jeremy O. Skog, "Using Conjoint Analysis to Apportion Patent Damages," 25 *Fed. Circuit B. J.* 581 (2016); Gregg Allenby et al., "Calculating Reasonable Royalty Damages Using Conjoint Analysis," 45 *AIPLA Q. J.* 233 (2017). An innovation in this literature is the idea that when people are surveyed or otherwise studied, they should compare an offering not just to an enhanced or narrowed item but also to items offered by other sellers, adjusted as they would be if the product in question has been without the patented piece. Another insight offered by

Their dogmatism suggests (6): a final-offer-arbitration rule (as reasonably suggested by one commentator[10]), asking the parties to (each) suggest an amount of damages, but promising to constrain the court to a choice between these two proposed amounts. This approach also aims to make the court's job easier, not by splitting something in half but rather by capturing the parties' private information, and encouraging reasonable claims by them, and perhaps settlement.

It is easy to be attracted to something approaching option (1), the maximum-value rule – perhaps without saying so in order not to be reversed by a higher court. There are several reasons for this sort of generosity to the infringed-upon party. First, there is the difficulty of extracting A from ABC. Second, there is the difficulty of recreating the bargain that would divide the gain from innovation between Cornell and HP. Most important, the prospect of high damages might be certain to deter the intentional taking of patented inventions. Still, it is important to see the danger of overdeterrence, which threatens a party like HP with disaster if it innovates. HP may well have known of Cornell's patent claim on A, but HP may have been uncertain about the legal viability of this patent, given that it could have considered Cornell's contribution to be an abstract idea rather than a process, machine, or article of manufacture.[11] Ideas alone are not protected. It is for this reason that I downplay the importance of the intentionality of HP's behavior. It may have been intentional; however, I describe HP as simply *knowing* of Cornell's claim, but thinking that the patent would eventually be found invalid. Another overdeterrence concern has already been noted; HP might have figured out the value of the ABC combination, and Cornell might have held out in negotiations in order to extract the value of the combination of its patented piece with BC. Law must not discourage HP (or in some cases Cornell) from innovating with its combinatory insight, even as it rewards Cornell for its invention, assuming it is eventually found to be novel and deserving.

To be sure, underdeterrence is also a concern. It is apparent that if HP must pay very little when it is sued for using patented material, inventors will learn that their

---

Sidak and coauthors is that the game changes when surveys ask about the future, when in fact the question is what would have happened in the past.

[10] Mark Lemley & Carl Shapiro, "A Simple Approach to Setting Reasonable Royalties for Standard-Essential Patents," 28 *Berkeley Tech. L. J.* 1135 (2013).

[11] Patents are limited to "any new and useful process, machine, manufacture, or composition of matter," to the exclusion of abstract ideas. See 35 U.S.C. § 101; see also *Diamond v. Chakrabarty*, 447 U.S. 303, 309 (1980) (citations omitted). However, despite its description as a process, Cornell's patent is not clearly viable under existing case law. In *Gottschalk v. Benson*, the Supreme Court denied the patentability of a binary code conversion process, stating that "[t]he mathematical formula involved here has no substantial practical application except in connection with a digital computer" and that its patent would in essence be "a patent on the algorithm itself" – something the court deemed an abstract idea. *Gottschalk v. Benson*, 409 U.S. 63, 71 (1972). Similar decisions were reached in *Parker v. Flook*, 437 U.S. 584 (1978) and *O'Reilly v. Morse*, 15 How. 62 (1854). Given these decisions, HP might have believed there was a reasonable argument for overturning Cornell's patent as too abstract and unconnected from application to be a "process" in the sense of 35 U.S.C. § 101.

outputs can be taken with no substantial reward to them, and as a result they may invest too little in inventive behavior. We do not know the optimal size of the monopoly-reward to grant inventors, but this is a job for Congress. A less apparent inefficiency, or problem, with under-compensation, is that users like HP may strategically mix in material under patent with other things in order to *create* a component valuation problem. ABC may actually be an inefficient way to build something, but HP will have an incentive to put these three things together in order to pay very little for the patented A, which would have been costlier for HP had it been used on its own or obtained through a proper bargain with Cornell. In short, it is reckless to allow anyone to avoid paying for the "value" of a patent by setting things up in order to benefit from a component valuation issue, but we should not unthinkingly prefer high damages, and certainly not some version of (1), the maximum-value rule, in order to penalize the apparent misbehavior, and discourage potential inefficient strategizing, by HP. Unsurprisingly, it would be nice to get the payment to Cornell just right, and limited to A, with or without a sweetener to deter knowing violations or court tests.

11.2 EVALUATING A SIMPLER CONGLOMERATED FEATURE

Consider an individual Y who owns a multilevel parking facility in one city and then is impressed by what he observes in a garage, owned by X, while visiting another city. The parking garage excites Y because it has features previously unknown to him; it includes painted numbers on the floor of each parking space, and it designates each floor of the facility with the name of a local sports team, and then plays the team's theme song near the elevator on that floor. These innovations make it easier for patrons to remember where they parked. Y returns home and copies these practices with some variation, because his garage is in a different town and is of a different style. The changes are fairly inexpensive to introduce, even if Y dutifully pays something to use any copyrighted music. Y might learn that X, or a supplier to X, claims a patent on these innovations, but Y has no fear of liability because these simple but clever features are mere ideas and, in any event, are probably obvious to many people who have thought about minimizing the number of patrons who need help locating their cars. Y regards the patent claim to be frivolous. In fact, and somewhat amazingly, a patent *has* been processed for the designation and musical accompaniment of floors in parking garages. The patent application, and the first decision accepting it, insisted that the music is not a mere idea because it is attached to a "machine," in the form of the computer directing the music.

The very idea of a patent for parking garage innovation is quite incredible to most observers, but here the point is simply that HP, like (the imagined) Y, may have misjudged the reach of patent law. And in terms of liability, the idea is that a high award might discourage innovation in garages owned by people like Y, as well as in computer programs developed by firms like HP. Note also that in the garage case it must be difficult to assess damages as directed by most of the possible rules sketched here. It is unlikely that a court would find convincing evidence of how many customers paid a few dollars more to park in the garage that had this extra music feature, and this is especially so given that it is combined with the painting of numbers on spaces – and no one claims that this feature is also patentable. For those of us who are mere patrons, it is puzzling why numbered spaces are not more common. A stingy but perhaps fair and workable approach to damages might be to see how many fewer calls for help customers made to the manager of Y's garage after it was improved; the value of the innovation to Y – even if his upgrades attracted no additional customers and did not enable an increase in prices (local taxes aside) – was the reduction in labor costs previously devoted to helping patrons find their vehicles. Note that even this approach fails to separate a single conglomerated feature.

11.3 MARKET SOLUTIONS

In the case of HP's knowing violation of Cornell's patent, how should damages be calculated? The garage example is instructive, but partly inapplicable. An attractive rule might call for a search for competitor firms, as suggested by Sidak and other authors,[12] that sold a product with BC but not with A. If there is such a set of sales, and especially a large set (in order to exclude that annoying problem of understanding the game normally described as the bargain between two parties) then we could compare the prices with HP's in order to get at the value of A.[13] Law could then use method (2) or (3), the value-added or estimated-bargain amount. Similarly, in the parking garage situation, there must be some garage owners who offer spaces designated with visible numbers but not with team (or country or show-tune) names and songs, and this could provide information about the value of the patented innovation. These pieces of information do not need to be in Y's city. In short, information can be provided by add-ons in similar markets. If there is a great deal of money at stake, as there was in the Cornell–HP case, we could even imagine a firm,

---

[12] See Allenby et al., "Valuation of Patented Product Features"; Sidak & Skog, "Using Conjoint Analysis to Apportion Patent Damages"; Allenby et al., "Calculating Reasonable Royalty Damages Using Conjoint Analysis."

[13] Patent law does on occasion use information from other sellers to assess values. See e.g. *Grain Processing Corp. v. Am. Maize-Products Co.*, 185 F. 3d 1341, 1351 (1999) (stating that "only by comparing the patented invention to its next-best available alternative(s) ... can the court discern the market value of the patent owner's exclusive right, and therefore his expected profit or reward, had the infringer's activities not prevented him from taking full economic advantage of this right"); *Georgia-Pacific Corp. v. U.S. Plywood Corp.*, 318 F. Supp. 1116, 1120 (1970) (noting that the "utility and advantages of the patent property over the old modes or devices" and the customary "selling price" may be used to establish reasonable royalty for a patent license).

perhaps at the direction of the court and at the expense of the litigants, creating a market for a computer with BC but not A, and then another in the same market with ABC, in order to see how much consumers would pay for the addition of A. The idea is to estimate a bargain between the infringer and the patent holder by looking for information in comparable markets and then awarding the differential value, or one-half of this value.

There will be markets – like the one with competing parking garages – in which the innovation does not generate higher prices. The market price may be dictated by first-time users who will simply search for the lowest prices or best locations near their destinations. The advantage to the innovator then comes in the form of more repeat customers, as users appreciate the added features. In this case, the damages for a wrongful taking of patented inputs are a function of the profit-per-customer times the increase in the number of patrons or the occupation rate. Meanwhile, it is sufficient to note that there are a number of ways of properly assessing damages in a patent law case like *Cornell v. Hewlett Packard*, and they all involve assessing the value of a component, whether through price, profit, or volume. Cornell, to its disadvantage, insisted that it obtain the maximum conceivable value of its patent, option (1) here, claiming that billions earned by HP should be turned over to the patent holder, Cornell, because of a single component, wrongfully used by HP, and contributing to its profit. At the very least, it needed to show evidence of the incremental impact on HP's profits from the inclusion of the patented and unlicensed component, simplified here as A. But it might also have pointed to an increase in sales, akin to the repeat customers in the parking garage case. The increase alone might seem to suggest something fairly close to the maximum conceivable value (1), but this ignores the fact that any increase likely comes from the combination of ABC, and presents the (now familiar) decoupling problem.

The garage example, though slightly contrived, also suggests a new method that may be transferable to marketing research. It is to sample some actual patrons as they enter the garage and ask them to identify features of the facility that attracted them to it. They are apt to mention location and price, but if they also refer to innovations that differentiate the garage from competitors, that would suggest increased business and revenue because of the named characteristics. It may even be possible to use this kind of retrospective survey to estimate the wrongful gain. On the other hand, if very few of these garage patrons, and especially repeat customers, can even identify the naming of levels or the accompanying music, it is more difficult to argue that the infringement should generate substantial damages. In sum, it is easy to see why an infringer may have known of the improvement but genuinely believed that it would not survive a legal challenge to its patent. It is also worth reiterating that a valid patent may increase the number of sales or other uses, but not the price of the product in which it is embedded along with other characteristics.

11.4 SURVEYS

Anyone schooled in marketing research will see both similarities and distinctions between "conjoined analysis" in marketing and the component valuation difficulty in assessing damages in patent law. Beginning with this important subject in marketing research, imagine an automobile manufacturer deciding whether to add a back-up mirror, two, four, or eight more airbags, and an auto-lane keeper to next year's model of one of its popular vehicles. The manufacturer knows the production cost of each feature but not the willingness of consumers to pay. Unlike innovations in many other industries, it is too costly to simply try out combinations and observe customer reaction. Trials are costly, and it is prohibitively expensive to fabricate and market prototypes. It is also impractical to offer models with every combination of options, and the after-market is unable to supply most of these bells and whistles. A restaurant can easily vary its menu in order to see what works, but a modern automobile manufacturer cannot do so. The decision-making problems are exacerbated by the fact that there is likely to be interplay among options, and this is what makes the problem interesting. For example, consumers will value an additional rear-seat airbag differently if the vehicle already has four airbags. A noise-absorbing fabric affects the value of an improved sound system, and so forth. The problem would be hard enough with five unrelated items in play, but given the importance of combinations, five items make for 120 possibilities. Even if the airbag choices are not interactive (one cannot have four as well as six airbags), there are plenty of possible combinations. Moreover, even when there is no physical connection between features, there is a price interaction, as consumers might pay more for a feature so long as the entire price of the vehicle does not exceed budgetary constraints. Given the cost and time of production, manufacturers turn to marketing experts, and their most popular approach is to survey a population resembling likely buyers. There is some literature that suggests the reliability of these surveys,[14] and this is not the place to take on that literature, tempting as I find the prospect of doing so with respect to marketing as it is with regard to the growing popularity of survey evidence in law. Most of the optimistic survey literature expresses concern for the danger that those who take the time to respond to surveys might not be representative of larger populations, but there are more serious problems. These surveys may not replicate; in some cases they ask consumers to imagine their future selves (with unknown family income and preferences) and even where this is avoided, they are often asking persons who are not actually buying a

---

[14] See generally Olivier Toubia, "Conjoint Analysis," in HANDBOOK OF MARKETING ANALYTICS 52 (Natalie Mizik & Dominique Hanssens eds., 2018); David Bakken & Curtis Frazier, "Conjoint Analysis: Understanding Consumer Decision Making," in THE HANDBOOK OF MARKETING RESEARCH: USES MISUSES AND FUTURE ADVANCES 288 (Rajiv Grover & Marco Vriens eds., 2006).

good and who might have very different responses when real money, family pressure, and other things are at stake.

The marketing literature is, unsurprisingly, sophisticated. It recognizes that survey respondents will not have the patience to evaluate 120 combinations and so it focuses statistical techniques on asking a manageable number of questions of the type "what would you pay for x" (where x contains a combination of features) or "please rank the importance to you of the following three features." The survey expert then estimates based on an assumption of linear functions and other ways of reasoning from several aggregated responses to creating a map of likely preferences for all combinations of the variables.[15] If we see that survey respondents will pay between $100 and $1,200 more for eight airbags than for two, but barely more if there is also a lane-keeper function in the package, then it is possible to interpolate to the demand for two additional airbags – assuming a linear, or other correctly specified, demand curve.[16]

An optimist might say that in the case of parking garages, and setting patent law aside, Y can simply go home and copy X's innovation, because X must have studied the costs and benefits, and decided that the innovations were worthwhile. And if Y learns that X innovated after seeing the features in yet another facility, owned by W, and X paid the patent holder before installing the system in X's garage, Y might free ride on X's decision-making; X must have decided that the patent was valid and worth accessing. Customers are unlikely to have very different valuations or memories just because they live in different cities, and patent law is also likely to be applied in similar fashion in different cities. The same strategy, or confidence in markets, might be used for automobiles. If another manufacturer includes two additional airbags and charges $Z more, then instead of paying for marketing research, a manufacturer might simply copy what it can see, and add two airbags, assuming the cost of doing so is less than Z. It might even extrapolate and imagine a demand function before offering four or five airbags at different prices, in order to attract consumers who prefer a lower price or more airbags than a competitor offers. A marketing expert might object to such an heroic assumption about perfect markets, but the same might be said about the expert's own assumptions regarding linear demand curves.

This sort of learning across disciplines runs in both directions. Patent lawyers and judges could learn some mathematics and engage in extrapolation, especially when there are no comparable firms to study.[17] If Cornell does not see other firms charging more because they provide BC (so that the value of A can be deduced),

---

[15] Bakken & Frazier, "Conjoint Analysis," 290–92, 295.
[16] The linearity assumption is common in the literature and probably uncalled for, but inasmuch as I warn of it in other work (titled *The Eventual Decline of Empirical Law and Economics*), I merely mention it here.
[17] Interdisciplinary learning is possible but unnecessary where firms and their lawyers have figured things out on their own. For example, marketing experts, and indeed run-of-the-mill

it could survey actual or likely buyers about the value of BC or ABC, and present this evidence in court. Following an idea advanced earlier, Cornell, or an expert designated by the court, might also ask actual customers what attracted them to HP's product, and with this tactic discover the importance of A compared to B and C. It would be surprising to find that customers had paid HP a substantial premium and yet could not even identify A, but stranger things have happened, and the cost of such an inquiry is low, as it is in both the parking garage and automobile cases.[18]

11.5 AN ANALOGY TO COMPARATIVE FAULT IN TORT LAW

Consider next the application of the doctrine of comparative fault in tort law. S drives too fast and is unable to stop in time to avoid hitting T, who is backing out of a driveway without pausing and taking due care. For many years, a wrongdoer like S was absolved of tort liability because T was contributorily negligent. The rule was not a bad one. Drivers like S could not foresee their victims' negligence, and they knew they would be liable for significant damages if their speeding caused an accident when the injured party was not negligent. Here, T's negligence is a kind of windfall for S, but it serves to motivate drivers like T to take care as well. Over time, and perhaps because most people's ethical intuition was that S should not be completely absolved, especially where S's behavior was intentional, law moved from contributory to comparative negligence. The move might also have been influenced by the further intuition that S should slow down even more in recognition of the fact that people like T might not be wearing a seatbelt or might pull out of a driveway too quickly. In any event, under the comparative negligence rule, the jury or judge is asked to "compare" S and T's fault, and then to divide the loss between them accordingly. There are many ways to interpret and carry out this instruction, but almost every one of these promotes (at least in theory) efficient behavior. As long as at least one driver is induced to take proper care, the others will also be motivated to take care, knowing that if they do not, they might be left to pay the entire loss.

Comparative negligence is especially, or even always, attractive when an innocent victim is injured by multiple wrongdoers. Imagine for instance that J, K, and L operate grossly polluting factories on a river's banks, and the combination of their pollutants damages downstream parties. Law wants the wrongdoers to pay, but how should payment be divided among JKL? Again, we wish we knew the marginal, or

---

business owners, regularly check out what competitors and their customers are doing, just as HP's gain from A is easily deduced if a competitor firm incorporates BC without A.

[18] After writing this paper, I was fortunate enough to run across a related, but perhaps even more unlikely, idea of using tax law (or really imagined transfer prices) to estimate hypothetical bargains in patent law, and then also to use patent law to estimate transfer prices for tax law's purposes. This is quite similar to the cross-discipline strategies advanced here. See Susan C. Morse, "Seeking Comparable Transactions in Patent and Tax," 37 *Rev. Litig. Brief* 201 (2018) (thoughtful and insightful discussion of borrowing in both directions).

incremental, contribution of each, but these are interconnected. Perhaps we would be harder on J if K and L were already on the river, and their wastes were absorbed harmlessly. After all, it was the third set of discharges that "caused" harm. This is an interesting problem, because a single owner of all three factories might find it most efficient to clean up the second or first factory. The marginal wrongdoer is easy to misidentify, just as denying recovery to one who "comes to a nuisance" is often inefficient. Here, there are increasing returns, which is to say harms, to scale, for the whole (harm) is greater than the sum of the parts.

The torts problem is analogous to the vexing problem in patent law, where we tried to reward the inventor, but also not to inhibit innovation, often in the form of combining patented and unpatented elements, by a user who may be an infringer. In both settings, the word "marginal" is misleading whether for gains (as in the patent cases) or losses (in the tort cases). In tort law, one possibility is to allocate liability in proportion to how much the wrongdoers saved by polluting, rather than behaving non-negligently and investing in scrubbers or taking waste products to designated dump locations. Another is to penalize intentional torts more severely than miscalculations.[19] But however this question is resolved, there is again the problem of component valuation.

11.6 PATENTS, MARKETING, AND TORTS CONJOINED

It may be that tort law has little to offer patent law and even less to give marketing and, in turn, tort law has little to learn from these other areas. This is so even though the three fields have component valuation problems in common. An important difference between torts and marketing begins with the observation that so long as the downstream victims are not overcompensated, there is little risk of overdeterrence. If J pays more than its fair share, whatever that might be, it can try to bargain with K and L in order to reduce their pollution and, consequently, the downstream losses. More important, if J's expected liability causes J to take precautions, or even over-care from an economic perspective, K and L will then learn that they will be entirely responsible for any downstream injury. After all, so long as liability is linked to law's usual negligence principle, J will be absolved, leaving the others to pay. Bargaining of the kind just described is even easier in patent law, where parties can bargain even if they have different estimates of the likelihood of a patent's viability, but bargaining means nothing to an automobile manufacturer struggling with a decision about improvements. It is tempting to say that patent law and marketing have more to learn from one another because the component problems they share are about dividing gains, while the comparative negligence setting is about dividing losses.

More optimistically, tort law and marketing may have more in common than first meets the eye. Recall the oblique reference to the Coase Theorem; one polluter

---

[19] See generally Richard A. Posner & William M. Landes, "An Economic Theory of Intentional Torts," 1 *Int'l. Rev. L. & Econ.* 127 (1981).

could pay another to cease polluting, or indeed could buy the other polluting firms and do the efficient thing all on its own, internalizing all the costs and benefits. Law could, rather bravely, require the polluters to make buy–sell offers on these prices, along the lines of the "you cut, I choose" method that children often use to divide a dessert, or partners might use when dissolving an investment that they value more than would an outside buyer. Similarly, just as a marketing expert can extrapolate after asking a set of potential customers what they would pay for a feature, or how they would rank combinations of features at a set price, so too law could ask each polluter what it would pay for the others to reduce pollution, or what it would pay for their factories. Honest answers would be encouraged by the fact that the law could require the parties to follow through and carry out the transaction at the specified price. There is much more to be said about the similarities and differences among these fields, but the aim here is to identify the connective fiber and the kinds of changes it might produce.

11.7 CONCLUSION: COMPONENT VALUATION ISSUES EVERYWHERE

Component valuation issues arise in private affairs as well as in legal matters, and not only in arenas where marketing expertise has been called into play. Thus, businesses must decide how much to invest in various assets and how much to pay key employees, while sellers of goods and services to these businesses are often trying to evaluate their worth to the buyers. In most settings, there is no opportunity for experiments or useful surveys, and parties are left to guess values, knowing that the answer is complicated by interactions with neighboring elements. For example, an athlete may be worth more to some teams than to others, largely because of practiced interactions with teammates. Similarly, political parties and donors learn that some legislators' campaigns are worth greater investment than others, because these candidates, if elected, will play important roles in close legislative votes or in committee deliberations. Unsurprisingly, the experts used by political candidates do work that is quite similar to that of marketing experts employed by manufacturers of consumer products, even though manufacturers want more sales or higher profits, while politicians often aim to attract bare majorities. Component valuation questions are found everywhere,[20] and I hope this chapter has encouraged readers to

[20] Other areas include disaggregation in pain and suffering calculations. I have already suggested that the division of benefits in corporate law's treatment of gains from mergers and, therefore, the well-known problem of dividing property in the breakup of partnerships (including marriage) present somewhat different problems. The problem discussed here is not quite the same as the familiar problem of dividing surpluses or thinking about Nash equilibria. Here we seek to disaggregate and identify the gains attributable to one cause, patent holder, or tortfeasor. If possible, the idea is to minimize the temptation to recreate the bargain between two or more specific parties. Some readers might wish to turn this into a game theory problem, but this is not the place for such a distraction.

think about them a bit differently in their own areas of law, business, and scientific research, and in mundane but equally challenging problems associated with disciplining children, evaluating leaders, and constructing investment portfolios. Most of these areas present "problems" that can be solved where there are numerous comparable transactions, identifiable parties who know their own preferences, or reasons to expect survey evidence or experiments to be revealing. It is tempting, but wrong I think, to say that the problem is just the same as dividing gains in all contracts or solving the "fair-shares" problem in mergers between affiliated corporations. In these situations there is a range of plausible answers and if the parties are left to bargain, we are presented with a manageable game theory problem. But the component valuation problem is more than a matter of dividing a pie, as for example when a nearby active market is available for comparison. I have tried to show that the questions addressed in the field of conjoined analysis in marketing research have much in common with problems in assessing damages in patent law and liability in comparative negligence cases in tort law. The marketing-patent law connection has been made in earlier literature, but the analysis here has shown that there is yet more to it. In any event, the similarities discussed here lead to the observation that the methods used in each of these (three) areas might help bring about progress in another. But the strongest conclusion is that by noticing the presence of component valuation problems in a few areas, and observing the ways in which they are or might be handled, we can improve our understanding of how to proceed in a variety of seemingly unrelated fields.

12

Marketing Analysis in Class Certification

Randolph E. Bucklin and Peter Simon[*]

12.1 INTRODUCTION: MARKETING AND CLASS CERTIFICATION

Marketing analyzes the behavior of buyers and sellers and often does so at the individual or segment level. Thus, differences among sellers or heterogeneity among buyers are often areas of focus for marketing analysis. Much of the class certification process involves assessments regarding the similarity – or lack thereof – in class members' situations. This has made marketing and its analytic tool kit for examining markets at the disaggregate level well suited to provide insight into key issues in class certification.

While the primary motivations for the behaviors of consumers and firms (as buyers and sellers) are often straightforward to discern, there is frequently a wide variety of reasons for specific decisions. In class certification, developing an in-depth understanding of decision-making processes across different groups or segments of consumers or firms can be quite useful. Quantitative analyses are now widely used to provide data-driven and statistics-based conclusions regarding key issues in class certification. Examples of these analytic techniques include cluster analysis, various types of regression analysis, clickstream data studies, and others.

This chapter is about the analytical, data-based techniques from marketing research that can be and have been used to address important issues in class certification. The chapter focuses on two aspects of class certification where marketing experts have played important roles: (1) establishing common harm and (2) establishing a common method for computing damages. We searched extensively for publicly available case records over the past decade in which marketing experts had applied analytic techniques to shed light on these two aspects. Our search yielded a series of recent examples from plaintiffs' and defendants' expert reports that pertain to both aspects. Collectively, these examples enable us to examine how marketing analysis has been applied to these topics in different case

[*] Excellent research support provided by Phuong Le, Haimin Zhang, and Chris Bosley.

situations and the insights that it can offer. We also discuss challenges and limitations involved in applying these analysis techniques in class certification.

This chapter proceeds as follows. First, we begin with a brief overview of the key legal concepts in class certification and how they intersect with marketing expertise. We next discuss the role of marketing analysis in ascertaining common harm among class members, illustrated by several recent case examples. We then turn to the role of marketing analysis in determining a common method for damages calculation, also illustrated by recent case examples. In both topics, we discuss implications of these techniques for marketing and class certification and then offer conclusions.

12.2 RELEVANT LEGAL CONCEPTS IN CLASS CERTIFICATION

An initial step in a class action lawsuit is the determination by a judge that a class is proper under the law. This is the process of "class certification." The Federal Rules of Civil Procedure, Rule 23(a) and Rule 23(b), dictate several criteria that a class must meet to be certified.[1] Specifically, Rule 23(a) requires that the proposed class satisfy requirements for numerosity (impractical to handle otherwise), commonality (questions of law or fact are common to class members), typicality (named plaintiffs properly represent the class), and adequacy (named plaintiffs do not have interests in conflict with those of the rest of the class).

Marketing expertise often comes to bear on the commonality requirement. A plaintiffs' expert might provide explanation and evidence that a method for determining harm (and damages) to consumers (or businesses) exists that can be applied to all potential class members. A defendant's expert might provide explanation and evidence that the proposed method would leave some class members unharmed or possibly even some with gains, or that the method would produce incorrect estimates of harm. Typicality of the named plaintiffs might also be examined by experts to provide examples in support of – or opposition to – the common method in question.

Though there are other provisions, Rule 23(b) effectively requires that the questions of law or fact common to class members *predominate* over questions affecting only individual members. Moreover, Rule 23(b) requires that a class action must be judged superior to other available methods for fairly and efficiently adjudicating the dispute. This requirement is known as the "predominance and superiority" or "manageability" criterion, requiring that class members be similarly situated both legally and factually. In other words, those unharmed by the defendant's alleged misdeeds factually differ from those who were. This rule also requires that all, or nearly all, class members were harmed.[2] Marketing expertise may be brought

---

[1] This section is necessarily an overview of class certification requirements. For a more in-depth discussion, see Christopher Chorba et al., "Expert Analysis of Class Certification Issues," Chapter 14 in LITIGATION SERVICES HANDBOOK (Roman L. Weil et al., eds., 6th ed.) (John Wiley & Sons, 2017).
[2] Ibid., p. 14.5.

to bear in the context of predominance by showing that class members were affected in the same way (in terms of being harmed) or were not affected in the same way.

Two key issues in class certification where marketing expertise and analysis have been frequently brought to bear are the following:

1. Common harm: were all (or nearly all) class members harmed by the alleged misconduct by the defendant?
2. Common method for damages: is there a suitable method available to calculate damages on a class-wide basis, without extensive inquiry needed into individual class members' situations?

The two issues intersect. For example, methods proposed for calculating damages may suggest that some class members were not harmed or even realized gains from the alleged misconduct. The next section discusses the role of marketing analysis in determining common harm and the subsequent section turns to the role of marketing analysis in establishing common methods for damage computation.

12.3 THE USE OF MARKETING ANALYSIS TO ADDRESS ISSUES OF COMMON HARM

Experts retained in the class certification phase of litigation may be asked to propose (for the plaintiff) or critique (for the defendant) a common method that could be used to show, on a class-wide basis, that class members were harmed by the alleged misconduct. A plaintiffs' expert might propose a statistical analysis to show that a substantial fraction of class members were adversely affected by the alleged behavior. For example, in a matter involving false or misleading advertising or product labeling, the plaintiffs' expert might propose to conduct a survey to measure purchasers' views on the effect of the label on purchase decisions. On the other hand, a defendant's expert might be asked to show that not all consumers were exposed to the at-issue advertising/label, or that not all consumers relied on the at-issue advertising/label in making their purchase decisions. In a class action brought by a group of businesses, the defendant's expert might be asked to show that not all businesses incurred lost profits as a result of the alleged misconduct.

A recurrent theme in such matters is the extent of *heterogeneity* among class members. As noted, marketing expertise and analysis are very well suited to explore the nature and extent of heterogeneity among putative class members. The heterogeneity could take several forms. First, there may be differences among class members in exposure to (or knowledge of) the alleged misconduct. Without exposure, harm is likely precluded for many consumers or businesses. Second, even if heterogeneity in exposure is not at issue, there may be differences in the extent to which class members relied upon the alleged misconduct in making their purchase decisions. If so, this could yield significant differences in harm – or some class members with harm and others with no harm. Third, even if exposure and decision process heterogeneity are not at issue, differences in the welfare or value that was lost could give rise to heterogeneity in harm. Welfare or monetary losses may not afflict all consumers in a class nor might all businesses in a class suffer impaired profits. Analyses of all of the above types of heterogeneity can draw from marketing expertise in examining markets at the disaggregate level (e.g. individuals or segments).

12.3.1 Heterogeneity in Exposure

In *Karim v. Hewlett-Packard Co.*, plaintiff Nad Karim alleged, on behalf of a putative class of California consumers, that Hewlett Packard (HP) misrepresented the capabilities of wireless cards included in certain HP laptop computers sold through HP's Home and Home Office (HHO) online store. Plaintiff claimed that the networking customization pages of the HHO website, which allowed buyers to specify and purchase a laptop with a customized wireless card, contained a false representation that certain wireless cards offered for sale were capable of dual-band operation. More specifically, he alleged that when a prospective purchaser configured the networking capabilities of his laptop computer on the HHO website, he could click on an embedded link that would then display a pop-up "Help Me Decide" (HMD) window explaining certain features of the offered wireless cards. It was on this optional HMD pop-up screen that the alleged misrepresentations were made.[3]

The defendant's expert, Dr. Tom Meyvis, analyzed clickstream data that anonymously captured the clicking behavior of visitors to the HHO website during an interval that included the putative class period. The clickstream data showed approximately 54 million visits to one or more configurator pages (where the features of a laptop computer could be customized before the computer was purchased) and approximately 4.9 million clicks on any of the HMD buttons. However, the data had important limitations. First, it did not distinguish between visits that resulted in a purchase from those that did not. Second, the data did not distinguish (a) HMD button clicks when the button was displayed as part of wireless card configuration (the "networking HMD button") from (b) clicks on any other HMD button, such as "Display," "Keyboard," etc. Lastly, it did not distinguish between clicks related to the laptops at issue from those not at issue in the case. As a result of these limitations, the clickstream data alone did not show what fraction of at-issue laptop purchasers clicked on the networking HMD button and might have been exposed to the allegedly false representation, if any.

To overcome these limitations, Dr. Meyvis combined the clickstream data with results from a survey he conducted in connection with the case.[4] His survey revealed

---

[3] Declaration of Dr. Tom Meyvis in Support of Defendant Hewlett Packard Co.'s Opposition to Plaintiff's Motion for Certification of a California Class, No. 4:12-cv-05240, *Karim v. Hewlett-Packard Co.* (N.D. Cal. June 1, 2015) (Meyvis HP Declaration), ECF No. 131-11 at ¶¶ 4–6.
[4] For more details on the survey design, see Meyvis HP Declaration at ¶¶ 29–79.

that clicks on the networking HMD button comprised only 2.1 percent of total HMD clicks. Given that there were a total of 4.9 million HMD clicks, the number of clicks on the networking HMD button would be estimated to be approximately 103,000.[5] The data also showed that there were about 687,000 transactions involving a purchase of an at-issue laptop. If one were to assume that *all* clicks on the networking HMD button were associated with a purchase then only 15 percent[6] of visits resulting in a purchase involved a click on the networking HMD button. Dr. Meyvis was then able to conclude that *at least* 85 percent of the proposed class members were not exposed to the allegedly false representation.

Dr. Meyvis' approach illustrates the use of clickstream data in conjunction with survey results to show that many proposed class members would not have been exposed to the alleged misrepresentation. Without exposure, purchase decisions could not have been influenced by the alleged misrepresentation and, consequently, those buyers were not harmed. The case also highlights some of the limitations that marketing experts confront when trying to use clickstream records that trace the search and purchase behavior of consumers online. As the case illustrates, oftentimes such data are incomplete or available at levels of aggregation too coarse to permit estimation of the actual exposure level. When this occurs, augmenting the clickstream data (e.g. with survey methods), can help to provide a basis for important findings regarding the heterogeneity in exposure among class members.[7]

12.3.2 *Heterogeneity in Decision-Making Processes*

A second important dimension in examining common harm is the extent to which class members relied upon the alleged bad actions in making decisions. For example, a close look at the factors influencing decision-making may reveal issues with respect to relevant similarities or differences among class members. The use of marketing analysis in this respect is illustrated in two recent class action cases. The first involves decision-making for retirement investments and the second involves consumer reliance on a product label claim.

In *Urakhchin v. Allianz Asset Mgmt. of Am., L.P.*, the plaintiffs brought a class action lawsuit against Allianz Asset Management of America, L.P. Plaintiffs alleged Defendants violated the Employee Retirement Income Security Act of 1974 (ERISA) by mismanaging the selection of investment options in the company's 401(k) retirement plan so as to favor company-owned funds as "core" investment

---

[5] 2.1% * 4.9 million = 102,900.
[6] 103,000 ÷ 687,000 = 0.15.
[7] Ultimately, the plaintiffs prevailed and the class was certified. See Order Granting Motion for Certification of a California Class, *Karim v. Hewlett-Packard Co.*, No. 4:12-cv-05240 (N.D. Cal. Dec. 18, 2015), ECF No. 139.

options within the plan.⁸ Plaintiffs alleged that participants in the plan (also the putative class) were harmed because these options often carried higher expenses and/or generated lower investment returns than passively managed index funds. The plaintiffs' expert, Dr. Steve Pomerantz, presented a list of Vanguard index funds that he proposed that the plan should have offered instead of the funds managed by the company. He calculated the weighted average of fees that the plan would have charged instead and presented this as the basis for common harm and damage estimation.⁹

The defendants' marketing expert, Dr. Randolph Bucklin, evaluated the investment choices made by individual plan participants and how they related to the participants' individual characteristics.¹⁰ Specifically, Dr. Bucklin examined the segmentation among class members in their investment selections. Two segmentation approaches were applied. The first grouped the plan's participants by known characteristics and analyzed individuals' behavior within those a priori segments.¹¹ The second clustered the plan's participants according to their observed investment choices, a post hoc segmentation.

In the a priori segmentation analysis, fund choices, and asset allocations differed significantly among the plan's participants along several dimensions. For example, participants who were classified as investment professionals selected different mixes of investments when compared with noninvestment professionals.¹² Participants with fewer assets in the plan made different investments than participants with greater assets.¹³ Participants whose account balances had not fully vested opted for different investments than participants with account balances that had.¹⁴ Lastly, participants who intensively used a self-directed option (Charles Schwab's Personal Choice Retirement Account, or PCRA) chose different investments from non-PCRA users.¹⁵ In sum, the revealed choices of participants showed considerable variation across segments based on observed characteristics. This suggested considerable heterogeneity among class members in their investing behavior and thus the potential for varying levels of harm, if any, to be present among participants.

Dr. Bucklin also took a second approach to the segmentation of the plan's participants by clustering class members by their investment allocations. The analysis grouped participants into eleven clusters representing various styles of allocation

---

⁸ First Amended Class Action Complaint For Damages, Injunctive Relief, and Equitable Relief, *Urakhchin v. Allianz Asset Mgmt. of Am., L.P.*, No. 8:15-cv-01614 (C.D. Cal. Jan. 6, 2016), ECF No. 28, ¶ 111.
⁹ Ibid., ¶ 7.
¹⁰ Confidential Expert Report of Randolph E. Bucklin, *Urakhchin v. Allianz Asset Mgmt. of Am., L.P.* (C.D. Cal. Mar. 31, 2017) (Bucklin Allianz Report), ¶ 8.
¹¹ Ibid., ¶¶ 24–25.
¹² Ibid., ¶¶ 44–47.
¹³ Ibid., ¶¶ 48–49.
¹⁴ Ibid., ¶¶ 50–52.
¹⁵ Ibid., ¶¶ 35–43.

decision-making.[16] The evident heterogeneity in participant choices in the 401(k) plan suggested that there may be meaningful differences in the individual situations of participants.[17] This highlighted the need for individual inquiry into participants' situations, including the role of assets held by participants outside of the plan in influencing investment decisions within the plan.[18]

In the *Urakhchin* case, relatively straightforward segmentation analyses were applied to available archive data to shed light on heterogeneity in class member decision-making. In other class action cases, like those involving widely distributed consumer products, such data may not be available to experts. Nevertheless, illuminating opinions regarding decision-making heterogeneity may be offered by relying upon marketing theory and literature. In *Briseno v. ConAgra Foods, Inc. (In re ConAgra Foods)*, the plaintiffs alleged that Wesson brand cooking oils marketed and distributed by ConAgra bore labels stating that the product was "100% Natural." The plaintiffs contended that, contrary to these representations, ConAgra used plants grown from genetically modified organism (GMO) seeds, engineered for greater yield and pesticide resistance. The plaintiffs asserted that the genetically modified organisms were not "100% natural," and that, as a result, ConAgra's labels and advertising were deceptive and likely to mislead consumers.

The plaintiffs' expert, Dr. Charles M. Benbrook, opined on whether Wesson brand cooking oils were "natural," based on his professional knowledge and expertise as an agricultural economist. To support his opinions, Dr. Benbrook reviewed a consumer survey conducted by Leatherhead Food Research, which found that thirteen attributes – including organic, no chemicals/artificial substances added, coming from nature, etc. – were most often mentioned in connection with a consumer's understanding of the term "natural."[19] Dr. Benbrook wrote that a genetically engineered crop is "fundamentally synthetic, in that it does not occur naturally and results in a product not found in nature."[20] Dr. Benbrook also reviewed a survey conducted by Hartman Group, which found that about 60 percent of respondents associated the phrase "absence of genetically modified food" with "natural."[21] He concluded that "when consumers choose foods labeled 'natural,' they expect that the foods are not derived from genetically engineered crops, nor

---

[16] Ibid., ¶ 54.
[17] Ibid., ¶¶ 55–57.
[18] Ibid., ¶¶ 58–60. The class in this case was certified by the district court, and the parties settled the matter: Order Conditionally Granting Plaintiff's Motion for Class Certification *Urakhchin v. Allianz Asset Mgmt. of Am., L.P.*, No. 8:15-cv-01614 (C.D. Cal. June 15, 2017), ECF No. 108; Final Judgment, *Urakhchin v. Allianz Asset Mgmt. of Am., L.P.*, No. 8:15-cv-01614 (C.D. Cal. July 30, 2018), ECF No. 186.
[19] Expert Declaration of Charles M. Benbrook, PhD, in Support of Motion and Motion for Class Certification and Appointment of Class Counsel, *In re ConAgra Foods, Inc.*, No. 2:11-cv-05379 (C.D. Cal. May 5, 2014) (Benbrook ConAgra Declaration), ECF No. 242, ¶¶ 38–41.
[20] Ibid., ¶ 42.
[21] Ibid., ¶¶ 43–44.

otherwise contain ingredients that were genetically engineered."[22] The plaintiffs alleged that "[a]ll members of the Classes were exposed to ConAgra's deceptive and misleading labeling and marketing of its Wesson Oils as '100% Natural' because that claim was on the label of every container of Wesson Oil sold."[23]

The defendants' marketing expert, Dr. Dominique Hanssens, discussed various factors that different consumers may consider when deciding whether or not to purchase a product. Drawing on multi-attribute theory and the concept of the marketing mix, he described a number of factors that influence various individual consumers' purchase decisions:

- Price can affect consumers' purchase decisions. As the price of a product goes up, more consumers would decide not to purchase the product.[24]
- Product characteristics such as taste, smell, and omega-3 fatty acid content would influence consumers' purchase decisions.[25]
- Brand can influence consumers' decision-making in different ways, depending on each consumer's preferences and characteristics. Some consumers tend to repeatedly purchase a brand's products, while others frequently switch brands.[26]
- "Place, or the retail environment, also impacts consumers' purchasing decisions."[27]
- Promotion – including advertising, sales promotions, and public relations – also affect product sales.[28]
- External factors such as the economy, competition, technology, and culture may impact a given consumer's decision to purchase a product.[29]

In principle, each of these mix elements or factors may carry different weights across consumers in their purchase decisions. This means that the extent to which different consumers rely upon an element of a product label in making a purchase decision will vary because consumers are heterogeneous in the weights they place on other factors. In addition, Dr. Hanssens cited academic literature on consumer information-seeking behavior. He noted that it can depend on many factors including familiarity with the product category.[30] Thus, the impact of the product label on

---

[22] Ibid., ¶ 45.
[23] Second Consolidated Amended Class Action Complaint, *In re ConAgra Foods, Inc.*, No. 2:11-cv-05379 (C.D. Cal. Dec. 19, 2012), ECF No. 143, ¶ 58.
[24] Declaration of Dominique M. Hanssens, PhD, in Opposition to Plaintiff's Motion to Certify Class, *In re ConAgra Foods, Inc.*, No. 2:11-cv-05379 (C.D. Cal. July 14, 2014) (Hanssens ConAgra Declaration), ECF No. 304, ¶ 21.
[25] Ibid., ¶ 22.
[26] Ibid., ¶ 22.
[27] Ibid., ¶ 25.
[28] Ibid., ¶ 26.
[29] Ibid., ¶ 27.
[30] Ibid., ¶¶ 23–24.

consumers' purchasing decisions also would depend on each consumer's prior experience with the product, another factor highly likely to vary across class members. Dr. Hanssens concluded that "[t]he variety of factors that influence consumer purchase decisions, and the different weight put on these factors by different consumers, means that there is a high degree of heterogeneity in the purchase decision process at the consumer level."[31] Dr. Hanssens also conducted a consumer survey, and found that the "100% Natural" Statement on Wesson brand cooking oils "did not have a material impact on consumer purchase intent or beliefs about GMO content."[32]

12.3.3 *Heterogeneity in Lost Value or Profits*

While the preceding case examples illustrate the issues of heterogeneity in exposure and in decision-making, another issue that can arise in ascertaining common harm is the potential for different outcomes across class members. For example, it may be possible that some class members actually benefited from the alleged misconduct of the defendant instead of being harmed. This might be examined using a variety of methods, including surveys, archival data, and consumer panel data. In a business-to-business setting, it might be evident in heterogeneity in the profit outcomes (i.e. positive or negative) stemming from the alleged misconduct.

In the *Google AdWords Litig.* case, two individuals and four firms sought class certification for a lawsuit against Google in 2010 alleging unjust enrichment in connection with Google's AdWords program. The plaintiffs alleged that Google failed to properly disclose that it placed AdWords ads on "parked domain" and "error page" websites (types of web pages considered to be unintended destinations for Internet users and which, therefore, may be ill-suited for presenting ads). The plaintiffs also claimed that ads on these websites received clicks that "result in far fewer conversions to advertisers, and therefore far less value, to plaintiffs and the class." As a result, the plaintiffs alleged that Google harmed class members by overcharging them for clicks from ads placed on these sites.[33]

Dr. Stan V. Smith, an expert for the plaintiffs, proposed to calculate damages by "comparing the actual price paid by advertisers for clicks on ads placed by Google on parked domains and error pages against the estimated 'but for' price for these same clicks had Google informed advertisers that these ads were indeed being placed on such low quality pages." His approach called for "re-pricing" the cost of the clicks advertisers paid for ads placed on parked domain and error pages.

---

[31] Ibid., ¶ 31.
[32] Ibid., 12. Ultimately, the class was certified: Order Granting in Part and Denying in Part Plaintiffs' Amended Motion for Class Certification, *In re ConAgra Foods, Inc.*, No. 2:11-cv-05379 (C.D. Cal. Feb. 23, 2015), ECF No. 545.
[33] Expert Report of Randolph E. Bucklin, *In re Google AdWords Litig.*, No. 5:08-cv-03369 (N.D. Cal. Oct. 4, 2010) (Bucklin Google AdWords Report), 4.

Damages would be computed as the difference between the prices paid by the advertisers in the class and the but-for prices. Dr. Smith proposed multiple methods for computing but-for prices, including a so-called "Smart Pricing Approach" in which an ad pricing formula used internally by Google would be applied to reprice the clicks in question.[34]

One of the defendant's experts, Dr. Randolph Bucklin, analyzed detailed Google ad metric data for the advertising campaigns run by the various named plaintiffs. While a number of limitations with Dr. Smith's damages method were discussed, an interesting result pertained to common harm. In particular, the advertising analysis showed that ads served on parked and error pages for one of the several named plaintiffs performed well in terms of conversion from clicks to purchases. When the cost per conversion was computed for the ads served on the pages in question, it turned out to be lower than for ads placed elsewhere. It was also lower than what would have been implied by the but-for analysis proposed by Dr. Smith, also raising questions about the proposed damages methodology.[35]

The *Google AdWords* case illustrates that the analysis of archival data at the individual level can show the potential for heterogeneity in profit outcomes across class members who are businesses. While this case involved advertisers on Google, similar analyses could be performed in other settings. Moreover, the analysis was limited to the archival data for just the named plaintiffs – which in this matter was sufficient for the defendant to challenge common harm. In other cases, such an analysis might be extended to a broader sample of class members or, with available data, to all class members.

12.4 MARKETING ANALYSIS TO ADDRESS ISSUES OF A COMMON METHOD FOR DAMAGES CALCULATION

One important role for marketing experts in class certification is to provide and evaluate methods of calculating class-wide damages arising from the alleged misconduct. Typically, the objective of the plaintiffs' expert is to offer a method applicable to all class members that is tied to the plaintiffs' theory of liability. The defendant's expert often critiques the proposed method (or methods) and attempts to show that it would lead to incorrect results or that the proposed method cannot be applied on a class-wide basis.[36]

---

[34] Rebuttal Expert Report of Randolph E. Bucklin, *In re Google AdWords Litig.*, 5:08-cv-03369 (N.D. Cal. Nov. 2, 2010), 4, 6.

[35] Class certification was denied, but that decision was reversed on appeal: Order Denying in Part Plaintiffs' Motion to Strike; Denying Plaintiffs' Motion to Certify Class, *In re Google AdWords Litig.*, No. 5:08-cv-03369 (N.D. Cal. Jan. 5, 2012), ECF No. 315; *Pulaski & Middleman, LLC v. Google, Inc.*, 802 F.3d 979 (9th Cir.2015); *cert. denied*, 136 S. Ct. 2410 (2016).

[36] Chorba et al., "Expert Analysis of Class Certification Issues," p. 14.4(c).

In class action cases involving falsely advertised characteristics or product-label misrepresentations, one of the commonly used metrics in the calculation of damages is the price premium. Specifically, the plaintiffs' expert might propose a method to estimate the price that consumers would have paid absent the false/misleading label, and thereby compute the "price premium" – the difference between what consumers actually paid and what they would have paid – as a measure of damages. The defendant's expert might typically be asked to evaluate the proposed method, whether misleading conclusions might be drawn from the price premium estimated, and whether the proposed method is applicable to all class members.

12.4.1 Hedonic Regression

One commonly proposed methodology to estimate the price premium is hedonic regression. Hedonic regression is an application of standard regression techniques that measures the value to consumers of various product attributes. It is based on the concept that each of a product's attributes has a different and measurable impact on aggregate consumer utility as measured by attributes' effect on price. The results of a hedonic regression express the price of a product as the sum of the values of the product's attributes. In this way, hedonic regression allows one to measure how much a particular attribute contributes to (or detracts from) the product's price. Each estimated regression coefficient provides the measure of this value for a particular attribute. The coefficient of the at-issue attribute can be interpreted as the price premium. To implement hedonic regression, a plaintiffs' expert typically proposes using data collected through the defendant's normal course of business, and/or independent market research data obtained from companies such as Nielsen or IRI. To illustrate, we discuss a recent example of the use of hedonic regression from class action litigation.

In *Belfoire v. Procter & Gamble Co.*, plaintiff Anthony Belfoire brought suit against Defendant Procter & Gamble Company (P&G) on behalf of a putative class of consumers in New York who had purchased Freshmates flushable toilet wipes (able to be disposed of in municipal sewer systems). The plaintiff alleged that he paid a premium for the flushable wipes over nonflushable moistened wipes.[37] The plaintiffs' expert, Dr. Colin B. Weir, proposed to use hedonic regression to calculate the price premium associated with the flushable characteristic, if any, on a class-wide basis.[38]

---

[37] Memorandum & Order, *Belfoire v. Procter & Gamble Co.*, No. 2:14-cv-04090 (E.D.N.Y. Oct. 5, 2015), ECF No. 149 at 5.

[38] Declaration of Carol A. Scott, PhD, *Belfoire v. Procter & Gamble Co.*, No. 2:14-cv-04090 (E.D.N.Y. Mar. 27, 2015) (Scott P&G Declaration), ECF No. 82 at ¶ 4.

The defendants' marketing expert, Dr. Carol A. Scott, evaluated Mr. Weir's proposed hedonic regression. Dr. Scott pointed out conceptual flaws in the hedonic regression approach. She explained that the ideal method of measuring a price premium in this case would be to compare the price charged for the Freshmates toilet wipes in the real world when the flushable characteristic was present on the package versus when it was not.[39] However, a "before" and "after" comparison was not possible in this case because the flushable characteristic had always appeared on the product packaging.

Because a "before" and "after" comparison was impossible here, a researcher using hedonic regression methods to analyze prices must look to competing products marketed with and without the flushable characteristic. This variation in prices could be used to identify the price premium associated with the flushable characteristic.[40] Dr. Scott pointed out that the price premium of the flushable characteristic would be the same for all brands with this characteristic, even though the flushable characteristic may have contributed differentially to the price of different brands.[41] Thus, the proposed hedonic regression would be unable to isolate the price premium associated with the flushable characteristic specific to the Freshmates product. It also could not "predict the behavior of consumers had the challenged statements not been present on the packages."[42]

The hedonic regression approach to estimating price premia for class-wide damages offers advantages and disadvantages. It is appealing because it can be implemented using actual, secondary data on prices and product attributes available from company records or syndicated providers. In doing so, it avoids the potential pitfalls of survey-based methods (discussed further in Sections 12.4.3 and 12.4.5) and is based upon the actual prices charged to consumers. Another advantage is that the methodology is relatively straightforward to present and understand. On the other hand, as the P&G case illustrates, it is limited to the observed data available for the product and its category. If there is insufficient variation in the occurrence of the product characteristic, it can be problematic to infer its contribution (or detraction) to price. It is also a method which relies on the difference in the market-clearing price of the product with and without the characteristic at issue. As such, it is vulnerable to critique on the basis of heterogeneity in the weights placed on the attribute across consumers. As Dr. Scott pointed out in her declaration in the P&G case, this can produce inaccurate or misleading damage estimates for class members. Lastly, the hedonic regression implicitly assumes that the but-for prices inferred from the historical data represent equilibrium outcomes – i.e. that competitor response to a change in the product characteristic is already reflected in the

---

[39] Ibid., ¶ 11.
[40] Ibid., ¶ 12.
[41] Ibid., ¶ 12.
[42] Ibid., ¶ 13. Ultimately, the district court ruled in favor of the plaintiffs' motion for class certification. *See* Memorandum & Order, *Belfoire v. Procter & Gamble Co.*

observed prices. This depends upon the nature of the variation available from the historical, secondary data.

12.4.2 Market Equilibrium Model

In addition to hedonic regression, another approach to estimate price premia is to construct a market equilibrium model. This approach is designed to overcome some of the limitations of hedonic regression by yielding estimates of price premia that reflect the response of competition to changes in product offerings or marketing claims. Such models require both estimates of demand and assumptions regarding relevant competitive forces and costs and are therefore considerably more complex undertakings. Experts can use a market equilibrium model to simulate counterfactual outcomes in which the allegedly offending action is absent (i.e. "but-for" the alleged misconduct).[43] Using such a model, the price premium becomes the difference between the market price under the simulated but-for condition and the price observed under the actual condition.

Conjoint analysis is a popular approach for estimating demand in a market equilibrium model. Conjoint analysis relies on a consumer survey designed specifically for the at-issue product and the at-issue characteristic. In a conjoint survey, respondents are typically asked to make a series of choices among different combinations of the attributes of a product. Such attributes include price and, for example, an at-issue package statement. By examining respondents' choices, a marketing expert can observe the trade-offs made by respondents, and infer the value (or utility) that respondents place on different attributes of the product or statements or claims made for the product. After obtaining survey responses, the expert uses statistical techniques to analyze the response data and to estimate consumer demand for the at-issue products under both the actual condition and the but-for condition. Following demand estimation, a model (or simulation) of the market would be constructed to simulate the decisions made by firms in the actual and but-for conditions, thus intending to reflect the outcomes that would hold in equilibrium. We now discuss case examples involving the estimation of demand and conduct of simulations in these modeling approaches.

12.4.3 Conjoint Analysis and Partworth Estimation using Hierarchical Bayes Regression

To estimate consumer demand using conjoint analysis, the first step is to estimate "partworths" – the partial contributions of various product feature levels to the overall utility associated with the product or what that "part of the product" is

---

[43] Greg M. Allenby et al., "Valuation of Patented Product Features," J. L. & ECON., 57(3), 629–63 (2014).

"worth" to a given consumer. Hierarchical Bayes regression is one of the most commonly used statistical techniques for such estimation.[44] Expert analyses in a recent consumer class action case illustrate the use of this technique but also highlight some of the challenges in applying conjoint to estimate damages without also carrying out market simulations that incorporate competitor reactions.

In *Hankinson v. R.T.G. Furniture Corp.* (R.T.G.), the defendant sold furniture with its ForceField Protection Plan. The ForceField Protection Plan stated that the furniture would be professionally treated with the defendant's ForceField fabric protectant, a fabric treatment that resisted common household food and beverage spills. The plaintiffs alleged that R.T.G. did not treat furniture sold with its ForceField Protection Plan with the ForceField fabric protectant in the advertised manner.[45] More specifically, the plaintiffs alleged that R.T.G. warehouse staff would often apply too little of the protectant, or fail to apply the protectant to all furniture surfaces, and/or would not allow the protectant to dry properly before packaging the furniture for delivery.[46]

The plaintiffs' expert, Mr. Steven P. Gaskin, designed and conducted a conjoint survey in an attempt to measure the value consumers attributed to the ForceField Protection Plan.[47] In each choice task of the survey, respondents chose among three purchase option profiles, each of which was composed of four features: (1) fabric protectant (this feature had four different levels, which varied in the amount of protectant applied and the length of dry time); (2) fabric stain warranty (this feature had four different levels, which varied in the type of stains covered and by the level of coverage); (3) order processing time; and (4) delivery.[48] Among the four features, fabric protectant and fabric stain warranty were the two key components of the ForceField Protection Plan, while order processing time and delivery were included as distractor features to disguise the purpose of the study.[49]

---

[44] Expert Report of Steven P. Gaskin, *Hankinson v. R.T.G. Furniture Corp.*, No. 9:15-cv-81139 (S.D. Fla. Oct. 3, 2016) (Gaskin R.T.G. Report), ECF No. 130-5, ¶¶ 17–18. The hierarchical Bayes regression method first assumes that (1) an individual's utility given a product profile is the sum of the partworths of the product profile, and (2) an individual's probability of choosing among product profiles is governed by a multinomial logit model. It then estimates the parameters underlying the distribution of partworths using the data generated from the conjoint survey. See *The CBC/HB System for Hierarchical Bayes Estimation Version 5.6*, SAWTOOTH SOFTWARE TECHNICAL PAPER SERIES, www.sawtoothsoftware.com/download/techpap/hbtech.pdf, pp. 5–7.

[45] Gaskin R.T.G. Report, ¶¶ 4–5.

[46] Plaintiffs also alleged that there were other problems with the ForceField Protection Plan, including the fact that the protectant had not been tested for efficacy, that it required annual reapplication, and that it could be purchased elsewhere for much less than the price charged by R.T.G. Ibid., ¶ 5.

[47] Ibid., ¶ 6.

[48] Ibid., ¶ 20.

[49] Ibid., ¶ 21.

After obtaining survey responses, Mr. Gaskin estimated a hierarchical Bayes regression to obtain individual-level partworths for each level of the four features. To go from the partworths to class-wide damages, Mr. Gaskin considered the total *market value* of the ForceField Protection Plan to be the sum of the highest partworth for fabric protectant and the highest partworth for stain warranty across all survey respondents. He then subtracted the partworths for different levels of fabric protectant and for different levels of fabric stain warranty from the total *market value*. He interpreted the difference in total partworth as the *reduction* in *market value* that consumers suffered due to the problems associated with the R.T.G. ForceField Protection Plan.[50]

The defendants' marketing expert, Dr. David Reibstein, identified several limitations of Mr. Gaskin's use of conjoint analysis. First, Dr. Reibstein pointed out that conjoint analysis by itself cannot measure the *market value* of a product feature because the market value of a product is the result of the interaction between supply and demand. Because conjoint analysis is limited to estimating only aspects of demand, it does not account for supply-side factors that help determine the market price of a product.[51] This critique highlights the challenges in attempting to estimate price premia damages based on demand estimation alone. Second, Dr. Reibstein noted that the results from Mr. Gaskin's hierarchical Bayes regression indicated substantial variation in respondents' underlying preferences.[52] This suggested significant differences in harm from the deficient use of protectant, if any, to each proposed class member and illustrates how an approach designed to estimate damages can also shed light on the extent to which there may or may not be common harm. Lastly, Dr. Reibstein criticized Mr. Gaskin's survey design, and discussed that a flawed, or unrealistic, survey design would likely bias the partworth estimation.[53]

---

[50] Mr. Gaskin calculated that, for example, the fabric protectant is worth 54.7 percent of the total market value of the ForceField Protection Plan, and 45.3 percent is accounted for by the stain warranty. Subtracting partworth for "2 ounces of protectant applied to all surfaces, 1 hr dry time" would reduce the market value of fabric protectant by 9.5 percentage points (54.7%–45.2%). Ibid., ¶¶ 6, 47, 49.

[51] Relevant supply-side factors not accounted for in a conjoint analysis conducted on consumers include the cost of providing the product, the availability of alternatives in the marketplace, and any competitive responses from these competing alternatives.

[52] For example, while Mr. Gaskin reports the average reduction in market value of 9.5 percent when going from 8 ounces of protectant and 24 hours of dry time to 2 ounces of protectant and 1 hour of dry time, the individual respondents' reductions range from 0.8 percent to 60.6 percent, with a median value of 7.4 percent.

[53] The district court granted the plaintiffs' motion to conditionally certify the class and preliminarily approve settlement: Order Granting Plaintiffs' Unopposed Motion to Conditionally Certify Class, Preliminarily Approve Settlement, Approve Class Notice, and Set Final Fairness Hearing, *Hankinson v. R.T.G. Furniture Corp.*, No. 9:15-cv-81139 (S.D. Fla. Aug. 4, 2017), ECF No. 204.

12.4.4 Random Coefficient Demand Estimation

As discussed earlier, partworth estimation obtained from conjoint analysis provides an estimate of consumers' valuation of certain features of an at-issue product. It alone cannot determine the market value of a product profile, or the market price of the at-issue feature. To account for supply-side factors, an expert can construct a market equilibrium model. In such a model, demand also needs to be first estimated. Another approach that can be used in these models is Random Coefficient Demand Estimation (RCDE).[54] The RCDE method assumes that a product is a bundle of characteristics, and that each of the characteristics influences consumer utility and demand for the product. The model also allows for consumer preferences to vary with individual characteristics; this permits the estimation to incorporate individual-level demographic information.[55] To complete the market equilibrium model, the supply side (costs and the actions of firms) can be represented with a multiproduct-firm differentiated product Bertrand model.[56]

In RCDE, each consumer's utility depends on the individual features and price of the product but in a way that randomly varies across consumers. Each consumer is assumed to purchase the product that yields the highest level of utility (including a no-purchase option). In that it is attribute based, the RCDE demand model shares similarities with conjoint-based demand estimation. However, it is well suited for estimation with secondary data as opposed to survey data. The model yields predictions for products' market shares and parameters are selected so that predicted shares best match actual shares. RCDE is a potentially powerful addition to the set of demand analytics marketing experts can draw from in class certification damages estimation. As the expert reports in a recent matter discuss, it has both potential and limitations.

In *Goldemberg v. Johnson & Johnson Consumer Cos.*, plaintiffs alleged that certain Johnson and Johnson (J&J) products were falsely labeled as "Active Naturals,"[57] which would make a reasonable consumer believe that the at-issue products do not contain harmful, synthetic, or unnatural ingredients. The at-issue products did, however, actually contain such ingredients. As a result, the plaintiffs alleged that consumers purchased more of, and/or paid more for, the at-issue products than they otherwise would have.[58]

---

[54] Aviv Nevo, "A Practitioner's Guide to Estimation of Random-Coefficients Logit Models of Demand," J. ECON. & MGMT. STRATEGY 9(4) 513–48 (2000).
[55] Ibid., 518–19.
[56] Ibid., n. 25.
[57] Expert Report of Dr. Jean-Pierre Dubé, *Goldemberg v. Johnson & Johnson Consumer Cos.*, No. 7:13-cv-03073 (S.D.N.Y. Sept. 17, 2015), ¶ 1.
[58] Declaration of Keith R. Ugone, PhD, *Goldemberg v. Johnson & Johnson Consumer Cos.*, No. 7:13-cv-03073 (S.D.N.Y. Nov. 13, 2015) (Ugone J&J Declaration), ECF No. 84, ¶ 1.

As part of the process of estimating the price premium, the plaintiffs' expert, Dr. Jean-Pierre Dubé, proposed to use RCDE to estimate the marginal utility consumers derived from each of the underlying product characteristics.

The defendant's expert, Dr. Keith R. Ugone, critiqued Dr. Dubé's proposed RCDE approach on a number of grounds. First, Dr. Dubé did not specify details sufficient to carry out an RCDE analysis in practice.[59] Dr. Ugone opined that such details are essential for evaluating whether Dr. Dubé's proposed approach could reliably determine class member damages. Second, the data necessary to execute Dr. Dubé's proposed RCDE analysis were likely to be unavailable,[60] casting doubt on whether the approach could ultimately yield a usable damages estimate. Lastly, Dr. Ugone noted that the RCDE approach proposed by Dr. Dubé depended on assumptions that did not apply in this matter and, as such, could yield unreliable results.[61]

Applying an RCDE model to estimate demand (as input into a market equilibrium analysis of damages) offers the marketing expert a way to estimate a sophisticated model of individual-level demand based on available historical, secondary data (e.g. Nielsen or IRI syndicated data). Because it is based on actual market outcomes, it avoids the sampling and survey-design limitations inherent in survey-based conjoint demand estimation. On the other hand, the model requires various assumptions about category specification and consumer purchase behavior. While these may represent reasonable approximations, they have already become fodder for detailed critiques of the proposed approach. More application of RCDE in litigation will be helpful in assessing how well it will be able to overcome these issues.

12.4.5 *Market Simulation and Price Premia*

We now turn to the simulation phase of a market equilibrium approach. In this step, the fully specified market equilibrium model is used to simulate the but-for

---

[59] Such details include (1) how he would categorize the ninety at-issue products for his RCDE analysis, (2) which competitor products he would include for each product category, (3) what product characteristics he would include, and (4) how he would define "markets" or the geographic area and time period. Ibid., ¶ 8.

[60] Dr. Ugone noted that the IRI data mentioned by Dr. Dubé did not include city-specific data, or data on specific retail outlets or distribution channels, or data on product characteristics. In addition, there are characteristics important to consumers but not easily measured or categorized in a RCDE framework, such as the fragrance of the products, the level of greasiness of the products, or how fast the product is absorbed into the skin. Ibid., ¶ 8.

[61] For example, Dr. Ugone noted that RCDE assumes that (1) consumers purchased a single unit of a particular product at each purchase decision, (2) consumers faced the same purchase price for the products within a market, and (3) every consumer would have the option to purchase each product included in the choice set (i.e. there were no products exclusive to certain sub-geographies). Ibid., ¶ 8.

Ultimately, the district court granted the plaintiffs' class certification motion: Opinion & Order, *Goldemberg v. Johnson & Johnson Consumer Cos.*, No. 7:13-cv-03073 (S.D.N.Y. Oct. 4, 2016), ECF No. 98.

condition (i.e. marketplace outcomes for the at-issue product in the absence of at-issue characteristics) and compare it to the actual condition.

In *Cobb, et al. v. BSH Home Appliances Corp.*, the plaintiffs alleged that certain Bosch and Siemens (Bosch) front-loading washing machines sold during the class period were prone to excessive biofilm buildup that can lead to mold and unpleasant odors. The plaintiffs alleged that Bosch failed to adequately inform consumers, prior to purchase, of the additional care steps (Bosch's Tasks) required to reduce the risk of mold growth and unpleasant odors.[62]

The plaintiffs' expert, Dr. Marc Rysman, estimated partworths of the features of the at-issue products using data generated by a conjoint survey and hierarchical Bayes regression.[63] He modeled how the disclosure of Bosch's Tasks would have affected consumer demand and, consequently, supply-side decisions by the defendant and its competitors.[64] Under Dr. Rysman's assumptions,[65] each producer would choose the price that maximizes profits. He then backed out the marginal cost of producing a washing machine. Dr. Rysman used these marginal costs to simulate a world in which Bosch's Tasks were disclosed, and to derive the but-for market price.[66]

The defendant's experts, Dr. William E. Wecker and Dr. Ran Kivetz, identified two principal limitations with the use of market simulation to estimate a but-for price in this case. The first was that the validity of the market simulation results rests on the validity of the underlying data and associated demand estimates. To the extent that the underlying conjoint analysis – from which data were generated and then used for demand-side calculations – was unreliable, the resulting damage calculations would also be unreliable. Second, even when conjoint surveys are designed and executed according to the principles and requirements of scientific surveys, the results should be closely scrutinized. Dr. Wecker's examination of the conjoint output showed valuations with wide variation and frequently nonsensical values.[67] Collectively, he

---

[62] Expert Report of Marc Rysman, PhD, *Cobb v. BSH Home Appliances Corp.*, No. 8:10-cv-00711 (C.D. Cal. Feb. 14, 2014) (Rysman BSH Report), ¶ 5. Bosch recommended that consumers perform extraordinary maintenance tasks such as (i) wiping the washer's rubber gasket following a wash cycle to remove biofilm and water, (ii) leaving the door ajar to allow the inside of the washing machine to dry, and (iii) running an empty, hot-water cycle using 1 cup of bleach every 3 months (collectively, Bosch's Tasks). Ibid., ¶ 10.

[63] Ibid., ¶ 34.

[64] Ibid., ¶ 37.

[65] Dr. Rysman made certain assumptions regarding the behavior of the producers: (1) they are profit-maximizing, (2) they compete on price, and (3) marginal costs are constant. Ibid., ¶ 37.

[66] Ibid., ¶¶ 35–42. He found that Bosch and Siemens front-load washers would have sold at a price approximately $113 lower than they were actually sold during the class period. Ibid., ¶ 44.

[67] For instance, for the first respondent, the estimated value of avoiding maintenance tasks range from a low of minus $54,305 to a high of $63,980, averaging –$196. The variability of the estimates and the fact that they fall both above and below zero, for all respondents, leads to the conclusion that an actual value of zero cannot be ruled out based on the statistical evidence. Moreover, the high frequency (18 percent) of negative values (indicating that the respondent prefers to pay more, rather than less, for a product that requires the maintenance tasks) suggests that the value estimates are not reliable.

opined that these issues cast doubt on the market simulation and resulting estimates for damages.[68]

12.5 CONCLUSION

Marketing analyses are being used more and more widely across a variety of class certification litigation. We review their use in this legal setting and discuss a number of examples drawn from recent case records. These were grouped into analyses to determine common harm versus analyses to determine class-wide damage estimates. A review of plaintiff and defendant expert reports from a variety of recent matters suggests that tensions frequently arise over the extent of meaningful heterogeneity among class members (common harm) and the most appropriate methods to obtain but-for estimates of market outcomes with which to compute price premia (common method for damages). As we have discussed, plaintiff experts may be challenged with respect to common harm when relying on methods that do not account for the underlying complexities of the class members' situation. Similarly, with respect to damages methods, defendant experts often point to limitations of available secondary data, flaws in survey methods, and reliance on demand-side models that do not incorporate supply-side decisions.

With respect to establishing common harm, several approaches are available to examine the relevant heterogeneity among class members. First, an expert might investigate whether all of the class members have actually been exposed to the alleged misconduct. Second, an expert might inquire into the differences among class members in the extent to which it was relied upon in decision-making. Finally, differences among class members in outcomes (value for consumers, profit for business) might be evident from survey methods or analysis of available data.

To address issues with respect to common methods for estimating damages, experts have used various analytic tools such as hedonic regression, conjoint analysis, and estimation of market equilibrium models. Table 12.1 presents a summary of these issues, tools, associated case examples, and case outcomes. The tools discussed here have frequently been applied to cases involving allegations of falsely advertised product characteristics or product label misrepresentations. Depending on the specifics of the at-issue products and the allegation, experts should weigh the pros and cons of each method, carefully scrutinize the assumptions, and evaluate whether the data – either collected from available data sources or through specially designed surveys – can provide the correct answer.

As class action litigation advances, the opportunities to apply marketing analysis to examine common harm and common damage estimation appear likely to expand.

---

[68] In this case, the district court ruled to grant the plaintiffs' class certification motion: Order Granting in Part Plaintiffs' Motion to Certify Class, *Tait* v. *BSH Home Appliances Corp.*, 8:10-cv-00711 (C.D. Cal. Dec. 12, 2012), ECF No. 166; the case caption was subsequently changed to *Cobb* v. *BSH Home Appliances Corp.*

TABLE 12.1. *Issues, methods, example cases, and outcomes*

Issue addressed	Method(s) used to address the issue	Case example where method(s) used	Outcome
Heterogeneity in exposure	Clickstream data analysis; surveys	Karim, et al. v. Hewlett-Packard Company	Class certified; settled while on appeal
Heterogeneity in decision-making processes	Consumer behavior within a priori and post hoc segments	Urakhchin, et al. v. Allianz Asset Management of America, L.P., et al.	Class certified; settled
	Surveys; multi-attribute theory and the concept of the marketing mix	Briseno, et al. v. ConAgra Foods, Inc.	Class certified; affirmed on appeal; settled
Heterogeneity in lost value or profits of businesses	Analysis of detailed Google ad metric data for the advertising campaigns run by named plaintiffs	Google AdWords Litigation	Class certification denied; reversed and remanded on appeal; settled
Common methods for damages calculations	Hedonic regression	Belfoire v. P&G	Class certified; settled
- Market equilibrium	Conjoint analysis and partworth estimation using hierarchical Bayes regression	Hankinson et al. v. R.T.G Furniture Corp, et al.	Class certified; settled
	Random coefficient demand estimation	Goldemberg, et al. v. Johnson & Johnson Consumer Companies, Inc.	Class certified; settled
- Market simulation and price premia	Conjoint analysis and partworth estimation	Cobb, et al. v. BSH Home Appliances Corporation	Class certified; settled

We hope that our discussion of the critiques of various analytic approaches has also highlighted the technical sophistication required of experts now working on these matters. As a result, class certification and marketing analytics together should make for an important and intellectually stimulating area of inquiry.

13

Damages Estimation in Consumer Deception Class Actions

Legal and Methodological Issues

August T. Horvath

13.1 INTRODUCTION

Class action damages used to be boring. Essentially an accounting exercise, they came at the end of the case, after resolution of the more interesting issues of what the defendant did and whether it was liable for doing it. And because trial rarely happens, especially in consumer class actions where jury awards can be untethered to damages estimates and potentially astronomical, the damages reports quietly served by the dueling expert witnesses near the close of discovery served mainly as a benchmark for pretrial settlement discussions.

This has changed. Because of legal developments discussed in this chapter, damages models in consumer class actions come into play much earlier in the case. Even before the damages study is completed, the plaintiff's damages expert's *proposed* damages model is considered by the court with a view to whether it could possibly support class certification. For defendants, the plaintiff's damages model is now the next best opportunity to dispose of many cases, once a defendant has lost its motion to dismiss at the initial pleading stages.

In one type of class action – false advertising and deceptive practices claims under various state statutes – damages models have been especially contentious. Since 2013, several major false-advertising class actions have run aground at the class certification stage because of deficiencies in their models for estimating class-wide damages. This chapter explains the importance of class damages models in recent false-advertising cases, describes the damages analyses that have been proffered and the issues raised with them, and analyzes the strategies that have been successful as of the time of writing.

13.2 LEGAL BACKGROUND

13.2.1 *Federal Rule of Civil Procedure 23 Requirements*

Rule 23 of the Federal Rules of Civil Procedure establishes the requirements for a federal civil suit to be maintained as a class action. In *Comcast v. Behrend*,[1] the Supreme Court held that at the class certification stage, a plaintiff seeking class-wide damages on a common basis must proffer a damages case that (1) can demonstrably calculate class-wide damages by common proof and (2) is consistent with its liability case. The Supreme Court directed that district courts "must conduct a rigorous analysis to determine whether that is so."[2]

The most universally accepted form of damages under these laws is restitution. The essence of the legal concept of restitution is that money or property that has been transferred, directly or indirectly, from the victim to the wrongdoer is to be returned to the victim. For restitution to be relevant, there therefore must have been an actual transfer of money or property. As explained by the California courts, "Restitution restores the status quo 'by returning to the plaintiff funds in which he or she has an ownership interest.'"[3]

> The proper measure of restitution in a mislabeling case is the amount necessary to compensate the purchaser for the difference between a product as labeled and the product as received. ... Restitution can ... be determined by taking the difference between the market price actually paid by consumers and the true market price that reflects the impact of the unlawful, unfair, or fraudulent business practices.[4]

As to each individual consumer, then, restitution in a typical false-advertising case equals the amount that the consumer paid minus the amount that the consumer would have had to pay to purchase the product in the but-for world where the false claim was not made. The consumer's "willingness" to pay is not directly relevant to the calculation. The relevant prices are the ones offered to the consumer by the market, and the recoverable "price premium" is the difference between the actual prices offered in the market and the price that would have been offered in the market absent the false advertising. For example, a product might have been priced at $5.00 without the falsely claimed feature and $7.00 with the feature, but an individual consumer might not care about the falsely claimed feature and might have been willing to pay $7.00 for either product. Or, the consumer may have valued the product at $10.00 without the falsely claimed feature and $12.00 with it,

---

[1] 569 U.S. 27, 133 S. Ct. 1426 (2013).
[2] Ibid., 133 S. Ct. at 1433.
[3] *Korea Supply Co. v. Lockheed Martin Corp.*, 29 Cal. 4th 1134, 1149 (2003).
[4] *Werdebaugh v. Blue Diamond Growers*, No. 12-CV-02724-LHK, 2014 WL 2191901 (N.D. Cal. Dec. 15, 2014), *22 (citing *Colgan v. Leatherman Tool Grp., Inc.*, 135 Cal. App. 4th 663, 700 (Ct. App. 2006)).

and feel that they got a bargain even at the price inflated by the false claim. None of this matters. The assumption of restitution theory is that the market price for the product actually sold with the falsely claimed feature was X, and if the market price had been lower, then all consumers who bought it for X would have been willing to buy it for X minus the premium. Those individuals transferred the premium to the seller on false pretenses, and should be able to get it back. Of course, at the lower price of X minus the premium, additional consumers presumably also would have bought the product who did not buy it in the real world, but those consumers have no cause of action because they didn't part with their money.

Restitution is distinct from "benefit of the bargain" damages. "Benefit of the bargain" is, as the term "bargain" implies, a concept most often employed in contract law. Where possible, in contract remedies where one side of a contract has not fully performed, the law seeks to make the aggrieved party whole by giving that party what was promised in the agreement. In some cases, a court awards "specific performance," forcing the nonperforming party to go through with the terms of the contract. More often, this is not feasible, and monetary compensation is substituted. This may be the cost of having someone else finish performing the contract or, if that too is not feasible, it may be the value to the plaintiff of what was promised. Whereas restitution seeks to restore the parties to where they were before the transaction was entered into, benefit-of-the-bargain damages seek to place the parties in the position where they would be if the transaction had been completed successfully with all promises kept.

Benefit-of-the-bargain damages differ for practical purposes from restitution damages in that the plaintiff did not necessarily have to pay the full value of the promised product to recover that value. The plaintiff may have paid less than market value for the product as promised, or even less than market value for the product as delivered, but is still entitled to the difference between the market value of what was promised and the market value of what was delivered.

"Willingness to pay," when used as a term of art in economics, is the maximum that a consumer will pay for a product or service. It is inherently an individual-level property, and can be described as the utility that an individual can obtain from a marketplace offering. When aggregated, willingness to pay has a direct logical relationship to the classical economic demand curve. When willingness to pay for a given population is aggregated, its frequency distribution is essentially the demand curve for the product or service within that population. There are wrinkles – for example, each individual consumer may be willing to buy more than one of a product or service, but not all at the same price, and thus have their own personal demand curve rather than just one data point to contribute to the aggregate – but in principle, willingness to pay is the driver of market demand.

Willingness to pay relates to both damages models described, but much more directly to the benefit-of-the-bargain conception, where we ask how much the consumer valued the product or service negotiated for. With respect to restitution damages, which are based on prices provided by the marketplace, the relationship between willingness to pay and the market prices of interest is more attenuated. The market conditions necessary for each individual consumer to be charged the maximum that they will pay for a given product or service, which requires not only a perfectly functioning market but also a perfect ability to sellers to price-discriminate, never exist. In the aggregate, any market price will be below some consumers' willingness to pay and above others'. A consumer whose willingness to pay is equal to the market price is the "marginal consumer" in that market. When considering willingness to pay in the context of false advertising, each consumer has two relevant willingnesses: (1) the most the consumer is willing to pay for the product or service assuming it has the falsely advertised benefit, and (2) the most the consumer is willing to pay for the product or service assuming that the non-existent attribute is not advertised or that the consumer is not deceived by the advertisement. Consumers who were willing to pay the price charged for the falsely advertised product even if it were not falsely advertised would have bought it anyway, but presumably would have been less happy with their purchases. Consumers whose willingness to pay for the falsely advertised product was at or above the price charged for that product, but whose willingness to pay for the product without the falsely advertised feature would have been below that price, would not have purchased the product absent the false advertising and would have spent their money elsewhere. Whether these consumers should be treated differently is an interesting philosophical question in false-advertising remedies.

Willingness to pay can be measured either directly, by the binding market transactions people enter into (revealed preference) or by asking them, in one form or another, what they would be willing to pay (stated preference). A central problem in economic consumer research is the validity of stated preferences as a proxy for revealed preferences. The most direct approach, of simply asking consumers what they would pay for a product or service, or for a specific advertised feature within a product or service, is not regarded as being accurately predictive of market behavior, although it is sometimes still used. Techniques such as conjoint analysis, with which much of this chapter will deal, are, in part, an attempt to address this.

13.3 BASIC METHODS

Because, as noted, the majority of significant US jurisdictions limit recovery for consumers deceived by false advertising to restitution damages, the basic objective of damages economists in false-advertising cases has been to find two numbers: (1) the market price of the product with the false advertising, i.e. the real-world price during the period of misconduct complained of,[5] and (2) what the market price of the

---

[5] For purposes of these economic analyses, it is usually assumed that every consumer understood the alleged false advertising in the same way and believed it to be true. In many false-advertising

product would have been but for the false advertising, i.e. the but-for world. The real-world price actually existed and can be measured, although, of course, there often isn't just one real-world price, either over time or across different selling outlets, geographic regions, and so forth. The but-for price may also have really existed, if there was a period before the false advertising began or after it ceased, when the product was also being sold, and other relevant conditions either were constant or can be measured and controlled for. Sometimes, the but-for price never existed or is otherwise inaccessible, and must be estimated. The difference between the real and but-for prices is the acceptable definition of the "price premium" which all consumers who purchased the falsely advertised price have a right to recover. Note, again, that in reality, the "price premium" is unlikely to have been just one constant price increase across all units of the product. Like the prices themselves, the premium is open to variation within the marketplace. Most damages analyses make the simplifying assumption that there was just one flat price premium. To date, there have not been negative consequences for this simplification, at least at the class certification stage.

13.3.1 *Econometric Time Series*

A time-series analysis is useful for damages estimation when there was a period of time before the offending conduct commenced that can be identified as the but-for world. Time-series analyses are commonly used to estimate damages in antitrust actions. The plaintiff identifies a point in time when a price-fixing cartel is alleged to have been organized. Pricing data are collected from periods before and after that moment. Normally, a time-series regression analysis is performed, with prices as the dependent variable. The chief independent variable is whether the price was charged during the conspiracy period or not. The regression analysis typically includes controls for seasonality and for known exogenous events that may have affected the prices.

Time-series analysis is not much used in false-advertising cases. It requires a particular set of circumstances to be viable. There has to be an identifiable period where the false advertising did not occur, whereas an advertising claim made for a consumer product often is made immediately upon introduction. It may also be difficult to collect historical pricing data for many products. And the life cycles of the consumer products at issue in false-advertising cases are often shorter than those for the components, raw materials, and standard commodities that frequently are the subject of antitrust cartels.

---

cases, both of these assumptions are very questionable. In principle, consumer survey research on perceptions of the advertising and belief in the alleged false claim could be incorporated into the econometric analysis, but this is rarely, if ever, done.

13.3.2 Hedonic Regression Analysis

In a hedonic regression analysis, different products in the marketplace are compared in an attempt to discern the price premium actually paid by consumers for the allegedly falsely advertised feature. The researcher selects products that have a range of features in an attempt to construct a feature-by-feature pricing model of a but-for product that has the characteristics of the falsely advertised product, but without the falsely advertised feature. When it works, a hedonic regression analysis can be an excellent method for estimating a real-world price premium. However, the marketplace often does not cooperate by furnishing a range of products with the necessary mixture of features to isolate the falsely advertised feature in the analysis.

13.3.3 Conjoint Analysis

Choice-based conjoint analysis has become the most favored method of damages estimation in class-action cases in recent years. Conjoint analysis is a technique for eliciting stated-preference[6] willingness-to-pay information from consumers. In a conjoint analysis, product features are systematically varied by constructing hypothetical products by the addition, deletion, and adjustment of these features. A specialized survey is administered to respondents, who are offered sets of products with varying features and asked to choose which of the set, if any, they would be willing to purchase. Respondents in a conjoint analysis are not directly asked what they would be willing to pay for a product or feature. Instead, price is introduced as one of the features of the products from which they are choosing, and the price level is varied. When enough respondents have indicated their preferences from among a large enough sample of choice alternatives, the survey data are ready for analysis.

The analysis of conjoint survey data is done by dedicated statistical software which also dictated the configurations of features presented to respondents. Using a logit-based model, the software can disaggregate the manipulated features of the products into the relative contribution each makes in the choice process for the product. These contributions are termed "partworths." Depending on the type of conjoint analysis that is performed, partworths for the features can be determined for individual respondents and also aggregated into estimates for the population from which the sample was drawn. In a false-advertising case the partworth for the allegedly

---

[6] Conjoint is sometimes characterized as a revealed-preference rather than a stated-preference measure. It depends on the definition of those terms. It is revealed preference in the sense that the consumer's preference emerges from a more holistic evaluation of competing products, rather than simply being queried as to the value of the particular feature. It is stated preference in the sense that respondents are only stating what they would buy, rather than committing their money. I lean toward considering conjoint a stated-preference method because it is not self-validating as to whether consumers actually would behave, in the marketplace, as their responses to a conjoint study indicate.

falsely advertised feature can be used to derive the willingness-to-pay price premium, i.e. the difference between what respondents would pay for the falsely advertised product if they believed the false claim and what they would be willing to pay for an otherwise identical product without the falsely claimed attribute.

Conjoint analysis was developed by mathematical psychologists in the 1960s, adapted for business use in the 1970s, and only more recently has been adapted for the types of litigation uses discussed in this chapter.[7] The technique has several features that set it apart from the regression methods discussed above. First among these is that it is not necessary to observe precise real-world prices to conduct a conjoint analysis. It is beneficial if the prices used as a varied attribute in the conjoint analysis approximate real-world prices, but since they are attached to hypothetical products, they need not and cannot be exact. The advantage to the researcher is that the pricing information can be created in an experimental setting without the need to go into the marketplace and gather actual pricing information, which is often difficult. The drawback is that the proponent of a conjoint analysis bears the burden of relating the willingness-to-pay estimates generated by the analysis to real-world pricing.

Conjoint analysis has other limitations as a research technique. The cognitive load that it places on respondents forces conjoint analysis to vary only a limited number of product features – often far fewer than actually vary from product to product. Attributes that are not varied can be explained to the subject and held constant, but the specification of which attributes should be varied in an analysis is critical.

The rest of this chapter describes how lawyers, expert witnesses, and courts have handled conjoint analysis, sometimes paired with hedonic regression analysis, as a damages model in an attempt to establish predominance for class certification purposes.

13.4 JUDICIAL REACTIONS

In the eight years since *Comcast* has been guiding the class certification predominance analysis, there has been noticeable evolution in the way courts have treated the commonly proffered damages models, especially conjoint analysis. Initially, claims made for the method were often accepted uncritically by courts. The distinction between willingness to pay and observed market prices was not fully elucidated, and deep scrutiny of the proffered analysis was relatively rare.

---

[7] Green, P. & Srinivasan, V., "Conjoint Analysis in Marketing: New Developments with Implications for Research and Practice," JOURNAL OF MARKETING, 54 (Oct. 1990), pp. 3–19 (reviewing developments in conjoint from the 1970s to 1990); Rao, Vithala R., *Applied Conjoint Analysis*, Springer Verlag, 2014.

One tactic that was successful in shielding conjoint analysis from close scrutiny was the characterization of these analyses as "conjoint surveys." Expert "surveys" have become something of a trigger word in judicial analysis. Judges have become accustomed to a particular kind of battle of experts in connection with survey research, in which two (or more) fully qualified survey experts perform surveys that fully meet the criteria for being done to the standards of expertise in the field, but come to opposite conclusions about the subject matter of the survey. The survey experts, or additional survey experts hired just to do critiques, then attack each other's surveys over what seem to the court like minor details of survey methodology that apparently make all the difference to what conclusions are reached. Understandably, when faced with motions under *Daubert v. Merrill Dow Pharmaceuticals*[8] to exclude such surveys, many courts have thrown up their hands and determined that, with respect to the specific category of surveys, once the expert witnesses and their work product have reached some minimal standard, criticisms of the survey methodology go only to the weight accorded to the survey evidence, and not to the admissibility of the survey.

A conjoint analysis starts with a survey for data collection, and that portion of the conjoint study certainly is subject to the many criticisms that can be raised about proper survey technique, such as the definition of the survey population, sampling, potentially leading questions, and so forth. But the distinctive feature of the conjoint study is the statistical analysis that leads to the computation of partworths, including the product attributes selected for variation. In principle, judicial examination of the statistical portion of the conjoint study could be no different than that of a time-series or hedonic regression analysis. But characterizing the conjoint study as a "survey" has led many courts to avoid these evaluations, and some courts have done so not only for *Daubert* admissibility purposes but also for what is supposed to be the more rigorous analysis dictated by *Comcast* at the class certification stage.

After the initial wave of generally approving judicial response to conjoint studies for class-action damages,[9] defense counsel began finding ways to highlight potential deficiencies with conjoint analysis as a damages estimation tool, and this led several courts, primarily in the 2015–2017 period, to reject these analyses and deny class certification. It appeared, for a time, that courts were reaching consensus on a point of view that a willingness-to-pay study, standing alone, cannot validly estimate real-world price premiums because its results are untethered to observed prices and cannot sufficiently account for the many market factors other than consumer willingness to pay that produce those prices. Various attempts were made to bolster

---

[8] 509 U.S. 579 (1993).
[9] Examples of cases that found conjoint analysis adequate without extensive analysis of its alleged shortcomings include *Guido v. L'Oreal, USA, Inc.*, No. 2:11-CV-01067-CAS, 2014 WL 6603730 (C.D. Cal. July 24, 2014); *Odyssey Wireless, Inc. v. Apple Inc.*, No. 15-CV-01735-H-RBB, 2016 WL 7644790 (S.D. Cal. Sept. 14, 2016); *Miller v. Fuhu Inc.*, No. 2:14-CV-06119-CAS-AS, 2015 WL 7776794, *21 (C.D. Cal. Dec. 1, 2015).

conjoint surveys with supplemental damages analyses, some of which were successful.

In 2017 and 2018, plaintiffs in several cases tried a technique for specifying the conjoint analysis, or else stating the assumptions made in conducting it, that purported to address market factors beyond consumers' willingness to pay. These plaintiffs contended that these alterations to the conjoint method can produce valid estimates of real-world price premiums even without deploying additional analyses that incorporate observations of actual prices. A few courts have accepted these arguments and found the conjoint studies acceptable for class certification purposes. As discussed in the next section, it is not clear that the experts propounding these analyses have done much more than assume away the deficiencies inherent in a willingness-to-pay analysis, and when courts are educated about these issues, they may return to a more skeptical posture. The case law concerning acceptable methods of damages estimation to meet the Rule 23 predominance requirement under *Comcast* is still in flux.

13.4.1 *Judicial Skepticism*

An early case in which plaintiffs proffering a conjoint analysis was defeated by the "supply-side" criticism was *Saavedra* v. *Eli Lilly and Co.*[10] This was a class action against pharmaceutical company Eli Lilly, which was accused of concealing the withdrawal risks associated with its antidepressant Cymbalta. Class certification was denied for failure to specify an adequate damages model on two occasions in this case. On the first try, the court criticized "Plaintiff's 'unusual' theory of injury and damages" in which, as the court characterized it in its second opinion, "Plaintiffs did not assert that they were injured by being overcharged; instead they asserted that they were harmed because they received 'a product that had less value than the value of the product as class members expected to receive it.'"[11] In other words, the plaintiffs sought benefit-of-the-bargain damages.

The *Saavedra* court held that in an efficient economic market, there might essentially be no supply-side constraints on a seller's pricing freedom, so that a seller could and would charge whatever the market would bear – i.e. the full amount of consumers' willingness to pay – for any product. In such a situation, a conjoint analysis might accurately reflect the actual market premium charged for the product feature, the court held. However, the court held, "the prescription drug market is quintessentially inefficient – characterized by monopolistic and monopsonistic behavior, which is further complicated by the role of insurance copayments."[12]

---

[10] No. 2:12-cv-9366-SVW (MANx), 2014 WL 7338930 (C.D. Cal. Dec. 18, 2014) (Order denying class certification); No. 2:12-cv-9366-SVW (MANx), (C.D. Cal. July 21, 2015) (second Order denying class certification).
[11] No. 2:12-cv-9366-SVW (MANx), (C.D. Cal. July 21, 2015) at 2.
[12] Ibid., 5.

These factors provided the court with ample reason to conclude that the pricing fluidity necessary for a willingness-to-pay differential found in a conjoint analysis to be reflected in a real-world price premium was utterly lacking in prescription drug markets. This all made sense, but the implication that, in most markets, price and value are linked closely enough for willingness to pay to be a good proxy for market price would work mischief in later cases.

On the second try, the *Saavedra* plaintiffs sought only statutory minimum damages, and not actual damages based on any economic conception at all. Still, however, under the laws of New York and Massachusetts pursuant to which they sought such damages, the plaintiffs were required to show some class-wide injury. Plaintiffs contended that they were forced to pay a price premium by Lilly's deception, but their analysis was again rejected for even this limited purpose.

In *In re NJOY, Inc. Consumer Class Action Litigation*,[13] a putative class of consumers sued NJOY, an e-cigarette manufacturer, for allegedly falsely representing that e-cigarettes pose lower health risks than traditional cigarettes. The plaintiffs offered both a conjoint analysis and a hedonic regression analysis to estimate consumers' evaluations of the value of the e-cigarettes with and without the disclosure of the health risks. NJOY successfully argued, with respect to the conjoint analysis, that "[a] consumer's subjective valuation of the purported safety message, measured by their relative willingness to pay for products with or without the message is not an accurate indicator of restitutionary damages, because it does not permit the court to calculate the true market price of N-JOY e-cigarettes absent the purported misrepresentations."[14] As to the hedonic regression analysis, the court found that this was one of those cases where the marketplace does not cooperate with the analysis by furnishing the appropriate range of products to permit the isolation of the attribute of interest. As the court held, the different brands of e-cigarettes at that time were too diverse and unique for a regression analysis to make a controlled comparison across brands.

Briseno v. ConAgra Foods, Inc.[15] was another California class action in which the plaintiffs alleged that ConAgra misleadingly marketed its Wesson brand cooking oils as "100% natural" even though they were extracted from genetically modified organisms (GMOs), which they alleged are not "natural." The *Briseno* plaintiffs advanced two damages models, a hedonic regression analysis and a conjoint analysis. The reason for the dual methodologies was not just to use hedonic regression as a backstop for conjoint analysis, as has been done in some cases. *Briseno* involved a particular wrinkle that should be taken into account more often in damages analysis. Technically, ConAgra's "100% natural" may not mean that the product was not

---

[13] 2016 WL 787415, *5–9 (C.D. Cal. Feb. 2, 2016).
[14] Ibid., *7 (emphasis in original).
[15] 674 Fed. Appx. 654, No. 15-55727 (9th Cir. Jan. 3, 2017), *cert. denied*, 138 S. Ct. 313 (2017), on appeal from *In re ConAgra Foods, Inc.*, 90 F. Supp. 3d 919 (C.D. 2015).

derived from GMOs, and may also mean many other things. Some consumers may understand this, while others may not. Doing a simple damages analysis presenting the product as "non-GMO" would have begged the question of how consumers are interpreting the advertising claim. If, say, only 50 percent of consumers understand the advertising claim in the way the attribute is presented to respondents, it has obvious implications for any price premium that can be charged. The *Briseno* plaintiffs dealt with this issue by first performing a hedonic regression analysis to estimate the total price premium resulting from ConAgra's "100% natural" claim. Such an analysis does not impose any particular interpretation of the claim; whatever consumers think of it is baked into the price premium they will accept. Next, a conjoint analysis sought to unpack different interpretations of the "100% natural" claim and determine the price premium attributable to the specific interpretation that it meant "not made with GMOs."

The court found that this application of the dual methodology approach was necessary and appropriate under the circumstances. The implication was that, if the marketing claim had been unambiguous, a hedonic regression analysis by itself might have sufficed. But it was initially rejected in the plaintiffs' first try at a damages model because of the marketing claim interpretation issue. In fixing their damages model using a second, appropriate technique, the *Briseno* plaintiffs provide an object lesson in how to marry diverse methodologies in a way that bears a sensible relationship to damages calculation under the particular circumstances of the case.

Zakaria v. Gerber Products Co.,[16] a putative class action in the Central District of California, concerned allergy prevention claims made by a manufacturer of infant formula. The plaintiffs contended that Gerber marketed its infant formulas with a general claim that they could prevent allergies, which consumers allegedly interpreted to mean later-onset childhood food and other allergies, instead of the infant allergies (chiefly skin rashes) that were all Gerber could substantiate that it could prevent. Class certification initially was granted based on a declaration by the plaintiff's expert that either or both of a conjoint analysis and/or a hedonic regression analysis could be performed to estimate the market price premium charged by virtue of Gerber's allergy claim. Later in the case, simultaneously with summary judgment, the court reconsidered, and ultimately decertified, the damages class. The decision was based on deficiencies with the plaintiffs' damages analysis, which ended up being only a conjoint study without a corroborating hedonic regression analysis.

In attacking the plaintiffs' conjoint analysis, Gerber argued that the analysis estimated only consumers' willingness to pay, failing to take account of any other market factors that may have caused them not to have to pay the calculated premium. Gerber asserted that it had not marked up the price of its infant formula when it added its allergy prevention claim, partly because, Gerber claimed, retailers

---

[16] No. 2:15-cv-00200-JAK-E (C.D. Cal. Aug. 9, 2017), *aff'd*, No. 0:17-cv-56509 (9th Cir. Nov. 14, 2018).

of infant formula maintain rigid price points at which they price competing infant formulas at parity. In addition, Gerber criticized the study's failure to use realistic market prices, took issue with several aspects of the study's execution such as the design of the hypothetical package stimuli and the omission of significant product attributes, and pointed to inconsistencies in the results.

The *Zakaria v. Gerber* court declined to exclude the plaintiff's expert witness under *Daubert*, but agreed with Gerber that the damages model failed to meet the Rule 23 standard of matching the plaintiff's theory of liability. The court accepted Gerber's argument that a conjoint analysis, standing alone, does not provide evidence that consumers were actually given the opportunity by "supply-side" market factors to pay the prices that the conjoint analysis indicates they are willing to pay. "The conjoint analysis is not sufficiently tethered to actual market conditions, including pricing and premiums,"[17] even if, as the plaintiff contended, the analysis used prices that closely approximated the prevailing prices in the market.

Similarly, the plaintiffs in the case of *Morales v. Kraft Foods Group, Inc.*[18] alleged that Kraft Natural Cheese Fat Free Shredded Cheese misrepresented itself as "natural." After initially certifying a class, the *Morales* court reconsidered and decertified the class after considering a renewed opposition submitted together with a motion for summary judgment. The plaintiffs relied on a conjoint study to assign an average willingness to pay for the "natural" claim. On review of the completed analysis, the court found that the conjoint analysis standing alone "did not determine the price premium that Kraft charged for the 'natural cheese' label, but rather 'measured customers' subjective willingness to pay, an academic and irrelevant exercise that is not consistent with Plaintiffs' theory of liability."[19]

13.4.2 A More Lenient Approach: *Dial Complete* and Subsequent Cases

The cases discussed, from the first few years of the application of *Comcast* to consumer deception class actions, seemed to signal trouble, if not a death knell, for the use of a conjoint analysis, standing alone, to estimate class-wide damages in the typical false-advertising case. Courts appeared to be converging on the conclusion that conjoint analysis simply measured the wrong thing. In terms of the various conceptions of injury discussed in Section 13.2, conjoint analysis estimates two hypothetical prices, neither of which is directly relevant to a restitution-based damages analysis: the values, defined as the maximum each consumer would be willing to pay, for a product with and without a falsely advertised attribute. Neither the amount actually paid for the product as advertised nor the amount that would have been charged and paid if the product had been accurately represented are

---

[17] Ibid.
[18] No. 2:14-CV-04387, 2017 U.S. Dist. LEXIS 97433 (C.D. Cal. June 9, 2017).
[19] Ibid., *66.

estimated. Observed prices actually paid can be incorporated into the analysis, but prevailing market prices in the but-for world of truthful advertising remain unknown.

As discussed, courts somewhat simplistically described the mismatch between willingness to pay and market prices in the but-for world as a failure to account for "supply-side" constraints on price setting. In the most recent developments in this field as of this writing, this simplistic formulation led some courts to accept simplistic patches to conjoint analysis as incorporating enough supply-side information to salvage the method from the standpoint of satisfying *Comcast*.

It all started innocently enough. In the *In re Dial Complete Marketing and Sales Practices Litigation*,[20] a putative class action filed by consumers in seven states alleged The Dial Corporation, a well-known personal care products company, of exaggerating the antibacterial efficacy of a foaming hand soap called Dial Complete. The District Court initially denied class certification in December 2015, finding that some of the claims asserted were incapable of class-wide proof, but granted leave to file an amended motion with a more detailed damages model.[21] The plaintiffs returned with a new expert witness and a conjoint analysis that they asserted could determine "whether the Plaintiffs and other Class Members had been deprived of a measurable monetary portion of the benefit-of-the-bargain they had struck with Dial by buying Dial Complete with a superior efficacy claim on the label but, in fact, receiving a product that did not provide the promised superior efficacy."[22]

The plaintiffs' expert in *Dial Complete* adopted an apparently more sophisticated conception of the purpose of the conjoint survey than some previous experts who had proffered such analyses in similar earlier cases. As quoted by the court, the expert wrote that "[t]o make consumers whole for the economic loss, every consumer would have to receive an additional payment sufficiently large to vertically shift the demand curve so that the demand curve for the product with the false claim plus additional compensation intersected with the supply curve in equilibrium for the product without the false claim."[23] To do this, the expert stated, the analysis must focus on the "marginal consumer in the market for the product without the false claim and compare the price she had paid to the price she would have paid for the product with the known-to-be-false-claim."[24]

The *Dial Complete* plaintiffs' expert discussed conjoint analysis not in terms of a restitution model of damages, but instead a benefit-of-bargain model. Consumers were to be "made whole" by being paid the amount by which they valued the falsely advertised antibacterial efficacy, even if they had not actually overpaid that amount,

---

[20] MDL Case No. 11-md-2263-SM (D.N.H. March 27, 2017) (Op. No. 2017 DNH 051, Order certifying class), www.nhd.uscourts.gov/sites/default/files/opinions/17/17NH051.pdf.
[21] Ibid., 2.
[22] Ibid., 5–6.
[23] Ibid., 6.
[24] Ibid., 6–7.

or any amount at all. However, it is not clear that the *Dial Complete* court grasped the difference between benefit-of-bargain and restitution damages. In its discussion of the definition of damages, the court smoothly transitioned from the benefit-of-bargain conception to the restitutionary formulation of prior cases such as NJOY: "Put another way, 'the proper measure of damages in this case is the difference between the market price actually paid by consumers and the true market price that reflects the impact of the unlawful, unfair, or fraudulent business practices.'"[25] This is, of course, not putting benefit-of-bargain damages another way; it is a different, restitutionary, conception of damages.

In any event, the plaintiffs' expert implemented the described analysis by first performing a conventional conjoint analysis, and then "running computer-based market simulations to convert willingness to pay into actual market value price premium." The exact nature of these simulations was unclear even to the court, which called the expert's description of the market simulation "somewhat opaque" and "generally difficult to follow" and wrote that his testimony on cross-examination was "unclear."[26] Dial and its experts opposed the analysis as fundamentally flawed. They noted the sleight-of-hand confusion between benefit-of-bargain and restitutionary damages, and protested that the plaintiffs' analysis had not, even putatively, estimated a difference between real and but-for market prices, because of failure to account for "supply-side" factors. The court, however, accepted the plaintiffs' argument that their expert's "market simulations" somehow accounted for these. In addition, the court cited the dictum in *Saavedra* for its conclusion that the hand-soap market, unlike the "highly regulated and often artificial pharmaceutical market," is "relatively stable," without any special complications that "might operate to sever the calculated relationship between price paid and value received."[27]

On the face of it, *Dial Complete* should not have been an influential case in damages estimation for consumer deception class actions. It is an unreported district court opinion. There is little detail in the opinion about the analysis that was conducted or how it purported to do what the expert claimed. It appears, from the court's opinion, that the plaintiff's expert mainly succeeded in confusing the court with a hypothetical market simulation and some economic jargon about market equilibrium. But the *Dial Complete* court made a significant assumption about the nature of markets that was almost completely unexamined: that, absent special circumstances such as heavy regulation, there are no "supply-side" constraints on seller price setting that need to be taken into account, and actual price will match consumers' willingness to pay.

---

[25] Ibid., 19, quoting *In re NJOY, Inc. Consumer Class Action Litig.*, No. CV 14-428-JFW (JEMX), 2016 WL 787415, at *5 (C.D. Cal. Feb. 2, 2016).
[26] Op. No. 2017 DNH 051, 7, 14, 25.
[27] Ibid., 24–25.

Another key assumption made by the plaintiff's expert in the *Dial* case was also mentioned by the court:

> [Plaintiff's] model is one in which quantity (the number of products with the offending claims actually sold) is held constant on the demand/supply graph in determining the likely market price of the product without the offending claim if sold in the actual market. His model seeks to calculate the highest price in the actual market at which Dial could have sold the same number of products without the challenged claim. The difference in price as calculated, then, would seem to capture the full measure of damages suffered by consumers who actually bought the allegedly misrepresented product.[28]

The expert assumed, for purposes of the analysis, that in the but-for world in which the advertiser abandoned its false-advertising claim, it would then reduce its price such that it sold the same quantity of the product as before. This is, of course, only one of many possible strategies, and whether it would be the profit-maximizing one depends on many things, including the defendant's cost structure. Effectively, the expert assumed that Dial's supply curve was a vertical straight line, i.e. it was willing to sell the same quantity of product at any price, and also assumed that no market factors constrained its pricing freedom. Playing the scenario backwards, suppose Dial initially was not making the false claim about its hand soap, but decided to introduce the false claim. Why would we assume that Dial would seek no additional sales from making the false claim, but merely higher revenues from the same number of sales? Given that (unlike a genuine product improvement) adding a false marketing claim to a product is almost costless, and there is no need to increase price to recover increased costs, it would seem at least as viable a strategy – even without retailer-constrained pricing or other market imperfections – not to increase price at all, but merely to sell more product at the existing margin.[29]

Did the plaintiff's expert in *Dial Complete* actually assume that in the real world, Dial would have elected to use the demand curve shift effected by introducing its false claim entirely to earn more margin on the same number of sales, and not at all to increase volume? Perhaps, but not necessarily. The assumption could be related to the expert's benefit-of-the-bargain orientation. If you are trying to quantify the mini-bargain that consumers make when they accept a promised new benefit for the product, arguably a valid strategy is to consider the consumers who already were buying that product, or who would have bought it, absent the promised new feature. Then, by asking what price increase would be needed to hold output constant after the introduction of the promised new feature, one is asking what those consumers,

---

[28] Ibid., 28.
[29] In the conventional equilibrium model with an upward-sloping supply curve and a downward-sloping demand curve, one expects that, if the demand curve shifts upward, the new equilibrium will climb the supply curve so that output is increased, and while price increases, it does so less than it would have if it met demand at the same level of output.

and no others, would accept as a price increase for the new feature. But while it may be a fair measure of benefit-of-the-bargain, this analysis has less relevance to the restitutionary damages that the court in *Dial Complete* was supposed to consider.

The short summary of the *Dial Complete* court's handling of the "supply-side" factors that had bedeviled other plaintiffs proffering conjoint analyses is that the court considered the plaintiffs to have "addressed" these factors merely by stating their assumptions regarding them, even if the assumptions were unjustified. The court admitted that this approach is "no doubt imperfect in some respects, weak in others, and subject to challenges on cross-examination,"[30] but it was sufficient to support class certification. This opened the way for other plaintiffs to argue that the willingness-to-pay estimates provided by conjoint analysis adequately reflected the difference between actual and but-for market prices, provided that (1) no unusual structural conditions prevailed in the marketplace for that particular product and (2) we assume that the quantity sold remains constant in the real and but-for worlds. In 2018, plaintiffs in at least two further false-advertising cases successfully pressed this argument.

The first case was *Hadley* v. *Kellogg Sales Co.*,[31] in which a consumer plaintiff sued the Kellogg cereal company in the District Court for the Northern District of California, alleging that the express and implied "healthy" claims made for various cereals and breakfast bars were false because of the added sugar in these products. The plaintiffs proposed three different damages models. These were a conjoint analysis, a hedonic regression analysis, and an "advantage realized model." In opposing the conjoint analysis, Kellogg cited *NJOY* and *Saavedra* as holding that such an analysis is inadequate where it ignores supply-side factors.[32] The court held, citing *Dial Complete*, that:

> [C]ourts have also found that conjoint analyses can adequately account for supply-side factors – and can therefore be utilized to estimate price premia without running afoul of Comcast – when (1) the prices used in the surveys underlying the analyses reflect the actual market prices that prevailed during the class period; and (2) the quantities used (or assumed) in the statistical calculations reflect the actual quantities of products sold during the class period.[33]

The *Hadley* court cited other cases that had reached the same conclusion, and in so doing, put the argument that the *Dial Complete* style conjoint analysis adequately addressed "supply-side" factors in the most concise form to date:

---

[30] Op. No. 2017 DNH 051, 29.
[31] 324 F. Supp. 3d 1084 (N.D. Cal. 2018).
[32] Ibid., 1104–5.
[33] Ibid., 1105. The court also cited *In re MyFord Touch Consumer Litigation*, 291 F. Supp. 3d 936 (2018), a product defect case brought mainly under various state warranty statutes, in which a conjoint analysis making the same no-change-in-quantity assumption as the analysis in *Dial Complete* was deemed to have adequately addressed supply-side factors for class certification purposes. See 324 F. Supp. 3d 1084.

[I]n *Fitzhenry-Russell v. Dr. Pepper Snapple Group, Inc.*, 2018 WL 3126385 (N.D. Cal. June 26, 2018), the court rejected the defendant's argument that the plaintiffs' proposed conjoint analysis ignored supply-side factors and "only considered a consumer's willingness to pay in the conjoint survey." *Id.* at *8. The court concluded that, contrary to the defendant's position, the proposed conjoint analysis "calculated the price premium consumers paid for the [challenged] claim, and not just a theoretical willingness to pay," because, among other things, the conjoint survey (1) "used actual *market-clearing prices* as the basis for the prices in the survey"; and (2) "took into account the *fixed quantity of supply* of [the product] because *those sales occurred in the past.*" *Id.* at *8 (emphases added [by the Court]) (internal quotation marks omitted [by the Court]).[34]

If this is the most concise description of the *Dial Complete* logic, it also calls to mind the most obvious objection. The mere use of actual prices and sales that "occurred in the past" from the real world, in which there was allegedly false advertising, supplies no evidence of what either prices or quantity of sales would have been in the but-for world where the product benefit was not claimed. The words that the *Hadley* court italicized as especially important in the above quotation appear to be meaningless buzzwords that reflected the plaintiff's arbitrary assumptions. This, in effect, ended up being the holding of the *Hadley v. Kellogg* case in accepting the plaintiff's conjoint analysis: that a willingness-to-pay damages model adequately addresses supply-side factors if it merely articulates arbitrary assumptions about them.

The analysis in *Hadley* also showed the consequences of the simplistic reduction of all other market factors besides the consumer's willingness to pay to the shorthand, "supply-side factors." Experts and courts began treating the deficiencies with stand-alone conjoint analyses as if they were nothing but a failure to describe the supply curve; that is, the quantity of a product producible at any given cost. This ignored the objections previously raised by plaintiffs about market factors not accounted for. For example, suppose, as was argued in *Zakaria v. Gerber*, that a manufacturer's pricing freedom is constrained by retailers who slot products into one or a few price points, so that the producer cannot raise price at will after making some product innovation, whether real or misrepresented. How does this affect the supply curve? It still costs the same to make any given amount of the product. It is "supply-side" in the sense that it is imposed on the consumer and prevents the consumer from being charged exactly as much as they are willing to pay, but from the maker's perspective, it is more of a demand-side factor, because it constrains what can be charged at retail, and presumably also at wholesale, for the product. Such market conditions are not accounted for merely by assuming that the quantity sold will always be the same. Indeed, in this hypothetical, they are contradicted by

---

[34] Ibid., 1105–6.

that assumption, because with price frozen, quantity is the only thing free to vary to capitalize on the innovation.

In *Hilsey v. Ocean Spray Cranberries, Inc.*,[35] a consumer alleged that Ocean Spray's claim of "no artificial flavors" on some of its juice drinks was deceptive because the beverages allegedly contained di-malic acid and/or fumaric acid. Again, as required by the California statutes under which the plaintiffs were suing, the necessary damages theory was restitution: "Plaintiff asserts that [Ocean Spray's] misrepresentations led consumers to pay more than they otherwise would have."[36] To assess the value of the alleged false advertising, the plaintiffs first presented a contingent valuation survey. Contingent valuation (CV), like conjoint analysis, is a survey-based technique for eliciting consumers' stated preferences about features of a stimulus, and produces a willingness-to-pay estimate. A full description of the differences between CV and conjoint analysis is beyond the scope of this chapter, but briefly, CV relies on direct statements by respondents of how much they would pay for specific feature sets rather than putting respondents to a choice of different feature-set configurations. Because it lacks certain methodological features of conjoint analysis,[37] CV has been less preferred than conjoint analysis for predicting market outcomes based on consumer evaluations of product features. However, these differences were immaterial for purposes of the *Hilsey* analysis, as the court found that "contingent valuation analysis is a reliable survey based methodology to determine price premium damages."[38]

The *Hilsey* analysis was a replay of that in *Hadley v. Kellogg*, in which the court cited *Hadley* repeatedly and reiterated the holding that "courts have found that the supply side of the conjoint analysis damages model is satisfied if the prices in the surveys reflect the actual market prices during the class period and the quantities used reflect the actual quantities of products sold."[39] The Hilsey court hinted that the justification for the assumption that output would remain the same in the but-for condition as in the real world was that "the supply remains constant as it is not

---

[35] Case No. 17cv2335-GPC(MDD) (S.D. Cal. Nov. 29, 2018) (Order Granting in Part and Denying in Part Plaintiff's on Motion for Class Certification and Appointing Class Counsel); see also Case No. 17cv2335-GPC(MDD) (S.D. Cal. Oct. 18, 2018) (Order Directing Parties to File Supplemental Briefing on Motion for Class Certification).

[36] Case No. 17cv2335-GPC (MDD) (S.D. Cal. Nov. 29, 2018).

[37] See M. Ben-Akiva, D. McFadden, & K. Train, "Foundations of Stated Preference Elicitation: Consumer Behavior and Choice-Based Conjoint Analysis," FOUNDATIONS AND TRENDS IN ECONOMETRICS 10 (1–2) (2019), pp. 9–10.

[38] Case No. 17cv2335-GPC (MDD) (S.D. Cal. Nov. 29, 2018), citing *Toyota Motor Corp. Hybrid Brake Mktg., Sales Practices & Prod. Liab. Litig.*, No. MDL 10-2172-CJC, 2012 WL 4904412, *1 (C.D. Cal. Sept. 20, 2012); *Dzielak v. Whirlpool Corp.*, Civ. No. 12cv89 (KM) (JBC), 2017 WL 1034197, *16–18 (D.N.J. Mar. 17, 2017); and *Miller v. Fuhu Inc.*, No. 2:14cv6119-CAS-AS, 2015 WL 7776794, *21 (C.D. Cal. Dec. 1, 2015).

[39] Case No. 17cv2335-GPC (MDD) (S.D. Cal. Nov. 29, 2018).

affected by the failure to disclose or not."[40] The implication seems to be that the defendant is capacity-constrained and could not produce any more product, although, of course, that is not especially relevant. The relevant question is whether the defendant could have, and more importantly would have found it profit maximizing to, sell *less* product in a but-for world where it faced a lower demand curve because it was not deceiving consumers. Nevertheless, the *Hilsey* v. *Ocean Spray* court became the latest to adopt the two-prong approach of (1) incorporating actual prices into the model and (2) assuming that output would be constant despite shifts in demand, so that only price is free to vary, as the way to address all market conditions adequately in a stand-alone conjoint analysis.

The *Dial Complete*, *Hadley* v. *Kellogg* and *Hilsey* v. *Ocean Spray* cases occurred within a short time span, and as of this writing, there has been little time for class action defense counsel to mount counterarguments. It is possible that defendants will learn how to explain the deficiencies of these models to courts, and that courts will begin requiring at least some justification for the assumptions they incorporate. Or it could also be that the shortcomings of a willingness-to-pay stated-preference damages model, which so recently created such a promising line of attack on the Rule 23 predominance requirement, have been put to rest in the minds of too many courts for the pendulum to swing back.

Researchers Allenby, Brazell, Howell, and Rossi, in a series of papers starting in 2014, proposed to address these issues by repurposing conjoint analysis.[41] They observed that the decisions of firms in pricing new product features are guided not merely by their expected impact on demand, but by their expected impact on the firm's profits. Therefore, they advocate employing conjoint analysis not merely to estimate willingness to pay, but as part of a model of the new market equilibrium that will emerge after the introduction of the features. Conjoint, as Allenby et al. note, can only go so far toward this end – indeed, not much farther than it has gone already, in terms of contributing just the demand component of the overall model. This is a welcome contrast to experts who have introduced conjoint studies in litigation with added features, such as some level of calibration with observed market prices, and then claimed that a conjoint study thus augmented can model supply-side factors. Allenby et al. recognize that a model that can adequately forecast actual market behavior requires "measures of costs, a demand system not only for the focal product but also for the major competing products, and an equilibrium concept."[42]

---

[40] Ibid., citing *Davidson* v. *Apple, Inc.*, Case No. 16cv4942-LHK, 2018 WL 2325426, *22 (N.D. Cal. May 8, 2018).

[41] G. Allenby, J. D. Brazell, J. R. Howell & P. E. Rossi, "Valuation of Patented Product Features," "THE JOURNAL OF LAW AND ECONOMICS", 57 (Aug. 2014), p. 629; G. Allenby, J. D. Brazell, J. R. Howell & P. E. Rossi, "Economic Valuation of Product Features," QUANTITATIVE MARKETING & ECONOMICS, 12 (Dec. 2014), p. 421.

[42] Allenby et al., "Valuation of Patented Product Features," 630.

But if all that were done, would the conjoint study, which seems like the easy part, still deserve star billing?

Part of the answer is that the conjoint study, and especially the parts of it that rely on good, old-fashioned survey technique for their validity, is not easy, and is critical to the entire exercise of marrying a conjoint survey with a market simulation. As Allenby et al. put it, "[p]ractitioners of conjoint have long been aware that conjoint is appealing because of its simplicity and low cost but that careful studies make all the difference between realistic predictions of demand and useless results," referencing traditional issues in questionnaire and survey design.[43]

Allenby et al. target their approach at a different task, "valuation" in patent litigation, or the "economic value of the patent" viewed from the perspective of the patent holder. Translated into deceptive advertising terminology, this would be the economic value of the falsely advertised claim to the false advertiser. This is related to, but not the same as, the pecuniary injury to consumers as conceptualized by false-advertising law. For one thing, to the extent that this economic value is extracted by the false advertiser from the marketplace, it might come, partly or wholly, at the expense of competitors rather than from consumers. This would happen, as discussed previously, if the false advertiser chooses to capture the value through increased sales, while offering putatively greater value (though actually just the same value) to consumers at the same price and margin. It might also happen in a more sophisticated scenario posited by Allenby et al. in which competitors lacking the falsely advertised price are forced to *lower* their prices to compete with the falsely advertised feature.[44] To the extent this occurs, consumers who continue to buy the competing products benefit from lower prices for the same goods; consumers who buy the falsely advertised product may either benefit or be injured, depending on the pricing of that product; and the false-advertising injury is visited primarily on competitors.

The general method advanced by Allenby et al. of incorporating choice-based conjoint into an equilibrium simulation, is increasingly being seen in false-advertising cases. Given enough information about the profitability of various alternatives and other supply-side factors, these analyses purport to be able to predict how firms will behave in response to the new market circumstances that will exist when they disseminate a false-advertising claim. This means that, as used in litigation, the models can purport not only to predict what premium the defendant *could* charge for the falsely advertised feature, but to describe what they *do* charge. Whether they do so, of course, is open to question. Allenby et al. note: "Our approach has been to compute equilibrium prices under the assumption that firms are fully informed regarding not only the form of the distribution of preferences but

---

[43] Allenby et al., "Economic Valuation of Product Features," 433.
[44] Allenby et al., "Valuation of Patented Product Features," 632.

also the parameters of this distribution."[45] Such an assumption would be amusing to many business executives. Rather, it is usually safe to assume that the company that introduces a new claim on a product, such as "made with real butter" on a packaged food, has little empirical notion what the consumer response will be, and even after some period of consumer reaction, knows little about the distribution of preferences as they relate to it. Likely the expert witness working on behalf of a plaintiff's law firm, if they have performed a conjoint study competently, will now know much more about the demand for the allegedly falsely advertised feature than the company that created it. This perhaps is a difference between the advertising and marketing context, where marketing claims are often very fluid and experimented with by trial and error in the marketplace, than the context of adding major, patent-protected product features that is the focus of much of the leading-edge research (and litigation) involving conjoint studies.

To create a model of market share and price equilibrium following the introduction of a falsely advertised feature, researchers must model not only the behavior of the advertising firm, but also that of its marketplace competitors. These firms, too, would have to know the preference distributions of the product feature. In other words, the researcher must make the somewhat heroic assumption that all firms in the market have access to their conjoint analysis.[46] This limits the applicability of the analysis: "Our view is that the valuation calculation based on profits in equilibrium with full information provides an approximation to a somewhat longer run view of firm profits [rather than an immediate optimal price calculation]." But is that appropriate for a false-advertising case, where the subject is not the "valuation" of a falsely advertised feature but, rather, the defendant's short-run pricing decisions?

So, has a plausible equilibrium model incorporating a conjoint survey ever been put forward in a false-advertising case? It is hard to say. As noted, the nature of class action litigation is such that at the class action stage, a plaintiff's expert witness need only describe how they intend to perform the analysis, and because the cases rarely reach later stages, the analysis never needs actually to be performed, or at least to be revealed. And even at the stage of summary judgment or trial, very little more than plausibility is required of the market-price estimates provided by the expert, especially if it is dressed in impressive technical language about the research process.

13.5 FUTURE APPLICATIONS OF CONJOINT IN FALSE-ADVERTISING CASES

The approach of Allenby et al., of incorporating conjoint into models of market equilibrium predicated on a profit-maximization assumption, has the virtue of modeling both of the ways in which increased demand resulting from a falsely

---

[45] Allenby et al., "Economic Valuation of Product Features," 440.
[46] Ibid. (conceding that this assumption can be unrealistic).

advertised feature might be realized – capture of more market share and increasing the price. This raises an issue in litigation, however, where, depending on whether the plaintiff is a competitor or a consumer class, the litigants are really only interested in one of these two things, and would very much like all of the value from the falsely advertised features to be captured in only one of these two ways. They tend to do this merely by assumption: for example, the assumption that has gotten recent conjoint-based damages models through the class certification process, that the defendant sells the same quantity of product in both the worlds with and without the false advertising. This is the opposite of the assumption used to pursue damages in the other major method of challenging false advertising: competitor suits under section 43(a) of the Lanham Act.[47] In Lanham Act suits, the primary mode of recovery by a competitor for false advertising is the recovery of "lost profits" from sales that the plaintiff did not make because the defendant's false advertising diverted those sales to the falsely advertised product. This can happen only if the false advertiser uses the demand impact of its falsely advertised claim, at least in part, to increase volume rather than margin. If the false advertiser raises its price by the exact amount needed to keep quantity constant, as assumed by the plaintiffs' experts in *Dial Complete*, *Hadley v. Kellogg*, and *Hilsey v. Ocean Spray*, then competitors' sales are unaffected, and the Lanham Act competitor plaintiff should be able to recover nothing. In the ideal case of Lanham Act false-advertising damages, the opposite happens: the false advertiser does not change its price, but merely increases its market share at the expense of its honest competitors.

Indeed, in a false-advertising class action in which damages are predicated on a model that assumes the defendant increased its price enough to keep quantity constant, then the plaintiffs should be required to present evidence that there was no increase in unit sales as a result of the false advertising. At the least, the defendant should be able to present evidence of increased sales. Such evidence would be adverse to the defendant in a Lanham Act competitor case, but would be exculpatory against a *Dial*, *Hadley*, or *Hilsey* damages model, amounting to prima facie evidence that the defendant did *not* charge the full "willingness-to-pay" premium that such an analysis would estimate. Such evidence, however, would not likely be considered by many courts at the class certification stage, where the analysis is more about whether a damages calculation method can compute class-wide damages in principle. The earliest that such evidence would likely be considered is on a summary judgment motion, and even then, because the causes of changes in sales volume can be disputed, it might have to wait until trial. And trials of false-advertising class actions are very rare.

The maturity of conjoint-based equilibrium studies, perhaps in the form proposed by Allenby et al. or in some other form, may give these techniques more utility in competitor false-advertising suits. It is striking, on reviewing the case law, that

---

[47] 15 U.S.C. § 1125(a).

conjoint-based techniques are now almost uniformly used in consumer class-action false-advertising suits, but rarely appear in Lanham Act competitor false-advertising suits, even though both involve assessing the market impact of false-advertising claims. The reason is clear enough. Plaintiffs in consumer suits want to show a price premium, and traditional willingness-to-pay studies are focused on this as an outcome. Plaintiffs in competitor suits want to show a gain in market share, and willingness-to-pay studies do not estimate this, unless combined with an equilibrium analysis or something similar. Thus, the more common approach in competitor suits is to look for an increase in sales or profits of the advertiser following the false advertising and to assume, without even considering the possibility that price was increased, that such sales and profits came out of the share of competitors. A conjoint study married to an equilibrium analysis could build a more robust model of gains in market share, based ultimately on consumer preference distributions, and be of utility in competitor cases. However, since injury and damages models in competitor suits are not subjected to the scrutiny that occurs under Rule 23 class certification procedures, it is not clear that there is demand in the litigation industry for a better mousetrap when it comes to damages estimation.

14

Taking a Second Look at Secondary Meaning

A Marketing Perspective on Circuit Court Factors

Peter N. Golder, Michael J. Schreck, and Aaron C. Yeater

14.1 INTRODUCTION

A brand element establishes secondary meaning when it becomes synonymous with the brand and serves as a source identifier for consumers. In legal parlance, secondary meaning has been defined as occurring when "in the minds of the public, the primary significance of a product feature or term is to identify the source of the product rather than the product itself."[1]

Secondary meaning has roots in both the legal and marketing literatures. It is important in both literatures because brands are valuable to consumers, and thus legal ownership rights to elements of brands are important. Brands are valuable, intangible assets because they lower search costs for consumers by helping them identify the source of goods and services they prefer, serve as signals of quality, and serve as the focal points for consumers' emotional attachments with specific products. In legal disputes about the use of branding elements, substantial consideration is given to direct evidence of consumer perceptions. However, the discipline of marketing recognizes that consumer perceptions do not exist in a vacuum. Rather, they are the result of a complex set of interactions, including marketing efforts by brands and consumers' experiences with those brands. We argue that conceptual principles and empirical methods from the marketing discipline provide useful insights into the conditions and challenges that companies face in attempting to create valuable brands, as well as insights for courts in assessing secondary meaning.

Companies invest substantial resources in developing their brand elements in an effort to have them recognized and appreciated by consumers. Ideally, these investments pay off in distinguishing the source of goods, such that the brand element becomes distinctive in the minds of consumers. But how can it be determined that a

---

[1] *Inwood Laboratories, Inc.* v. *Ives Laboratories, Inc.*, 456 U.S. 844, 1982, n. 11.

brand element has become distinctive? This question lies at the heart of many litigations regarding protection of trademarks or trade dress.

For more than seventy years, the Lanham Act has provided the statutory foundation for protecting brand elements as trademarks, which it defines as "any word, name, symbol, or device, or any combination thereof [used or intended to be used] to identify and distinguish [a producer's] goods ... from those manufactured or sold by others and to indicate the source of the goods."[2] While the Lanham Act includes provisions for companies to register brand elements as trademarks with the US Patent and Trademark Office, such registration does not guarantee that a brand element will remain protected in a litigation challenge. Nor does a lack of registration imply a lack of protection. Rather, the key to protecting a brand element in litigation is establishing that it is distinctive.

Courts have identified two paths to establishing a brand element's distinctiveness. Some brand elements can be distinctive by their very nature (termed "inherently distinctive" according to the law). The second path is *acquiring* distinctiveness by making impressions in the minds of consumers. In this second path, a brand element is said to have acquired secondary meaning, indicating that, *empirically*, consumers understand the brand element as a source identifier. As we discuss further in Section 14.2.1.1, this path typically involves the brand element having an original, primary meaning to consumers that is not source identification but which is later overwritten in the minds of consumers by a meaning of source identification (e.g. Burberry's "check" pattern). The focus of our chapter is this second path to distinctiveness – secondary meaning.

Given the importance of brands in an increasingly complex communication environment, disputes over brands are common. Over the years, circuit courts have set forth a variety of tests intended to evaluate the presence or absence of secondary meaning. We summarize these tests in Table 14.1. Interestingly, though they all seek to answer the same question, the twelve circuits that have put forth formal tests of secondary meaning agree on only one factor:[3] exclusivity, manner, and length of use of the mark. The first six factors in Table 14.1 are recognized by a majority of the courts. The remaining factors are recognized by four or fewer of the twelve circuit courts. However, some of these minority factors (e.g. advertising expenditures, size, and prominence of the company) relate to the majority-held factors (e.g. amount and manner of advertising, amount of sales, and number of customers).

The concepts underlying these circuit court tests – use of the mark, advertising, sales, customers, consumer testimony – are fundamental to the marketing discipline. So, too, is the definitional focus of secondary meaning on the minds of consumers. We thus argue that marketing-based principles and empirical methods are

---

[2] 15 U.S.C. §1127.
[3] The DC Circuit is the only circuit for which we were unable to locate a formal set of secondary meaning factors.

TABLE 14.1 *Factors considered by circuit courts in secondary meaning tests*

	Factor	Circuit												Total circuits	Barrier?	Action?	Outcome?
		1	2	3	4	5	6	7	8	9	10	11	Fed.				
1	Exclusivity, manner, and length of use of a mark	*	*	*	*	*	*	*	*	*	*	*	*	12	X		
2	Consumer survey evidence	*		*	*	*	*	*	*	*	*	*		10		X	X
3	Amount and manner of advertising		*	*	*	*	*	*	*	*	*	*		10	X		X
4	Amount of sales and number of customers			*	*	*	*	*	*	*	*	*	*	10			X
5	Proof of intentional copying by the defendant			*	*	*	*	*	*	*	*	*	*	10			+
6	Direct consumer testimony	*		*		*	*	*	*	*	*			8			X
7	Established place in the market			*			*	*	*					4	X		X
8	Unsolicited media coverage of the product				*	*			*				*	4			X
9	Efforts to promote a conscious connection, in the public's mind, between the name or mark and a particular product or venture	*								*	*			3		X	
10	Advertising expenditures	*	*											2	X	X	
11	Size and prominence of the company			*								*		2		X	X
12	Degree of actual recognition by public that name designates proprietor's product or service											*		1			X
13	Actual confusion			*										1			X
14	Use of the mark in trade journals				*									1			X
15	Association of the trade dress with a particular source by actual purchasers												*	1			

Notes: We present the circuit court factors as literally conveyed by each circuit. We note that, conceptually, there may be overlap between factors listed separately in this table. For example, the Federal Circuit does not list consumer survey evidence as an individual factor, but does note that such surveys are a typical way to measure the individual factor "Association of the trade dress with a particular source by actual purchasers."

According to a recent Federal Circuit ruling, the DC Circuit is the only circuit court that has not developed a multifactor test of secondary meaning.

[+] See the chapter text for discussion of how the factor "Proof of intentional copying by the defendant" may or may not relate to our marketing-based framework, depending on the nature of the "proof."

Sources: American Intellectual Property Law Association, "Legal Standards of the Federal Circuit Courts – 2017 Update"; *Converse, Inc. v. International Trade Commission*, Case 16-2497, Oct. 30, 2018 Decision, US Court of Appeals for the Federal Circuit.

particularly relevant to these circuit court factors. The objective of our chapter is to provide a marketing perspective that integrates and implements the circuit court factors for secondary meaning. We propose that these circuit court factors can be consolidated into an organizing framework rooted in marketing principles. In addition, we draw on the marketing literature to elaborate on circuit court factors and to propose additional empirical approaches to inform these factors, including application of the historical research method.[4]

Our framework consists of the following categories:

1. *Barriers* to creating secondary meaning;
2. *Actions* to promote the creation of secondary meaning, and to sustain it; and
3. *Outcomes* reflecting marketplace results indicative of success in creating secondary meaning.

The framework must be employed with appropriate expertise. In that context, it has several desirable qualities. First, while viewing secondary meaning through a marketing lens, it is consistent with secondary meaning factors identified by circuit court precedent. Second, it is not biased toward plaintiffs or defendants. Third, it provides insights for fact-finders interested in assessing whether secondary meaning exists, as well as for companies attempting to create secondary meaning. Finally, the framework has been used in expert testimony accepted by courts in multiple cases.

The framework makes multiple contributions. First, it provides a way of thinking about secondary meaning rooted in marketing principles that organizes the disparate circuit court tests into a consistent analytical approach. Second, it provides multiple empirical approaches beyond surveys for assessing companies' success (or lack thereof) in creating secondary meaning, including approaches that can provide insight on nonrecent infringement, which surveys can have difficulty addressing. Third, it emphasizes companies' actions and challenges in seeking to establish secondary meaning, and provides crucial contextual insights for interpreting empirical evidence of secondary meaning.

14.2 FRAMEWORK

In this section, we discuss our barriers–actions–outcomes framework. At the outset, it is important to note that this chapter does not contain an exhaustive list of all items that could be considered by a marketing expert examining a particular context. However, we believe the exemplars we provide are sufficiently comprehensive to illustrate considerations that arise frequently in litigation.

---

[4] Golder, Peter N., "Historical Method in Marketing Research with New Evidence on Long-Term Market Share Stability," *Journal of Marketing Research*, Vol. 37(2), May 2000.

The first column of Table 14.2 lists the exemplars of the barriers–actions–outcomes framework that we discuss in the following sections. The second column of Table 14.2 links these exemplars to legal factors assessing secondary meaning that have been endorsed by the circuit courts. These exemplars can link to other circuit court factors as well, but in this table we list relevant linkages.

TABLE 14.2 *Barriers, actions, and marketplace outcomes: exemplars and related circuit court factors*

Barriers	
Exemplar	Related circuit court factor(s)
Nature of the element	Manner of use
Advertising of functional benefits	Amount and manner of advertising
Marketplace noise due to third-party use	Exclusivity of use
Extent of exposure to consumers	Manner and length of use; amount of sales and number of customers
Preexisting and/or coexistent source-identifying brand elements	Manner of use; amount and manner of advertising

Actions	
Exemplar	Related circuit court factor(s)
Internal marketing documents discuss intent, execution plans, and progress evaluations	Manner of use; amount and manner of advertising
Allocate marketing resources to promote the element	Amount and manner of advertising
Police use of the brand element by third-party competitors	Exclusivity of use

Marketplace outcomes	
Exemplar	Related circuit court factor(s)
Consumer metrics	Consumer survey evidence
Media recognition	Unsolicited media coverage
Customer testimonials	Direct consumer testimony
Consumer search data	Direct consumer testimony; degree of actual recognition by public that name designates proprietor's product or service
Litigation surveys	Consumer survey evidence
Recognition by competitors	Proof of intentional copying by the defendant

14.2.1 Barriers

This section outlines potential barriers to achieving secondary meaning. The greater these barriers are for a given brand element, the more difficult it will be for the element to achieve secondary meaning. Lower barriers indicate a relatively easier path to achieving secondary meaning.

14.2.1.1 The Intrinsic Nature of the Element

As discussed in the introduction, some brand elements are inherently distinctive, whereas others must acquire their distinctiveness through developing secondary meaning. This fundamental difference stems from how consumers are likely to initially interpret the element, which we call its "primary meaning." Elements that are not inherently distinctive have a primary meaning that is unrelated to source identification. For the secondary meaning of source indication to take root, it must displace this primary meaning in the minds of consumers.[5] For example, a consumer might initially interpret the all-brown color of a delivery truck as an aesthetic choice, or as a functional choice to make dirt harder to see. For the consumer to instead interpret the all-brown design as indicative of a particular delivery company, this primary meaning must be overridden. In contrast, when a consumer sees the word "Kodak" on a camera, there is no other primary meaning that would impede the role of "Kodak" as a source identifier. Unlike the Kodak example, the case of brown on the delivery truck poses a barrier to secondary meaning that must be overcome.

This distinction can arise even when both brand elements consist of words. Consider a hypothetical coffee shop named "Tasty Coffee" versus one named "Left–Right Coffee." When asked, "Have you had any Tasty Coffee lately?" in the form of a spoken question, a consumer may well recall a flavorful cup brewed at home or at another coffee shop. A different reaction would likely ensue if the consumer were asked, "Have you had any Left–Right Coffee lately?" The distinction here is driven by the primary meaning already manifested in the words "tasty coffee." The "Tasty Coffee" moniker has a barrier to achieving secondary meaning in the form of a primary meaning that must be displaced; "Left–Right Coffee" does not have the same barrier.

The difference in the above scenarios can be understood through the marketing lens of the "basic" versus "augmented" product. A basic product is one that adequately performs the product functions intended to deliver benefits that satisfy customers' needs or wants,[6] whereas the augmented product includes the basic

---

[5] Cohen, Dorothy, "Trademark Strategy," *Journal of Marketing*, Vol. 50(1), Jan. 1986.
[6] Keller, Kevin L., *Strategic Brand Management: Building, Measuring, and Managing Brand Equity*, 4th ed., Global ed., Pearson, 2013.

product as well as that product's brand positioning.[7] For example, a tool's stripe design could be part of the basic product (as it relates to the consumer's aesthetic perception of the product), while the "Kodak" name is part of the augmented product but not the basic product. Similarly, coffee that is "tasty" satisfies a basic customer need, whereas "Left–Right" can be interpreted only as an augmentation of the basic product. In this way, elements that are part of the basic product face a higher barrier to secondary meaning.

While elements that constitute part of the product design will, more commonly, be part of the basic product, this is not necessarily the case for all nonword elements. Logos – unlike elements of product design – typically do not play a role in directly satisfying customers' needs or wants. For example, adding a small depiction of a whale to an article of clothing may not be interpreted as a contribution to the aesthetics or function of the clothing. As a result, the whale logo faces a lower barrier to secondary meaning than a stripe pattern might on the same clothing.

The marketing intuition conveyed in the above examples – that the primary meaning of an element can vary based on the element and the context of its use – is consistent with established standards in the legal context. For example, in assessing distinctiveness of word marks, courts seek to classify the mark into one of the following categories:

1. *Generic*: synonymous with the product category; "the genus of which the particular product is a species."[8]
2. *Descriptive*: literally descriptive of the goods on offer, but not to the point of being generic; "conveys an immediate idea of the ingredients, qualities or characteristics of the goods."[9]
3. *Suggestive*: requiring "imagination, thought and perception to reach a conclusion as to the nature of the goods."[10]
4. *Arbitrary*: possessing no discernible relationship to the goods on offer.[11]
5. *Fanciful*: invented words with no dictionary or linguistic meaning.[12]

A word mark is generic when it is synonymous with the product category; accordingly, a generic mark cannot take on a secondary meaning that links it to one particular company.[13] This is intuitive from the marketing perspective, as being synonymous with the product category implies a strong primary meaning. At the

---

[7] Kotler, Philip and Kevin L. Keller, *Marketing Management*, 13th ed., Pearson, 2009, p. 318.
[8] *Abercrombie & Fitch Co. v. Hunting World, Inc.*, 537 F.2d 4, United States Court of Appeals for the Second Circuit, Jan. 16, 1976.
[9] Ibid.
[10] Ibid.
[11] Ibid.
[12] "Protecting Your Trademark Enhancing Your Rights through Federal Registration," United States Patent and Trademark Office, Feb. 2020, www.uspto.gov/sites/default/files/documents/BasicFacts.pdf.
[13] *Abercrombie & Fitch Co. v. Hunting World, Inc.* (1976).

other end of the spectrum, fanciful words (such as "Kodak"), as pure invention, have no primary meaning. Arbitrary words lack a primary meaning in the context of the goods on offer, even though they have a primary meaning more generally. For example, when used generally in the 1980s, the word "Amazon" likely brought to mind a depiction of a long river or vast rain forest but had no primary meaning to consumers in the context of bookselling. Between the extreme ends of the spectrum are the intermediate categories of "Descriptive" and "Suggestive," which effectively differ by how much mental processing is needed to connect the word mark to the offered product. Just as it sounds, a descriptive mark literally describes the product, but not to the point of being generic (e.g. "Fresh 'n Juicy Peaches" versus the generic "Fresh Peaches"), whereas more thought is required to connect a suggestive mark to its product (e.g. "Juicy Bite" as a name for a company selling peaches). The legal literature emphasizes that across these categories "the lines of demarcation ... are not always bright,"[14] and, critically, that "a term that is in one category for a particular product may be in quite a different [category] for another."[15] Moreover, even holding constant the product, a term may shift categories over time or across groups of users.[16]

The law has characterized potential trademark protection for word marks along these categories. Fanciful, arbitrary, and suggestive word marks are *inherently distinctive*, meaning their "intrinsic nature serves to identify a particular source."[17] Accordingly, a showing of secondary meaning is not required to receive trademark protection. Descriptive word marks are not inherently distinctive, but can be protected if they *acquire* distinctiveness, i.e. if secondary meaning is developed. This is consistent with the notion that, relative to arbitrary, fanciful, and suggestive word marks, descriptive word marks have a stronger primary meaning related to the product and therefore face a greater initial barrier toward the consumer understanding them as a source indicator. Generic marks, being synonymous with the product category, can never be the exclusive property of a single company and are therefore not protectable.

The legal approach for assessing distinctiveness of nonword marks is also consistent with marketing principles. As a first matter, the law does not hold all categories of nonword marks to the same standard. In particular, symbol marks (e.g. Nike's Swoosh, the Vineyard Vines whale) are understood as separate from trade dress.[18] Even within the category of trade dress, product packaging is assessed differently from product design. These distinctions are articulated in *Wal-Mart Stores, Inc. v. Samara Brothers, Inc.*, in which the Supreme Court considered whether it was

---

[14] Ibid.
[15] Ibid.
[16] Ibid.
[17] *Wal-Mart Stores, Inc. v. Samara Brothers, Inc.*, 529 U.S. 205, 120 S. Ct. 1339, 146 L. Ed. 2d 182, 2000.
[18] Ibid.

possible for product design to be inherently distinctive. The court firmly rejected that notion, stating that "product design almost invariably serves purposes other than source identification,"[19] specifically to "render the product itself more useful or more appealing."[20] Consequently, the court ruled that "a product's design is distinctive ... only upon a showing of secondary meaning."[21] In marketing terms, the court's position reflects the notion that product design is part of the basic product, not the augmented product, and thereby tends to have a primary meaning unrelated to source identification. At the same time, the court made clear that product *packaging*, a different type of trade dress, was capable of being inherently distinctive, but in cases where the packaging was not inherently distinctive, acquiring secondary meaning would also be required for protection.[22] This intrinsic difference between product design and product packaging is reflected in the fact that, according to marketing principles discussed earlier, design is part of the *basic* product (via its satisfaction of consumer needs or wants) while packaging is not. The court's discussion in *Samara* is consistent with the view that packaging is often part of the *augmented* product, owing to its "predominant function [being] source identification."[23] Accordingly, product design faces higher barriers to secondary meaning.

Combining the insights offered by the marketing and legal literatures, elements that face relatively lower barriers to distinctiveness are those with weaker primary meanings, such as fanciful or arbitrary elements. The stronger the primary meaning, such as with product design or with descriptive word marks, the greater the barrier to achieving distinctiveness. Specific assessment of barriers will depend on the circumstances of the case, including the nature of the element in question.

14.2.1.2 Advertising Functional Benefits and/or Aesthetic Benefits

Consumers do not form their impressions of brand elements in isolation or solely by the intrinsic nature of the brand element. Marketing and advertising shape consumer perceptions, and in so doing, may increase the barriers to secondary meaning. This is particularly true if marketing and advertising serve to reinforce the primary meaning of the element as something other than a source indicator. A classic example of this is advertising that touts the functional benefits of a product design feature. For example, advertising that highlights the durability of a backpack's double stitching will reinforce the primary meaning of the stitching to consumers as providing a functional benefit as opposed to identifying a brand. Similarly, advertising that calls out the aesthetic appeal of a design will reinforce consumers'

---

[19] Ibid.
[20] Ibid.
[21] Ibid.
[22] Ibid.
[23] Ibid.

inclination not to treat this design as a source indicator. Companies that engage in these types of advertising, despite promoting the element itself, exacerbate the barriers to secondary meaning.

The law recognizes that consumer understanding of a mark as functional cuts against the mark's ability to function as a source identifier: "The person who asserts trade dress protection has the burden of proving that the matter sought to be protected is not functional."[24]

14.2.1.3 Marketplace Noise Due to Third-Party Use

Regardless of the intrinsic nature of the brand element, a company will face a significant barrier to achieving secondary meaning to the extent that other uses of the element are present in the marketplace. Consider, for example, a black stripe down the handle of a tool. To the extent that other makers of tools use striped designs, it will be more difficult for any one company to convince consumers that a striped design is indicative of only one company. Noncompetitor third parties may also use the element, such as artists or media that use the element in a nonbranded context, or companies that use the element in an unrelated product category or context. Such uses create "marketplace noise" that detracts from the notion that the element points to only one source. Notably, even historical third-party use, or prior use, can pose a barrier to secondary meaning, as consumer impressions can persist over time.[25] The amount of marketplace noise may depend on the extent to which third-party use has been advertised and promoted by those third parties.[26]

Wide use of an element inhibits a company's ability to establish secondary meaning. For example, as the court ruled in one well-known case involving guitar design, "[G]iven the similarity of applicant's configuration to that of other guitars, applicant has a heavy burden to demonstrate acquired distinctiveness."[27] Third-party use could become common enough to render a brand element generic. In these situations, there is no way to overcome the barrier.

14.2.1.4 Extent of Exposure to Consumers

Time is a barrier for companies seeking to establish secondary meaning for a brand element. Sales often require time to manifest in substantial amounts. Effective

---

[24] 15 U.S.C. §1125(a)(3).
[25] Mitra, Debanjan and Peter N. Golder, "How Does Objective Quality Affect Perceived Quality? Short-Term Effects, Long-Term Effects, and Asymmetries," *Marketing Science*, Vol. 25(3), 2006.
[26] We note that Table 14.2's exemplars of barriers, actions, and outcomes may relate to more circuit court factors than those identified in the table. For example, Table 14.2 links marketplace noise with "Exclusivity of use," but as we discussed earlier, marketplace noise may also relate to "amount and manner of advertising."
[27] *In re Gibson Guitar Corp.*, Trademark Trial and Appeal Board, Dec. 19, 2001, p. 13.

marketing communications require time to plan, execute, and evaluate. Consumers rely on their past perceptions of products and take time to update their beliefs. For example, while quality is important to consumers, it takes six years, on average, for consumers to update their perceptions of a product's quality.[28] Designing, delivering, and measuring the effectiveness of advertising communications is a challenging, complex, complicated, fragile, multistep process requiring clear messages, reinforcement, and a long-term approach.[29]

Time is not the only determinant of consumer exposure. Consumers are exposed to products in a variety of ways – sales, sales displays, advertising, usage, observation, etc. Some products are inherently more observable by consumers than others. For example, handbags are more visible in their usage than shoe insoles. Hence, while time on the market is often an important factor for courts to consider, the impact of that time may require consideration of additional factors. Even after a marketing campaign is developed and executed, it takes time for those messages to influence consumer perceptions.

14.2.1.5 Preexisting and/or Coexistent Source-Identifying Brand Elements

Another form of marketplace noise can be created when a company attempts to establish secondary meaning for an element in the context of a preexisting source identifier, as with a design feature on a product that already has a logo. In such cases, consumers may focus on the recognizable preexisting brand elements and pay less attention to others when determining source.[30]

14.2.2 *Actions*

Whether facing high barriers or low barriers to acquiring secondary meaning, a company can take action to overcome those barriers. The necessary actions are proportional to the extent and size of the barriers. As explained in this section, these actions should reflect a comprehensive, coordinated marketing strategy by the company to establish the element as indicative of source.

Lower barriers make it relatively less difficult to achieve secondary meaning for brand elements, while higher and more numerous barriers increase this difficulty. But difficult is not impossible, and companies accomplish difficult objectives all the time. The key to creating any valuable asset is to invest sufficiently and wisely.

There is a prescribed way to go about the investments needed to create secondary meaning. Trademark strategy consists of planning, implementation, and

---

[28] Mitra and Golder, "How Does Objective Quality Affect Perceived Quality?, p. 230.
[29] Keller, Kevin L., "Brand Synthesis: The Multidimensionality of Brand Knowledge," *Journal of Consumer Research*, Vol. 29(4), Mar. 2003.
[30] Fiske, Susan T. and Shelley E. Taylor, *Social Cognition: From Brains to Culture*, 2nd ed., Sage, 2013.

control.³¹ Cohen's article is worthy of investigation for greater detail on this topic. Similarly, the Kotler and Keller framework "Steps in Developing Effective Communications" is worthy of investigation for additional details. For example, effective communications with consumers require identifying the target audience, determining objectives, designing communications, etc.³²

Next, we discuss several specific exemplars of actions that companies can undertake in attempting to overcome the barriers to establishing secondary meaning.

14.2.2.1 Internal Marketing Documents Discussing Intent, Execution Plans, and Progress Evaluations

Given the difficulties of establishing secondary meaning, a company's internal marketing planning documents should clearly indicate an intention to establish a brand element as source identifying. Effective marketing and advertising strategy calls for establishing objectives and measuring results against those objectives.³³ This approach is important in developing a "consistent and coherent message" to be communicated externally.³⁴ Then companies must police their internal activities to root out inappropriate or inconsistent uses of the trademark internally. To the extent that internal employees do not uniformly understand that a specific brand element is a source identifier, it may be difficult for external customers to achieve this understanding. In order to accomplish this internal understanding, companies should clearly articulate all brand elements along with their proper usage through brand manuals.

Another aspect of internal policing for brand names "requires the use of the generic name of the product with the trademark,"³⁵ for example, using the generic "adhesive bandages" with the "Band-Aid" brand name. Otherwise, the trademark could potentially become generic.³⁶

After companies have allocated these efforts toward the objective of establishing secondary meaning, the final step in this part of the process is to measure whether these objectives are being carried out and whether they are having an effect. Marketers "should supervise the manner in which the trademark is used in promotion."³⁷ Then, companies can measure not only secondary meaning per se, but also

---

[31] Cohen, "Trademark Strategy," pp. 61–62.
[32] Kotler, Philip and Kevin L. Keller, *Marketing Management*, 14th ed., Pearson, 2012, pp. 482–84.
[33] Kotler and Keller, *Marketing Management*, 13th ed., p. 498.
[34] Cohen, Joshua and Rex Donnely, "Deliberate Differentiation: Strategies for Creating and Protecting Iconic Designs (How Planning Trumps Serendipity in Pursuit of the Real Thing and other True-Life Stories of Design Protection)," *Trademark Reporter*, Vol. 105(6), Nov.–Dec., 2015, p. 1444.
[35] Cohen, "Trademark Strategy," p. 64.
[36] Ibid.
[37] Ibid., p. 64.

other dimensions of consumer perception, such as awareness, recall, recognition, and association.

14.2.2.2 Allocation of Marketing Resources

Once company plans are in place, the next step is to promote the brand element aggressively while ensuring consistency between a company's brand guidelines and its externally communicated message. There is an expectation that "firms spend extensively to advertise and promote their trademarks."[38]

Companies seeking to establish secondary meaning for product design features must undertake "concerted advertising efforts to show that the design or design feature is being treated as a brand."[39] One particular form of advertising is especially informative with respect to a company's attempts to establish secondary meaning: "look for" advertising.[40] "Look for" advertising refers to "advertising that directs the potential customer in no uncertain terms to look for a certain feature to know that it is from that source."[41] Advertisements containing "look for" concepts "may be particularly probative on the issue of whether a product design functions as a source identifier."[42] Importantly, the advertisements must parse out the particular features as unique and distinct from the product as a whole; "look for" advertising "does not refer to advertising that simply includes a picture of the product or touts a feature in a non-source-identifying manner."[43] Advertising of a product design feature as "famous," "iconic," "exclusive," etc. may constitute "look for" advertising that indicates a desire to associate the design feature with the brand as opposed to the design's functional or aesthetic purpose.[44]

Consistency in the company's external communications efforts is also important. A company must avoid marketing and advertising messages that undermine its effort to create secondary meaning. When attempting to establish and reinforce association between product design features and the brand, companies should market the design features consistently over time.[45] For a design mark, it can be helpful to use the mark consistently across different product lines (e.g. three stripes by adidas on different styles of shoes).

---

[38] Ibid., p. 64.
[39] Luchs, Michael G., *Design Thinking: New Product Development Essentials from the PDMA*, Wiley-Blackwell, 2015, p. 378; Cohen and Donnely, "Deliberate Differentiation."
[40] Luchs, *Design Thinking*, p. 378.
[41] In re Koninklijke Philips Electronics N.V., Trademark Trial and Appeal Board, Sept. 26, 2014, p. 16.
[42] Ibid.
[43] Ibid.
[44] Jacoby, Jacob, "The Psychological Foundations of Trademark Law: Secondary Meaning, Genericism, Fame, Confusion and Dilution," *The Trademark Reporter*, Vol. 91(5), Sept.–Oct. 2001.
[45] Keller, *Strategic Brand Management*, p. 249.

Even if company marketing and advertising efforts do not reinforce the primary meaning of a brand element, they can nevertheless act as a barrier to achieving secondary meaning. Advertisements using inconsistent language or inherently confusing language to refer to the brand element may counteract any intention of the advertisement to establish secondary meaning of the brand element in the minds of consumers.

14.2.2.3 Policing Use of the Brand Element by Third-Party Competitors

Another company action indicative of efforts to establish secondary meaning is aggressive policing of the asserted trademarks. Companies are expected to invest in external policing to eliminate infringing uses of the trademark by third parties, since these create additional barriers for the company.[46] Lack of policing suggests that the company may not be committed or even intend for the asserted brand element to be source identifying.

A legal strategy of policing use of an asserted trademark is a poor substitute for a clear, well-executed marketing strategy to establish secondary meaning. In other words, policing alone will not overcome significant barriers to achieving secondary meaning because such acquired distinctiveness must reside in the minds of consumers, not in companies' legal briefs or cease-and-desist letters.

14.2.3 *Marketplace Outcomes*

A thorough assessment of barriers and actions is directly informative about several of the circuit court factors used to determine secondary meaning (see Table 14.2). These barriers and actions set the conceptual context for understanding whether secondary meaning is more or less likely to have been established. The final section details qualitative and quantitative empirical marketplace outcomes that are useful indicators of whether a company's marketing actions have been successful in overcoming barriers to establishing secondary meaning. Secondary meaning is most likely when barriers are low, company actions are well planned and well executed, and empirical marketplace outcomes indicate that consumers view the brand element as a source identifier.

Several of the measures described below are outgrowths of the historical research method. The historical method is a well-established and detailed approach to analyzing archival records. One of this chapter's authors has published a full explication of this method[47] and has submitted, as primary author with eleven other marketing professors from leading business schools as co-signatories, an amicus brief to the US Supreme Court regarding the relevance of archival records for addressing

---

[46] Cohen, "Trademark Strategy," pp. 61–74; Keller, *Strategic Brand Management*, p. 171.
[47] Golder, "Historical Method in Marketing Research."

issues of consumer usage and perception.[48] A primary benefit of archival data is that it exists independent of researchers' efforts to investigate a specific research question. In contrast, survey researchers create the stimuli and contexts used to generate new data with a specific objective already in mind. Another benefit of archival data is that it can inform judgments about whether secondary meaning existed years ago, including time periods too remote for survey responses to be considered reliable or valid. Overall, the approaches below should be thought of as a nonexhaustive set of useful complements to survey research.

14.2.3.1 Consumer Metrics Collected in the Ordinary Course of Business

Because secondary meaning exists in the minds of consumers, company efforts to assess how consumers perceive their brand can be informative as to secondary meaning. Many companies proactively track consumer perceptions in the ordinary course of business as a means of actively measuring progress towards achieving aspects of brand equity.[49] The survey method is a particularly popular tool for conducting internal market research. Surveys have been used to assess brand awareness (in the form of aided recognition and unaided recall of the brand), reported liking of the brand, purchase intent, and likelihood of recommending the brand.

When considering consumer metrics collected in the ordinary course of business, it is important to assess the extent to which the metric actually relates to consumer perceptions of the at-issue brand element. For example, a survey that tracks purchase intent for a product *as a whole* may be uninformative as to whether consumers view a *particular element* of the product's design as a source identifier. On the other hand, consumer responses to open-ended questions about the product as a whole could potentially call out the at-issue brand element. It can be helpful, therefore, to analyze consumer metrics generated by the company's market research even if source identification was not the prescribed *ex ante* focus of the research.

14.2.3.2 Customer Testimonials

Direct measures of consumer perceptions may also be available outside of the company's internal records, in the form of customer testimonials. While some customer testimonials are solicited in affidavit form as part of the litigation process, many are publicly available as archival data (e.g. online customer reviews). Systematic textual analysis of such reviews may provide an opportunity to assess

---

[48] Brief of Professor Peter N. Golder, PhD, and other marketing academics as amici curiae in support of respondent, *United States Patent and Trademark Office, et al. v. Booking.com B.V*, Supreme Court of the United States, 140 S. Ct. 2298 (2020) (No. 19-46).
[49] Keller, *Strategic Brand Management*, p. 293.

the prominence of the at-issue brand element in the minds of consumers. When assessing such prominence, it may be informative to compare metrics for the at-issue brand element against benchmark brand elements that have or have not achieved secondary meaning, as determined in prior court decisions. In addition to online customer reviews, consumer social media postings may also be informative (e.g. Facebook, Instagram, Twitter).

14.2.3.3 Media Recognition

Textual analysis can also be used to quantify the extent of media recognition of the at-issue brand element. Using well-designed search criteria, a sample of media articles mentioning the relevant product can be collected. Analysis of the sample may involve assessing the extent to or manner in which the media articles discuss the at-issue brand element or, more significantly, describe it with such terms as "iconic," "classic," or "signature." Here, too, it may be informative to compare metrics for the at-issue brand element against benchmarks with and without secondary meaning, as determined in prior court decisions.

From a marketing perspective, different types of media recognition may have differing relevance for secondary meaning. Unsolicited media recognition, for example, may indicate that the product or at-issue brand element (if highlighted) has attained some level of popularity sufficient to warrant coverage to the respective audience. Solicited media recognition may also have this potential, but in cases where the company paid to have its product or brand element promoted, this may be more reflective of a marketing action than a marketplace outcome. Though some courts emphasize only unsolicited media recognition, from a marketing perspective, both types of media recognition are relevant for consideration.

14.2.3.4 Consumer Search Data

Online search queries generated by consumers may also be informative for assessing secondary meaning. If the at-issue brand element has a searchable name and consumers actually search for it, this suggests consumer awareness of the element. However, awareness does not necessarily indicate that consumers associate the element with a *single* source. Careful analysis of search data, therefore, is important when investigating its relevance for secondary meaning, and may include benchmark comparisons.

14.2.3.5 Litigation Surveys

Surveys are a common tool for assessing secondary meaning in litigation. A primary benefit of surveys is their creation of data via questions regarding the at-issue brand elements that are posed directly to consumers. To yield reliable insights, a survey must be properly designed, executed, and analyzed.[50] Yet even then, survey insights have limits. For example, assessments of secondary meaning in litigation are concerned with the state of consumers' impressions *at the first instance of alleged infringement*. To the extent that the survey timing trails this alleged infringement, the survey's relevance can be diminished.[51] Further, even when conducted proximate to the alleged infringement, a survey that yields findings consistent with secondary meaning is typically silent as to *how* this secondary meaning was achieved. For these reasons, and notwithstanding their popularity, surveys constitute only one piece of the puzzle in the empirical assessment of secondary meaning.

14.2.3.6 Recognition by Competitors

Some courts have highlighted the importance of *intent* when considering copying of the at-issue brand element by competitors. From a marketing perspective, consumers would not be expected to observe or be influenced by such intent. Therefore, for intent to matter, it would have to be reflective of preexisting consumer perceptions. Analysis of competitors' internal documents may thus be helpful for determining whether these competitors identified the at-issue brand element as desirable based on consumer perceptions or, in the alternative, based on its aesthetic or functional properties.

14.3 CONCLUSION

The concept of secondary meaning has dual roots in both the legal and marketing literatures. Given the prominence and economic significance of brands, legal disputes over brands arise frequently. These disputes often center on brand elements that are not inherently distinctive, i.e. those at-issue brand elements that must establish secondary meaning in order to become source identifiers in the minds of consumers. Circuit courts have developed multifactor tests for assessing secondary meaning (see Table 14.1).

The purpose of this chapter was to provide a marketing perspective that integrates and implements the circuit court factors on secondary meaning. More specifically, we have proposed that these circuit court factors can be consolidated into an organizing framework rooted in marketing principles and empirical approaches that inform these factors. Our framework can provide courts with a deeper, richer,

---

[50] Diamond, Shari S. and Jerre B. Swann, *Trademark and Deceptive Advertising Surveys*, 1st ed., American Bar Association, 2012.
[51] For example, the Federal Circuit recently held that "surveys are sometimes difficult to use as evidence of historic secondary meaning" and that "survey results were probative, at best, of the public's perception five years after the survey was conducted." *See Converse, Inc. v. International Trade Commission*, Case 2016-2497, United States Court of Appeals for the Federal Circuit, Oct. 30, 2018, pp. 19, 21.

TABLE 14.3 *Conceptual favorability of establishing secondary meaning*

	Low barriers	High barriers
High actions	FAVORABLE	NEUTRAL
Low actions	NEUTRAL	UNFAVORABLE

marketing-based understanding of these factors and an expanded toolkit for applying them in specific case contexts.

Our framework consists of barriers that determine the ease or difficulty of establishing secondary meaning, company actions that attempt to overcome these barriers, and marketplace outcomes that provide measures of success in establishing secondary meaning. Table 14.3 illustrates how barriers and company actions provide conceptual context for understanding the relative favorability or unfavorability of establishing secondary meaning.[52] The four conditions depicted are the result of high and low barriers crossed with high and low company actions.

In the upper-left quadrant, low barriers combined with high company actions make it relatively easier for a company to establish secondary meaning. Examples that could fit into this quadrant might include the brand name "Apple" for technology products and Sinclair's use of a green dinosaur in connection with gas stations.[53] The lower-right quadrant depicts the converse: high barriers and low company actions make it less likely that a company will be able to establish secondary meaning. Examples that could fit into this quadrant might include Samara's children's clothing[54] and Converse Chuck Taylor's midsole sneaker design. The remaining quadrants (lower left and upper right) indicate neutral (i.e. not necessarily favorable or unfavorable in the context of case-specific barriers and actions) conditions for establishing secondary meaning. For these quadrants with neutral favorability, careful application of the empirical methods portion of our framework will have particular importance for reaching a determination of likelihood of secondary meaning.

---

[52] Here we use the term "favorability" in an a priori sense; that is, prior to assessing empirical marketplace outcomes. As we discuss in this chapter, empirical marketplace outcomes are useful indicators of whether a company's marketing actions have been successful in overcoming barriers to establishing secondary meaning.

[53] A complete analysis would be required to make a determination of the extent of barriers and actions as well as the likelihood of secondary meaning in any particular case.

[54] *Wal-Mart Stores, Inc. v. Samara Brothers, Inc.* (2000).

Overall, companies hoping to create secondary meaning and courts assessing secondary meaning need to consider the barriers, company actions attempting to overcome those barriers, and the relevant marketplace outcomes. These marketing principles and methods will enhance courts' ability to reach sound determinations of secondary meaning.

15

Social Media Evidence in Commercial Litigation

Tom Wesson, Erich Schaeffer, Brenda Arnott-Wesson, Mark Pelofsky, David Heller, and Bree Glaviano

This chapter demonstrates that analyzing what people post on social media sites can yield powerful evidence for use in commercial litigation. This kind of analysis is a natural way of listening in on people's conversations about products, services, brands, trademarks, and patents, all of which are often the subject of high-stakes lawsuits. An argument is made that an expert who could commission an opinion survey could now also commission a social media analysis, which will contribute to a more persuasive and often more time-appropriate body of evidence upon which to rely. Examples of the use or potential use of social media in litigation are presented, including cases that used social media evidence, such as the US government's lawsuit against Lance Armstrong; a case involving a meat byproduct sometimes referred to as "pink slime"; a case centering on an allegedly deceptive Super Bowl beer advertisement; and many cases involving disputes having to do with intellectual property. Finally, we compile and discuss a number of issues relating to the use of social media in litigation. These issues include questions about social media's authenticity, the best way to preserve it, and several other analytical and legal questions. The chapter concludes with a discussion of how social media analysis can migrate from the periphery of litigation evidence toward having a more central role.

15.1 SOCIAL MEDIA EVIDENCE: THE LANCE ARMSTRONG DOPING CASE

In January 2013, Lance Armstrong, the cyclist who won seven Tour de France titles during the 1990s and 2000s, went on national television and admitted to Oprah Winfrey that he had used banned performance-enhancing drugs (PEDs) throughout his cycling career.[1] The admission was both the culmination of years of acrimonious

---

[1] Throughout this chapter, we discuss what role social media evidence could play in a variety of legal cases. We may or may not have performed work in connection with these matters. We

accusations and denials and the cementing of Armstrong's legacy as perhaps the most famous tainted athlete of all time.

Even today, years after Armstrong won his last race, his name comes up every time a new sports doping scandal occurs: "So @MariaSharapova is tennis' Lance Armstrong now. She publicly denounced drugs in the sport, but ended up getting caught herself lol smh," wrote one commenter, on Twitter.

Armstrong's doping legacy was the key issue in the much-publicized case that pitted Armstrong against his former teammate turned whistleblower, Floyd Landis, and the United States Postal Service (USPS). Armstrong was accused of defrauding the government by accepting over $30 million from the USPS to sponsor his cycling team from 1998 through 2004. The USPS sought to recoup this money, along with associated damages and penalties.[2] One of the USPS's claims in the case was that the audience that it had hoped to influence positively with the sponsorship was now drawing a connection between the USPS and the most infamous sports cheater of all time:[3] "The USPS specifically stated in 2000 that the reason it was sponsoring the USPS team was to 'positively impact customer perceptions of the Postal Service' and improve its own employees' sense of pride.' Doping of athletes and cheating to win athletic events is plainly inconsistent with these objectives."[4]

A major challenge the USPS faced in its lawsuit was how to demonstrate that the goals of the sponsorship, which ended in 2004, were being undermined by Armstrong's admission of doping nearly ten years later. One way to do this was to catalog the media coverage after the admission that linked Armstrong, the scandal, and the Postal Service. Indeed, the USPS's media expert took precisely this approach. In his work on the case, he determined that the USPS was connected to Armstrong's doping scandal in 41,912 Internet articles and 3,825 print articles, which together accounted for more than 150 billion impressions.[5] Clearly, there is little doubt that USPS's target audience had access to many reminders that the Postal Service sponsored the now-disgraced Armstrong, even more than a decade after the termination of the sponsorship.

make no claim to have full knowledge of what evidence was presented in a case or why evidence may have been held back. In all cases, only publicly available information is presented and, as such, what is presented in the chapter may not offer a complete representation of the case issues or strategy. Consequently, examples presented in this chapter are for illustrative purposes only, we offer no opinion as to whether or not social media evidence would be, or would have been, appropriate in the cases discussed.

[2] Complaint, *Landis v. Tailwind Sports Corporation et al.*, 1:11cv976, US District Court – District of Columbia, June 10, 2010, pp. 57–61.
[3] The complaint also alleged that Mr. Armstrong and his cycling team had violated the terms of the contract, among other things.
[4] Complaint, *Landis v. Tailwind Sports Corporation et al.*, p. 50.
[5] Defendant Lance Armstrong's Notice of Motion to Exclude Testimony of Larry Gerbrandt, Brian Till, and Jonathan Walker, *Landis v. Tailwind Sports Corporation et al.*, 1:11cv976, US District Court – District of Columbia, June 9, 2017, p. 14.

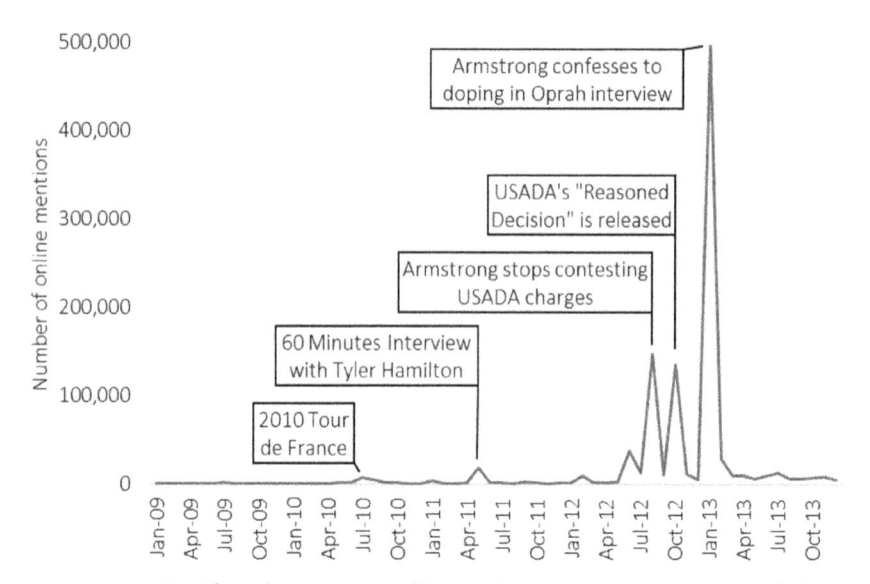

FIGURE 15.1. Social media mentions of Lance Armstrong in connection with doping allegations

But is counting news stories persuasive? Is the fact that the USPS's target audience had the *opportunity* to see thousands of news articles potentially linking it to the scandal sufficient to show that people made that link and that the goals of the sponsorship were undermined? In one of its pretrial motions, Armstrong's legal team argued that "Simply counting allegedly 'negative' impressions tells you nothing. There is no evidence that it actually impacted any target audience."[6] Social media, on the other hand, can provide precisely this kind of evidence.

In particular, social media analysis can provide insight into how consumers gathered and shared information about the story, as well as how they reacted to the scandal and to the USPS's role in it; and, crucially for a case unfolding more than ten years after the events in question, social media evidence can reveal how consumer engagement and response evolved over time. The pattern of social media activity can shed light not only on whether and how much social media users associated Armstrong and the USPS with the scandal, but how this association changed over time and, specifically, whether the association persisted until the time of the case.

An analysis of posts that link Lance Armstrong and doping shows that the volume of posts increased during key events in the doping scandal, culminating with the Oprah Winfrey interview. In fact, there were nearly 300,000 posts linking Armstrong and doping published in the seven days following Armstrong's confession to Oprah. Figure 15.1 illustrates the reaction on social media to key events in the case.

---

[6] Ibid., p. 8.

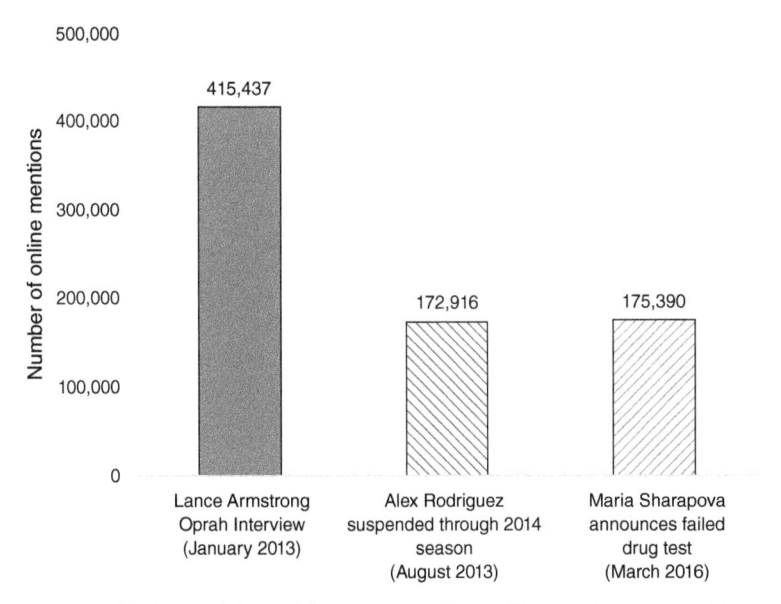

```
                                  415,437
       500,000

       400,000

       300,000

       200,000                                     172,916              175,390

       100,000

             0
                          Lance Armstrong      Alex Rodriguez       Maria Sharapova
                          Oprah Interview    suspended through 2014  announces failed
                          (January 2013)          season               drug test
                                              (August 2013)          (March 2016)
```

FIGURE 15.2. Peak monthly social media mentions of Lance Armstrong, Alex Rodriguez, and Maria Sharapova in connection with doping allegations

Social media analysis also shows how the Armstrong scandal differed in both scale and substance from comparable athlete stories, such as Alex Rodriguez's (baseball) and Maria Sharapova's (tennis) doping scandals. A comparison of the peak number of posts published in a one-month period linking each athlete to PEDs shows that the peak of Armstrong's doping scandal was more than twice as large as both Rodriguez's and Sharapova's (see Figure 15.2).

It is also informative to look at the percentage of all posts mentioning Lance Armstrong linking him to doping. The data shows that social media users strongly linked Armstrong to doping allegations for a very long time, even through to the present. Further, by analyzing a random sample of posts that mention Lance Armstrong, LanceArmstrong, or @LanceArmstrong from each year from 2009 through 2019, it is possible to compare the association of Armstrong with doping to his association with benchmark topics before, during, and after the peak of the scandal (see Figure 15.3). In particular, we measured the number of posts that linked Armstrong to one of the following topics: (1) the doping scandal; (2) Livestrong or any association to Armstrong being a cancer survivor; (3) motivational quotes attributed to Armstrong; (4) Armstrong's family or any of his romantic relationships; and (5) Armstrong's new brand, WEDU, and his two podcasts, The Forward and The Move (formerly, Stages).[7]

---

[7] We did not find any other general topics linked to Armstrong that were more commonly discussed on social media during our review of the posts.

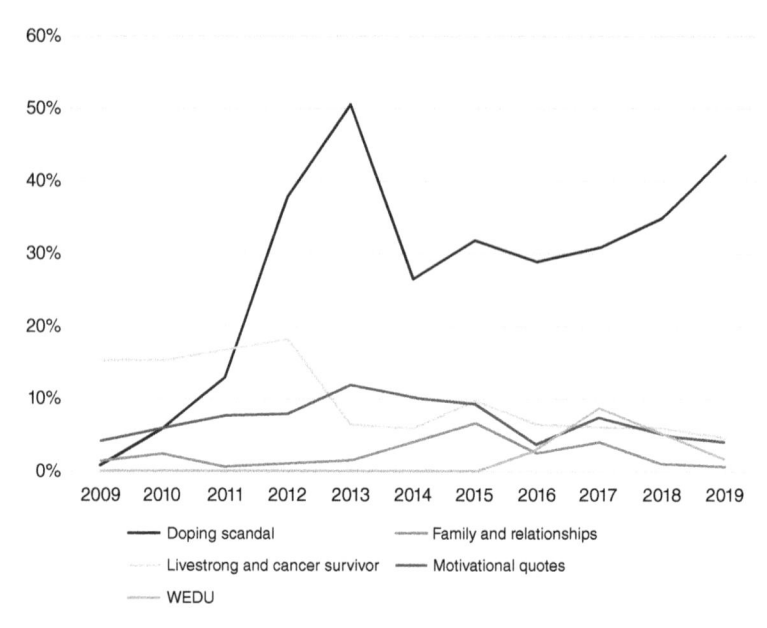

FIGURE 15.3. Percentage of all online conversations connecting Armstrong to doping allegations compared to other benchmark topics

These benchmarks demonstrate the strength of the associative link between Armstrong and doping. A review of the data shows that starting in 2011, the doping scandal took over the general conversation about Armstrong. Starting in 2012, the share of posts linking Armstrong to doping never declined below 31 percent of the overall conversation. In comparison, no other topic accounted for more than 18 percent of the overall conversation at any point. In fact, since the peak of the scandal in 2013, the share of conversations related to most of the benchmarks has steadily declined. Meanwhile, the percentage of posts linking Armstrong to doping has been increasing steadily since 2014 and has nearly reached the same share today as it held in 2012. Even as the overall number of posts linking Lance Armstrong to doping has declined, it is clear that the associative link between Lance Armstrong and doping has not. To the extent that consumers continue to talk about Armstrong, the most common topic of conversation is his doping past.

Taken together, these three graphs demonstrate that the negative publicity arising from Armstrong's transgressions was substantial and long-lasting, both in absolute terms and relative to other doping scandals.

While these data show that consumers associated Armstrong with doping, the USPS still needed to demonstrate that consumers associated Armstrong's doping with the USPS. In traditional media, that link was made through images and video (e.g. by including pictures of Armstrong in the USPS jersey in an article or showing clips of Armstrong racing in the USPS jersey in a TV broadcast) rather than through text.[8] The same sort of pattern appears on social media. While the number of mentions of the USPS in the text of posts about Armstrong is relatively low, a review of Instagram[9] posts featuring #LanceArmstrong published in the last quarter of 2014 found that 7 percent included a picture displaying the USPS logo, indicating that the consumers continued to associate Armstrong with the USPS ten years after sponsorship ended.

The Armstrong example shows how social media reflects the sort of informal reactions and conversations that consumers have always had among friends and family. However, social media conversations differ from those verbal conversations in two important ways: they have the potential to involve a much larger group of people, and they are recorded as retrievable data.

While quantitative analyses of social media increase the robustness of the findings, individual posts can be very useful at trial because they are often highly evocative. These anecdotes can break through the monotony of trial procedures, add color to a body of evidence that may otherwise fail to capture a jury's full attention and understanding, and make a lasting impression on jurors – and judges. In the Armstrong case, there were many attention-grabbing posts in which consumers disparaged Armstrong and linked the USPS to the scandal. As the following examples show, some posts demonstrate clearly and memorably the connection between Armstrong's use of PEDs and the USPS in the minds of consumers:

- "Since US Postal Service sponsored #Lance Armstrong and his drug buddies, maybe USPS could get drugs for postal carriers and speed up service."
- "After this admission by Lance Armstrong, I honestly don't see how I can ever use the US Postal Service again."
- "So if we sent things through USPS, did we help Lance Armstrong cheat since he was sponsored by them? We are all to blame, people!"

Had the case gone to trial,[10] Armstrong's attorneys would almost certainly have argued, among other things, that the audience had long ago forgotten the connection between the USPS sponsorship (that ended in 2004) and Armstrong by the time of his admission during the Oprah Winfrey interview (2013). Had the government presented this social media evidence, the jury might have concluded otherwise.

---

[8] For instance, an analysis of TV news broadcasts archived by the TV News Archive found approximately 1,200 broadcasts that linked Armstrong, doping, and the USPS. In over 1,000 of these broadcasts the connection to the USPS was created visually.
[9] Unfortunately, collecting historical data from Instagram is difficult, meaning it is not possible to conduct a more comprehensive analysis of the kind of images Instagram users were sharing during the height of the doping scandal.
[10] Armstrong paid the USPS $5 million to settle the case in the spring of 2018, just before the trial was scheduled to begin.

15.2 APPLYING SOCIAL MEDIA EVIDENCE IN LITIGATION

The Lance Armstrong case demonstrates that measures of the potential impact of an event on the wider population, such as the number of articles written about it, can be enhanced by direct measures of the online activity generated by the event, such as how many people commented, liked, followed, or retweeted. These online actions by people provide insight into what they are thinking. The Internet and social media have given us the ability to better understand how others see things, beginning nearly instantaneously after the event in question. We can also look back into the recent past and discover what people were thinking about a particular topic at a particular point in time. The ability to listen in on so many casual conversations, past and present, has created countless opportunities to gain new insights in business, politics, and the social sciences. One of the last places to take advantage of the new social listening has been commercial litigation. This opportunity to apply social media to the law is the subject of this chapter.

15.2.1 *Social Media as Organic Evidence for Commercial Litigation*

Over the last ten years or so, firms have learned to harness the power of social media to understand and appeal to consumers' interests. At the same time, social media has allowed consumers to provide near-constant feedback to firms, other consumers, and any other interested party who cares to look at their posts. Through these interactions, social media now plays an important role in shaping consumer–brand relationships.

The growth in social media mirrors a fundamental shift in the role of the Internet in daily life.[11] Because for many people the Internet and social media are deeply embedded in their day-to-day life, social researchers no longer consider social media data to be novel. Social media data are regularly collected to shed light on people's opinions, feelings, and concerns.[12]

The data generated through people's social media use are a form of "naturally occurring evidence."[13] Because social media are forums where people vent their feelings and seek social support,[14] social media content tends to be highly reactive and expressive. Despite the public nature of most social media, because social media tends to be composed of less formal forms of communication, social researchers

---

[11] Graham, L. T., Gosling, S. D., and Wilson, R. E., "A Review of Facebook Research in the Social Sciences," *Perspectives on Psychological Science*, Vol. 7, No. 3, May 2012, pp. 203–20.

[12] Chen, X., Vorvoreanu, M., and Madhaven, K., "Mining Social Media Data for Understanding Students' Learning Experiences," *IEEE Transaction on Learning*, Vol. 7, No. 3, July–Sept. 2014, pp. 246–59.

[13] Johnson, T. P., and Smith, T. W., "Big Data and Survey Research: Supplement or Substitute?" In *Seeing Cities through Big Data*. Springer, 2017, pp. 113–25.

[14] Chen, Vorvoreanu, and Madhaven, "Mining Social Media Data for Understanding Students' Learning Experiences."

consider people's activity on social media to be more authentic than responses to formal research prompts (such as opinion surveys).[15] It is because of its "organic" or "naturally occurring" character and authenticity that social media data can serve effectively as evidence in commercial litigation. Online posts constitute a living archive, in the sense that posts made over time can be accessed in order to understand what consumers were thinking in the past and how that thinking evolved as events unfolded.

15.2.2 Social Media Analysis as a Complement to Survey Evidence

Legal cases in which understanding consumers' thoughts, beliefs, or sentiments is important typically rely on traditional approaches to assess public opinion to develop that understanding (interviews, focus groups, consumer surveys, etc.). These traditional methods, foremost among them consumer surveys, while valuable, have limitations.

As mentioned, the nature of social media as "organic" or "found" data (as opposed to data generated *post facto*) underlies a fundamental difference between social media analysis and surveys. Schober et al. describe three major differences between the use of social media data and surveys for social measurement: how participants understand the activity (responding to questions versus posting); the nature of the data; and practical and ethical considerations.[16] These fundamental differences make social media analysis a potentially useful complement to traditional methods (such as consumer surveys). The two methods, then, provide converging evidence that can be effective in either an affirmative or rebuttal context.[17]

In surveys, researchers can ask narrow questions, specifically addressing the issues they believe to be relevant in a case. For example, if a particular feature of a product is allegedly being infringed upon, survey respondents can be shown an image of the feature and asked questions about it. In social media analysis, however, the researcher uses the posts themselves to determine which issues are relevant to consumers. This is referred to as a "bottom-up" approach "that makes no

---

[15] Ibid.
[16] Schober, M. F., et al., "Social Media Analyses for Social Measurement," *Public Opinion Quarterly*, Vol. 80, No. 1, 2016, pp. 180–211.
[17] For example, in the case *Juul Labs, Inc. v. 4X Pods* (2020), Juul alleged that 4X Pods infringed on its trademarks and trade dress in their marketing of 4X Pods, creating a likelihood of confusion. Juul put forth a consumer survey for likelihood of confusion and provided a handful of isolated examples of confusion from consumers on social media. The New Jersey District Court ruled that even scant anecdotal social media evidence was compelling in the context of the survey, stating, "All in all, while direct evidence is scant, I must consider it in the context of the consumer surveys, which are robust and significant. Juul has made a fair showing on the actual confusion factor. Because this factor is important in a compatibility assurance case, and because such evidence is usually hard to come by, Juul's showing weighs heavily in my decision." *Juul Labs, Inc. v. 4X Pods*, Civ. No. 18-15444 (KM)(MAH) (D.N.Y. Dec. 22, 2020).

assumptions about which variables are likely to be relevant."[18] In survey research, the investigator determines the topic of discussion and analysis. In social media analysis, on the other hand, discussion topics are chosen by consumers, and the analysis emerges from the content of the data. While its organic nature can make social media data particularly compelling, it also means that social media, by itself, is sometimes unable to provide all the insight necessary in a case. Online posts may not address the specific issues that are relevant to the case. For example, the presence or lack of secondary meaning attached to stripes around the outside of a shoe might be a key legal issue. Consumers, however, might not discuss these stripes specifically when posting online.

While surveys are useful for collecting consumer opinion and thoughts in a reliable, verifiable, and statistically quantifiable manner, they can be subject to bias and problems stemming from their retrospective nature. When using surveys in litigation, it is not unusual for a researcher to ask consumers to report on what they believed or what they were thinking two or three or more years previously. For example, to be useful in the Armstrong case, any survey would have required respondents to recall how they reacted to Armstrong's doping admission some three years after it occurred and more than ten years after the termination of the sponsorship at issue in the case. Opinion surveys, to be accurate and useful in litigation, require respondents both to remember events that might have seemed insignificant when they occurred and to ignore all subsequent events and information that might bias their recollection. This is a tall order.

On the other hand, social media and other online posts are records of spontaneous, contemporaneous communications of what people are thinking and saying in real time in a real-world environment. Social media data are unique in that they are created as events are unfolding and are preserved as an artifact of the event. These data are not created long after the fact based on respondents' memories as prompted by survey questions. The temporal characteristics of social media data can also allow for a more fine-grained analysis of the data than surveys typically can. In most instances, a researcher can identify the exact instant a social media post was created. This detail can allow researchers to see the immediate impact of specific events in much more detail than is possible based on survey respondents' memory of past events. Furthermore, in surveys, the researcher determines the time period under consideration in advance and asks questions about that period. In social media analysis, the researcher can use the data themselves to identify the timing of significant events that drive consumer opinion. Both these strengths of social media analysis are illustrated in the Lance Armstrong example discussed earlier. Figure 15.1 shows, quite unequivocally, the huge impact of the Oprah interview on the social media discussion about Lance Armstrong.

---

[18] Schober et al., "Social Media Analyses for Social Measurement."

Another potential source of bias in surveys is the fact that participants often endeavor to please the surveyor, especially during in-person interviews. This inclination to please can be problematic in litigation, where the specific nature of the questions asked can make the purpose of the survey clear to respondents or allow respondents to guess the purpose of the survey and modify responses with that assumed purpose in mind.[19] Survey responses can also be affected by constraints imposed by the survey environment itself, such as: time constraints; the linear nature of most survey designs; the use of multiple-choice and other closed-ended question formats to facilitate statistical analysis; and a lack of opportunity for respondents to provide information outside the scope of the questions asked.

In contrast, when consumers post to social media, they are doing so of their own volition, on their own schedule, and for their own audience. A typical user rarely considers that the data they generate will be used for public opinion or social measurement purposes. On the other hand, a common criticism of social media research is that there is no reason to believe that its findings are representative of the views of the population as a whole;[20] whereas, in survey research, samples are typically designed to ensure that they are representative of a full population. With social media data there is no reason to assume that any specific population is represented, except that of the "social media user."[21] The trust placed in surveys is based in large part on their claim to be representative of the population as a whole. While this claim may at times be called into question, if we take it at face value, we can think of social media analysis as complementing survey data by providing insight into specific subsets of the general population.

As one considers these differences, what is important to bear in mind is that they are simply that – differences. Social media data are different from other types of data, particularly survey data, in important ways. These differences mean that neither one is a substitute for the other nor is one superior to the other, but rather that they complement each other. Therefore, attorneys might be wise to consider complementing survey data by incorporating social media data sources into the discovery process and the potential applications of social media evidence to their case.

A recent example demonstrates how social media can work in support of a survey. In *MillerCoors, LLC* v. *Anheuser-Busch Companies, LLC*, the plaintiff claimed that the defendant's Super Bowl commercial and the subsequent advertising campaign, which focused on the plaintiff's use of corn syrup in the beer brewing process, was

---

[19] Diamond, S. S., "Reference Guide on Survey Research," *Reference Manual on Scientific Evidence*, National Academies Press, 2011, pp. 389–91 and 410–11; Nichols, A. L., and Maner J. K., "The Good-Subject Effect: Investigating Participant Demand Characteristics," *The Journal of General Psychology*, Vol. 135, No. 2, 2008, pp. 151–66.

[20] See, for example, "Social Media and Public Opinion," *Langer Research Associates*, Aug. 2013, p. 2.

[21] Schober, M., et al., "Research Synthesis: Social Media Analyses for Social Measurement," *Public Opinion Quarterly*, Vol. 80, No. 1, Spring 2016, p. 194.

misleading and likely to deceive consumers. MillerCoors contended that a Bud Light advertising campaign led consumers to believe that corn syrup is present in the final product of its beers, even though corn syrup (like any other fermentable sugar) is consumed by yeast during the fermentation process. To support its case, MillerCoors retained an expert who conducted a survey to measure the degree to which consumers who saw the allegedly misleading commercial believed that corn syrup was actually present in the final product. The survey found that an "economically meaningful and statistically significant" percentage of consumers surveyed believed that corn syrup was actually present in the final product.[22]

MillerCoors' expert produced a separate social media analysis to "confirm" (among other things) the results of his survey.[23] Like the survey, the social media analysis examined whether social media users believed that corn syrup was in the final product. The results from the social media analysis were consistent with the survey: "28.6% of consumer posts include information that indicates the author holds the mistaken belief that corn syrup used in brewing is present in the final product (the beer itself)."[24] Ultimately, the court found the social media analysis compelling even if it was not definitive. In a ruling partially granting the plaintiff a preliminary injunction, the court found that the social media evidence "provides anecdotal evidence to support the survey results."[25]

In this case, social media was also used to provide insights that are not available through traditional litigation surveys. For instance, the study examined the volume of posts in which consumers discussed corn syrup and a specific MillerCoors product. Comparing the volume of posts before and after the Super Bowl demonstrates the extent to which the defendant's allegedly misleading advertising campaign created a new conversation around the presence or absence of corn syrup in MillerCoors and Anheuser-Busch products.

15.2.3 *Rigorous Demands for the Research and Analysis of Social Media Used in Commercial Litigation*

Social media data are an example of "big data." Marketers use "big data" techniques to mine social media posts in order to track brand positions and standing over time and in relation to competitors.[26] The "big data" label highlights the volume of social

---

[22] Report of Yoram (Jerry) Wind, PhD, *MillerCoors, LLC. v. Anheuser-Busch Companies, LLC*, 19-cv-218-wmc, US District Court – Western Wisconsin, Mar. 27, 2019.
[23] Ibid., p. 37.
[24] Ibid., p. 54. Only 6.9 percent of posts indicated the author understood that corn syrup was not present in the final product, meaning users expressed mistaken beliefs in more than four times as many posts. In the rest of the posts, the user did not express a clear opinion.
[25] Ibid., p. 43.
[26] Tellis, J., and Tirunillai, S., "Mining Marketing Meaning from Online Chatter: Strategic Brand Analysis of Big Data Using Latent Dirichlet Allocation," *Journal of Marketing Research*, Vol. LI, Aug. 2014, pp. 463–79.

media data, but it is not only sheer volume that makes such data complex to research and analyze. Social media data also have high "velocity," which means the posts are created quickly and conversations move rapidly among users, both in general and around specific events.[27] Social media data appeal to marketers in part because the speed of social media tends to align more closely with the speed of business decision-making than do other means of assessing consumer sentiment.[28] Social media data also come in a great variety of forms. Facebook posts, Tweets, Instagram posts, bulletin board posts, and product reviews are all structured differently, and there is a wide variety of posts even within each group. The volume, velocity, and variety of social media posts create unique challenges in addition to the opportunities they generate.

One of the complications in social media analysis is that it can be difficult to identify relevant posts because of the variety and irregularity of language used.[29] Language used in social media often contains slang, sarcasm, misspelling, and ambiguous meaning.[30] Moreover, many social media posts are about several things all at once. A post mentioning a low-priced sneaker imitating a famous brand could be primarily about money concerns but might also mention various other topics ranging from the price of real estate to the quality of McDonald's food. Similarly, social media posts sometimes imply which product feature the post is about, without explicitly mentioning the feature. For example, a poster who admires the contrasting colors on a shoe might be referring to the look of a white midsole and toe cap on a plain black shoe without referring to either of these features explicitly. A keyword search of posts could easily miss such a post.

Along with these general challenges of social media analysis, the particular context of commercial litigation poses additional challenges: It is an adversarial process requiring a very high degree of rigor to produce results that can withstand the scrutiny of opposing counsel and experts. The tools and techniques typically employed in social media analyses for use in business and marketing have not been designed to withstand this high level of scrutiny. In marketing, algorithmic approaches, in particular machine learning, can be effective at "cleaning the data," removing false positives, commercial activity, bots, and spam. In litigation, however, these techniques may not be sufficient because even small errors or omissions can be used to call entire analyses into question. Further, automated tools often must be specifically trained and validated with enough hand-coded data to be reliable with different content, data sources, or periods of time. The one-off nature of litigation does not always allow for the development of purpose-built tools. In the context of

---

[27] Japec, L., et al., "Big Data in Survey Research: AAPOR Task Force Report," *Public Opinion Quarterly*, Vol. 79, No. 4, Winter 2015, pp. 839–80.
[28] Ibid., p. 866.
[29] Chen, Vorvoreanu, and Madhaven, "Mining Social Media Data for Understanding Students' Learning Experiences."
[30] Ibid.

litigation, sophisticated techniques such as random sampling, human review, and verification of intercoder reliability may be needed to ensure that analyses of social media data meet the evidentiary standards required by the courts.

15.3 PINK SLIME: USING SOCIAL MEDIA ANALYSIS TO ADDRESS CAUSALITY

A recent case involving a substance commonly referred to as "pink slime" provides another useful example of how social media analysis can be used by both sides in a commercial lawsuit. The case demonstrates how litigants and counsel who approach social media evidence proactively and creatively can use it to support their positions on a broad range of issues, including the fundamental issue of causality.[31]

15.3.1 *Case Background*

From March 7, 2012, to April 2, 2012, ABC aired eleven TV segments and published fourteen online news stories reporting on a beef product it referred to as "pink slime." Pink slime, properly known as lean finely textured beef (LFTB), is a beef product added to ground beef. It is made by spinning beef trimmings in a centrifuge to separate lean meat from fat. According to Beef Products, Inc. (BPI), the manufacturer of 70 percent of the LFTB sold in the United States at the time of ABC's reporting,[32] LFTB lowers the fat content of meat, lowers the cost of meat to consumers, and allows an additional 10–20 pounds of meat to be processed per animal.[33] ABC described LFTB as a "cheap filler," "once only used in dog food and cooking oil."[34] ABC also quoted a United States Department of Agriculture (USDA) whistleblower who described the presence of LFTB in ground beef as "economic fraud."[35]

For BPI, ABC's reporting was a direct attack on its business. Following ABC's reporting, multiple grocery stores stopped selling ground beef that included LFTB, leading to a precipitous decline in sales for BPI. Prior to ABC's coverage, BPI sold

---

[31] The analysis below is intended to be an example showing the application of social media evidence in a high-stakes case. While the various illustrative analyses are based on real data, they may not be sufficiently robust to stand up to the rigors of litigation.

[32] Complaint, *Beef Products, Inc. et al. v. American Broadcasting Companies, Inc. et al.*, 4:12cv4183, US District Court – Southern South Dakota, Oct. 24, 2012, p. 26.

[33] Ibid., pp. 1–2.

[34] Avila, J., "70 Percent of Ground Beef at Supermarkets Contains 'Pink Slime,'" *ABC News*, Mar. 7, 2012, https://web.archive.org/web/20120310052604/https://abcnews.go.com/blogs/headlines/2012/03/70-percent-of-ground-beef-at-supermarkets-contains-pink-slime/; "ABC World News with Diane Sawyer," *ABC*, Mar. 7, 2012, https://archive.org/details/WJLA_20120307_233000_ABC_World_News_With_Diane_Sawyer/start/960/end/1020.

[35] "Whistleblowers Expose 'Pink Slime' in Widespread Ground Beef," *ABC7*, Mar. 9, 2012, https://abc7.com/archive/8574471/.

5 million pounds of LFTB per week; following the coverage, BPI was selling only 2 million pounds per week.[36] As a result, BPI had to close three facilities and lay off 300 employees.[37]

In September 2012, BPI filed a lawsuit in South Dakota against ABC seeking $400 million in damages (which would be tripled under South Dakota's Agriculture Food Products Disparagement Act).[38] BPI alleged that ABC's reporting "intentionally maligned" BPI and LFTB by "recast[ing] and renam[ing]" LFTB as "pink slime,"[39] misleading consumers about LFTB in a variety of ways and interfering with BPI's business. In June 2017, three weeks into the trial, ABC and BPI settled for a reported $177 million.[40,41]

As in the Armstrong case, a social media analysis is especially appropriate in the pink-slime case because consumer perceptions are at issue. BPI contended that ABC's reporting led consumers to believe false and disparaging information about LFTB.[42] To make its case, it was not sufficient for BPI to show that ABC's reporting was inaccurate or that consumers had negative beliefs about LFTB. BPI had to show that ABC's reporting had an impact on consumer perceptions of LFTB and that the change in consumer perceptions harmed BPI. Through the analysis of contemporaneous online commentary related to LFTB and ABC's reporting, it is possible to show the impact that ABC's reporting had on consumer beliefs about LFTB. An interesting conclusion from the analysis of social media in the LFTB case is that both sides could have gathered useful evidence from social media data.[43]

15.3.2 Using Social Media Evidence to Support the Plaintiff's Case

Applying social media evidence to support BPI's claims in the pink-slime case is relatively straightforward. There was a clear increase in posts mentioning pink slime

---

[36] Complaint, *Beef Products, Inc. et al. v. American Broadcasting Companies, Inc. et al.*, pp. 7–8.
[37] Ibid., pp. 7–8.
[38] Ibid., p. 256.
[39] Ibid., pp. 53–58.
[40] Kludt, T., "ABC Settles Suit over What It Had Called 'Pink Slime,'" *CNN Business*, June 28, 2017, https://money.cnn.com/2017/06/28/media/abc-bpi-settlement/index.html.
[41] Hauser, C., "ABC's 'Pink Slime' Report Tied to $177 Million in Settlement Costs," *New York Times*, Aug. 10, 2017, www.nytimes.com/2017/08/10/business/pink-slime-disney-abc.html.
[42] BPI did include anecdotal consumer comments in the Complaint (see pp. 106–12 and Appendices 3–6). Unfortunately, the Appendices to the Complaint are not publicly available. Further, the number of comments included in the body of the Complaint is minimal and the comments are all from ABC Online. As we will show, analyzing large numbers of posts from a variety of sources can provide more compelling evidence.
[43] BPI did hire an expert witness to opine on, among other things, the nature and impact of ABC's reporting on social media. According to press reports from the trial, BPI's expert opined that ABC's coverage was "intensive" and "unprecedented," and that its coverage was the "primary driver of consumer concern." Unfortunately, BPI's expert's report is not publicly available. See Dockter, M., "ABC Stories Called 'Unprecedented' by BPI Expert Witness," *Sioux City Journal*, June 26, 2017, p. A.3.

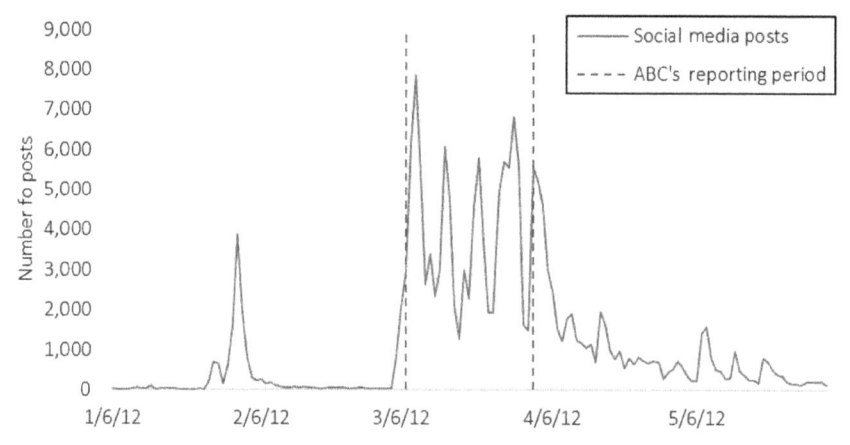

FIGURE 15.4. Number of social media posts mentioning "pink slime"
A manual review of a sample from the dataset found that approximately 5 percent of the dataset is composed of false positives and another 4 percent have an indeterminate meaning (e.g. a user simply posts #Pinkslime with no further comment or context). The majority of the false positives were generated in response to producer and rapper Pharrell and deceased rapper Mac Miller announcing an EP titled *Pink Slime* in June 2014, after ABC's reporting period.

and LFTB during ABC's reporting of the story (see Figure 15.4). For the two-month period prior to ABC's reporting, there was an average of 272 posts per day about pink slime published on multiple social media platforms. During ABC's reporting period, there was an average of 4,027 posts per day, a nearly fifteen-fold increase. Additionally, pink slime remained a topic of conversation following the reporting period, suggesting that ABC's reporting had a lasting impact. For the two-month period after ABC's reporting, there was an average of 900 posts per day about pink slime. The increase in mentions of pink slime demonstrates that consumers paid attention to ABC's reporting and supports BPI's first charge against ABC – that ABC's reporting recast LFTB as "pink slime."

In addition to its on-air reporting, ABC published multiple posts on its social media platforms publicizing its pink-slime coverage. There was a very high level of consumer engagement with these stories, as indicated by the numbers of comments left on posts about pink slime published on ABC's Facebook pages.[44]

During its reporting period, ABC posted twelve stories about pink slime to its ABC News and ABC World News Facebook pages. ABC's pink-slime posts consistently generated more comments than almost all other content posted on the pages (see Figures 15.5 and 15.6). From December 2011 to July 2012, ABC published a

---

[44] Owners of social media accounts, in this case ABC, have access to even more fine-grained engagement metrics, such as clicks, impressions, reach, and page views. Depending on the platform, they may also have access to posts that are not available publicly. BPI could have asked for this content in discovery.

Linked story	Date posted	Number of comments	Percentile rank (# of comments)
Where You Can Get "Pink-Slime"-Free Beef	March 9, 2012	271	87%
"Pink Slime" Will Be a Choice for Schools	March 15, 2012	216	80%
"Pink Slime" Taste Test	March 16, 2012	217	82%
Safeway to Stop Selling "Pink Slime" Textured Beef	March 21, 2012	181	75%
Safeway, SUPERVALU and Food Lion to Stop Selling "Pink Slime" Beef	March 21, 2012	505	97%
"Dude, It's Beef!": Governors Tour Plant, Reject "Pink Slime" Label	March 29, 2012	279	87%
Average:		278	84%

FIGURE 15.5. Consumer engagement with posts about pink slime on the ABC News Facebook page

Linked story	Date posted	Number of comments	Percentile rank (comments)
70 Percent of Ground Beef at Supermarkets Contains 'Pink Slime'	March 7, 2012	173	98%
'Pink Slime' Will Be a Choice for Schools	March 15, 2012	58	82%
Safeway to Stop Selling 'Pink Slime' Textured Beef	March 21, 2012	41	69%
Where to Get 'Pink-Slime'-Free Beef	March 22, 2012	45	73%
'Dude, It's Beef!': Governors Tour Plant, Reject 'Pink Slime' Label	March 29, 2012	37	65%
'Pink Slime' Maker AFA Files for Bankruptcy	April 2, 2012	59	82%
Average:		69	78%

FIGURE 15.6. Consumer engagement with posts about pink slime on the ABC World News Facebook page

total of 2,625 posts on its ABC News Facebook page, and 1,593 posts on its ABC World News page. During that period, the pink-slime stories on average generated more comments than 84 percent of posts published on the ABC News page, and 78 percent of posts published on the ABC World News page. Clearly, consumers found ABC's pink-slime posts more engaging than almost anything else ABC published during that timeframe. This high level of engagement supports BPI's claim that ABC's coverage had an impact on consumer perceptions of LFTB.

In addition to claiming that the ABC stories were the reason that the product was tagged with the name "pink slime," BPI alleged that ABC intentionally misled

False assertion	Keywords
Not meat or beef	Not meat, not beef, filler, pump up, substitute, trimmings
Not safe for consumption	Waste, dog food, lurking, fecal, pathogens, bacteria, contaminant, ammonia spray
Not nutritious	Low grade, scrap, connective tissue, gelatin, fat, nutritious, additive, adulterant
Committed fraud and/or acted improperly	Fraud, deceptive, beef industry, whistleblower

FIGURE 15.7. Social media posts spreading ABC's allegedly damaging and misleading claims about BPI and LFTB

consumers by implying that (1) LFTB was "not meat or beef,"[45] (2) LFTB was "not safe for public consumption,"[46] (3) LFTB was "not nutritious,"[47] and (4) "BPI engaged in improper conduct with the USDA."[48] An analysis of social media posts using a set of keywords based on the language used throughout ABC's reporting revealed more than 17,000 posts that spread each of the allegedly misleading claims BPI identified from ABC's reporting (see Figure 15.7 for a list of the keywords used). These posts support BPI's claims that ABC's allegedly misleading claims had an impact on consumers.

15.3.3 Using Social Media Evidence to Support the Defendant's Case

While there is clearly social media evidence supporting BPI's claims in the pink-slime case, ABC could also have used social media to challenge some of BPI's claims. For example, a review of posts discussing or mentioning pink slime shows that LFTB was referred to as "pink slime" *before* ABC's reporting period. In fact, there were more than 16,500 posts in which LFTB was referred to as "pink slime" in the two-month period before ABC first reported on it (see Figure 15.8). One story, in particular, generated a lot of buzz on social media before ABC's reporting began. In January 2012, McDonald's and other fast-food chains announced that they would stop using beef that contained pink slime. This story alone generated thousands of posts in a fifteen-day period starting in late January 2012. After it was reported (two days prior to ABC's reporting) that the USDA purchased 7 million pounds of LFTB for school lunches, thousands more posts mentioning pink slime were published.

---

[45] Complaint, *Beef Products, Inc. et al. v. American Broadcasting Companies, Inc. et al.*, pp. 62–66.
[46] Ibid., pp. 73–77.
[47] Ibid., pp. 90–95.
[48] Ibid., pp. 100–102.

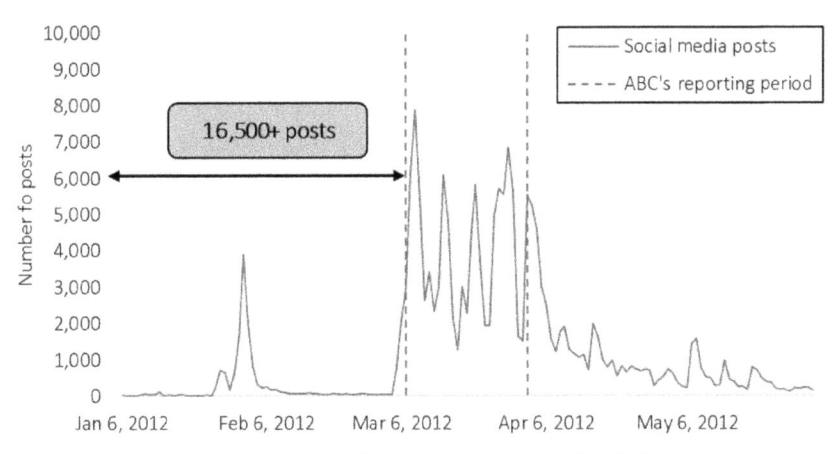

FIGURE 15.8. Number of social media posts mentioning "pink slime"

While this volume of posts is certainly lower than it was during ABC's reporting period, the use of the term "pink slime" was still widespread before it was ever used by ABC. ABC neither coined nor first popularized the term.

Notably, discussion of the USDA's decision continued into ABC's reporting period, potentially confounding any attempt to measure the impact ABC's reporting had on the volume of pink-slime posts that were generated.[49]

Further, evidence from ABC's Facebook pages indicates that consumers' interest in pink slime was fleeting. On June 6, 2012, ABC published two pink-slime stories to its ABC News and ABC World News Facebook pages. While these posts were published only two months after ABC's reporting period, consumer engagement with these posts was considerably less than it was with the posts published during ABC's reporting period. Specifically, the story published on the ABC News page generated only fifty-two comments (28th percentile), and the story published on the ABC World News page generated only nine comments (19th percentile). While ABC's pink-slime reporting did create a spike in consumer engagement, the spike may not have been long-lasting.

Finally, even before ABC's reporting, consumers overwhelmingly referred to LFTB as "pink slime" on social media. From January 6, 2012, to March 6, 2012, fewer than 300 posts referred to LFTB by some version of its proper name (e.g. lean finely textured beef, finely textured beef, boneless lean beef trimmings, ammoniated beef, or LFTB). In contrast, more than 16,500 posts contained the term "pink slime," meaning 98 percent of all posts about LFTB prior to ABC's reporting mentioned the term "pink slime."

---

[49] Separating posts about the USDA decision from those caused by ABC's reporting is challenging and can only be accomplished with a combination of sophisticated automated techniques and human review.

15.3.4 *Pink Slime: Conclusions*

Clearly, BPI could have used social media evidence to bolster its case, and ABC could have used it to provide a rebuttal. For BPI, social media evidence shows that ABC's coverage generated a tremendous volume of social media discussion and an extraordinary level of consumer engagement, leading to tens of thousands of posts repeating the allegedly false and misleading claims reported by ABC. For ABC, a social media analysis shows that ABC did not coin the term "pink slime" and that there was significant online discussion of pink slime before it picked up the story. An analysis of social media evidence by one or both parties would have provided the trier of fact with additional information upon which to base its conclusions. Social media analysis would have offered contemporaneous evidence about consumers' beliefs that would have been very difficult, if not impossible, to acquire through alternative means.

15.4 EXAMPLES OF USING SOCIAL MEDIA ANALYSIS IN INTELLECTUAL PROPERTY CASES

The Armstrong and pink slime examples focus on social media use in cases centered on highly publicized events that, predictably, generated voluminous social media activity. It is important also to discuss the role that social media evidence can play in less newsworthy cases. Social media evidence is especially helpful in intellectual property cases, where it can overcome some of the limitations inherent in survey data.[50] Direct consumer commentary can be extremely helpful for demonstrating whether consumers are confused by the similarities between marks, whether a trademark is generic or distinctive (possessing "secondary meaning"), or whether harm is likely to occur (or has occurred) because of the alleged infringement.

In the remainder of this section, we present a few examples of real-world-use cases for social media evidence in intellectual property litigation. It is important to note that these are complex and, in some cases, ongoing matters. Therefore, for each, we only offer a general overview of evidence (which is subject to change) and important rulings.

15.4.1 *Using Social Media Posts to Demonstrate Likelihood of Confusion*

A key element in many trademark cases is the need for the plaintiff to demonstrate that the defendant's use of the mark in question is likely to cause consumer confusion. Likelihood of confusion is demonstrated through a multifactor test that includes, among other things, an examination of the degree of similarity between the design of the junior and senior marks and whether there exists evidence of actual

[50] Schober et al., "Research Synthesis."

confusion (i.e. consumers mistakenly believe the infringing product or service bearing the mark originated from or is somehow associated with the trademark owner). Social media evidence can shed light on both these questions.

In 2014, Converse Inc. (Converse) filed a complaint against thirty-one footwear manufacturers and retailers at the International Trade Commission (ITC), claiming the defendants were "knocking off" its trademarked Chuck Taylor All Star design (known colloquially as "Chucks"). Due in part to the complexity of the supply chain and the fungibility of overseas footwear manufacturers, Converse was seeking a General Exclusion Order (GEO) against the importation of any products that infringed on one or more of its trademarks. To support its claims of infringement, Converse included evidence in the complaint from online posts to demonstrate that (1) consumers found the imitations to be confusing (as defined in the preceding paragraph); and (2) the availability of imitations caused Converse to lose sales it otherwise would have received.

The most common type of confusion present in this case was "post-sale confusion"[51] – confusion that occurs when a consumer sees a "knock-off" product in the real world and mistakes it for the genuine product. Evidence of this type of confusion is observable on social media. For example, one consumer titled her review of an imitation product as: "$12 Chuck Taylor knock-off review." In the review, the author stated, "all good on the knockoff front – people compliment me on my 'Chucks.'" Although clearly, the writer of the post was not confused, others (those who complimented the poster) were. Numerous other consumer reviews of the imitation shoes feature a consumer stating that they had received compliments or was asked by confused consumers if they were wearing Chucks.

Posts revealing that Converse lost sales to imitation manufacturers are also present on social media. Individuals wrote that their plans to buy Converse shoes changed when they saw imitations at a lower price point, and they chose those instead. Others expressed that they were glad they had not paid a premium price for Chucks when they could buy imitations for much less. These types of posts not only demonstrate that Converse lost sales as a direct result of defendants' underselling, but also serve to highlight the downward price pressure the imitations placed on the entire product category.

In another case, this one filed in the US District Court for the Western District of Texas in 2015, YETI Coolers, LLC (YETI), a manufacturer of premium-priced coolers, sued another manufacturer, RTIC Coolers, LLC (RTIC), that produced a product nearly identical to its own in shape, design, color scheme, and hardware. The defendant's advertising focused on comparing the two companies' products and, of course, the price difference between them. YETI alleged that RTIC's coolers

---

[51] Initial Determination on Violation of Section 337 and Recommended Determination on Remedy and Bond, *In the Matter of Certain Footwear Products*, 337-TA-936, US International Trade Commission, Nov. 17, 2015.

infringed on its trade dress and, as such, were likely to cause confusion in the marketplace.

Consumer posts support YETI's allegations for two factors in the likelihood-of-confusion analysis: similarity of design and actual confusion. In terms of similarity of design, many consumers expressed their opinion that RTIC's designs were similar, if not identical, to YETI's. Examples of posts supporting this claim include:

- "All my buddies ... are ordering one now after seeing mine yesterday. They couldn't believe how much like a YETI it was."
- "That thing looks exactly like a YETI. Looks identical except for the name."
- "Looks to me like a direct rip off of the YETI."
- "As for the Rtic coolers, they are certainly a YETI clone, right down to the color options."

There are also multiple instances of actual confusion, including rumors circulating online that RTIC was owned by YETI or that the two manufacturers were somehow connected. For example:

- "The guys that started Yeti, started RTIC."
- "As far as the RTIC knock offs go. Some people in the industry think that it's a subsidiary of YETI. Kind of like Keystone Light vs COORS light. The coolers and web page are identical to YETI. Why would they just sit back and let a company undercut them unless they owned said company?"
- "It seems odd to me that these RTIC coolers look almost exactly like the YETI coolers. Looks like just a few minor tweaks ... Oh, and go to the websites and tell me they don't use the very same web design outfit. LOL! ... Looks like YETI going for the lower end market."

As these and many other similar posts demonstrate, social media can be a relevant source of corroborating evidence for multiple factors in the multifactor test for determining likelihood of confusion.[52]

Additionally, courts have ruled that social media posts demonstrating potential confusion are admissible. The case *OraLABS, INC. v. Kind Group LLC* concerned an infringement dispute between the makers of lip-care products "Lip Revo" (OraLABS) and "eos" (Kind Group). The US District Court ruled that the evidence was admissible, saying: "The Twitter posts that Kind Group seeks to admit are even

---

[52] Other examples of cases where social media have supported one or more factors in the multifactor test include *You Fit v. Pleasanton Fitness LLC*, where anonymous Yelp reviews confusing the at-issue products were determined by the court to weigh in favor of confusion, and *Bulman v. 2bkco, Inc.*, where the court found that Twitter posts asking for help with the plaintiff's app but directed at the defendant's social media account were probative in demonstrating a likelihood of confusion.

more direct than accounts of third-party statements. Kind Group provides the statements themselves. These statements are not hearsay and are properly considered as evidence of actual confusion."[53]

In another confusion case, the issue wasn't the social media posts but the use of hashtags in advertising. Juul Labs, Inc., sued Eonsmoke, alleging, among other things, trademark and trade-dress infringement.[54] Eonsmoke's advertisements on Instagram and other social media included a list of hashtags,[55] many of which were related to Juul, such as #juulgang, #juulnation, and #juul. Eonsmoke argued that it should be allowed to use these hashtags because they were only meant to inform consumers about compatibility with Juul products. The court ruled against this argument, stating:

> [T]here are multiple posts using Juul hashtags. This bespeaks a coordinated strategy. One post with Juul hashtags among many unoffending posts could be written off, but that is not the case here. Given how many Juul-related hashtags were used and in how many posts, Eonsmoke stretched its usage of the Juul wordmark beyond nominative fair use.[56]

There are three important take-aways from this ruling. First, courts are acknowledging that a brand's use of hashtags must be considered as part of its advertising strategy. Second, quantitative analysis of the use of hashtags is useful in cases of allegedly systematic bad acts. Third, we can expect courts to rule that hashtags constitute part of a marketing strategy when the matter comes up in relation to other issues, such as false advertising.

15.4.2 Using Social Media Posts to Address Distinctiveness/Genericness

Social media can also be used to demonstrate whether a trademark or trade dress has acquired distinctiveness or is viewed as generic by consumers. The issue of distinctiveness sits at the core of many trademark-related lawsuits. For example, since 2010, there has been an ongoing series of cases centered on whether the term "Pretzel Crisps" is distinctive, and therefore eligible for trademark protection.[57] In 2017, the Trademark Trial and Appeal Board (TTAB) upheld its previous ruling that Pretzel Crisps is generic and that the Pretzel Crisps mark is not distinctive.[58] In November

---

[53] *OraLabs, Inc. v. Kind Group LLC*, Civil Action No. 13-cv-00170-PAB-KLM (D. Colo. Aug. 12, 2015) p. 2.
[54] *Juul Labs, Inc. v. 4X Pods*, Civ. No. 18-15444 (KM)(MAH) (D.N.Y. Dec. 22, 2020).
[55] Ibid., p. 1.
[56] Ibid., p. 9.
[57] *Princeton Vanguard, LLC v. Frito-Lay North Am., Inc.*, 786 F.3d 960, 114 U.S.P.Q.2D (BNA) 1827, US Court of Appeals – Federal Circuit, May 15, 2015; *Frito-Lay N. Am., Inc. v. Princeton Vanguard, LLC*, 124 U.S.P.Q.2D (BNA) 1184, 2017 TTAB LEXIS 300, Trademark Trial and Appeal Board, Sept. 6, 2017.
[58] *Frito-Lay N. Am., Inc. v. Princeton Vanguard, LLC*.

2017, Snyder's, the owner of the canceled trademark, filed a suit asking the court to consider new evidence to prove distinctiveness for Pretzel Crisps.[59]

Snyder's could decide to offer social media evidence among the new evidence it cites to support its claim that the term "Pretzel Crisps" has acquired distinctiveness.[60] A brief analysis of online posts suggests there may be compelling evidence showing that consumers view Pretzel Crisps as a brand. This evidence would refute the TTAB's finding of genericness. Some consumers list the brand (Pretzel Crisps) first, followed by the specific flavor they are referencing, such as in the following example: "The Pretzel Crisps pretzel crackers in the buffalo wing flavor is so good." In other posts, consumers argue that "Pretzel Thins" do not compare to Pretzel Crisps, which they refer to as "the real deal." Both posts appear to be evidence of a consumer who views the term Pretzel Crisps as a brand, not a generic term.[61] Ultimately, Snyder's was unsuccessful in defending its trademark. In June 2021, a district court judge ruled "that, on balance, consumers primarily perceive "pretzel crisps" to be a common/generic name."[62]

15.4.3 Other Applications of Social Media Evidence in Trademark Litigation

Social media posts have been offered as evidence in cases involving fame and dilution claims. In *Chanel, Inc. v. Jerzy Makarczyk*, the Chanel fashion house opposed a real estate developer's attempt to register the "Chanel" mark for use in "real estate development and construction of commercial, residential and hotel property."[63] Chanel claimed that the defendant's use of the mark was likely to cause dilution of its famous mark. In its finding that the Chanel mark was famous, the court cited both Chanel's overall social media presence and, more specifically,

---

[59] Complaint, *Snyder's-Lance, Inc. et al. v. Frito-Lay North America, Inc.*, 3:17cv652, US District – Western North Carolina, Nov. 6, 2017.

[60] Snyder's did put forth social media evidence in the case. A non-attorney staff member of the plaintiffs reviewed social media mentions of "Pretzel Crisps" on Twitter from April 1, 2018, through October 24, 2018 and concluded that a majority of tweets (63 percent) "referenced the PRETZEL CRISPS brand in a non-generic fashion." The court found the evidence unconvincing as Snyder's did not submit the coding results or an explanation of how the coder reached his conclusion, included Tweets published fourteen years after the initial trademark application, and included Tweets published by the plaintiffs. Additionally, the judge criticized Snyder's for counting all tweets with plaintiffs' twitter handle (@pretzelcrisps), the hashtag #snackfactory, that reference "Snack Factory," or include an image of Snack Factory products as a reference to the Pretzel Crisps brand. These criticisms reinforce the need for litigants to carefully consider the methodology of a social media analysis. (Opinion, *Snyder's Lance, Inc. v. Frito-Lay North America, Inc.*, 3:17cv652, US District – Western District of North Carolina, Charlotte Division, June 4, 2021.)

[61] We have not attempted to identify posts where consumers use the pretzel crisp term generically and are not offering an opinion as to the volume of such conversation.

[62] Opinion, *Snyder's Lance, Inc. v. Frito-Lay North America, Inc.*

[63] *Chanel, Inc. v. Jerzy Makarczyk*, Opposition No. 91208352, Serial No. 85600670, Trademark Trial and Appeal Board, May 27, 2014.

advertising of the brand on social media. In particular, the court noted that Chanel's Facebook page had 9.5 million fans and was ranked fifth among all fashion brands.

Similarly, in *Bath & Body Works v. Summit Entertainment*, Bath & Body Works sought a declaratory judgment regarding its right to use the term "Twilight" on its personal care products.[64] The defendant, Summit, is a producer and distributor of motion pictures, including the *Twilight* franchise. Summit presented more than 500 blog posts citing actual association of the two brands. The court found that these posts weighed in favor of dilution by blurring.

Consumer complaints posted on social media have also been offered in support of claims of irreparable harm. In *Life Alert Emergency Response v. Lifewatch*, the plaintiff offered social media complaints it received from consumers who had received robocalls from the defendant that made use of the plaintiff's slogan.[65] The appellate court noted that these complaints helped substantiate the threat to the plaintiff's reputation and goodwill and thus supported a finding of irreparable harm.

15.4.4 Quantitative Analysis of Social Media Posts

The cases described primarily demonstrate how qualitative social media posts – anecdotes representing the voice of the consumer – can be compelling evidence in trademark litigation. However, as in the Lance Armstrong and pink-slime cases, *quantitative* analyses of online posts can also be probative in trademark cases. In one recent case, a regional retail chain was attempting to stop a competitor with a similar name from opening stores in its home region. To demonstrate that its trademark was widely recognized by local consumers, the plaintiff commissioned an analysis of social media. About 350,000 posts were identified that mentioned the name of the incumbent retailer, nearly all from its home region. The sheer volume of posts, coupled with individual user comments, provided compelling evidence that the trademark was widely recognized and distinctive throughout the plaintiff's home region.

Some courts have even gone so far as to suggest that a social media analysis is an expected input in the measurement and determination of the strength of a mark. In *Kibler v. Hall*,[66] the musician DJ Logic alleged that another musician who performed under the name "LOGIC" infringed on his trademarked name. The court faulted the plaintiff for failing to present evidence of a substantial following on

---

[64] *Bath & Body Works Brand Mgmt., Inc. v. Summit Entm't, LLC*, 11 Civ. 1594(GBD)(JLC), 2014 US Dist. LEXIS 37700, US District Court – Southern District of New York, Mar. 21, 2014.

[65] *Life Alert Emergency Response, Inc. v. Lifewatch, Inc.*, 2:08-cv-02184-CAS(FFMx), 2014 US Dist. LEXIS 69984, US District Court – Central District of California, May 19, 2014.

[66] Complaint, *Kibler v. Hall, et al.*, 2:14-cv-10017, US District Court – Eastern District of Michigan, Dec. 27, 2013.

Twitter and Facebook, stating that a convincing case should have included evidence from those social media platforms, including counts of "likes," "followers," and "reposts." The court also noted that "promotion on platforms such as Twitter and Facebook not only constitute marketing but is among the most popular and effective advertising strategies today."[67]

In another recent case, *Paramount Farms* v. *Keenan Farms*,[68] the court found that while Facebook popularity did not *conclusively* demonstrate recognition of the associated trade dress, the nearly 300,000 "likes" on the Paramount Farms' Wonderful Pistachios Facebook page lent credibility to the other evidence of fame presented by Paramount Farms.

These examples, and others like them, demonstrate that social media data provide a living and accessible archive, from which data can be marshaled as qualitative and/or quantitative evidence to support or refute the various arguments set forth in intellectual property disputes. The nature of this archive, in terms of its sheer volume and unique temporal qualities, allows it to be leveraged to tell a compelling and understandable narrative to support a litigant's position in many trademark disputes.

15.5 ISSUES TO BE RESOLVED TO MOVE SOCIAL MEDIA ANALYSIS FROM THE PERIPHERY TO THE CENTER OF LITIGATION

15.5.1 *Litigation Applications Lag Developments in the Academic Community and Present New Issues That the Academic Community Has Yet to Solve*

As mentioned, researchers who work with social media data face several challenges that are amplified when the analysis is for use in litigation, where the acceptable margin of error is slim and the degree of scrutiny is high. Today, analyzing social media data with the degree of accuracy to be considered probative in litigation requires at least some time-consuming human assessment of individual posts. In the future, as natural-language-processing techniques to algorithmically draw meaning from language are improved, it may become possible to perform a social media analysis with only minimal human assessment.

An ongoing challenge is that the court's establishment of standardized practices for applying marketing tools in litigation, like those that govern consumer surveys, has not yet occurred for social media. Decisions such as how to identify a suitable population of posts and select a representative sample from this population must still

---

[67] Opinion, *Kibler* v. *Hall, et al.*, 2:14-cv-10017, US Court of Appeals – Sixth Circuit, Dec. 13, 2016, p. 7.

[68] *Paramount Farms Int'l LLC* v. *Keenan Farms Inc.*, 2:12-cv-01463-SVW-E, 2012 US Dist. LEXIS 190634, US District Court – Central District of California, Nov. 28, 2012.

be defended on a case-by-case basis. As the use of social media data in litigation becomes more common and standard practices emerge, litigants will encounter decreased risk of an analysis being excluded for methodological deficiencies.

As previously discussed, social media evidence speaks to the same issues as surveys – consumer perception, opinion, and action – but measures them from a different perspective. Surveys offer structured responses that directly address the key questions in a case from respondents who are pre-screened to ensure they are among the relevant consuming public. Social media analysis offers unstructured data from a wide variety of consumers who might not discuss issues in a manner that is directly probative for the case at hand. Measures of reliability in surveys, such as the demographic representativeness of the sample, will have to be adapted or abandoned altogether when evaluating the reliability of social media evidence.[69]

Part of the standardization process is the development of a concordance between the language of the consumer and the standards of litigation. There is a variety of situations in which questions asked by the courts about consumer opinion, perception, and action do not align with how consumers typically think or speak in the real world. Unsurprisingly, existing marketing research tends not to focus on these types of questions. Consider, for example, the issue of secondary meaning. The legal standard for secondary meaning is as follows: "A developed association in the public's mind between the mark, name, or trade dress of a product and a specific manufacturer originating it that renders the mark, name, or trade dress protectable under trademark law."[70]

Consumers rarely, if ever, discuss brands in a manner that speaks directly to their perception of the origin of the product. However, this does not mean social media is of no value in answering this question. Rather, meaning can be deduced by looking at online conversations that relate to some of the same issues. For instance, in an online post a consumer might mention features of a product that they enjoy, might identify a product in a photo even though there is no brand name visible, or might state their recognition of features only available on one brand's product. Each of these types of comments is suggestive of secondary meaning. For example, the Converse and YETI posts discussed earlier clearly illustrate that the trade dress of these products has acquired secondary meaning.

It is worth noting that the mismatch between the way consumers think and post about products and brands on the one hand, and the legal questions typically asked about consumer beliefs and sentiment on the other, also applies to surveys and other

---

[69] For instance, Schober et al. explicitly differentiate between population coverage, the "extent to which all members of the population are potentially able to be sampled," and topic coverage, the extent to which the data analyzed accurately cover the topics under study. They argue that social media may adequately achieve topic coverage without achieving population coverage. See Schober et al., "Research Synthesis."

[70] "Secondary Meaning," *FindLaw*, https://dictionary.findlaw.com/definition/secondary-meaning.html.

measures of consumer perception. Despite the court's establishment of clear guidelines for survey formats and questions, it is still difficult to design, implement, and interpret a survey that is invulnerable to significant criticisms raised by the opposing side.

15.5.2 Potential Threats to the Growth of Social Media Evidence's Role in Commercial Litigation

Over the last fifteen years, there has been consistent growth in both the breadth and volume of US consumer social media usage.[71] The emerging ubiquity of social media has brought with it increased scrutiny of the privacy practices of companies with large volumes of consumer data, like Facebook and Twitter. Adding to consumers' concerns are the many substantial data breaches suffered by large organizations, such as Equifax (2017), Adobe Systems (2013), Under Armour (2018), JP Morgan Chase (2014), and the US Military (2018). Facebook, in particular, has been caught in the center of multiple privacy scandals, most notably the 2018 Cambridge Analytica data leak.[72]

Although the long-term effects of scandals like this are unknown, Facebook and Instagram have taken steps to limit third-party data access in reaction to the revelations. Facebook, Instagram, and Twitter have frequently changed their policies towards data access, often without public notice. This erratic approach makes it difficult to access data regularly and reliably. Newer networks, such as TikTok, have also launched with more restrictive data access than any of the other major platforms. It is unclear whether this is the beginning of a larger, industry-wide trend towards more restrictions on third-party access to social data.

Changing political and business conditions, regulatory rulings, technological advancements, and shifting consumer attitudes are also factors that could alter the amount and makeup of data available in the long term.[73] For instance, in the runup to, and following, the 2020 presidential election, social media platforms took several

---

[71] Perrin, A., "Social Networking Usage: 2005–2015," *Pew Research Center*, Oct. 2015, www.pewinternet.org/2015/10/08/2015/Social-Networking-Usage-2005-2015/. See also Smith, A., and Anderson, M., "Social Media Use in 2018," *Pew Research Center*, Mar. 2018, www.pewinternet.org/2018/03/01/social-media-use-in-2018/.

[72] Granville, K., "Facebook and Cambridge Analytica: What You Need to Know as Fallout Widens," *NY Times*, Mar. 19, 2018, www.nytimes.com/2018/03/19/technology/facebook-cambridge-analytica-explained.html.

[73] In the wake of the data breaches, new regulations have been implemented such as the *EU General Data Protection Regulation* (GDPR) and the *California Consumer Privacy Act* (CCPA) to elevate the protection of personal data. The GDPR went into effect in May 2018 and defines personal data broadly and puts the individual at the center of data protection. It is designed to give EU residents the right to know and decide how their personal data is being used, stored, protected, transferred, and deleted. Individuals have the right to restrict further processing and to request that all their data be erased, known more commonly as "the right to be forgotten." The CCPA grants California consumers similar rights but defines personal

steps that limited access to social media content: Instagram limited users' ability to search for recent posts when searching for specific hashtags;[74] Facebook removed posts it believed were promoting misleading information;[75] and Twitter suspended many high-profile accounts (most notably, President Trump's) and more than 70,000 accounts that it determined were spreading misinformation associated with the QAnon conspiracy theory.[76] It is too early to tell what short-term and long-term impact these measures had and will have on the way consumers engage with these platforms and on third parties' access to data.

Any sustained effort to limit third-party access to social data will limit its value in commercial litigation. However, rulings involving third-party access will not prevent parties from demanding access to one another's social media history, including consumer communications and comments, in the discovery process. While some platforms such as Facebook and Google have developed sophisticated advertising models that limit clients' direct exposure to data, it is important to note that the business models of other social media platform providers depend on their ability to provide third-party access to at least aggregate or anonymized data, so there is some convergence of interests around the goal of maintaining data access.

The courts have become involved in some cases where third-party organizations have had their data access revoked by a social media platform. Although a number of these types of cases have been decided in trial, there remains no clear consensus on what limits social media platforms can place on third-party data access.[77]

information more explicitly including any "inferences drawn from any of the information identified."

[74] Carman, A., "Instagram Nixes the 'Recent' Tab from Hashtag Pages ahead of Election," *The Verge*, Oct. 30, 2020, www.theverge.com/2020/10/30/21541939/instagram-recent-hashtag-tab-election-2020; https://twitter.com/InstagramComms/status/1321957713476280320.

[75] Guy, R., "Our Preparations ahead of Inauguration Day," *Facebook*, Jan. 11, 2021, https://about.fb.com/news/2021/01/preparing-for-inauguration-day/; Guy, R., "Our Response to the Violence in Washington," *Facebook*, Jan. 6, 2021, https://about.fb.com/news/2021/01/responding-to-the-violence-in-washington-dc/.

[76] "An Update Following the Riots in Washington, DC," *Twitter*, Jan. 12, 2021, https://blog.twitter.com/en_us/topics/company/2021/protecting-the-conversation-following-the-riots-in-washington-.html.

[77] Two of the most important decisions were issued in a pair of cases involving major social media networks: Facebook in *Facebook* v. *Vachani*, and LinkedIn in *hiQ Labs* v. *LinkedIn*. In *Facebook* v. *Vachani*, a long-running dispute regarding the right for a social aggregator, Power.com, to scrape Facebook user data, the court found in favor of Facebook, stating that Power "accessed Facebook's computers 'without authorization' within the meaning of the CFAA and is liable under that statute." (*Facebook, Inc.* v. *Power Ventures, Inc.*, 844 F.3d 1058, 2016 US App. LEXIS 21944, US Court of Appeals – Ninth Circuit, Dec. 9, 2015.) In *hiQ Labs* v. *LinkedIn*, a more recent case that focused similarly on a third party's right to scrape user data from social media platforms, an appeals court twice affirmed the lower court's order and found in favor of hiQ Labs' claim that LinkedIn had tortiously interfered with hiQ Labs' customer contracts by attempting to block hiQ Labs' access to LinkedIn data. However, in November 2022, the United States District Court for the Northern District of California dismissed hiQ Labs' claim of tortious interference on the technical basis of litigation privilege. On the other

Consumer use of and attitude towards social media in the long term are also potential threats to the availability and quality of social media data. Privacy concerns may lead consumers to shift away from public channels of communication (such as a Twitter post on a public account) to semiprivate (such as a Facebook post on a friend's wall) or private channels (such as a direct message sent on Instagram or Snapchat, or messaging platforms such as Telegram). Consumers also may opt to "protect" public accounts such that only approved users can view their content.[78]

A final consideration is the extent to which consumers continue to post publicly but do so under a pseudonym. Online forums like Reddit typically display no personally identifying information alongside a post, and other more traditional social media sites like Twitter do not require users to create accounts linked to their real identities. Anonymized content can still be a valuable measure of consumer opinion, especially when viewed in the aggregate. However, the analysis of anonymous posts poses unique challenges. Perhaps the most pervasive issue is that of authenticity – how can an anonymous online post be traced back to a genuine consumer who is expressing a genuine opinion?[79]

The proliferation of influencers and other kinds of undisclosed promotional activity, such as fake reviews,[80] can call into question whether a post or product review represents a user's independent judgment or is simply the product of a brand's marketing campaign. Similarly, the issue of whether or not a post can be traced back to a genuine consumer has received widespread media coverage after Russian social media campaigns were found to have attempted to influence the 2016 US presidential election.[81] While Twitter claimed in 2020 that they have seen

---

hand, the court denied a motion for summary judgment on a counterclaim of breach of contract by LinkedIn that asserted that hiQ Labs had violated LinkedIn's terms of service. While the court granted LinkedIn's summary judgment with respect to hiQ Lab's use of fake accounts ("turkers") as part of its scraping operations, it denied the motion with respect to hiQ Lab's scraping and using of scraped data because the court found that there remained genuine disputes of material facts regarding hiQ Labs' affirmative waiver and estoppel defenses. The two parties reached a confidential settlement on December 6, 2022, leaving case law related to data scraping unsettled.

[78] Major social media platforms do not release data on the split between public and private communications, so it is unclear to what extent, if any, this type of shift is occurring.

[79] In *QVC v. Your Vitamins*, the court outlined the issue succinctly, stating that "blog posts ... may be more reliable than broad-based surveys, insofar as they represent direct feedback from consumers specifically interested in the product(s) at issue, although concerns regarding such posts' authenticity are not ill-founded." (*QVC, Inc. v. Your Vitamins, Inc.*, Civ. No. 10-094-SLR, 714 F. Supp. 2d 291, 2010 US Dist. LEXIS 76073, July 27, 2010.)

[80] See, for instance, Schoolov, K., "Amazon Is Filled with Fake Reviews and It's Getting Harder to Spot Them," *CNBC*, Sept. 6, 2020, www.cnbc.com/2020/09/06/amazon-reviews-thousands-are-fake-heres-how-to-spot-them.html; and Proserpio, D., et al., "How Fake Customer Reviews Do – and Don't – Work," *Harvard Business Review*, Nov. 24, 2020, https://hbr.org/2020/11/how-fake-customer-reviews-do-and-dont-work.

[81] See, for example, Confessore, N., et al., "The Follower Factory," *New York Times*, Jan. 27, 2018, www.nytimes.com/interactive/2018/01/27/technology/social-media-bots.html.

"significant gains in tackling" the "malicious use of automation,"[82] an estimate from 2017 found that between 9 and 15 percent of active Twitter accounts were bots.[83] Unfortunately, there is no agreed-upon definition of what constitutes a bot,[84] making it difficult to evaluate different claims about the prevalence of bots on Twitter and other social media platforms.

However, the challenge of demonstrating the authenticity of evidence is not a problem that is unique to social media. Consumer surveys, especially those conducted online, are vulnerable to consumers who misrepresent themselves or do not offer thoughtful and truthful responses. Most surveys now employed in commercial litigation involve no person-to-person contact between the survey taker and survey administrator. Furthermore, the nature of survey questions in litigation is such that respondents are often able to surmise the purpose of the survey from the questions. This can bias their responses toward ones that they believe will please the survey administrator.[85] Respondents are also known to provide responses designed to make themselves look good.[86]

Of course, all measures of consumer opinion are potentially subject to bias from outside influences. Attempts to bias consumer opinions existed long before the Internet or social media came to be. For example, the practice of "astroturfing" has a long history.[87] Astroturfing has expanded well beyond organizations simply taking sides on an issue without revealing who is backing them and driving their

[82] Roth, Y., and Pickles N., "Bot or Not? The Facts about Platform Manipulation on Twitter," *Twitter*, May 18, 2020, https://blog.twitter.com/en_us/topics/company/2020/bot-or-not.html
[83] Varol, O., et al., "Online Human–Bot Interactions: Detection, Estimation, and Characterization," *International AAAI Conference on Web and Social Media*, Montreal, Quebec, May 15–18, 2017. Twitter has testified that roughly 5 percent of its accounts are run by bots. Facebook has estimated that 2 percent of its average monthly users may be fake and that 10 percent are duplicate accounts, meaning they are not a user's main account. See Essaid, R., "Commentary: The War against Bad Bots Is Coming. Are We Ready?" *Fortune*, Feb. 26, 2018, http://fortune.com/2018/02/26/russian-bots-twitter-facebook-trump-memo/.
[84] Orabi, Mariam, et al., "Detection of Bots in Social Media: A Systematic Review," *Information Processing & Management*, Vol. 57, No. 4, 1–23, July 2020. See also Roth and Pickles, "Bot or Not?"
[85] This is known as subject or participant bias. See, for discussion, Diamond, "Reference Guide on Survey Research," pp. 410–11.
[86] This is known as social desirability bias. Paulhus, D. L., "Measurement and Control of Response Bias." In J. P. Robinson, P. R. Shaver, and L. S. Wrightsman (Eds.), *Measures of Social Psychological Attitudes, Vol. 1. Measures of Personality and Social Psychological Attitudes*, Academic Press, 1991, pp. 17–59.
[87] Astroturfing refers to the practice of making a sponsored message appear as if it originated at the grassroots level. Shakespeare refers to this practice of falsely creating the impression of a grassroots movement in *Julius Caesar* (Act 1, Scene 2), where Cassius writes fake letters from the public to convince Brutus to assassinate Caesar. In business, the practice dates back to at least the early 1900s, when Dixie Cup anonymously circulated a pamphlet called *The Cup Campaigner* warning of the dangers of drinking from public drinking cups. Another well-known example of astroturfing was the National Smokers Alliance, which was formed in 1993 by the tobacco industry to oppose regulations limiting the ability of adults to smoke freely. Beder, S., "Public Relations' Role in Manufacturing Artificial Grass Roots Coalitions," *Public Relations Quarterly*, Vol. 43, No. 2, 1998, pp. 21–23.

agendas. Organizations have used such tactics as buying expert opinion and hiring individual citizens to express the organization's view in public. In fact, today it is even possible for an organization to hire an entire crowd to express its views and create the illusion of grassroots support for its position.[88] One goal of these illusory grassroots movements is to influence general public opinion, which will, in turn, show up in such measures of public opinion as surveys and social media analyses.

Given this history, courts have long needed to assess the authenticity of evidence about public opinion, including who may have clouded public opinion about an issue with misleading and disingenuous contributions to public discussions. Similarly, witnesses have lied, and paper documents have been forged, altered, or misrepresented since the first courts began taking evidence. Thus, developing the means to demonstrate the authenticity of social media evidence is but the latest step in the long process of evidentiary standard setting.

It is possible to mitigate some of the challenges in identifying and removing inauthentic content in the context of litigation. Depending on the nature of the case, the veracity and origin of individual posts may be important. In these instances, it is often possible to find details about a user that increase the degree of confidence in a post's authenticity or relevance from metadata or an account's historical activity. Of course, for large-scale analyses, it is not feasible to apply a high degree of scrutiny to each post, so other techniques such as statistical sampling with manual review and machine learning can be useful for identifying automated or inauthentic content.[89] The release of the Federal Trade Commission's disclosure guidelines specifically for social media influencers can also help to limit the proliferation of inauthentic content. The guidelines require users to disclose whether they have a "financial, employment, personal, or family relationship with a brand."[90] Platforms have also developed tools that make it easier to identify promoted content[91] and have worked to remove fake content.[92] Additionally, it can be helpful to confirm

---

[88] See, for example, https://crowdsondemand.com.

[89] For a review of different techniques used to identify automated content on social media, see Orabi et al., "Detection of Bots in Social Media." Some companies, such as Botometer and Bot Sentinel, have released publicly available tools that claim to identify Twitter bots using machine learning. Before relying on these tools or attempting to develop their own, researchers should understand the assumptions and operational definitions built into the development of these tools, what labeled data was used to develop a supervised or semi-supervised machine-learning algorithm or to validate the efficacy of the tool, and whether a tool is appropriate across different platforms.

[90] "Disclosures 101 for Social Media Influencers," *Federal Trade Commission*, Nov. 2019, www.ftc.gov/system/files/documents/plain-language/1001a-influencer-guide-508_1.pdf.

[91] "Branded Content Tools on Instagram," *Instagram Business*, https://business.instagram.com/a/brandedcontentexpansion; Salem, M., "A New, Optional Feature for Paid Promotion Disclosure," *YouTube Official Blog*, Oct. 4, 2016, https://blog.youtube/news-and-events/a-new-optional-feature-for-paid.

[92] Tung, L., "Fake Reviews: Facebook and eBay Ban Dozens of Groups after Watchdog Probe," *ZDNet*, Jan. 8, 2020, www.zdnet.com/google-amp/article/fake-reviews-facebook-and-ebay-ban-dozens-of-groups-after-watchdog-probe/; Schiffer, Z., "Amazon Is Trying to Crack Down on

through discovery that litigants have not seeded social media with inauthentic content and, if they have, what specific content should be removed from any analysis of genuine consumer posts.

Clearly, social media analysts must be vigilant in establishing reasonable safeguards to identify and remove inauthentic content and take care to remain apprised of new developments for doing so in the academic, business, and social-research communities. As marketers, social researchers, data scientists, and attorneys collaborate to address these problems in the world of high-stakes litigation, they may develop techniques that are useful well beyond the confines of litigation. While litigation is, perhaps, the context in which confirming the veracity of social media data is most crucial, all types of users of social media data will benefit from these efforts, including the marketing community as a whole.

15.6 CONCLUSION

For the first time in human history, we can listen in on millions of past and current consumer conversations, thanks to the phenomenon of social media. Social media sites collect posts that reveal people's reflections, motivations, and reactions. Readers of these posts can understand other people's thinking in a way that has never been possible before. Naturally, the business and political worlds have jumped on this new power. Marketers use social media to broadcast their messages but also to listen to their customers. Politicians have aggressively used social media to communicate with their followers within moments of any event, to gauge voter and opposition reaction and, of course, to raise money.

As perhaps ought to be the case, the courts have moved a little more deliberately in embracing social media. As social media becomes better understood and more widely studied and used, its use in litigation will almost certainly broaden. However, as with any other kind of evidence, the usefulness of social media evidence will be dictated by the science behind its analysis and the quality of the analysis (and analysts) employing it. And in that regard, social media evidence is no different from fingerprinting, DNA testing, or opinion surveying. All these types of evidence have become more common, perhaps even commonplace, but not before being proven reliable. And still, none of these three is above vigorous debate and rebuttal.

In any legal case in which evidence about the opinions or thinking of people would be useful, social media evidence might be able to provide powerful insights, as it is spontaneous, natural, and unsolicited. While it can be tainted by "bots" and deliberate manipulation, there are increasingly clever ways to detect and remedy any taint. And, as a failsafe, social media evidence will always be open to scrutiny from

Fraudulent Reviews. They're Thriving in Facebook Groups," *The Verge*, Oct. 2, 2020, www.theverge.com/2020/10/2/21497416/amazon-crack-down-fraudulent-reviews-facebook-wechat-groups; Roth and Pickles, "Bot or Not?,"

the opposing party, which, increasingly, will employ its own social media experts to provide just such a rebuttal.

Furthermore, there are now lawsuits being filed that can be thought of as pure social media matters. For example, we know of a case involving a well-known entertainment executive in which the claim is that he was defamed on Twitter. In this case, and others like it, evidence of harm (or lack of harm) is largely drawn from social media. In such cases, the parties have no choice but to consider social media evidence.

There remain, however, challenges to be overcome. Applying social media analysis to the sometimes esoteric questions that are currently asked in litigation remains a difficult process that may best be solved by an overhaul to the very questions themselves. As these complex techniques mature and start to be relied upon by litigants, the courts will need to develop a thoughtful system to differentiate reliable social media evidence from junk science.

The science of social media analysis is progressing at a rapid pace, and its use in court is expanding. Litigants ignore the use of social media at their peril. Furthermore, the choice of how to use social media evidence and the skill with which the analysis is executed are critical to its usefulness and persuasiveness. Eventually, perhaps, social media evidence will be as common as opinion surveys in cases involving consumer opinion and behavior. Given the large and diverse group of people who are now expressing themselves through social media on an ever-increasing range of topics and to larger and larger audiences, the power of listening in on the electronic conversations captured in social media has become irresistible. The question now is not whether to listen, but how.

PART IV

How the Law Protects

16

Law as Persuasion

Bert I. Huang[*]

When does the law persuade us about what is right or wrong – and when does it not? On topics ranging from racial equality to abortion to same-sex marriage, historians have debated and puzzled over the law's persuasive force on our collective moral intuitions. Meanwhile, other scholars have sought out individual-level insights into the psychology of law's persuasion, under the microscope of controlled experiments.

This chapter presents evidence of the law's influence on our moral intuitions in a survey experiment based on a classic dilemma known as the "trolley problem," in which someone must make a choice about whether to turn a runaway train, actively harming one person but saving more people by doing so. This sacrificial dilemma is a familiar reference in legal and policy discussions of harm–harm trade-offs, or "tragic choices."[1] Such a scenario is also well-suited for studying the law's possible influence, as it is not an easy moral call, and "[e]specially under conditions of uncertainty, people look for information in their environment that provide credible clues for making judgments."[2] In the trolley problem, such uncertainty occurs not because our moral intuitions are weak or amorphous; rather, it is because forceful intuitions are set in contest: we must save more people, and yet we must not actively cause anyone harm.

In this study, survey subjects are presented with an identical story posing a trolley-like dilemma; the only thing that varies in what they read is information about what

---

[*] I wish to thank Andrew Bradt, Jacob Gersen, Michael Gilbert, Maeve Glass, Mark Greenberg, Scott Hemphill, William Hubbard, Jason Scott Johnston, Frances Kamm, Daryl Levinson, Trevor Morrison, Anne Joseph O'Connell, Adam Samaha, Lior Strahilevitz, Kathryn Tabb, and workshop participants at Berkeley, Columbia, Harvard, New York University, the Paul & Daisy Soros Conference, the University of Chicago, and the University of Virginia for helpful suggestions and for the chance to present this work at earlier stages. For research support I thank Columbia Law School and the Parker School Global Innovation Award; and for excellent research assistance, I thank Rebecca Arno, Thomas Enering, and Tim Wang.
[1] See e.g. GUIDO CALABRESI & PHILIP BOBBITT, TRAGIC CHOICES (1978).
[2] Kenworthey Bilz & Janice Nadler, *Law, Psychology, and Morality*, 50 PSYCHOL. OF LEARNING AND MOTIVATION 101, 108 (2009).

the law says: some are told that the law requires turning the train, others that the law forbids it. Extending prior work using a similar design to present evidence that the law can influence our moral intuitions about such a dilemma,[3] this experiment introduces new variations aimed at drawing out further insights about when and how such persuasion is likely, or not. In particular, these variations differ in the law's morally relevant content (for example, one is a law that does not address the issue of harm) and in how the law is characterized (some conditions name specific crimes, while others describe liability in a more abstract way).

The findings show that telling subjects about the law can influence their moral intuitions about this sacrificial dilemma. Comparing results across the variations, however, suggests inferences that run counter to a simplistic account of how persuasive we might expect a law to be. First, there is evidence of law's influence on moral intuitions even when the law does not expressly address harm, which is the core issue in the dilemma. Second, there is more evidence of influence for the conditions that describe liability in an abstract way than for those that name specific crimes; and, based on the subjects' responses about which laws they deemed "unfair," one might speculate that for some subjects the specific-crime characterization prompted more of an adverse reaction. Future study of such potentially anti-persuasive reactions may draw guidance both from the legal literature on the legitimacy or moral credibility of the law, as well as from an allied framework in the consumer psychology literature, focusing on the concept of reactance.

16.1 THE EXPERIMENT

Each survey subject is presented with a vignette that is identical except for a randomized segment describing what the law says. The scenario begins, for all subjects:

> Michael is a railroad engineer. One day, while he is working near the train tracks, he notices a freight train approaching. The train seems out of control. Michael can see that the driver is slumped over, unconscious.
>
> There are two workmen on the tracks ahead. The train is now rushing towards them. They don't see the train coming, and Michael can't get their attention. He yells at them, but the construction noise is too loud. He waves his arms, but they are looking the other way.
>
> Michael happens to be standing near a railroad switch. He can reach it easily, and he knows that pulling the switch will turn the train onto a side track before it hits the two workmen.
>
> However, there is another workman on this side track. He also doesn't see or hear the train coming, and Michael can't get his attention either.
>
> Michael can choose to pull the switch, or he can choose not to do anything.

[3] Bert I. Huang, *Law and Moral Dilemmas*, 130 HARV. L. REV. 659 (2016).

If Michael pulls the switch, he knows that the man on the side track will be seriously injured by the train.

If Michael doesn't do anything, he knows that the two men on the main track will be seriously injured by the train.

A single randomized statement about the law is then appended to the end of the scenario. The law conditions are phrased as follows (without the title shown in brackets below). First, there are three conditions that state legal liability in a more abstract way, as "breaking the law":

{**Don't harm**}
There is a law saying that Michael (who works for the railroad) must not cause harm to anyone on the tracks. This means that if he pulls the switch, he will be held liable for breaking the law. If he doesn't do anything, he won't be held liable.

{**Not authorized**}
There is a law saying that Michael (who works for the railroad) must not change the path of a train without prior authorization. This means that if he pulls the switch, he will be held liable for breaking the law. If he doesn't do anything, he won't be held liable.

{**Duty to act**}
There is a law saying that Michael (who works for the railroad) must try to reduce casualties from accidents. This means that if he does nothing, he will be held liable for breaking the law. If he pulls the switch, he won't be held liable.

There are also two conditions that state legal liability in a specific way, naming the exact crime:

{**Criminal assault**}
There is a law saying that Michael (who works for the railroad) must not cause harm to anyone on the tracks. This means that if he pulls the switch, he will be held liable for criminal assault and battery. If he doesn't do anything, he won't be held liable.

{**Criminal negligence**}
There is a law saying that Michael (who works for the railroad) must try to reduce casualties from accidents. This means that if he does nothing, he will be held liable for criminal negligence. If he pulls the switch, he won't be held liable.

After reading this story, with the law condition appended, each subject is then asked to evaluate the morality of pulling the switch, by answering whether it is "morally prohibited," "morally permissible," or "morally required." These three options follow standard terminology in moral philosophy,[4] and this choice set has been used in prior experimental work.[5]

---

[4] See e.g. FRANCIS M. KAMM, THE TROLLEY PROBLEM MYSTERIES (2015).
[5] Huang, *supra* note 3.

16.2 MECHANISMS OF PERSUASION

The {Don't harm}, {Not authorized}, and {Criminal assault} conditions are legal prohibitions against pulling the switch, and the {Duty to act} and {Criminal negligence} conditions are legal requirements to pull the switch. The most natural opposing pairs with parallel phrasing are the {Don't harm} and {Duty to act} conditions, which state liability in more abstract terms; and the {Criminal assault} and {Criminal negligence} conditions, which name specific crimes. Note, however, that I did not include a bureaucratic duty to set against the bureaucratic prohibition, {Not authorized}, because I did not settle on a phrasing that I thought subjects would likely find to be a plausible rule requiring the engineer to turn the train for a technical reason;[6] still, the {Not authorized} condition can be contrasted with the {Duty to act} condition, given their parallel abstract phrasing of liability.

The main prediction for these comparisons between paired opposing legal conditions is that the law will exert an influential pull on moral judgments in the direction aligned with the law's command. This influence could appear in the observations in two ways: First, it could appear as a greater share of subjects saying that pulling the switch is "morally prohibited" in the {Don't harm} and {Not authorized} conditions than in the {Duty to act} condition; and, likewise, more saying so in the {Criminal assault} condition than in the {Criminal negligence} condition. Second, it could appear as a greater share of subjects answering "morally required" in the {Duty to act} condition than in the {Don't harm} and {Not authorized} conditions; and more saying so in the {Criminal negligence} than in the {Criminal assault} condition. There are no obvious expectations about the share answering "morally permissible" because each directional influence can both increase and decrease that share (depending on how many people shift in from "morally required" versus how many shift out to "morally prohibited," or vice versa).

Various psychological mechanisms of persuasion may play a role in law's influence on people's moral intuitions about such a dilemma. What follows is a rough-and-ready articulation of possible mechanisms, drawn from the literature on compliance effects as well as on attitude change,[7] and grouped for convenience

---

[6] One might imagine, for instance, that the central character Michael was already tasked with pulling the switch because the side track is actually the correct path for the train; however, this would sound odd in the context of a train running out of control and might introduce a mystery about why the "correct" track still has a worker obliviously standing on it.

[7] See e.g. Bilz & Nadler, *supra* at note 2; Robert Cooter, *Expressive Law and Economics*, 27 J. OF LEGAL STUD. 585 (1998); Dan M. Kahan, *Social Influence, Social Meaning, and Deterrence*, 83 VA. L. REV. 349 (1997); Richard H. McAdams, *The Origin, Development, and Regulation of Norms*, 96 MICH. L. REV. 338 (1997); Cass R. Sunstein, *Social Norms and Social Roles*, 96 COLUM. L. REV. 903 (1996); TOM R. TYLER, WHY PEOPLE OBEY THE LAW (2006).

in a way that corresponds to differing modes of persuasion. Before proceeding, it is worth emphasizing upfront that people likely vary in their responsiveness to the various mechanisms;[8] the outcomes in this study can only reveal aggregate net effects.

1. **Informational.** The potential mechanisms in this group should only be active when the content of the law directly concerns the regulation of harm, and is thus relevant to the harm–harm trade-off at the core of the moral dilemma.

* *Law offers direct moral guidance.*
* *Law supplies morally relevant reasoning.*
* *Law serves as social proof or an indicator of societal norms.*

2. **Functional.** A second group are those that operate because the law is the law, and may be active even if the law does not concern the regulation of harm in a way directly relevant to the dilemma.

* *Law defines social roles, acting as a coordination device.*
* *Law sets a default about what is normally expected to happen.*
* *Obeying the law is morally good.*
* *The suffering of liability is a morally relevant cost.*

3. **Arbitrary.** One further possibility is that the law condition mindlessly breaks the tie, as a coin flip might. Should such an undiscerning mechanism be important, there should be signs of influence in all of the law conditions.

If one assumes that the informational or functional mechanisms differ in strength among the conditions, then comparisons among the conditions' effects may offer suggestive evidence for sorting among the mechanisms. For example, it seems a plausible assumption that the {Not authorized} prohibition is less likely to be viewed by subjects as providing direct moral information about the harm–harm trade-off. Thus, if the primary pathways of law's influence are those in the informational group, then the {Not authorized} condition should show less influence than the {Don't harm} condition, or possibly none at all. But if the {Not authorized} condition does show some influence, this may be a sign that other mechanisms are at work; for example, the functional group of mechanisms may be engaged.

It also seems sensible to expect that both the informational and functional groups of mechanisms would be active in the {Don't harm}, {Duty to act}, {Criminal

---

[8] Moreover, the subjects who are near one margin (say, those torn between saying "morally prohibited" and "morally permitted") may respond differently than those at the other (those torn between saying "morally permitted" and "morally required").

assault}, and {Criminal negligence} conditions, but that some of these mechanisms might be engaged more by the specifically criminalized conditions. If so, it may be possible to sort between the two groups or even among the mechanisms within each group. For instance, the law conditions imposing criminal liability may induce subjects to weigh the moral cost of liability more than the law conditions stating liability abstractly might.[9] Or, it may be plausible to assume that the expressly criminalized liability of the {Criminal assault} or {Criminal negligence} conditions would send a stronger signal of societal norms than the {Don't harm} or {Duty to act} conditions, respectively – but may not offer more morally relevant reasoning, given that the underlying harm principle is the same.

16.3 PRIOR IMPRESSIONS

A further condition included in this experiment is the train scenario on its own, without any additional statement about the law. The subjects' moral judgments in this {No statement} condition can be understood as reflecting the background impressions about the law they may already be holding even when not told anything. Note that this condition should *not* be understood as stating that no relevant laws exist, or of stating that there will be no liability. Rather, the differences between the moral judgments in the {No statement} condition and those in the various law conditions should be interpreted as the effect of telling subjects what the law says, relative to leaving them to their own prior impressions about what the law says. There are no useful predictions to be made, for comparisons between this condition and the others, because interpreting these responses depends on what prior impressions subjects may be holding about the law when not told anything more; rather, it is more sensible to view these results as an indicator of where those prior impressions lie.

16.4 SURVEY POPULATION

The survey subjects are adults in the United States recruited by the survey firm SurveyMonkey, which approximated age and gender distributions based on the census. They were paid neither a piece rate nor a time-based wage; however, they were rewarded with either a small donation to a charity or an entry in a sweepstake for a small prize. The following subjects were excluded: anyone who did not complete the survey or who said that they could not take it seriously; anyone who had taken another survey recently about a similar trolley-problem dilemma; anyone

---

[9] Results from a prior experiment suggested the possibility that the law's influence on moral judgment may be more pronounced when the law condition says that liability will follow than when it says that the law will not be enforced. Huang, *supra* note 3, at 694–95.

TABLE 16.1. *Saving two by sacrificing one*

	Morally prohibited	Morally permissible	Morally required	N
Breaking the law				
Don't harm	18.8%	56.8%	24.4%	176
Not authorized	17.5%	55.2%	27.3%	194
Duty to act	4.1%	51.8%	44.1%	195
Specific crime				
Criminal assault	12.9%	63.2%	23.9%	209
Criminal negligence	5.8%	62.8%	31.4%	191
Prior impressions				
No statement	12.9%	59.1%	28.1%	171

who failed a comprehension question; and anyone who had attended law school or and taken courses in moral philosophy.

16.5 RESULTS

The outcomes are seen in Table 16.1. Two basic sets of comparisons are analyzed here. The first considers whether varying the content of the law makes a difference in people's moral judgments – this is the primary indicator of law's influence. The second considers the subjects' preexisting background impressions about the law, by seeing which conditions' statements about the law seem to shift subjects' moral judgments relative to leaving them with their prior impressions.

1. **Comparing across laws.** The observed differences across law conditions can be interpreted as evidence that informing people about different legal commands results in different distributions of moral intuitions – in other words, it matters what the law says. The reported differences are statistically significant at the conventional level unless otherwise noted.

To begin with pairwise contrasts among opposing laws, first we may consider the three law conditions that phrase liability in a more abstract way (as "breaking the law"). Between the {Don't harm} and {Duty to act} conditions, the share of subjects saying that pulling the switch is "morally prohibited" falls from 19 percent to 4 percent;[10] and "morally required" rises from 24 percent to 44 percent.[11] Between the {Not authorized} and {Duty to act} conditions, the share saying "morally

---

[10] $\chi^2(1, N = 371) = 20.19, p < 0.001$.
[11] $\chi^2(1, N = 371) = 15.782, p < 0.001$.

prohibited" falls from 18 percent to 4 percent;[12] and "morally required" rises from 27 percent to 44 percent.[13] Turning to the conditions in which specific crimes are named: between the {Criminal assault} and {Criminal negligence} conditions, the share saying "morally prohibited" falls from 13 percent to 6 percent.[14] Yet, although the share saying "morally required" seems to rise from 24 percent to 31 percent, we cannot say so with conventional statistical confidence;[15] this result will be discussed in more detail later in this chapter.

2. **Comparing with prior impressions.** Comparing the law conditions with the {No statement} condition tests for differences between subjects' moral judgments when they are told about a specific legal command, relative to their moral judgments as possibly informed by any original impressions they may have about the law. Again, note that the {No statement} condition should not be seen as representing the subjects' "pure" moral sense, as if absent any influence from preexisting impressions about the law – to the contrary, this measure reflects those prior impressions, whether consciously or unconsciously held.[16]

Not surprisingly, it appears that the subjects' moral judgments as informed by their original impressions about the law lie somewhere in between their judgments as influenced by the legal extremes presented in the experimental conditions. The 13 percent share saying "morally prohibited" in the {No statement} condition does not differ in a statistically significant way from any of the law conditions against pulling the switch; but there are significant drops to the 4 percent in the {Duty to act} condition,[17] and to the 6 percent in the {Criminal negligence} condition,[18] the conditions requiring pulling the switch. Similarly, the 28 percent share saying "morally required" shows a statistically significant difference only with the {Duty to act} condition, rising to 44 percent.[19] Given these measurements, one might speculate that the subjects' prior impressions about the law on average lie somewhat closer to expecting that the law prohibits pulling the switch. But other speculative interpretations are also possible; for instance, the duty-imposing law conditions may tend to exert more influence for the subjects who find them informative.

---

[12] $\chi^2(1, N = 389) = 18.194, p < 0.001$.
[13] $\chi^2(1, N = 389) = 11.928, p < 0.001$.
[14] $\chi^2(1, N = 400) = 5.95, p = 0.015$.
[15] This difference is not statistically significant, under the conventional $p = 0.05$ cutoff. $\chi^2(1, N = 400) = 2.808, p = 0.094$.
[16] Note, however, that even if a subject would express a different moral judgment in the {No statement} condition than in a specific law condition, this does not necessarily mean that the subject's prior impression about the law differs from the specific legal command; another possibility is that the strength of the law's influence is altered by drawing conscious attention to it.
[17] $\chi^2(1, N = 366) = 9.297, p = 0.002$.
[18] $\chi^2(1, N = 362) = 5.499, p = 0.019$.
[19] $\chi^2(1, N = 366) = 10.091, p = 0.001$.

16.6 PERSUASION – AND REACTANCE?

Overall, the contrasts between opposing law conditions offer evidence that telling people different things about the law can influence their intuitions about this moral dilemma. Two findings are worth exploring in more depth, as one offers suggestive evidence about the possible mechanisms of persuasion at work, and the other may generate hypotheses for future study relating to the possibility of psychological reactance.

First, the {Not authorized} condition shows as much evidence of influence as {Don't harm}, even though the former's rationale is not expressly related to the core issue in the dilemma, the harm–harm trade-off. Second, the contrasts between the conditions naming specific crimes, {Criminal assault} and {Criminal negligence}, offer less evidence of law's influence on moral intuitions than do the contrasts involving the {Don't harm}, the {Not authorized}, and the {Duty to act} conditions, all of which phrase legal liability in a more abstract way (as "breaking the law").

1. Mechanisms? The {Not authorized} condition does not purport to offer any moral guidance or reasoning about the harm–harm trade-off, much less supply any signal about relevant societal norms. And yet its impact seems similar to that of {Don't harm}, in that their contrasts with the opposing {Duty to act} condition are similar.[20] One might thus speculate that one or more persuasive mechanisms in the functional group are active.[21] For instance, some subjects may defer to such a law as defining the actor's role within the system, or as a coordination device that helps to ensure overall safety; such deference might seem especially sensible in the unfamiliar context of a railroad engineer's decision. Or some subjects may count the threat of sanctions or other collateral consequences as a proper part of the actor's own moral calculus (maybe thinking of the harm to his family should he lose his job). Or some subjects may feel it is moral to obey the law, even when the law is based on a procedural technicality.[22]

---

[20] But there is statistical uncertainty around each point estimate, of course, and there is not enough statistical power given this sample size to say that these estimates are "close" in a statistically meaningful way (such as showing a narrow confidence interval around zero for their difference).

[21] Note that although the {Not authorized} versus {Duty to act} contrast does provide evidence of the law's influence, allocating each condition's contribution to the gap would require a measure of the subjects' "natural" moral judgments in the absence of any preexisting influence from prior impressions about the law; no such measure is presented here. (Again, the {No statement} condition does not provide such a measure; to the contrary, it captures those prior impressions.) Thus it is possible that only the {Duty to act} condition is responsible for the gap; the discussion above relies on the pure assumption that the {Not authorized} and {Don't harm} conditions also contribute.

[22] For some subjects, this condition may engage the moral value of respect for authority or hierarchy. See Jonathan Haidt, *The New Synthesis in Moral Psychology*, 316 SCIENCE 998 (2007).

An alternative interpretation, however, is that some subjects may see the {Not authorized} condition as morally informative about harm (though it does not expressly address harm) on the assumption that the rule is rooted in a concern that unauthorized changes to the path of a train can create dangerous risks. I did not take this possibility into account when choosing the phrasing for this condition, which is an oversight worth addressing in future extensions.

2. **Reactance?** There is more evidence that the law conditions stating liability in abstract terms ("breaking the law") influence the subjects' moral judgments, than there is for the law conditions naming specific crimes ("criminal assault and battery" and "criminal negligence").[23] If one had expected that the vividness of a specific criminalized description of liability should activate certain mechanisms of persuasion more than would the more abstract phrasing, or if one had expected that the criminalized labeling would be perceived as stronger social proof of societal norms, then this leaves something to be explained.[24] One possibility is simply that such expectations were incorrect – that naming specific crimes does not necessarily communicate more vividly (for example, some subjects may be unfamiliar with the terms "criminal assault and battery" or "criminal negligence," or the technicality of such phrasing may dampen its impact), and that such descriptions do not necessarily enhance a perception of social proof of societal norms.

Another possibility is that one (or both) of the specific-crime conditions exerts less net influence on moral judgments than does its abstractly phrased counterpart, due to a countervailing reaction to the criminalized phrasing among some subjects. A rough diagnostic is available in a follow-up question asked after the subject has already answered the central moral judgment question. It asked subjects how they felt about the law information they were given, including allowing them to choose the options "the law was fair in this situation" or "the law was unfair in this situation." These answer options were included to detect whether some subjects might feel that criminalization was illegitimate, when applied to the actions of someone confronted – through no fault of their own – with such a tragic choice to make.

---

[23] More precisely put, we can infer with greater confidence that there are differences on both the "morally prohibited" and "morally required" margins, in the comparisons among the {Don't harm}, {Not authorized}, and {Duty to act} conditions. In the comparison between the specific-crime conditions, the difference on the "morally required" margin falls short of the conventional $p = 0.05$ level, as noted above.

[24] Moreover, the conditions with the phrasing "breaking the law" do not specify whether the liability is civil or criminal, leaving it to the subjects' imagination. In early-stage presentations, I had used the shorthand "civil" as a characterization for the {Don't harm} and {Duty to act} conditions. But I stand corrected, with thanks to those workshop participants who persuaded me that such a shorthand might both obscure the possibility of understanding the phrase "breaking the law" as indicating possible criminal liability, and also distract from what is interesting about that phrasing – that it describes liability in an abstract way.

Overall, more subjects say that the laws prohibiting turning are "unfair": 63 percent for {Criminal assault}, 53 percent for {Don't harm}, and 48 percent for {Not authorized}. Fewer say that the laws requiring turning are unfair: 25 percent for {Criminal negligence} and 25 percent for {Duty to act}. Likewise, fewer said that the laws prohibiting turning are "fair": 6 percent for {Criminal assault}, 9 percent for {Don't harm}, and 12 percent for {Not authorized}. And more said that the laws requiring turning are fair: 25 percent for {Criminal negligence} and 33 percent for {Duty to act}.[25]

The high proportion of subjects (63 percent) in the {Criminal assault} condition saying that the law is unfair is notable, even relative to the other two prohibition conditions. Among those subjects, 90 percent also say that turning the train is "morally permissible" or "morally required" (contrary to the law's command). It seems sensible to speculate that the harshness of imposing liability for criminal assault and battery may have dampened the responsiveness of the subjects' moral intuitions to this law condition.[26] Could the {Criminal assault} condition have lost some net influence because it seems especially disproportionate or even illegitimate, prompting a countervailing impulse for some subjects? Did more subjects discount the moral information, or the social proof, to be gained from such a law in such a situation?[27] These possibilities correspond to what the legal psychology literature has theorized as a loss of moral credibility when a law becomes uninformative about what is morally right,[28] which in the extreme may even lead to the possibility of a perverse behavioral response – "flouting the law" – as observed in prior experimental work.[29]

Such adverse reactions have also been examined closely in the literature of consumer psychology and marketing,[30] including health

---

[25] Both the variation among law conditions in these evaluations and the apparent differences among the pairwise comparisons in evincing law's influence tend to reduce the plausibility of the "arbitrary" mechanism (likened to a mindless coin-flip, above). Both sorts of nonuniformity suggest that subjects view the conditions with discernment and differentiation.

[26] This is not to suggest that any criminalized phrasing might do so; here, both the fairness and unfairness responses for the {Criminal negligence} condition seem close to those for its abstractly phrased counterpart, the {Duty to act} condition.

[27] Although the discussion suggests the possibility of sorting among the mechanisms within the informational group based on the assumption that naming specific crimes may convey societal norms more convincingly, it is ambiguous what lesson is learned from the fact that the criminal-phrasing comparison shows less evidence of law's influence. It could be, for example, that social proof of societal norms is not an important mechanism relative to the others; or it could be that societal norms are quite important but some subjects simply discount the informative value of the {Criminal assault} condition, given what they perceive to be its implausibility.

[28] See e.g. Paul H. Robinson & John M. Darley, *Intuitions of Justice: Implications from Criminal Law and Justice Policy*, 81 S. CAL. L. REV. 1 (2007).

[29] See Janice Nadler, *Flouting the Law*, 83 TEX. L. REV. 1399 (2005).

[30] See e.g. Gavan J. Fitzsimons & Donald R. Lehmann, *Reactance to Recommendations: When Unsolicited Advice Yields Contrary Responses*, 23 MARKETING SCI. 82 (2004); Mark

communications.³¹ In this literature, these effects are commonly described as instances of "psychological reactance theory."³² Although the exact scope of reactance as a concept depends on whom one asks, it generally is said to mean "a motivational state that is hypothesized to occur when a freedom is eliminated or threatened with elimination."³³ Such a threatened freedom is "defined broadly to include actions as well as emotions and attitudes ... in other words, freedom to do, freedom to feel, or freedom to hold a particular evaluation, or not"; and thus reactance is the theory "most frequently called upon to give account" of both "boomerangs and failure to persuade."³⁴ Among the proposed effects of reactance are "an increase in the attractiveness of the constrained behavior and a decrease in the evaluation of the source of the restriction," as reactance is "a motivational state directed toward reattaining the restricted freedom."³⁵ This literature on marketing and consumer psychology, not surprisingly, has devoted much attention to the possibility that overt persuasion attempts may generate reactance.

Several key features of stimuli that are thought to generate reactance map readily onto legal commands. As relevant here, the mapping seems to make the {Criminal assault} condition a likely candidate for reactance theory: Such a law is likely to be seen initially as a "credible source," such that "increased threat arises because the decision maker is likely to increase the attention to and weight on recommendations provided by the credible source."³⁶ Moreover, it is likely to be seen as a "persuasion attempt" from a credible source, in that criminal law tends to convey a moral message.³⁷

Wendlandt & Ulf Schrader, *Consumer Reactance against Loyalty Programs*, 24 J. OF CONSUMER MARKETING 293 (2007); Peter Wright, *Factors Affecting Cognitive Resistance to Advertising*, 2 J. OF CONSUMER RES. 53 (1975).

³¹ See e.g. Marissa G. Hall, Paschal Sheeran, Seth M. Noar, Kurt M. Ribisl, Marcella H. Boynton & Noel T. Brewer, *A Brief Measure of Reactance to Health Warnings*, 40 J. BEHAV. MED. 529 (2017); Joseph Grandpre, Eusebio M. Alvaro, Michael Burgoon, Claude H. Miller & John R. Hall, *Adolescent Reactance and Anti-Smoking Campaigns: A Theoretical Approach*, 15 HEALTH COMM. 349 (2003); Steven R. Graybar, David O. Antonuccio, Lynn R. Boutilier & Duane L. Varble, *Psychological Reactance as a Factor Affecting Patient Compliance to Physician Advice*, 18 COGNITIVE BEHAV. THERAPY 43 (1989).

³² See e.g. SHARON S. BREHM & JACK W. BREHM, PSYCHOLOGICAL REACTANCE: A THEORY OF FREEDOM AND CONTROL (1981); Mona A. Clee & Robert A. Wicklund, *Consumer Behavior and Psychological Reactance*, 6 J. OF CONSUMER RESEARCH 389 (1980); James P. Dillard & Lijiang Shen, *On the Nature of Reactance and Its Role in Persuasive Health Communications*, 72 COMM. MONOGRAPHS 144 (2005); Zakary L. Tormala & Richard E. Petty, *Source Credibility and Attitude Certainty: A Metacognitive Analysis of Resistance to Persuasion*, 14 J. OF CONSUMER PSYCHOL. 427 (2004).

³³ BREHM & BREHM, *supra* note 32, at 98.

³⁴ Brian L. Quick, Lijiang Shen & James P. Dillard, *Reactance Theory and Persuasion*, in THE SAGE HANDBOOK OF PERSUASION: DEVELOPMENTS IN THEORY AND PRACTICE 167, 167 (James P. Dillard & Lijiang Shen eds., 2013).

³⁵ Fitzsimons & Lehmann, *supra* note 30, at 83.

³⁶ *Id.* at 84.

³⁷ See Tormala & Petty, *supra* note 32.

This study was not designed to test for reactance as fully conceptualized in this literature on the psychology of persuasion. Yet the responses about whether the stated law is "unfair" might be interpreted as expressing resistance to the law's attempt at persuasion – that is, as a possible indicator for reactance. In particular, contesting the law's command as "unfair" seems a close fit for the psychological strategies of "counterarguing" and "source derogation" that have been considered classic mechanisms of reactance.[38] It is fortuitous that a measure meant to capture what the legal psychology literature might call legitimacy also corresponds to certain dimensions of what the consumer psychology literature might call reactance; this overlap seems worthy of further analysis and potential synthesis.[39]

16.7 LIMITATIONS AND EXTENSIONS

Several limitations are worth emphasizing and offer guidance for future work. First, experiments based on vignettes share the common limitation that how subjects react to a story might not reflect their responses to actual events. This study's findings, for example, may be overstated because the law is told directly to the subject, relative to a natural-setting study in which people might not have heard about the law. Yet these findings might be understated because what it says about the law may readily be dismissed as fictional, relative to a study based on actual laws that are verifiable or common knowledge; or one might even imagine some subjects showing a sort of reactance against a survey that appears to be pressing a certain viewpoint.

Second, this study makes progress, but only in a limited way, toward sorting among the possible mechanisms. It suggests that mechanisms within the functional group are likely to be engaged; by contrast, the arbitrary tiebreaking mechanism does not track the findings. But by no means does this study rule out mechanisms in the informational group. Do some subjects find direct moral guidance in what the law says? Do some see the law as social proof of societal norms? These remain open questions. Moreover, the listed psychological pathways seem likely to be incomplete, likely to vary from person to person, and also likely to interact in complex ways with other influences on our moral intuitions.

Third, this study has not been designed to test reactance theory, but rather identifies it ex post as generating hypotheses worthy of investigation in future work. To state what may be obvious, reactance theory has potential explanatory power not only for boomerang effects but also for weakened signs of persuasion.[40] It seems

---

[38] See e.g. Clee & Wicklund, *supra* note 32; Quick, Shen & Dillard, *supra* note 34; Tormala & Petty, *supra* note 32; Wright, *supra* note 30.

[39] The notion of legitimacy has been considered within the reactance literature. See e.g. Sandra Sittenthaler, Christina Steindl & Eva Jonas, *Legitimate vs. Illegitimate Restrictions – A Motivational and Physiological Approach to Investigating Reactance Processes*, 6 FRONTIERS IN PSYCHOL. 1 (2015).

[40] See Quick, Shen & Dillard, *supra* note 34.

appropriate to consider such a possibility especially in studies where outcomes take the form of aggregate net effects among groups of heterogeneous subjects, and there is reason to believe that positive persuasion is occurring for some subset of subjects, as is the case in this study. In such a context, it seems sensible to ask whether an adverse reaction among some other subset of subjects is plausibly at work (even if that subset is not large enough to flip the sign of the net outcomes).

Reactance theory may thus serve as a guide in generating and refining predictions for future work on law's influence on moral judgments. One might, for example, design studies comparing subgroups of subjects who are less or more likely to show an adverse reaction to a given sort of command by the law.[41] Complementarily, the legal literature on legitimacy and moral credibility can offer insights about what sorts of threats to one's freedom of moral evaluation – that is, what sorts of laws – might generate the most reactance.

---

[41] See e.g. Fitzsimons & Lehmann, *supra* note 30; Yael Zemack-Rugar, Sarah G. Moore & Gavan J. Fitzsimons, *Just Do It! Why Committed Consumers React Negatively to Assertive Ads*, 27 J. OF CONSUMER PSYCHOL. 287 (2017).

17

The Coca-Cola Bottle

A Fragile Vessel for Building a Brand

Jacob E. Gersen and C. Scott Hemphill*

The Coca-Cola bottle is among the most famous product packaging in the world. Consumers everywhere instantly recognize the distinctive curvy bottle and understand what it represents. It has been celebrated as a design classic and featured prominently by artists ranging from Norman Rockwell to Andy Warhol. The bottle is not only a cultural icon but also a triumph of branding, its goodwill built up over time by the Coca-Cola Company's heavy investments in advertising and other forms of marketing.

Central to this success has been a multipronged strategy to secure legal protection for the fruits of these investments. For more than a century, the bottle has been a pillar of that strategy, alongside Coca-Cola's secret formula and the Coca-Cola name itself. Today, the bottle is arguably the world's most famous example of "trade dress," a form of federal trademark law that protects product packaging that serves as a designator of source.[1] No one doubts the existence of so-called secondary meaning, that consumer association between the bottle and the Company as a product source. When Supreme Court Justices ranging from Stephen Breyer to Antonin Scalia have written about trade dress, the bottle has served as a primary point of reference.[2]

Despite the bottle's importance, the story of how it reached this exalted position is surprisingly neglected. This chapter is an effort to fill that gap. We seek to recover the early history of the bottle with a view to understanding the interplay of law and

---

* We thank Barton Beebe, Sarah Burstein, Noam Elcott, Jeanne Fromer, Mark McKenna, and workshop audiences at Harvard and NYU for helpful comments. Antara Joardar, Ryan Knox, Sam Koenig, Fred Wang, and Victoria Yu provided outstanding research assistance.

[1] See e.g. Mark A. Lemley, *The Modern Lanham Act and the Death of Common Sense*, 108 YALE L.J. 1687, 1700 (1999) (describing bottle as "classic example" of product trade dress); MCCARTHY ON TRADEMARKS AND UNFAIR COMPETITION § 7.94 (5th ed. 2017) (acknowledging recognition of bottle as "indisputable paradigm" of container trade dress).

[2] See *Qualitex Co. v. Jacobson Products Co.*, 514 U.S. 159, 162 (1995) (Breyer, J.); *Wal-Mart Stores, Inc. v. Samara Bros.*, 529 U.S. 205, 215 (2000) (Scalia, J.).

marketing that enabled its present success. We draw upon a variety of sources, including the prosecution history of relevant patents, the proceedings of an early infringement suit, and the numerous settlements of litigation initiated by the Company against other soda producers. The latter were collected in a Company-sponsored publication called *Opinions, Orders, Injunctions, and Decrees Relating to Unfair Competition and Infringement of Trade-Mark*.[3] *Opinions and Orders* eventually grew to three volumes and was styled to resemble an authoritative bound compilation of case law such as the Federal Reporter.

As we explain, intellectual property protection in the early years was fragile and contingent.[4] The story begins in 1914, when the Company's top lawyer spearheaded the effort to develop a new bottle. We examine the two main forms of legal protection available to the Company during this period. *Design patents* could protect the new bottle as a novel ornamental design. If successful, the Company would have exclusive rights to the design. *Unfair competition* law, a precursor to modern protection of trade dress, could protect the bottle as an identifier of source. If successful, rivals would be prohibited from using a confusingly similar bottle to "pass off" their colas as the real thing. Design patent law offered only short-term protection, given that a design patent expired fourteen years from issuance.[5] Unfair competition law offered long-term, effectively permanent protection once secondary meaning was established.

The Coca-Cola Company was not the first to employ these legal tools. Others had used design patents to protect packaging or had asserted unfair competition claims against rivals. The Company's efforts stood out, however, in their aggressiveness and sophistication. For example, it obtained not one but three design patents, which purported to protect the bottle from imitators for about thirty-six years. It avidly sued rivals and published the results in *Opinions and Orders*. A quotation from Justice Oliver Wendell Holmes adorned the spine as a kind of warning to rivals. Writing for a unanimous Supreme Court, Justice Holmes had declared that the Coca-Cola name "means a single thing coming from a single source, and well known to the community."[6] By thus establishing that the name had achieved secondary meaning, the quotation simultaneously celebrated the cultural importance of Coca-Cola and handed the Company an important legal victory.

By contrast, the Company's early efforts to protect the bottle were haunted by problems and risks. Its problems began with the first design patent, which covered a prototype that was significantly altered en route to production. That difference left

---

[3] THE COCA-COLA COMPANY, OPINIONS, ORDERS, INJUNCTIONS, AND DECREES RELATING TO UNFAIR COMPETITION AND INFRINGEMENT OF TRADE-MARK (1923 & 1939) (hereinafter OPINIONS & ORDERS). Volume 1 was published in 1923. Volumes 2 and 3 followed in 1939.

[4] Cf. Robert Brauneis, *Copyright and the World's Most Popular Song*, 56 J. COPYRIGHT SOC'Y U.S.A. 335 (2009) (arguing that, notwithstanding its commercial success as a purportedly copyrighted work, the song "Happy Birthday to You" lacks copyright protection).

[5] The term was later lengthened to fifteen years. See 35 U.S.C. § 173 (2018).

[6] *Coca-Cola Co. v. Koke Co. of America*, 246 U.S. 143, 146 (1920).

the Company vulnerable because the scope of the patent would not necessarily stretch to cover an alleged infringer that adopted the same shape as the production bottle. Worse, the Company revealed its weak position in an ill-advised patent suit against another soft drink maker. The court in that case construed the patent narrowly, providing a road map for avoidance by others.

The Company's later patents were no help either. The second design patent essentially covered the production bottle. However, the Company waited more than five years after production began to file an application. The resulting patent might well have been invalid given its close resemblance to the earlier production bottle. In any event, the patent could not have been applied retroactively to prevent copying of the production bottle. The surprising implication of these patent missteps is that other firms were probably legally free to use the hourglass shape as soon as the first bottle came off the production line in 1916.[7]

The patents played an important role in helping the Company transition to long-term protection under unfair competition principles. They bought time for the bottle to develop secondary meaning, which was a necessary part of any unfair competition claim. Scholars have considered how unfair competition (and later trade dress) might be used as a tool for extending protection beyond the expiration of a design patent.[8] Patented product designs, such as the famous pillow shape of the shredded wheat biscuit, have been the principal focus. The Coca-Cola bottle offers a notable example of the same strategy being employed in the context of product packaging.

Unfortunately for the Company, the patents' flaws put the development of secondary meaning at risk. Had rivals exploited the flaws, the unfair competition claim might have failed as well. The use of design patents to facilitate the development of secondary meaning also gave rise to an additional source of uncertainty. Early case law treated design patents as a bargain between the patentee and the public, in which the design was dedicated to the public once the patent expired. Courts rejected efforts to convert short-term patent exclusivity into long-term unfair competition protection. This hostility posed a threat to the viability of unfair competition as a means to protect the bottle from imitators.

Our discussion proceeds in four parts. Section 17.1 describes the severe challenge posed by copycat colas and the Company's development of a novel, distinctive bottle as a response. Section 17.2 examines the Company's design patent strategy and its shortcomings. Section 17.3 explains unfair competition law as a means to exclude rivals, including the central role played by secondary meaning. Section 17.4 explores the interaction between design patents and unfair competition, particularly the risk that short-term protection using design patents might undermine the Company's long-term interest in protection under unfair competition principles.

---

[7] At least in the short run. If and as secondary meaning was achieved, the Company would have an unfair competition claim against rivals.
[8] See e.g. Mark P. McKenna, *(Dys)Functionality*, 48 HOUSTON L. REV. 823 (2011).

Along the way, we identify significant modern echoes of the Company's strategies, including the pursuit of multiple patents to extend the duration of protection and the use of design patents as a way to buy time for the development of secondary meaning.

17.1 THE BOTTLE: A SHORT HISTORY

In the 1880s, the Coca-Cola Company faced a major challenge. Copycat colas with similar names and bottle labels were everywhere. Noka-Cola and Coke-Ola, among many others, openly free-rode on the popularity of Coca-Cola. The Company responded with a flurry of lawsuits. Pursuing competitors one by one, however, was very difficult, given the sheer number of imitations. Moreover, as soon as one copycat was taken off the market, another one popped up elsewhere.

In response, the Company devised a second tool to deter imitations: the distinctive product delivery system and packaging that we know today as the Coca-Cola bottle. The idea of a distinctive bottle was not itself new. For decades, special bottles had been used to identify the drugs contained therein, and entire glassworks were devoted to manufacturing distinctive bottles for exactly this purpose.[9] The Company held a design contest with a $500 reward.[10] The idea was to devise a bottle that, in the words of a leading bottler, was identifiable "even when feeling it in the dark" and "so shaped that, even if broken, a person could tell at a glance what it was."[11]

Eight glass manufacturers accepted the challenge. A team from the Root Glass Company visited the local library in Terre Haute, Indiana, to find images of coca and kola – ingredients in the original formulation of Coca-Cola – to somehow incorporate into their design. The team found nothing suitable; instead, legend has it, they found a picture of a cocoa pod on a nearby page of the Encyclopedia Britannica. Cocoa is used to make chocolate; it has nothing to do with coca. Nevertheless, the distinctive bulge of the cocoa pod was incorporated into the bottle design, resulting in the hourglass shape that we know today.

The new bottle was a potentially useful tool against copycats. Consumers would come to recognize the bottle by sight and by touch and to associate it with Coca-Cola. Armed with this association, consumers could successfully distinguish the real thing, no matter what the imitators named their beverage or how similar the soda itself looked. For this strategy to work, however, the Company had to solve two

---

[9] See Peter D. Schultz et al., *The Dating Game: William Walton, Whiteman Brothers, and the Warren Glassworks*, BOTTLES & EXTRAS, July–Aug. 2010, at 46; GEORGE GRIFFINHAGEN & MARY BOGARD, HISTORY OF DRUG CONTAINERS AND THEIR LABELS (1999).

[10] *The History of the Coca-Cola Contour Bottle: The Creation of a Cultural Icon*, COCA-COLA Co., www.coca-colacompany.com/company/history/the-history-of-the-coca-cola-contour-bottle (hereinafter Coca-Cola History).

[11] NORMAN L. DEAN, THE MAN BEHIND THE BOTTLE 105 (2010) (quoting Benjamin Franklin Thomas).

challenges: adoption and exclusivity. In other words, it was important that Coca-Cola be sold in the new bottle rather than a different bottle, and that competitors must be prevented from selling their cola in a bottle with this shape. Neither outcome was a foregone conclusion.

Adoption was not automatic because the Company did not do the bottling. Fountain Coca-Cola was the Company's initial focus, bottles an afterthought. Company founder Asa Candler thought bottles were low-class and left the bottling task to others, even going so far as to enter into a perpetual contract for syrup at a very low price because he was so dubious of the enterprise. Syrup was sold to bottling franchisees all over the country. Candler miscalculated, as bottle sales soon outpaced fountain sales. Even Americans who would never find themselves seated at the soda fountain could buy a bottle of Coca-Cola for a nickel.[12] While Candler's decision left huge profits on the table, the profitability of bottling had the happy side effect of encouraging entrepreneurs to spread the Coca-Cola gospel. Bottling turned out to be one of the main driving forces behind consumer diversification and mass consumption. In hindsight, this misjudgment may well have been a major factor in achieving ubiquity of the product.

The Company needed the bottlers' cooperation to make the switch to a new bottle. Early bottles could be any shape or color, required by contract merely to have diamond-shaped paper labels bearing the Company's name in capital letters.[13] Making the switch was costly. Moreover, as agents of the Company, some bottlers were faithless in the early days, furtively adulterating the syrup with saccharine,[14] suggesting that they might be a reluctant partner in the quest to stamp out free-riders. Harold Hirsch, the Company's general counsel, exhorted the bottlers to accept a new design "that we can adopt and call our own child."[15] In appealing to the bottlers' ambition, he also revealed his own: "We are not building Coca-Cola alone for today. We are building Coca-Cola forever, and it is our hope that Coca-Cola will remain the National drink to the end of time."[16] What must have seemed bombastic at the time also proved prophetic. In the end, the bottlers went along.

Exclusivity was important because otherwise, competitors could simply sell their soda in a bottle of identical shape. Conceivably, the higher cost of a specially manufactured glass bottle raised the costs of rivals seeking to market an imitation. But at heart, exclusivity depended crucially upon IP protection. When the Company introduced the new bottle, it stated its goal plainly in a newspaper ad

---

[12] Constance L. Hays, The Real Thing: Truth and Power at the Coca-Cola Company 22 (2004).
[13] Id. at 20. The traditional rule prohibiting the licensing of trademarks – since abandoned – may have complicated the Company's challenge.
[14] Mark Pendergrast, For God, Country and Coca-Cola: The Definitive History of the Great American Soft Drink and the Company That Makes It 79 (2d ed. 2000).
[15] Id. at 103.
[16] Id.

that it furnished to its bottlers. "We've Bottled Up the Pirates of Business," the headline ran; "they cannot imitate the new Coca-Cola bottle – it is patented."[17]

Legal exclusivity, once secured, facilitated the Company's heavy investments in marketing – investments that would have made free-riding even more tempting if it were permitted. By 1927, the Company claimed to have spent more than $20 million marketing the bottle,[18] and bottlers spent millions more.[19] These marketing efforts went far beyond advertising. For example, the Company worked with a range of artists to fashion the Coca-Cola image and infuse it into popular culture. Norman Rockwell's well-known "Out Fishin" (1935) portrayed a young boy fishing from his stoop on a tree stump, with his pole, his dog, and a bottle of Coca-Cola. Haddon Sundblum forever stamped his (and Coke's) mark on American cultural consciousness with his soon-to-be iconic Coca-Cola Santa – plump, jolly, dressed in Coca-Cola red and white, and drinking from the bottle.

The investments paid off. Today, the bottle is famous, ubiquitous, and nearly synonymous with the product itself. Heavy marketing has inspired brand loyalty and, with it, a willingness to pay a premium for Coca-Cola. For some consumers, the taste of a Coke and its packaging might be said to have merged.[20] We now turn to the IP protection that made this success possible.

17.2 DESIGN PATENTS

Design patents were the Company's first line of defense, particularly important in the short run. A design patent protects the visual appearance of a product, including its overall shape and surface ornamentation.[21] Design patents are similar in important respects to the utility patents that cover useful inventions. Whereas a utility patent "protects the way an article is used and works," a design patent "protects the way an article looks."[22] To receive patent protection, a design must satisfy not only

---

[17] DEAN, *supra* note 11, at 105–06.
[18] Transcript at 22, *Coca-Cola Co. v. Whistle Co.*, 20 F.2d 955 (D. Del. 1927) (hereinafter Whistle Transcript) (opening of plaintiff) ("$23 million have been expended in advertising this bottle in conjunction with other advertising of Coca-Cola in the past five years."). Trial testimony associated this figure with a longer time frame – 1915 to 1926 – and was arguably ambiguous on whether the full $23 million was spent on the bottle. See *id.* at 79–80 (testimony of W. A. Landers, comptroller of Coca-Cola Co.) (testifying that $23,300,000 was spent on "advertising by the Coca-Cola Company").
[19] *Id.* at 79 (testifying, in 1927, that bottlers spent $2,152,000 on advertising "between 1921 and to date [sic]").
[20] Cf. Rebecca Tushnet, *Gone in Sixty Milliseconds: Trademark Law and Cognitive Science*, 86 TEX. L. REV. 507, 508–09 (2008) ("It's well known that people like Pepsi better than Coke until they know what it is they're drinking, at which point preferences shift to Coke. Part of what people are drinking is the trademark").
[21] U.S. PAT. & TRADEMARK OFF., MANUAL OF PATENT EXAMINING PROCEDURE § 1502 ("Definition of a Design").
[22] *Id.* §1502.01. Of course, "the utility and ornamentality of an article are not easily separable." *Id.*

specific rules that are unique to design patents, but also rules initially developed for utility patents.[23]

To be patentable, a design must be novel, nonobvious, and ornamental.[24] One modern formulation of the novelty test is that an ordinary observer, familiar with existing designs – in legal jargon, "prior art" – would not regard the new design to be "substantially the same" as any existing design.[25] The obviousness inquiry begins by identifying a single preexisting "primary reference" whose "design characteristics . . . are basically the same" as the new design.[26] Only if a primary reference can be found may secondary references be used, in conjunction with the primary reference, to arrive at a design with "the same overall visual appearance" as the claimed design.[27] These tests are lenient, making it difficult for the Patent Office to reject design patent claims.[28]

Coca-Cola was hardly the first firm to seek a design patent for an ornamental bottle. An early example is the 1890 patent for a "peculiar square-shaped, bulging-necked bottl[e]," used for rye whiskey by Cook & Bernheimer Co.[29] Novel bottle designs had also been patented for perfume and salad dressing, among other products. Thus, seeking design patent protection for the Coca-Cola bottle was very much part of a convention at the time.

The Company's efforts were notable, however, in their aggressiveness. It secured a series of three patents, granted in 1915, 1923, and 1937, that collectively spanned nearly thirty-six years – more than double the fourteen-year duration of protection for a single patent. Patent #1, granted in 1915, covered the Root Glass prototype that won the design contest.[30] As shown in Figure 17.1, the design had a large bulge in the middle – so large that the bottle was unstable when placed on a surface. The production bottle, manufactured starting in 1916, was significantly slimmed down

---

[23] See 35 U.S.C. § 171(a), (b) (2018) (requiring that patentable designs be "new, original[,] and ornamental," and that provisions applicable to utility patents also apply to design patents); see also Jason J. Du Mont & Mark D. Janis, *The Origins of American Design Patent Protection*, 88 IND. L.J. 837, 841–42 (2013).

[24] 35 U.S.C. §§ 102–03; see Sarah Burstein, *Visual Invention*, 16 LEWIS & CLARK. L. REV. 169, 175–76 (2012).

[25] See *International Seaway Trading Corp. v. Walgreens Corp.*, 589 F.3d 1233, 1239–40 (Fed. Cir. 2009); Sarah Burstein, *Is Design Patent Examination Too Lax?*, 33 BERKELEY TECH. L.J. 607, 613 (2018).

[26] *High Point Design LLC v. Buyers Direct, Inc.*, 730 F.3d 1301, 1311–12 (Fed. Cir. 2013). Obviousness is evaluated from the standpoint of "a designer of ordinary skill who designs articles of the type involved." *Id.* at 1312.

[27] *Id.*

[28] See Burstein, *supra* note 25, at 610, 611, 616 (reporting an allowance rate well in excess of 80 percent); *Design Data June 2022*, U.S. PAT. & TRADEMARK OFF., www.uspto.gov/dashboard/patents/design.html (reporting an allowance rate, "[c]umulative for fiscal year 2022," of approximately 84 percent).

[29] Design Pat. 19,726 (filed Feb. 15, 1890; granted Mar. 25, 1890). The quoted description of the bottle is from *Cook & Bernheimer Co. v. Ross*, 73 F. 203, 205 (C.C.S.D.N.Y. 1896).

[30] U.S. Pat. No. D48,160 (issued Nov. 16, 1915).

| Patent #1 | Production Bottle | Patent #2 | Patent #3 |
| (1915) | (1916) | (1923) | (1937) |

FIGURE 17.1. Coca-Cola patents and the 1916 production bottle.
Source: United States Patent and Trademark Office; the High Museum of Art.

compared to the prototype. Patent #2, granted in 1923, was nearly identical to the production bottle, with a slight change in the "ribs."[31] Patent #3, granted in 1937, was a further slight variant on the design in Patent #2.[32]

It bears emphasis that the Company did not secure a timely patent on the production bottle itself. Patent #1 covered a design that differed substantially from the production bottle. Patent #2 closely hewed to the production bottle, but the Company waited for more than five years after production had begun to file an application. The consequences of this oversight are examined in the following.

Patents in hand, the Company sued rivals for infringement. Patent #1 was the primary and typically the sole focus of these cases. The successful results were collected in the pages of *Opinions and Orders*.[33] A typical injunction prevented the use of any bottle "covered by" or "embodying the invention" of Patent #1. Often, the injunction also prohibited use of the Coca-Cola mark, likely reflecting an additional assertion of trademark infringement of the Coca-Cola name. Some also

[31] U.S. Pat. No. D63,657 (issued Dec. 25, 1923).
[32] U.S. Pat. No. D105,529 (issued Aug. 3, 1937).
[33] See e.g. *Coca-Cola Co. v. D. J. O'Connell* (Ga. Super. Ct. Apr. 15, 1918), in I OPINIONS & ORDERS, supra note 3, at 630–31; *Coca-Cola Co. v. M. L. Valverde*, No. 3888 (Miss. Ch. 1920), in I OPINIONS & ORDERS, supra note 3, at 608–09; *Coca-Cola Co. v. Glazier*, No. 384 (N.D. Tex. 1924), in II OPINIONS & ORDERS, supra note 3, at 193–95.

prohibited the use of the Company's actual bottles, presumably because the defendant was reusing empties.[34] In some cases, the defendant was also required to pay costs, which likely served as an additional deterrent to would-be infringers.

The Company's patent strategy faced its most significant test in 1927, when it sued the Whistle Company, a seller of brightly-colored soda, for infringement of Patent #1.[35] The Company identified, as the "characteristic feature" of the patent, that "line known to art and architecture as the 'line of beauty,' or ogee curve. It consists of a double or reverse curve, convex and concave."[36] Whistle's bottle also used a double curve but was different from the patented design in other respects, and indeed was covered by a design patent of its own. As shown in Figure 17.2, the Whistle design was tall and slender, whereas Patent #1 was short and bulging, and it lacked the ripples of the Coca-Cola design.

Viewed in hindsight, the Company's decision to sue Whistle is puzzling. Whistle was not a copycat or obvious free-rider on Coca-Cola's success. The Company did not even attempt an unfair competition claim. So far as appears, Whistle posed no real threat to Coca-Cola's business. Moreover, the success of the suit was far from assured, given the substantial differences in Whistle's design. There was also real potential downside if the court invalidated the Company's flagship patent or construed it narrowly.

Whistle went to trial rather than settling. At trial, the parties sparred over the meaning of the Supreme Court's test for infringement, announced in *Gorham Co. v. White*: "[I]f, in the eye of an ordinary observer, giving such attention as a purchaser usually gives, two designs are substantially the same, if the resemblance is such as to deceive such an observer, inducing him to purchase one supposing it to be the other, the first one patented is infringed by the other."[37] The Company tried to establish the necessary resemblance to an ordinary observer along dimensions other than the visual appearance of the two designs. Counsel argued, for example, that the designs would be difficult to distinguish by touch: an "ordinary dealer digging down into a tub of ice water at night" would have trouble distinguishing the two.[38] Counsel also arranged for Coca-Cola to be sold to consumers in Whistle bottles, to show that consumers didn't notice the switch, prompting the judge to

---

[34] At least as to patent law, a suit complaining of the reuse of empties would likely fail on exhaustion grounds. See *Mitchell v. Hawley*, 83 U.S. 544, 547 (1872) ("[A] patentee [that] construct[s] a machine and s[ells] it without any conditions…must be understood to have parted to that extent with all his exclusive right"). Such a suit might have a better chance under trademark law or unfair competition principles.

[35] *Coca-Cola Co. v. Whistle Co.*, 20 F.2d 955 (D. Del. 1927) (entering judgment for Whistle after a trial). In its complaint, the Company also asserted Patent #2 and an additional patent that it had acquired as part of a settlement with an alleged infringer. These claims were dropped before trial.

[36] *Id.* at 956.

[37] 81 U.S. 511, 528 (1871).

[38] Whistle Transcript, *supra* note 18, at 21.

370 Jacob E. Gersen and C. Scott Hemphill

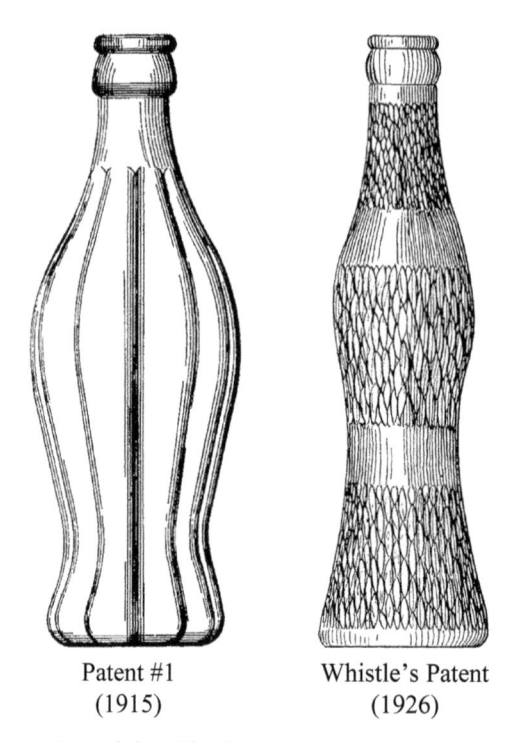

Patent #1 Whistle's Patent
(1915) (1926)

FIGURE 17.2. Patent #1 and the Whistle patent.
Source: United States Patent and Trademark Office.

muse that the same was likely true for a wide variety of bottle designs that didn't arguably infringe. The Company's overarching theme at trial was that an adverse ruling would devastate its business and render the design patent law a dead letter.

Whistle won the case. The court relied heavily on the fact that the prior art was full of other designs with double curves, including the designs shown in Figure 17.3. Thus, assuming that Patent #1 was valid despite the prior art, it must be narrow. The court's approach was in tune with an understanding of the ordinary observer test in which the comparison is made "in the context of the prior art."[39] In light of the prior art, the court concluded that the use of a double curve was not a basis for finding infringement.[40]

Whistle revealed a significant flaw in the Company's patent strategy. Suppose another firm had decided in 1916 to sell a bottle that was identical in shape to the production bottle. Would this bottle infringe Patent #1? The answer is far from

---

[39] *Egyptian Goddess Inc. v. Swissa Inc.*, 543 F.3d 665, 676 (Fed. Cir. 2008) (en banc); see Rebecca Tushnet, *The Eye Alone Is the Judge: Images and Design Patents*, 19 J. INTELL. PROP. L. 409, 419–20 (2012) (explaining the benefits of a comparison that pays attention to the prior art).
[40] *Whistle*, 20 F.2d at 956 ("Obviously, if the assumption of validity of plaintiff's patent is to be persisted in, in the light of the prior art, the characteristic feature of [Patent #1] must be discovered elsewhere than in the use by him of the ogee curve").

D755 (1856)   D16,802 (1886)   D19,107 (1889)

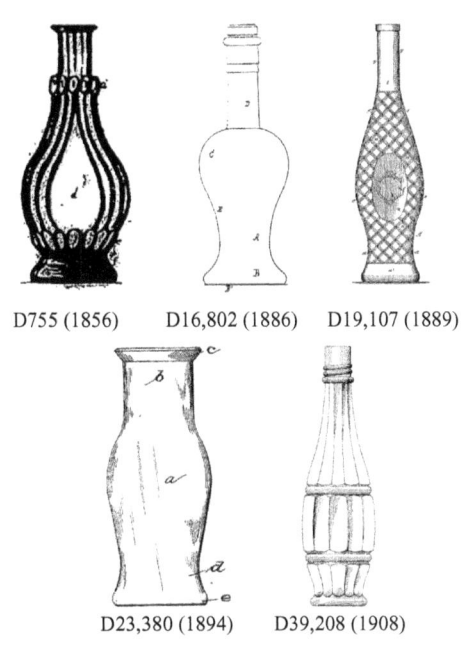

D23,380 (1894)   D39,208 (1908)

Source: United States Patent and Trademark Office.

FIGURE 17.3. Prior art patents cited in *Coca-Cola Co. v. Whistle Co.*.
Source: United States Patent and Trademark Office.

clear. A savvy defendant could make the same arguments that carried the day in *Whistle*: that the patent (if valid) was narrow in light of the prior art, and that *Gorham* did not require the court to ignore the prior art. The use of a double curve – what the Company described as the "outstanding characteristic" of the patent – would not be enough to infringe.

The defendant would also emphasize important differences compared to Patent #1. Just as in *Whistle*, the dimensions of defendant's bottle would be recognized as substantially different: tall and slender, rather than short and bulging.[41] The defendant would likely emphasize a further difference. The defendant's design, in adopting the shape of the production bottle, would contain a smooth panel on which the name of the product could be blown. Patent #1 is missing such a panel.[42]

---

[41] This difference was similarly emphasized in the application process for another design patent, in order to overcome the objection that it was too similar to Patent #1 to merit a separate patent. See Prosecution History, U.S. Patent No. D54,241 (Feb. 10, 1919) ("The shape of Samuelson's bottle [i.e. the design in Patent #1] is chunky, thick set and wholly devoid of the dainty slenderness and simple grace of outline which marks the applicant's design ... It appeals to the sense of the bizarre, the grotesque and the ridiculous. It is fat and funny"). D54,241 was not a Company design, but was eventually acquired by the Company as part of a settlement of patent infringement and initially asserted in the litigation against Whistle.
[42] This point was made in the prosecution of U.S. Patent No. D54,241. See *id.*

To be sure, this hypothetical case is more difficult than *Whistle* in some respects. The differences between Patent #1 and the Whistle bottle are greater than the differences between Patent #1 and the shape of the production bottle. If another firm used not only the same overall shape but also the ripples present in Patent #1 (and in the actual production bottle), the case would be closer still. Either way, the relevant question is whether the shape of the production bottle is different enough, such that the designs are not "substantially the same." Here, the fact that the production bottle effectively received its own patent (i.e. Patent #2), despite the existence of Patent #1 in the prior art, might tend to reinforce a conclusion of substantial difference.[43] Moreover, the Company's pursuit of Patent #2 might reflect an awareness that Patent #1 did not extend far enough.[44]

Taken as a whole, a strong case can be made that Patent #1 did not stretch to cover the shape of the production bottle.[45] Our conclusion is reinforced by a candid moment toward the end of the *Whistle* trial. The Company's counsel argued that if the patent was so narrow that Whistle did not infringe, then neither would a copy of the production bottle.[46] The point of the argument was to present a parade of horribles to the court – that a narrow construal would open the door to imitation of the bottle. We believe that the Company counsel's argument is essentially correct. If we are right about that, then others could have used the same design as the production bottle – or, at minimum, the same shape – immediately upon its introduction in 1916.

If another firm had taken this approach, Patent #2 could not rescue the Company from its predicament due to a basic principle of patent law: a patent cannot remove prior art from the public domain. That is, Patent #2 (granted in 1923, applied for the previous year) could not apply retroactively to remove the preexisting (1916) design of the production bottle from the public domain. Thus, competitors were free to use the design, provided that no earlier patent covered it. If Patent #1 did not stand in the way, as discussed, then the production bottle could have been used immediately. If (contrary to our argument) Patent #1 was infringed, then the production bottle could have been used, at the latest, when Patent #1 expired in 1929.

Patent #2 had the additional problem that it might well have been invalid, given its near identity to the prior art production bottle.[47] Near identity is reflected in

---

[43] See *International Seaway Trading Corp. v. Walgreens Corp.*, 589 F.3d 1233, 1239–40 (Fed. Cir. 2009) (holding that the same standard applies to anticipation and infringement).
[44] Dean points to Patent #2 as a possible effort to cure the defect. See DEAN, *supra* note 11, at 132. As we discuss, the later patent could not cover the production bottle, which was part of the prior art.
[45] Dean similarly suggests that the production bottle might be too different from Patent #1 to infringe. See *id*.
[46] Whistle Transcript, *supra* note 18, at 166–67.
[47] A similar issue arose in *Kellogg Co. v. National Biscuit Co.*, 305 U.S. 111 (1938), a famous Supreme Court case about shredded wheat discussed in Section 17.4. See *id*. at 119 n. 4 (noting that a court had previously held a pertinent design patent to be invalid because the design was in public use more than two years before a patent application was filed).

Coca-Cola's own public history of the bottle, which mistakenly describes Patent #2 as a "renew[al]" rather than a new patent.[48] Indeed, the designer reportedly was given instructions to make only small tweaks to the production bottle in developing the design that was the subject of Patent #2.[49] The Patent Office took nearly two years to issue the patent, initially rejecting the application on the ground that "the slight differences over [the prior art] are for either old features" or insufficiently novel to warrant a grant.[50] The prior art in question was yet another bottle patent; so far as appears, the production bottle was never discussed during the application process.[51]

We recognize that even small differences from the prior art may be sufficient to support the grant of a fresh design patent. Nevertheless, the near identity of Patent #2 to the prior art raises serious doubts about validity. The patent's invalidity, if established, would be an independent reason why it would not block other bottles with the same shape. Invalidity could have a further consequence if the Company was aware of it, stemming from the Company's decision to mark its bottles with Patent #2 ("PAT'D DEC. 25, 1923") once Patent #1 expired.[52] Marking a bottle in this fashion when the bottle was in fact unpatented, "for the purpose of deceiving the public," would violate the patent-marking statute, subjecting the Company to civil damages.[53]

The Company's aggressive use of multiple patents to extend protection over time has an important modern echo. In the pharmaceutical industry, branded drug makers frequently secure multiple patents on a drug in an effort to extend the duration of patent protection and keep lower-priced generic drugs out of the market. The later-expiring patents are frequently challenged successfully by generic entrants, on the grounds (among others) that the patent is too narrow to cover the allegedly infringing product or else invalid in light of the prior art.[54] Fortunately for the Company, apart from the *Whistle* case, the bottle patents appear not to have been subjected to much scrutiny, preserving them as a tool to stop and deter would-be copyists.

---

[48] Coca-Cola History, *supra* note 10 ("In 1923, the patent for the bottle was renewed").
[49] DEAN, *supra* note 11, at 148, describes the work of his father, a designer at Root Glass: "Dean was instructed to make the change so minor that it would not be noticeable to preserve the integrity of the highly successful design."
[50] Prosecution History, U.S. Pat. No. D63,657 (Sept. 2, 1922).
[51] *Id.* (rejecting application in light of U.S. Pat. No. D21,524 (issued May 10, 1892)); cf. Bill Lockhart & Bill Porter, *The Dating Game: Tracking the Hobble-Skirt Coca-Cola Bottle*, BOTTLES & EXTRAS, Sept.–Oct. 2010, at 46, 55 (attributing lengthy pendency to prior art production bottle as a basis for doubts about patentability).
[52] DEAN, *supra* note 11, at 132.
[53] Section 39 of the Patent Act of 1870 prohibited the marking of "any unpatented article" with the word "patent," "for the purpose of deceiving the public." Patent Act of 1870, ch. 230, § 39, 16 Stat. 198, 203 (1870) (current version at 35 U.S.C. § 292).
[54] See e.g. *Eli Lilly & Co. v. Barr Labs. Inc.*, 251 F.3d 955 (Fed. Cir. 2001); see also C. Scott Hemphill & Bhaven N. Sampat, *Evergreening, Patent Challenges, and Effective Market Life in Pharmaceuticals*, 31 J. HEALTH ECON. 327 (2012) (finding that generic entrants disproportionately challenge lower quality and later expiring patents).

17.3 UNFAIR COMPETITION

Design patents were at best only a short-term solution to the problem of copycats. The long-term source of protection for the bottle was unfair competition law (and ultimately federal trade dress protection). As noted in the introduction, the bottle has been repeatedly invoked as the paradigmatic example of federal trade dress. How did we get here?

Much as a trademark and trade dress today are protected from misappropriation by a counterfeiter, product packaging and design were similarly protected from copycats under the common law. Protection was administered by a mix of state and federal courts. A private party could sue in federal court, claiming that a competitor was creating consumer confusion by selling a product with the same design or packaging as the plaintiff. Often, the particular claim was that the defendant had engaged in "product simulation." Such unfair competition cases were a precursor to and form of modern trademark law.

Prior to the introduction of the Coca-Cola bottle, firms relied upon unfair competition law to enjoin competitors from using confusingly similar bottles. For example, in the late 1890s, Hires' Root Beer was known by its "peculiar" bottle: cylindrical with "high shoulders and short neck."[55] The distinctive shape was the purchaser's "principal method of identification."[56] Hires secured an injunction preventing a competitor from selling soda in a similarly shaped bottle. As the court of appeals explained, "[t]he defendant is not deprived of the right to market its root beer, but, at its peril, must see to it that its product is not dressed in the clothes of another."[57] The *Hires* court considered allowing the defendant to use the same shape but with a different label, and rejected this alternative as insufficient.[58] In another case around the same time, a federal court granted similar relief for the "square-shaped [and] bulging-necked" bottle for rye whisky discussed in Section 17.2.[59] In the related context of product design (as opposed to product packaging), courts sometimes, though not always, granted an injunction.[60]

---

[55] *Charles E. Hires Co. v. Consumers' Co.*, 100 F. 809, 809–10 (7th Cir. 1900).
[56] *Id.* at 810.
[57] *Id.* at 813–14.
[58] *Id.* at 813 ("Any restraint . . . that did not include the form of bottle . . . would be ineffective to stay the wrong").
[59] *Cook & Bernheimer Co. v. Ross*, 73 F. 203, 205–06 (C.C.S.D.N.Y. 1896). There was no imitation of the label, notwithstanding some similarity: "Complainant's case rests solely on the form of package, which it claims has been so imitated as to make out a case of unfair competition." *Id.* at 204. Cf. Thomas R. Hendershot, *Principal Trademark Registration and Patent Policy: An Inherent Conflict Which Requires Denial of Registration to Container Designs*, 16 VILL. L. REV. 533, 537–38 (1971).
[60] Compare *George C. Fox Co. v. Hathaway*, 85 N.E. 417, 418 (Mass. 1908) (bread), and *Enterprise Mfg. Co. of Pa. v. Landers, Frary & Clark*, 124 F. 923, 924 (C.C.D. Conn. 1903) (coffee mill), with *Flagg Mfg. Co. v. Holway*, 59 N.E. 667, 667 (Mass. 1901) (zithers; no injunction). See also McKenna, *supra* note 8, at 837–39 (collecting product design cases that reached conflicting results and arguing against injunctive relief).

In other instances, the defendant had imitated both the bottle and the labeling, and the court enjoined the comprehensive imitation without suggesting that a mere change in labeling would solve the problem. For example, in one case that reached the Supreme Court, the plaintiff sold bitter water in "a straight bottle with a short neck" and a particular label,[61] and the court reinstated a decree enjoining the use of an imitative bottle and label. The court explained that the plaintiff had "the right to require that her competitors shall be forced to adopt a style of bottle which no one with the exercise of ordinary care can mistake for hers."[62] Cases about bottles (and labels) for olives and Benedictine cordial reached a similar result,[63] as did a variety of non-bottle cases.[64]

The Company filed suit under the unfair competition approach to stop and deter imitation of its new bottle.[65] Its settlements, duly recorded in *Opinions and Orders*, often prohibited the defendant from "imitat[ing] ... the distinctive bottle adopted and long used" by Coca-Cola.[66] Critically, establishing protection under unfair competition principles depended upon proof of secondary meaning: that consumers associated the design or packaging with a particular source. As the Supreme Court explained in a word mark case, the producer "must show that the primary significance of the [mark] in the minds of the consuming public is not the product but the producer."[67] As applied here, the Company would need to show that consumers understood that the bottle signaled that the product contained therein came from Coca-Cola.

---

[61] *Saxlehner v. Eisner & Mendelson Co.*, 179 U.S. 19, 30, 37 (1900).

[62] *Id.* at 41.

[63] See e.g. *Gulden v. Chance*, 182 F. 303, 319–20 (3d Cir. 1910) (olives); *A. Bauer & Co. v. La Société Anonyme de la Distillerie de la Liqueur Bénédictine de l'Abbaye de Fécamp*, 120 F. 74, 76–78 (7th Cir. 1903) (Benedictine cordial).

[64] See e.g. *Sterling Remedy Co. v. Spermine Med. Co.*, 112 F. 1000, 1002–03 (7th Cir. 1901) (medicine); *Globe-Wernicke Co. v. Brown & Besley*, 121 F. 90, 91–92 (7th Cir. 1902) (letter files); *William Wrigley, Jr., Co. v. L. P. Larson, Jr., Co.*, 195 F. 568, 569–70 (C.C.N.D. Ill. 1911) (chewing gum).

[65] An example is *Coca Cola Co. v. Glazier*, a 1924 case decided in Texas federal court. *Glazier* was discussed at length during the *Whistle* trial. According to Whistle's counsel, not contradicted by the Company, the *Glazier* suit was contested mainly on unfair competition grounds. See Whistle Transcript, *supra* note 18, at 6–7, 10, 35, 102, 104, 105–06, 166–67, 178. The *Glazier* complaint is missing from the National Archives case file, but Glazier's answer is available and confirms the presence of an unfair competition claim. See Answer at ¶ 7, *Coca-Cola Co. v. Glazier*, No. 384 (N.D. Tex. Jan. 3, 1924) (asserting that "no reasonable person could be deceived or misled into believing that the product of defendant was the product of complainant"). The final decree, reproduced in *Opinions and Orders* (see *supra* note 33), contains no explicit mention of unfair competition concerns.

[66] See e.g. *Coca-Cola Co. v. Bogue*, No. 166 (S.D. Tex. 1925), *in* II Opinions & Orders, *supra* note 3, at 213–14; *Coca-Cola Co. v. Queen City Bottling Co.*, No. 457 (S.D. Ohio 1927), *in* II Opinions & Orders, *supra* note 3, at 814–16; *Coca-Cola Co. v. J. Pabst Sons Co.*, No. 480 (S.D. Ohio 1927), *in* II Opinions & Orders, *supra* note 3, at 826–28; *Coca-Cola Co. v. B. J. Head*, No. 41 (S.D. Ga. 1930), *in* II Opinions & Orders, *supra* note 3, at 956–57; *Coca-Cola Co. v. Gold Seal Creamery*, No. E-9083 (D. Or. 1930), *in* II Opinions & Orders, *supra* note 3, at 959–63.

[67] *Kellogg Co. v. National Biscuit Co.*, 305 U.S. 111, 118 (1938).

Secondary meaning was also important in a later period, as a basis for modern trade dress protection. As a technical matter, it might not be strictly necessary for the Company to establish secondary meaning for the bottle. Some marks and some trade dress are "inherently distinctive": their "intrinsic nature serves to identify a particular source."[68] KODAK for film is a famous example of an inherently distinctive mark. Certain forms of trade dress, including product packaging, can be inherently distinctive as well. Product design, by contrast, cannot. Whether the Coca-Cola bottle is product packaging, as opposed to product design, is unclear. The Supreme Court opinion that held that product designs cannot be inherently distinctive pointed to the Coca-Cola bottle as the paradigmatic "hard cas[e] at the margin" between the two:

> a classic glass Coca-Cola bottle, for instance, may constitute packaging for those consumers who drink the Coke and then discard the bottle, but may constitute the product itself for those consumers who are bottle collectors, or part of the product itself for those consumers who buy Coke in the classic glass bottle, rather than a can, because they think it more stylish to drink from the former.[69]

In any event, even if secondary meaning were not strictly necessary for protectability, it would be helpful, since a stronger association translates to broader scope of protection for the trade dress.[70]

The Company was also highly familiar with efforts to demonstrate secondary meaning from its trademark cases against rivals. As noted in Section 17.1, it sued numerous competitors with similar names, including a copycat called Koke. The case eventually reached the Supreme Court, and the central issue addressed by the court was whether the Coca-Cola name was understood by consumers as a signifier of source, as opposed to a description of the products' ingredients. This was important because as a description, the name was a failure. Originally, the name was descriptively accurate. Coca leaf gave the product its original cocaine kick, and the kola nut was known as a source of caffeine. The Company played up the connection with illustrations of coca leaves and kola nuts on bottle labels and advertisements. But times changed and the product was reformulated. Cocaine was removed from the "soft" drink,[71] and the kola nut was only used in trace amounts.

The inaccuracy gave Koke an opening. Koke argued that the Company had "unclean hands" for using a misleading mark. Unclean hands is an equitable

---

[68] *Two Pesos, Inc. v. Taco Cabana, Inc.*, 505 U.S. 763, 768 (1992).
[69] *Wal-Mart Stores, Inc. v. Samara Bros.*, 529 U.S. 205, 215 (2000).
[70] See Barton Beebe & C. Scott Hemphill, *The Scope of Strong Marks: Should Trademark Law Protect the Strong More than the Weak?*, 93 N.Y.U. L. REV. 1339 (2017) (describing and criticizing the broad scope granted to strong marks).
[71] It was apparently removed around 1903. See Bart Elmore, *What Coke's Cocaine Problem Can Tell Us about Coca-Cola Capitalism*, OUPBLOG (Mar. 21, 2014), blog.oup.com/2014/03/coke-cocaine-coca-cola-capitalism-business-strategy.

doctrine that prevents a plaintiff from successfully invoking the equitable powers of the court if the plaintiff itself is engaged in certain forms of legal wrongdoing. Because the relief sought in all of these trademark suits was injunctive – an order for the defendant to stop marketing its product with the confusing or deceptive name – the Company's wrongdoing could prevent legal remedy entirely.

The potency of such an accusation of misbranding was brought home by another (non-IP) case, quaintly named *United States v. Forty Barrels & Twenty Kegs of Coca-Cola*.[72] The Food and Drug Administration complained that because Coca-Cola contained "no coca and little if any cola," it was misbranded, in violation of the federal pure food law of 1906. The Company was in a no-win legal situation. If Coca-Cola *had* contained cocaine, the Company would have been in trouble for the cocaine, which became illegal to distribute without a doctor's prescription in 1914. Yet, absent cocaine and kola, its mark was misleading and arguably its product misbranded.[73] The FDA's complaint, which ultimately settled, showed the Company's vulnerability to a misbranding claim.

The Company's trademark suits eventually escaped the specter of misdescription, in large part because of the success of its marketing campaigns and the ubiquity of the product in the popular imagination. In 1920, the Supreme Court decided that it didn't matter that the Coca-Cola name was once misleading, because consumers had come to understand the name as a signifier of source. Thus, the Holmes quotation in the introduction: "The name now characterizes a beverage to be had at almost any soda fountain. It means a single thing coming from a single source, and well known to the community."[74] Put differently, the name Coca-Cola, although descriptively misleading (arguably to the point of unlawfulness), came to signify the source of the soda rather than a claim about the nature of the soda. Rather than running afoul of the law, by being a widely successful product the name came to be protected as a trademark.

17.4 THE BENEFITS AND RISKS OF DUAL PROTECTION

The Company's dual approach to bottle IP – design patent protection in the short run, unfair competition (and later federal trade dress) in the long run – had some distinctive benefits and risks. First, and most obviously, every little bit helps. IP rights are generally probabilistic and uncertain; one never knows when a suit might fail. A design patent might be deemed too narrow to exclude a rival; a particular unfair competition suit might result not in an injunction but in a weaker remedy, such as

---

[72] 241 U.S. 265 (1916).
[73] The litigation also included an allegation of adulteration, which was prohibited under the Pure Food and Drug Act of 1906 and the subsequent Food, Drug, and Cosmetic Act of 1938.
[74] *Coca-Cola Co. v. Koke Co. of America*, 254 U.S. 143, 146 (1920).

requiring the defendant merely to affix a clarifying label. Perhaps better, then, to take a belt-and-suspenders approach.

The design patents also reinforced the unfair competition claims in an important way. Secondary meaning takes time to develop. If a design is copied quickly, before secondary meaning emerges, secondary meaning might never be achieved. This is not a merely theoretical concern. Today, designs that are copied before secondary meaning has a chance to develop are out of luck, insofar as trade dress protection is concerned.[75] Here, the Company's design patents provided it with more than three decades of protection during which it was able to invest heavily in marketing. Without patent protection, it might not have been possible to convince imitators to stay out of the market for long enough to establish secondary meaning. If a rival had shown that Patent #1 did not cover the production bottle, much as it did not cover Whistle's, secondary meaning might never have developed.

At the same time, the design patents posed a significant threat to the Company's unfair competition claims. Intellectual property doctrine and policy reflects a long-standing concern with bootstrapping: that one type of claim might be used to compensate for a weakness or deficiency in another, and thereby extend the protection beyond its proper bounds. A particularly potent version of this concern involves patent law. Patent law provides powerful legal protection, but only for a limited time. The bargain between the patentee and the public is that after expiration, the patented invention or design is dedicated to the public. If time-limited patent protection could be converted to indefinite protection as a matter of unfair competition or trademark, the public would not receive the full use of the invention or design.

This concern with bootstrapping was reflected in the case law well before the Company launched its new bottle. In the late 1800s, Singer, the dominant manufacturer of sewing machines, excluded competitors by means of utility patents on various aspects of its design. After the patents expired, Singer sued a competitor that made sewing machines with an identical "size, shape, ornamentation, and general external appearance" as Singer's.[76] Singer argued that the competitor had done so in order to "induc[e] the belief" that the machines were actually made by Singer. This was an unfair competition claim that effectively sought to preserve exclusivity beyond the point of patent expiration.

The Supreme Court accepted the unfair competition concern in principle, but rejected the implication that a competitor could be enjoined from selling a product with the identical form. Such an injunction would violate the bargain the patentee had made with the public:

---

[75] See e.g. *Laureyssens v. Idea Group, Inc.*, 964 F.2d 131 (2d Cir. 1992).
[76] The case also included allegations about use of the Singer name, but here we focus on the shape of the machine.

It is self-evident that on the expiration of a patent the monopoly created by it ceases to exist, and the right to make the thing formerly covered by the patent becomes public property. It is upon this condition that the patent is granted. It follows, as a matter of course, that on the termination of the patent there passes to the public the right to make the machine in the form in which it was constructed during the patent. We may therefore dismiss without further comment the complaint as to the form in which the defendant made his machines.[77]

The court accommodated the unfair competition concern to a limited degree by requiring the competitor to take steps to clarify to consumers that it, and not Singer, made the machines.

Singer signaled a potential problem for the Company's use of both patent law and unfair competition law to protect the bottle from competitors. The patents would create space for secondary meaning to develop, but at the potential cost of threatening the Company's ability to enjoin competitors' use of the bottle. A court might order the rival to merely label its bottles to clarify that the product was not Coca-Cola. Labeling was an imperfect solution that would presumably defeat the purpose of having distinctive bottles in the first place. To be sure, it fell short of the Company's aspiration to have a bottle that was identifiably associated with Coca-Cola, even by feel or broken into pieces. Implementation of a remedy short of injunction, moreover, was highly uncertain in practice. Paradoxically, to the extent these risks were recognized, that might have created extra pressure on the Company to pursue additional design patents.

The Company's strategy differed from Singer's, in that the bottle was protected by design patents, rather than utility patents. However, arguably this was a distinction without a difference. A design patentee equally reaches a bargain made with the public. So the Second Circuit appeared to conclude in a 1918 case, not long after the first bottle design patent was granted and the bottle went into production. *Shredded Wheat Co. v. Humphrey Cornell Co.*[78] was a case about the shape of shredded wheat cereal biscuits. Henry Perky had developed the biscuits after being prescribed a diet of mushed wheat that he found inedible unless he baked it to a crisp. The product was protected not only by a utility patent on the biscuit, but also a design patent on the pillow shape. After the patents expired, a rival made a biscuit "identical in substance and appearance with the plaintiff's."[79] The plaintiff sued in unfair competition, alleging that secondary meaning had been acquired in the appearance of the biscuit.

The court applied *Singer*, concluding that upon patent expiration, the form of the product – i.e. the pillow shape – had been dedicated to the public and could therefore be copied freely. Moreover, Judge Learned Hand's opinion for the court

---

[77] *Singer Mfg. Co. v. June Mfg. Co.* 163 U.S. 169, 185 (1896).
[78] 250 F. 960 (2d Cir. 1918).
[79] *Id.* at 962.

explicitly connected this dedication to the public with the expiration of the *design* patent.[80] As in *Singer*, the court then proceeded to assess to what extent the plaintiff's secondary meaning might be protected by requiring the defendant to alter its biscuit in other respects, such as color or size.

Twenty years later, the Supreme Court came to a similar conclusion in another shredded wheat case. Nabisco, having acquired Perky's interests, sued Kellogg, which was manufacturing biscuits with the same shape. Nabisco argued, once again, that copying the pillow shape amounted to unfair competition – that Kellogg was thereby "passing off" Kellogg biscuits as Nabisco's.[81] The court once again sided with the entrant, pointing to the expiration of utility patents (on the product and on machinery) and a design patent:

> The plaintiff has not the exclusive right to sell shredded wheat in the form of a pillow-shaped biscuit – the form in which the article became known to the public. That is the form in which shredded wheat was made under the basic [utility] patent. The patented machines used were designed to produce only the pillow-shaped biscuits. And a design patent was taken out to cover the pillow-shaped form. Hence, upon expiration of the patents the form ... was dedicated to the public.[82]

The *Kellogg* Court then recited *Singer*'s discussion about the patent bargain. As with *Singer* and *Cornell*, the Court once again recognized the unfair competition claim in part, insisting that the entrant market the pillow-shaped biscuit "in a manner which reasonably distinguishes its product from that of plaintiff" and analyzing at length the scope of its responsibility.[83]

Taken together, these cases suggested that the Company would be unable to assert an unfair competition claim that blocked others' use of the bottle once the design patents had expired. The logic of the bargain theory applied with equal force to utility and design patents, and had been explicitly applied to design patents in *Cornell* and *Kellogg*. That said, the Company's lawyers might have hoped to distinguish the Coca-Cola bottle, as an example of product packaging, from the product design at issue in *Cornell* and *Kellogg*. Packaging, they might argue, has a stronger claim to indefinite protection as an indicator of source, and raises less concern that such protection deprives the public domain of an important resource. A court that accepted this distinction might fully embrace an unfair competition claim founded on an expired design patent covering product packaging, even if it

---

[80] "As to form, the plaintiff appears to us finally concluded by its own design patent ... [T]he plaintiff's formal dedication of the design is conclusive reason against any injunction based upon the exclusive right to that form, however necessary the plaintiff may find it for its protection." *Id.* at 964.

[81] As in *Singer*, the broader case included allegations about use of the product name.

[82] *Kellogg Co. v. National Biscuit Co.*, 305 U.S. 111, 119–20 (1938).

[83] See also *id.* at 120 (describing "obligation to identify its product lest it be mistaken for that of the plaintiff").

resisted doing so as to product design.[84] Ultimately, however, doctrine went in a different direction. Alongside the bargain approach, a second line of thinking emerged that more tightly connected the "no bootstrapping" principle solely to utility patents, thereby leaving space for design patents to receive different treatment. The argument was that an incumbent should not be allowed the advantage of a *functional* feature – that is, a product feature that results in lower costs or higher quality – on a permanent basis. This argument appeared in *Kellogg*, which rested in part on the functional concern that a rival would be placed at a permanent practical advantage if it were denied access to the pillow shape. The court opined that the "cost of the biscuit would be increased and its high quality lessened if some other form were substituted for the pillow shape."[85] The same concern also could be found in *Cornell*, which similarly evaluated possible changes to the defendant's product in light of higher cost or lower quality.[86] This same point was hinted at in *Hires*, which noted that plaintiff's distinctive bottle served no functional purpose, but rather sought to identify the source of the product, which suggested in turn that the defendant's use of the distinctive bottle shape could serve no other purpose but fraudulent imitation.[87] Today, this concern about functionality is central to modern trademark doctrine, which denies trade dress protection to functional features.

A concern with functionality provides a basis for distinguishing design patents from utility patents. Utility patents protect functional features, whereas design patents protect ornamental features. Thus, an unfair competition claim directed to a particular shape that had been the subject of a utility patent is likely to implicate functional concerns. Indeed, in modern trade dress doctrine, the existence of an expired utility patent is "strong evidence" of functionality.[88] Such concerns about functionality are unlikely to be present for design patents.

Ultimately, this second approach carried the day. Functionality, and a version of functionality confined to utility patents, is the principal doctrine that mediates the interaction between patent and trade dress. Today, an expired design patent is generally held to pose no barrier to continued trade dress protection or injunctive relief.[89] It is common for counsel to advise clients to follow the path blazed by the

---

[84] See John A. Diaz & Warren H. Rotert, *Principal Registration of Contours of Packages and Containers under the Trademark Act of 1946*, 49 TRADEMARK REP. 13, 20 (1959) (suggesting such a distinction).

[85] *Kellogg*, 305 U.S., at 122.

[86] *Shredded Wheat Co. v. Humphrey Cornell Co.*, 250 F. 960, 965 (2d Cir. 1918) ("The question is always commercial; we ought not to impose any burdens which, either by changing the appearance of the article itself, or by imposing expense upon its production, will operate to give the plaintiff such advantage in the market as will substantially handicap his competitors").

[87] See *Charles E. Hires Co. v. Consumers' Co.*, 100 F. 809, 812 (7th Cir. 1900) (noting that any functional justification for the imitation was "pretentious").

[88] See *TrafFix Devices, Inc. v. Mktg. Displays, Inc.*, 532 U.S. 23, 29 (2001).

[89] See e.g. *Nabisco Brands, Inc. v. Conusa Corp.*, 14 U.S.P.Q. 2d 1324 (4th Cir. 1989) (Life Savers); see also *In re Mogen David Wine Corp.*, 328 F.2d 925, 933 (C.C.P.A. 1964) (wine decanter).

Coca-Cola Company: to secure a design patent and thereby facilitate the acquisition of secondary meaning, all with a view to enjoying trade dress protection down the line.[90] In this respect, as in so many others, Coca-Cola was ahead of its time.

17.5 CONCLUSION

The Coca-Cola bottle has become a ubiquitous signifier of the product and, by providing uniformity of quality, price, and access, an equalizing force in society. The bottle embodies part of why Warhol celebrated Coca-Cola as an American cultural icon:

> What's great about this country is that America started the tradition where the richest consumers buy essentially the same things as the poorest. You can be watching TV and see Coca-Cola, and you know that the President drinks Coke, Liz Taylor drinks Coke, and just think, you can drink Coke, too. A Coke is a Coke and no amount of money can get you a better Coke than the one the bum on the corner is drinking. All the Cokes are the same and all the Cokes are good. Liz Taylor knows it, the President knows it, the bum knows it, and you know it.[91]

Today, the bottle has retained its powerful hold on the public imagination, even as its actual use as a container for the product has waned. The Company eventually shifted from glass packaging to aluminum cans and plastic bottles, while continuing to feature the bottle in advertising.[92] In the 1990s, the bottle made a big return in plastic bottles that adopted a version of the hourglass shape. In the 2000s, the Company introduced a new aluminum bottle. As the Company noted in advertisements touting the bottle's return, sounding an almost apologetic note: "Certain things belong in certain packages. Anything else just doesn't seem right."[93] The silhouette appears pervasively in advertising and as an image printed on bottles and

---

[90] See e.g. Charles F. Reidelbach, Jr., *Protect Your Product Design Using Both Patents and Trademarks*, HIGGS FLETCHER MACK (Aug. 9, 2001), higgslaw.com/protect-your-product-design-using-both-patents-and-trademarks ("In establishing secondary meaning, the design patent may be used as a source of protection from others using a similar design allowing the patented design the time needed to acquire secondary meaning... [A]n individual can obtain a design patent that protects the item for 14 years during which time the trade dress of the product develops secondary meaning"); Matthew Warenzak, *The Intersection of Trade Dress and Design Rights in Product Design*, SMITH GAMBRELL RUSSELL, www.sgrlaw.com/the-intersection-of-trade-dress-and-design-patents-in-product-design (Nov. 15, 2018) ("[W]hen a new product design is developed, trade dress is not available as there is no way to establish that it has acquired secondary meaning... [T]o protect the new design, a design patent can be filed... [T]he design patent provides more than enough time for the product design to acquire the secondary meaning needed to become eligible for trade dress protection").

[91] ANDY WARHOL, THE PHILOSOPHY OF ANDY WARHOL (FROM A TO B AND BACK AGAIN) 100–01 (1975).

[92] DEAN, *supra* note 11, at 110.

[93] *Id.* at 113.

cans, often near the curvy "dynamic ribbon device," which is a further visual echo of the bottle's shape.

The bottle's success has been built on the legal ability – or at least the perceived ability – to exclude and thereby deter imitations. Legal protection provides a way to secure a return on enormous investments in marketing and branding. And yet, as we have shown, the basis for excluding rivals was surprisingly thin and historically contingent in the early days. Perhaps this very weakness was part of the impetus to strengthen and broaden IP protection for packaging in subsequent decades.[94]

The design patents' flaws meant that the shape might have been available to others from the start. The Company was lucky that the defects were apparently not recognized. Had the flaws been discovered and probed at the time, secondary meaning might never have developed. Similarly, had the public-bargain approach to patent expiration carried the day, the design might have been freely used by others. Thus, there is a good chance that, with scores of competitors using an identical bottle to deliver their beverages, the bottle would have been no more associated with Coca-Cola than an ordinary wine bottle is with Chateau Lafite Rothschild.

---

[94] Cf. Ross D. Petty, *The Codevelopment of Trademark Law and the Concept of Brand Marketing in the United States before 1946*, 31 J. MACROMARKETING 85 (2011) (describing the pressure to expand trademark protection to cover new descriptive marks and prohibit noncompeting uses).

18

Poor Consumer(s) Law

The Case of High-Cost Credit and Payday Loans

Shmuel I. Becher, Yuval Feldman, and Orly Lobel[*]

18.1 INTRODUCTION

"It's Better to be Wealthy and Healthy than Poor and Ill"[1]

There is a long-standing consensus on the need to fight poverty and eliminate it. Some fifty-five years ago, the American President Lyndon B. Johnson launched a "War on Poverty" in his 1964 State of the Union Address. Nevertheless, poverty is still a striking problem. In the United States, more than 46 million Americans lived in poverty in 2012.[2] Worldwide, billions live on less than eight US dollars a day,[3] and hundreds of millions on less than one dollar a day.[4] Poverty is a complex, multifaceted, and persistent problem.[5]

---

[*] We thank Haung Bert, Jake Gersen, Jim Hawkings, Saul Levmore, Mark Pelofsky, Michel Pham, Jacob Russell, Joel Steckel, Joel Urbany, the participants at the Legal Applications of Marketing Theory (Harvard Law School, 2019) and the Australasian Consumer Law Roundtable (Curtin Law School, 2018) for their helpful comments on earlier drafts, William Britton for excellent research assistance, and Victoria Business School for kind financial support.

[1] Alluding to a title of a satiric tragi-comedy movie (1992).

[2] With the rates of state poverty ranging from 10 to 24.2 percent. See POLICIES TO ADDRESS POVERTY IN AMERICA (Melissa S. Kearney & Benjamin H. Harris eds., 2014), 5–6.

[3] See GILLIAN K. HADFIELD, RULES FOR A FLAT WORLD: WHY HUMANS INVENTED LAW AND HOW TO REINVENT IT FOR A COMPLEX GLOBAL ECONOMY (2017), p. 281. Hadfield also notes that "more than half of the global population still lives on incomes of less than the equivalent of $3,000 a year"; id.

[4] See e.g. WHO, World Health Statistics 2013 (WHO, Geneva, 2013); World Bank Group, Poverty and Shared Prosperity 2016 – Taking on Inequality, p. 35 ("The global poverty estimate for 2013 is 10.7 percent of the world's population, or 767 million people living on less than US$1.90"). In the United Kingdom, one-third of the population "spent at least one year in relative income poverty between 2011 and 2014"; Kizzy Gandy et al., Poverty and Decision-making: How Behavioural Science can Improve Opportunities in the UK, at 7 (Oct. 2016), www.locarla.com/pdf/JRF-BIT-Poverty-and-decision-making-Final.pdf.

[5] See e.g. PETER H. SCHUCK, ONE NATION UNDECIDED: CLEAR THINKING ABOUT FIVE HARD ISSUES THAT DIVIDE US (2017), at 25 (explaining that the chapter that deals with

The Sustainable Development Goals (SDGs), a United Nations strategic plan which came into effect in January 2016, delineates seventeen key goals to be achieved by 2030.[6] The plan, aimed to sustainably improve life, defines "No Poverty" as its first goal. Other goals, such as those that relate to hunger, housing, education, and equality, further illustrate that the SDGs put poverty eradication "at the heart of the 2030 Agenda."[7] Likewise, the World Bank Group's mission is depicted in its slogan "Our Dream is a World Free of Poverty."[8]

Focusing on poverty and aspiring to eliminate it make perfect sense. We have come to realize that poverty may be a significant contributor to some of our most pressing social and policy problems.[9] Poverty is correlated with higher levels of crime and drug addiction, health problems, violence, reduced social mobility, homelessness, lower levels of trust, lack of social cohesion, less attentive parenting, low productivity, lack of opportunities, and counterproductive economic behavior.[10] Poverty is also is often correlated, and compounded, with other markers such as ethnicity, race, gender, and immigration status.[11]

Furthermore, very low levels of income are associated with low life satisfaction, which may be due to an objective lack of financial means, and because low-income earners compare themselves to those who are more fortunate.[12] Low income is also associated with shorter life expectancy.[13] Overall, and in line with Maslow's (contested) hierarchy of needs,[14] the poor are more likely to find it hard to

---

poverty "is the longest chapter in the book, as befits its importance, its complexity, and the enormous amount of social science research devoted to it".)

[6] See Sustainable Development Goals, www.undp.org/content/undp/en/home/sustainable-development-goals.html.

[7] See id. (citing UNDP Administrator Achim Steiner, who says that "Poverty eradication is at the heart of the 2030 Agenda, and so is the commitment to leave no-one behind").

[8] See the World Bank webpages on poverty, www.worldbank.org/en/topic/poverty/overview.

[9] SCHUCK, supra note 5, at 24.

[10] See e.g. Anandi Mani et al., Poverty Impedes Poverty Function, 341 SCI. 976, 976 (2013); Mark M. Kishiyama et al., Socioeconomic Disparities Affect Prefrontal Function in Children, 21 J. COGN. NEUROSC. 1106 (2008); SCHUCK, supra note 5, at 24; POLICIES TO ADDRESS POVERTY IN AMERICA, supra note 2.

[11] See Randall Hansen, The Poverty of Postnationalism: Citizenship, Immigration, and the New Europe, 38(1) THEORY SOC. 1–24 (2009). For an econometric perspective with a critical evaluation of the impact of immigration on low-income wages see Steven Raphael & Eugene Smolensky, Immigration and Poverty in the United States, 99(2) AM. ECON. REV. 41–44 (2009).

[12] See e.g. Johannes Haushofer & Ernst Fehr, On the Psychology of Poverty, 344 SCI. 862, 864 (2014) (reviewing studies that suggest "causal links between poverty, psychological well-being, and stress levels"); CAROL GRAHAM, HAPPINESS FOR ALL? UNEQUAL HOPES AND LIVES IN PURSUIT OF THE AMERICAN DREAM (2017) (associating poverty in the United States with unhappiness, stress, and low levels of hope).

[13] See e.g. Haushofer & Fehr, supra note 12 (noting that "Economic poverty means living in squalor, dying early, and raising children who face similar prospects").

[14] Abraham H. Maslow, A Theory of Human Motivation, 50 PSYC. REV. 370 (1943).

experience belonging, be accepted and valued by others, or reach self-actualization.[15]

There is a large body of literature on poverty, with experts disagreeing over many aspects. The very definition of poverty is the subject of debate.[16] Moreover, experts contest how to measure poverty, what its origins are, and what the best way to deal with it is. However, it is generally agreed that poverty has multiple erratic behavioral, sociological, educational, cultural, historical, and economic causes.[17]

From a psychological perspective, poverty affects people's economic choice patterns and decision-making processes. A growing body of literature suggests that people who face poverty are likely to make bad economic choices.[18] Some of this literature indicates that it is not so much that bad choices lead people to poverty, but rather that poverty can lead people to make bad choices.[19] Suboptimal behavior, in turn, can deepen or perpetuate poverty. An example of this suboptimal behavior, which sometimes reinforces the poverty cycle, is the use of high-cost credit.[20]

Alleviating poverty requires holistic and innovative policies,[21] and the law has a vital role in this battle. Yet despite the diverse literature on poverty, the legal literature does not systematically address the links between decision-making and

---

[15] For discussing the link between basic need satisfaction and psychological health see Shaun Saunders, Don Munro & Miles Bore, *Maslow's Hierarchy of Needs and Its Relationship with Psychological Health and Materialism*, 10 S. PACIFIC J. PSYC. 15 (1998).

[16] For one discussion see Gandy et al., *supra* note 4, at 17–18. Shuck, for instance, regards poverty as "a condition of deprivation that causes suffering among those who endue it (and among many of us who observe it), and it is conventionally assessed against some measure of well-being"; SCHUCK, *supra* note 5, at 30. We use terms like poor people and poverty more loosely, at times interchangeably.

[17] For instance, Schuck delineates a list of causes which include "bad luck, bad choices, family breakdown, educational deficits, dysfunctional and self-reinforcing cultural patterns, social and neighborhood isolation, immigration, discrimination, mass incarceration, and economic dislocations," while noting that "most of those causes are also its effects." SCHUCK, *supra* note 5, at 25. For highlighting family structure as an important cause see Gandy et al., *supra* note 4, at 19 (in the United Kingdom, single parents are at high risk to experience poverty, amounting to 25 percent of working age adults).

[18] See e.g. SENDHIL MULLAINATHAN & ELDAR SHAFIR, SCARCITY: THE NEW SCIENCE OF HAVING LESS AND HOW IT DEFINES OUR LIVES (2013); Haushofer & Ernst Fehr, *supra* note 12; Gandy et al., *supra* note 4.

[19] See MULLAINATHAN & SHAFIR, *supra* note 18.

[20] See e.g. Marcus Banks et al., *"In a Perfect World It Would Be Great if They Didn't Exist": How Australians Experience Payday Loans*, 24 INT'L. J. SOCIAL WELFARE 37 (2015); Allison Daminger et al., *Poverty Interrupted: Applying Behavioral Science to the Context of Chronic Scarcity*, 42 IDEAS (2015), at 18 (explaining that for the poor "payday lenders with usurious interest rates are used to bridge the gap between paychecks but also trap families in debt cycles for months or years"); Anandi Mani et al., *supra* note 10, at 976 (noting that counterproductive behaviors "are ... particularly troubling because they can further deepen poverty" and explaining that "Predatory lenders in poor areas, for example, may create high interest-rate borrowing").

[21] See e.g. Gandy et al., *supra* note 4, at 9, 20 (advocating for not only economic and human capital, but also "environmental capital, social capital, character capital and cognitive capital").

poverty. Decisions made by individuals can make a significant difference to their poverty status.[22] At the same time, the way we structure choices – i.e. "choice architecture" – using laws and regulation can significantly influence such decisions.[23] In this chapter we examine how consumer law, equipped with behavioral insights, can better serve to alleviate poverty.

Due to its prevalence and importance, this chapter focuses on borrowing practices, with specific emphasis on high-cost credit. In particular, we ask how legal policy should be crafted in order to inform policy and nudge poor people toward better economic decisions.[24] In answering this question, we take the view that improving people's lives, especially those who are disadvantaged, is a legitimate and desired goal of legal policy.[25]

The remainder of this chapter is organized as follows: Section 18.2 introduces behavioral biases that may lead people to over-borrow or use high-cost credit. In the first three subsections we respectively address the following three general biases: the optimism bias, the present bias, and the (behavioral) economics of information. Section 18.2.4 then focuses on the psychology of poverty and scarcity. It explains how scarcity affects decision-making and thus why poor people are prone to make erroneous economic choices. Section 18.3 is policy oriented. Here we discuss various ex post and ex ante policies that are better tailored to assist the poor in making financial decisions. Section 18.4 briefly notes some of the challenges for the implementation of our proposals. It also considers how the framework we propose in this chapter can be further implemented in additional contexts.

18.2 HIGH-COST CREDIT AND BORROWING: KEY BEHAVIORAL CONTRIBUTORS

One would assume that important economic decisions are based on a careful and rational analysis of economic factors. The reality, however, is different. Consumers, though not all of them,[26] often make dubious financial decisions.

---

[22] See e.g. Gandy et al., *supra* note 4, at 16.
[23] See RICHARD THALER & CASS SUNSTEIN, NUDGE: IMPROVING DECISIONS ABOUT HEALTH, WEALTH, AND HAPPINESS (2008).
[24] We use the term "poor people" to refer to people who experience poverty. "Poor people" constitute dynamic group, since some people may enter and exit poverty in various points in time. See also Gandy et al., *supra* note 4, at 19.
[25] For one view of what constitutes an improvement in people's life *see* John Bronsteen, Christopher Buccafusco & Jonathan S. Masur, *Welfare as Happiness*, 98 GEO. L. J. 1583 (2010).
[26] Consumers, of course, are heterogenous. While some borrowers may be subject to cognitive biases and other behavioral phenomena, others may use loans wisely. For suggesting rules that attempt to separate "good" from "bad" borrowers while discerning tastes from circumstances see Jacob Russell, *Misbehavioral Law and Economics: Heterogeneous Preferences and Consumer Regulation*, 51 U. MICH. J. L. REFORM 549 (2018).

In one famous study, a bank offered its clients a big loan by sending them a letter, while randomizing a few of its aspects. Some of the letters included photos, varied by race and gender, of bank employees. Some of the letters offered customers a chance to win a cell phone in a lottery, should the client inquire about the loan. The letters also presented the financial information in varying degrees of complexity. Some included a deadline as well. The results indicated that any one of these variants had a significant economic effect. Perhaps most strikingly, a photo of an attractive woman had the same positive impact on demand by men as reducing the interest rate by five points.[27] This, of course, indicates that people deviate from rationality when responding to information and other stimuli.

Many poor people take loans with extremely high interest rates, also known as payday loans. In the United States, for instance, the typical annual interest rate on such loans is 300–400 percent. This can lure some consumers into a debt trap.[28] Payday loans do provide credit to poor people who face pressing needs and who typically cannot obtain this money elsewhere. But access to payday loans can, on average, undermine well-being. Such loans can hurt borrowers by tempting them to overconsume, spend more on nonessentials, and spend less on life necessities such as housing and food.[29]

The history of the rise of payday lenders and the introduction of credit cards gives some insight into the behavioral aspects of consumer lending. In the mid-1950s, marketers hypothesized that Americans preferred borrowing money from loan sharks and other sketchy institutions at an irrationally high interest rate, rather than from an established bank, because banks were respectable institutions. Consumers therefore viewed the face-to-face interactions with bankers as similar to the judgment of a father figure: "Shady lenders were preferred because of their seditious nature. They were closer in kind to those who needed money, and they lacked the moral authority to judge financial failure."[30] Realizing this psychology, marketers made recommendations to banks to reframe loans as overdraft and credit, which removed the moral judgment from taking out a bank loan.

---

[27] Marianne Bertrand et al., *What's Advertising Content Worth? Evidence from a Consumer Credit Marketing Field Experiment*, 125 QUARTERLY J. ECON. 263 (2010).

[28] For an accessible account of how payday loans turn into a debt trap see Michael McCormack, *CFPB Rule Could Protect Low-Income Households from Predatory Short-Term Lending*, THE CENTURY FOUNDATION (Oct. 6, 2016). It should be noted, however, that in spite of these figures there is no consensus on the exact impact of payday loans. For one cautious view see Paige Marta Skiba, *Regulation of Payday Loans: Misguided?*, 69 WASH. & LEE L. REV. 1023 (2012). See also Neil Bhutta et al., *Payday Loan Choices and Consequences*, 47 J. MONEY, CREDIT & BANKING 223 (2015); Piotr Danisewicz & Ilaf Elard, *The Real Effects of Financial Technology: Marketplace Lending and Personal Bankruptcy* (2018), https://papers.ssrn.com/sol3/papers.cfm?abstract_id=3208908 (finding that decreased access to some forms of credit increased personal bankruptcy filings, particularly among poor consumers).

[29] See Christine Dobridge, *For Better and for Worse? Effects of Access to High-Cost Consumer Credit*, FEDS Working Paper (2016), https://ssrn.com/abstract=2810054.

[30] ORLY LOBEL, YOU DON'T OWN ME (2017).

Today, although lenders are subject to mandated disclosure – obliging them to disclose payments, fees, and interest rates – such rules have not removed the high-cost credit market.[31] In fact, the market for payday and other loans is flourishing, and such loans are extremely commonplace. It is estimated that in the United States alone there are more than 10 million borrowers annually,[32] with more than 23,000 payday lender branches.[33] According to the Consumer Financial Protection Bureau (CFPB), over 80 percent of payday loans are rolled over or renewed within fourteen days, and half are in sequences of at least ten loans.[34]

Overborrowing is often also reflected in late utility payments or credit card debt, for those consumers who can afford credit cards.[35] For many others, rent-to-own transactions are another source of expensive purchases and financial hardship.[36] The same is true with respect to lottery tickets, which poor people tend to purchase disproportionally.[37] These behaviors often come at the expense of saving more for the future and consuming in a way that is more aligned with long-term aspirations and preferences.[38]

This section presents behavioral biases that may lead people to overborrow and conduct their financial affairs in ways that undermine their own preferences and welfare. In the following sections we first discuss three general behavioral phenomena: the optimism bias, the present bias, and the behavioral economics of information. We then address the psychology of the poor. Understanding the dynamics

---

[31] For a general critique of information disclosures see e.g. CARL E. SCHNEIDER & OMRI BEN SHAHAR, MORE THAN YOU WANTED TO KNOW: THE FAILURE OF MANDATES DISCLOSURES (2014). We return to this issue in more detail below.

[32] JOHN CASKEY, PAYDAY LENDING: NEW RESEARCH AND THE BIG QUESTION (2010).

[33] MULLAINATHAN & SHAFIR, supra note 18, at 107.

[34] Kathleen Burke et al., CFPB Data Point: Payday Lending (CFPB Office of Research, 2014).

[35] See e.g. MULLAINATHAN & SHAFIR, supra note 18, chapter 5 (discussing deferral of utility bills); YVETTE HARTFREE & SHARON COLLARD, POVERTY, DEBT AND CREDIT: AN EXPERT-LED REVIEW, pp. 18–31 (2014) (discussing credit and poverty relationship in the United Kingdom).

[36] See e.g. Paul Ali et al., Consumer Leases and Indigenous Consumers, 20 AUSTRALIAN INDIGENOUS L. REV. 154 (2017) (noting that "recent studies illustrate that the price ultimately paid to hire goods under a consumer lease contract will generally exceed the retail value of the goods hired and that it is the most expensive form of finance available" and that this reality "forces ... [consumers] into even greater financial distress"); Jim Hawkins, Renting the Good Life, 49 WM. & MARY L. REV. 2041, 2044 (2008) (arguing that "[t]he overall cost for the merchandise ends up doubling or tripling the cost of purchasing it outright at another store").

[37] See e.g. Emily Haisley, Romel Mustafa & George Loewenstein, Subjective Relative Income and Lottery Ticket Purchases, 21 J. BEHAV. DEC. MAKING. 283, 287 (2008) (poor people spend more on lottery tickets); Andrew Weinbach & Rodney Paul, Running the Numbers on Lotteries and the Poor: An Empirical Analysis of Transfer Payment Distribution and Subsequent Lottery Sales, 36 ATL. ECON. J. 333, 343 (2008) (lottery spending increases soon after welfare payments are made).

[38] See e.g. Daminger et al., supra note 20, at 20 (explaining that "a payday loan may be a plainly bad financial choice in the long run, but the immediate tradeoff of no electricity or food can trump that long-term loss").

that influence the mind of the poor when making financial decisions will make crafting effective policies more likely.

Before addressing particular behavioral biases, the concept of dual reasoning – a central notion that stands at the heart of our analysis – should be introduced. Dual reasoning reflects the idea that individuals depart from rational decision-making models in systematic and predictable ways.[39] The behavioral literature differentiates between two thinking processes.[40] One is a fast, automatic, intuitive, effortless, and mostly unconscious process – dubbed System 1. The other is a controlled, attentive, voluntary, and deliberative process, labeled System 2.[41] While System 2 represents long-term planning, calculating, analytical thinking, and self-control, System 1 represents automatic and sometimes hasty behavior, focused on present needs and desires.[42]

This concept regarding the role of automaticity in decision-making now lies at the heart of much research in behavioral law and economics.[43] As we demonstrate in the following, some borrowers are liable to use – and lenders are likely to target – System 1, hence bypassing System 2. The traps of System 1, which can too often lead people astray, are often dubbed "behavioral biases."

As Hanson and Kyser note, policymakers should be aware of "the possibility that other actors will take advantage of ... [psychological phenomena] to influence individual preferences for their own gain."[44] Indeed, firms are liable to "respond to market incentives by manipulating consumer perceptions in whatever manner maximizes profits."[45] Furthermore, competitive markets can lead to a reality where firms "*must* exploit consumers' imperfect rationality ... [thus, firms] that do not take

---

[39] DANIEL KAHNEMAN, THINKING, FAST AND SLOW (2001). See also Orly Lobel & On Amir, *Stumble, Predict, Nudge: How Behavioral Economics Informs Law and Policy*, 108 COLUM. L. REV. (2009).

[40] For an important review *see* Jonathan St. B. T. Evans, *Dual-Processing Accounts of Reasoning, Judgement, and Social Cognition*, 59 ANN. REV. PSY. 255 (2008).

[41] KAHNEMAN, *supra* note 39, at 13. Kahneman notes that "[t]he distinction between fast and slow thinking has been explored by many psychologists over the last twenty-five years." *Id*. See also Lobel & Amir , *supra* note 39.

[42] There is an enormous body of literature discussing the dual reasoning model, documenting the variation in controllability, malleability, and awareness. See e.g. IN TWO MINDS: DUAL PROCESSES AND BEYOND (Jonathan Evans & Keith Frankish eds., 2009); Jonathan Evans, *Dual Processes, Evolution and Rationality*, 10 THINKING & REASONING 405, 405 (2004). See also Gerd Gigerenzer & Daniel G. Goldstein, *Reasoning the Fast and Frugal Way: Models of Bounded Rationality*, 103 PSY. REV. 650 (1996). However, the paradigm of intuitive versus deliberate processes has also been debated and criticized. See e.g. Arie W. Kruglanski & Gerd Gigerenzer, *Theoretical Note: Intuitive and Deliberate Judgments Are Based on Common Principles*, 118 PSY. REV. 97 (2011).

[43] Plentiful papers and books have been published in this tradition. For a recent excellent example see EYAL ZAMIR & DORON TEICHMAN, BEHAVIORAL LAW & ECONOMICS (2018).

[44] Jon D. Hanson & Douglas A. Kysar, *Taking Behavioralism Seriously: Some Evidence of Market Manipulation*, 112 HARV. L. REV. 1420, 1426 (1999).

[45] Jon D. Hanson & Douglas A. Kysar, *Taking Behavioralism Seriously: The Problem of Market Manipulation*, 74 N.Y.U. L. REV. 630, 743 (1999).

advantage of consumer biases ... would not succeed in the marketplace."[46] In the subsequent sections we provide a few concrete examples relevant to our context.

18.2.1 The Optimism Bias

The optimism bias is one of the most robust findings in the behavioral literature.[47] This literature demonstrates that people display unrealistic optimism in various ways. People are overly optimistic about their future, underestimating their risks and overestimating their chances to experience positive life events.[48] For instance, the majority of people believe they are less likely than others to face accidents, health problem, and diseases.[49] Kids, teens, adults, and the elderly all display overoptimism, and overoptimism is represented in a vast majority of the population.[50]

Being unrealistically optimistic can lead people to take risks based on a mistaken perception regarding their relative immunity from harm. In our context, a consumer who contemplates a loan may exhibit overoptimism by erroneously overestimating the likelihood of enjoying a stable income. Consumers also underestimate the risks of facing economic crises that would make repayments difficult or impossible. Therefore, consumers may fail to correctly predict their chances to experience an inability to repay their loans on time.[51]

Such behavioral patterns have been observed in a variety of contexts. In one study, students demonstrated overoptimism by underestimating the time it would take to pay off their loan while overestimating their future income.[52] In another study, more optimistic consumers tended to choose credit cards, which were suboptimal for their actual borrowing behavior.[53] Data from the United Kingdom also shows that

---

[46] This is so since consumers would fail to appreciate the value of the products and services that are being offered by those firms that do not exploit consumers' biases. See OREN BAR-GILL, SEDUCTION BY CONTRACT (2012), at 54.
[47] See e.g. Neil D. Weinstein, *Unrealistic Optimism about Future Life Events*, 39 J. PERSONAL. SOC. PSYCHOL. 806 (1980); Ola Svenson, *Are We All Less Risky and More Skillful than Our Fellow Drivers?*, 47 ACTA PSYCHOL. 143 (1981).
[48] See e.g. Neil Weinstein, *Optimistic Biases about Personal Risks*, 246 SCI. 1232 (1989); Lynn A. Baker & Robert E. Emery, *When Every Relationship Is Above Average: Perceptions and Expectations of Divorce at the Time of Marriage*, 17 LAW HUM. BEHAV. 439 (1993); Neil D. Weinstein & William M. Klein, *Unrealistic Optimism: Present and Future*, 15 J. SOC. CLIN. PSYC. 1 (1996).
[49] See e.g. Weinstein, *supra* note 48. People are also overly optimistic regarding their general abilities, skills and success. See Baker & Emery, *supra* note 48.
[50] It is estimated that about 80 percent of the population exhibit overoptimism. See e.g. TALI SHAROT, THE OPTIMISM BIAS: A TOUR OF THE IRRATIONALLY POSITIVE BRAIN (2011), 59.
[51] Brigitte C. Madrian et al., *Behaviorally Informed Policies for Household Financial Decisionmaking*, 3 BEHAV. SCI. POL. 27, 32 (2017).
[52] See Hamish G. W. Seaward & Simon Kemp, *Optimism Bias and Student Debt*, 29 NEW ZEALAND J. PSYC. 17 (2000).
[53] See Sha Yang, Livia Markoczy & Min Qi, *Unrealistic Optimism in Consumer Credit Card Adoption*, 28 J. ECON. PSYC. 170 (2007).

consumers with more optimistic financial expectations incur more debt.[54] As Bar-Gill points out, overoptimism can be a significant driver of excessive borrowing in suboptimal conditions.[55] This may be further exacerbated by the possibility that some people in poverty may actually choose high-cost loans "as a way of imposing discipline on themselves to pay it back faster."[56] Given the high rates of payday loan rollovers,[57] this may result in rather serious financial problems.

18.2.2 The Present Bias

The present bias reflects the general tendency to overvalue relatively small rewards in the present and prefer them over larger future rewards that require self-regulation. From a cognitive perspective, immediate benefits or costs loom larger and disproportionately outweigh future ones. Therefore, people will prefer immediate benefits even if these benefits will come at a greater cost in the future.[58] The terms "myopia" and "time/hyperbolic discounting" also describe this kind of behavior.[59] Put simply, myopic consumers "care more about the present and not enough about the future."[60] This is also related to (bounded) willpower, where people's limited ability to delay their need for immediate satisfaction causes them to make repeated mistakes in regard to their economic choices.[61]

---

[54] Sarah Brown et al., *Debt and Financial Expectations: An Individual-and Household-Level Analysis*, 43 ECON. INQUIRY 100 (2005).

[55] BAR-GILL, *supra* note 46. Yet this is not to say that all borrowers are overly optimistic in all respects. See Ronald Mann, *Assessing the Optimism of Payday Loan Borrowers*, 21 SUP. COURT ECON. REV. 105 (2013) (finding that 60 percent of payday loan borrowers were able to accurately predict the length of repayment). See also Kathryn Fritzdixon et al., *Dude, Where's My Car Title? The Law, Behavior, and Economics of Title Lending Markets*, 2014 U. ILL. L. REV. 1013, 1042 (2014) (discussing the optimism of title lending customers). For a discussion of the optimism of payday landers' advertisements see Jim Hawkins, *Are Bigger Companies Better for Low-Income Borrowers? Evidence from Payday and Title Loan Advertisements*, 11 J.L. ECON. & POL'Y 303 (2015).

[56] Gandy et al., *supra* note 4, at 27 (referring to Morduch, 2009).

[57] As noted below, more than 80 percent of payday loans in the United States are rolled over within a month.

[58] Ted O'Donoghue & Matthew Rabin, *Doing It Now or Later*, 89 AM. ECON. REV. 103 (1999).

[59] See e.g. Ted O'Donoghue et al., *Time Discounting and Time Preference: A Critical Review*, 40 J. ECON. LIT. 351 (2002); David Laibson, *Golden Eggs and Hyperbolic Discounting*, 112 QUAR. J. ECON. 443 (1997); Robert H. Strotz, *Myopia and Inconsistency in Dynamic Utility Maximization*, 23 REV. ECON. STUD. 165 (1955).

[60] BAR-GILL, *supra* note 46, at 21.

[61] There is a rich literature in developmental psychology, on how poverty, especially in childhood, affects people's ability to regulate their self and cope with the need to delay gratification. Gary W. Evans & Pilyoung Kim, *Childhood Poverty, Chronic Stress, Self-Regulation, and Coping*, CHILD DEVELOPMENT PERSPECTIVES 7(1) 43–48(2013). Interestingly, these effects could also be manipulated in the lab: Lei Liu, Tingyong Feng, Tao Suo, Kang Lee, & Hong Li. *Adapting to the Destitute Situations: Poverty Cues Lead to Short-Term Choice*, PLOS ONE 7 (4) e33950 (2012).

The bias toward the present can lead to suboptimal and counterproductive behaviors. Such behaviors may include, for instance, drinking soft drinks rather than water, spending more money at present rather than saving for the future, not flossing teeth, watching a movie at home rather than going to the gym, or procrastinating when facing a task that requires work. Delaying gratification and avoiding temptation is not easy, and people tend to surrender to the demands of the "present self" at the expense of the "future self."

While the present bias is a universal phenomenon, young, poor, and less educated consumers are most likely to suffer from it.[62] Poor people face immediate and pressing needs, such as paying rent or utilities, forcing them to focus on the present. Studies have demonstrated that, when processing resources are limited, people are more liable to prefer an alternative that is more momentarily pleasurable over the one that is cognitively superior (e.g. cake over fruit).[63] In our context, as will be further elaborated, chronic scarcity makes it harder for poor people to plan for the future. This may lead to counterproductive financial decisions, such as using a payday loan to alleviate pressing needs at the expense of future welfare.[64]

At this point it is important to note that poor families are not disinterested in planning for the future. It is that such families typically lack the necessary information for planning ahead. Instead, the urgent needs of the present cause a "decision fatigue." In other words, our present needs undermine our mental ability.[65] We return to this notion in more detail in Section 18.2.4, where we discuss scarcity and the psychology of the poor.

18.2.3 The (Behavioral) Economics of Information

Standard economics posits that people are rational agents who base their beliefs, preferences, and actions on information. Information, therefore, can valuably enhance decision-making and is essential for making well-informed choices. According to this line of reasoning, imperfect or asymmetric information can lead to market failures. As Akerlof famously pointed out nearly fifty years ago, asymmetric information can lead to a market for "lemons," where only low-quality products are offered (for low prices).[66]

---

[62] Joseph G. Eisenhauer & Luigi Ventura, *The Prevalence of Hyperbolic Discounting: Some European Evidence*, 28 APPL. ECON. 1223 (2006).

[63] Baba Shiv & Alexander Fedorikhin, *Heart and Mind in Conflict: The Interplay of Affect and Cognition in Consumer Decision-making*, 26 J. CONS. RES. 278 (1999). At the same time, enjoying a high income may give people a stronger sense of control over the future (and therefore be less liable to the present bias); Gandy et al., *supra* note 4, at 27 (referring to Joshi & Fast, 2013).

[64] MULLAINATHAN & SHAFIR, *supra* note 18, at 108–10.

[65] See e.g. Banks et al., *supra* note 20, at 20.

[66] George A. Akerlof, *The Market for "Lemons": Quality Uncertainty and the Market Mechanism*, 84 Q.J. ECON. 488 (1970).

However, behavioral findings suggest that people approach information in a different way, and it is definitely not a matter of fact that "the more, the better."[67] First, too much information can cause "information overload."[68] The term "information overload" is used to recognize that people exhibit limited processing capacity and can become overwhelmed by a deluge of information or choices. Information overload can sometimes result in suboptimal decisions, where subjects ignore (at least part of) the information at hand.

While information overload stems from limited cognition, other informational biases come from a belief-based utility. For instance, confirmation bias causes people to look for and overvalue information that supports their existing beliefs or desires. As its name implies, confirmation bias leads individuals, when forming an opinion, to search for data that confirms their existing opinion, rather than information that may challenge or contradict it.[69] Therefore, if a consumer has reached a decision to take a specific course of action – such as using high-cost credit – they are more likely to search for reinforcing indications to buttress their decision.

The confirmation bias can explain why even those consumers who do read disclosures and loan information are not likely to evaluate that content rationally. According to the confirmation bias, people process information in a way that strengthens their already existing viewpoints.[70] Hence, even if consumers read information regarding their loans, they should not be expected to always evaluate such information objectively.[71] As a result, a poor consumer who believes that expensive credit will end up improving their long-term financial situation is likely to overvalue information that supports their desire or belief. At the same time, the consumer likely to ignore or discredit contradicting information or evidence that could have served as warning cues.

Behavioral biases might also prevent borrowers from reading relevant information and disclosures in the first place. Realistically, consumers do not expect disclosure

---

[67] See e.g. Charles E. Davis & Elizabeth B. Davis, *Information Load and Consistency of Decisions*, 79 PSYCHOL. REP. 279, 279 (1996) ("While there may be a belief that 'more is better,' decision-makers often complain of 'information overload' or an inability to respond to the abundance of information available").

[68] Naresh K. Malhotra, *Reflections on the Information Overload Paradigm in Consumer Decision-Making*, 10 J. CONS. RES. 436 (1984).

[69] See e.g. SCOTT PLOUS, THE PSYCHOLOGY OF JUDGMENT AND DECISION-MAKING 233 (1993) ("[The confirmation bias] usually refers to a preference for information that is consistent with a hypothesis rather than information that opposes it").

[70] See ARTHUR S. REBER, THE PENGUIN DICTIONARY OF PSYCHOLOGY 151 (2nd ed., 1995) (defining confirmation bias as "the tendency to seek and interpret information that confirms existing beliefs").

[71] Hillman and Rachlinski use the term "motivated reasoning" to illustrate this idea in the context of consumer form contracts. See Robert A. Hillman & Jeffery J. Rachlinski, *Standard-Form Contracting in the Electronic Age*, 77 N.Y.U. L. REV. 429, 453 (2002) ("Because consumers usually encounter standard terms *after* they have decided to purchase the good or service, they will process the terms in the boilerplate in a way that supports their desire to complete the transaction").

materials to further denote that the transaction they are about to enter is a favorable one. This may trigger "active information avoidance," which is another form of biased information processing and information interpretation.[72]

Information avoidance leads people to not obtain relevant information, even when they know that such information is available and free. This behavior is closely related to the "ostrich effect" or "ostrich problem,"[73] and its incentive is rooted in hedonic preferences. The motivation for this behavior is self-preservation by evading psychological pain or suffering.[74] People prefer not feeling bad, and avoiding information may allow subjects to stay optimistic, reduce anxiety, prevent dissonance, and avoid experiencing regret. Alternatively, people may avoid information in order to prevent having to behave contrary to their current preferences.[75] Indeed, people who exhibit active information avoidance may be willing to pay to avoid unfavorable information they do not wish to learn.[76]

As an interesting example, empirical data shows that investors are less likely to seek information regarding their investment portfolios when the stock market declines.[77] Information avoidance, when applied to our context, entails that some people who face a decision to take an expensive loan are unlikely to actively seek information relating to the loan if this information is likely to be unfavorable and difficult to handle. Likewise, they are not liable to pay proper attention to disclosures and warnings. Moreover, those who do come across negative information are more likely to forget this information.[78]

At times, financial information concerning debt is likely to threaten one's beliefs and emotions, and may require unattractive courses of action.[79] Avoiding financial information is, therefore, a "common, pathological and detrimental approach that people adopt in relation to their finances and debt."[80] This entrenched behavior, which is difficult to overcome, deprives people of potentially valuable information.[81] Naturally, such information can sometimes be imperative for good decision-making and improving future behaviors.

---

[72] Russell Golman et al., *Information Avoidance*, 55 J. ECON. LIT. 96 (2017).
[73] T. L. Webb et al., *'The Ostrich Problem': Motivated Avoidance or Rejection of Information about Goal Progress*, 7 SOC. PERS. PSYCHOL. COMPASS 794 (2013).
[74] Golman et al., *supra* note 72.
[75] Ben Harkin, *Improving Financial Management via Contemplation: Novel Interventions and Findings in Laboratory and Applied Settings*, 8 FRONT. PSYCHOL. 327 (2017).
[76] Anada Ganguly & Joshua Tasoff, *Fantasy and Dread: The Demand for Information and the Consumption Utility of the Future*, 63 MANAG. SCI. 4037 (2016).
[77] See Nachum Sicherman et al., *Financial Attention*, 29 REV. FINANC. STUD. 863 (2016).
[78] Golman et al., *supra* note 72, at 103.
[79] Harkin, *supra* note 75 (Summary).
[80] *Id.*
[81] *Id.*

18.2.4 The Psychology of Poverty and Scarcity

"One cannot take a vacation from poverty."[82]

The biases discussed in the previous sections are universal, and as such, they are generally relevant to all consumers. Nonetheless, poor people are more likely than others to make bad economic choices. As noted, poor people frequently take loans with very high interest rates and are frequently engaged in other types of suboptimal borrowing and spending (such as rent-to-own transactions and credit card debt). In this Section, we examine some unique causes that may lead poor people to bad financial decision-making. As we demonstrate below, this also may explain why poor people make counterproductive choices in other domains, such as the consumption of unhealthy foods and other products.

Most importantly, the psychology of scarcity teaches us that poor people suffer from an additional distinct problem, one that interacts with the above-mentioned behavioral patterns and, at times, exacerbates them. The problem, in essence, is that poor people often make bad decisions merely because they are poor.[83] Impulsive financial behavior and poor decision-making may, in fact, be the products of a persistent sense of scarcity. Marketers may recognize this reality and prey on the poor for certain services and products.

The state of poverty reduces the capacity to overcome temptations and to exercise planning.[84] Scarcity is likely to make people myopic: it directs people to further focus on present needs and overvalue immediate gains.[85] Scarcity means that the mind is clouded and more prone to error.[86] Let us delineate this imperative idea in some more detail.

System 2 thinking requires cognitive bandwidth in the form of mental processing capacity. Our attention, self-control, and long-term planning abilities are bounded.[87] Poverty means less cognitive bandwidth. The multiple disadvantages of poverty – including financial worries, time pressure, negative stereotypes, and emotional distress – tax cognitive capacities. This, in turn, can negatively affect the quality of judgments and decisions.[88]

---

[82] MULLAINATHAN & SHAFIR, *supra* note 18, at 148.
[83] *Id.*, chapter 5.
[84] Haushofer & Fehr, *supra* note 12, at 862 ("poverty appears to affect decision-making by rendering people susceptible to the willpower and self-control depleting effects of decision-making").
[85] MULLAINATHAN & SHAFIR, *supra* note 18, at 52–60.
[86] Interestingly, scarcity may also improve decision-making, since it forces people to focus on pressing needs and recognize the trade-off they face. See Anuj K. Shah et al., *Scarcity Frames Value*, 26 PSYC. SCI. 402 (2015). However, additional research is needed to identify whether scarcity can potentially protect poor consumers against various biases; *id.*
[87] Frank Schilbach et al., *The Psychological Lives of the Poor*, 106 AM. ECON. REV. 435 (2016).
[88] MULLAINATHAN & SHAFIR, *supra* note 18, chapter 7.

People on low income often have fewer opportunities to refill or rest their cognitive resources.[89] As Mullainathan and Shafir put it, "[o]ne cannot take a vacation from poverty."[90] Low socioeconomic status typically involves the disadvantages that come with a noisy urban environment without green spaces, which result in enhanced mental fatigue.[91] Often poor people cope with negative feelings associated with job loss and stigma, while facing the need to make many critical decisions – such as complying with the conditions of welfare payments or coordinating irregular shift-work with childcare.[92] On top of that, experiencing low self-esteem can lead to a stronger desire to acquire high-status goods.[93] In other words, status purchases are sometimes a compensatory behavior, meant to quiet an injured ego.[94] This may become more acute where income and health inequalities are large and conspicuous, which is likely to be the case in materialistic societies.[95]

Overall, there is no evidence of significant difference in cognitive abilities between people with high and low incomes. When people were prompted to think about money worries prior to taking a fluid intelligence test, however, the subsequent scores of the low-income subjects dropped dramatically.[96] These results were repeated in a real-world setting: Indian sugarcane farmers' effective IQ scores correlated with fluctuation in their financial situation, which was dependent on the planting cycle. Before a harvest, when they were poor, their scores were 9–10 points lower than after the harvest, when they were relatively well off. This constitutes a dramatic difference.[97]

In short, scarcity has been shown to significantly reduce bandwidth and thus has implications on other cognitive activity.[98] This helps to explain why people in disadvantaged circumstances may make worse decisions that at times seem irrational and counterproductive.[99] In particular, it suggests that, for poor people who

---

[89] Schilbach et al., *supra* note 87, at 439.
[90] MULLAINATHAN & SHAFIR, *supra* note 18, at 148.
[91] Frances E. Kuo, *Coping with Poverty: Impacts of Environment and Attention in the Inner City*, 33 ENV. BEHAV. 5 (2001).
[92] Daminger et al., *supra* note 20.
[93] See e.g. Niro Sivanathan & Nathan C. Pettit, *Protecting the Self through Consumption: Status Goods as Affirmational Commodities*, 46 J. EXP. SOC. PSYCOL. 564 (2010).
[94] *Id.*; see also Derek D. Rucker & Adam D. Galinsky, *Desire to Acquire: Powerlessness and Compensatory Consumption*, 35 J. CONS. RES. 257 (2008).
[95] Income inequality in the United States is among the highest. See Income Inequality (indicator), OECD (2018), https://data.oecd.org/inequality/income-inequality.htm#indicator-chart. Poverty rates in the United States are also among the highest. See Poverty rate (indicator), OECD (2018), https://data.oecd.org/inequality/poverty-rate.htm#indicator-chart.
[96] Mani et al., *supra* note 10.
[97] The equivalent of going from a borderline intellectually challenged to average. MULLAINATHAN & SHAFIR, *supra* note 18, at 161.
[98] Mani et al., *supra* note 10.
[99] See e.g. Schilbach et al., *supra* note 87, at 439 (noting that "when you are poor, economic challenges are more than just economic, they are also cognitive").

experience scarcity, "borrowing is an obvious feature."[100] Furthermore, a "feedback loop in which poverty reinforces itself through exerting an influence on psychological outcomes ... may prolong the climb out of poverty for poor individuals."[101] Therefore, interventions that impose additional cognitive costs on low-income groups are problematic.

Interestingly, this is in line with recent neuroscience studies which indicate that modern experiences may cause a cognitive divide between the haves and the have-nots.[102] Low income and low levels of wealth can negatively impact brain dynamics. More generally, part of the problem may have deep roots that date back to childhood. Remarkably, child poverty has adverse effects on the development of the brain because it sets it on a particular path. Children who are born into poverty will hear 30 million fewer words by the time they turn four.[103] While this number is staggering, the difference in exposure is significant in both quantity and quality.

The first three years of childhood are crucial for the development of the brain.[104] Research also shows that the prefrontal cortex, the part of the brain that is critical for attention and problem solving, is negatively altered in children of low socioeconomic status.[105] Living in poverty impacts one's identity and leads to feelings such as shame, self-blame, and abnormality.[106]

All of this means that placing the burden and the responsibility solely on poor consumers to improve their decision-making processes is problematic. Hence, policymakers should give special attention to preventing exploitative marketing strategies and aiding poor consumers in their endeavor to make good economic choices. We turn to this next.

18.3 THE ROLE OF LAW AND POLICY

"Anyone who has ever struggled with poverty knows how extremely expensive it is to be poor."[107]

It may be tempting for people who are financially stable to look down on those with low income or who are living in poverty. Our culture often emphasizes the messages of merit and logic to social and economic status and downplays the role of luck and

---

[100] MULLAINATHAN & SHAFIR, *supra* note 18, at 148.
[101] Haushofer & Fehr, *supra* note 12, at 866.
[102] For an interesting discussion see *All in the Mind: Brain Diversity and Modernization*, https://overcast.fm/+CYGCMMq8.
[103] DANA SUSKIND, 30 MILLION WORDS: BUILDING A CHILD'S BRAIN (2015).
[104] *Id.*
[105] See e.g. Kishiyama et al., *supra* note 10. The study found that brain measures of attention were reduced in low-socioeconomic-status children in a way that resembled patients with brain damage.
[106] See e.g. MATT HELMER, HOW POVERTY AND COGNITIVE BIASES CAN IMPACT DECISIONS AND ACTIONS (2015).
[107] James Baldwin, *Fifth Avenue, Uptown: A Letter from Harlem*, ESQUIRE (July 1960).

history.[108] Social capital undermines people's willingness to help others.[109] It may as well be hard to fully understand the circumstances and hardships that scarcity and poverty entail. Wealth leads to more independence, which in turn decreases empathy emotions and prosocial behavior.[110] Furthermore, brain scans reveal that pictures of people in poverty can activate the part of the brain associated with feelings of disgust, therefore denying poor people humanity.[111] But as the previous section illustrates, it would be erroneous to put the blame on the poor. It would also be unwise to assume that poor people can easily and simply learn from their mistakes and improve their decision-making processes.

Furthermore, firms often tailor their tactics and marketing efforts to their target audience. Some firms have specialized in targeting and luring poor or vulnerable consumers, offering services and products such as payday loans, rent-to-own transactions, and uninvited sales.[112] It is thus unsurprising to find a positive correlation between the number of payday lenders and the percentage of youngsters, minorities, and the poverty rate.[113] If anything, with the aid of big data and sophisticated algorithms, this trend is likely to become even more persistent.

To be sure, poverty has not been left unnoticed. Thoughtful, expensive, and expansive social programs have been designed to assist poor people. Legal rules and regulations have been implemented. However, such rules and programs are often not fully tailored to the problem and do not address its origins.

Although such interventions sometimes fall short,[114] policymakers tend not to engage in a consistent and long-term examination of their effects.[115] Therefore, it is of little surprise that current tools can not only be unhelpful but also counterproductive. Such tools may provide the poor with a false sense of protection, which makes them ever more tempted by, and comfortable in, making bad decisions.

In this section, we propose three types of policy recommendations. First, we focus on general policies and large-scale policy measures that may alleviate the scarcity

---

[108] As noted, race, gender, and ethnicity may impact one's wealth and opportunities. Minorities and women are disproportionately among the poor, and their social mobility is rather limited.

[109] Lene Aarøe & Michael Band Petersen, *Crowding Out Culture: Scandinavians and Americans Agree on Social Welfare in the Face of Deservingness Cues*, 76 J. POLITICS 684 (2014).

[110] Paul K. Piff et al., *Having Less, Giving More: The Influence of Social Class on Prosocial Behavior*, 99 J. PERS. SOC. PSYC. 771 (2010).

[111] Susan T. Fiske, *From Dehumanization and Objectification, to Rehumanization: Neuroimaging Studies on the Building Blocks of Empathy*, 1167 ANN. N.Y. ACAD. SCI. 31 (2009).

[112] For an interesting complaint along these lines with respect to overdraft fees that allegedly disproportionally affect the poor see *In re Checking Account Overdrafting Litig. (Lopez, et al. v. JPMorgan Chase Bank, N.A.)* Case No. 1:09-MD-02036-JLK, 2012 BL 428918 (S.D. Fla. May 24, 2012).

[113] As well as negative correlation to income and education level. See James R. Barth et al., *Banks and Payday Lenders: Friends or Foes?* 21 INT'L ADV. ECON. RES. 139 (2015).

[114] See e.g. Ali et al., *supra* note 36 (arguing that "despite regulatory reforms and enforcement actions, Indigenous communities continue to be vulnerable consumers").

[115] See generally Shmuel I. Becher, *Unintended Consequences and the Design of Consumer Protection Legislation*, 93 TULANE L. REV. 105 (2018), sections III.B–III.C.

mindset or enhance alternatives to payday loans. Second, we look at borrowers. Here, we discuss some behavioral best practices that may debias consumers and improve their decision-making process. We also further examine how consumers' heterogeneity may impact legal policy, proposing a more personalized approach to legal intervention. Finally, we look at lenders and inquire how legal regulation may enhance responsible lending. While some of our suggestions may help consumers in general, others are more specifically tailored to poor consumers and payday loan borrowers.

18.3.1 *General Policy and Ex Ante Fixes*

People overvalue treatment but undervalue prevention. Prevention, however, is often preferable. In our context, prevention might be achieved in two main ways: (1) encouraging alternative lending mechanisms and (2) preventing the negative consequences of scarcity by changing macroeconomic policies.

There are a few alternative services with lower costs, which can substantially mitigate a consumer's need to use payday loans and high-cost credit. Banks and credit unions already offer competitive financial products at a lower cost.[116] Another emerging alternative is employer-based loans and payday advances. It has been reported that an increasing number of "U.S. employers are teaming up with financial institutions ... to offer small personal loans to their workers."[117] This may not only be a humane and socially responsible move, but also a beneficial one. This is because such loans may increase employees' work satisfaction and improve retention rates.[118] A further option to consider is modern Postal Banking, which exists in many countries, but not currently in the United States. The idea, in essence, is that local post offices – building on their financial, democratic, and human infrastructure – will offer microloans and other fundamental financial services.[119] Subprime credit cards may provide yet another superior alternative to payday loans.[120]

Moreover, governments offer significant support programs to poor consumers.[121] These may include, for example, job training, tax benefits, food/nutrition aid,

---

[116] Madrian et al., *supra* note 51, at 33.
[117] Yuka Hayashi, *New Workplace Perk: Loans for Low-Income Employees*, WALL STR. J. (Nov. 2, 2017).
[118] *Id.* (citing a chief executive stating that "If you could help an employee whose car breaks down or water heater is broken, you are going to have an employee come to work in better shape" and referring to his observation that "the loan program helped the company boost its employee retention rate").
[119] See MEHRSA BARADARAN, HOW THE OTHER HALF BANKS: EXCLUSION, EXPLOITATION, AND THE THREAT TO DEMOCRACY (2015), chapter 7 (Postal Banking).
[120] Mike Calhoun, *Think There's no Good Alternative to Payday Loans? Think Again*, WASHINGTON POST (June 29, 2016).
[121] See e.g. SHUCK, *supra* note 9, at 64–86 (discussing antipoverty programs in the United States).

security income, and temporary assistance programs. However, many eligible poor households do not take advantage of these programs,[122] which leads to two unfortunate and interrelated results. First, households lack financial resources, therefore tempting them to turn to payday loans. Second, the lack of financial support bolsters the problematic aspects of scarcity. In effect, a vicious cycle is in place.

Policymakers should take more proactive steps to increase awareness of such programs among poor consumers.[123] The current approach – triggering warnings only when consumers attempt to take out a loan – may be too late to aid financial planning behavior. Advertising the alternatives, such as bank services, and their benefits may lead to fewer consumers taking out payday loans.[124] Policymakers should also make sure that such alternatives are easily accessible,[125] and should simplify and standardize related procedures and enrollments.[126] Simplicity and coherence can help the poor make better decisions,[127] freeing cognitive bandwidth and thus elevating "helpful programs into transformative ones."[128]

Additionally, third parties can have an essential role in mitigating some of the challenges that poor people face. For starters, aid organizations would be wise to offer poor consumers accessible assistance with procedures and with the filing process. More broadly, objective third parties could also produce a voluntary "Fair Trade'" standard or stamp of approval, which would be awarded to lenders that employ fair practices.[129] This may serve to mitigate the negative consequences of payday loan marketing.

---

[122] Madrian et al., *supra* note 51, at 34.

[123] This issue brings to mind the question of how credit, aid programs, and payday loans advertisements should be regulated. We briefly touch upon this issue later.

[124] Firms are far more likely to engage in aggressive marketing campaigns, while far less advertising is done for plans and programs which can assist poor people. See Marianne Bertrand et al., *Behavioral Economics and Marketing in Aid of Decision-Making among the Poor*, 25 J. PUB. POL. MARKETING 8 (2006).

[125] Madrian et al., *supra* note 51, at 35 (suggesting the implementation of "a universal portal through which claimants can both verify eligibility for and complete enrollment in a range of programs").

[126] See e.g. RUTGER BREGMAN, UTOPIA FOR REALISTS – AND HOW WE CAN GET THERE (2017), 96 (arguing that social services and aid plans require "claimants to demonstrate their shortcoming ... Otherwise your benefits are cut. Forms, interviews, checks, appeals, assessments, consultations, and then still more forms – every application for assistance has its own debasing, money-guzzling protocol ... This isn't a war on poverty; it's a war on the poor"); Madrian et al., *supra* note 51, at 35.

[127] Cf. HADFIELD, supra note 3, at 290–91 (discussing the argument that complexity and high demands prevent poor people in poor countries from using the formal infrastructure and legal institutions). Numerous field studies demonstrate that one of the main mechanisms to increase cooperation of individuals is to make things as simple as possible. This is naturally more likely to be needed for people that are, on average, less educated.

[128] Colleen Briggs, *How Boosting Cognitive Bandwidth Can Fight Poverty* (Aug. 17, 2017), www.jpmorganchase.com/corporate/news/insights/cbriggs-kdavis-boosting-cognitive-bandwidth.htm.

[129] For a thorough discussion of this idea in the general context of consumer standard form contracts *see* Shmuel I. Becher, *A "Fair Contracts" Approval Mechanism: Reconciling*

Moreover, third parties can also offer – and be encouraged to offer – valuable microfinance programs.[130] In short, microfinance is often regarded as a cutting-edge financial innovation that may alleviate poverty and empower poor consumers, especially women.[131] Research on the impact of microfinance is at times conflicting and still partial in scope; its potential, however, should be examined carefully.[132]

People rarely consider more than one option at a time – a behavior called "cognitive rigidity." Cognitive rigidity "gets amplified when we feel threatened by time pressure, negative emotions, exhaustion, and other stressors."[133] However, having a few options in mind is likely to yield a better decision. Keeping options open should be especially valuable to borrowers who experience scarcity and consider payday loans. Accordingly, other possible strategies include informing single-program users of the existence of other programs.[134] A further possibility is automatically enrolling eligible individuals into some programs.[135] Promotion of these programs, or verifying that consumers indeed use them, could also be a prerequisite for the execution of a payday loan.[136]

18.3.2 *Improving Consumers' Financial Decision-Making*

Many consumer markets are characterized by market failures that prevent market forces from maximizing welfare. However, we cannot simply replace failed market forces through regulation. First, it is highly doubtful that the legislature is equipped with the expertise, knowledge, resources, and information necessary to determine optimal products and contracts. Consumer heterogeneity makes it harder on

---

Consumer Contracts and Conventional Contract Law, 42 U. MICH. J. L. REFORM 747 (2009).

[130] See e.g. the Grameen America initiative, www.grameenamerica.org; Elmira Bayrasli, Microfinance in America? FORBES (Mar. 26, 2012).

[131] See e.g. HADFIELD, *supra* note 3, at 311–18.

[132] For a careful and nuanced attitude see e.g. Frithjof Arp et al., Microfinance for Poverty Alleviation: Do Transnational Initiatives Overlook Fundamental Questions of Competition and Intermediation?, 24 TRANSNATIONAL CORPORATIONS 103 (2017). See also Abhijit Banerjee et al., The Miracle of Microfinance? Evidence from a Randomized Evaluation, 7 AM. ECON. J. APPLIED ECON. 22 (2015).

[133] See e.g. Jack B. Soll et al., Outsmart Your Own Biases, HARV. BUS. REV. (May 2015).

[134] This can be done, for instance, by linking application procedures and eligibility prerequisites across various support programs.

[135] Madrian et al., *supra* note 51, at 34. In light of the status quo bias and the power of inertia this has been done with success in other domains. For one famous example *see* Richard H. Thaler & Shlomo Benartzi, Save More Tomorrow™: Using Behavioral Economics to Increase Employee Saving, 112 J. POL. ECON. S164 (2004).

[136] While these alternatives address lending institutions, there are more ambitious yet highly contested proposals that focus on broad (macroeconomic) policy measures. One alternative is to increase minimum wages. Another is to promote Universal Basic Income (UBI). Both options, which are beyond the scope of this chapter, may improve mental health and reduce financial stress, thus making poor people less inclined to make counterproductive financial decisions.

legislatures to set optimal regulation, and having this flexibility is generally one of the advantages of the market. Second, it is not at all clear that the legislature's purpose is indeed maximization of consumer or social welfare. Often the legislature is influenced by pressure applied by corporations (political capture). These often push forward legislation maximizing the firms' profits at the expense of the consumers' interest.[137]

Keeping that in mind, behavioral economics proposes soft paternalistic approaches. "Asymmetric paternalism" and "libertarian paternalism" are examples of more subtle approaches, which take consumer heterogeneity into account. Asymmetric paternalism calls for rules that advance the welfare of the less shrewd consumers while not significantly hurting the more sophisticated ones.[138] For instance, disclosing (in our context, financial) information can be beneficial for those consumers who lack this information, yet it does not impose an excessive cost on sophisticated consumers who can gather this information elsewhere. Along similar lines, libertarian paternalism seeks to advance protections that preserve the individual's ability to choose what they would choose absent legal intervention.[139] For example, default rules that encourage saving (e.g. social deductions from wages) can still allow those who are not interested in this arrangement to opt out.[140] Whenever possible, we recommend considering protections that follow this logic.

As illustrated, multiple biases and challenges may lead people to make imprudent financial decisions. To tackle that, two types of interventions that may improve consumers' financial behavior come to mind. The first is to utilize System 1 nudges. The other is to prime consumers to make more use of System 2.

18.3.2.1 System 1 Nudges

Defaults. Defaults are known to have a strong impact on people's behavior. In payday loans, it is worth considering making the default of full repayments, where consumers do not roll over their loans, a sticky one. For instance, if a borrower wants to opt out of full payment, they should be required to fill out forms, physically submit them to the lender, and perhaps answer a detailed questionnaire that will guarantee full awareness of the financial consequences. Moreover, if full payment

---

[137] For a basic public choice theory account see DANIEL A. FARBER & PHILIP P. FRICKEY, LAW AND PUBLIC CHOICE: CRITICAL INTRODUCTION 12–37 (1991).

[138] For a development of the idea see Colin Camerer et al., *Behavioral Economics and the Case of "Asymmetric Paternalism,"* 151 U. PA. L. REV. 1211 (2003).

[139] See Cass R. Sunstein & Richard H. Thaler, *Libertarian Paternalism Is not an Oxymoron*, 70 U. CHI. L. REV. 1159 (2003); Richard H. Thaler & Cass R. Sunstein, *Libertarian Paternalism*, 93 AM. ECON. REV. 175 (2003). For a more extensive discussion see RICHARD H. THALER & CASS R. SUNSTEIN, NUDGE: IMPROVING DECISIONS ABOUT HEALTH, WEALTH, AND HAPPINESS (2008).

[140] A default rule like this utilizes the fact that many tend, by inertia, to stay with the status quo. This does not prevent others from choosing a different alternative.

cannot be made and the consumer needs to deviate from said default, perhaps there should be another default of a significant partial repayment. A warning should also be displayed as borrowers opt out of desirable defaults.

Reminders and Kind Messages. Let us illustrate the idea of reminders by referring to nudge banking – a new concept aimed at helping consumers in achieving their long-term financial goals. In one instance, bank customers were given a Nudge app, which includes thirty-eight types of short messages.[141] Customers using this app received, among other things, notices regarding their spending. The app can detect increased spending or inform users how much they would save by changing their behavior (e.g. eating at home instead of dining out). It can also tell consumers when their spending is not in line with the way other consumers behave.

A similar application, which can utilize behavior insights that may nudge people toward better decisions, could be used in respect to payday loans (for those borrowers who own a smartphone). Such an application can send payment reminders, be used to pay loans, propose making small payments in the middle of the borrowing cycle, and provide borrowers with comparative information regarding other borrowers' payments.[142] Downloading and using such an application can even be a mandatory (or a default) prerequisite for loan issuance. This application may also serve as a platform that will exploit human biases to increase savings among low-income earners.[143] Such savings can buffer against the need to use a high-cost credit/loan.

Information Presentation. Information presentation should be in line with current findings of how people process information. To begin with, information should be presented in an accessible and easy way, which should also account for borrowers' levels of education and language proficiency. For example, empirical studies examining the readability of payday loans in general and arbitration clauses in particular found that these were not in line with consumers' (let alone poor consumers') levels of literacy.[144]

Moreover, information presentations can make a better use of visual cues – such as font, size, color, and frames – to enhance their effectiveness. Since people are strongly influenced by comparisons and loss aversion, showing the actual price in

---

[141] See *Banking Innovations Here and Around the World - from the Blog: Would You Like to Experience the Benefits of "Nudge" Banking?*, UNICREDIT BULBANK (Jan. 26, 2016), www.unicreditbulbank.bg/en/about-us/news/banking-innovations-here-and-around-the-world-from/.

[142] See Cara Feinberg, *The Science of Scarcity – A Behavioral Economist Fresh Perspective on Poverty*, HARVARD MAGAZINE (May–June 2015) (noting "a 20 percent improvement in timely rent payment simply by sending postcard reminders and creating a monthly raffle for tenants who paid on time").

[143] A somewhat similar move has been successfully taken by Walmart. See Rob Walker, *How to Trick People into Saving Money*, THE ATLANTIC (May 2017).

[144] CONSUMER FIN. PROT. BUREAU, ARBITRATION STUDY: REPORT TO CONGRESS (2015), at 27–29; Brenna A. Sheffield, *Pre-Dispute Mandatory Arbitration Clauses in Consumer Financial Products: The CFPB's Proposed Regulation and Its Consistency with the Arbitration Study*, 20 NORTH CAROLINA BANKING INSTITUTE 219, 242, 251 (2016).

fees of a payday loan compared with the price of other existing alternatives may make payday loans seem less attractive.[145] Framing and word choice may also play a role, as people respond differently to "dollars owed" than to interest percentages.[146] Along these lines, the fees and interest the borrower has to pay can be presented as a "fine" and charged at the time the loan is issued. Making this payment a present penalty, rather than a future payment, may nudge borrowers into better realizing the true costs of their financial decision.

18.3.2.2 Encouraging the Engagement of System 2

Interestingly, "[e]asy convenient process/little paperwork" is cited as a key motivation that leads borrowers to use payday loans.[147] Since the psychology of scarcity induces people to take the easier path involving minimal effort, this makes perfect sense. However, people need some moderate degree of stress to behave optimally when making decisions.[148]

Hence, promoting a deliberative environment around high-cost credit transactions can be very beneficial. Regulation should ensure that payday loan paperwork is not overly simplified – i.e. simplified in a way that conceals important information and gives the borrowers a false sense of a mundane and trivial decision. This can be furthered by requiring payday borrowers to participate in a counseling session.[149]

We can further increase the likelihood of borrowers using System 2 by asking them to assume they cannot have a payday loan and then requiring them to think of the other alternatives to a payday loan.[150] Moderate levels of stress can yield another benefit: reducing the optimism bias. Thus, it is worthwhile to make sure that the lending environment is structured in a way that will not overly reduce – and perhaps even increase – levels of stress. Lenders should be required to conspicuously disclose and highlight the likelihood of having a future rollover. To make these disclosures

---

[145] Gandy et al., *supra* note 4, at 28.
[146] Feinberg, *supra* note 142.
[147] Elliehausen Gregory, *An Analysis of Consumers' Use of Payday Loans*, Financial Services Research Program Monograph No. 41, Board of Governors of the Federal Reserve System (2009).
[148] See generally IRVING LAW JANIS & LEON MANN, DECISION-MAKING: A PSYCHOLOGICAL ANALYSIS OF CONFLICT, CHOICE, AND COMMITMENT 62 (1977) (specifying conditions for vigilant decision-making). See also Gloria Phillips-Wren & Monica Adya, *Risky Decisions and Decision Support: Does Stress Make a Difference?*, 9 PROCEEDINGS OF JAIS THEORY DEVELOPMENT WORKSHOP. SPROUTS: WORKING PAPERS ON INFORMATION SYSTEMS (2009); MULLAINATHAN & SHAFIR, *supra* note 18, at 142–43. For a more reserved view and for suggesting that this issue merits additional research see Haushofer & Fehr, *supra* note 12, at 866.
[149] See e.g. Lauren E. Willis, *Financial Education: Lessons Not Learned & Lessons Learned*, LIFE-CYCLE INVESTING: FINANCIAL EDUCATION AND CONSUMER PROTECTION 125 (Zvi Bodie et al., eds., 2012).
[150] This is known as "the vanishing options test", see CHIP HEATH & DAN HEATH, DECISIVE: HOW TO MAKE BETTER CHOICES IN LIFE AND WORK (2013).

more powerful and prevent potential mistakes, individualized use-pattern information should be mandated.[151] Where such information does not exist, lenders should disclose use patterns of consumers with similar traits.

Research has demonstrated that relatively simple interventions in the setting of decision-making can improve financial mismanagement for consumers "with complex and negative financial histories."[152] For example, asking people to think about reasons for avoiding debt-related information will probably reduce the likelihood of information avoidance.[153] Additionally, long-term planning can be encouraged by employing questionnaires and videos. Such questionnaires and videos can ask people to contemplate information avoidance and explain its origins and negative consequences. Videos may prove to be a powerful tool because they can present information in a more intuitive and entertaining way. Such videos can be produced by governmental entities (such as the CFPB) or pro-consumer organizations. They can then become a mandatory and integral component of loan issuance.

It may also be beneficial to include a worksheet in the loan process that will help consumers make a concrete plan for loan repayment. First, this will induce a more serious environment and make payday loans less hassle-free, and therefore less misleadingly attractive. Second, including a worksheet has been proven to be a successful intervention that reduces the problem of underestimating expenditure.[154] Third, channeling consumers' attention to future repayments may make the links between the current decision to borrow and its future consequences clearer. Thus, it may reduce borrower's present bias.

Finally, policymakers may want to consider providing borrowers with a cooling-off period during which they may cancel the loan within a specific time frame.[155] The cooling-off period can induce more rational thinking by allowing the consumer to consider the transaction at their convenience. While doing so, the consumer should be able to consider more information about the loan and the existing alternatives in the market. Thus, we should make sure that during the cooling-off period, the videos, tutorials, and infographics discussed earlier will be at the borrower's disposal for further review. It might be important to certify that contracts are drafted using plain language as well, to ensure they are compatible with consumers' level of literacy.

As an additional positive side effect, a cooling-off period may change the incentives that the lender has ex ante. A cooling-off period will make the lender hesitate a

---

[151] See Oren Bar-Gill & Franco Ferrari, *Informing Consumers about Themselves*, 3 ERASMUS L. REV. 93 (2010).
[152] Harkin, *supra* note 75.
[153] *Id.*
[154] *Id.*
[155] Cooling-off periods, however, are not a panacea and can at times backfire and harm consumers. See Shmuel I. Becher & Tal Z. Zarsky, *Open Doors, Trap Doors, and the Law*, 74 LAW CONTEMP. PROBS. 63 (2011).

while before acting slyly or presenting the transaction dishonestly or misleadingly.[156] The very knowledge that the customer can reflect on the loan ex post and terminate the transaction after it has been formed is likely to weaken the dealer's incentive to manipulate the customer in the first place.

18.3.2.3 Taking Personalization and Differentiated Regulation Seriously

While some interventions have been found to be productive in general, different populations and groups may require different treatments. Firms, however, tend to adopt a generic and universal approach to compliance with consumer protection measures, which may harm poor consumers.[157] Therefore, it is imperative to move beyond "one-size-fits-all" types of regulation and consider more individually tailored and nuanced interventions.[158] According to this line of reasoning, personal and demographic characteristics should be taken into account in order to better align the protections afforded to the needs and preferences of borrowing consumers.

Interestingly, consumer heterogeneity is evident in the results of some policy interventions. In our context, there is growing evidence that social programs may well have diverse effects on different groups. For instance, the parent academy – an interesting intervention to help poor families in Chicago Heights –helped White and Hispanic people, but not Blacks.[159] The same varied effects may be true regarding different age groups. In this context, it has been argued that "[a]ntipoverty programs vary in their effectiveness, with the elderly benefiting most and being affected least by the work disincentives built into many of the programs."[160] All this further demonstrates that the solution to complex problems – such as the regulation that should govern payday loans – is not likely to be the same for everyone.[161]

First, we may consider personalized disclosures, reminders, and messages. With the rise of big data, sophisticated algorithms, artificial intelligence, and machine learning, legal scholars have started exploring the idea of personalized laws.[162] In the context of disclosures in consumer law, it has been suggested that "[i]mpersonal information duties and standardized notices could be replaced by granular legal norms which provide personalized disclosures based on informational needs of an

---

[156] *Id.*, at 1240.
[157] See Paul Ali et al., *Financial Hardship Assistance behind the Scenes: Insights from Financial Counsellors*, 52 AUST. J. SOC. ISS. 241 (2017).
[158] Yuval Feldman & Orly Lobel, *Behavioral Trade-Offs: Beyond the Land of Nudges Spans the World of Law and Psychology*, in NUDGE AND THE LAW: A EUROPEAN PERSPECTIVE (Alberto Alemanno & Anne-Lise Sibony eds., 2015).
[159] Roland G. Fryer Jr., Steven D. Levitt & John A. List, *Parental Incentives and Early Childhood Achievement: A Field Experiment in Chicago Heights*, NBER Working Paper No. 21477 (2015).
[160] SCHUCK, *supra* note 5, at 25–26.
[161] Cf. Russell, *supra* note 26.
[162] See e.g. Anthony Casey & Anthony Niblett, *Self-Driving Law*, 66 U. TORONTO. L. J. 430 (2016).

individual and personal preferences."[163] Tailoring disclosures in such a way will promote their effectiveness while optimizing costs. The same is true in regard to reminders and messages, which can be personalized based on each borrower's characteristics and circumstances. Along similar lines, "the Consumer Financial Protection Bureau could identify particular default contractual provisions that are well suited to particular types of consumers and require firms to offer the terms to customers with those profiles."[164]

Second, consider overoptimism. While this bias is relevant to people from different backgrounds and ages, it is in its lowest rates at midlife. This may entail that policy intervention can be tailored according to age. Thus, young borrowers will deserve an extra-vigilant approach, intended to ensure the engagement of System 2. Such an approach may necessitate using premortems,[165] where borrowers will be asked to imagine a future failure to repay, and then asked what may have caused such a failure. Similarly, borrowers may be informed about overall failure rate (of other borrowers) and asked to consider whether and why this rate is different than their own personal estimation.[166] The need to justify one's optimism when confronted with challenging data may also reduce overoptimism.

Third, fair lending may require lenders to assess the borrower's ability to pay. The basic idea here is to ensure that borrowers can repay their loans. While there are legal limitations that prevent people from using certain attributes of individuals from being considered by lenders,[167] with abundant information and big data systems, lenders can consider a large variety of aspects and information that are not based on forbidden discriminatory proxies relatively easily.[168] Thus, regulators should stay vigilant as to what is, and is not, being considered in this respect. Hopefully, such a personalized approach may yield more just results, where borrowers are not discriminated against based on color or ethnicity.[169]

---

[163] Christoph Busch, *Implementing Personalized Law: Personalized Disclosures in Consumer Law and Privacy Law*, 86 CHI. L. REV. 309 (2018).

[164] Ariel Porat & Lior Jacob Strahilevitz, *Personalizing Default Rules and Disclosure with Big Data*, 112 MICH. L. REV. 1417, 1440 (2013). See also Yuval Feldman & Yotam Kaplan, *Big Data and Bounded Ethicality*, 29 CORNELL J.L. & PUB. POL'Y 39 (2019) (detailing the advantages of using big data in dealing with problematic situations).

[165] See e.g. Soll et al., *supra* note 133.

[166] *Id.*

[167] Yan Zhang, *Assessing Fair Lending Risks Using Race/Ethnicity Proxies*, 64 MANAG. SCI. (2016).

[168] For a general discussion of the potential of big data for decision such as those of creditors, see Liran Einav & Jonathan Levin, *The Data Revolution and Economic Analysis*, 14(1) INNOV. POL. ECON. 1–24 (2014). For a more detailed discussion of the potential problems in big data analysis of borrowers' history see Mikella Hurley & Julius Adebayo, *Credit Scoring in the Era of Big Data*, 18 YALE J.L. TECH. 148 (2016).

[169] For discussing lending discrimination based on mortgage data *see* Robert Bartlett et al., *Consumer Lending Discrimination in the FinTech Era* (Dec. 7, 2017), https://papers.ssrn.com/sol3/papers.cfm?abstract_id=3063448.

18.3.3 Responsible Lending: Revisiting Lenders' Obligations

So far, we have mainly focused on borrowers. We discussed their cognitive biases, and the effects of scarcity and poverty more generally. We then recommended policy and legal measures that may provide borrowers with tools and an environment to make better financial decisions.

We now shift our focus to lenders and their ability to mitigate counterproductive behavior and improve borrowers' decision-making. We first discuss lenders' responsibility ex ante – i.e. before a loan is issued. We then propose that courts review lenders' responsibility and behavior ex post, utilizing the doctrine of unconscionability.

18.3.3.1 Ex Ante Measures

According to Richard Cordray, the CFPB's director, "consumers are being set up to fail with loan payments that they are unable to repay."[170] To mitigate that reality, the CFPB proposed in 2016 a new federal rule[171] that requires high-cost credit lenders to examine customers' ability to pay back loans.[172] The suggested rule also forbids lenders from offering new loans to pay off the old ones. This is of key significance, because according to the CFPB more than 80 percent of such loans are rolled over within a month, making them a snowball trap.

As part of responsible lending, regulators can require lenders to verify that borrowers take advantage of government assistance programs. Additionally, as is the case under New Zealand law, lenders could have a duty to make reasonable inquiries to assure that the credit they provide will meet the borrowers' requirements and objectives.[173] We should also consider more intrusive interventions, such as requiring lenders to inquire about the loan's purpose. If the borrower's intent is to pay for utilities, a medical bill, or other necessity, the lender can deposit the loan directly to the relevant account or otherwise ensure the money is used for the stated purpose. Lastly, we can require lenders to demonstrate that borrowers understand

---

[170] CPFB, *Consumer Financial Protection Bureau Proposes Rule to End Payday Debt Traps* (June 2, 2016), at 2.

[171] PAYDAY, VEHICLE TITLE, AND CERTAIN HIGH-COST INSTALLMENT LOANS, 12 C.F.R. § 1041 (2016).

[172] Integrating "pre-agreement" assessment as part of responsible lending has been experienced in various jurisdictions. See e.g. C. M. Van Heerden & Reinhard Steennot, *Pre-Agreement Assessment as a Responsible Lending Tool in South-Africa, and Belgium: Part 1*, 21 POTCHEFSTROOM ELECT. L. J. (2018). It has also been employed in other domains. See Joseph Sanders & Vijay Raghavan, *Improvident Student Lending*, 2018 UTAH L. REV. 919 (2018).

[173] Responsible Lending Code (Minister of Commerce and Consumer Affairs, 2015), www.consumerprotection.govt.nz/assets/PDFs/responsible-lending-code.pdf

"key pertinent costs, benefits, and risks of the financial products they have been sold."[174]

At the same time, if it is not a necessity that drives the loan, that may serve as a warning sign. In such cases, the lender may be required to report the loan further (e.g. to community or aid services). Alternatively, the borrower may be asked to watch a special tutorial and answer some written questions prompting further thought. Additionally, we may require the buyer to reflect during an ex ante cooling-off period – asking them to fill out the relevant forms and return in a few days to execute the loan.

Lenders' responsibility and their assessment of borrowers' ability to repay can be measured ex post by examining, for instance, the rate of rollovers. Where this rate exceeds a specific threshold – to be determined by experts – lenders will have to refute a presumption that their business policy is improper. Another possibility is measuring whether the credit indeed achieved the borrower's goal; i.e. if the loan indeed helped the borrower in line with their ex ante plans. All these measures will be published and generally accessible.

This, in turn, may result in two positive outcomes: first, it will inform borrowers, policymakers, and aid organizations; second, the mere fact that there is a public and legal surveillance ex post is likely to induce more careful and fair business behaviors ex ante.[175] At the second stage, this data should be aggregated to form some grade or ranking. If this becomes a salient aspect for consumers, businesses will align their behaviors accordingly so as not to undermine their reputations. Of course, there should be additional economic incentives, such as fines and loan forgiveness, when lenders do not comply with the law.

18.3.3.2 Ex Post: Revisiting the Doctrine of Unconscionability

The unconscionability doctrine was incorporated in the Uniform Commercial Code (UCC) Section 2-302, titled "Unconscionable Contract or Clause." The prevailing opinion regarding the doctrine of unconscionability is that courts can and should use the doctrine to review both substantive and procedural contractual aspects.[176] As the famous case of *Williams v. Walker-Thomas Furniture Co.*[177]

---

[174] Lauren E. Willis, *The Consumer Financial Protection Bureau and the Quest for Consumer Comprehension*, 3 Russ. Sage Found. J. Soc. Sci. 74 (2017).

[175] Paul R. Kleindorfer, *What if You Know You Will Have to Explain Your Choices to Others Afterwards? Legitimation in Decision-Making*, The Irrational Economist – Making Decisions in a Dangerous World (2010), at 72.

[176] See Melvin A. Eisenberg, *The Bargain Principle and Its Limits*, 95 Harv. L. Rev. 741, 752–54 (1982); Robert A. Hillman, *Rolling Contracts*, 71 Fordham L. Rev. 743, 749 (2002); Daniel T. Ostas, *Postmodern Economic Analysis of Law: Extending the Pragmatic Visions of Richard A. Posner*, 36 Am. Bus. L. J. 193, 228 (1998).

[177] *Williams v. Walker Thomas*, 350 F.2d 445 (D.C. Cir. 1965), rev'g, 198 A.2d 914 (D.C. 1964).

illustrates, courts use the unconscionability doctrine to protect an allegedly weak party from being exploited by a stronger party.

In *Williams*, the court dealt with the conscionability of a repossession clause in a rent-to-own contract, which purported to lease the purchased items to the appellant, a poor credit borrower, for monthly rent payments. The federal court of appeals explained that "unconscionability has generally been recognized to include an absence of meaningful choice on the part of one of the parties together with contract terms which are unreasonably favorable to the other party."[178] Section 208 of the *Restatement*, titled "Unconscionable Contract or Term," reflects a similar idea.

The doctrine of unconscionability could also be used by courts to assess, ex post, high-cost credit transactions.[179] Indeed, unconscionability has been regarded as "the Law of the Poor."[180] Most prominently, the doctrine is an important judicial tool for coping with transactions entered into with imperfect information and lack of meaningful choice.[181] At least one court has followed this path while acknowledging cognitive biases that may put borrowers at risk.[182]

Similarly, courts have developed a "reasonably communicated" test in order to ensure that the weaker party had a reasonable chance to observe the importance and meaning of a specific contractual clause.[183] Assuming no ex ante regulation of payday loan contracts, courts may consider, among other things, the readability of these contracts.[184] Given the psychology of scarcity, unconscionability and similar or related doctrines can play a more significant role in judicial scrutiny of high-cost credit transactions.

18.3.3.3 Summary

As a quick overview, Table 18.1 depicts the main behavioral phenomena we have been discussing, how they can negatively impact financial decision-making, and how we suggest mitigating or de-biasing these negative impacts.

---

[178] *Id.* at 449.

[179] Baird, for instance, explains that important contractual aspects should be undertaken in "an environment that allows for reflection and deliberation." Douglas G. Baird, *The Boilerplate Puzzle*, 104 MICH. L. REV. 933, 944 (2006).

[180] Ann Fleming, *The Rise and Fall of Unconscionability as the Law of the Poor*, 102 GEO. L. J. 1383 (2013).

[181] Cf. Shmuel I. Becher, *Asymmetric Information in the Market for Contract Terms: The Challenge That Is Yet to Be Met*, 45 AM. BUS. L. J. 723 (2008). Moreover, the flexibility of the unconscionability doctrine allows the creation and development of other related doctrines, such as unfair surprise, which courts use to refrain from enforcing contract provisions that violate the reasonable expectations of a contracting party. See e.g. Donald B. King, *Standard Form Contracts: A Call for Reality*, 44 ST. LOUIS U. L.J. 909, 911 (2000).

[182] See *State ex rel. King v. B&B In. Grp., Inc.*, 2014-NMSC-024.

[183] Such as forum selection clauses. See generally Kaustuv M. Das, *Note & Comment: Forum-Selection Clauses in Consumer Clickwrap and Browsewrap Agreements and the "Reasonably Communicated" Test*, 77 WASH. L. REV. 481, 492–96 (2002).

[184] As noted, payday loan contracts are written in a language that prevents a typical borrower from being able to read and understand them. See supra note 144 and accompanying text.

TABLE 18.1. *Behavioral phenomena, their impact and mitigating/de-biasing tools*

Behavioral phenomenon	Effect on financial decision-making	Proposed remedies
Optimism bias	Excessive borrowing and suboptimal precaution taking	1. Third parties and intermediaries to offer alternatives and assist consumers
Present bias	Limited ability to delay satisfaction in spite of possible negative long-term effects	2. Defaults to increase likelihood and stickiness of superior options
Limited self-control	Experiencing difficulties to resist temptations	3. Reminders on nature of spending and options to save
Scarcity-related cognitive limitations	Limited ability and availability to deal with complex decisions	4. Diversifying and improving information presentation
Cognitive rigidity	Focusing only on one option	5. Encouraging deliberative reasoning (usage of spreadsheets, cooling-off periods)
Information overload	Ignoring important information	6. Incentivizing, ex post and ex ante, responsible lending
Confirmation bias	Searching for, and overvaluing, information that supports preexisting beliefs	7. Personalizing the regulatory treatment (utilizing past behavior, big data, etc.)
Ostrich effect	Avoiding reading disclosures and financial information	

18.4 CONCLUDING REMARKS

"Poverty is like punishment for a crime you didn't commit."[185]

Poverty is a serious problem with far-reaching consequences. Tackling poverty requires a cross-disciplinary understanding, useful data, a systematic evidence-based analysis, and a holistic approach. Alleviating poverty demands ongoing and deep commitment toward building human capital, individual capabilities, and supporting society. This cannot be done effectively without addressing the causes and consequences of poverty throughout the life course. Nonetheless, policymakers often channel their attention to short-term financial fixes, which appeal to the public and enhance their image or reputation.[186]

Though merely one piece of a significant and challenging puzzle, consumer finance plays an important role in poverty policy.[187] Indeed, one of the pillars of

---

[185] Attributed to Eli Khamarov, Stanford Center on Poverty and Inequality.
[186] For a detailed discussion in the context of consumer law see Becher, *supra* note 115.
[187] Cf. Norman I. Silber, *Discovering That the Poor Pay More: Race Riots, Poverty, and the Rise of Consumer Law*, 44 FORDHAM URB. L. J. 1319 (2017) (discussing David Kaplovitz's book *The Poor Pay More*, the importance of consumer finance, and the recommendation to address social grievances through legal revisions).

poverty eradication is minimizing costs. This can be achieved by taking out low-cost credit and accumulating savings that can serve as a safety net and a buffer.

Along these lines, this chapter focused on borrowing practices from a consumer law perspective. It explained the biases that may lead people to overborrow and overspend. It also reviewed the unique psychological and cognitive forces that can induce poor consumers to make counterproductive financial decisions. With that in mind, it examined policy interventions that may be better tailored to cope with the genuine sources of the problem.

The policy interventions discussed in this chapter may raise a few legitimate concerns. One such concern relates to inadvertent consequences, such as stereotyping and negative reinforcement. Unfortunately, sometimes well-intended social programs can severely backfire. If poor people are treated differently, they might be reminded repeatedly of their low socioeconomic status. Such reminders may cause negative identity priming and enhance a sense of helplessness.[188] This can further one's worries, which may reinforce weaknesses and problems, instead of solving them.

Studies show that intellectual performance can be impaired by internalizing negative stereotypes such as ethnicity and social class. In the context of poverty, one study found that priming low-income students by asking them to provide demographic information led to worse performance on a test, when compared to the performance of low-income students who were not primed in that direction.[189] This is a stereotype threat: concerns about one's identity create a mental load which saps the cognitive system and working memory, thus leading to suboptimal performance.[190]

Another important concern is personal privacy. One set of our recommendations discussed tailoring the legal treatment of poor consumers. This entails using consumers' personal information. When it comes to indigent consumers, this should be carefully viewed given the argument that marginalized populations enjoy merely "weak versions" of privacy.[191]

More generally, and in spite of the concerns noted, we hope that the framework outlined in this chapter may be applicable to other financial contexts of impoverished people. Consider gambling and lotteries, which disproportionally affect the poor, or the consumption and regulation of unhealthy products such as soft drinks,

---

[188] Cf. HELMER, *supra* note 106, at 31.
[189] Bettine Spencer & Emanuele Castano, *Social Class Is Dead. Long Live Social Class! Stereotype Threat among Low Socioeconomic Status Individuals*, 20 SOC. JUST. RES. 418 (2007).
[190] Jean-Claude Croizet et al., *Stereotype Threat Undermines Intellectual Performance by Triggering a Disruptive Mental Load*, 30 PERS. SOC. PSYC. BULL. 721 (2004); Sian Beilock, *Stereotype Threat and Working Memory: Mechanisms, Alleviation, and Spillover*, 136 J. EXP. PSYCOL. GEN. 256 (2007).
[191] See KHIARA M. BRIDGES, THE POVERTY OF PRIVACY RIGHTS (2017) (discussing the privacy of poor mothers).

fast food, alcohol, and tobacco. In these and other domains, such as housing and schooling, poverty has an impact on decision-making processes, and legal policy should look for ways to facilitate a better reality. Introducing psychological and behavioral insights into this process may result in policies that are more effective, which will lead to a more compassionate society. Following this reasoning, the psychology of scarcity can shed further light on other nonfinancial domains.[192]

Ineffective interventions provide the poor with a false feeling of protection – which may tempt them even more to make bad decisions. It further provides the wealthy and the fortunate a false sense of empathy regarding the underprivileged and prevents them from taking effective action to aid the poor. Regulators can help improve the financial situation of the poor by understanding how financial decisions are made and adopting behaviorally informed interventions. We hope this chapter takes a modest step toward that end.

---

[192] University entry and academic scholarships may be additional contexts where policies can be changed in order to accommodate the psychology of scarcity. If poverty or scarcity explain why poor people do worse in their exams and assessments, this may provide an additional angle (and justification) for policies that benefit the poor.

19

Eating Law

Stephen Ansolabehere and Jacob E. Gersen

19.1 INTRODUCTION

In 2014, two titans in the food industry squared off in the Supreme Court of the United States. POM Wonderful, LLC is a well-known beverage producer, largely credited with ushering in America's love affair with pomegranate juice. POM Wonderful produces a number of pomegranate-based beverages. One such beverage is a "Pomegranate Blueberry" juice that consists primarily of, well, pomegranate and blueberry juice. Not to be left out of the bourgeoning pomegranate juice market, the Coca-Cola Company began manufacturing and selling its own version of a pomegranate blueberry juice drink: Minute Maid Enhanced Pomegranate Blueberry Flavored 100% Juice Blend. It consists of 99.4 percent apple juice.

Neither POM nor Coke is known in the food industry for its fear of litigation.[1] So it was not altogether surprising when, in 2008, POM filed suit against Coke under the false-advertising provision of the Lanham Act,[2] as well as under California's Unfair Competition Law[3] and False Advertising Law.[4] Among other things, the Lanham Act authorizes suit by plaintiffs whose commercial interests have been harmed through false or misleading representations about goods.[5] Challenging the drink's labeling, marketing, name, and advertising, POM argued that Coke misled consumers to believe that Coke's pomegranate blueberry juice consisted primarily of pomegranate and blueberry juices.[6]

---

[1] As an illustration, consider the three volume compendium of Coca-Cola Law. *Opinions, Orders, Injunctions, and Decrees Relating to Unfair Competition and Infringement of Trade-Mark*.
[2] 15 U.S.C. § 1125(a).
[3] Cal. Bus. & Prof'l Code § 17200 *et seq.*
[4] *Id.*
[5] 15 U.S.C. § 1125.
[6] In ruling on Coke's motion to dismiss, the district court determined, among other things, that POM's state law claims were expressly preempted by the FDCA to the extent that the Unfair

A food company's product names and labels must meet requirements established by the Food, Drug & Cosmetic Act (FDCA) and implementing regulations established by the Food and Drug Administration (FDA). But the FDCA does not provide a private right of action for enforcement. The FDA may issue a warning letter to noncomplying companies or seek to seize foods because they are deemed adulterated or misbranded according to the Act, but the ordinary consumer cannot generally sue a food company for failing to comply with applicable FDA regulations. So, a consumer who purchased Coke's version of the juice thinking it contained lots of – or indeed virtually any – juice derived from either pomegranates or blueberries could not sue, even if Coke's product name or claims violated FDA requirements. Nor could the ordinary consumer sue under the Lanham Act. The Lanham Act does, however, provide a right of action for competitors harmed by the fraudulent or deceptive trade practice. The issue before the Supreme Court in POM Wonderful v. Coca-Cola was whether the FDCA precludes a competitor suit pursuant to the Lanham Act. In short, what is the relationship between the FDCA and the Lanham Act when both might reasonably be applied to the same underlying conduct?

Not surprisingly, POM argued that the Lanham Act permits such a lawsuit, calling its case against Coke a "classic Lanham Act false advertising case."[7] POM also cited a survey that found 36 percent of consumers believed the Minute Maid-branded juice contained mainly pomegranate and blueberry juice.[8] POM emphasized that while FDA regulations may not expressly bar Coke's pomegranate-blueberry label, the FDA has also not explicitly approved the label.[9] POM contended that there is no textual basis – in either the Lanham Act or the FDCA – to exempt FDA-compliant labels from Lanham Act challenges. Thus, according to POM, such an exception could be made, if at all, by implication. POM argued that the presumption against "implied repeals" is strong, and thus that both statutes should be given effect unless they are in "irreconcilable conflict."[10] Coke, POM urged, could have complied with both the Lanham Act and FDA regulations. FDA regulations did not require Coke to choose a misleading label.[11] POM moreover argued that because FDA "does not have anywhere near the resources necessary to police food labeling," barring Lanham Act challenges would create "a significant enforcement gap that Congress could not have desired."[12]

Competition Law and False Advertising Law imposed obligations different from those imposed by the FDCA. However, POM amended its complaint to avoid the preemption ruling, adding a misbranding claim under California's Sherman Law, which is identical to the FDCA.

[7] Brief for Petitioner at 8, *Pom Wonderful* v. *Coca-Cola*, 573 U.S. 102 (2014) (No. 12-761), 2014 U.S. S. Ct. Briefs LEXIS 772, at *18.
[8] *Id.* at 10.
[9] *Id.* at 14.
[10] *Id.* at 15.
[11] *Id.*
[12] *Id.* at 18.

Coke, on the other hand, argued that POM could not sue under the Lanham Act because FDA regulations "specifically authorize" Coke's label. To allow such Lanham Act suits by competitors would "disrupt the national uniformity Congress has required in the naming and labeling of food and juice products" via the FDCA and the Nutrition Labeling and Education Act of 1990 (NLEA).[13] Coke predictably asserted that the text, structure, and purpose of the NLEA and FDCA show an overriding congressional intent to achieve uniformity in labeling and to bar private lawsuits undermining that goal.[14] Furthermore, Coke contended that the court has long held that specific federal statutes can limit the application of other, more general federal statutes, even when neither statute expressly says so. Limiting earlier, more general laws based on later, more specific laws is not "implied repeal," but rather "a classic judicial task."[15] And in any event, private lawsuits are not the appropriate solution to agency resource problems.[16]

Beyond providing good fodder for certain first-year law school classes, the oral argument revealed a fault line in the emerging litigation battles about food – a fight that at last count involved several hundred lawsuits, many of them class actions, against the major food companies. At argument, none of the justices seemed particularly taken with Coke's argument and many recognized that most claims about food are not exactly tightly overseen. Justice Ginsburg queried:

> I would like you to respond to this question: In the real world, the FDA has a tremendous amount of things on its plate, and labels for juices are not really high on its list. It has very limited resources. You are asking us to take what it has said about juice as blessing this label, saying it's not misbranding, when its regulations aren't reviewed by the Court, when there is no private right of action, and say that that overtakes the Lanham Act. It's really very hard to conceive that Congress would have done that.[17]

Chief Justice Roberts and Justice Ginsburg suggested that the Lanham Act and the FDCA might serve different purposes, such that a label could comply with FDA regulations and still mislead "on the entirely different question of commercial competition ... that has nothing to do with health."[18]

Various commentators noted the justices' evident discomfort with the notion that ruling in Coke's favor might leave companies like POM with no recourse for competitors' misleading labels, as long as those labels comply with FDA

---

[13] Brief for Respondent at 1, *POM Wonderful v. Coca-Cola*, No. 12-761 (Mar. 26, 2014), http://sblog.s3.amazonaws.com/wp-content/uploads/2014/03/12-761-bs-Coca-Cola.pdf.
[14] *Id.* at 15.
[15] *Id.* at 14.
[16] *Id.* at 17.
[17] *Id.* See also Transcript of Oral Argument at 42–43, *Pom Wonderful v. Coca-Cola*, 573 U.S. 102 (2014) (No. 12-761).
[18] Michael Bobelian, *In* POM v. Coca-Cola, *Supreme Court Could Shake Up Food Labeling*, FORBES (Apr. 22, 2014, 3:06 PM), www.forbes.com/sites/michaelbobelian/2014/04/22/supreme-court-asked-to-referee-dispute-between-coca-cola-and-pom/.

regulations.[19] As Justice Kennedy said during oral argument, "You want us to write an opinion that said that Congress enacted a statutory scheme because it intended that no matter how misleading or how deceptive a label it is, if it passes the FDA, ... there can be no liability? That's what you want us to say?"[20]

This notion that the FDA does health and the Lanham Act (and perhaps the Federal Trade Commission (FTC)) does commercial competition and consumer confusion is, of course, not quite right precisely because today names and claims about foods are often an attempt to invoke a sentiment about health. Indeed, POM Wonderful has been both credited and criticized for its attempts to tout the health benefits of pomegranate juice. Whether the juice is sold with an express or implied health claim, part of the pomegranate juice mystique is that it is supposed to be good for us. Presumably that is part of the reason Coke sought to sell apple juice as pomegranate blueberry juice.

The formal legal question that the justices were called upon to answer was about the relationship between two potentially overlapping federal statutes that delegate authority to two different agencies with jurisdiction over claims about food. As the justices' questions illustrate, however, the answer to that question is at base a question about who, if anyone, is really in charge of truth when it comes to food. As Justice Kennedy added at one point, "it's relevant for us to ask whether people are cheated in buying this product."[21]

Without delving too deeply into waters that are best skimmed across, FDA's food-naming rules authorize the use of terms such as "Pomegranate" and "Blueberry" in the name of a product so long as the term "flavored" is used in the name as well. That is, a "pomegranate blueberry flavored blend of five juices" complies with FDA's food naming requirements so long as the blend of five juices "tastes like" or is "flavored with" pomegranate and blueberry. This is so even if the product contains virtually no pomegranate or blueberry juice.

Consider the colloquy between the bench and Kathleen Sullivan, former Dean of Stanford Law School, who was representing Coke before the court.

Ms. Sullivan: We don't think consumers are quite as unintelligent as POM must think they are. They know when something is a flavored blend of five juices ... the non-predominant juices are just flavor.

Justice Kennedy: Don't make me feel bad just because I thought this was pomegranate juice.

---

[19] Elaine Watson, *POM v. Coke at the Supreme Court: Who Came Out on Top?*, FOOD NAVIGATOR (Apr. 21, 2014), www.foodnavigator-usa.com/Regulation/POM-v-Coke-at-the-Supreme-Court-Who-came-out-on-top.

[20] Coke responded at oral argument that companies opposing a competitor's labeling regime should "go to the FDA and seek FDA's change of its rulemaking." Transcript of Oral Argument at 39, *supra* note 17.

[21] *Id.*

Ms. Sullivan:	Justice Kennedy – Justice Kennedy it's pomegranate-blueberry-flavored blend of five juices. I've found that oftentimes – well –
Justice Scalia:	He sometimes doesn't read closely enough.

(Laughter.)[22]

A unanimous court went on to hold that the Lanham Act suit could go forward in the lower courts. But beyond the standard challenges of statutory interpretation lurk more basic ones: would the justices have been confused or deceived by Coke's juice? Is the answer really that they should have read more carefully? Should consumers have to pore through the Federal Register to know what's in their juice? And ought the law respond to the gap between what is reasonably understood about a food product and – for lack of a better word – the truth about it?

One constant during the past century and before is the need to understand how ordinary people make judgements and inferences about the foods they consume. Our project is founded on a belief that the best approach to the legal regulation of food depends, in part, on the empirical reality of consumer behavior. There is an intuitive appeal to the Justice Kennedy model of the reasonable consumer: If I, the judge would be confused then it is deceptive because who is the reasonable consumer, if not me?

Our goal in this project is to make some headway on this question. To do so, we start with several recent controversies involving claims and beliefs about food. Some are drawn from active litigation including class action lawsuits against food companies claiming that consumers were misled by a product name or claim. Others involve recent actual and proposed changes to the labeling regimes governing genetically modified foods on the one hand and added sugars on the other. Methodologically, we analyze these questions mainly using experiments involving online survey instruments. Section 19.2 provides a brief overview of the relevant legal regime. Section 19.3 focuses on GMO disclosure regulation and related controversies. Section 19.4 focuses on the disclosure of sugar content. And Section 19.5 concludes by returning to the *POM* v. *Coke* controversy.

19.2 SOME MODEST PUZZLES ABOUT FOOD AND LAW

19.2.1 *Protecting Who?*

Traditionally, the law of food marketing is broken into two parts: labeling and advertising. The two policy domains are closely related, but the sources of law that regulate each are different. As a result, the lead agencies that administer each domain differ as well. The Federal Trade Commission is responsible for policing

---

[22] *Id.*

food advertising. The FDA and the United States Department of Agriculture (USDA) regulate food labeling for food products that fall within their respective jurisdictions. The Federal Meat Inspection Act (FMIA) gives authority to the USDA's Food Safety and Inspection Service (FSIS) to implement and enforce food labeling requirements with respect to meat and poultry products derived from domestic animals, poultry products derived from domestic birds, and liquid egg and liquid egg products produced in cracking plants. Pursuant to the 1938 FDCA, the FDA has jurisdiction to regulate food labeling with respect to all foods that enter commerce in the United States that are not regulated by the USDA. Thus, a food label for a food product in interstate commerce is regulated either by the FDA or by the USDA. As with any split jurisdiction scheme, conflicts and confusion can arise.[23] In the main, however, the agencies tend to share information and coordinate whenever possible.

The FTC's jurisdiction over food advertising derives from sections 5 and 12 of the FTC Act, which broadly prohibit unfair or deceptive commercial acts or practices and specifically prohibit the dissemination of false advertisements for foods, drugs, medical devices, or cosmetics. The FTC has issued two policy statements that articulate the agency's views on deception. The Deception Policy Statement was appended to *Cliffdale Assocs., Inc.*,[24] and the Statement on Advertising Substantiation was appended to *Thompson Med. Co.*[25] According to these policies, in identifying deception in an advertisement, the FTC considers the representation from the perspective of a consumer acting reasonably under the circumstances: "The test is whether the consumer's interpretation or reaction is reasonable."[26] To implement the standard, the FTC "examines the overall net impression of an ad and engages in a three-part inquiry: (1) what claims are conveyed in the ad; (2) are those claims false or misleading; and (3) are those claims material to prospective consumers."[27]

The FDA's general statutory authority to regulate food labeling derives from section 403(a)(1) of the FDCA, which deems a food misbranded if its labeling is false or misleading. Unlike the reasonable consumer standard adopted by the FTC in its Deception Policy, courts in the first half of the twentieth century often interpreted the FDCA to protect not the reasonable consumer, but rather "the ignorant, the unthinking, and the credulous" consumer.[28] For example, an FDA

---

[23] See Jacob E. Gersen, *Overlapping and Underlapping Jurisdiction in Administrative Law*, 2006 SUP. CT. REV. 201 (2007).
[24] 103 F.T.C. 110, 174 (1984).
[25] 104 F.T.C. 648, 839 (1984).
[26] 103 F.T.C. at 177.
[27] *Kraft, Inc. v. F.T.C.*, 970 F.2d 311, 314 (7th Cir. 1992).
[28] See, e.g., *United States v. El-O-Pathic Pharmacy*, 192 F.2d 62, 75 (9th Cir. 1951); *United States v. An Article of Food ... Manischewitz ... Diet Thins*, 377 F. Supp. 746, 749 (E.D.N.Y. 1974). But see *United States v. 88 Cases, Bireley's Orange Beverage*, 187 F.2d 967, 971 (3d Cir. 1951) (act requires evaluation of claims from the perspective of the ordinary person or reasonable consumer).

order condemning "Diet-Thins Matzos" manufactured by Manischevitz was upheld, in part, because the dieting consumer is often not reasonable at all:

> the test is not the effect of the label on a "reasonable consumer," but upon "the ignorant, the unthinking and the credulous" consumer. Even a technically accurate description of a food or drug's content may violate 21 U.S.C. § 343 if the description is misleading in other respects. *United States v. An Article – Nuclomin*, 482 F.2d 581 (8th Cir. 1973). Thus, whether or not the side panel of the Diet-Thins label may accurately describe its virtues for certain special diets which do not appear to involve weight control, the misleading nature of the front panel still justifies condemnation of the seized articles. . . .
>
> Purchasers of diet products are often "pathetically eager" to obtain a more slender figure. There can be no doubt that the weight-conscious consumer may be led to believe that Diet-Thin Matzos are lower in calories than ordinary matzo crackers.[29]

For several decades courts oscillated between allowing condemnation of foods with labels that would trick only the reasonable consumer or trick only the ignorant, unthinking, or credulous consumer. The FDA remained comparatively silent on the issue. Ultimately, however, in the early 2000s, the FDA sought to harmonize its approach to food labels with the FTC's approach to advertising.[30] In 2002, the FDA decided that the reasonable consumer was the appropriate standard to use in determining whether a claim in the labeling of a dietary supplement or conventional food is misleading.

> The reasonable consumer standard more accurately reflects FDA's belief that consumers are active partners in their own health care who behave in health-promoting ways when they are given accurate health information. In addition, the reasonable consumer standard is consistent with the governing first amendment case law precluding the Government from regulating the content of promotional communication so that it contains only information that will be appropriate for a vulnerable or unusually credulous audience. *Cf. Bolger v. Youngs Drug Prods. Corp.*, 463 U.S. 60, 73–74 (1983) ("the government may not 'reduce the adult population . . . to reading only what is fit for children.'") (quoting *Butler v. Michigan*, 352 U.S. 380, 383 (1957)).
>
> Based on the FTC's success in policing the marketplace for misleading claims in food advertising, FDA believes that its own enforcement of the legal and regulatory requirements applicable to food labeling will not be adversely affected by use of the "reasonable consumer" standard in evaluating labeling for dietary supplements and conventional foods. Explicit FDA adoption of the reasonable consumer standard

---

[29] *An Article of Food . . . Manischewitz . . . Diet Thins*, 377 F. Supp. at 749 (internal citations omitted).
[30] Lewis Grossman, *FDA and the Rise of the Empowered Consumer*, 66 ADMIN. L. REV. 627 (2014).

will rationalize the regulatory environment for food promotion while both protecting and enhancing the public health.[31]

As should be clear, the choice between the reasonable consumer standard and the ignorant, unthinking, and credulous consumer (IUC) standard is in part a choice about which portion of the consumer population to protect. If the reasonable consumer is the median consumer, then allowing labels or marketing into the marketplace that will trick the IUC consumer entails that some (unreasonably) deceptive food names and labels will remain on store shelves. If a substantial minority of citizens behave more like the IUC consumer than the reasonable consumer, the law will tolerate substantial confusion and misunderstanding in the food marketplace.

19.2.2 *Naming, Blaming, and Claiming*[32]

19.2.2.1 Command and Control

The transition toward focusing on the reasonable consumer dovetails with a move away from what might be thought of as command-and-control regulation of food identity.[33] For example, many areas of food law replicate a basic problem: is the consumer getting (and eating) what the consumer thinks they are getting? Is it milk or colored water? Is it natural honey from bees or synthetic honey produced in a lab? Is it 12 ounces of food or only 10 ounces of food and 2 ounces of fill? Is it tuna or some other non-fish? And so on.

For many years, one of the major legal solutions to this problem was the use of strict *standards of identity*,[34] a tool authorized by the 1938 FDCA. A standard of identity requires that any food lawfully sold as a given standardized food must meet strict ingredient requirements. A food that purports to be or is represented as a regulated food either must meet the standard or it may not be sold because it is "misbranded."

For example, if a food is sold as ice cream, it must meet strict ingredient or recipe requirements. These are specified in the standard of identity regulation for "ice cream and frozen custard."[35] If the food looks, tastes, and is marketed as ice cream

---

[31] Guidance for Industry: Qualified Health Claims in the Labeling of Conventional Foods and Dietary Supplements, 67 Fed. Reg. 78,002, 78,003 (Dec. 20, 2002).

[32] With apologies to Professors Felstiner, Abel, and Sarat. See William L. F. Felstiner, Richard L. Abel & Austin Sarat, *The Emergence and Transformation of Disputes: Naming, Blaming, Claiming . . .*, 15 LAW SOC. REV. 631 (1980).

[33] Cf. Grossman, *supra* note 30 (discussing rise of the "empowered consumer" model at the FDA).

[34] The standard of identity model remained dominant throughout the 1960s. See Federal Food, Drug, and Cosmetic Act § 401, 21 U.S.C. § 341 (1970).

[35] 21 C.F.R. 35.110.

but does not contain the precise recipe in the FDA standard of identity, it may only be marketed as "imitation ice cream."[36] By the 1950s, it was estimated that more than half of all foods sold were subject to FDA-mandated standards of identity.[37] A more recent example involves the product named "Just Mayo" – a mayonnaise-like product that does not contain eggs.[38] Mayonnaise, according to the Code of Federal Regulations, contains eggs. Just Mayo does not contain eggs, so it may not lawfully be sold as mayonnaise.[39] Mayo, in the FDA's view, is short for Mayonnaise and so the name Just Mayo runs afoul of the rules.

In terms of the regulatory toolkit, the standard-of-identity program is a version of centralized command and control. If a food is to be sold as mayonnaise, it must be produced in a way that conforms to a pre-specified government recipe. As such, the regime requires relatively little involvement from consumers. No extensive disclosures about ingredients are required because everyone knows what ingredients must be contained in the food. Indeed, the early years of the standards-of-identity program involved little information for consumers and little flexibility for companies.[40] Note that the centralized recipe model was intended to remove the possibility of fraud, deception, or consumer confusion. But because the statute prohibits the sale in interstate commerce of a nonconforming food that "purports to be or is represented as" a standardized food, the question of consumer confusion remains.[41] A relevant legal question is always whether a consumer would understand that a given food purports to be or is represented as being a standardized food.

[36] See Richard A. Merrill & Earl M. Collier, Jr., *"Like Mother Used to Make": An Analysis of FDA Food Standards of Identity*, 74 COLUM. L. REV. 561 (1974)..
[37] Id. at 561 (citing Robert W. Hamilton, *Rulemaking on a Record by the Food and Drug Administration*, 50 TEX. L. REV. 1132, 1141 (1972); *Developments in the Law – The Federal Food, Drug, and Cosmetic Act*, 67 HARV. L. REV. 632, 660 n. 211 (1954)).
[38] The standard of identity for mayonnaise is contained at 21 C.F.R. 169.140.
[39] See U.S. Food & Drug Admin., Warning Letter to Hampton Creek Foods (2015):

> Your Just Mayo and Just Mayo Sriracha products are misbranded within the meaning of section 403(a)(1) of the Act [21 U.S.C. § 343(a)(1)] in that they purport to be the standardized food mayonnaise due to the misleading name and imagery used on the label, but do not qualify as the standardized food mayonnaise as described under 21 CFR 169.140. The name "Just Mayo" and an image of an egg are prominently featured on the labels for these products. The term "mayo" has long been used and understood as shorthand or slang for mayonnaise. The use of the term "mayo" in the product names and the image of an egg may be misleading to consumers because it may lead them to believe that the products are the standardized food, mayonnaise, which must contain eggs as described under 21 CFR 169.140(c). Additionally, the use of the term "Just" together with "Mayo" reinforces the impression that the products are real mayonnaise by suggesting that they are "all mayonnaise" or "nothing but" mayonnaise. However, your Just Mayo and Just Mayo Sriracha do not meet the definition of the standard for mayonnaise. According to the labels for these products, neither product contains eggs. Additionally, the products contain additional ingredients that are not permitted by the standard of identity for mayonnaise, such as modified food starch.

[40] Merrill & Collier, Jr., *supra* note 36, at 567–78.
[41] Id., at 571–75.

19.2.2.2 Decentralized Disclosure

While the FDA continues to administer the standards-of-identity program, there was a marked shift in the approach to food identity in the 1970s.[42] Experts and later FDA employees sought to enhance the introduction of new foods to the marketplace, increase flexibility in the marketing of foods, and reduce reliance on strict standards of identity.[43] Scholars of regulatory policy may note that this was part of a general trend away from command and control to somewhat more decentralized tools such as performance standards. Nevertheless, the agency all but stopped issuing new standards, and stopped requiring the term "imitation" so long as the substitute for a standardized food was not nutritionally inferior.[44]

Food labels in 1950s and 1960s also bore little resemblance to the labels that we see on food today. Little information was provided, in part because standards of identity were so strict. The shift to greater flexibility was paired with new food labeling regimes. Producers could, by and large, put whatever they wanted into a food product, but more information was disclosed to the consumer on the label. The FDA urged disclosure of all nonstandardized ingredients on the label and if a company made a representation about nutrient content, the FDA's 1973 rule required that the comprehensive nutrition labeling must be provided in a standardized format.[45]

This transition was consummated in the Nutritional Labeling Health and Education Act of 1990.[46] The statute requires the ubiquitous Nutrition Facts Panel on most foods and authorized the FDA to define some common food terms such as "reduced fat" or "low sodium."[47] The Nutrition Facts Panel is fixed across foods. Yet, as anyone who has visited a grocery store recently will know, food labels now also contain an extraordinary number of related terms and claims. Some, such as health claims or the term organic, are tightly regulated by federal regulation. Others, like Natural or Fresh, are currently not. Today's food marketplace is confusing not so much because food names, ingredients, labels, and marketing are unregulated, but at least in part because some of those things are tightly controlled and others barely at all.

---

[42] Grossman, *supra* note 30, at 642–43; Merrill & Collier Jr., *supra* note 36, at 619–21.
[43] White House Conference on Food, Nutrition and Health, Final Report 122 (1969).
[44] Grossman, *supra* note 30, at 644.
[45] *Id.*; PETER BARTON HUTT, RICHARD A. MERRILL & LEWIS A. GROSSMAN, FOOD AND DRUG LAW: CASES AND MATERIALS 391–92 (3rd ed. 2007); Label Designation of Ingredients for Standardized Foods, 38 Fed. Reg. 2137 (Jan. 19, 1973).
[46] Nutrition Labeling and Education Act (NLEA) of 1990, Pub. L. No. 101-535, 104 Stat. 2353 (codified as amended at 21 U.S.C. § 343(q) (2012)).
[47] FDCA § 403(r), 21 U.S.C. § 343(q)(1)(D) (2012). See generally Grossman, *supra* note 30, at 643–44.

TABLE 19.1. *What do people care about when deciding about food?*

Care most about	
Nutritional value	25.1%
Your weight	15.1%
Price of food	**51.4%**
Eating a healthy diet	**31.1%**
Allergies to food	4.6%
Like or taste good	**40.7%**
Organically grown	6.9%
Fair trade/pay of growers	2.5%
Food scarcity	2.3%
Religious/moral code	2.2%
Question. When it comes to food, which of the following do you think about the MOST or pay MOST attention to? Please choose up to 2.	

Source: Stephen Ansolabehere, Harvard Modules HUA and HUB, Cooperative Congressional Election Study 2018, https://cces.gov.harvard.edu/data, N = 2,000.
Note: Bold indicates significantly different at the .05 level.

19.2.3 *Food, Information, and Consumption*

Food is a product with some attributes that can be observed prior to sale, some attributes – like taste – that can be learned about after the sale, and some attributes that can only truly be revealed after many years of exposure – such as health risks and benefits. A company may advertise that its hamburger tastes great, but in a world where repeat business matters – if customers learn that the hamburger "tastes awful" – lies and deception are unlikely to be a successful long-term business strategy. Companies, moreover, should want to provide consumers with the information they want. Such information varies across a heterogeneous population, of course, but when asked what they care about when deciding about food, survey respondents offer fairly consistent responses: price, nutrition, taste, and health, as illustrated by Table 19.1.

To oversimplify a bit, the problem for a consumer is to relate what they know or can observe about a product to these underlying product attributes that consumers care about and ultimately drive their decisions about what to buy and eat. From the perspective of institutional design, the challenge is to first accurately understand how consumers reason from features of a food product – the food name, words used to describe food, the label, nutrition facts, a particular advertisement, and so on – to the desired information. And, second, to design a set of legal rules that ameliorates rather than exacerbates the gap between what consumers think about a food and what is true about it.[48]

---

[48] For a full model, see STEPHEN ANSOLABEHERE & JACOB E. GERSEN, A CONSUMPTION MODEL OF FOOD (2017).

At first blush, labels and names may be informative about the characteristics of a given product in two ways. First, they may be directly informative. That is, products often have explicit claims such as "healthy" or "GMO-free" or "nutritious." Consumers may believe such claims or not; they may make strong or weak inferences about the precise underlying product attribute – be it taste, health, cooking properties, or price – being claimed. Those claims may be true or false and direct inferences may be correct or incorrect.

Product names or labels are also often indirectly informative about other aspects of food that consumers value. That is, consumers may draw indirect inferences from a claim about one product attribute to other underlying product attributes. When a product is labeled as containing GMOs or is described as GMO-free, consumers may also infer that the product tastes worse (better), is healthier, or cheaper. That is, one aspect of a food product (e.g. an all-natural product name) may create *halo* or *anti-halo* effects on consumer beliefs about other product attributes. These indirect inferences too may naturally be correct or incorrect.

To make headway on these issues, we designed a series of experiments in which we varied the information about a food product provided to respondents. The variations were developed to observe whether labels can affect preferences for products, what inferences consumers draw from labels, and how inferences about various aspects of products affect preferences to purchase products. In constructing these experiments, we used actual products and followed the labeling information as closely as possible.

19.3 GMOS, DISCLOSURE, AND FEAR

19.3.1 *Legal Background*

In the summer of 2016, Congress passed a bill that requires some form of labeling of foods containing genetically engineered (GE) materials. The measure preempts state laws, like Vermont's, that required different labels than those mandated by the federal measure. The federal law requires companies to disclose any genetically engineered materials, but does not necessarily require them to disclose that fact on the label or product itself. Rather, if companies choose, they can simply put a bar code or QR code that consumers could scan with a smart phone to retrieve the relevant information. Smaller companies will be allowed to include only a phone number that consumers could call to receive information about any genetically engineered foods.

As far as labeling laws go, this one hardly qualifies. It is a bit like Congress passing a law without words, but only a QR code that citizens can scan to find out the content of the law. The law requires not so much disclosure of GE materials on the label, but disclosure of the disclosure of GE materials on the labels. The call-me-later approach to food labeling is more than a bit unusual. At the moment, neither activists who worked tirelessly for mandatory GMO labeling, nor states like Vermont that wanted their own labeling regime, nor maybe even industry are all that thrilled. Various commentators have thrown around their own label: sham. Yet, as an approach to information disclosure, the measure also reflects our own confusion and even ambivalence about the actual and potential harms from genetically engineered materials.

The truth is that scientists are almost uniform in their belief that there is no inherent human health risk from consuming foods containing genetically engineered materials. We have been eating cross-bred fruits and vegetables for many years. And, in the United States at least, virtually no corn that is produced is not genetically engineered. To the extent that there is scientific consensus on anything these days, there is a pretty good one that there is nothing about foods containing GE materials that renders them riskier or less healthy than their non-GE counterparts. Some have urged that GE crops that are herbicide-resistant increase the use of herbicides and damage the environment – a plausible and important claim but one that is not about human safety directly.

So, why require disclosure?[49] The honest answer is that consumers care; they care a lot. At a moment when the electorate is deeply fractured and political parties can agree on virtually nothing, consider that roughly 90 percent of survey respondents support mandatory GMO labeling. But the typical response when consumers want to know something about a desirable product attribute is for companies to tell them. If consumers want low-sodium tomato sauce, some company will start making and labeling low-sodium tomato sauce. If consumers want to know that products contain no GMOs, companies can always just voluntarily say so. But other companies are rightly worried that if their competitors say "GMO free" and they don't, then consumers will infer something bad about their product and either not buy it or pay less. There is also likely to be a difference between an affirmative statement that a food "contains GMOs" versus allowing companies to say "GMO free."[50] Company fear is certainly warranted, as our results show. GMO disclosure seems to create not just consumer aversion, but also an anti-halo effect that creates negative consumer beliefs about taste, quality, health, and nutrition. What fear or anxiety exists around GMOs seems to spread to other non-GMO-related product attributes, as we discuss in the next section.

19.3.2 Cooking Oils and Class Action

ConAgra is currently being sued in a class action lawsuit alleging that consumers were deceived by a "100 percent natural" product claim about cooking oil that

---

[49] For a comprehensive discussion of the GMO labeling regime and attendant issues, see Cass R. Sunstein, *On Mandatory Labeling, with Special Reference to Genetically Modified Foods*, 165 U. PENN. L. REV. 1043 (2017).
[50] *Id.* at 1055.

contained GMOs. That is, plaintiffs allege that members of the class made an incorrect indirect inference from the phrase 100 percent natural to GMO-free. In January 2017, the Ninth Circuit concluded that the lawsuit could go forward.

In our cooking oil experiment, we start by varying the terms of the labels on two cooking oils – Wesson All Natural Canola Oil and Mazola Canola Oil. A sample of 1,000 respondents was divided into four groups. Each group was shown two labels – a variant of the Wesson Oil label and a variant of the Mazola label. The labels are presented side-by-side on a computer screen. In one group, the labels both say "Contains No GMOs." In a second group, the Wesson All Natural label says "Contains GMOs" and the Mazola Canola Oil label says "Contains No GMOs." In a third group, the Wesson label says "Contains No GMOs" and the Mazola label says "Contains GMOs." And, in a fourth group, both labels say "Contains GMOs." After observing the pair of product labels, respondents are asked a series of questions about their views of product attributes and which product they would prefer to purchase.

19.3.2.1 Direct Effects and GMOs

Our cooking oil experiments first allow for a simple test of consumer aversion to GMOs. Our data indicate that the label "Contains GMOs" has a substantial and significant effect on consumers' purchasing preferences. The intent to buy product A was statistically indistinguishable from the intent to buy product B in both the first (both contain GMOs) and fourth groups (neither contains GMOs). Specifically, the purchasing preferences were statistically indistinguishable between the group shown two labels each indicating that both products contain no GMOs and those shown two labels each indicating that both products contain GMOs. Although there was a slight preference for the Wesson product, it was not significantly different from the preference for the Mazola product.

The group shown a label indicating that the Wesson product contains GMOs but the Mazola product does not contain GMOs were about 15 percentage points more likely to purchase the Mazola product. The group shown a label indicating that the Wesson product contains no GMOs but the Mazola product contains GMOs expressed about a 15 percentage point higher preference for the Wesson product. Both are significantly different from the baseline groups (in which both products contain no GMOs or both products contain GMOs).

These results are consistent with another experiment (discussed further in Section 19.3.2.3) in which consumers are shown two milk labels. One label contains the phrase "Contains Bovine Growth Hormone" and the other contains the phrase "Contains No Bovine Growth Hormone." The labels are otherwise identical. By a statistically significant margin of fifty-eight to forty-two, survey respondents said they prefer the product with no bovine growth hormone.

The "Contains GMOs" label is sufficient to shift purchase preferences away from a product, but the effects are in the range of 8–15 percentage points. It is not the case that all consumers refuse to purchase a product containing GMOs; many are still happy to do so. Presumably, some consumers simply do not care about GMOs or that the product choice is subtler than simply liking or disliking GMOs. A food, much like most other products, is actually a bundle of underlying product attributes – taste, nutrition, cost, GMOs – and some consumers will, of course, care more about one product attribute than another.

19.3.2.2 Mediating Effects and Indirect Inference

While consumers have an aversion to products containing GMOs, the GMO label also produces an important mediating effect on inferences about other product attributes. One way of describing this effect is as an *anti-halo* effect.

As noted, in our basic model of consumer decision-making, a desire to purchase food is a function of preferences about underlying product attributes. On this admittedly imperfect view of food, the food product is an aggregation of the set of largely unobservable or partially observable attributes such as taste, nutrition, price, and other features that subsets of consumers care about (e.g. geographic origin, methods of production, labor conditions, and so on). Note that there is an infinite number of potential food product attributes that any given consumer might care about and because a label contains limited information, it is often perfectly reasonable for consumers to make inferences about unobserved product attributes based on observed attributes.

Put differently, a food product label does two things. First, it communicates direct information. Second, it allows consumers to make indirect inferences about other information not disclosed. Our experiments illustrate how the presence of GMOs on food labels generate intermediate effects on purchase decisions as the presence of GMOs affects consumer beliefs about various other attributes of each product.

For the cooking oil experiments, we focus on four underlying attributes: healthfulness, price, taste, and cooking effectiveness. Table 19.2 presents the differences between the percentage of respondents who said product A (Wesson) and product B (Mazola) was superior on each attribute. A value of 1 means all people thought product A (Wesson) was better and a value of –1 means that all people thought that product B (Mazola) was better. For each of the product attributes, the presence of GMOs on the label produced significantly different beliefs.

First, consider price. Most people (on average 55 percent) said that there was no price difference between product A and product B. However, those beliefs vary significantly depending on the GMO content label. Consumers believe that products with GMOs are cheaper. When neither product was labeled as containing GMOs, about 17 percent more of respondents thought that Mazola was cheaper (10 percent said Wesson and 27 percent said Mazola). When both products were labeled as containing GMOs the difference was 14 points (5 percent said Wesson was cheaper and 19 percent said Mazola). The substantial effect on price beliefs emerges upon showing that one of the products has GMOs and the other does not.

TABLE 19.2. *Effects of GMOs on price, taste, cooking, healthiness, and purchase*

	Price (%A lower minus %B lower)	Taste (%A better minus %B better)	Cooking (%A better minus %B better)	Health (%A better minus %B better)	Buy (A)
Brand A: $4 Brand B: $3	−0.19	+0.08	+0.05	+0.08	57%
Brand A: Contains rBGH Brand B: No rBGH	+0.18	−0.15	−0.26	−0.35	39%
Brand A: $4 + BGH Brand B: $3 + No BGH	−0.29	+0.28	+0.34	+0.51	69%
Brand A: $3 + BGH Brand B: $4 + No BGH	−0.15	−0.01	+0.04	+0.04	51%

Source: Stephen Ansolabehere, Harvard Module HUF, Cooperative Congressional Election Study 2015. https://cces.gov.harvard.edu/data. N = 1,000; 250 per treatment group (each row of table)

When the Wesson oil is shown to have GMOs and the Mazola product is shown not to, 37 percent say the Wesson oil is cheaper and 17 percent say the Mazola product is cheaper. When Wesson oil is shown to have no GMOs and Mazola is shown to have GMOs, the pattern reverses: 51 percent said the Mazola product was cheaper and 12 percent said the Wesson oil was cheaper.

Table 19.2 also illustrates that similarly significant shifts occur for beliefs about which product is healthier, which is better to cook with, and which tastes better. Unlike price, on which people inferred the GMO product was more desirable (cheaper), for taste, cooking, and health, the GMO product was deemed less desirable. Again, when neither product is shown to have GMOs or when both do, respondents expressed approximately the same beliefs about the products on each of these attributes. When the Wesson product was shown to have GMOs and the Mazola product not, respondents said the Wesson product was less healthy, did not taste as good, and was less good to cook with. The opposite pattern holds when the Mazola product is shown to contain GMOs and the Wesson product does not.

Three findings are worth underlining. First, there is a clear aversion to GMOs. Second, GMOs are perceived to be cheaper so as to produce a positive effect on willingness to purchase. Therefore, third, respondents' beliefs move in opposing directions. Their beliefs about price make the GMO product more desirable, but their beliefs about taste, cooking, and healthfulness make it less desirable. Which of these beliefs dominates depends on the relationship between each of these characteristics and purchasing preferences, a relationship that will itself vary enormously across individual consumers.

The results from a multiple regression (probit) are reported in Table 19.3. The first model (column) in Table 19.3 presents the estimated differences between

TABLE 19.3. *Probit estimates relating beliefs about products to purchase preferences*

	Model 1	Model 2
Group 1 (v. 4)	0.018 (0.114)	0.035 (0.123)
Group 2 (v. 4)	−0.379 (0.115)**	−0.105 (0.125)
Group 3 (v. 4)	0.259 (0.116)**	−0.251 (0.143)
Price belief		0.470 (0.090)**
Taste belief		0.657 (0.140)**
Cooking belief		0.769 (0.125)**
Health belief		0.715 (0.128)**
Nutrition belief		0.424 (0.145)**
A organic		−0.024 (0.142)
B organic		0.248 (0.150)
Education	0.035 (0.031)	0.040 (0.036)
Income	−0.025 (0.014)	−0.024 (0.016)
Gender	0.104 (0.081)	0.108 (0.095)
Age	0.002 (0.002)	0.002 (0.003)
Number of observations	1,000	1,000
Pseudo-R-squared	0.027	0.210

Source: Stephen Ansolabehere, Harvard Module HUF, Cooperative Congressional Election Study 2015. https://cces.gov.harvard.edu/data. N = 1,000
Note: ** indicates that the coefficients are statistically different from 0 at the .05 level.

Group 1 and 4, Group 2 and 4, and Group 3 and 4, controlling for education, income, age, and gender. The second model adds to the first the measures of beliefs about which product is better on each of the following attributes: price, taste, nutrition, health, and cooking. The model also includes beliefs about whether each product is thought to be organic.

We interpret the second model as measuring the mediating effects of each of the attributes. The assumption we make is that the coefficients on the attributes do not change with the experiment, but the mean levels of the attributes do. One concern is that the attributes are measured post-treatment (i.e. after the experiment), and the coefficients may be endogenous. To evaluate this proposition, we looked for interaction effects between the treatments and the variables measuring beliefs. We found no substantial interactions and nearly all were statistically indistinguishable from 0. (Other experiments following vary information about the attributes directly.) The coefficients on the main effects are statistically insignificant after including the mediating variables. This suggests the experimental effects work through shifts in the means of the mediating variables.

All five attributes included in Model 2 have substantial and statistically significant effects. The demographic variables do not. Importantly, the marginal effects of beliefs about price are about half as large as the effects of nutrition and health and taste. In expressing their purchasing preferences, then, people are more responsive to beliefs and information about the qualities of the consumer product than they are to the price in this model.

As we will see, consumers consistently respond to new information about taste and health. And consumers are more responsive to these characteristics of products than they are to other characteristics. Price is a somewhat different attribute, as price becomes the metric of the value that consumers place on the other attributes.

19.3.2.3 Consumer Willingness to Pay to Avoid GMOs

Our next experiment attempts to gauge the willingness to pay to avoid GMOs. This experiment manipulated the price and label of two brands of milk (one gallon). The price treatments indicated that one gallon cost $3.75 and the other $4.25, or showed no price. The GMO treatments labeled one gallon as containing bovine growth hormone (BGH) and the other as containing no BGH, or no BGH information on either. Recombinant bovine growth hormone (rGBH) is a synthetic hormone made in a lab using genetic technology. It is used by dairy farmers to increase milk production in cows. It is banned in the European Union and Canada, but has been approved in the United States since 1993. Milk produced from cows raised with rGBH contains genetically engineered products.

The experimental design was as follows. Group 1 was shown Brand A, with a price of $4.25, and Brand B, with a price of $3.75. Group 2 was shown Brand A, with a label indicating "Contains Bovine Growth Hormone," and Brand B, with a label stating "Contains No Bovine Growth Hormone." Group 3 was shown Brand A, with a price of $4.25 and a label stating "Contains Bovine Growth Hormone," and Brand B, with a price of $3.75 and a label stating "Contains No Bovine Growth Hormone." And Group 4 was shown Brand A, with a price of $3.75 and a label stating "Contains Bovine Growth Hormone," and Brand B, with a price of $4.25 and a label stating "Contains No Bovine Growth Hormone."

A straightforward measure of the preference for products without BGH is contained in Group 2. Respondents were presented with a choice between Brand A milk, which contains BGH, and Brand B milk, which contains no BGH. The milk labels were otherwise identical. If the BGH label did not affect preference, then we expect that 50 percent would choose A and 50 percent would choose B. In fact, 42 percent chose A and 58 percent chose B, a result statistically significantly different from 50–50. Consumers were somewhat averse to genetically engineered milk.

Further inspection of Row 2 of Table 19.4 reveals that respondents inferred many different attributes of the product from the BGH label. Those respondents in Group 2 inferred the brand with BGH was less healthy, less nutritious, and less tasty – but also somewhat less expensive. Again, inferences about price and quality work in opposite directions with GMO labels.

TABLE 19.4. *Effects of bovine growth hormone (BGH) label on price, taste, nutrition, healthiness, and purchase preferences*

	Price (%A lower minus %B lower)	Taste (%A better minus %B better)	Nutrition (%A better minus %B better)	Health (%A better minus %B better)	Buy (A)
Brand A: $4 Brand B: $3	−0.69	+0.00	+0.04	+0.01	19%
Brand A: *Contains BGH*, Brand B: *No BGH*	+0.20	−0.15	−0.15	−0.36	42%
Brand A: $4 + *BGH*, Brand B: $3 + *No BGH*	−0.61	−0.18	−0.22	−0.42	10%
Brand A: $3 + *BGH*, Brand B: $4 + *No BGH*	−0.81	+0.15	+0.19	+0.39	49%

Source: Stephen Ansolabehere, Harvard Module HUR, Cooperative Congressional Election Study 2015. https://cces.gov.harvard.edu/data. N = 1,000; 250 per treatment group (each row of table)

Adding a GMO label makes consumers believe the product is cheaper. The difference in price was about 20 percentage points; the difference in health was 36 percentage points. It turns out, however, that in expressing a purchasing preference, only respondents' beliefs about taste and health mattered. That is, consumers do make an inference about nutrition and price from the presence of GE materials, but that inference does not affect their decision about whether to purchase the milk.

A second comparison provides another measure of the effect of BGH labels on purchase preference, but this comparison holds price constant. Recall that Group 1 is shown that Brand A costs $4.25 and Brand B costs $3.75, a 50 cent difference. Group 3 is shown that same price difference but that Brand A contains BGH and Brand B contains no BGH. By comparing the dynamics of Group 1 to the dynamics of Group 3, we can isolate the relationship between GMO labels and price.

Of respondents in Group 1, 19 percent chose Brand A, the more expensive brand. Of respondents in Group 3, only 10 percent chose Brand A, the more expensive brand, labeled as containing BGH. The 9-point difference is statistically significantly different from 0, and the effect is due entirely to the introduction of the BGH information. Note also that this difference is almost identical to the 8-point effect of simply stating that a product has BGH without listing a price. Analysis of Group 2 and the comparison of Groups 1 and 3 reveal that there is a preference among consumers to avoid milk containing BGH. That information alone can lower consumers' willingness to purchase a milk container by about 8–9 percentage points compared with a container that says that the product contains no BGH.

A final way to gauge consumer attitudes toward BGH is to ask how willing people are to pay to avoid products that contain BGH. Group 3 and Group 4 offer respondents a choice between milk with BGH and milk without BGH. The groups differ in the prices shown. Group 3 is shown the gallon of milk with BGH and a price of $4.25 and the gallon of milk without BGH and a price of $3.75. Group 4 presents the milk with BGH and a price of $3.75 and the milk without BGH and a price of $4.25. The 50 cent price difference was chosen to be substantial but not unrealistically large. The total price difference or price swing between Groups 3 and 4 is $1.00 and represents a swing of 25 percent – a $1.00 change over a $4.00 gallon of milk.

Only 10 percent of respondents in Group 3 chose the milk with BGH and the higher price. That is a very low willingness of consumers to buy the product; if consumers were indifferent, we would expect 50 percent to buy Brand A. But as we saw in the comparison of Groups 2 and 3, most of the reluctance to buy Brand A among Group 3 respondents is due to the price differential. When the prices are reversed, and the BGH brand is shown to cost 50 cents less than the milk containing no BGH, willingness to buy the BGH brand rises by 40 percentage points. Forty-nine percent of Group 4 respondents said that they would buy the product with BGH but that cost 50 cents less.

Group 4 is intriguing for two reasons. First, Group 4 is indifferent between the BGH and no BGH milk. Quite by accident we seem to have found that pricing BGH milk at $3.75 compared with no BGH milk at $4.25 makes consumers indifferent between the two products. This suggests that the price differential at which there is no loss of market share for milk that contains BGH is about 12.5 percent (50 cents out of $4). Second, it is surprising that Group 4 does not swing more strongly toward the BGH milk given the price sensitivity of consumers. Although the price swing is symmetric around $4.00 between Groups 3 and 4, the consumer preference is far from symmetric around 50–50. Only 10 percent of those in Group 3 chose the BGH milk when it was priced more expensively. But those in Group 4 only rise to 50 percent preferring the cheaper BGH milk. Nor is the shift in preferences symmetric around the group that was shown no price information. Among Group 2, 42 percent chose the BGH milk. This suggests that the curve indicating the willingness of consumers to pay for BGH milk might be asymmetric and nonlinear, and the presence of BGH might create considerable reluctance among consumers.

19.3.2.4 What Does GMO Mean, to You?

With the findings in Table 19.4, we now probe more deeply the interpretation and meaning that people ascribe to GMOs. Our results suggest that many consumers treat the GMO label much as they would a long and complicated list of ingredients like hydrogenated oils. Returning to the cooking oil experiments, we show respondents two ingredient lists. One, for Product A, lists three types of oils and a variety of other ingredients. Another, for Product B, shows canola oil as the only ingredient.

TABLE 19.5. *Cooking oil experiment effect summaries*

	All natural ingredients (group n = 500)	Artificial ingredients (group n = 250)	Contains GMOs (group n = 250)
Buy	+0.3%	−32.0%**	+4.1%
Organic	+0.2%	−50.3%**	+2.9%
Nutrition	−0.2%	−49.1%**	+14.6%*
Health	−3.7%	−69.5%**	−1.0%
Taste	−8.2%*	−37.7%**	+4.9%
Fresh	+2.4%	+14.4%**	−2.0%
Cooking	−0.9%	−57.5%**	+4.4%
Price	−8.3%* (more expensive)	+11.4%*	+21.0%**

Cell numbers are the difference between the percentage of people who think Product A has the characteristic and the percentage of people who think Product B has the characteristic. 0 means that half of the respondents think Product A has the attribute and half think Product B has the attribute.
Source: Stephen Ansolabehere, Harvard Module HUF, Cooperative Congressional Election Study 2015. https://cces.gov.harvard.edu/data. N = 1,000
Note:** indicates that the coefficients are statistically different from at the .05 level

Product A	Product B
INGREDIENTS:	**INGREDIENTS:**
Canola Oil, Cottonseed Oil, Hydrogenated Canola Oil. Less than 2% of: Salt, Mono- and DiGlycerides and Polyglycerol Esters of Fatty Acids, Soy Lecithin, Natural and Artificial Flavors, Medium Chain Triglycerides, TBHQ (Preservative), Colored with Beta Carotene	Canola Oil

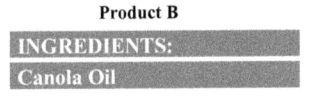

FIGURE 19.1. Comparison of cooking oil ingredient lists

The easiest way to think about the cooking oil experiment is that we are providing three treatments: (1) use of the phrase "All Natural"; (b) presence of GMOs; and (c) a complicated ingredient list. We vary exposure to those treatments, mix them up across the two products and then ask respondents which product they are more likely to buy. We then ask a series of questions about which product respondents think is more nutritious, healthier, better tasting, better to cook with, more expensive, contains GMOs, and so on. The results are summarized in Table 19.5.

First focus on the ingredient treatment, first row. Consumers shown the scary ingredient list were 32 percent less likely to say they would purchase that product. Or, more precisely, the difference between the proportion of people who said they would purchase A and those who said they would purchase B is 32 percent. Second, note that the "All natural" treatment produces very few meaningful effects. Most are small and not statistically significant. Consumers do think all natural means more expensive. And, interestingly, all natural actually seems to create an anti-halo for taste. That said, it is a small effect and we would not put much weight on it. Still, more respondents thought the product that is not all natural would taste better.

With respect to the GMO treatment in the third column, positive effects mean that respondents think the GMO product is less likely to have the relevant attribute. Respondents were 14 percent more likely to think GMOs are less nutritious, 21 percent less expensive, and 5 percent less good. These are meaningful effects, but the magnitude of the ingredient list effects is much larger. From the legally mandated ingredient list, people are drawing much more meaningful indirect inferences than from terms like "all natural" or even "GMO-free."

When the longer, scarier, but real ingredient list is shown, respondents are 50 percent less likely to think the product is organic, 49 percent less likely to be more nutritious, almost 70 percent less likely to be healthier. But, interestingly, 14 percent are more likely to think the product is fresh – perhaps inferring that some scary ingredients are preservatives. All told, respondents were 32 percent more likely to say they would purchase the product without the scary ingredient list. Interestingly, while company fear about GMO disclosure is warranted, the other ingredients in a food play as large a role in driving consumer preference.

19.3.2.5 More Oil, Now with Vinegar

To this point, our results suggest that consumers are responsive to product names, terms, and claims. Consumers accurately make direct inferences from such descriptions. Consumers also make indirect inferences, creating the possibility for halo and anti-halo effects of product names, ingredients, and marketing phrases. As a way of replicating the results on cooking oil and also further clarifying the underlying inference process, we ran a variant of the above experiments using salad dressing. By design, the cooking oil experiments allow consumer beliefs to vary in an unconstrained way. For the purpose of designing legal institutions or regulatory strategy, however, we need to know how consumers respond to more specific disclosure interventions. Thus, in the salad dressing experiments we attempt to fix or at least impose some structure on beliefs about a particular product attribute. Lest the discussion get too abstract too quickly, we explain through illustration.

As above, respondents are shown two products – Brand A: Annie's Natural Tuscan Italian Dressing, an ingredient list, and a nutrition facts panel; Brand B: Ken's Italian Dressing, ingredients, nutrition facts. Rather than asking respondents which product they think is more expensive, tastes better, or is healthier, we now simply provide them with information about the product's price, taste, and health. So, we make one product more expensive and give the respondents the price differential. We tell respondents that *Cook's Illustrated* has ranked Product X as best tasting or worst tasting on a scale of 1–8. We also indicate that Product X has received a health grade of A or D. The combinations of products, price, taste, and health ratings are then all varied.

TABLE 19.6. *Consumer beliefs about product attributes after information disclosure*

Outcome variable	Price treatment	Taste treatment	Health treatment	R-square
Which product is cheaper?	0.815**	0.067	−0.099*	0.202
	(0.042)	(0.042)	(0.042)	
Which product tastes better?	0.037	0.458**	0.493**	0.311
	(0.043)	(0.043)	(0.043)	
Which product is healthier?	−0.031	−0.030	1.153**	0.403
	(0.036)	(0.036)	(0.036)	
Which product is more nutritious?	−0.021	−0.025	1.106**	0.343
	(0.040)	(0.040)	(0.040)	
Which product is safer?	−0.005	0.001	0.943**	0.311
	(0.036)	(0.036)	(0.036)	
Which product would you buy?	0.129**	0.180**	1.015**	0.277
	(0.043)	(0.044)	(0.044)	

Source: Stephen Ansolabehere, Harvard Module HUY, Cooperative Congressional Election Study 2016. https://cces.gov.harvard.edu/data. N = 1,500

This structure allows us to verify that consumers are making correct, sensible inferences based on the information shown in the experiments. Do respondents update their prior beliefs about a product's taste, health, and cost? In a word, yes. More respondents always think the right product is more expensive, healthier, and better tasting, as evidenced by the bolded coefficients in Table 19.6. That is reassuring, both for our research, and also for various rating agencies and organizations. It is also good for law, as it suggests mandatory disclosures produce reasonably accurate updating of beliefs.

Now that we have fixed or locked in beliefs about these product attributes, we can focus on what might be thought of as *residual* indirect inferences. What else do consumers infer from price? As the first column of Table 19.6 indicates, consumers infer price from price, but not much else. Price is the only statistically significant effect. The same is true of taste, as evidenced by the second column. Consumers infer taste from information about taste, but nothing about the product's other underlying attributes such as safety, health, or nutrition. But a good taste grade makes respondents a bit more likely to buy.

However, the results are quite different for the health treatment. Respondents infer taste, safety, nutrition, and price from the health rating of A or D. And note that the health information has a huge effect on purchasing decisions: eight to nine times larger than the price and taste information.

In Table 19.7, each row summarizes a comparison of two particular product bundles of price, taste, and health. For example, the first row (T1) compares Brand A as Annie's Dressing at a price of $4, a health grade of A, and a taste rating of 1 (best) to Brand B of Ken's Dressing at a price of $6, a health grade of D, and a taste

TABLE 19.7. *Summary of product, price, health, and taste bundles*

	Brand A: Annie's	Brand B: Ken's	No Diff	N
T1: A: $4; A; #1 B: $6; D; #8	73%	22%	2%	175
T2: A: $4; D; #1 B: $6; A; #8	17%	72%	3%	190
T3: A: $4; A; #8 B: $6; D; #1	67%	25%	3%	214
T4: A: $4; D; #8 B: $6; A; #1	17%	71%	5%	198
T5: A: $6; A; #1 B: $4; D; #8	73%	23%	2%	190
T6: A: $6; D; #1 B: $4; A; #8	20%	73%	2%	186
T7: A: $6; A; #8 B: $4; D; #1	50%	39%	8%	187
T8: A: $6; D; #8 B: $4; A; #1	17%	78%	3%	161

Source: Stephen Ansolabehere, Harvard Module HUZ, Cooperative Congressional Election Study 2016. https://cces.gov.harvard.edu/data. N = 1,500

rating of 8 (worst). Given those two bundles of product attributes, 73 percent would prefer to buy Annie's.

Now consider row 2 (T2). Product A costs $4, received a health grade of D, and a taste ranking of 1. Product B costs $6, received a health grade of A, and a ranking of 8 (last) for taste. That is, the only product attribute that has changed between row 1 and row 2 is that the health grade has been switched. Only 17 percent will buy A, even though it is cheaper and better tasting.

Now compare T2 and T8. In T8, Product A costs $6, received a health grade of D, and a tasting rating of 8. Product B costs $4, received a health grade of A, and a tasting rating of 1 (best). That is, all product attributes *except* health have now been reversed, yet the same 17 percent prefer to buy Product A. Essentially, the impact on buying preference is made by the health claim.

Lastly, note that we can drive respondents to indifference, as we see in T7. Here, Product A costs $6, gets a health grade of A, and a taste rating of 8. Product B costs $4, gets a health grade of D, and a taste rating of 1. That is, we drive a wedge between price, taste, and health. Now, half the respondents go for Product A and half go for Product B. That means that companies can counteract some of the negative inferences or anti-halos by generating positive inferences in the other direction.

Part of the impetus for the mandatory GMO labeling law was the (accurate) claim that consumers want to know whether their food contains GMOs. Our work, however, suggests that manufacturers of GMO food are right to fear disclosure. This is so not merely because people fear GMOs, which they do, but also because consumers make additional negative inferences about other attributes of the food. These attributes may not in fact actually be correlated with GMO presence. The disclosure requirement, therefore, produces a doubly negative effect. That said, our finding also suggest that consumers treat the GMO disclosure much as they do a list of artificial-sounding ingredients. These effects, however, apparently can be counteracted with credible ratings or rankings from third-party organizations.

19.4 SUGAR AND SPICE AND EVERYTHING NICE

While Congress was debating GMO labels, the FDA was engaged in making another rule on food labeling and mandatory disclosures. Although questions about calories, font, and serving size all had their day, the issue that took center stage was sugar. Most of us have seen, if not exactly studied, the Nutrition Facts panel on the back of foods. It tells us how many calories are in a serving, how many servings are in a package, and the percentage of the daily recommended value (DRV) of things like salt, fat, and various vitamins the food contains. Anyone who has carefully studied rather than simply glanced at the Nutrition Facts panel might recall that the amount of sugar in the food is listed in grams – but unlike all other items on the panel – not as a percentage of the daily recommended value. The amount is expressed without a reference point.

In the spring of 2016, the FDA decided to separately require the listing of "added sugars" and also express those amounts as percentages of the DRV. This move was hailed as long overdue by food activists and the hope was that by finally exposing how much sugar is added to US foods in products ranging from yogurt, to bread, to tomato sauce, to soda, two things would happen. First, consumers would start avoiding foods with an unhealthy amount of added sugars. Second, and related, food producers would start adding less sugar to these products in order to keep consumers. This would make individual dietary choices better and also render the entire US food supply healthier.

There is no question that there is a lot of sugar added to our food. Nor is there any doubt that we consume vastly more sugar than is recommended. A single bottle of soda typically contains 133 percent of the recommended sugar intake for an entire day. Yet the premise and therefore promise of the new nutrition label is more than a bit uncertain. The idea seems to be that by focusing on *added* instead of *total* sugars and by anchoring consumers on the *percentage* of Daily Value (DV), shifts in consumer and producer behavior will follow – shifts that have not occurred by simply requiring the disclosure of total grams of sugar on the package. Although scattered evidence is consistent with the premise, our data suggest reason for concern.

We focused on two foods: juice and yogurt. Juice has a lot of naturally occurring sugars and yogurt traditionally has a lot of sugar added. One cup of juice has around 23 grams of sugars. The World Health Organization has recently dropped its daily recommended intake to around 25 grams a day. Similarly, many common yogurts contain between 25 and 50 grams of sugar. Unlike soda, however, fruit juice and yogurt have traditionally been understood as healthy. Thus, a change in behavior seems most likely to be observed for surprisingly high-sugar foods that are commonly thought to be healthy.

19.4.1 *Juice*

We showed our respondents two kinds of juice, one made by POM Wonderful and the other made by Minute Maid. We broke our respondents into four groups and varied the information shown on the product labels along two dimensions. We varied which product was shown to have more sugar (alternating between 30g and 15g) and also varied whether the label expressed the amount of sugar as a percentage of the DV (using 35 grams as the DV).

Table 19.8 summarizes the effects. The final column contains the percentage of respondents that were inclined to buy the POM Wonderful product instead of the Minute Maid product. First, note that all four groups in our sample had a baseline preference for POM, although by varying the amount of sugar contained in each product, we are able to induce consumers to near indifference.

Second, the amount of sugar seems to have a big effect on willingness to purchase. Compare Groups 3 and 4 (the bottom two rows). When POM is shown

TABLE 19.8. *Effect of sugar content and sugar percentages*

		Price	Taste	Health	Buy A
1	Pom 30g, % MM 15g, %	0.087	+0.068	0.216	55%
2	Pom 15g, % MM 30g, %	0.328	−0.369	0.560	74%
3	Pom 30g MM 15g	0.136	−0.097	0.410	59%
4	Pom 15g MM 30g	0.181	−0.339	0.451	72%

Source: Stephen Ansolabehere, Harvard Module HUF, Cooperative Congressional Election Study 2015. https://cces.gov.harvard.edu/data. N = 1,000

to contain 30g of sugar and Minute Maid 15g, 59 percent of respondents say they would purchase POM. When POM is shown to contain 15g and Minute Maid 30g, that number jumps 13 percentage points to 72 percent. Sugar matters. Comparing rows 1 and 2 illustrates a similar shift. Swapping the amount of sugar contained in the two products dramatically affects their desirability. When POM contains half the sugar of Minute Maid, the average probability of purchasing POM shifts from 55 to 74 percent, a very sizable difference of 19 percentage points.

But recall that even absent the percentage DV information, we observed a 13 percent shift from the sugar volume alone (row 3 vs. row 4). Including the percentage DV information yields approximately an additional 6 percent marginal change. This is not a trivial effect and it suggests that including the percentage DV information for sugar may change behavior, but it is not a massive effect.

Now consider Groups 1 and 3 (rows 1 and 3 respectively). These groups of respondents are shown identical information, except that Group 1 is also shown the amount of sugar, expressed as a percentage of the DV. Groups 2 and 4 (rows 2 and 4) are also shown identical information, except for the additional percentage DV information. Thus, by comparing the effects in Groups 1 and 2 versus the effects in Groups 3 and 4, we can isolate the independent effect of presenting the amount of sugar as a percentage of DV. Comparing rows 1 and 3, adding the percentage information produces a drop of 4 percentage points in the willingness to buy POM. Comparing rows 2 and 4 produces only a 2 percentage point shift. The largest change in willingness to buy derives from the sugar volume disclosure, not the expression as a percentage of the DV. Moreover, the difference in the percentage value here was quite large: 85 vs. 42 percent. We suspect that for smaller differences, an even greater relative portion of behavioral change will derive from the amount of sugar rather than the form of its expression.

The other columns in Table 19.8 contain information on consumer views about the comparative price, taste, and health of the two juice products. Numbers close to zero mean that, on average, respondents did not perceive a difference between the two products on that dimension. Positive numbers mean that respondents thought POM cost more, tasted better, or was healthier. Negative numbers mean that consumers thought Minute Maid cost more, tasted better, or was healthier. Comparing Groups 1 to 2 and Groups 3 to 4, respondents associate more sugar with better taste, but the size of that inference does not depend on whether the percentage DV is presented.

19.4.2 Yogurt

To this point, we have suggested that the amount of sugar has a significant impact on consumer choice among juice products. And we have shown that adding the percentage DV has a genuine, but modest, effect on the desirability of goods. The juice experiments allow consumers to make an inference about the relationship

TABLE 19.9. *Yogurt, sugars, and price*

		Price	Taste	Health	Buy A
1	15g; 30g	−0.114	+0.029	0.299	66%
2	$1.50, $1	−0.570	−0.057	0.468	54%
3	$1.25, $1	−0.400	−0.060	0.337	64%
4	$1, $1	−0.055	+0.056	0.427	69%

Source: Stephen Ansolabehere, Harvard Module HUR, Cooperative Congressional Election Study 2015. https://cces.gov.harvard.edu/data. N = 1,000

between the product, sugar content, and price, but we did not provide actual pricing information. Because price is obviously an enormous driver of consumer decisions – about food and otherwise – we now introduce pricing information directly.

Yogurt is another food product with a lot of sugar, most of it added to make it taste better. Most yogurts (other than the Greek variety) contain between 19 and 50 grams of sugar. In our yogurt experiment, we again break our respondents into four groups. None of the groups are shown the percentage DV. The first group is shown two yogurt labels. Product A contains 15g of sugar; Product B contains 30g of sugar. Group 1 is given no price information. Group 2 is shown the identical products, but also given price information: Product A is $1.50 and product B is $1.00. Instead of a $0.50 difference, Group 3 is shown a $0.25 price difference, again with Product A being higher priced. Group 4 is shown the same products but with no price difference; each product is $1.00.

Table 19.9 shows that, in the baseline group without price information, 66 percent of respondents prefer the yogurt with the lower sugar content. But the 50 cent price difference (or a 50 percent price difference at this price point) in row 2 makes consumers almost indifferent. Now, only 54 percent favor Product A. These respondents prefer lower sugar and make use of the sugar content information, but their willingness to pay for less sugar is obviously not infinite.

When we reduce the price difference to $0.25 (row 3), about 64 percent of consumers prefer the more expensive, less sugary yogurt. And when we provide price information but remove any price differentials across the products (row 4), roughly the same number of respondents prefer the low-sugar-content yogurt as when no price information is provided – 69 percent versus 66 percent. Overall, the data present a fairly simple and consistent portrait of consumer willingness to pay to avoid sugar.

The rest of the coefficients in Table 19.9 are summaries of how caring a lot about price, taste, and health impacts purchasing preferences for the two yogurts. For example, focusing on row 1, respondents who say they care a lot about price are less likely to purchase the low-sugar yogurt. Respondents who care a lot about taste are pretty much indifferent (the coefficient is close to zero). Respondents who care a lot about health are about 30 percent more likely to purchase the low-sugar yogurt.

Now focus on the bottom row, the group that has the price information but no price differences across the products. Consumers that care a lot about price are indifferent (the coefficient is near zero), as they should be because there is no price difference. There is still virtually no effect of taste preferences, but the health effect is quite large. Respondents who care a lot about health are now 43 percent more likely to purchase the low-sugar yogurt. There is a clear trade-off between health concerns and price concerns, as shown by comparing Group 1 and Group 4.

Groups 2 and 3 further reveal this trade-off. Those who care a lot about price are nearly 60 percent less likely to buy the low-sugar, high-price yogurt. And those that care a lot about health are 47 percent more likely to purchase the low-sugar, high-price yogurt. The price effect is strong (40 percent) but lower when the price difference drops to a quarter. Overall, our results suggest that consumers care about sugar content in a rational and predicable way, trading health benefits off against price.

19.5 *POM V. COKE* REVISITED

We left the oral argument in *POM Wonderful* v. *Coca-Cola* with a basic question: would reasonable (or credulous) consumers be confused by Coca-Cola's Enhanced Pomegranate Blueberry Flavored 100% Juice Blend even though the product name

FIGURE 19.2. Comparison of POM Wonderful and Coca-Cola juice bottles

TABLE 19.10. *Consumer views about POM and Minute Maid juices*

Which drink ...	POM	Minute Maid
Tastes sweeter?	15%	41%
Tastes better?	29%	25%
Is more nutritious?	43%	15%
Costs more?	57%	14%
Is organic?	30%	7%
Is authentic pomegranate juice?	61%	10%
Would you buy?	58%	42%

Source: Stephen Ansolabehere, Harvard Module HFD, Cooperative Congressional Election Study 2014. https://cces.gov.harvard.edu/data. N = 1,500

is consistent with FDA rules about product names? We now return to that question. We first showed respondents the two juice products with their trade names: POM Wonderful Pomegranate Blueberry 100% Juice, and Minute Maid Enhanced Pomegranate Blueberry Flavored 100% Juice Blend.

We then asked respondents a series of questions about respondent perceptions of the two juices. Table 19.10 summarizes the results. Because we use the actual trade name and bottle images, it is not possible for us to differentiate preexisting views of the products from newly formed views. Nevertheless, respondents in our survey did not seem particularly confused. Only 10 percent thought the Minute Maid juice was an authentic pomegranate juice drink. Only 15 percent thought the Minute Maid juice was the more nutritious of the two products. Only 7 percent thought Minute Maid was organic. Consumers also seemed to understand the price trade-off. Only 14 percent thought that Minute Maid would cost more than POM. And, interestingly, respondents seemed to have only weak views about which juice would taste better.

What about purchasing preferences? Table 19.11 contains coefficients from a basic regression model. A positive coefficient can be interpreted as follows: if a respondent thinks that POM Wonderful is the real pomegranate juice (row 1), then they are 10 percent more likely to prefer to purchase POM. In row 2, for example, consumers that believe Minute Maid is the real pomegranate juice are about 13 percent less likely to purchase POM. Consumers that thought POM would taste better were about 22 percent more likely to prefer POM. And consumers that thought POM was the more nutritious drink were about 18 percent more likely to say they would purchase POM. All told, our respondents did not seem particularly confused. They did not treat the two juices as identical, equivalent, or even similar. The juice survey is also consistent with the story we have been telling. Respondents make fairly consistent inferences from what they can observe about a product to what they want to know about the product: price, taste, and health.

TABLE 19.11. *Relationship between beliefs about juice attributes and purchasing preference*

Question: Which product are you more likely to buy? (Pom or Minute Maid)

Attribute	Effect of attribute on probability of buying Pom (v. Minute Maid)
Pom is authentic pomegranate juice	0.098 (0.026)**
Minute Maid is authentic pomegranate juice	–9.101 (9.025)**
Which tastes sweeter?	–0.037 (9.028)
Which tastes better?	0.464 (0.029)**
Which costs more?	0.023 (0.031)
Which has more nutritional value?	**0.395 (0.032)****
Pom is organic	–0.011 (0.024)
Minute Maid is organic	0.023 (0.031)
Number of observations	1,491
R-squared	0.367

Source: Stephen Ansolabehere, Harvard Module HFD, Cooperative Congressional Election Study 2014. https://cces.gov.harvard.edu/data. N = 1,500
Note:** indicates that the coefficients are statistically different from at the .05 level and bold indicates that it is significantly different at the .05 level

19.6 CONCLUSION

In recent years, the food marketplace has been swamped with products, names, claims, advertising, and marketing that seem intended to create and profit from consumer confusion. Food itself has been transformed as more and more staples are produced using genetic modification. In terms of regulatory strategy, the United States has seen a transition from centralized command-and-control standards of food identity, to mandatory ingredient disclosure, to mandatory nutrition facts, to an acknowledgement that even truthful claims may be confusing and deceptive. By and large, our regime is a permissive one unless a claim would be deceptive or confusing to the reasonable consumer.

It does not take much training in statistics, however, to recognize that a significant portion of the citizenry will not quite live up to this standard. The old approach of protecting the ignorant, unthinking, and credulous had something to it, particularly if a substantial portion of the population is ignorant, unthinking, or credulous. Regardless, the questions increasingly being asked by regulators, judges, and juries adjudicating claims of deception and fraud are really empirical ones about how real consumers process actual product claims and make inferences about the food they buy. Our goal in this project has been to fill in some of these empirical gaps and create a stronger tether between consumer decisions on the ground and the legal strategy of regulation.

Our story is a simple one in which consumers reason from the observable characteristics of a food to the unobservable attributes about which they care most. While consumers may make mistakes, there is little in our data to suggest ignorance or irrationality. It is possible for companies to benefit from incorrect inferences and also to create ambiguity about whether a product has desirable attributes. But our findings suggest that consumers are doing reasonably well and that the best regulatory response is likely to focus on disclosures on attributes that consumers value most. Rather than leaving consumers to make inferences from observable or disclosed attributes to taste and health, regulators (or companies themselves) might do well to rely on trustworthy third-party rating agencies. Indeed, within the food industry such ratings are becoming an increasingly common tool of food producers and sellers. We pursue the problems and puzzles associated with such organizations in future work.

For EU product safety concerns, contact us at Calle de José Abascal, 56–1°, 28003 Madrid, Spain or eugpsr@cambridge.org.